Language in South Asia

South Asia is a rich and fascinating linguistic area, its many hundreds of languages from four major language families representing the distinctions of caste, class, profession, religion, and region.This comprehensive new volume presents an overview of the language situation in this vast subcontinent in a linguistic, historical, and sociolinguistic context. An invaluable resource, it comprises authoritative contributions from leading international scholars within the fields of South Asian language and linguistics, historical linguistics, cultural studies, and area studies. Topics covered include the ongoing linguistic processes, controversies, and implications of language modernization; the functions of South Asian languages within the legal system, media, cinema, and religion; language conflicts and politics; and Sanskrit and its long traditions of study and teaching. *Language in South Asia* is an accessible interdisciplinary book for students and scholars in sociolinguistics, multilingualism, language planning, and South Asian studies.

BRAJ B. KACHRU is Center for Advanced Study Professor of Linguistics and Jubilee Professor of Liberal Arts and Sciences Emeritus at the University of Illinois.

YAMUNA KACHRU is Professor Emerita of Linguistics at the University of Illinois.

S. N. SRIDHAR is Professor and Chair at the Department of Asian and Asian American Studies, State University of New York at Stony Brook.

Language in South Asia

Edited by
Braj B. Kachru, Yamuna Kachru, and S. N. Sridhar

CAMBRIDGE UNIVERSITY PRESS
Cambridge, New York, Melbourne, Madrid, Cape Town, Singapore, São Paulo

Cambridge University Press
The Edinburgh Building, Cambridge CB2 8RU, UK

Published in the United States of America by Cambridge University Press, New York

www.cambridge.org
Information on this title: www.cambridge.org/9780521786539

First published 2008

Printed in the United Kingdom at the University Press, Cambridge

A catalogue record for this publication is available from the British Library

Library of Congress Cataloguing in Publication Data

Language in South Asia / edited by Braj B. Kachru, Yamuna Kachru, and S. N. Sridhar.
p. cm.
Includes bibliographical references and index.
ISBN-13: 978-0-521-78141-1 (hardback : alk. paper)
ISBN-10: 0-521-78141-8 (hardback : alk. paper)
ISBN-13: 978-0-521-78653-9 (pbk. : alk. paper)
ISBN-10: 0-521-78653-3 (pbk. : alk. paper)
1. South Asia–Languages. 2. Sociolinguistics–South Asia. 3. Multilingualism–South Asia. 4. Language planning–South Asia. 5. Indic philology. I. Kachru, Braj B. II. Kachru, Yamuna. III. Sridhar, S. N. IV. Title.

P381.S58L36 2007
306.4′40954–dc22
2006037011

ISBN 978-0-521-78141-1 hardback
ISBN 978-0-521-78653-9 paperback

In Memoriam

William Bright (1928–2006)
Suniti Kumar Chatterji (1890–1977)
Murray B. Emeneau (1904–2005)
Charles A. Ferguson (1921–1998)
Sumitra Mangesh Katre (1906–1998)
Prabodh B. Pandit (1923–1975)
A. K. Ramanujan (1929–1993)
Ravindra N. Srivastava (1936–1992)

Contents

Figures

Maps

Tables

Preface

This volume is the sixth in the series initiated by Cambridge University Press twenty-six years ago. The first book in the series was *Language in the USA*, edited by Charles A. Ferguson and Shirley Brice Heath (1981). The inspiration for the present volume on *Language in South Asia* came from Ferguson and Heath's pathbreaking contribution. It was the late Professor Ferguson who, in his inimitably persuasive way, suggested to one of the editors of the present volume the desirability and importance of a book on *Language in South Asia*. That was in the late 1970s, when *Language in the USA* was in the final stages of publication.

Charles A. Ferguson, affectionately called Fergi, was a committed scholar in South Asian linguistics in more than one sense. Thom Huebner, once a faculty colleague of Ferguson at Stanford University, succinctly summarizes Ferguson's "longest standing interests" in South Asia that goes back to 1945. It was then that Ferguson published his first article on South Asian linguistics. Since then, adds Huebner,

> he has published nearly twenty others, he has co-edited a major volume on the topic (Ferguson and Gumperz, 1960), and there has been at least one volume of South Asian linguistics dedicated to him (Krishnamurti, 1986). In "South Asia as a Sociolinguistic Area," Ferguson highlights some features of language use that make South Asia unique. In the process he demonstrates how features of language use just as well as language structure can cluster in real relationships. Not only does the paper deepen the reader's understanding of the region, it also suggests that this type of research into the language situation of a larger geographical region can have implications for theories of language change and cultural diffusion in general. (1996: 21)

Huebner explains that what is characteristic of Ferguson's "uniquely Fergusonian" contribution and quality is derived from:

> his solid training in Sanskrit, Greek, Latin and Oriental languages at the University of Pennsylvania, in descriptive linguistics there under Harris, and in the interest not only in language but also in the people who use it. That perspective is one that consistently looks for the relationship between diachronic language change and language development, phonology and syntax, social conventionalization and cognitive processing, and language universals and individual differences. (12)

In his research and teaching, Ferguson was not committed to just one theory or methodology. That was evident in his unparalleled gift of academic leadership internationally. This volume is a modest attempt to celebrate Ferguson's contribution to South Asian linguistics as a teacher, as a researcher, and, indeed, as one of the promoters of linguistics in the subcontinent.

We express our gratitude and thanks to Indian linguists who trained a generation of South Asian linguists in the 1950s and beyond, following the Deccan College and Rockefeller Foundation initiatives of the 1950s for the teaching of, and research in, linguistics in the region. These include Ashok Kelkar, Bh. Krishnamurti, Prabodh B. Pandit, and Ravindra N. Srivastava. It is now the generation of their *śiṣyas*, encouraged and trained by them, who are in the forefront of South Asian linguistics, not only in South Asia, but internationally, and continue the *guru–śiṣya paramparā*.

We also want to celebrate the memory of those linguists who had initiated a new direction in South Asian linguistics in the 1960s in what was then East Bengal – a part of Pakistan. These linguists, along with other intellectuals and scholars, were cruelly assassinated in Dacca University during the Bangladesh Liberation War against Pakistan (1971). A generation of Bangladeshi linguists was lost.

We are grateful to many colleagues and friends who provided insights, suggestions, and critiques in planning *Language in South Asia* at the University of Illinois at Urbana-Champaign, the United States, and at the University of Delhi and Jawaharlal Nehru University in New Delhi, India.

The chapters in this volume understandably do not cover all the dimensions of language in South Asian societies. *Language in South Asia* provides some selected facets of the issues that are articulated in current debates. It is our hope that this book, like the proverbial palimpsest that has been written over and over again, is yet another attempt in that direction.

References

Ferguson, Charles A. 1945. "A chart of the Bengali verb." *Journal of the American Oriental Society* 65, 1, 54–5.

Ferguson, Charles A. 1992. "South Asia as a sociolinguistic area," in *Dimensions of Sociolinguistics in South Asian. Papers in Memory of Gerald Kelley*, edited by Edward C. Dimock, Jr., Braj B. Kachru, and Bh. Krishnamurti New Delhi: Oxford and India Book House, pp. 25–36.

Ferguson, Charles A. and John J. Gumperz. 1960. *Linguistic Diversity in South Asia (International Journal of American Linguistics* 26, 3, 2*)*. Bloomington: Indiana University Press.

Huebner, Thom (ed.) 1996. *Sociolinguistic Perspectives: Papers on Language in Society, 1959–1994*. Oxford: Oxford University Press.

Krishnamurti, Bh. (ed.) 1986. *South Asian Languages: Structural Convergence and Diglossia*. New Delhi: Motilal Banarsidass.

Acknowledgments

Chapter authors in this volume acknowledge the helpful advice, suggestions, and support of their colleagues, students, and assistants in the preparation of their contributions in this volume.

Karumuri V. Subbarao, the author of Chapter 2, is thankful to Mimi Kevichusa for the Angami data, Van Lal Bapui for the Hmar data, Sarju Devi and Geeta Devi for the Manipuri data, and Teresa Sundi, Bir Singh Sinku, and C. B. Deogam for the Ho data. The author is also thankful to the editors Braj B. Kachru and S. N. Sridhar, to the anonymous reviewers, and to Ronald Asher for their valuable comments.

Anvita Abbi, the author of Chapter 7, is thankful to Yogendra Yadav for supplying her information on Nepal, and Tariq Rahman, Joan Baart, and Carla Radloff for information on Pakistan.

Ashok Aklujkar, the author of Chapter 9, is grateful to Mahes Raj Pant and Diwakar Acharya, who caught the author's attention in his oversights in the first draft of this chapter, and to Tej K. Bhatia, Peter E. Hook, Madhav M. Deshpande, P. R. Subramanian, S. N. Sridhar, and James Nye, who supplied the necessary bibliographical information when the sources accessible proved to be inadequate.

S. N. Sridhar, the author of Chapter 11, is grateful to Braj B. Kachru and Hans H. Hock for their comments on an earlier version of this chapter that appeared in *Lingua* 53 (1981), 199–220.

Ian Smith, the author of Chapter 12, is grateful to B.A. Hussainmiya for the Sri Lanka Muslim Tamil and Sri Lanka Malay data, and to Sonny Lim for the Bazaar Malay data.

Rama Kant Agnihotri, the author of Chapter 13, is thankful to Rimli Bhattacharya, Shahid Amin, Anvita Abbi, and Kumar Sahani for their suggestions, and is grateful to Vandana Puri, Uddipan, and Ketawala Buddhasiri for their help.

S. N. Sridhar, the author of Chapter 16, is thankful to E. Annamalai, Mark Aronoff, Bh. Krishnamurti, K. Marula Siddappa, K. V. Narayana, and Ki Ram Nagaraja for helpful comments.

Tej K. Bhatia and Robert J. Baumgardner, the authors of Chapter 19, are thankful to Bader Masood of the Australian High Commission for providing materials on Pakistan, and to Vindya Pinnaduwa for providing materials on Sri Lanka.

Tamara M. Valentine, the author of Chapter 22, is grateful to the American Institute of Indian Studies and National Endowment for the Humanities for their support to conduct field research in India during the academic year 2000–2001.

Kamal K. Sridhar, the author of Chapter 26, is grateful to Tony Polson and Soma Phillipos for help in collecting Malayali data and to Hema Shah for the Gujarati data.

Abbreviations

Chapter 2

1, 2, 3	first/second/third person
acc	accusative
adjr	adjectivalizer
agr	agreement
comp	complementizer
dat	dative
decl	declarative
def	definite
det	determiner
dm	deictic marker
DO	direct object
dub	dubitative
emph	emphatic
epen	epenthetic
erg	ergative
fem	feminine
fut	future
inch	inchoative
incl	inclusive
inf	infinitive
io	indirect object
IO	indirect object
masc	masculine
mkr	marker
neut	neuter
nm	nonmasculine
nom	nominative
noz	nominalizer
O	object
obj	object
P	place adverbial

perf	perfect
pl	plural
pred	predicate
pres	present
prog	progressive
pron	pronominal
pst	past
q	question
S	subject
SALs	South Asian languages
sg	singular
sub	subject
sx	suffix
T	time adverbial
tr	transitive
V	verb
vr	verbal reflexive
vrec	verbal reciprocal
y/n qm	yes/no question marker

Chapter 3

asp	aspirated
caus.	causative
dbl. tr.	double transitive
dir.	direct
f.	feminine
hon.	honorific
intr.	intransitive
m.	masculine
obl.	oblique
pl.	plural
poss.	possessive
sg.	singular
tr.	transitive
unasp	unaspirated
vd	voiced
vl	voiceless
voc.	vocative

Chapter 5

SA	South Asia

Chapter 7

DNT	Denotified Tribes

Chapter 11

3rd	third person
B	Brahman
H-U	Hindi–Urdu
id.	–
Ka.	Kannada
Ma.	Malay
NB	non-Brahman
neut.	neuter
pej.	pejorative
Pkt.	Prakrit
S.Dr.	South Dravidian
sing.	singular
Skt.	Sanskrit
Ta.	Tamil
Te.	Telugu
Tu.	Tulu

Chapter 12

1st pers.	first person
2nd pers.	second person
3rd pers.	third person
ACC	accusative
DAT	dative
DET	determiner
fem.	feminine
fut	future
GEN	genitive
HABIL	habilitative

hon	honorific
INFIN	infinitive
INST	instrumental
masc.	masculine
NEG	negative
PAST	past
pl	plural
Ptg.	Portuguese
sg	singular
NONFUT	nonfuture
Si.	Sinhala
SL Malay	Sri Lanka Malay
SLM Tamil	Sri Lanka Muslim Tamil
SLP	Sri Lanka Portuguese
Std.	standard
Ta.	Tamil

Chapter 14

C	Consonant
V	Vowel

Chapter 16

1S	first person singular
3SN	3rd person, singular, neuter
ACC	accusative
DAT	dative
hon	honorific
INF	infinitive
PASS	passive
PST	past
REL.PTPL.	relative, participle

Chapter 17

hon.	honorific
P-A	Perso-Arabic
S	Sanskrit

Chapter 21

MSA	Modern South Asian
SA	South Asian

Chapter 24

acc.	accusative
Adj.	adjective
decl.	declarative
excl.	exclamation
hon.	honorific

Chapter 25

A	Awadhi
B	Bhojpuri
Be	Bengali
E. Hn	Eastern Hindi dialects
Eng	English
FH	Fiji Hindi
GB	Guyanese Bhojpuri
Hn	Hindi
IB	Indian Bhojpuri
M	Magahi
Ma	Marathi
MB	Mauritian Bhojpuri
OBH	overseas varieties of Bhojpuri-Hindi
SB	South African Bhojpuri
SH	Suriname Hindustani
Std Hn	Standard Hindi
TB	Trinidad Bhojpuri
UP	Uttar Pradesh
W. Hn	Western Hindi dialects

Note on Transcription

The contributors to this volume have used more than one transcription system to represent the sounds of South Asian languages. For example, long vowels are represented either by a length mark over the letter or a colon after the letter, retroflexes are represented by the International Phonetic Association (IPA) symbols or by a dot under the letter, or a capital letter. Since all of these different systems will be encountered by readers as they go to primary sources, we have retained the different systems used by the contributors as long as they represent one of the more widely used systems.

Introduction: languages, contexts, and constructs

Braj B. Kachru

There are multiple constructs of South Asian language contexts. The region has been characterized, in great exasperation, as a linguistic "problem area," a proverbial Tower of Babel. These metaphors apply to South Asia as a whole, to the State of India, and to each distinct region. A penetrating observer of Indian society and culture, V. S. Naipaul, portrayed this land of his ancestors as "a country of a million little mutinies." But the crises of the mutinies, reassures Naipaul, "were the beginning of a new way for many millions, part of India's growth, part of its restoration" (1990: 517–18). Naipaul, of course, was not specifically thinking of the region's language conflicts, but if he were, he would not be entirely wrong. Those linguistic mutinies, the long history of the subcontinent tells us, have ultimately proved to be creative conflicts in many ways.

The Indian subcontinent comprises seven sovereign states: India (population 1,095,351,995), Pakistan (165,803,560), Bangladesh (147,365,352), Nepal (28,287,147), Sri Lanka (20,222,240), Bhutan (2,279,723), and Maldives (359,008).[1] But linguistically speaking, these political divisions cloud the extensive underlying – and deeply shared – chronicles of literary and sociolinguistic histories of the present seven states of the subcontinent.[2] The major language families of South Asia are Indo-Aryan, Dravidian, Tibeto-Burman, and Munda. The region's diversity also manifests itself in religious pluralism, representing Buddhism, Christianity, Hinduism, Islam, Jainism, Sikhism, and Zoroastrianism.

The South Asian region comprises almost 25 percent of the global population. This number, however, represents only a part of the linguistic reality of the subcontinent. In their historical and functional contexts, the South Asian languages exhibit an extended tradition of diffusion, mutual contact, and convergence.

This earlier, and ongoing, linguistic convergence (*Sprachbund*) between and among typologically distinct languages is also evident in their literatures,

[1] These figures are taken from www.cia.gov/cia/publications/factbook/geos/us.html

[2] In earlier linguistic and literary studies the term "India" does not necessarily refer to the present territorial and political map of post-1947 India. The concept is used in a wider sense of shared identities and linguistic histories of the region that now includes several other states.

folk traditions, and three major linguistic impacts, those of Sanskritization, Persianization, and Englishization. These processes of convergence continue to be evident in contemporary languages in their linguistic hybridizations and fusions in every region of South Asia. These contact phenomena are evident in what may be described as linguistic "look-alikeness" in the languages of the region beyond the lexical level: the areal characteristics of the South Asian languages have been studied, discussed, and illustrated in convergence processes in grammar, phonology, discourse, and literary creativity. It is on the basis of such evidence that India/South Asia has been characterized as a linguistic, literary, and sociolinguistic area. For example, Kannada, a Dravidian language, has a long history of mutual convergence with Marathi, an Indo-Aryan language. This type of productive process is also evident in other Dravidian languages, such as Tamil, Telugu, and Malayalam. There is indeed an extensive and much-discussed body of research on such convergence, termed the *Indo-Aryanization* of Dravidian languages and *Dravidianization* of Indo-Aryan languages (See, e.g. Emeneau 1956; Ferguson 1992; B. Kachru 1976; Masica 1976; Mukherjee 1981; Nadkarni 1975; Pandit 1977; Ramanujan and Masica 1969; S. N. Sridhar 1981).

The ten parts of *Language in South Asia* are very selective. They present overviews of various selected facets of the language situation in the vast subcontinent in the three areas mentioned above: linguistic, historical, and sociolinguistic. In Part 1, "Language History, Families, and Typology," Ronald E. Asher and Karumuri V. Subbarao provide a backdrop for contextualizing the histories of South Asian language families and their typological characteristics. Part 2, "Languages and Their Functions," locates selected languages in contexts of history and their domains of functions. The languages discussed are "Hindi–Urdu–Hindustani" (Yamuna Kachru), "Persian in South Asia" (S. A. H. Abidi and Ravinder Gargesh), "Major Regional Languages" (Tej K. Bhatia), "Minority Languages and Their Status" (Rakesh M. Bhatt and Ahmar Mahboob), and "Tribal Languages" (Anvita Abbi). Part 3, "Sanskrit and Traditions of Language Study," provides fresh perspectives on "Sanskrit in the South Asian Sociolinguistic Context" (Madhav Deshpande), and on the long traditions of the study and teaching of the Sanskrit language in "Traditions of Language Study in South Asia" (Ashok Aklujkar).

The three chapters in Part 4, "Multilingualism, Contact, and Convergence," address the manifestations and implications of the three core issues of South Asia's linguistic pluralism: "Contexts of Multilingualism" (E. Annamalai), "Language Contact and Convergence in South Asia" (S. N. Sridhar), and "Pidgins, Creoles, and Bazaar Hindi" (Ian Smith). In Part 5, "Orality, Literacy, and Writing Systems," Rama Kant Agnihotri focuses on "our linguistic and cultural behavior in response to changes in interactional situations," and Peter T. Daniels on South Asian writing systems of major and minor languages.

The one chapter in Part 6, Language Conflicts, (Robert B. King), addresses the most explosive, provocative, and still unresolved concerns – those of "Language Politics and Conflicts." Part 7, "Language Modernization in Kannada," again a solo chapter by S. N. Sridhar, outlines the linguistic processes, controversies, and implications of language modernization. Part 8, "Language and Discourse," brings together five distinct functional domains of language: "Language in Social and Ethnic Interaction" (Yamuna Kachru), "Language and the Legal System" (Vijay K. Bhatia and Rajesh Sharma), "Language in the Media and Advertising" (Tej K. Bhatia and Robert Baumgardner), "Language in Cinema" (Wimal Dissanayake), and "Language of Religion" (Rajeshwari V. Pandharipande).

The three chapters in Part 9, "Language and Identity," outline and illustrate the strategies applied to constructs of gender (Tamara Valentine) and to the traditionally marginalized – and generally ignored – topic of Dalit literature and language (Eleanor Zelliot). The last chapter in this section, by Rukmini Bhaya Nair, is a pioneering exploration of language and youth culture.

The concluding part, Part 10, "Languages in Diaspora," provides perspectives on selected diasporic locations of South Asian languages – their histories, their altered contexts and acculturations, and linguistic impacts of the dominant languages of the regions: Rajend Mesthrie writes about South Africa, where the relocated South Asian population is now estimated to be over one million, and Kamal K. Sridhar that of the United Kingdom and the United States with estimated populations of over two million and one-and-a-quarter million, respectively, that is, the combined South Asian population of over three-and-half million.[3]

Languages of wider functions

In this tapestry of typologically related – and unrelated – families of languages and their subvarieties that represent distinctions of caste, class, profession, religion, and region, it is, however, the network of languages of *wider communication* that cut across linguistic and geographical boundaries and facilitate communication in various pan-South Asian functions across the subcontinent.

[3] The sources for the figures quoted here are the following:
For South Africa, Simelane, Sandie E. (2002). Note that Simelane gives figures only for Indians: 1,045,597 (2.6 percent). No mention is made of Pakistan, Bangladesh, or any other country of the region. For the UK www.movinghere.org.uk/galleries/histories/asian/origins/local1.htm, accessed July 7, 2006. For the year 2001, the population figures are India (1,028,539), Pakistan (706,752), Bangladesh (275,250), Total South Asia (2,010,541). No mention is made of Sri Lanka and other countries of the region. For the USA www.migrationinformation.org/USfocus/display.cfm?ID=378, accessed July 7, 2006.

See Dixon 2006. India (1,022,552), Pakistan (223,477) [data based on US Census Bureau, 2000]. The total cited above includes minimum numbers for Bangladesh, Sri Lanka, and other countries of the region.

It is the languages of *wider functions* that link regional, ethnic, and linguistic populations of the pluralistic subcontinent. These languages are used in varying degrees of functional effectiveness and communication, in administrative, commercial, and religious contexts, and in cross-linguistic situations, and often as languages of status, power, and identity construction.

This section briefly contextualizes the role of three such languages that resulted in Sanskritization, Persianization, and Englishization of South Asian languages. The volume does not include a chapter on South Asian English. This Introduction, however, contextualizes the earlier phase of introduction of English in South Asia and provides a selected bibliographical narrative of what is now characterized as South Asian English(es), in the voices of administrators, educators, and journalists.[4]

Chapters 8 (Madhav M. Deshpande) and 9 (Ashok Aklujkar) discuss the functions that Sanskrit has performed in a variety of domains. There has been, and continues to be, a distinct impact of Sanskritization in philosophical and metaphysical discourses, rituals, and literary creativity in almost every genre in all major South Asian languages and literatures.[5] The later, gradual but marked, Persianization of South Asian languages introduced yet another dimension to the linguistic and literary contexts of South Asia, as outlined in Chapter 4 by Abidi and Gargesh.

Sanskritization

The emergence of modern South Asian languages after 1000 CE did not diminish the impact of Sanskrit. Chaitanya insightfully summarizes this ongoing impact of the language:

> when the modern Indian languages began to emerge as literary vehicles, the influence of Sanskrit was in no way diminished, although there was a change in the form of that influence. (1977: 30)

The altered form of the impact of Sanskrit is characterized in the following terms: (1977: 30)

> If the cultured people began to compose increasingly in the regional languages, the great majority of them derived their inspiration from the Sanskrit tradition, many of them wrote in Sanskrit also in addition to the vernacular, and the bulk of the early literature in all these languages is mostly translation of Sanskrit classics.

[4] See, for example Das 1991 for a detailed and insightful discussion on the impact of Western education on Indian literatures and literary creativity. See also B. Kachru 1994.

[5] See, for example Chaitanya 1977; Das 1991.

Sanskritization, as is well documented (1977: 30):

> Powerfully influenced even the Dravidian group of languages and the texture of Telugu, Kanarese and Malayalam is today indistinguishable from that of Bengali or Marathi as far as the Sanskrit derivation of the bulk of the vocabulary is concerned.

And concerning the resistance of Tamil to Sanskritization of its written form, Chaitanya adds (1977: 30):

> If Tamil resisted the Sanskritization of its alphabet, we must recall that Agastya who lived in the second century B.C. and his disciple who wrote the *Tolkappiyam*, took ample inspiration from Yaska, Panini and Indra Dutta in laying the foundations of Dravidian grammar and rhetoric.

And Chaitanya explains:

> Further, the eighth century works of Jains in Tamil, like the *Sri Purana*, *Nilakesi*, *Samaya Divakara*, etc., use as highly Sanskritized a language as the Manipravalam works of Malayalam.

In conclusion, Chaitanya says:

> Above all, even if the Tamil language resisted dominance by Sanskrit, the contribution of Tamilnad to Sanskrit studies has in no way been less than that of any other region. (30–1)

Persianization

The Persian language was introduced, as discussed in Chapter 4, at the time of Mahmud of Ghazni (1001–1026 CE). The implantation, spread, and impact of Persian, has been a controversial topic with a variety of constructs. The American historian Stanley Wolpert observes that the Mughuls "spread Perso-Arabic poetry and prose with their swords of Islamic conquest and conversion" (1991: 185). With the gradual stabilization of Mughul power, Persian became the language of courts, administration, and literary creativity in several regions of South Asia. The domination, diffusion, and social penetration of the Persian language cultivated a distinct literary and intellectual culture that left a deep impact on South Asia's major languages, literatures, and a variety of administrative and legal genres.

An illustrative case of Persianization is the state of Jammu and Kashmir in India. In Kashmir, the ancestral Sanskrit language was gradually reduced primarily to Hindu ritualistic functions. The pandits of Kashmir, with altered political dynamics of the region, switched to Persian. The Persian language was then established as the language of power, politics, status, and literary recognition. The pandits used the medium of Persian to impart their religious, cultural, and ritualistic texts, such as the *Mahābhārata*, *Bhāgvata*, *Rāmāyaṇa*, and *Shivpurāṇa*. The Kashmiri Pandits produced their religious and ritualistic texts in the Perso-Arabic script so that Hindus knowing Persian could read them and not depend on the Devanagari or the now almost extinct Sharada scripts. These included the texts of *karmakāṇda* (Hindu rituals), *jyotiṣ śāstra* (astrology), and *āyurveda* (the indigenous medical system).

In her treatise, *The Way of the Swan*, Cook further elaborates this point when she observes:[6]

> ... the pandits [of Kashmir] composed a new Shaiva literature in Persian verse. The classical Persian *gazal* became the ode to Shiva, Lord of the La Makan, Spaceless Space. The technical vocabulary of Erfan suited their purposes perfectly, and morning prayers were conducted in a Persian which listening neighbors could not distinguish from songs of the "Orafa." Whatever position they won for themselves in India when forced out of Kashmir by Persian-speaking invaders, the pandit emigrés continued to compose their Persian Shaiva odes. (1958: 8–9)

It is, therefore, understandable that the Persian classics, such as the *Mathnavi* of Moulana Rumi, the *Shāhnāma* of Firdusi, and the *Sikandarnāma* of Nizami, were taught in the *maktabs* (schools for Koranic instruction) which were, as the Kashmiri scholar Pushp observes, often run by Kashmiri Pandit *akhuns* "who had no inhibition in popularizing Persian handbooks" (Pushp 1996: 22).

The Persianization of Kashmir was not a unique case; it provides just one example of the linguistic, cultural, and political impact of Persian. Chaitanya, in contextualizing the introduction and diffusion of the Persian language in wider Indian political and social contexts, says: "With the consolidation of Muslim power in North India, Persian became a formidable rival to Sanskrit for the patronage of the Imperial court." And Chaitanya further reminds us:

> But we must not forget that Akbar and that ill-fated son of Shah Jahan, Dara Shikoh, were great patrons of Sanskrit. Bairam Khan, the Great Khan (Khan Khanan) who was the general of Akbar, was also a Sanskrit scholar. Further, the competition of Persian was felt only in the Moghul court. The culture of most of the vassal states was Hindu and every dynasty patronized Sanskrit. (1977: 31)

Englishization

The numbers of South Asian users of English now exceed the combined population of the Inner Circle of English – the United States, the United

[6] See, Cook 1958.

Kingdom, Canada, Australia, and New Zealand. The Asian continent, particularly South Asia and China, have altered the international profile of world Englishes.[7]

The location of the English language in South Asia, and its gradual, extensively argued, debated, and reconstructed diffusion, in this subcontinent is closely linked with the firm political control of various regions by what was the British Empire. The political control that lasted for over two hundred years, ending in the 1940s, did not include the end of the linguistic legacy of the Raj – the English language.

In tracing the relationship of the empire and its antecedents, it is said that the first English-knowing person to visit India may have been an emissary of Alfred the Great in 882 CE. According to the Anglo-Saxon Chronicle, he visited the subcontinent with gifts to be offered at the tomb of St. Thomas. Speculating about the antecedents of English in the subcontinent, the late Samuel Mathai, a distinguished professor of English studies in India, wonders:

> . . . who first spoke English in India. When Sir Thomas Roe presented his credentials as Ambassador of James I at the court of Jehangir in Delhi in 1615, the East India company, which had been in India already for some fifteen years, had established factories at Surat and other places, and had brought the English language to the shores of India. Sir Thomas was Ambassador to the Great Moghul for three years. ([1979] 2004: v)

And Mathai observes: "[d]uring these years there must have been a small English-speaking community in Delhi" (ibid.).

The recorded history thus shows that significant contacts with English started in the seventeenth century, which gradually led to the maneuvering toward strategic control of various regions of the subcontinent. This mission was almost accomplished by the eighteenth and nineteenth centuries. The process of the introduction of English was slow and much debated by the managers of the Raj, church groups, and native intellectuals, and politicians. The subsequent unprecedented functional and social penetration of the English language may be viewed in four overlapping phases: Exploration, Implementation, Diffusion, and Institutionalization. It was through these controversial and celebratory strategies that the English language acquired an unparalleled position in its social, linguistic, literary, and ideological impact on the subcontinent.

The first phase of exploration was dominated by missionary organizations, with initial support from the government, which played an important role in the debate on the future status of English in South Asia. In a study on *Promotion of*

[7] See, B. Kachru 2005, section entitled "The heart of the matter", pp. 205–7. See also Kachru, Kachru and Nelson 2006, pp. 90–129.

Learning in India by Early European Settlers, Narendra Nath Law summarizes the main object of the missionaries as "the propagation of the Gospel." And in further elucidation, he observes that, "they [the missionaries] were directed purely to religious education . . . through their native language which the Europeans tried to master, as also the spread of Western education among the Indians in order to enable them to appreciate better the Christian values" (1915: 6–7).[8]

The "missionary clause" that was added to the Charter of the East India Company in 1698 lasted until 1765 when direct support and encouragement of the missionary activities was discontinued. There was a well-documented, violent reaction, particularly from the Clapham sect. Charles Grant (1746–1823) expressed concern about the morals of the people in the subcontinent and provided the following remedy:

> The true curse of darkness is the introduction of light. The Hindoos err, because they are ignorant and their errors have never fairly been laid before them. The communication of our light and knowledge to them, would prove the best remedy for their disorders (Grant, 1831–1832: 60–1).

In 1813, it was therefore determined that:

> Measures ought to be introduced as may tend to the introduction among them [the natives of the subcontinent] of useful knowledge, and of religious and moral improvement. That in furtherance of the above objects sufficient facilities shall be afforded by law to persons desirous of going to, or remaining in India (Parliament Debate, 26).

The point of "religious and moral education" was further emphasized before Parliament in rather stronger words by William Wilberforce, then Foreign Secretary, when he proposed to "exchange its [India's] dark and bloody superstition for the genial influence of Christian light and truth." It was through such initiatives that the missionary activities were revived. The initiatives provided additional stimulus and motivation for the teaching of English, which was already in the curriculum of the missionary schools.

In prepartition India, the phase of implementation began over one hundred and seventy years ago. It was then that Thomas Babington Macaulay's (1800–1859) controversial Minute was introduced in Parliament, on February 2, 1835. This much-debated Minute provided a blueprint for undivided India's educational strategies and policy. A debate still continues on the motives and ultimate success of Macaulay's mission of creating "a class of persons, Indians in blood and

[8] For details about the period of exploration, see, for example for India, Sherring 1884; Richter 1908; Law 1915; for Sri Lanka, Ruberu 1962; and for Pakistan, Rahman 1996a, Chapters 3 and 4, and 1991a, b.

colour, but English in taste, in opinions, in morals and in intellect." In Macaulay's view, India's native languages were "poor and rude" and the learning of the East was "a little hocus-pocus about cusa-grass and the modes of absorption into the Diety" (Bryant 1932: 56–7). This statement was made, in spite of his also often-cited arrogant confession that "I have no knowledge of either Sanskrit or Arabic. But I have done what I could to form a correct estimate of their value."

In presenting this Minute for approval to the Supreme Council of India, Macaulay unambiguously indicated to the Council "his intention of resigning if they [his recommendations] were not accepted" (ibid.: 56). The Minute received the Seal of Approval from Lord William Bentick (1774–1839) on March 7, 1835. A distinguished British educator and linguist, John Rupert Firth (1890–1960), who taught during the end of the British Raj in Lahore (now in Pakistan), held "superficial Lord Macaulay" responsible for "the superficiality characteristic of Indian education" (Firth, 1930: 210–11).

There was, one must add, also a socially active Indian group who desired "the natives of India" to be instructed in mathematics and sciences, led by Rammohan Roy (1772–1833), who were, as Roy says (1823: 99–101):

> Filled with sanguine hopes [that] European gentlemen of talents and education would instruct the natives of India in mathematics, natural philosophy, chemistry, anatomy and other useful sciences which the natives of Europe have carried to a degree of perfection that has raised them above the inhabitants of other parts of the world.

Macaulay's vision of a "class of persons . . . English in taste, in opinions, in morals and in intellect" that the introduction of English education was to have achieved succeeded only partially. In reality, the opinions, values, and vision that South Asian English users nurtured and presented through the English medium were not consistent with the beliefs of the architects of the Minute. The medium instead turned into "a linguistic weapon" that articulated *mantras* (messages) that the architects of English education did not foresee and did not put on their agenda for the language plans of the Raj.

In the linguistically pluralistic subcontinent, the English language became a mobilizing medium that was rediscovering, as it were, the subcontinent. The Bengali writer Bankim Chandra Chatterjee reflects on this pragmatic reality of the subcontinent when he says:

> There is no hope for India until the Bengali and the Panjabi understand and influence each other, and can bring their influence to bear upon the Englishman. This can be done only through the medium of English. (cited in Wolpert 1991: 187)

The history, motivations, and intended educational, ideological, and political goals in the context of Ceylon (now Sri Lanka) were not much different from the Indian subcontinent (for references, see B. Kachru 1994, 2005).

Constructs of English (1854–1976)

Chatterjee's above statement was indeed just one construct of English, the medium and what it conveys. What follows is a selected bibliographical narrative of multiple voices, those of the colonizers and the colonizees, from 1837 to 1976. These many voices represent a variety of faces, attitudes, and agendas about locating the language in the subcontinent and about its South Asianization.

One of the earlier studies, by Alexander Duff (1837) of the General Assembly's Mission, Calcutta (now Kolkata), presents his vision of a "New Era of the English Language and English Literature in India." This study provides a context for understanding the colonial debates during the Raj and the linguistic turbulence that continues to surface in post-Raj South Asia.

David O. Allen (1854), a missionary of the American Board of India, provides yet another prescient view. It appears to Allen that

> from the designs of Providence as developed in the course of events, that English is to be the language generally used in North America, and that in a few generations it will be vernacular over a larger part of the world and among a larger population than has ever yet used a common language . . . that the English language is hereafter to exert an influence in the world far beyond any other language, ancient or modern (p. 265).

David Allen asks: "the English possessions in Southern Asia appear likely to be yet further extended. It becomes therefore an interesting question, how far are these conquests likely to extend the knowledge and use of the English language in those countries?" Allen further analyzes this question from the perspectives of "several facts" and "circumstances" (p. 265).

Nilmani Cowar (1859) discusses Macaulay's Minute of 1835. The question Cowar asked, almost a century and a half ago, continues to vibrate even now, not only in South Asia but also beyond this subcontinent: "Can English be the language of India [South Asia]?" In concluding his arguments, Cowar says: " . . . whatever direction we may choose to view the subject, we cannot be persuaded to believe that the home-grown languages of India will be superseded by the English" (12).

Alexander Allardyce (1877) provides socially realistic construct of "the Anglo-Indian tongue."[9] The question he addressed in 1877 has continued to be discussed in linguistic literature about, for example, "code-mixing", and "code-switching" in South Asian English and other varieties of world Englishes. "What right, says someone, can our unnatural countrymen in India have to desecrate their mother tongue in this fashion?" Allardyce's linguistically appropriate answer is: "The mixture of English and native words, which we call

[9] The word "Anglo-Indian" originally referred to a British person in India but "was officially adopted in 1900 to describe persons of mixed descent, then known as Eurasians" (Allen 1975: 21).

Anglo-Indianisms, constitutes an idiom in the speech of the governing clan, and really forms a bond of union between them and the governed" (p. 541). The example he provides is:

I'm dikk'd to death! The khansamah had got chhutti, and the whole bangla is ulta-pulta. The khidmatghars loot everything, and the masalchi is breaking all the surwa-basans; and when I give a hokhm to cut their tallabs they get magra, and ask their jawabs. And then the maistries are putting up jill-mills, and making such a gol-mol, that I say darwaza band to everybody. But when all is tik, I hope you will tiff with us.

Presenting a functionally appropriate aside about the example, Allardyce adds: "To those whose lives have been passed upon this side of Suez, a speech like the above will seem somewhat puzzling; but it would be perfectly intelligible in a Calcutta [now Kolkata] drawing-room." And to illustrate the difference between Queen's and Company's English, Allardyce provides a "translation" of the above illustration, which, says the author, "we have supposed a fair hostess saying to some morning caller":

I'm bothered to death! The butler has got leave, and the whole house is turned upside down. The table-servants steal everything, and the scullion is breaking all the soup-plates; and when I order their wages to be cut, they all grow sulky and give warning. And then the carpenters are putting up venetians, and making such an uproar, that I am obliged to say 'not at home' to everybody. But when all is put to rights (sic.), I hope you will lunch with us (p.541).

Is this *desecration* of language by "our unnatural countrymen in India?" Allardyce's answer is:

The mixture of English and native words, which we call Anglo-Indianisms, constitutes an idiom in the speech of governing class, and really forms a bond of union between them and the governed.

Allardyce's was one of the first attempts to place Indian functions of English and its hybridization in a socially realistic functional context. This insightful study concludes:

It is almost touching to see how two old Anglo-Indians are drawn together by the familiar talk, and to hear what wonderful stories, couched in how unintelligible language, they have got to tell. It is getting the fashion nowadays for purists to sneer at Anglo-Indianisms; but no one who is really acquainted with Anglo-Indian society will have any fault to find with a dialect that so admirably serves to express its wants and ideas (p. 551).

Ellis Underwood (1885) brings yet other imagined constructs of Indian [South Asian] creativity in English. His "little book" provides "a brief sketch of some of the chief characteristics of the Native of India, as indicated and illustrated by the style and the feelings displayed in his compositions in the English language." The author aptly reminds us: "If 'the apparel oft proclaims the man,' much more does his style and diction" (pp. 7–8).

Underwood's first chapter is essentially about "magniloquence of style," illustrated with examples from Indian writing of the period. The chapter on poetry tells us (p. 21):

> [t]here are some enterprising Natives – happily their number is at present comparatively few – who have ventured to make excursions into the field of English verse.

These are divided into two categories: the *magniloquent* and *painfully prosaic*. The illustrative texts, for example, are by: The Head Clerk of a Sadr Post Office and author of an Urdu Moral Book who wrote, "[A] welcome to His Excellency the Right Hon'ble Edward Robert Lytton Bulwer, Viceroy and Governor General of India, for the Imperial Durbar"; and another poem by "[A] Parsee gentleman in the spirit of loyalty" to the Duke and Duchess of Connaught on their visit to Bombay (now Mumbai). On "Phrases and Quotations; Slang," Underwood observes:

> It is the delight of the Oriental in a patch-work of gaudy colours and a cheap profusion of finery for his holiday decorations, carried into the domain of literature; in his diction, as at his festivals, he is apt to mistake garishness for splendour, tinsel for ornament. (p. 30)

The chapter on "Dependence of Character" focuses on, for example, "a spirit of complaisance," "an over-eager desire to please," which are, says the author, "an essential characteristic of the Oriental temperament" (43), and "to the most ordinary query – a reply almost unrivalled in its mingled caution and servility." This stylistic submission, says Underwood, "is not one that we can afford to contemplate with indifference, much less with satisfaction; and that (apart from general moral considerations)" (p. 45). In concluding the chapter, Underwood expresses his agony in these words:

> If such is the temperament prevailing among the educated and English-speaking classes of the Indian community, what must be that of the great mass of the Indian peoples with their old and long traditions of unresisting submission to the authority – a nation who have been "all their life-time subject to bondage," whether under Native or alien rule? (p. 51)

In the chapter on "Petitions and Appeals" Underwood turns his attention to this special register that was gradually developing in English in India, which reflects "this *ma–bap* attitude of mind," that is, the mind-set of total dependency, as that of a child on parents: *ma* (Hindi *mā̃*, mother) and *bap* (Hindi, *bāp*, father, p. 52).

In the final section, "Moral Principle; Sentimentalism," Underwood in the first part, refers to the duties of "a man and a citizen," and issues related to "secular education." But then he realizes that "our readers will have had enough of a rather unpleasant topic, and we pass on to the last characteristic" (p. 76). That is "the sensibility – the susceptibility to emotion – which is so marked a feature of the Indian temperament" (pp. 76–77). This trait, the author believes, is combined with that of "naivety". And he provides what he considers "an excellent example of how the Indian mind loves to gloat over its sorrows, and seems to take almost an artistic delight in 'piling up agony'" (pp. 78–79). And, finally, Underwood reassures his readers with a disclaimer:

In bringing to a conclusion this light, and by no means exhaustive, sketch of a not unimportant subject, we would disclaim any inclination on our own part to view Native character on its darker side. If its weaknesses and defects rather than its excellencies have formed our topic, the reason is intimately connected with the subject which we have chosen, and which naturally lends itself to such treatment. (p. 81)

The two reviews by Henry Yule (1886) and George Birdwood (1887) provide another view of the cultural penetration and assimilation of Indian (South Asian) English, its hybridization, and its social currency in multiple functions and registers.[10] By 1880, the linguistic processes of hybridization, fusion, and nativization were being noticed, analyzed, and discussed in education centres and the media, not only by British educators, administrators, and visitors, but also by "native" observers.

Yule (1886) and Birdwood (1887) provide descriptions of Yule's much-celebrated, and unparalleled, glossary of Anglo-Indian words and phrases. Yule's essay was written on his and Burnell's work at the request of the editor of *Asiatic Quarterly* "to provide some account of the work" (p. 119).

The esoteric title of the glossary has its own history: *Hobson-Jobson: A Glossary of Colloquial Anglo-Indian Words and Phrases, and of Kindred Items, Etymological, Historical, Geographical and Discursive* is discussed in detail by Yule in this review:

Hobson-Jobson, though now rare and moribund, is a typical and delightful example of that class of Anglo-Indian terms which consists of Oriental words highly assimilated, perhaps by vulgar lips, to the English vernacular, and seemed especially fitted to our book . . . (p. 131).

10 As an aside, it might be mentioned here that lexical compilations of Indian (South Asian) Englishes have a long history that dates back to 1653; see Yule 1886: 120; B. Kachru 1980 and later, particularly 2005, Chapter 27. Yule warns us: "The subject, in fact, had taken so comprehensive a shape that it was becoming difficult to say where its limits lay, or why it should ever end, except for an old reason, which had received such poignant illustration: *ars longa, vita brevis*" (Yule 1886: 120). See also, Hawkins 1976, 1984; B. Kachru 1980, 1994; Lewis 1991; and Muthiah 1991.

Over a hundred years later, this "legendary dictionary" is considered by Salman Rushdie "eloquent testimony to the unparalleled intermingling that took place between English and the languages of India" (1991: 81–3).

This awareness is evident in the writing of Hyde Clarke (1890) and Michael Macmillan (1895), who raise a variety of issues that continue to be discussed even now. Clarke's study is a panegyric of "[T]he English language in India and the East," which, he says, "binds together a great part of the population of the world, of many races and religions, but of which," he reminds us, "the English element is the original and main constituent" (p. 149). This study is not only an eulogy of the language, but also of the empire on which the Sun never set. Clarke claims that English-speaking populations "constitute the great organization for promoting the culture and advancement of mankind, for extending civilization, morality, and freedom" (p. 150). What a heavy burden and responsibility for the English speech community of the United Kindom!

Clarke provides a profile of the world's major languages and concludes that "[s]o far as language is concerned, it is evident that we [English speakers] are beyond competition by European languages," or Chinese – or any one of its dialects (p. 150). We are, asserts Clarke, "in possession of a great instrument of civilization . . . " (p. 150). But his main concern is that "Englishmen are so satisfied with the value of their language that they do not make it a boast nor take any measures for its diffusion" (p. 153). He sees linguistic challenges, in terms of language spread and diffusion, in Russia's "Russifying everything" (p. 155) and in "an aggressive institution," the *Alliance Française*, whose aim is the diffusion of the French language.

In Clarke's view, for a long period, Persian, Urdu, and Sanskrit have been encouraged, and they are all foreign languages in India, as much as is English; Sir William Jones "led the way, and when Sanskrit was a decaying language, its study has been revived" (p. 157); some day Sanskrit will be "an instrument against us"; and that until recently English has been "subjected to special discouragement" (p. 157).

Clarke is unhappy about India's "pseudo-universities and colleges" (p. 157) in which "school-masters' studies of Shakespeare only provide other feeders of baboo-English" (p. 157). What is the remedy? Clarke's answer is: "What is wanted for the development of India is work and workmen, and not Oxford and Cambridge schoolmasters with high salaries and great pretensions" (p. 158). The agony of the author is that "we do not . . . look after ourselves, or turn our advantages to the best account. We allow others to crow over us, and we neglect our own people" (pp. 161–62).

Michael Macmillan (1895), a Utilitarian Fellow of Bombay University and Professor of English Literature at Elphinstone College, Bombay (now Mumbai), provides an extremely well-illustrated and insightful discussion on "[t]he philological results" of the British Empire in India. These results have three manifestations: the incorporation of Indian words in English and of English words in India's languages, and the fact that several English words and several Indian words have assumed new senses and new combinations, owing to the social intercourse between Englishmen and natives of India (p. 78).

This linguistic process of contact and convergence, argues Macmillan, resulted earlier in the coalescing of Norman French and Anglo-Saxon over a period of time into one language, as did the fusion of Arabic and Persian, which resulted in an Indian language, Hindustani. In his view:

> We have, at the present time, the first steps of a similar fusion between the English language and the vernaculars of India, a process which, if continued for a century or two, would produce a new composite language, partly of Eastern and partly of European origin. (pp. 77–78)

The analysis of selected processes of "Anglo-Indian words and phrases" is discerning and profusely documented with those words which have been "admitted into full English citizenship," or are still "struggling" for such citizenship (p. 79). Macmillan's objective is "to show that the same principles of philology that rule the formation of the great literary languages of the world are clearly exemplified even in such a humble hybrid dialect as Anglo-Indian" (p. 114).

At the beginning of the new century, a variety of sociopolitical, educational, and hegemonic issues began to be articulated. A. P. Sen (1902) asks: "Does English education breed sedition in India?" The view that the Indian educational system had turned into a "breeding ground of sedition" was expressed not only in India but also in England. What was "sedition" for the agencies of the Raj in England and India was perhaps the beginning of the vision of the widely-cited letter by Raja Rammohan Roy to Lord Amherst in 1823, quoted earlier in this chapter. Sen provides the history of the charge of "sedition": it was considered, observes Marshman in his *History of Bengal*, "bad policy to enlighten them (the Indians) because their ignorance was regarded as a kind of security of the continuance of our Empire" (cited in Sen 1902: 168).

In his discussion, Sen methodically unfolds a variety of aspects of sedition: the implication of the meaning of the term "sedition," and the questions of "disloyalty" and "loyalty" of the educated class and of the "illiterate masses." And he raises the core question: is English education the cause of sedition? After discussing a variety of other aspects, he concludes that the "balance of advantages" is in favor of English (p. 176). Sen argues "[t]hat the system of Indian education has many shortcomings and stands in need of reforms no one can doubt ... But education on Western methods is practically still in its infancy in India." He wonders: "What young system has ever been perfect?" (pp. 176–7). His coda, with which many may agree today, is: "... whatever may be the defects of the present system of education, no impartial observer will deny that its advantages more than counterbalance its disadvantages" (p. 177).

Sen has a long list of advantages of English education, a position still debated, "interrogated," "problematized," and argued by scholars and politicians. I cannot resist the temptation to quote Sen here (p. 177):

> It [English] has been instrumental in stimulating the best energies of the country. It has produced a very large number of distinguished judges, learned and acute lawyers, efficient doctors of medicine, erudite scholars, eminent professors of science, of philosophy, and of mathematics, the highest and the ablest native executive officers of the Government, and the most helpful of Viceroy's native councillors.

And about English education, Sen observes (p. 177):

> English education has vastly reduced the expenditure of the Indian administration by equipping a large number of Indians for the Government service, which was at one time the monopoly of Europeans, and has thus saved India from financial ruin. It has minimised the possibility of mutiny and civil war through panic and ignorance.

Sen is equally articulate about the media and their impact (p. 177):

> It has created public press and public opinion, which, however misguided at times, have increased the increasing purity of Indian administration by exposing abuses of authority and official oppression and jobbery, and by placing the native views before the Government. It has chastened the native service.

In contextualizing English in South Asian sociopolitical contexts, Sen observes (p. 177):

> It has forged a link of knowledge and intimacy between the rulers and the ruled, so wide asunder by race and religion. It has developed fellow feelings between the various and strange races of India by creating a common language for them all. It has a tendency to make one nation out of the numerous – and, at one time, antagonistic – nations of India. It has rendered Indians less servile and fawning and more self-respecting than before. It has developed powers of self-government which it is the professed aim of the British policy to create and nourish.

Sen is on the mark in his conclusion when he says (p. 177), "Perhaps some of these very advantages constitute the real grievances of the opponents of English education in India!"

Raymond C. Goffin (1934) and A. F. Kindersley (1938), respectively, cover almost identical territories on Indian English. They provide a variety of specimens of the prescriptivist school that flourished during that period. An exponent of that school is Smith-Pearse (1934), whose examples are extensively explicated by Goffin.

There are three major problems with the prescriptivists' studies: they do not recognize the contextual appropriateness and sociolinguistic relevance of linguistic innovations; their exclusive norm for correctness is an *external* one with which the Indian (South Asian) learners are not familiar and which is not, in the majority of cases, functionally appropriate in South Asian contexts; and they do not make a distinction between what may be termed "error," "deviation" and "innovation."

Goffin appropriately makes a distinction between "Anglo-Indian" and "*educated* Indian English speech":

> Anglo-Indian is, after all, merely a jargon, a few scattered limbs of speech; whereas Indian English, though it began as, and still mainly consists of 'ignorant English', does yet show signs of assuming an individual body, or at least a sort of ghostly life – an English far exiled from home. (p. 21)

> 'Indian English', then, is in the main the outcome of the English educational system established in India. And, according to the degree to which the Indian student has assimilated his learning in the schools, so his English approximates 'purity'. In the vast majority of cases, as is only natural, the influence of his native idiom is never completely subdued. In some it is scarcely subdued at all, and from such emanate the perpetrations universally recognized as 'babu English' .... (pp. 22–23)

Som Nath Chib (1936) addresses three major linguistic concerns of the 1930s. These concerns, in their present *avatāras*, continue to be debated in South Asian political, linguistic, and educational discourses. One major question is: "how far can English replace our vernaculars?" Chib addressed three issues subsumed within this question: First, the dilemma of Hindustani; second, Indian vernaculars and universities; and finally, the most explosive linguistic issue, which continues to erupt in language riots in South Asia, that of the languages of minorities. Hindustani continues to be a functional reality in many parts of India, but the debate about providing it a status in the linguistic hierarchy of South Asia is almost over. It died before the assassination of its enthusiastic proponent, the late Mahatma Gandhi (1869–1948), in 1948.

Chib is passionate about the future of English (19): "[English] will remain the official language as long as we are governed by the British Government, and a suitable common language for business purposes, for a long time to come." In his conclusion, Chib confronts the political realities of India by asserting (pp. 58–59):

> It is relevant to our present discussion to state that this movement [the Pan Islamic movement] will blight the growth of the new language, Hindustani, which we wish to create out of Urdu and Hindi. As long as Muslims look to countries outside India for inspiration and Hindus look backwards to antiquity and both of them follow a policy of aggressive communalism under the disguise of self-defence and safeguarding their

rights, the idea of having a common language as a result of the fusion of Urdu and Hindi must remain as remote as the Greek calends.

In chronological order, Kindersley (1938) supplements Goffin's prescriptive study. His presentation is rather sketchy, but he provides additional data, collected by the author Kindersley himself, who, as a note says, spent twenty-four years in the Indian Civil Service, traveled and worked as a consultant in most of the major provinces, and focused on "the English of those who have learnt the language in schools" (p. 25). A cline of terms is used to characterize the subvarieties of Indian English: *normal English*, *dog English*, *adventurous kind of English*, and *Indianisms*.

The most discussed – and "amusing" – variety of Indian/South Asian English is termed *babu* (*baboo*) English. "Babu" is, as Yule and Burnell explain (1886: 44): "Properly a term of respect attached to a name, like Master and Mr., and formerly in some parts of Hindustan applied to certain persons of distinction. Its application as a term of respect is now almost or altogether confined to Lower Bengal." As regards the uses of the term, Yule and Burnell explain (p. 49):

> In Bengal and elsewhere, among Anglo-Indians, it is often used with a slight savour of disagreement, as characterizing a superficially cultivated, but too often effeminate Bengali. And from the extensive employment of the class, to which the term was applied as a title, in the capacity of clerks in English offices, the word has come often to signify "a native clerk who writes English."

The term, Baboo English, has by now, crossed the regional boundaries and continues to have currency all over India, including Southern India, Bangladesh, Nepal, and Pakistan. It is now not restricted to the style of administrative English; the style is indicative of profuse stylistic ornamentation and politeness. This style of communication – written or spoken – has been the focus of attention, discussion, and linguistic entertainment for centuries. Schuchardt ([1891] 1980) provides the following example of such officialese:

> The extreme stimulus of professional and friendly solicitations has led me to the journey of accomplished advantages to proceed with these elucidating and critical comments; wherein no brisking has been thrown apart to introduce prima facie and useful matters to facilitate the literary pursuits of lily-like capacities. If the aimed point be embraced favourably by the public, all in all grateful acknowledgement will ride on the jumping borders from the very bottom of my heart.

Two studies on this fascinating topic were published just one year apart: one by T. W. J. (1890) and the second by Arnold Wright (1891). The long title of T. W. J.'s book is "*Baboo English*"; *Or, Our Mother-Tongue as Our Aryan brethren understand it. Amusing specimens of composition and style, or, English as written by some of Her Majesty's Indian subjects.*

In the specimens that are extensive, T. W. J. provides glimpses of a wide range of language functions in a variety of interactions. The author says (ii), "[M]ost of the letters, etc., ... have been selected from a number which have passed through my hands during a quarter of a century's residence in India." The selections from these letters include topics such as an employer who had ordered his clerk to buy a cane tiffin basket, an incident of a dog bite, a petition of a beef hawker, a judgment by a native magistrate, a rare specimen of English composition, a leave application on account of a wife's death, the four little girls in manhood, and a complaint of savage dogs being kept by Europeans.

The editor makes it clear to his readers that "several of the accompanying productions have emanated from men who have passed the University Examinations in which English is a *compulsory* subject ..." (p. ii).

This variety of Baboo English, therefore, cannot be compared, argues the editor, with English men and women who "make equally ridiculous mistakes when using Hindustanee, or other Eastern languages." They are different, because, he explains, "they have picked up scraps of the vernacular from native servants, and do not profess to understand the idioms, or grammar of the language" (ii).[11]

The second study, by Arnold Wright (1891), provides extensive genre-specific specimens of "Baboo English" from Indian newspapers "as 'Tis Writ." The informative first chapter is a "sketch of the Indian Press" which is "in some respects the oldest, in others the youngest, Press upon the face of the globe" (p. 7). The native press, as opposed to the Anglo-Indian press, says Wright (pp. 16–17), "is young, but it is a vigorous product, and it has wisely followed on the lines of Anglo-Indian journalism in matters distinct from policy." He continues:

> The chief organs of native opinion – I speak now of those printed in English, such as *The Hindoo Patriot* of Calcutta, the *Indian Spectator* of Bombay, and *The Hindu* of Madras – are conducted in a scholarly manner and written in irreproachable English. Their editorial matter, when not disfigured by race prejudice or religious narrowness, might often be transferred bodily to their Anglo-Indian contemporaries without the difference being detected. There is, perhaps, a tendency to favour bombast and grandiloquence in treating of questions, but, on the whole, from a purely literary point of view, they afford little ground for criticism.

The subgenres of the newspaper register are discussed with introductory notes: editorials, the "free-and-easy" style of journalism, the "customary style" of announcements, "Quack advertisements" and obituaries, "native

[11] See also relevant sections on Goffin in Hosali 2000; Hunt 1931a, b; B. Kachru 1983a, b, 2005; Labru 1984; Lewis 1991; Roberts 1800; and Schuchardt, 1891.

descriptive reports," native humor and poetry, petitions and begging letters. The last chapter, "The contents of an Anglo-Indian Editorial box," are the letters that "find their way into the Editor's Box." In Indian journalism, says the author (p. 62), "[T]here are no columns of witty sayings or jokes such as are common to most English papers, and on the rare occasions that the Indian writer does condescend to be frivolous, there is invariably a political object underlying his humour."

These two studies provide abundant specimens of text from the earlier period of creativity and nativization of the English language in the multilingual contexts of India. Baboo English, as the two studies show, is one major source for our better understanding of the development and stabilization of this variety of South Asian English.

Two more studies, by George C. Whitworth (1907) and G. Subba Rao (1954), provide perspectives about the attitudes and analysis of Indian English almost half a century apart. Whitworth and Rao reflect the distance in time and in sociopolitical, linguistic and attitudinal changes during the period. Whitworth, a former Indian Civil Service officer, had earlier published a 350-page dictionary titled *An Anglo-Indian Dictionary: A Glossary of Indian terms used in English, and of such English or Other Non-Indian terms as have attained special meanings in India* (1885), which had been received with understandable excitement. His later book, published fifty-two years after the dictionary, is written with the hope that "no one will take up this little book expecting to find an amusing collection of those linguistic flights to which imaginative Indians occasionally commit themselves" (p. 5). These "linguistic flights," however, do not provide the overall picture of the competence of Indians in English. In explaining the situation, Whitworth tells us (pp. 5–6):

> I have been struck with the wonderful command which Indians – and not only those who have been to England – have obtained over the English language for all practical purposes. At the same time, I have often felt that what a pity it is that men exhibiting this splendid facility should now and then mar their compositions by little errors of idiom which jar upon the ear of the native Englishman . . . it seems well worth while to try and render them a small service by showing them how their admirable knowledge of our language may be made still more complete.

The eleven chapters in Whitworth's volume are an attempt in that direction, "to render a small service" (p. 6): The Articles; Adverbs; Prepositions; Conjunctions; Nouns; Pronouns; Adjectives; Verbs; Syntax; Metaphors; Vocabulary.

Rao's study (1954) is the first scholarly attempt to discuss English in India (South Asia) within the context of "Indo-British cultural and linguistic relations." This study has a broader focus and discusses linguistic (phonetic, grammatical, and semantic), sociocultural, and historical contexts. In his

"Introductory Note" to the volume, W. A. Craigie makes a futuristic observation which, as time and history has shown, was unwarranted:

> It is obvious that the recent changes in the administration of India, and the separation of Pakistan, may have some effect in lessening the number of Indian words that may be retained, or hereafter adopted, in English. It is also possible that the penetration of English into the Indian languages may be lessened by the ultimate adoption of Hindi as the recognized language of India (p. vii).

On both these counts, post-independence India, and South Asia in general, has provided surprises, and a new linguistic history of the region is in the making.

The two books discussed below represent the two faces of the post-British imperium studies: linguistic celebration and agony. The first is the celebration of the result of the much-cited pleas by Raja Rammohan Roy to Lord Amherst to provide funds for English education in India. The second is that of agony expressed – with a variety of ideological constructs – about "superficial" Lord Macaulay's induction of the Raj's language in the Indian Empire, *The Great Debate: Language Controversy and University Education*, edited by a distinguished Indian thinker, A. B. Shah (1968). This collection provides a unique perspective on the most debated and often violent linguistic issues that have confronted India and other South Asian countries.

In his Foreword to *The Great Debate*, India's Judge of the High Court of Judicature, Bombay (now Mumbai), V. M. Tarkunde, expresses appreciation for English in these words (p. v): "By our good fortune English has been the common language of higher education throughout India. Whatever might have been the defects and inequities of foreign rule, it was during the British regime that India was welded into a nation." He expresses his agony in these moving words: "It appears, however, that we did not deserve this good fortune. A narrow nationalist sentiment, which was generated during the struggle for independence, led a growing number of people to look upon English as a foreign language." His following message is loud and clear (p. vi):

> *A little thought would show that whereas a nation may have a language, a language has no nationality. Like any other acquisition in the field of knowledge, the English language belongs to those who know it and like it.* Nationalist sentiment has blinded many of us to this simple truth. (Emphasis added)

Shah's anthology aims to provide "an outline of contextual background" and "authoritative presentation of each important point of view" (p. xiii). *The Great Debate*, as Shah rightly claims, is "for the enlightened lay citizen . . . to weigh the various arguments . . . to decide for himself which policy or combination of policies will best serve the short- and long-term interests of his own and of countrymen, and to ensure through democratic means that his voice is heard in clear terms in the councils of nations" (p. xii).

The reproduced – or specially commissioned – chapters are from "highly qualified persons having practical experience in the field of university education" (x). What Shah desires to present is "a dispassionate reappraisal of the present language policy on academic standards" (p. x).

The four parts of the book bring together insightful perspectives contextualized in terms of thematically organized sections: "The Policy" (Chs. 1–3); "Aspects of the Question" (Chs. 4–19); "A Minister Reigns" (Chs. 20–24); "The Press, the Professions and the Public" (Chs. 25–34); and finally, an Appendix on "Recommendations of the Education Commission" on the study of language (pp. 187–209).

The content of the book justifies the title, *The Great Debate*, which represents the voices of academics, politicians, and social activities, and also of what in India's political parlance are called *aam aadmii* ("the general public"). A number of these are included in "The Letters to the Press." (See also B. Kachru 2005).

The study by Kalyan K. Chatterjee (1976), a perceptive academic, brings a variety of interpretations to this intriguing topic. He rightly reminds us that the introduction and presence of English in India "can indeed be called a historical phenomenon and a classical subject for interdisciplinary studies. And yet there is hardly any scholarly work to provide historical perspective to the introduction of English in India" (ix). Chatterjee confronts the facts as they were in the 1970s and continue to be in the new century: English is not losing its hold in India, the university programmes in English continue to draw larger numbers, Indian writing in English has "now a sizeable audience," (p. ix) writers in different Indian languages have shown no willingness to part with their English connection, and so on. He concludes (p. x), "All these lead us to recognize that English has struck roots in India: . . . " and he believes "it is coterminous with our institutional and social objectives."

This, then, is the issue of conflict between "tradition and modernity." Chatterjee discusses this issue with elegance and deep insight. The "enlightened first-generation nationalists . . . did not want India to ever deny the new modernity coming from Europe; they wanted her to assimilate and transform Western ideas, but her real Renaissance, as Aurobindo said, must come 'from the roots of our being'" (p. xi). The "first-generation nationalists" included Rabindra Nath Tagore (1861–1941), Aurobindo Ghosh (1872–1950), and Balgangadhar Tilak (1856–1920). Then there is a list of "conflicting questions" which all Indians confront. These questions are (pp. xi–xii):

> How can we repudiate English without having to part with much that continues to make India what she is today? How can we shed our doubleself, our alien 'epipsyche' without shedding our self-consciousness and missing an all-important step in the growing internationalization of the world?

If English gives way, what takes its place? Could English be limited in its use in our educational institutions, or be given a specifically utilitarian role?

This extensive study, Chatterjee concludes, is "not so much to find definitive answers to these questions as to make clear their historical contexts" (p. xii).[12]

The above narratives of English in South Asia, from 1837 to 1976, are only part of the story, and only a part of the constructs of the language.[13] Macaulay's much-maligned – and much-celebrated – Minute was just the beginning of a linguistic turbulence that has still not abated.

The narratives and strategies used for implanting English in earlier education and administration in Ceylon (now Sri Lanka) are not much different from the story of pre-partition India. The features of "Lankan English" are, as Hickey observes (2004: 554), "largely those of southern India in general. Influence by the structure of the Dravidian language Tamil is in evidence in the north and northwest of the island, while the Indo-Aryan language Sinhala is the major substrate influence on the remainder of Sri Lanka."

The *Swabhasha* (indigenous language policy) entailed a shift from English after political independence. The implementation of that policy in Sri Lanka resulted in a chain of other complex problems from which Sri Lanka has yet to recover.[14]

The above constructs of English indeed present only part of the story, about the motivations for implanting English in the subcontinent, the channels of its diffusions, and the social hierarchies the language created. There are yet other evolving and often-articulated stories voiced in all South Asian regions. These stories provide yet other constructs of, what I have termed, the "victimology of English" in social, educational and literary contexts. There is thus a rethinking about English studies, its "ownership" and its functions.

We must remind ourselves that, in South Asian social and linguistic contexts, the concept of languages of "wider communication" is functionally a misnomer. In the north of India there is a saying that *pą̃c kos par pānī badle, bīs kos par bhāshā* ("The water changes after every ten miles, and

[12] The titles of the nine chapters cover this challenging territory with stimulating discussions: 1. "Issues and Events: How It All Came About," 2. "Utilitarian Concern: Useful Knowledge and a Rational Morality," 3. "Macaulayism: Response and Reaction," 4. "The Renaissance Analogy: The spread of an Idea," 5. "The Moral Concern and the Pursuit of the Millenium," 6. "The Orientalist Vision: Synthesis and Indigenization," 7. "Orientalism in Action: Translation and the Comparative Manner," 8. "The Evangelist Thesis: Fide et Bonis Litteris," and 9. "Time's Morro: What are the Roots that Clutch." See also Frykenburg, 1988; and for earlier postindependence futuristic views of English in India, see Anand 1948 and Wadia 1954.

[13] The papers and books briefly discussed above are reprinted in full in Bolton and Kachru 2006a (6 vols.). In 1887, two short papers on "Anglo-Indianism" were published by D. W. Ferguson.

[14] For further details and references see, e.g. Barnes 1932; Halverson 1966; B. Kachru 1994, 2005; Kandiah 1964.

languages after every forty miles"). The language differences are determined by a variety of sociocultural and linguistic variables – those of caste and religion, and a range of distinctions of "high," "low," and "popular" in literature. (See, e.g., Shapiro and Schiffman 1981: 164–73.) The range of literary styles includes two or more varieties: *granthika*, the literary variety, and *vyāvhārika*, the colloquial variety, in the case of Telugu (a Dravidian language), and *sādhubhāshā*, the literary variety, *calitbhāshā*, the colloquial in the case of Bengali (an Indo-Aryan language). These variety distinctions have implications for education, the media, and literary creativity, as discussed in, for example, Krishnamurti (1978). The two major transplanted languages in the subcontinent, Persian and English, have also developed multiple varieties, as has the Sanskrit language.

Language Research Paradigms and the 1950s

In his critique of general linguistics in South Asia, Ashok R. Kelkar (1969: 533) observes:

> South Asia presents a rather depressing picture when one surveys the current trends in language studies generally and in general linguistics specifically – only slightly less depressing than the late V. S. Sukhthankar (1941: 595–6) found it to be in addressing the Philological Section of the 10th All India Oriental Conference.
> "We read with pardonable pride," he says, "the encomiums lavished by foreign scholars on the great grammar of Pāninī, and we are complacent enough not to realize that these very encomiums are at the same time the most crushing indictment of his unworthy descendants, who have shamefully neglected the study of this important subject" – and while saying this, he has both "medieval and modern times in mind." (1969: 532)

It was much later, in the late 1950s, that gradually South Asia drifted from essentially European paradigms – those of England, Germany, and France – and finally opened up to what Kelkar calls "the Saussure-Sapir-Bloomfield revolution in linguistics." At the deliberation of a conference, presided over by the late Sir Ralph Turner (1888–1983), the Deccan College-Rockefeller Foundation Linguistic Project was initiated. The Project was overseen by the late Sumitra Mangesh Katre (1906–1998), a far-sighted and dynamic academic visionary (see Katre, 1957). At the Summer and Autumn schools organized under the auspices of the project several senior American linguists came to India. This long list includes Edward C. Dimock (1930–2001), Gordon H. Fairbanks (1913–1985), Charles A. Ferguson (1921–1998), John J. Gumperz (b. 1922), Henry A. Gleason (b. 1917), Henry Hoenigswald (1915–2003), Gerald B. Kelley (1928–1987), Uriel Weinreich (1926–1967), and Norman Zide (b. 1928). There were also some Europeans such as John Burton-Page (1921–2005) from the School of Oriental and African Studies, London.

The schools started at Deccan College, Poona (now Pune), then moved to different university campuses in other parts of India. At these schools many Indian and South Asian scholars also had an opportunity to attend seminars conducted by, for example, Suniti Kumar Chatterjee (1890–1977), Phiroz A. Dustoor (1898–1979), Bh. Krishnamurti (b. 1928), T. P. Meenakshisundaram (1901–1980), Prabodh B. Pandit (1923–1975), Baburam Saksena (1897–1989), Sukumar Sen (1900–1992), and T. N. Srikantaiya (1906–1966), and to meet scholars such as J. S. Taraporewala (1885–1956).

These institutes moved to other parts of India over a period of several years, providing opportunities to young aspiring linguists from India and other South Asian countries to study and research about South Asian linguistic pluralism and regional language issues and South Asia's linguistic "problems."

R. N. Srivastava (1936–1992), one of the first Indian scholars trained in the Russian tradition of linguistics at Leningrad, considers "the application of linguistic theories and models developed in the West to the description of Indian vernaculars" as one of the trends of modern Indian linguistics. The scholars trained in new paradigms, Srivastava adds, "demonstrated that the concept of coexistent subsystems which operate partly in harmony and partly in conflict is not merely a hypothetical linguistic construct, but in fact exists in the verbal behavior of Indian speech communities" (1992: 330). And to illustrate his point, he refers to the research of Ferguson (1959), Gumperz (1961), and Ferguson and Gumperz (1960).

In other words, serious attempts in model-oriented, socially realistic analyses of South Asian languages were initiated. The impact of this linguistic "self-awareness," in Srivastava's view (1992: 332–3), resulted in the study of "linguistic heterogeneity and cultural complexity"[15] the enormously complex situation of multilingual and pluri-registral verbal interaction[16] methodological concerns about the functions of and innovations in codes in contact, which gave rise to the notion of "bilingual creativity"[17] and language minorities, conflicts, policy, and planning.[18]

15 e.g. D'souza 2001; B. Kachru 1978b and later; Krishnamurti 1986; Khubchandani 1983 and later; Pandit 1972; Pattanayak 1981, 1990; Saghal 1991; Singh 1985; K. Sridhar 1989; Srivastava 1980.

16 e.g. "verbal repertoire," "code-switching," "conventions of speaking and writing"; see, e.g. Bhatt 1996; Gumperz 1968; Y. Kachru 1993, 1996; Pandharipande 1983, 1992b; S. N. Sridhar and K. Sridhar 1980.

17 e.g. B. Kachru 1965, 1983a, b.

18 e.g. Abbi 1995b; Bhatia 1982; Bright 1990; J. Das Gupta 1970; P. Das Gupta 1993; B. Kachru 1982b; Y. Kachru and T. Bhatia 1978; Krishnamurti and Mukherjee 1984; Singh 1992; G. N. Srivastava 1970; for English, see relevant chapters in Thumboo 2001.

The First Pakistan Conference of Linguistics was organized in 1962 by Anwar S. Dil, who was also the founder of Linguistic Research Group of Pakistan. At that time, as Dil says:

> Pakistani linguistics today is not an organized academic discipline [. . .] Recent contributions to linguistic science are not commonly known among Pakistani language scholars, and very little theoretical and experimental research is being done at present by Pakistani linguists. (1969: 678–80; see also Dil 1966)

This concern is not much different from that which Sukthankar (1941) expressed about India in the 1940s.

The publications of Tariq Rahman (1991a, b, 1996a) provide some idea of the current directions in Pakistani linguistics and the frustrations that "force scholars in the Third World to remain peripheral" (1996a: xvii). The recent studies in Pakistani linguistics include, for example, Ali 1996; Bashir 2006; Baumgardner 1992, 1993; Baumgardner *et al.* 1993; Ghaffar 1990; Haque 1993; Omar 1986.

An outline of earlier research on linguistic studies on Sinhalese and Tamil in Sri Lanka (earlier Ceylon) are presented in D. E. Hettiaratchi (on Sinhalese, 1969: 736–51) and by A. Sathasivam (Tamil in Sri Lanka, 1969: 752–9), respectively. Sri Lankan scholars, such as Suresh Cangarajah, Thiru Kandiah, and Arjun Parakrama, have critically contributed toward our better understanding of world Englishes in the Outer Circle, particularly Sri Lanka. (See also Fernando 1996; Halverson 1966; Kandiah 1991, 1996.)

The ongoing political and economic turmoil in Nepal has made research on language a nonpriority item, though various governments have participated in UNESCO-led efforts at planning for language education. Yadava (2006), however, provides some information on linguistic activities in Nepal in recent years (1999–2005; see also Verma 1996).

There continues to be a dearth of surveys and research materials on Bhutan and the Maldives.

Current issues and directions

In the 1950s–60s a national network of summer and winter schools with participation of young scholars from a variety of disciplines generated an unprecedented intellectual excitement in linguistics in several Indian universities. The excitement was evident in across the subcontinent – particularly in India. It was evident in discussions of contemporary linguistic theories, methodologies, and contextually relevant applications of the linguistic sciences.

In India, two major steps were taken by establishing the Central Institute of English in Hyderabad in 1958. The Institute was later renamed, for political reasons, the Central Institute of English and Foreign Languages, and in August 2007, it was granted the status of a Central University and renamed the English and Foreign Languages University. However, in contrast to the Central Institute of English, the Central Institute of Indian Languages in Mysore was established much later – in 1969.

In retrospect, it is evident that the post-1950s excitement about primary focus on South Asian languages and linguistics gradually took a new direction in the 1970s. This direction reminds one of what may be called the "Dixon hypothesis," articulated by Robert M. W. Dixon in the 1990s concerning "major myths in modern linguistics" (1997: 133). Dixon's concern was primarily about most linguistics programs in the West, but to some extent it does apply to South Asia, too.

This myth, as summarized by B. Kachru (2005: 168), relates to what

> ... has now divided linguistics into DESCRIPTIVISTS and THEORETICIANS. This dichotomy has ultimately impacted university linguistics departments, and there is no attention paid to writing descriptive grammars of languages – living or dying. In most linguistics programs in the West, says Dixon, linguists are generally trained without any training in field linguistics, which, Dixon comments, is 'rather like a group of "surgeons," none of whom has ever actually performed an operation, giving courses on principles of surgery' (Dixon 1997: 133). Perhaps Dixon has somewhat overdramatized the point, but he certainly has articulated a vital topic that is of concern to us all.

The late Ravindra N. Srivastava, provides a futuristic agenda to deal with this myth when he contextualizes the linguistic study and research in the following words:

> ... the "bright" aspects of linguistic studies in India have to be integrated in order to develop theories appropriate to our Indian reality and tradition ... we have to make linguistics a socially meaningful activity and more viable and relevant. (1992: 336–37)

And in conclusion, Srivastava refers to William Labov's insightful and relevant questions raised in 1982, in his paper entitled 'Objectivity and commitment in linguistic science: The case of the Black English trial in Ann Arbor'. Srivastava asserts: "we cannot absolve ourselves from questions related to objectivity and commitment in linguistic sciences and, hence, have to seek answers to two questions – What is linguistics about? and what is it good for?"

These are some of the questions the *Language in South Asia* has attempted to address.

Further Reading

See, e.g. Agnihotri and Khanna 1997; Canagarajah 1999; Cohn 1985; P. Dasgupta 1993; Dharwadkar 2003; Dissanayake 1985; Ferguson 1996;

B. Kachru 1983a, b; Y. Kachru and Nelson 2006; Kandiah 1984, 1995; Krishnaswamy and Brude 1998; Mehrotra 1998; Ram 1983; Viswanathan 1987, 1989. See also Nagarajan's critique of Mehrotra 2003; Parakrama 1995; Singh 1998. The constructs representing such voices are not restricted to South Asia but come from users of world Englishes across cultures (see, e.g., B. Kachru, Y. Kachru and Nelson, eds. 2006).

Part 1

Language history, families, and typology

1 Language in historical context

R. E. Asher

Introduction

South Asia is often described as a linguist's paradise. While it is not the only region of the world to merit such a label, there are several clear reasons for this: the number of different languages spoken is very large (though less than the figure of 1,652 listed in the 1961 Census for India and even than the 1,018 classified by the same Census as indigenous); there are linguistic records, in the form of both inscriptions and texts, going back considerably more than three millennia; there are the inscribed remains, from the ancient civilization of the Indus valley, of a language that has yet to be deciphered to the full satisfaction of the world of scholarship; there are literary languages side by side with languages that lack a writing system; two dozen writing systems are in use; many of the languages exhibit diglossia; and there is, and has long been, widespread bi- and multilingualism, both individual and geographical. Indeed, bilingualism, rather than monolingualism, is the norm.

It is impossible to be at all precise about either the number of languages spoken in the region or the number of speakers of each. There are several well-rehearsed reasons for this: the status of a given language variety – whether it is more appropriately regarded as a language in its own right or as one of a number of dialects of a language – is not always clear; some languages still may remain to be discovered; available statistics vary in quality, reliability, and date; there has been a tendency in recent national censuses to disregard figures for languages with less than a certain minimum of recorded speakers; political factors may be involved in the question of which languages are recognized and in the manner in which different language varieties are grouped together. Certain things can, however, be asserted with confidence: the total number of languages is not less than 300. Some of these are at risk of dying out;[1] some are among the most widely spoken languages in the world. The last group comprises the great literary languages of South Asia, six of which fall in the group of the world's top twenty languages in this respect (and two in the top five).

[1] See van Driem 2007.

Historical factors

Language variety both makes history and reflects history. There are two principal ways in which historical developments have contributed to the rich linguistic scene in South Asia. First is the movement of populations at different times into the area from outside. Second is the divergence within a language over time when different groups of speakers have become relatively isolated from each other, and the consequent emergence of forms of speech that need to be considered different languages. Yet the passage of time has seen not only divergence but also convergence; the typological differences that are among the factors differentiating members of the different language families represented are less than what might have been expected – the result of contact between speakers. The possibility of contact has been increased by historical factors. Though it is the case that South Asia has only been close to being a single political unit during the period of British rule, there have been several periods when the greater part of the subcontinent has been politically united, as in the times of the Mauryan Empire (under Ashoka) in the third century BCE, the Gupta Empire (fourth to sixth centuries CE), the Delhi Sultanates (fourteenth to sixteenth centuries) and, most notably perhaps, the Moghul Empire (sixteenth to eighteenth centuries).

While historians can confidently provide dates for political developments as represented by this succession of empires, the dating – and indeed the ordering – of the movements of the populations that provided the current language mix is shrouded in considerable obscurity.

Four language families are widely represented, namely Indo-European (through its Indo-Iranian branch), Dravidian, Sino-Tibetan (primarily through its Tibeto-Burman branch) and Austro-Asiatic (primarily through the Munda branch). In addition, Kam-Thai is represented by four languages, and four members of the Andamanese family are still extant. There is at least one language isolate. Since all of the four large families apart from Dravidian are unquestionably more widely represented outside South Asia, there is an assumption that they had an earlier homeland elsewhere. No dating of the assumed population movements is possible with regard to Sino-Tibetan and Austro-Asiatic, but the arrival from the northwest of the group of Indo-Europeans known as Aryans can be put at approximately the middle of the second millennium BCE.

Many have speculated on where the Dravidians might have come from, but unless Dravidian can convincingly be shown to be related to some other language or language family, the question is unanswerable. Many proposals, with very varying degrees of plausibility, have been made for links with languages spoken in many different parts of the world, among them Basque, Japanese, Korean, and Swahili. Even the most well-argued case, for a genetic relationship with Elamite (McAlpin 1981), is not entirely persuasive. There are reasons to assume that, before the arrival of the Aryans, the population of the greater part of South Asia was Dravidian-speaking. For, along with the heavy concentration of Dravidian speech in the southern parts of India, there are several areas, quite often relatively quite isolated, further north where minor Dravidian languages are spoken. These include Orissa, Madhya Pradesh, Maharashtra, Bihar, and West Bengal in India, as well as Pakistan, Bangaladesh, and Nepal.

If the Dravidians are to be taken as having their origin outside South Asia, then the question of the language spoken in the great urban-based civilization that flourished in the Indus Valley between 2500 and 1500 BCE becomes an important part of the argument. Given that this civilization preceded the advent of the Aryans and given the likelihood that Dravidians before their time covered most of the subcontinent, it is a reasonable hypothesis that those who inhabited the cities of Harappa and Mohenjodaro spoke an ancestor of Dravidian languages spoken today. Deciphering the linguistic remains that have come down to us – the clay seals – is by no means straightforward, above all because of the lack of any bilingual text. That the language could be Dravidian, however, has been meticulously demonstrated (Parpola 1994).

Language families in South Asian countries

The statistical expectation that the language families that in terms of their recorded history can be regarded as indigenous to the region will be unevenly represented is borne out by the facts. Moreover, the hierarchy of numbers of speakers for the four dominant families – Indo-Iranian > Dravidian > Austro-Asiatic > Tibeto Burman – is different from that of the number of languages recorded for each: Tibeto-Burman > Indo-Iranian > Dravidian > Austro-Asiatic. Minimum figures, estimated very conservatively, for each dimension are as follows.[2]

	Number of languages	Number of speakers (m)
Indo-Iranian	110	1,000
Dravidian	35	250
Austro-Asiatic	25	12
Tibeto-Burman	150	11

Note: m = million.

Indo-Iranian

The world's most widely spoken family of languages, in terms both of numbers of speakers and of geographical distribution, is Indo-European, of which

[2] These figures are based on data provided by national censuses and by Singh and Manoharan 1993.

Indo-Iranian is one of ten branches. Indo-Iranian itself is now seen as having three branches: Iranian, Indo-Aryan, and Nuristani. Languages belonging to the last of these three are spoken in the Afghan Hindu Kush, that is to say, outside the region of South Asia as defined in this book (though a small number of speakers are found in northeast Pakistan). As far as the other two are concerned, in terms of geographical coverage and numbers of speakers, the Indo-Aryan or Indic sub branch of Indo-Iranian dominates over Iranian, which is largely confined to western Pakistan, though Persian has been important in the social and political history of language in the region, particularly in the centuries preceding British rule. The history of Iranian can be traced back to at least the sixth century BCE in the form of texts in Old Persian, a southwestern dialect of Iranian, and the northeastern Avestan, the language of the Avesta, the sacred text of Zoroastrianism. Modern representatives of Iranian in South Asia are found in Pakistan, with Baluchi (1998: 4.7 million speakers) and Waneci (1998: 95,000), spoken in Baluchistan, Pashto (1981: 13.1 million), spoken in the North-West Frontier Province, Ormuri (1,000), spoken in Wazirstan, and Wakhi (1981: up to 60,000) and Yidgha (6,000),[3] spoken in the northernmost valleys of the country. Pashto, Waneci, Wakhi and Yidgha belong to the South-East branch of Iranian, and Baluchi and Ormuri to the North-West branch. The position of Indo-Aryan is much more complex and the classification of the languages of this subfamily has been the subject of much difference of opinion,[4] since the criteria on which any classification might be based are in conflict. One controversy that does appear to have been resolved relates to the position of "Dardic," one member of which grouping is Kashmiri. Dardic had been thought (e.g. by Grierson[5]) to form a separate group within Indo-Iranian along with Iranian and Indo-Aryan. The term is now used for a subset of languages within the set, which are allocated to Indo-Aryan, the remainder being taken to be distinct and to belong to Iranian. The grouping together of languages on the basis of perceived similarity in phonological and morphological structure turns out in most cases to correspond closely to geographical distribution, and proposed groups are in almost all cases given geographical labels, such as Northern (Dardic), North-Western (including, say, Sindhi and Punjabi), Central (with Hindi the main member), Western (including Bengali, Assamese, and Oriya) and Southern (commonly including Gujarati, Marathi, and Sinhalese[6]). Accounts differ in two main respects: the position at which lines are drawn between different groups and the matter of whether two speech varieties should be considered to be two different languages or merely dialects of one language.

3 Backstrom and Radloff (1992: 61).

4 The different views are neatly summarized by Masica (1991: 446–63).

5 See Masica (1991: 461–3).

6 Also referred to as Sinhala.

Thus, in the 1961 Census of India, Rajasthani and Bihari were listed separately, but in 1981 were, along with several other languages, subsumed under Hindi.

In the realm of language and dialect differentiation, the status of Hindi raises another question, namely that of its relationship to Urdu. At the level of spoken, conversational language the two are barely distinguishable and, on the basis of purely linguistic criteria, could not even be considered distinct dialects. However, there are sociocultural reasons for regarding them as different entities, a fact that is reflected in the use of the Devanagari script for writing Hindi and the Perso-Arabic script for Urdu. Moreover, there is divergence in the case of more formal language, whether it be spoken or written, in that Sanskrit is taken as the principal source for neologisms in Hindi, whereas Urdu draws on Persian or Arabic.

Indo-Aryan has a long recorded history, the earliest texts being the Vedas, of which the first, the Rigveda, dates back to the middle of the second century BCE. Vedic is variously described as a predecessor of Sanskrit and as an early form of it. The importance of Sanskrit in India today as the country's oldest classical tongue and as the language of the sacred texts of Hinduism is recognized by its being the only one of the "scheduled" languages listed in the Constitution of India that is not a modern spoken language. Vedic and classical Sanskrit form Old Indo-Aryan. The later forms subsumed under Middle Indo-Aryan are first attested in inscriptions containing edicts of Ashoka representing a variety of spoken dialects, the so-called "Prakrits," of the third century BCE. Pali, the language of the Buddhist canon, belongs to the same period. New Indo-Aryan is generally deemed to begin in approximately 1000 CE, and it is with the languages that make up New Indo-Aryan that the remainder of this section is concerned.

In most of the countries of South Asia – Pakistan, Nepal, India, Bangladesh, Sri Lanka, the Maldives – the majority of inhabitants speak an Indo-Aryan language and the homeland of this subfamily stretches over a vast area in the northern part of the region. Starting at the most northeasterly point, we have the Dardic languages. Those spoken in Pakistan include Khowar (200,000), Bashkarik, Maiya, Chilis, Gauro, Kandia, Ushojo, Torwali (60,000), Dameli, Phalura, Gawar-Bati and Kalasha, spoken in the extreme north, and Shina (1981: 300,000), spoken mainly around the higher reaches of the Indus. Across the frontier, in the Kashmir valley, is Kashmiri (3,174,684 speakers recorded in 1981). Other major North-Western Indo-Aryan languages spoken in Pakistan are Hindko (1981: 2.4 million), a name applied with no great precision to a range of related languages/dialects spoken in the North-West Frontier Province and in the city of Peshawar; Siraiki (1998: 13.9 million) in the eastern part of Baluchistan; Punjabi (1998: 58.4 million) in the Punjab; and Sindhi (1998: 18.7 million) in Sind. There are Sindhi speakers in India (1991: 2,122,848) too, mainly in Gujarat, where the variety spoken in Kutch, adjacent to the Pakistani province of Sind, is sometimes referred to as Kacchi. Urdu (1998: 10.0 million), not associated with any particular province, but important in Pakistan, in spite of its minority status, as the language of the central government and administration and as a widely used lingua franca. Two other Central Indo-Aryan languages, Gujari and Domaki, are spoken in northern Pakistan.

Across the frontier, in the Kashmir valley, is Kashmiri, the most widely spoken Dardic language (3,174,684 speakers recorded in 1981). In the south of the Kashmiri-speaking area, there are other Dardic languages with much smaller numbers of speakers: Kashtawari (21,000), Doda Siraji, Rambani and Poguli, all of which are sometimes considered to be dialects of Kashmiri. To the south and east of Kashmir is found a group of languages known under the general name of Pahari or Northern Indo-Aryan, further divided into Western and Central Pahari. Furthest to the west is found Dogri (1981: 1,520,889), Bhadrawahi and Padari are spoken in southern Kashmir, while Pangwali, Chameali (1991: 63,408), Kului, Satlej, Mandeali, Handuri, Kiunthali, Baghati, Sadochi, Jaunsari and Bharmauri belong to Himachal Pradesh.

In Nepal, 85 percent of the population have an Indo-Aryan mother tongue. The four most widely spoken are Nepali (2001: 11,053,255), spoken in all regions; Maithili (2001: 2,797,582), spoken in Eastern Terai and Central Terai; Bhojpuri (2001: 1,712,536), in Central and Western Terai; and Tharu (2001: 1,331,546), in East, Mid-West, and Far-West Terai. Northern Indo-Aryan languages closely related to Nepali are Palpa and Jumeli. Other Indo-Aryan languages spoken in Nepal – mainly in the Terai areas – that have considerable numbers of speakers are the North-Western Danuwar (2001: 31,849) and Darai (2001: 10,210), the Central languages Urdu (2001: 174,840), Hindi (2001: 105,765) and Marwari (2001: 22,673), and the East Central languages Awadhi (2001: 560,744), Bhajjika (2001: 237,947) and Angika (2001: 15,892). An eastern dialect of Nepali known there as Lhotshamkha, is also spoken in southern Bhutan (perhaps 160,000 speakers). This is similar to the variety spoken in India in the south of Sikkim and in the Darjeeling District of West Bengal. The total number of Nepali speakers in India, where the language is also called Gorkhali, in 1991 was 2,076,645.

Returning to the West we come back to Punjabi (1991: 32,753,676), spoken in the Indian state of Punjab. In an easterly direction from there are the states of Rajasthan, Haryana, Uttar Pradesh, Madhya Pradesh, and Bihar, which together constitute the Hindi region of India in the sense that in these states Hindi (1991: 337,272,114) is the language of local administration and education. Such a statement, however, provides an oversimplified picture of the situation, in that there is a case for recognizing a number of different languages – more than 50 – within this figure, and if the numbers from these are subtracted, the total for Hindi becomes 233,432,285. Thus in Haryana we find Haryanvi (362,476). For Uttaranchal, there are Garhwali (1,872,578) and Kumauni (1,717,191); for

Rajasthan, Rajasthani (13,328,581), Mewari (2,114,622), Harauti (1,235,252), Mewati (102,916), Marwari (4,673,276), Bagri (593,730) and Dhundhari (965,006); for Uttar Pradesh, Awadhi (481,316) and Bhojpuri (23,102,050); for Madhya Pradesh, Bagheli (1,387,160), Nimadi (1,420,051), Malvi (1,142,478) and Bundeli (1,657,473); for Bihar, Maithili (7,766,597) and Magahi (10,566,842); for Jharkhand, Sadani (1,569,066); and for Chhattisgarh, Chhattisgarhi (10,595,199) and Surgujiya (1,045,455). Other Central Indo-Aryan languages not included in the grand total for Hindi are Bhili (5,572,308), spoken at the junction of Rajasthan, Gujarat and Madhya Pradesh, and Khandeshi (973,709), immediately to the south of this. Bhili is also the language of more than half of the inhabitants of Dadra and Nagar Haveli. A distinct dialect of Bhili, Varli (1991: 91,753), is spoken in the Thana District of Maharashtra. It is in Uttar Pradesh that is found the greatest concentration of speakers of Urdu (1991: 43,406,932), which is also spoken in Hyderabad, the capital of Andhra Pradesh, in its southern form, Dakhini.

The remaining languages to the east are included in one subgroup by all analysts. Bengali, the second most widely spoken language in South Asia, straddles the border between India (1991: 69,595,738 in West Bengal) and Bangladesh (1991: 110,000,000, or 90 percent of the population of the country). Spoken in Bangladesh and closely related to Bengali are Chittagonian (14 million speakers) and Sylheti (7 million). In the same group of Indo-Aryan and spoken mainly in India are Rajbangshi (1991: 2,839,481) and Bishnupriya (75,000). Assamese (1991: 13,079,696) is the principal language of the Indian state of Assam. Oriya (1991: 28,061,313) has the same status in Orissa. A widely used lingua franca throughout Nagaland and in parts of Arunachal Pradesh and Manipur is the Assamese-based pidgin, Nagamese.

There remains what is generally classified as the Southern or South-Western group of Indo-Aryan languages. Gujarati (1991: 40,673,814) is the language of Gujarat. Much further south, in the Tamil Nadu city of Madurai, a dialect of Gujarati known as Saurashtri (1991: 220,126) is spoken by a community of silk weavers. The state language of Maharashtra is Marathi (1991: 62,481,681). In the south of this state there are speakers of a variety of Konkani (1991: 1,760,607), the language of Goa and also spoken further south in Karnataka, round about the city of Mangalore, and in Dadra and Nagar Haveli. Halabi (1991: 534,313) is spoken in the south of Chhattisgarh and in the east of Madhya Pradesh.

The third major language commonly included in the South-Western group is Sinhalese (2001: 13,865,245, or 74 percent of the total population of the island), the national language of Sri Lanka, to where speakers of Indo-Aryan migrated in the fifth century BCE. Because of its long separation from other Indo-Aryan languages, Sinhalese has developed on somewhat different lines from other members of the family, with the result that it is sometimes considered to constitute a separate subgroup. One other Indo-Aryan language is spoken only in Sri Lanka, namely Vedda,[7] the language of a small aboriginal group (1963: 411) and one that is in serious danger of extinction. Related to Sinhalese is Maldivian or Divehi, the language of the Republic of the Maldives, spoken by the vast majority of the population of 270,101 (2000).

Dravidian

It is Dravidian which, among the language families of South Asia, that most closely rivals Indo-Iranian in terms of the extent of its geographic distribution, with populations speaking one or another member language in Pakistan, Nepal, India, Bangladesh, and Sri Lanka. As has already been indicated, it is the second largest in terms of numbers of speakers. Its earliest records are in the form of Tamil inscriptions in the Brahmi script[8] from the time of Ashoka (3rd century BE) and poems of the so-called "Sangam" age belonging to approximately the same period. Any conclusions about the situation of the family before then can only be based on methods of comparative reconstruction taking account of Dravidian languages as spoken today and of texts in some of those languages that have been preserved from earlier periods.[9] In the case of the other three major languages, Kannada, Telugu, and Malayalam, such texts, while lacking the antiquity of the earliest Tamil ones, go back several centuries, with the earliest inscriptions in Kannada, for instance, dating from the 5th century.

The dating of the succession of splits that led from proto-Dravidian to the languages of today is not easy to determine, though it is likely that some instances of divergence that led to the appearance of new languages took place during historical times rather than in the prehistoric period. Certainly, the major languages were established as separate languages by the end of the first millennium of the present era. Agreement about the composition of the different groups within Dravidian is closer than in the case of Indo-Aryan, though it is by no means absolute. Languages that are most closely related genetically are, as tends to be the case, also closer in terms of their geographical homeland, and the descriptive labels reflect this. They will be discussed here under the grouping North, Central, South-Central, and South, with the latter two being taken as more closely related to each other than to either of the other two. The number of Dravidian languages is uncertain, for reasons similar to those given with respect to Indo-Aryan. New languages were discovered in the closing decades of the twentieth century, and the reanalysis of data collected earlier has sometimes led

[7] An alternative possibility that has to be allowed for is that Vedda "is a creole which has arisen through many years of language contact between the original Vedda language and Sinhalese" (Dharmadasa 1990: 85).

[8] The most recent as well as the most authoritative study of these inscriptions is Mahadevan 2003.

[9] For the fullest account of such reconstruction, see Krishnamurti 2003.

to different conclusions about what speech variety should be regarded as a separate language.[10]

The heaviest concentration of Dravidian speech is in the four southern states of India – Karnataka, Andhra Pradesh, Kerala, and Tamil Nadu – and, indeed, the name by which the family is known is derived from the Sanskrit word for "south." However, Dravidian speech communities are spread across the north of South Asia. Furthest to the west is Brahui (1981: 1.2 million[11]), spoken in the Baluchistan province of Pakistan and to a lesser extent in Sind. The most widely spoken member of the North Dravidian group is Kurukh[12] (1991: 1,426,618), spoken in Bihar, Madhya Pradesh, Orissa, and West Bengal in India and also by a small number in Bangladesh. A somewhat different variety, known as Dhangar Kurukh, is spoken in the Eastern Terai in Nepal (2001: 28,615). Mainly in Bihar, but with some speakers in West Bengal and in Bangladesh, is Malto (1991: 108,148).

Central Dravidian languages each have somewhat smaller numbers of speakers than the three principal members of the Northern Group, though Kolami (1991: 98,281), spoken principally in Maharashtra but also in Andhra Pradesh and Madhya Pradesh, comes close to Malto. The other members of the Central group are spoken in the Koraput District of Orissa. It has been argued (Burrow and Bhattacharya 1962–1963) that Ollari and Gadaba, formerly taken to be separate languages, might more appropriately be described as dialects of the same language.[13] Two closely related members of the same group are Naiki and Naikri.

It is in the combined Southern and South-Central group that are located the four major literary languages of the family, Telugu, Kannada,[14] Tamil, and Malayalam. Each is the language of administration and education of one of the four southern states and is very much the majority language there, but each has considerable numbers of speakers in other states. Telugu, with the largest

10 Appended to Krishnamurti 1993 from another source, for instance, is a "Language list" containing eighty names, but the body of the article does not go beyond stating that "[m]ore than twenty-five languages of the Dravidian family are spoken in India, Pakistan and Sri Lanka" and notes that "genetic classification is not established for all languages in the list."

11 This figure from the 1981 Census of Pakistan is thought by some commentators to be a considerable exaggeration of the number of actual speakers. Many people classified as Brahuis are bilingual in Baluchi, and possibly even more speak only Baluchi. On the other hand, the total number of Brahui speakers would be increased if those living in Afghanistan and Iran were added.

12 One of a number of alternative spellings is Kurux, and the language is also known as Oraon/Uraon.

13 No reliable estimate of the number of speakers is available. There may be between 10,000 and 20,000 of the two together. The imprecision stems from the fact that the 1981 Census of India lists 28,027 speakers of Gadaba, but this figure includes speakers not only of the Dravidian language but also of the Austro-Asiatic language with the same name spoken not only in the same district but also in Madhya Pradesh and Andhra Pradesh.

14 Also known, particularly in earlier accounts, as Kanarese or Canarese.

number of speakers of any Dravidian language (1991: 66,017,615), is the language spoken in Andhra Pradesh and is the principal member of the South-Central group. Other members of this group are located somewhat to the north of Telugu. Gondi (1991: 2,124,852), of which there are several distinct varieties, is spread over a large area of Madhya Pradesh, eastern Maharashtra, southern Orissa, and northwestern Andhra Pradesh. Closely related to Gondi, to the extent that some scholars regard it as a Gondi dialect, is Koya (1991: 270,994), speakers of which are found in Andhra and Orissa. One other South-Central language has a large number of speakers, namely Kui[15] (1991: 641,662), spoken primarily in southern Orissa, but also in Andhra Pradesh, Madhya Pradesh, and Tamil Nadu. Often confused with this because of the similarity of their names and through their being spoken by various tribal groups, again with similar names, is Kuvi (1991: 220,783),[16] also centered in Orissa, but with some speakers in Andhra Pradesh too. Konda[17] (1991: 17,864) is found in the Visakhapatnam District of Andhra Pradesh and the Koraput District of Orissa where Pengo (1961: 1,254) too is spoken. Manda, spoken in the Kalahandi district of Orissa, is now considered a distinct language from Pengo. Also spoken in Kalahandi, and in Koraput, is Awe or Indi, with perhaps 10,000 speakers.

Karnataka is the home of three South Dravidian languages. First in importance is the state language Kannada (1991: 32,753,676). In South Kanara district, in the coastal region in the south of the state, but with some speakers over the border in Kerala, is Tulu (1991: 1,552,259). A neighbor of Tulu is Kodagu (1991: 97,011), spoken in Coorg.[18] Treated by recent Censuses of India as a dialect of Kannada, Badaga (1991: 134,187) has a good claim to be considered a separate language. Its home is in the northwest of Tamil Nadu. Close to the area where Badaga is spoken are to be found, high up in the Nilgiri Hills in the northwest of the state, two South Dravidian languages which have barely two thousand speakers between them and so are now disregarded by census takers. They are Toda (1971: 790) and Kota (1971: 1,269). Again in the same area is Irula, with perhaps 50,000 speakers, now generally recognized as a separate language rather than as a dialect of Tamil. Kerala is closer than any other India state to being monolingual in terms of the mother tongue of its inhabitants, with 96 percent speaking Malayalam (1991: 30,377,176). A dialect of Malayalam is also the main language of the Laccadive Islands (Lakshadweep). We come finally, in the extreme south of the region, to Tamil itself (1991: 53,006,368), the Dravidian language with the longest continuous recorded history and the

15 Other names that have been used for the language include Kandh and Khond.

16 This is one of a number of cases where it is difficult to differentiate between the number of people in a set of scheduled tribes and the number of people speaking a given language. Kuvi has also been referred to as Kuvinga, Kond and Khondi, among other names.

17 Also known as Kubi.

18 From which it gets one of its alternative names, Coorg.

official language of the state of Tamil Nadu. It also has an important position in Sri Lanka, where it is the language of the majority in the northern and eastern provinces (1981: 3,752,447). Along with Sinhalese, it is one of the country's two official languages. It is the language of a number of different communities – Sri Lanka Tamils, Indian Tamils, and Sri Lanka Muslims, who together make up a quarter of the population.

Austro-Asiatic

Though no early Austro-Asiatic texts are available from ancient times for the languages in the family that have their home in South Asia, and the position is therefore very different from the one that applies in the cases of Indo-Aryan and Dravidian, it is likely that their presence in the region is at least of equal antiquity with that of Dravidian. Certainly, their presence there predates the arrival of Indo-Aryan speakers, and Austro-Asiatic can reasonably be regarded as being in principle one of the candidates for consideration as the language of the Indus Valley civilization, though no serious work appears to have been done to test this hypothesis. Unlike Dravidian, Austro-Asiatic has many manifestations outwith South Asia. Indeed, more languages in the family are spoken outside the region than within it. On the other hand, it is the case that the branch of the family most strongly represented in India is not represented elsewhere.

The Austro-Asiatic family as a whole is spread over a wide area stretching from central through western India, Burma, peninsular Malaysia, Laos, Cambodia, and Vietnam. There is general agreement that there are within it two principal groups, namely Mon-Khmer and Munda, with the subdivisions of the former being considerably more complex than those of the latter. Munda is largely confined to South Asia, while most Mon-Khmer languages belong to mainland South-East Asia.

Two of the twelve or so recognized divisions of Mon-Khmer have their home in India, namely Khasi and Nicobarese. Khasi (1991: 912,283) is the official language of Meghalaya. Two varieties, Pnar or Syntang (1991: 169,388) and War (1991: 26,735), are sufficiently distinct to be generally regarded as separate languages.

Nicobarese (1991: 26,261) languages fall into three main groups. In the northern Nicobar Islands is Car Nicobarese, also known as Pu. In the central islands is Nancowry, with Great Nicobarese, also known as Southern Nicobarese, in the southern islands. Further subdivisions have been proposed, with the speech variety of individual islands (e.g. Chaura, Teressa/Bomboka) being given the status of separate languages. In the interior of Great Nicobar, members of a tribal group, probably numbering less than a hundred, speak Shom Peng.

The score or so of Munda languages are scattered over much of north-eastern, central, and eastern India, Nepal, and Bangladesh, in a somewhat similar way to the nonliterary Dravidian languages. The total number of speakers exceeds six million, though statistics for individual languages cannot be taken to be at all precise, partly because the Census of India (where the majority of speakers live) lists a substantial number simply under Munda (1991: 413,894). It is generally accepted that there are two major divisions, northern and southern, with the larger number of both languages and speakers belonging to the northern branch.

Within North Munda, the major division is between Korku (1991: 466,073), spoken in the southern part of Betul District in Madhya Pradesh and also in northern Maharashtra, and the rest. The other subgroup, sometimes labeled Kherwari, again has two major divisions, Mundari (also the name of a language in the subgroup) and Santali. It is Santali that is credited with the largest number of speakers for any Munda language (1991: 5,216,325 in India, with a further 40,193 (2001) in Nepal and perhaps 150,000 in the Rajshahi division of Bangladesh). Within India, the largest numbers are in West Bengal and Bihar, but with others in Assam, Tripura, and Orissa. Closely related to Santali is Turi (1961: 1,562). Among the languages in the Mundari subgroup are Ho (1991: 949,216) in the Singhbhum District of Bihar and also further south in Orissa, with some speakers also in the northwest of Bangladesh; Mundari (1991: 816,378 in the Ranchi District of Bihar and also in Madhya Pradesh, West Bengal, Assam, Tripura, and Orissa); Bhumij (1991: 45,302 in the Mayurbhanj District of Orissa and in Bihar); Koda/Kora: (1991: 28,200 in West Bengal and Orissa); Korwa (1991: 27,485 in Madhya Pradesh and in Maharashtra, Uttar Pradesh, and Bihar); Asuri (1961: 4,540 in Maharashtra, Madhya Pradesh, Bihar, West Bengal, and Orissa); and Birhor (1961: 590 in Bihar).There are other North Munda languages that have not been placed confidently in either subgroup, namely Agariya (1961: 98 in Maharashtra, Madhya Pradesh, Bihar, and Orissa) and Birjia/Bijori (1961: 2,395 in Maharashtra, Madhya Pradesh, Bihar, and West Bengal).

The two main subgroups of South Munda are made up of Kharia and Juang on the one hand, and Sora/Savara and Gadaba/Gutob on the other (the last of these not to be confused with the Dravidian language Gadaba). Kharia: (1991: 225,556 in India) is spoken chiefly in the Ranchi District of Bihar but also in Madhya Pradesh, West Bengal, Assam, and Orissa, with some speakers in Nepal also. Juang (1991: 16,858) belongs almost entirely to the Keonjhar District of Orissa. Savara/Sora (1991: 273,168) is spoken predominantly in the Ganjam, Koraput, and Phulbani districts of Orissa, but there are speakers in all the states bordering on Orissa and as far away as Assam. Gadaba (1991: 28,158) belongs mainly to the Koraput District of Orissa, but there are some speakers in Andhra Pradesh also.

Tibeto-Burman

Though the total number of speakers of Tibeto-Burman languages in South Asia is relatively small, their situation can be said to be more complex than that of any other of the principal language families represented in the region, and only a brief sketch can be attempted here. Their geographical spread in South Asia itself is confined to the northern and eastern edges of the region. However, Tibeto-Burman as a whole covers an area stretching from the northeastern part of Pakistan through Burma and southern China to the northwestern parts of Thailand, Laos, and Vietnam.

There is no clear consensus in respect of the divisions of this subfamily of Sino-Tibetan and the relationships holding between its members.[19] For the Tibeto-Burman languages spoken in Pakistan, India, Nepal, Bhutan and Bangladesh, account needs to be given of the following groups: Western or Bodic (further subdivided into Bodish and Himalayan), Central (with subdivisions Lepcha, Western Arunachal, Adi-Mising-Nishi, Mishmi and Dhimalish), North-East India[20] (with subdivisions Bodo-Garo, Northern Naga, Jinghpaw, Luish and Kuki-Chin-Naga) and South-Eastern (Mru and Burmish-Ngwi).

Of the major groupings listed above, Bodic has the greatest extent in South Asia – from Pakistan, through, northern Nepal, Sikkim, Bhutan, and into eastern India – and South-Eastern the least, being included only to account for two languages spoken where India and Bangladesh border on Burma.

Bodish languages belong to the western end of the northern fringes of South Asia. Balti (1981: 223,622) is the principal language of Baltistan District of the Northern Areas of Pakistan. It is closely related to Ladakhi (1981: 72,587),[21] the majority language of Ladakh across the border in Jammu and Kashmir where Purik (45,000), a distinct dialect of Balti, and Zanskari (5,000), a dialect of Ladakhi, too, are spoken. To the south of these, in the Indian state of Himachal Pradesh, are Spiti (10,000), Tod (1,700), Ranglo (1,000), Nyam (12,000), Lahauli (1991: 22,027), Kanashi and Kinnauri (1991: 61,794[22]). Uttaranchal is the home of Jad (300), Rangpa (7,500) Darmiya (2,000), and the closely related Chaudangsi (3,000) and Byangsi (2,000).

The speech areas of Chaudangsi and Byangsi spread over into the Far Western Region of Nepal. In the Mid-Western Region are speakers of Humli Tamang, Khan, Karmarong, Dolpo (5,000), Rengpungmo, Tichurong (2,000) and Kaike

[19] The account that follows is based principally on Bradley 1997, where details of further recognizable subclassifications may be found.

[20] Also known as Sal languages because the word for ‘sun’ in most of them can be traced back to a reconstructed *sal.

[21] Figures preceded by a date are from the national Census of the country in question for that year. Others are taken from Bradley 1997 or from Gordon 2005.

[22] Including Kinashi also.

(2001: 794). Bodish languages spoken in the Western Region are: Chantel (2001: 5,912), Thakali (2001: 6,441), Gurung (2001: 338,925), Dura (2001: 3,397), Ghale (2001: 1,649), Manang (4,000), Nar (500), Nubri (3,200) and Tsum (3,000). In the southern parts of these two regions are the Himalayan languages Magar (2001: 770,116), Kham (30,000), Raute/Raji (2001: 518), Chepang (2001: 36,807) and Bujheli/Gharti (2001: 10,733). The Central Region is home to the Bodish languages Jirel (2001: 4,919) and Sherpa (2001: 129,771), and to the Himalayan languages Newari (2001: 825,458), Thami/Thangmi (2001: 18,991), Bhramu/Baram (2001: 342), Hayu (2001: 1,743), Sunuwar (2001: 26,611), Surel and Jerung (2001: 271). The largest concentration of Tibeto-Burman languages in Nepal is found in the Eastern Region, where the following are spoken: Lhomi (2001: 4), Halung, Langtang, Kachad, and Danjong – from the Bodish group – and Chaurasia (5,000), Tilung (2001: 310), Bahing (2001: 2,765), Thulung (2001: 14,034), Khaling (2001: 9,288), Dumi (2001: 5,271), Kohi (200), Sotang, Nachering (2001: 3,553), Chukwa, Sangpang (2001: 10,810), Puma (2001: 4,310), Bantawa (2001: 371,056), Chamling (2001: 44,093), Chintang (2001: 8), Lohorong (2001: 1,207), Chulung (2001: 1,314), Parali, Mewahang (2001: 904), Yamphe, Yamphu (2001, combined with Yamphe: 1,722), Yakkha (2001: 14,648), Lumba (1,000), Belhare (500), Chatthare Limbu and Athpare (2,000) – from the Himalayan group. Limbu is spoken in eastern Nepal (2001: 333,633) and in the southwest of the Indian state of Sikkim (1991: 28,174). Of the Dhimalish group, Dhimal (2001: 17,308) is spoken in the southeastern corner of Nepal, and Toto (20,000) in the north of the Indian state of West Bengal.

India has a substantial immigrant Tibetan population (1991: 69,416), and Sikkim is host to a substantial proportion of these. Lepcha spans the borders of Sikkim and West Bengal in India (1991: 39,342) and Bhutan.

The language situation in Bhutan is the least documented of any South Asian country. It is clear, however, that apart from the southern fringes of the country, where Lhotshamkha is spoken, the dominant language family is Tibeto-Burman, and within that the Tibetan subgroup of Bodish. The national language is Dzongkha (160,000)[23] and this, in a range of dialect forms, is the language of the west of the country. Bumthankha (30,000), the language of the central district of Bumthan, Khengkha (40,000), spoken to the south of this, and Kurthopkha (10,000), to the northeast, all appear to be quite closely related. Sharchopkha, also known as Tshangla (138,000), which is spoken in the southeast of the country, belongs to a different subgroup of the family and is very similar to Monpa, spoken over the border in the Indian state of Arunachal Pradesh (1991: 43,226).

Arunachal Pradesh and the other eastern states of India, along with parts of south-east Bangladesh, are predominantly Tibeto-Burman-speaking. In the northern region bordering on China are found the Western Arunachal languages

[23] The estimated figures in this paragraph are for 1991, and are taken from van Driem (2001).

Sulung (1991: 5,443), Bugun (1991: 1,046), Hruso (4,000), and the Adi-Mising-Nishi languages Nishi/Dafla (1991: 173,791), Apa Tani (23,000), Hill Miri (10,000) Adi (1991: 159,409) and Mising (1991: 390,583). At the eastern end are the Mishmi languages (1991: 29,000). Small pockets of Jinghpaw speech are found here and in the eastern part of Assam.

Across the whole of northern Assam, Bodo (1991: 1,221,881) dominates. Other languages of the Bodo-Garo branch of the family spoken in Assam are Rabha (1991: 139,365), Lalung (1991: 33,746), Dimasa (106,000), Hojai, and Deori (1991: 117,901). Bodo and Rabha are also spoken in West Bengal. The principal language of the eastern half of Meghalaya is Garo (1991: 675,642). Round the edge of this area are dialects of Koch (1991: 26,179).

In the northern half of Nagaland are the Northern Naga languages Khyam-nyungan (1991: 23,544), Chang (1991: 32,478), Phom (1991: 65,350), Konyak (1991: 137,722), Wancho (1991: 39,600), Nocte (1991: 30,441) and Tangsa (1991: 28,121). In the southern half of Nagaland and in the north of Manipur are languages of the Southern Naga subgroup of Kuki-Chin-Naga: Ao (1991: 172,449), Sangtam (1991: 47,461), Lhota (1991: 85,802), Yimchungru (1991: 47,227), Rengma (1991: 37,571), Sema (1991: 166,157), Angami (1991: 97,631), Khezha (1991: 13,004), Chakhesang (1991: 30,985), Maram (1991: 10,144), Zeliangrong (1991: 35,079) and Zemi (1991: 22,634). Other Kuki-Chin-Naga languages spoken in Manipur are the principal language Meithei or Manipuri (1991: 1,270,216), which until 2003 had the distinction of being the only language outside the Indo-Aryan and Dravidian families to be listed among the eighteen in Schedule VIII of the Constitution of India,[24] Anal (1991: 12,156), Kom (1991: 13,548), Chawte (3,000), Mayol (3,000), Tangkhul (1991: 101,841), Maring (1991: 15,268), Kuki/Thado (1991: 107,992), Mao (1991: 77,810), Kabui (1991: 68,925), Zemi (1991: 22,634) and Mizo. The last of these, also known as Lushai, is the most widely spoken language of Mizoram (1991: 538,842), where the related Paite (1991: 49,237), Vaiphei (1991: 26,185), Zou (1991: 15,966), Lakher (1991: 22,947) and Hmar are also spoken. There are speakers of Hmar (1991: 65,204) and Langrong/Hallam (1991: 29,322), a member of the same subgroup, in the south-east of Assam and in Tripura. In Tripura, the most widely spoken language is Kokborok or Tripuri (1991: 694,940), a Bodo-Garo language.

Many of the Tibeto-Burman languages of the eastern states of India have speakers in Bangladesh. It has been estimated that there are approaching 100,000 speakers each of Garo (in Jamalpur, Mimensingh, and Tangail districts) and Manipuri (in Sylhet) and perhaps half as many of Tripuri, again in Sylhet. Most of the speakers of languages of this family, however, are concentrated in the districts of Bandarban and the Chittagong Hill Tracts. Kuki-Chin languages

[24] In 2003 Maithili, Dogri (both Indo-Aryan), Santhali (Austro-Asiatic) and Bodo (Tibeto-Burman) were added.

include Bawm (1981: 5,733), Laizo, Khumi (1981: 1,188), Lushai (1981: 1,041), Pankhu (1981: 2,278) and Mizo (1981: 1,041). The Luish language Sak is spoken in the south-east corner of the country. From the South-Eastern group of Tibeto-Burman, the Mru subgroup is represented by Mru, and Burmish-Ngwi by Arakanese (1981: 122,735) and Lisu. There are Arakanese speakers in India also (1971: 12,378).

Kam-Thai

Kam-Thai, which along with Kadai forms one of the two main components of Tai-Kadai – languages which are spoken over an area stretching from southern China to south-east Asia, is represented in South Asia by languages belonging to the Southwestern subgroup of Thai, which are spoken in the Indian states of Assam and Arunachal Pradesh. These are Khamti (perhaps 11,000 speakers in India in addition to the 59,000 in northwestern Burma), Khamyang (50), Aiton and Phake (2,000 speakers each).

Austronesian

A further language family, belonging mainly to southeast Asia and the western Pacific, namely Austronesian, is represented in the official statistics found in censuses conducted in Sri Lanka. This is Malay (1981: 46,963), a member of one of the two subgroups of the western branch of the family.[25]

Andamanese

The languages that were spoken in the Andaman Islands have no known genetic relationship with any other language family. In the mid-nineteenth century, there were as many as thirteen languages split into three groups, Northern, Central, and Southern, the first two of these together making up Great Andamanese. But with the diminishing size of the population from an estimated 3,500 in 1858 to a few hundred in the late 20th century, only four languages remain, one, A-Pucikwar belonging to the Central group and the other three to the Southern. Speakers reported for these in 1981 were: A-Pucikwar 24, Onge 106, Jarawa 250 and Sentinelese 50 (Bradley 1981).

Language isolates

One South Asian language that has not been shown convincingly to be genetically related to any other language or language family is Burashaski. Its

[25] It has been proposed that Austronesian is in a position of remote relationship with Kam-Thai but the view is not universally accepted.

two distinct dialects are spoken in the most northerly part of Pakistan, in the Hunza-Nagar valleys and in the Yasin valley (the latter dialect being known as Werchikwar). The total number of speakers may approach 55–60,000.[26] Nihali, which has some 2,000 speakers in the Indian state of Maharashtra is generally also regarded as an isolate, though a strong Munda influence on its vocabulary has been recognized.

Western Indo-European

The period of West European dominance in much of South Asia has left an impact, and it is with a brief acknowledgement of this that this survey of the languages of South Asia ends. In Sri Lanka, one of the communities listed in censuses is that of the Burghers (2001: 75,283), who speak a creole based on Portuguese and Dutch with some input from Sinhalese and Tamil also. In India, French continues to have some importance in Pondicherry. The biggest legacy by far, however, is that of English (with, for instance, 178,598 native speakers recorded for 1991).

Conclusion

Certain generalizations emerge from the miscellaneous facts presented above. The most obvious is that the countries of South Asia are essentially multilingual, with the Republic of the Maldives being the obvious exception. The extent of multilingualism does nevertheless vary considerably among the others, with the situation in Sri Lanka being the simplest among them. If the others are put on an increasing scale of linguistic complexity, a possible sequence is Sri Lanka, Bhutan, Bangladesh, Pakistan, Nepal, and India (though there is room for some doubt about the relative position of Nepal and Pakistan).[27] Qualifications of such statements are always possible. Bangladesh, for example might be allocated a different position in the sequence if the dominant position of Bengali were to be considered, for the minority languages are spoken by less than 1 percent of the population as a whole.

Multilingualism also involves a mingling of language families. Of the four major families represented, all have groups of speakers in Nepal, India, and Bangladesh. In Pakistan, all but Austro-Asiatic are found. In Bhutan and Sri Lanka the languages belong to two families: Tibeto-Burmese and Indo-Aryan in the case of Bhutan and Indo-Aryan and Dravidian in the case of Sri Lanka. Indo-Aryan is the one (sub)family to be represented in all the countries of the area.

[26] Backstrom and Radloff (1992: 37). Berger (1998: 3) estimates a possible 40,000 each in Hunza and Nagar.

[27] The number of living languages listed in Gordon (2005) for countries of South Asia is: Maldives 1, Sri Lanka 7, Bhutan 24, Bangladesh 39, Pakistan 72, Nepal 123, India 415.

This mingling and the fact of contact between different languages and language families has had certain clear effects – effects that have been all the stronger because over the centuries, partly as a result of centralized rule, linguistic boundaries have not also been political boundaries. Important among these effects has been a certain reduction of the differences of a typological nature that at one stage differentiated languages belonging to different families in the region. South Asia is in this sense a linguistic area, a point that is taken up in some detail in later chapters.

The linguistic history of the area is particularly well documented, and for this there are two principal reasons. The first is the use of writing, adopted throughout the area some centuries before the beginning of the present era. The second is the existence of early grammatical treatises, of which the best known are the Sanskrit grammar of Panini in the north, who probably lived in the fifth century BCE, and the Tamil grammar of Tolkappiyanar, of possibly the second century BCE. The grammatical tradition has been continuous through to modern times and is present in all the major literary languages.

One dichotomy in the language situation in South Asia which has not been made explicit but which will be apparent from what precedes is that the languages of the area fall into two groups, one formed by those with a long and still thriving literary tradition and one formed by those which either have not been reduced to writing or do not have a writing system that has been adopted for everyday use. In simple terms, it can be said that the languages with the largest numbers of speakers are the ones that are literary languages in this sense. In the most populous countries of the region (the obvious exceptions being Bhutan and the Maldives) this means those used by populations of more than, say, ten million.[28] From this it follows that most of the languages of the area do not possess a literary tradition.[29] On the other hand, the vast majority of the inhabitants of the countries of South Asia speak a language that does have such a tradition. Moreover, writing systems have in modern times been developed for many of the more widely spoken minority languages. Such topics are among those discussed in later chapters of this book.

28 The formula is not totally applicable, in that Tulu (1981: 1,376,306), for instance, has a literary tradition going back to the nineteenth century. Similarly, it excludes Manipuri/Meithei, for which both Devanagari and roman scripts have been used. However, a lower figure would take in languages with higher numbers of speakers than Tulu but with more dispersed populations.

29 Such easy generalizations ignore the existence of traditions of oral poetry even among very small groups. See, for example, Emeneau (1971).

2 Typological characteristics of South Asian languages

Karumuri V. Subbarao

Introduction

Linguistics as a discipline is concerned with discovering language universals and coming up with an explanation for them in order to characterize the human linguistic faculty. There are two major approaches that linguists have followed in their explanation for language universals (Comrie 1981). One is associated with the innateness hypothesis formulated by Chomsky and his followers, and the other with linguistic typological research as proposed by Greenberg (1966). The first approach adopts the methodology of studying of a small number of languages in-depth and providing a statement of language universals in terms of very abstract structures. The assumption is that discovering general principles of linguistic organization and constraints that operate on them is necessary and sufficient to characterize the innate human linguistic ability. According to this view, all the human beings have the innate capability to acquire language. All languages share a set of common principles that are called *language universals*. These universals are not language specific. These common principles constitute what is called the *Universal Grammar* (UG). UG is genetically endowed and hence is embedded in the human mind. UG is prior to experience (i.e. exposure of the child to any specific language). Further, UG is species specific. In the words of Chomsky (1981: 7), "Universal Grammar may be thought of as some system of principles common to the species and available to each individual prior to experience." While languages share a set of principles, they do differ from each other not in innumerable number of ways, but in a limited number of ways and this phenomenon is referred to as *parametric variation*. One of the parameters where languages differ from each other, for example, is the deletion of pronouns in subject, direct object, indirect object, and oblique object (locative, ablative, or instrumental) positions in a set of languages while such deletion is not permitted in the other set of languages. Such a phenomenon is referred to as the pro-drop parameter.

The second approach questions the methodological soundness of formulating language universals based on the study on a small number of languages and relying on very abstract structures and general constraints to account for observed variation in languages. It emphasizes investigating data from a wide range of languages and stating language universals in terms of relatively concrete structures, and thus, the emphasis is on a more empirically based approach. One of the ways in which universals can be formulated under this approach is based on word order in a sentence. Depending upon the position of the verb in a sentence, there are three major word order types that are found in human languages: subject–object–verb (SOV), subject–verb–object (SVO), and verb–subject–object (VSO). Examples of languages with SVO word order are English, French, and Russian. Examples of languages with VSO word order are Arabic, Hebrew, and Irish. Examples of languages with SOV word order are Japanese, Korean, and almost all the South Asian languages (hereafter SALs). Based on the order in which the constituents, subject, object, and verb, occur in a sentence, certain generalizations called implicational universals can be made. For example, if the verb (V) occurs in the nonfinal position in a language, the auxiliary verb invariably precedes the main verb. That is, a non-SOV order implies precedence of occurrence of the auxiliary in relation to the main verb. (Greenberg 1966). Languages that share a number of implicational and nonimplicational universals, irrespective of their genetic inheritance, may be grouped into types. The typological classes seem to emphasize differences between groups of languages rather than lead to an appreciation of what is universal. However, the two approaches are not opposed to each other; they are complementary (Subbarao 1998a; Subbarao and Saxena 1987). Linguists interested in linguistic universals are also interested in linguistic typology, and researchers in typology are careful to document which of the seemingly universal structures may be reasonably claimed to be so as opposed to being unfalsifiable and therefore invalid.

Logically, subject (S), object, (O), and verb (V) can occur in the following orders: SVO, SOV, OVS, OSV, SOV, VOS, and VSO. Investigations in typology attempt to determine which of these orders actually can be attested in human languages. Based on the position of the verb in a sentence, specific generalizations concerning the order of occurrence of other constituents can be made. These generalizations may be absolute or may not be absolute.

If the generalizations are not absolute, they are labeled statistical universals (Comrie 1981). Within the same language the order of constituents might vary: there may be languages that exhibit SOV order in most structures but have SVO as the preferred order in some structures. One such language is Kokborok, a Tibeto-Burman language spoken in Tripura.

Another example of an implicational universal is that if a language has SOV order, it will also have the following features in the nominal expressions: modifying expressions such as adjectives, possessive-genitive phrases and relative clauses precede the head noun, whereas postpositions follow the head noun. Needless to mention, such implicational universals need not be absolute, either.

Languages may also differ in terms of case marking on the subject and object. For instance, the subject may be case marked by the nominative case in some languages or it may be case marked by an ergative case marker. The former is called nominative-accusative type (e.g., French, German, and English) and the latter as ergative-absolutive type (e.g., Georgian, Hindi–Urdu, and Punjabi). In an ergative language, the subject of the intransitive verb and the object of a sentence with a transitive verb are case marked identically and the subject is ergative case marked. The ergative subject normally exhibits the syntactic properties of a subject.

Typology of South Asian languages

The typological features of SALs have been discussed earlier in several insightful studies (e.g., Emeneau 1956; Masica 1976; Ramanujan and Masica 1969). Emeneau's (1956) work was seminal in its conceptualization of the subcontinent as a linguistic area.[1] This chapter recapitulates the earlier research and presents additional data[2] and evidence in support of the notion "South Asia as a linguistic area" from major and "minor" languages. In view of the limitation of space, the notions of South Asia as "a sociolinguistic area" (D'souza 1987; Pandit 1972) and "literary area" (B. Kachru 1992a) will not be discussed here (see, however, Chapter 17).

South Asia, along with the Balkans, is a paradigm example of the rather rare phenomenon known as "sprachbund," (Trubetzkoy 1928) or "linguistic area" (Emeneau 1956) or "convergence area" (first suggested in Weinreich 1958; see also Hock 1991: 494).[3]

1 Emeneau (1956: 16 n.28) defines a linguistic area as "an area which includes languages belonging to more than one family but showing traits in common which are found not to belong to the other members of (at least) one of the families."

2 Data presented in this chapter from Tibeto-Burman languages were collected in Shillong, Meghalaya, and Halflong, Assam and from Ho, a Mundari language, in Chaibasa, Jharkhand. Due to limitations of space the case of Kashmiri (see Bhatt 1999; Wali and Koul 1997) and Khasi is not discussed. There have been a number of scholars from specific regions who have provided me data for a variety of languages. I have identified their names and the language names. I have also expressed my gratitude for comments and suggestions from several scholars, including the editors of this volume, on an earlier version of this paper. See Acknowledgment, p. xvii, of this volume for the names of all to whom I owe a debt of gratitude.

3 Weinreich (1958) in his paper in *Word* 14, 374–9 was the first to use the phrase "convergence area." The term "convergence" has been in use ever since to characterize the phenomenon observed in language contact situations which results in changes at the level of phonology, morphology, syntax, and semantics. It is not clear, however, who first used the specific term "convergence." For a discussion of Trubetzkoy's work, see Velten (1943).

In the South Asian subcontinent, languages belonging to different genetic groups exhibit common structural traits largely owing to two main reasons: (1) thousands of years of prolonged language contact amongst languages because of intense bi- and multilingualism, and (2) the fact that all these languages (except Khasi, which is verb medial and Kashmiri, which is a V2 language) are verb final and verb finality plays an instrumental role in the manifestation of many identical structural traits.

In this chapter the focus is on the following aspects of the typology of South Asian languages. We shall first discuss some significant features at the level of phonology shared by the languages of the South Asian subcontinent. We shall then focus our attention on some word order universals found in SALs and some significant features of the syntax of SALs (see also Butt *et al.* 1994).[4] The features discussed below are based on the study of the syntax of these languages and there is no psychological or functional explanation in support of the observed similarities.

Phonology

At the level of phonology, all SALs exhibit a contrast between front unrounded vowels *i* and *e* and the rounded back vowels *u* and *o*. Length is phonemic in most of the languages. SALs have the stops *p, t, ṭ,* and *k* and their voiced counterparts *b, d, ḍ,* and *g*, which exhibit phonemic contrast except in Tamil. In most of the Indo-Aryan and Dravidian languages, except Brahui, retroflexion is phonemic and thus, there is a contrast between *t* and *ṭ*, and *d* and *ḍ*, respectively. It is believed that retroflexion developed in Indo-Aryan spontaneously in the environment of *r* and retroflex vowels, and went through rapid diffusion as a result of contact with Dravidian languages. Retroflex sounds, however, do not occur in Garo, the Naga languages, Kachin (Tibeto-Burman), and Khasi (Mon Khmer), and the one Indo-Aryan language in close proximity to them, Assamese (see Ramanujan and Masica 1969 for further details). In addition to the bilabial, dental, retroflex, and velar stops, most Indo-Aryan languages also have a palatal affricate series (*c, j,* etc.) which patterns identical to the stops. Along with voicing, aspiration is also phonemic in most Indo-Aryan languages. Thus, for example, Bengali, Gujarati, Hindi, Marathi, and others have four bilabial

[4] According to Comrie, language typology is concerned with "differences among languages" and "with the study of variation." (1981: 30–1). The most commonly found types of languages are verb final, verb medial and verb initial in which the verb occurs in the final or medial or initial position, respectively, of a sentence. In the studies on word order typology depending on the position of a verb (head) in a sentence certain common structural characteristics amongst languages are abstracted. These common characteristics are generally called word order universals (cf. Greenberg 1966 for details). A study of word order universals of SALs demonstrates how similar or different the languages are that belong to four different language families of the subcontinent.

stops: *p, ph, b,* and *bh*. The same is true of the dental, palatal, retroflex, and velar stop series. Punjabi, an Indo-Aryan language, went through a stage of loss of voiced aspirates and developed phonemic tone to compensate for the loss. Sindhi, an Indo-Aryan language, has voiced implosives ɓ, ɗ, ʄ, and ᶑ although it does not have the corresponding voiceless implosive stops. Aspiration is phonemic only in Sanskrit borrowings in Dravidian languages.

In Tibeto-Burman languages tone is phonemic. According to Benedict (1972: 85), "Tones probably occur in most Tibeto-Burman languages, yet our information on this point is meagre." Some of the Tibeto-Burman languages, such as Hmar, Mizo, Paite, and Aimol, have voiceless liquids and nasals. Most of the Tibeto-Burman and Munda languages have a glottal stop.

Most of the Munda languages and Khasi have checked (unreleased) consonants in the final position of a word.

Syntax

All SALs except Khasi, which is a verb-medial language, share common structural characteristics at the level of sentence and as mentioned earlier, it could mainly be because of either or both alternative reasons.

(1) Since all SALs except Khasi are verb-final languages, they share a number of word order universals of SOV languages.
(2) All SALS have been in intense language contact with each other for a long period of time thus giving rise to the creation of a "linguistic area" or "sprachbund" which literally means "language league" (see Trubetzkoy 1943 and, with reference to South Asia, see Emeneau 1956 and Hock 1991).

We shall first examine the former alternative. It is generally agreed in the studies on word order typology (see note 4) as well as in recent theoretical frameworks that it is the position of the verb (head, as it is generally labeled) in a sentence that plays a crucial role in the order of occurrence of elements in a sentence. For example, the position of occurrence of adpositions (prepositions and postpositions) to the right or left of a noun phrase in a language depends upon whether the language is verb final or non-verb final. Since all SALs except Khasi have been consistently verb final, it could be the main factor that resulted in similar structural traits.

Recall that a majority of languages in the world are of the following three types: verb final, verb medial, and verb initial. The order of constituents in a verb-final language, as has been said earlier, is subject (S), object (O), verb (V), or (SOV), in a verb-medial language subject (S), verb (V), object (O), or (SVO), and in a verb-initial language verb (V), subject (S), object (O), or (VSO).

We shall now examine the second alternative. In the South Asian subcontinent multilingualism is not an exception but a norm (Agnihotri 1992, 2001b) and contact between different languages is not an obstacle but a facilitator in communication (Pandit 1972). Thus, multilingualism implies intense language contact as a result of which characteristic features of one language family or language may be "transferred" to another language. Such a phenomenon is labeled "convergence" (see Arora 2004; Gumperz and Wilson 1971; Hock 1991).

We shall now discuss the syntactic features that are shared by verb-final SALs.

Basic word order

An example of a sentence from Hindi–Urdu reflecting SOV word order is given in (1a).

Hindi–Urdu (Indo-Aryan)

(1a)	aap	ne	muj^{h}e	dek^h-	aa	t^{h}aa
	subject		object	verb		
	you	erg	me	see	perf	pst

"You had seen me."

In most SALs the verb occurs in the final position of a sentence as in the above example. However, in Khasi, an Austro-Asiatic language, spoken by 628,846 people in the state of Meghalaya in the northeastern part of India, the verb occurs in the medial position and in Kashmiri (Bhatt 1999; Raina 2002), an Indo-Aryan language, where the finite form of the verb – may it be the main verb or the auxiliary – occurs in the second position in a sentence as in German and Dutch. This is generally referred to as the V2 position.

Lexical constituents in a sentence can freely be moved/scrambled in Indo-Aryan, Dravidian, and Munda languages while such movement is permitted in Tibeto-Burman languages when the noun phrase is followed by postpositions. The following examples from Hindi–Urdu are illustrative:

(1b)	muj^{h}e	aap	ne	dek^h-	aa	t^{h}aa
	me	you	erg	see	perf	pst

(1c)	dek^h-	aa	t^{h}aa	aap	ne	muj^{h}e
	see	perf	pst	you	erg	me

(1d)	muj^{h}e	dek^h-	aa	t^{h}aa	aap	ne
	me	see	perf	pst	you	erg

Such movement is due to bringing a specific constituent in a sentence into focus for the sake of emphasis (see Gambhir 1981 for further details).

Position of the auxiliary verb

The auxiliary verb follows the main verb. In (1a) above the perfect aspect marker *-aa* and past tense marker *t^haa* follow the verb stem *dek^h* "see." There is, however, an exception to this generalization: in Kashmiri, the finite form of the verb occurs in the second position in a sentence and thus, it may precede the main verb as in (2) below.

Kashmiri (Indo-Aryan)

(2)	raaman	dits	*ʃaamas*	*kitaab*
	Ram-erg	give-pst	Sham-dat	book

"Ram gave Sham a book."

(3)	raaman	c^hu	*ʃaamas*	*kitaab*	*divaan*
	Ram-erg	be-pres	Sham-dat	book	give-prog

"Ram is giving a book to Sham." (Raina 2002: 114)

In (2) above, the finite form of the verb *dits* ("gave") carries the finite past tense marker and in (3) *c^hu* ("be-pres") carries the finite present tense marker. Examples (2) and (3) are ungrammatical if the finite form of the verb occurs in the final position in the sentence to the right of the object as (2a) and (3a) illustrate.

(2a)	*raaman	*ʃaamas*	*kitaab*	dits
	Ram-erg	Sham-dat	book	give-pst

"Ram gave Sham a book."

(3a)	*raaman	*ʃaamas*	*kitaab*	divaan	c^hu
	Ram-erg	Sham-dat	book	give-prog	be-pres

"Ram gave Sham a book." (Raina 2002: 114)

Order of indirect object and direct object

The indirect object (IO) precedes the direct object (DO) in the unmarked (canonical) word order of most SALs. The IO and DO are in italics in the following example.

Hindi–Urdu

(4)	saliim	ne	*salmaa*	*ko*	*kitaab*	dii
	Salim	erg	Salma	to	book	gave

"Salim gave a book to Salma."

Postpositions

While verb-medial languages such as English and French have prepositions that occur to the left of the noun, all verb-final SALs have postpositions that follow the noun. This phenomenon accords with the implicational universal of language typology mentioned above, though Persian which is verb final has prepositions as well as postpositions. (Greenberg 1966). However, the implicational universal that all non-verb-final languages have prepositions is an absolute universal in the sense that it has no exceptions. Khasi is an example for such universal.

Angami (Tibeto-Burman)

(5) miza gi
table on
"On the table"

Position of the genitive

If the language has postpositions, the genitive precedes the head noun as predicted by the implicational universal for verb-final languages.

Manipuri (Tibeto-Burman)

(6) pritam gi lairik
"Pritam of book"

Comparison

Comparative and superlative constructions in SALs use a postposition, comparable to *than* in English, to mark the standard of comparison. Most SALs lack bound comparative and superlative morphemes, comparable to the *-er* and *-est* of English. As expected, the marker of comparison follows the standard of comparison; see, for example, the following:

Hindi–Urdu

(7) rag^{h}u raad^{h}aa se lambaa hai
Raghu Radha than tall is
"Raghu is taller than Radhaa."

(8) rag^{h}u sab se lambaa hai
Raghu all than tall is
"Raghu is the tallest of all."

Some Tibeto-Burman languages such as Angami (78,995 speakers), Hmar (5,000 speakers), and Sema (95,630 speakers) do have a bound marker for comparison. For example, in Hmar *saang* is "tall", *saang-lem* is "taller", and *saang-tak* is "tallest."

Hmar (Tibeto-Burman)

(9)	hi	naupangtepa	hi	kha	naupangtepa	kha	*nekin*	a-	saang-	*lem*
	this	small boy	this	that	small boy	that	than	3sg	tall	-er

"This small boy is taller than that small boy."

(10)	lalaa	(cu)	an-	pool-	a	a-	in-	saang-	*tak*
	Lala	def	their	class	in	3sg	vr	tall	-est

"Lala is the tallest in their class." (Subbarao 1998b)

Time and place adverbials

Time adverbials (T) precede place adverbials (P). Thus, the order of their occurrence is TP as in Angami in (11). In contrast, in Khasi, a non-verb-final language, it is PT just as in English and French.

Angami (Tibeto-Burman)

(11)	a-	e	vɔr-	ke-	tyɔ	khrə-	u-	nu	deli-	nu	n-	ze	kese-	tyɔ
	I	nom	come	inf	fut	month(T)	def	in	Delhi(P)	in	you	with	meet	fut

"I will meet you in Delhi next month." (Kevichusa 1996)

Order of time and place adverbials

Time and place adverbials occur in *descending order* (Subbarao 1984). By descending order we mean the superordinate chunk of place or time occurs first, then a subordinate chunk, and then a chunk subordinate to that follows. See, for example:

Time adverbials

Telugu (Dravidian)

(12)	2002	samwatsaram	janawari	nela	loo	padiheenoo	taariikhu
	2002	year	January	month	in	fifteenth	date

raatri-	ki	enimidi	ganṭala-	ki
night	to	eight	hours	dat

"At 8 pm on the fifteenth of January in 2002."

Place adverbials

Hindi–Urdu (Indo-Aryan)

(13)	banaaras	mẽ	wiʃwanaat^h	mandir	ke	dwaar	par
	Benaras	in	Vishwanath	temple	of	gate	on

"At the gate of the temple of Kashi Vishwanath in Benaras."

Complementizer

The complementizer (comparable to the sentential linker *that* in English), consistent with the implicational universal of SOV word order, follows the clause in all the Dravidian languages and in some Indo-Aryan languages such as Nepali, Assamese, and Sinhalese. In Kashmiri, Punjabi, and Hindi-Urdu, the complementizer occurs to the *left* of the subordinate clause as in French and English. In some of the Indo-Aryan languages, such as Bengali, Oriya, Marathi, and Konkani as well as in Manipuri (a Tibeto-Burman language), there are two complementizers: a particle comparable to *that* of English and *ki* of Hindi, which precedes the subordinate clause and a quotative, a form of the verb "to say," that follows the subordinate clause. The quotative is consistent with the SOV word order while the complementizer comparable to *ki* of Hindi is not. All the Tibeto-Burman languages except Manipuri have only a postsentential complementizer consistent with the SOV word order.

Preclausal complementizer

Hindi–Urdu (Indo-Aryan)

(14)	ramyaa	ne	kahaa	t^{h}aa	*ki*	[vah	t^{h}aɳɖe	paanii	se	nahaa	saktii	hai]
	Ramya	erg	said	had	comp	she	cold	water	with	bathe	can	pres

"Ramya said that she could bathe in cold water."

Postclausal complementizer

Telugu (Dravidian)

(15)	ramyaa	[tanu	canniiɭɭa-	loo	snaanam	ceyya-	galanu]	*ani*	ceppindi
	Ramya	she	cold water	in	bath(noun)	do	can	comp	said

"Ramya said that she could bathe in cold water."

The postclausal complementizer, a participial form of the verb *say*, has acquired a variety of other functions such as a purposive marker, reason adverbial marker, a marker for naming and labeling and with onomatopoeic expressions, and so on. See Emeneau (1956), Y. Kachru (1979), Kuiper (1967), S. N. Sridhar (1990), and Subbarao *et al.* (1989) as in the following examples.

As a purposive marker

Telugu (Dravidian)

(16)	meemu	taajmahalu	cuuddamu-	*ani*	welleemu
	we	Tajmahal	will see	in order to	went

"We went to Agra *in order to* see the Taj Mahal."

As a reason marker

Telugu (Dravidian)

(17)	ramana	ki	tana	bhaaryaa	aalasyam gaa	leecindi	*ani*	koopam	waccindi
	Ramana	dat	his	wife	late	got up	because	anger	came

"Ramana got mad *because* his wife came home late."

Naming-labeling

Telugu (Dravidian)

(18)	indiraa	*an-ee*	maniʃi
	Indira	said	person

"A person called Indira."

With onomatopoeic expressions: The onomatopoeic expression in (19) is *dhan* and the quotative *ani* occurs to its right.

Telugu (Dravidian)

(19)	illu	*dhan*	m-	*ani*	paḍipooyindi
	house	onomatopoeic	epen	comp	fell

"The house fell with a thud."

Sequence-of-tense phenomenon

A distinct feature of SALs is that the principle of Tense Harmony between the verb of the matrix clause and subordinate clause is not observed. In other words, the tense of the main clause and the embedded clause do not have to agree. The matrix verb and the embedded verb may both have their own independent tenses as a result.

Hindi–Urdu (Indo-Aryan)

(20)	saritaa	ne	kahaa	t^haa	ki	[maĩ	aap-	se	kal	miluungii]
	Sarita	erg	said	had	comp	I	you	with	tomorrow	will meet

(Literal) "Sarita told (me) that I will meet you tomorrow."
"Sarita had told me that she'd meet me tomorrow."

Though the matrix verb carries the past tense marker and the embedded verb carries the future tense marker, the sentence is grammatical. In English and some other languages the sequence-of-tense is observed rather strictly and extends to time adverbials as well (e.g., as in 21b). The tense marker and the time adverb are in italics.

English

(21a) *Sarita had told me that she'*ll* meet me *tomorrow*.
(21b) Sarita had told me that she'*d* meet me *the next day*.

Unlike in English and many other languages, the pronominal forms of the subjects of matrix and embedded clause do not have to be identical in shape in indirect speech in SALs. This is due to the fact that the speaker is quoting verbatim. Hence, the postsentential complementizer is labeled as a quotative (For a detailed discussion of the quotative, see Emeneau 1956; Y. Kachru 1979; Kuiper 1967; and Subbarao *et al.* 1989). However, significantly in Hindi–Urdu, Kashmiri, Bengali, Oriya, and Marathi the same phenomenon of tense mismatch and retention of the pronominal forms of the direct speech are found though the complementizer occurs in a preclausal position.

We shall now discuss modifiers of a noun phrase (adjectives, determiners, and relative clauses).

Adjectives

Position of occurrence

The position of adjectives in SALs is that, in Indo-Aryan and Dravidian languages the adjective always precedes the head noun.

Hindi–Urdu (Indo-Aryan)

(22) kʰuubsuurat laṛkii
beautiful girl
"A beautiful girl."

In Tibeto-Burman languages the adjective may precede or follow the noun and it is language specific. For example, in Manipuri (980,896 speakers), the adjective may precede as well as follow the head noun.[5]

[5] The occurrence of an adjective either to the left or to the right of a noun clearly demonstrates that there is no correlation between the position of the adjective and the word order in language. An SVO language such as English permits adjectives to its left. See Dryer 1992 for further details.

Manipuri (Tibeto-Burman)

(23)	phəzəbə	nupi
	beautiful	girl

"A beautiful girl."

(24)	nupi	phəzəbə
	beautiful	girl

"A beautiful girl."

Determiners

Position of determiners

In Indo-Aryan and Dravidian languages determiners precede the head noun whereas in some Tibeto-Burman languages determiners follow the head noun.

Hindi–Urdu (Indo-Aryan)

(25)	vah	laṛkii
	that	girl

"That girl"

Angami (Tibeto-Burman)

(26)	themie	hau
	man	this

"This man"

Split determiner

Some Tibeto-Burman languages have a split determiner system where the determiner consisting of two parts precedes and follows the noun phrase. We label them as det1 and det2.

Hmar (Tibeto-Burman)

(27)	hi	par	hi	a-	mɔi
	det1	flower	det2	3sg	beautiful

"This flower is beautiful."

Relative clauses

Relativization is a process in which there is a noun phrase in the main clause and there is a corresponding relative pronoun identical with the head noun that occurs in the subordinate clause. Indo-Aryan and Dravidian languages have two types of relative clauses: full clause and participial. They have a specific construction that is labeled "relative-correlative" construction in which the relative pronoun in the subordinate clause functions like a modifier as in (28) below.

In Indo-Aryan languages the embedded relative clause may either precede the head noun (prenominal) or follow the head noun (postnominal-1) or occur to the right of the verb of the matrix clause (postnominal-2). The head noun is in italics.

Prenominal

Hindi–Urdu (Indo-Aryan)

(28)	jo	laɽkaa	vahãã	k^{h}aɽaa	hai	*vah*	meraa	b^{h}aaii	hai
	which	boy	there	standing	is	he	my	brother	is

"The boy who is standing there is my brother."

Postnominal-1

Hindi–Urdu (Indo-Aryan)

(29)	*vah*	*laɽkaa*	jo	vahãã	k^{h}aɽaa	hai	meraa	b^{h}aaii	hai
	that	boy	who	there	standing	is	my	brother	is

"The boy who is standing there is my brother."

Postnominal-2

Hindi–Urdu (Indo-Aryan)

(30)	*vah*	*laɽkaa*	meraa	b^{h}aaii	hai	jo	vahaãã	k^{h}aɽaa	hai
	that	boy	my	brother	is	who	there	standing	is

"The boy who is standing there is my brother."

The relative pronoun and the question word have different forms in Indo-Aryan languages unlike in English where they are homophonous.

Hindi–Urdu (Indo-Aryan)
(31)

Relative pronoun	Question word
jo "who"	*kaun* "who"
jis ko/jise "whom" (accusative-dative)	*kis ko/kise* "whom" (accusative-dative)
jahãã "where"	*kahãã* "where"
jab "when"	*kab* "when"
jis tarah "which way"	*kis tarah* "how"

Note that the relative pronoun starts with the consonant *j-* (as in *jo, jis, jab*, etc.) and the question word always starts with *k-* in Indo-Aryan languages. In contrast, in Dravidian languages the question word and the relative pronoun are homophonous.

Telugu (Dravidian)
(32)

Relative pronoun	Question word
ewaru "who"	*ewaru* "who"
ewari-ki "whom" (dative)	*ewari-ki* "whom" (dative)
ewari-ni "whom" (accusative)	*ewari-ni* "whom" (accusative)
ekkaḍa "where"	*ekkaḍa* "where"
eppuḍu "when"	*eppuḍu* "when"
elaagu "which way"	*elaagu* "which way"

The relative clause occurs only to the left of the head noun in Dravidian languages just as in other verb-final languages such as Japanese and Korean in contrast to Indo-Aryan languages where it may precede or follow the head noun. The frequency of occurrence of relative clauses in Dravidian languages is very low.

Most of the Tibeto-Burman languages do not have a relative pronoun as such and hence do not have a full relative clause as in English, French, German, or Hindi–Urdu. The modifying clause, which is a participial clause, may occur to the left of the head noun as in (33) or to its right as in (34). Recall that adjectives too may occur to the left of the head noun as in (23) or to its right as in (24). Since the head noun phrase *nupamaca* "boy" occurs in the main clause, examples in (33) and (34) are instances of an externally headed relative clause. We have marked the embedded clause in brackets in the examples.

Manipuri (Tibeto-Burman)

(33)	[phurit	angangba	litpə]	*nupamaca*	adu	ngasi	laki
	shirt	red	wearing	boy	that	today	came

(34)	*nupamaca*	[phurit	angangba	litpə]	adu	ngasi	laki
	boy	shirt	red	wearing	that	today	came

"The boy wearing a red shirt came today."

Internally headed relative clauses

Tibeto-Burman languages have a construction labeled as internally headed relative clause where the head occurs internally in the embedded clause and the main clause does not contain any identical noun phrase. Note that the head *leʃəda* ("book") occurs in the embedded clause to the left of the embedded verb in (35) in Angami below. The embedded clause is marked by [ ] in (35).

(35)	[nɔ	leʃəda	puo	pie	a	tsə-	ʃə-	ke-	cə-u]	ʃə	se
	you	book	one	acc	me	give	ob	noz	dmdef	thick	very

"The book which you gave me is very thick."

Free relatives

When the head of the relative clause is indefinite, nonspecific, and hypothetical, the clause is labeled a free relative clause. In Dravidian languages and in some Tibeto-Burman languages the main clause and the subordinate clause in such cases are linked by a marker called the "dubitative marker" (dub mkr) in traditional grammars. The dubitative marker is in italics in (36) and the embedded clause is marked by its enclosure in square brackets.

Telugu (Dravidian)

(36)	[reepu	ewaru	raa	dalucu-	konnaar-	*oo*]	waaḷḷu	raa	waccu
	tomorrow	who	come	wishes to	vr-3pl	dub mkr	they	come	may

"Whoever wants to come tomorrow may come."

Tamil (Dravidian)

(37)	[nii	engenge	pooriy-	*oo*]	angellam	naanum	varuveen
	you	where where	go-	dub mkr	there-all	I also	will come

"I too will come wherever you go."
(The glosses have been slightly altered). (see Annamalai 1997a)

Angami (Tibeto-Burman)

(38)	[suomie	sɔdu	vɔr	nɪ	ba-	*si*]	siko	vɔrlierivi
	whoever	tomorrow	come	want	pres	dub mkr	they	may come

"Whoever wants to come tomorrow, may come."

Sema (95,630 speakers), another Tibeto-Burman language, too has the dubitative marker *kieno* performing identical functions as a marker to express the hypothetical entity as head of a relative clause just as in Dravidian languages. Dakhini Hindi–Urdu, spoken in southern India, and Konkani, spoken in Mangalore, too, have a marker *ki* that performs identical functions as the dubitative marker in Dravidian and Tibeto-Burman does. Based on such correlations, it is argued in Subbarao (2000: 104) that such correlations reflect "the cognitive capability" of the human mind to transcend "genetic barriers" and effect linguistic convergence.

Negative

The negative occurs postverbally in Tibeto-Burman and Dravidian languages. In some Indo-Aryan languages (e.g., Bengali, Marathi) it occurs postverbally and in some such as Hindi–Urdu and Punjabi, preverbally.

Preverbal negative

Hindi–Urdu (Indo-Aryan)

(39)	ve	log	yah	kaam	*nahĩĩ*	kar	paaye
	those	people	this	work	not	do	could

"They could not do this work."

Postverbal negative

Bengali (Indo-Aryan)

(40)	ora	ajke	dilli	jete	parlo	na
	they	today	Delhi	go	could	not

"They could not leave for Delhi today."

The negative in Dravidian languages and in some Indo-Aryan languages (e.g., Marathi) behaves like a verb and exhibits agreement with the subject.

Postverbal negative exhibiting subject agreement

Marathi (Indo-Aryan)

(41)	te	yethe	naahii-	t
	they	here	not	pl

"They are not here." (Pandharipande 1997: 186)

(42)	tilaa	aambe	nako-	t
	she-dat	mangoes	do-not want	pl

"She does not want mangoes." (Pandharipande 1997: 186)

Postverbal negative exhibiting agreement[6]

Telugu (Dravidian)

(43)	nee*nu*	aa	pani	ceyya-	lee-	*nu*
	I	that	work	do	cannot	1sg

"I cannot do that work."

[6] See Krishnamurti, Bh. and J. P. L. Gwynn 1985 for further details.

(44)

meem*u*	aa	pani	ceyya-	lee-	*mu*
we	that	work	do	cannot	1pl

"We cannot do that work."

The agreement of the negative with the subject in Marathi could be due to contact with Dravidian languages. In Ho (Munda) the negative carries subject agreement marker and it occurs in the preverbal position.

Affirmative

Ho (Mundari)

(45)

a-ko	musing-	musing-	ko	unung-	ta-	n-	a
they	often	often	3plsub agr	play	pres	[-tr]	decl mkr

"Often they play." (Koh 2003)

Preverbal negative exhibiting subject–verb agreement

(46)

a-ko	musing-	musing	ka-	*ko*	unung-	ta-	n-	a
they	often	often	not	3pl sub agr	play	pres	[-tr]	decl mkr

"Not often do they play." (Koh 2003)

Interrogatives

Position of the question word

Question words occur *in situ*, that is, in the same position as the constituent that is being questioned; there is no obligatory movement of the question word. Question words can be scrambled (moved to the left or right) in a sentence while in some Tibeto-Burman languages such scrambling is not preferred. Question words questioning various constituents in a sentence can occur in a row.

Telugu (Dravidian)

(47)

ewaru	eppuḍu	enduku	elaagu	eedi	ewari-ki
who	when	why	how	what	whom
istaaḍ-	oo	naaku	teliyadu		
will give	dub mrk	to me	not known		

"I do not know who will give when, why, how, what, to whom." (literal translation)

Position of yes/no question markers

Yes/no question markers occur preverbally in some Indo-Aryan languages and postverbally in other SALs.

Hindi–Urdu

(48)	kyaa	aap	kal	aagre	jaa	sakenge
	y/n q m	you	tomorrow	Agra	go	can

“Can you (polite) go Agra tomorrow?”

Ho (Mundari)

(49)	am	aɳ	concoɽe-	m	manating-	taɖi-	ɳ-	a-	*ci*
	you	me	intelligent	2sg sub agr	consider	pres	1sg obj agr	decl mkr	yes/no qm

“Do you consider me intelligent?” (Subbarao, fieldnotes)

Note that the *yes/no* question marker *ci* does not carry any agreement marker in Ho.

Mizo (Tibeto-Burman)

(50)	pro	i-	dam-	*εm*
	you	2sg agr	alright	tag q mkr

“How are you?” (Are you alright?) (literal)

Pro stands for the pronoun that is deleted which is discussed below.

Pronoun deletion

Languages that have a rich subject–verb agreement or morphologically uniform inflectional paradigms (Jaeggli and Safir 1989) permit the deletion of pronouns (pro-drop) *optionally* in a sentence. Most of the Indo-Aryan languages and Dravidian languages except Malayalam exhibit a rich agreement system and a pronoun (pro) functioning as subject, object, indirect object, and oblique objects is freely dropped.

Tibeto-Burman languages such as Angami (78,995 speakers), Manipuri (980,896 speakers), Rabha (112,424 speakers), and Tangkhul (79,887 speakers) do not exhibit subject–verb agreement and they have morphologically uniform inflectional paradigms in the sense that agreement markers are not present in all persons and numbers. Hence, they permit pro-drop of the subject in a simple as well as in an embedded sentence. In some cases unless the embedded subject is pro-dropped, the sentence is ungrammatical (Subbarao 2000: 102–3).

Hindi–Urdu (Indo-Aryan)

(51)	raajuu	ne	kahaa	t^{h}aa	ki	pro	kal	aa-	ũũgaa
	Raju	erg	said	had	that		tomorrow	come	will

“Raju had said that he’d come the next day.”

The absence of the pronominal is indicated by pro in (51).

Anaphora

By anaphora we mean back reference, that is, items referring back to their antecedents in a sentence. By anaphors we mean reflexive (*myself, yourself, themselves*, etc.) and reciprocal (*each other, one another*, etc.) expressions. Most of the SALs have simple as well as complex anaphors (reflexives and reciprocals). All Dravidian languages, except Malayalam, and a few Indo-Aryan languages, such as Marathi, Sinhala, Gujarati, and some Tibeto-Burman languages also have a verbal device to express reflexivity and reciprocity. The verbal reflexive and reciprocal may or may not be homophonous. The verbal device also functions as an inchoative (intransitive marker that detransitivizes a verb), as a self-benefactive and in the formation of specific lexical items. (See Lust *et al.* 2000 for details). Munda languages, such as Ho, Mundari, So:ra: (Savara), and Santali have only a verbal anaphor and there is no nominal anaphor in these languages.

Complex form as DO

In (52) and (53) below from Hindi–Urdu the pronoun *use* "her" cannot refer back to the subject; it has only a discourse referent (Davison 2000; Y. Kachru and Bhatia 1977).

Hindi–Urdu (Indo-Aryan)

(52)	saritaa-	ne	*apne*	*(aap)*$_{i,*j}$-	*ko/*	usee$_{*i,j}$	saraah-	aa
	Sarita	erg	self's	self	acc	she-acc	praise	pst

"Sarita praised herself$_i$/her$_{*i,j}$"

(53)	raad^{h}aa$_i$-	*ne*	*apne*	*(aap)*$_{i,*j}$-	*ko/*	usee$_{*i,j}$	ʃiiʃee	mẽ	dek^{h}aa
	Radha-	erg	self's	self	acc	she-acc	mirror	in	saw

"Radha$_i$ saw/looked at herself$_i$/her$_{*i,j}$ in the mirror." (The glosses have been slightly modified.) (Davison 2000: 408)

Complex form as IO

(54)	raad^{h}ikaa$_{i,*j}$-	*ne*	*apne*	*(aap)*$_{i,*j}$-	*ko/*	usee$_{*i,j}$	tohfaa	diyaa
	Radhikaa	erg	self's	self	acc	she-acc	gift	gave

"Radhika gave a gift to herself."

Simple form as DO

(55) raad^{h}ikaa *ne* *apne* *ko* aaine mẽ dekhaa
Radhika erg self's acc mirror in saw
"Radhika looked at herself in the mirror."

Simple form as IO

(56) raad^{h}ikaa ne *apne* *ko* tohfaa diyaa
Radhika erg self's acc gift gave
"Radhika gave a gift to herself."

Unlike in Hindi–Urdu, in Kashmiri the reflexive pronoun does not carry any case marker and is in the absolutive case though it occurs in the direct object position. Note that the reflexive in example (57) is case marked by ø whereas the reflexive in the example from Telugu in (58) is case marked accusative.

Kashmiri (Indo-Aryan)

(57) saliim- an vuc^{h} ***panunpaan-*** ø əanas- manz̨
Salim erg saw self- absolutive mirror in
"Salim saw himself in the mirror." (Wali *et al.* 2000: 483)

Telugu (Dravidian)

(58) kamala tana- ni- tanu eppuḍuu poguḍu- *kon-* *ṭun-* di
Kamala self's acc self always praise vr prog- 3sgfem
"Kamala always praises herself."

Most of the Munda languages, such as Ho, Santali, and Mundari, do not have a nominal anaphor at all and they only have a verbal reflexive and reciprocal marker. These languages thus contrast with all the languages of the other families of the subcontinent and with many other languages of the world that have a nominal anaphor.

In Ho there is a marker *-n-* that occurs with intransitive verbs. It is the same marker that functions as a verbal reflexive. This indicates that the verbal reflexive "detransitivizes" the verb. Since the nominal reflexive is absent, we have indicated this by a ø.

Ho (Munda)

(59) am arsi- re- m ø *nel-* ke- n- a
you mirror in subj agr mkr self see pst vr decl mkr
"You saw yourself in the mirror."

The verbal reciprocal is *-pe-* which is infixed in the verb *nel* ("see") in Ho. Thus, *ne-pe-l* imparts the meaning of "see each other." Since the verbal reciprocal *-pe-* is infixed in the verb *nel* ("see"), it is glossed *ne-* as "see1" and *–l* as "see2." The absence of the nominal reciprocal is indicated by a ø.

Ho (Munda)

(60) alang ø *ne-* *pe-* *l-* aka- n- a
we(dual) each other see1 vrec see2 pres perf vr decl mkr
"We two have seen each other."

The verbal reflexive/reciprocal functions as an inchoative (intransitive) marker. For example, the verbal reflexive/reciprocal in Mizo is *-in-* and it also functions as a detransitivizer as can be seen in (61) in contrast to (62) in which the detransitivizer *-in-* is absent.[7]

Mizo (Tibeto-Burman)

(61) konkhaay$_I$ a$_i$- *in-* hon
door 3sg inch opened
"The door opened."

In (62) *-in-* cannot occur because the verb *hon* ("open") is [+transitive].

Mizo (Tibeto-Burman)

(62) lali$_i$- n konkhaay a$_i$- -ø hon
Lali erg door 3sg inch opened
"Lali opened the door." (Lalitha Murthy and Subbarao 2000: 788)

Clefts

The cleft construction is permitted in Dravidian and in some Tibeto-Burman languages and not permitted in Indo-Aryan languages except in Sinhalese. The constituent that is clefted occurs to the right of the sentence as the final constituent.

An example of a question in (63) shows that the question word *ewaru* ("who") occurs in preverbal position.

Telugu (Dravidian)

(63) ninna mii inṭi- ki *ewaru* wacc- ee- ru
yesterday your house to who come pst 3pl
"Who came to your house yesterday?"

[7] For more evidence from Mizo, a Tibeto-Burman language, see Lalitha Murthy and Subbarao 2000.

An example of a cleft in (64) shows that the question word *ewaru* ("who") occurs in postverbal position at the end of the sentence as the last constituent.

Telugu (Dravidian)

(64)	ninna	mii	in*ṭi*-	ki	wacc-	in-	a-	di	*ewaru*
	yesterday	your	house	to	come	pst	adjr	3sg nm pron sx	who

"Who is it that came to your house yesterday?"

We provide an example of a simple statement (65) and a cleft (66) from Sinhala (Gair 1998: 155–7). It is the adverb that is clefted in sentence (66) in Sinhala.

Sinhala (Indo-Aryan)

(65)	mamə	ee	gamə-	*ṭə*	giyaa
	I	that	village	to	went

"I went to that village." (Shubhani Amaradeo, personal communication)

(66)	mamə	ee	giy-	ee	gamə-	*ṭə*
	I	that	go-pst-	emph	village	to

"I went to that village." (Gair 1998: 155)

Note that in Sinhala too the clefted adverb *gaməṭə* ("village-dat") occurs as the final constituent in the sentence.

When a negative occurs in a clefted sentence, it occurs to the right of the clefted constituent and thus the clefted constituent becomes a penultimate constituent as (67) from Telugu shows.

Telugu (Dravidian)

(67)	ninna	miiru	cuus-	in-	di	puli	kaadu
	yesterday	you	see	pst	3 sg pron sx	tiger	not

"It is not a tiger that you saw yesterday."

The noun phrase *puli* ("tiger") is clefted and the negative *kaadu* ("not") follows it as the negative must always occur as the final constituent.

Ergativity

Indo-Aryan languages,[8] such as Gujarati, Hindi–Urdu, Marathi, Punjabi, and Kashmiri, and Tibeto-Burman languages, such as Mizo, Hmar, Aimol, and

[8] The subject (S) of an intransitive verb and the object (O) of a transitive verb carry "the same morphological marker (absolute), while a different marker is used for A (ergative) subject." (Comrie 1978: 333).

Kom, have syntactic split ergativity and some languages, such as Assamese, Nepali (Indo-Aryan), Manipuri, Sema, and Angami (Tibeto-Burman), have morphological ergativity. Austro-Asiatic and Dravidian languages do not exhibit this phenomenon at all.

Hindi–Urdu (Indo-Aryan)

(68)	rag^{h}u	ne	prasaad	ko	kitaab	dii
	Raghu (masc)	erg	Prasad (masc)	dat	book (fem)	gave (fem)

“Raghu (masc) gave a book (fem) to Prasad (masc).”

Manipuri (Tibeto-Burman)

(69)	thomba-	na	thombi-	bu	u-	i
	Thomba	nom mkr	Thombi	acc	look at	pres

“Thomba looks at Thombi.”

Ho (Mundari)

(70)	soma	gapa	eu-	ta?a-	i	seno-	a
	Soma	tomorrow	there	to	sub agr	go	decl mkr

“Soma will go there tomorrow.”

Agreement

In most of the SALs the verb agrees with the subject and in ergative languages with the object under certain conditions. In a small number of languages the verb agrees with indirect object and oblique object. For example, in Hmar (Tibeto-Burman) the verb exhibits agreement with the subject and animate indirect object.

Hmar (Tibeto-Burman)

(71)	lali/$_i$-	n	i-	koma/$_j$	lekhabu	a/$_i$-	pek-	ce/$_j$
	Lali	erg	you	for	book	3sg(sub)	give	2sg(io)

“Lali gave you a book.”

There are some Tibeto-Burman languages in which there is no subject–verb agreement. These include Manipuri, Kokborok, and Sema (see Subbarao 2001 for further details). Malayalam is the only Dravidian language that does not exhibit subject–verb agreement. Khasi and Munda languages too exhibit agreement. An example of the absence of subject–verb agreement is given below from Manipuri (Tibeto-Burman). Note that the verb does not carry any first person agreement marker that indicates that the subject is *ai* “I.”

Manipuri (Tibeto-Burman)

(72)

ai-	na	caobi-	bu	thagat-	li
I	nom	Chaobi	acc	praise	[-fut]

"I praised Chaobi." (Sarju Devi and Subbarao 2003)

The dative subject construction

With psychological predicates or when the logical subject is a possessor, the subject (possessor or experiencer) carries dative or genitive or locative postposition. The verb in such cases agrees with the possessed noun phrase (theme or patient) (see Bhaskararao and Subbarao 2004; Y. Kachru 1970, 1990; S. N. Sridhar 1979a; Verma and Mohanan 1990; for further details). All Dravidian and Indo-Aryan languages have this construction while it does not occur in most of the Tibeto-Burman and Austro-Asiatic languages.

Hindi–Urdu (Indo-Aryan)

(73)

rad^{h}aa	ko	kavitaa	aur	kahaanii	donõ	pasand	hãĩ
Radha(sg)	dat	poetry	and	story	both	pleasing	are (pl)

"Radha likes both poetry and stories."

Note that though the subject in (73) is in third person singular, the verb exhibits plural agreement as the possessed noun phrase is in plural. A similar phenomenon is observed in Telugu.

Telugu (Dravidian)

(74)

maa-	daggara	ḍabbu	leedu
we-pl	near	money -sg	not-sg

"We don't have any money."

Conjunctive participles

SALs have a nonfinite construction generally labeled "the conjunctive participial construction." In this construction the sentence carries only one finite verb and all the subordinate clauses carry a participial form of the verb which is *nonfinite*. This construction occurs in languages such as Hindi–Urdu, Punjabi, and Kashmiri (for Hindi–Urdu, see Y. Kachru 1981a). The conjunctive participle has a finite ending (a past tense marker to be precise) in Dravidian languages (Lalitha Murthy 1994). Some of the functions of the conjunctive participle include imparting the meaning of a coordinating conjunction indicating sequential action, a concessive interpretation if used with an inclusive particle and a negative, and the interpretation of an alternative action in the sense of "instead of" (Y. Kachru 1981a).

Coordinating conjunction signaling sequential action

Hindi–Urdu (Indo-Aryan)

(75)

ramyaa	g^{h}ar	jaa	kar	kapṛe	badal	kar	k^{h}aanaa
Ramya	home	go-	having-en	clothes	change	having-en	food

k^{h}aa	kar	so	gayii
eat	having+en	sleep	went

"Ramya went home, changed her clothes, had her dinner, and slept."

Telugu (Dravidian)

(76)

maanasi	palahaaram	cees-	i	*ṭii*	taag-	i	snaanam	cees-
Manasi	breakfast	do	having-en	tea	drink	having-en	bath	do

i	office-	ki	weḷḷ-	in-	di
having-en	office	to	go	pst	3sg nm

"Manasi had her breakfast, drank tea, had her shower, and then went to her office."

Manner adverb

Hindi–Urdu

(77)

saare	bacce	aaj	skuul	dauṛ	kar	pahũce
all	children	today	school	run	having-en	reached

"All the children reached the school running today."

Reason adverb

(78)

itnii	raat	gaye	vahãã	jaa	kar	kyaa	faaydaa
so much	night	past	there	go	having-en	what	benifit

"What is the use of going so late at night?"

Concessive use

(79)

itnii	mehnat	kar	ke	b^{h}ii	saritaa	kaamyaab
so much	hard work	do	having-en	also(inclusive particle)	Sarita	successful

ho	nahĩĩ	paayii
be	not	could

"Even though she worked so hard, Sarita could not be successful."

Negative conjunctive participle

Hindi–Urdu (Indo-Aryan)

(80)	rag^{h}u	g^{h}ar	na	pahũc	kar	aur kahĩĩ	pahũc	gayaa
	Raghu	home	not	reach	having +-en	somewhere else	reach	went

"Instead of reaching home Raghu went somewhere else."

The interaction of the negative with the conjunctive participle in SALs deserves special mention. When the negative occurs in the matrix clause, the effect (scope) of the negative may be on the matrix verb or on the embedded verb and hence, such sentences are ambiguous. The following example from Hindi–Urdu is illustrative.

(81)	ravi	riʃvat	le	kar	kaam	nahĩĩ	kartaa
	Ravi	bribe	take	having+ en	work	not	does

(1) "Ravi does not take bribes and does the work."
(2) "Ravi takes bribes and (still) does not do the work."

In (1) the scope of the negative is on the conjunctive participle and in (2) it is on the matrix verb. Such ambiguity is found in most of the SALs.

Reduplication

Reduplication and echo formation are two characteristics associated with SALs. Pronouns, adjectives, question words, verbs, and adverbs all have reduplicated forms (cf. Abbi 1992; Emeneau 1956). Reduplication normally provides emphasis or imparts distributive meaning.

Pronoun

Telugu (Dravidian)

(82)	manam	manam	okaṭi
	we(incl)	we(incl)	one

"We are all together" (Subbarao and Lalitha Murthy 2000: 224)

Reduplication of adjectives and adverbs yields an intensive (e.g. *lal-lal kamiiz* "red red shirt" and *d^{h}iire d^{h}iire calnaa* "slowly slowly drive") or distributive meaning, as in the following:

Adjective

Hindi–Urdu (Indo-Aryan)

(83)	is	dukaan	mẽ	acchii	acchii	kitaabẽẽ	miltii	hãĩ
	this	shop	in	good	good	books	available	are

"Good books are available in this shop."

Adverb

(84)

g^har	g^har	mẽ	diwaalii	manaayii jaatii	hai
house	house	in	Diwali	celebrated	is

"The Diwali festival is celebrated in every house."

Manner adverb

A reduplicated noun may function as a manner adverb. The reduplicated noun *khuʃii khuʃii* ("happiness happiness (literally)") functions like the manner adverb *khuʃii se* ("happily").

(85)

ham log	is	g^har	mẽ	rah	lenge	k^huʃii	k^huʃii
we people	this	house	in	live	will take	happiness(noun)	happiness(noun)

"We'll stay in this house happily."

A reduplicated expression may impart meaning entirely different from its nonreduplicated (simple) counterpart. In Hindi–Urdu *jaldii* has the meaning of "early" or "quickly." However, *jaldii jaldii* imparts the meaning of "in a hurry." The following examples are illustrative.

(86)

aaj	mãĩ	daftar	jaldii	aa	gayaa
today	I	office	early	come	went

"I came to the office early today."

(87)

aaj	mãĩ	daftar	jaldii jaldii	aa	gayaa
today	I	office	in a hurry	come	went

"I came to the office in a hurry today."

In some SALs reduplication plays a crucial syntactic role. One such instance is the partial reduplication of the verb or adjective in the formation of *yes/no* questions in Kokborok (Tibeto-Burman) spoken in Tripura. Kokborok is a verb-final language but it exhibits verb-medial structures too, in the unmarked order as can be seen in sentence (88) below.

Kokborok (Tibeto-Burman)

(88)

akung	tini	*malai-*	kha	khumti-	bai
(subject)		(*verb*)		(direct object)	
Akung	today	meet	pst	Khumti	acc

"Akung met with Khumti today."

The verb *malai* ("meet") is partially reduplicated in a *yes-no* question as in (89). We have glossed the verb *ma-malai* as meet1 and meet2.

(89)

akung (subject)	ki	tini	ma-	malai	kha	khumti- (direct object)	bai
Akung	y/n qm	today	meet1	meet2	pst	Khumti	acc

"Did Akung meet with Khumti today?"

Another example of reduplication as a syntactic process is the case of anaphors in Dravidian (cf. example (58) from Telugu) and Manipuri (Tibeto-Burman) as in sentence (90) below.

Manipuri (Tibeto-Burman)

(90)

caoba-	na	masa-	na	mas-	bu	thagat-	ce-	i
Chaoba	nom	himself	nom	himself	acc	praise	vr	pst

"Chaoba praised himself." (Sarju Devi and Subbarao 2003: 61)

Echo words

Echo words result from a partial reduplication of words where an initial consonant or syllable is replaced in the reduplicated word. Each language has its preferred consonant or syllable for such formations; in Hindi–Urdu, it is *w*-, in Kashmiri, *ʃ*-, and in Telugu, *g*- .

Hindi–Urdu (Indo-Aryan)

(91) caay "*tea*" caay waay "*tea and the like*"
k^haanaa "food" k^haanaa waanaa "*food and the like*"

Telugu (Dravidian)

(92) puli "*tiger*" puli gili "*tiger and the like*"
ceruku "*sugarcane*" ceruku giruku "*sugarcane and the like*"

Conclusion

In this chapter I have provided a brief description of the major typological features of SALs. Though the languages of the subcontinent belong to four genetically different language families, their syntactic features are almost identical. This is because of the following: (1) they are all verb-final languages which partially explains their shared features, and (2) they have been in close contact with each other for thousands of years. These common syntactic features provide a strong support to the notion of "India as a linguistic area" proposed by Emeneau (1956), articulated earlier by Chatterji (1926) and Bloch (1934), and elaborated in Masica (1976) and others. There are however certain features that appear to be language family or language specific. For example, the absence of the nominal anaphor in Munda languages and the infixation of an intranisitive marker to mark the coindexation of the subject noun phrase with a null element in the direct object postion is not found in any other family of the subcontinent. Another example is the partial reduplication of the verb or adjective in the formation of *yes/no* questions in Kokborok (Tibeto-Burman).

In spite of the parametric differences, the fact that many syntactic processes are shared by the languages of the subcontinent indicates that there is linguistic unity in diversity.

Part 2

Languages and their functions

3 Hindi–Urdu–Hindustani

Yamuna Kachru

Introduction

Hindi is a New Indo-Aryan language spoken in the north of India. It belongs to the Indo-Iranian branch of the Indo-European family of languages. It is spoken by more than two hundred million people either as a first or second language in India, and by peoples of Indian origin in Trinidad, Guyana, Fiji, Mauritius, South Africa, and many other countries. It is the official language of India, and English is the associate official language. In addition, Hindi is the state language of Bihar, Chattisgarh, Jharkhand, Haryana, Himachal Pradesh, Madhya Pradesh, Rajasthan, Uttarakhand, and Uttar Pradesh.

Urdu, a language closely related to Hindi, is spoken by twenty-three million people in India and approximately eight million people in Pakistan as a mother tongue. It is the official language of Pakistan, the state language of Jammu and Kashmir, and additional state language of Bihar and Uttar Pradesh in India.

Hindi and Urdu have a common form known as Hindustani which is essentially a colloquial language (Verma 1933). This was the variety that was adopted by Mahatma Gandhi and the Indian National Congress as a symbol of national identity during the struggle for freedom. It, however, never became a language of literature and high culture (see Bhatia 1987 and Rai 1984 for an account of the Hindi–Urdu–Hindustani controversy in the late nineteenth and early twentieth centuries).

Background

It is difficult to date the beginnings of the New Indo-Aryan languages of India. Scholars generally agree that the development of Indo-Aryan languages of India took place in three stages. The Old Indo-Aryan stage is said to extend from 1500 BCE to approximately 600 BCE. The Middle Indo-Aryan stage spans the centuries between 600 BCE and 1000 CE. The Middle Indo-Aryan stage is further subdivided into an early Middle Indo-Aryan stage (600–200 BCE), a transitional stage (200 BCE–200 CE), a second Middle Indo-Aryan stage (200–600 CE), and a late Middle Indo-Aryan stage (600–1000 CE). The period between 1000–1200/1300 CE is designated the Old New Indo-Aryan stage because it is at this stage that the changes that began at the Middle Indo-Aryan stage became established and the New Indo-Aryan languages such as Hindi, Bengali, and Marathi assumed distinct identities.

Before proceeding with a description of Hindi–Urdu, it may be useful to sketch briefly the sociolinguistic situation of Hindi–Urdu in the Indian subcontinent (Rai 1984). The name Hindi is not Indian in origin; it is believed to have been used by the Persians to denote the peoples and languages of India (Verma 1933). Hindi as a language is said to have emerged from the patois of the market place and army camps during the period of repeated Islamic invasions and establishment of Muslim rule in the north of India between the eighth and tenth centuries AD. The speech of the areas around Delhi, known as *khari boli* [*kʰəɽī bolī*], was adopted by the Afghans, Persians, and Turks as a common language of interaction with the local population. In time, it developed a variety called Urdu (from Turkish *ordu* "camp").

As far as the labels are concerned, the term Urdu was not used for the language before the end of the eighteenth century, as Faruqi, Rai, and others agree. Hindustani as a label for language was used at least since the time of the Mughal Emperor Babur (ruled between 1526–1530) and even before that (Srivastava 1994: 90). The most common names used by Amir Khusrau (1253–1325) and other writers were Hindi, Hindvi, or Rexta (mixed language), and later Dakhini. The early form of the language developed at the market place and the army camps, naturally, had a preponderance of borrowings from Arabic and Persian. Consequently, it was also known as *Rexta* ("mixed language").

The speech of the indigenous population, though influenced by Arabic and Persian, remained relatively free from large-scale borrowings from these foreign languages. In time, as Urdu gained some patronage at Muslim courts and developed into a literary language, the variety used by the general population gradually replaced Sanskrit, literary Prakrits and Apabhramshas as the literary language of the midlands (*madhyadesha*)[1] This latter variety looked to Sanskrit for linguistic borrowings and Sanskrit, Prakrits, and Apabhramshas for literary conventions. It is this variety that became known as Hindi. Thus, both Hindi and Urdu have their origins in the *khari boli* speech of Delhi and its environs although they are written in two different scripts (Urdu in Perso-Arabic and

[1] A recent book by Faruqi (2001) claims that Urdu was never a court language and expresses doubt that a form of Hindi devoid of Arabic–Persian influence was ever the common language of the so-called "Hindi" area. Faruqi's claims are puzzling in view of the fact that Urdu replaced Persian as the court language of the last Mughal Emperor Bahadur Shah Zafar, himself a well-known poet of Urdu (see ch. 4 in this volume), and a form of Hindi devoid of Persianization and Sanskritization is attested in many of the poets of medieval period, including Amir Khusrau (1253–1325), Kabir (fifteenth century), and Abdul Rahim Khankhana (sixteenth century).

Hindi in Devanagari). The two languages differ in minor ways in their sound system, morphology, and syntax. These differences are pointed out at appropriate places below.

Both Urdu and Hindi have been in use as literary languages since the twelfth century. The development of prose, however, begins only in the eighteenth century under the influence of English, which marks the emergence of Hindi and Urdu as fully fledged literary languages.

Phonology

The segmental phonemes of Hindi–Urdu are listed in Table 3.1. The phonemes that occur only in the highly Sanskritized or highly Persianized varieties are given in parentheses. The two noteworthy features of the inventory of consonant phonemes are the following: Hindi–Urdu still retains the original Indo-European distinction between aspirated and unaspirated voiced plosives (cf. Indo-European **ghṛdho* and Hindi *gʱər* ("house")). It retains the distinction between aspirated and unaspirated voiceless plosives that emerged in Indo-Aryan, that is, the distinction between *kal* ("time") and *k'al* ("skin"). Another Indo-Aryan feature, that of retroflexion, is also retained in Hindi–Urdu, cf. *tota* ("parrot") and *ṭoṭa* ("lack"). These two features, that is those of aspiration and retroflexion, are mainly responsible for why Hindi–Urdu sounds so different from its European cousins.

Oral and nasal vowels contrast, for example *ak* ("a plant") and *ãk* ("draw, sketch"); hence, nasalization is distinctive. Short and long consonants contrast, for example *pəta* ("address"), *pətta* ("leaf"); hence, length is distinctive.

The contrast between aspirated and unaspirated consonants is maintained in all positions, initial, medial, and final. The distinction between tense *i* and lax *ɪ* and tense *u* and lax *ʊ*, however, is lost in the final position except in very careful and formal speech in the highly Sanskritized variety.

Stress is not distinctive in Hindi–Urdu; words are not distinguished on the basis of stress alone. For instance, a word such as *kəla* ("art"), whether stressed *kə́la* or *kəlá*, means the same. The tense vowels are phonetically long; in pronunciation the vowel quality as well as length is maintained irrespective of the position of the vowel or stress in the word. For instance, the word *muskərahəṭ* ("smile") can either be stressed as *múskərahəṭ* or *muskəráhəṭ*; in either case, the vowel quality and length in the syllable *ra-* remains unaffected. Words such as *jamata* ("son-in-law") are pronounced with three successive long vowels although only the first or the second syllable is stressed. Stressing and destressing of syllables is tied to syllable weight in Hindi–Urdu. Syllables are classified as one of the three measures of weight: light (syllables ending in a lax, short vowel), medium (syllables ending in a tense, long vowel or in a lax, short vowel followed by a consonant), and heavy (others). Where one syllable in a

Table 3.1. *Phonemes of Hindi–Urdu*

Vowels			*Front*		*Central*		*Back*	
High			ī				ū	
Mid High			i				u	
Mid Low			e		ə		o	
Low			ɛ		ɑ		ɔ	
Consonants			Labial	Dental	Retroflex	Alveo-Palatal	Velar	Back Velar
Stop	vl	unasp	p	t	ʈ	c	k	q
		asp	p'	t'	ʈ'	c'	k'	
	vd	unasp	b	d	ɖ	j	g	
		asp	b'	d'	ɖ'	j'	g'	
Nasal			m	n	ɳ	ɲ	ŋ	
Flap	vd	unasp			ɽ			
		asp			ɽ'			
Lateral						ɭ		
Fricative	vl		(f)	s	(ʂ)	ʃ	(x)	
	vd			(z)		(ʒ)	(ɣ)	
Semi-vowels			w(v)			y		

word is of greater weight than others, the tendency is to place the word stress on it. Where more than one syllable is of maximum weight in the word (i.e. there is a succession of medium or heavy syllables), usually the last but one bears the word stress. This stress pattern creates the impression of the staccato rhythm that speakers of English notice about Hindi–Urdu.

The predominant pattern of penultimate stress in Hindi–Urdu is inherited from an earlier stage of Indo-Aryan, that is, the Middle Indo-Aryan stage. Old Indo-Aryan had phonemic accent of the pitch variety and there is evidence for three pitches in Vedic: *uddātta* ("high, raised"), *anudātta* ("low, unraised"), and *svarita* ("high falling, falling"). At a later stage of Old Indo-Aryan, Classical Sanskrit does not record accent. By late Old Indo-Aryan, pitch accent seems to have given way to stress accent. There are different opinions about stress accent in Middle Indo-Aryan. It is generally believed that stress occurred on the penultimate syllable of the word, if long, or on the nearest preceding syllable, if the penultimate was not long. In words with all short syllables, stress occurred on the initial syllable.

Syllable boundaries in Hindi–Urdu words fall as follows: between successive vowels, for example *pa-e* ("legs"), *a-i-e* ("come") (hon.), *nə-ī* ("new") (f.), and *so-i-e*, ("sleep") (hon.); between vowels and following consonants, for example *ro-na* ("to cry"), *pə-ta* ("address"), and *ũ-ca* ("tall, high"); and between consonants, for example *səṛ-kẽ* ("roads"), *pət-la* ("thin"), and *hin-dī* "*Hindi* language").

As has already been said, Hindi is written in the Devanagari script, which is the script used by Sanskrit, Marathi, and Nepali also (see Table 3.2). On the basis of the evidence obtained from the ancient inscriptions, it is clear that Devanagari is a descendant of the Brahmi script. Brahmi was well established in India some time before 500 BCE. Despite some controversy regarding the origin of the Brahmi script, it is generally believed that its sources lie in the same Semitic script which later developed into the Arabic, Hebrew, Greek, and Latin scripts. The scripts used for the New Indo-Aryan and the Dravidian languages of India are believed to have developed from the northern and southern varieties of Brahmi.

There are minor differences between the scripts used for Hindi, Sanskrit, Marathi, and Nepali. For instance, Hindi does not have the retroflex lateral /ḷ/ or the retroflex vowels /ṛ, ḷ/ and their tense counterparts. It uses the retroflex vowel symbol /ṛ/ and the symbol for weak aspiration /:/ only in words borrowed from Sanskrit. Although written as /ṛ/, the vowel is pronounced as a combination of /r/ and /i/.

In general, there is a fairly regular correspondence between the script and the pronunciation. The one notable exception is the pronunciation of the inherent vowel ə. The Devanagari script is syllabic in that every consonant symbol represents the consonant plus the inherent vowel ə, thus, क represents the sound *k* plus ə, or *kə*. Vowels are represented differently according to whether they comprise entire syllables or are parts of syllables, that is, are immediately preceded by a consonant: thus, the symbol इ represents the syllable *i* but in the syllable *ki*, it has the shape ि, which is adjoined to the symbol for *k*, resulting in कि. Even though each consonant symbol represents a consonant plus the inherent vowel, a word written as कल, that is, *kələ,* is not pronounced as such, it is pronounced as *kəl* ("yesterday, tomorrow"). That is, all the final inherent vowels are dropped in pronunciation. The rules regarding the realization of the inherent vowel in pronunciation are as follows; in two or three syllable words, the penultimate inherent vowel is pronounced when the final one is dropped, and in words of four syllables, both the final and the antepenultimate inherent vowels are dropped while the others are pronounced. Thus, *səməjʹə* is pronounced as *səməjʹ* ("understanding"), *mehənətə is* pronounced as *mehnət* ("hard work"). These general principles, however, do not apply to words containing medial *h*, loanwords, compounds and words formed with derivational suffixes. For instance, *səməjʹ* with the inflectional suffix of perfective *-a* is pronounced as *səmjʹa* ("understood"), but with the derivational agentive suffix *-dar* is pronounced *səməjʹdar* ("sensible") (see Ohala 1983 for details of ə-deletion).

Table 3.2. *Devanagari script*

Vowels
Independent

अ	आ	इ	ई	उ	ऊ	ऋ
ə	ɑ	ɪ	i	ʊ	u	rɪ
ए	ऐ	ओ	औ	अं	अ:	
e	ɛ	o	ɔ	əm	əh	

Following Consonant

ा	ि	ी	ु	ू	े	ै	ो	ौ	ं	ः
ɑ	ɪ	i	ʊ	u	e	ɛ	o	ɔ	əm	əh

Consonants

क	ख	ग	घ	ङ			
kə	khə	gə	ghə	ŋə			
च	छ	ज	झ	ञ			
čə	čhə	ǰə	ǰhə	ñə			
ट	ठ	ड	ढ	ण			
ṭə	ṭhə	ḍə	ḍhə	ṇə			
त	थ	द	ध	न			
tə	thə	də	dhə	nə			
प	फ	ब	भ	म			
pə	phə	bə	bhə	mə			
य	र	ल	व	श	ष	स	ह
yə	rə	lə	və	šə	ṣə	sə	hə
क़	ख़	ग़	ज़	फ़			
qə	xə	γə	zə	fə			

Although most derivational and inflectional morphology of Hindi is affixal in nature (i.e. Hindi mostly utilises prefixes and suffixes), there are remnants of the morphophonemic ablaut alternation of vowels of the *guṇa* and *vṛddhi* types in a substantial number of verbal roots and nominal compounds in Hindi. These are the most frequent and regular of vowel changes for derivation as well as inflection in Sanskrit. A *guṇa* vowel differs from a simple vowel as it results from a vowel combining with another according to the usual rules given below; a *vṛddhi* vowel, by a further lengthening of a *guṇa* vowel is its own *guṇa* and *a* remains unchanged for both *guṇa* and *vṛddhi.* The series of corresponding degrees is as follows (Kellogg 1875):

Chart of *guṇa* and *vṛddhi* increments[2]

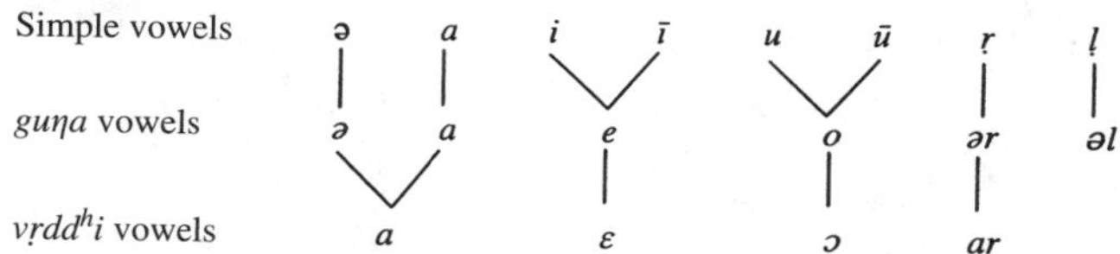

The *guṇa* increment is an Indo-European phenomenon, the *vṛddhi* increment is specifically Indian in origin. These processes are still utilized to some extent in coining new compounds of borrowings from Sanskrit for modernizing Hindi. Some examples of the verbal roots that exemplify these processes are pairs such as *kʰul* ("open") (intr.) and *kʰol* ("open") (tr.); *kəṭ* ("cut") (intr.) and *kaṭ* ("cut") (tr.); *dikʰ* ("be visible") and *dekʰ* ("see"); and some examples of nominal compounds are *pərəmə + iʃvər = pərmeʃvər* ("Supreme God"); *məha + īʃə = maheʃ* ("Great God") (a name of Lord Shiva); and *səda + evə = sədɛv* ("always"). Some examples of modern vocabulary coined on the same principles are *sərvə + udəy = sərvodəy* ("universal welfare"), *mətə + ɛky = mətɛky* ("unanimity of opinion"), and *ʃubʰə + icchu = ʃubʰecchu* ("well-wisher").

To the extent that it shares a basic vocabulary with Hindi, the *guṇa* and *vṛddhi* phenomena are applicable to Urdu as well. The Urdu writing system, however, is based on the Perso-Arabic script. As is clear from Table 3.3, the script lacks adequate vowel symbols but has an overabundance of consonant symbols for the language. Table 3.3 lists the independent forms only.[3]

Morphology

A brief description of Hindi–Urdu nominal and verbal morphology follows (for a detailed discussion of derivational and inflectional morphology, see Bailey (1956, 1982), Bhatia (1996), McGregor (1972), Russell (1980), Schmidt (1999), Sharma (1958), and Singh and Agnihotri 1997 among others).

Nominal

Forms of Hindi–Urdu nouns undergo changes in order to indicate number, gender, and case. There are two numbers, *singular* and *plural*; two genders, *masculine* and *feminine*; and three cases: *direct, oblique*, and *vocative.*

[2] In Indo-European linguistics, *vṛddhi* has become a term for the lengthened grade of the *ablaut* vowel gradation, a well-known characteristic of the Indo-European languages.

[3] The letter *alyf* is pronounced as *a* following a consonant; *ayn* is either not pronounced at all or given the value of *ə* or *a* following a consonant. It is pronounced as a glottal stop only in High Urdu.

Table 3.3. *Persian script*

Letter	*Pronunciation*	*Urdu Name*
ا	a*	əlyf
ب	b	be
پ	p	pe
ت	t	te
ٹ	ṭ	ṭe
ث	s	se
ج	ǰ	ǰim
چ	č	če
ح	h	he [/bəṛi he/]
خ	x	xe
د	d	dal
ڈ	ḍ	ḍal
ذ	z	zal
ر	r	re
ڑ	ṛ	ṛe
ز	z	ze
ژ	ž	že
س	s	sin
ش	š	šin
ص	s	swad
ض	z	zwad
ط	t	to, toe
ظ	z	zo, zoe
ع	*	əyn
غ	γ	γəyn
ف	f	fe
ق	q	qaf
ک	k	kaf
گ	g	gaf
ل	l	lam
م	m	mim
ن	n	nun
و	v	vao
ه	h	he [/choṭi he/]
ی	y	ye

Note: əlyf is pronounced as *ā* following a consonant; əyn is either not pronounced at all or given tha value of *a* or *ā* following a consonant. It is pronounced as a glottal stop only in High Urdu.
Source: Comrie (1987): 476.

Nouns are declined differently according to the gender class and the phonological property of the final segment in the word. Given here are paradigms of the major classes of masculine and feminine nouns.

Paradigm of masculine nouns ending in -a

	Sg.	*Pl.*
Dir.	ləɽkɑ "boy"	ləɽke
Obl.	ləɽke	ləɽkõ
Voc.	ləɽke	ləɽko

Masculine nouns ending in -ī

Dir.	mɑlī "gardener"	mɑlī
Obl.	mɑlī	mɑliyõ
Voc.	mɑlī	mɑliyo

Nouns ending in -ū

Dir.	sɑɽ'ū "wife's sister's husband"	sɑɽ'ū
Obl.	sɑɽ'ū	sɑɽ'uõ
Voc.	sɑɽ'ū	sɑɽ'uo

Nouns ending in a consonant

Dir.	nɔkər "servant"	nɔkər
Obl.	nɔkər	nɔkrõ
Voc.	nɔkər	nɔkro

Certain masculine nouns ending in -ɑ such as such as *raja* ("king"), *pita* ("father"), *caca* ("father's younger brother"), and *mama* ("mother's brother") are exceptions in that they do not change for direct plural and oblique singular.

Paradigm of feminine nouns ending in -ī

	Sg.	*Pl.*
Dir.	ləɽkī "girl"	ləɽkiyɑ̃
Obl.	ləɽkī	ləɽkiyõ
Voc.	ləɽkī	ləɽkiyo

Nouns ending in -ɑ

Dir.	mɑtɑ "mother"	mɑtɑẽ
Obl.	mɑtɑ	mɑtɑõ
Voc.	mɑtɑ	mɑtɑo

Nouns ending in -ū

Dir.	bəhū "daughter-in-law"	bəhuẽ
Obl.	bəhū	bəhuõ
Voc.	bəhū	bəhuo

Nouns ending in a consonant

Dir.	bəhən "sister"	bəhnẽ
Obl.	bəhən	bəhnõ
Voc.	bəhən	bəhno

In Perso-Arabic borrowings, High Urdu keeps the Perso-Arabic plural markers, for example *kaɤəz* ("paper"), and *kaɤzat* ("papers").

The oblique case forms are used whenever a noun is followed by a postposition, for example *ləɽke ko* ("to the boy"), *g'ərõ mẽ* ("in the houses"), and *ləɽkiyõ ke sat'* ("with the girls").

The adjectives occur before the noun and agree with their head noun in number, gender, and case. They do not, however, exhibit the full range of forms. This can be seen in the paradigm of *əcc'A* ("good") (A is a cover symbol for the various inflections).

Adjective: əcc'A ("good")

Masculine

	Sg.	*Pl.*
Dir.	əcc'a	əcc'e
OR	əcc'e	əcc'e
Voc.	əcc'e	əcc'e

Feminine

	Sg.	*Pl.*
Dir./Obl./Voc.	əcc'ī	əcc'ī

The adjectives that end in a consonant, for example *sundər* ("beautiful"), and in a vowel other than *-a* for example *nəklī* ("false, artificial"), are invariant, for example *sundər lərɽka /lərɽkī* ("handsome boy/beautiful girl"), *nəklī dãt* (*m.*) / *bãh* (*f.*) ("artificial teeth/arm").

The main postpositions that indicate case relations such as accusative, dative, instrumental and so on are the following: *ne* ("agentive, marker of a transitive subject in the perfective"), *ko* ("accusative/dative"), *se* ("instrumental/ablative/comitative"), *mẽ, pər* ("locative"), *kA* ("possessive/genitive"), and *ke liye* ("benefactive"). There are several other postpositions that indicate location, direction, and so on such as *ke pas* ("near"), *kī or* ("toward"), *ke samne* ("in front of"), *ke pīc'e* ("behind"), *ke bahər* ("out (of)"), *ke əndər* ("inside"), *ke par* ("across"), *ke bina* ("without"), *ke sat'* ("with") and *ke hat'/dvara* ("through").

The pronouns have more case forms than the nouns, as is clear from the following paradigm:

	1st		*2nd*		*3rd*	
	Sg.	*Pl.*	*Sg.*	*Pl.*	*Sg.*	*Pl.*
Dir.	mɛ̃	həm	tū	tum	yəh/vəh	ye/ve
Obl.	muj'	həm	tuj'	tum	is/us	in/un
Poss.	merA	həmarA	terA	tumhɑrA	iskA/uskA	inkA/unkA

The third person pronominal forms are the same as the proximate and remote demonstratives, *yəh* ("this") and *vəh* ("that"), and their inflected forms.

The possessive form of the pronouns behaves like an adjective and agrees with the possessed noun in number, gender and case, for example *mere beṭe ko* ("to my son"), *tumharī kitabõ mẽ* ("in your books"), and *unkī bəhnõ ke sat'* ("with their sisters"). The oblique forms are used with the postpositions except that the first and second person pronouns are used in their direct case forms with the agentive postposition *ne*. The third person plural pronouns have special combined forms when they are followed by the agentive postposition, for example *in + ne = inhõne* and *un + ne = unhõne*. All the pronouns listed above have special contracted forms when followed by the accusative/dative postposition, for example *muj' + ko = muj'e, tuj' + ko = tuj'e, is/us + ko = ise / use, həm + ko = həmẽ, tum + ko = tumhẽ, in / un + ko = inhẽ / unhẽ*.

In addition to the pronouns listed above, Hindi–Urdu has a second person honorific pronoun *ap* which is used with both singular and plural reference for both male and female addressees. The honorific pronoun has the same form in all numbers and cases, that is, it is invariant. The possessive is formed by adding the postposition *kA* to *ap*. To make the plural reference clear, the item *səb* ("all") or *log* ("people") may be added to the form *ap*, for example *ap səb/log*.

Hindi–Urdu also has a reflexive pronoun *ap* ("self") which has an oblique form *əpne* and a possessive form *əpnA*. The form *ap is* used for all persons. There is a reduplicated form of *ap, əpne ap,* which is also used as the reflexive pronoun in Hindi–Urdu, for example *ram ne əpne ko / əpne ap ko ʃīʃe mẽ dek'a* ("Ram looked at himself in the mirror").

The two interrogative pronouns, *kɔn* and *kya* are used for human and nonhuman respectively. The oblique forms of these pronouns are *kis* in the singular and *kin* in the plural. The possessive is formed by adding the possessive postposition *kA* to the oblique. Similar to the third person pronouns, these pronouns also have combined forms such as *kinhõne, kise*, and *kinhī̃*.

The devices of reduplication and partial reduplication or echo-compounding are used for expressing various meanings. For instance, reduplication of adjectives has either an intensive or a distributive meaning, as in *lal-lal saṛī* ("very red saree"), *taza-taza dūdʹ* ("very fresh milk"), *kale-kale bal* ("jet-black hair"), *ū̃ce-ū̃ce pəhaṛ* ("tall mountains"). Echo-compounding of adjectives, nouns and verbs has the meaning "and the like", for example *sundər-vundər* ("pretty and such"), *cay-vay* ("tea and other such things"), and *milna-vilna* ("meeting and other such activities"). Echo-compounding usually tones down the meaning of the adjective; it, however, adds to the meaning of other words; for instance, *cay-vay* means not only tea but snacks that go with it. Another device used extensively is that of compounding two words with related meanings: *hə̃sī -xuʃī* ("laughter and happiness") (pleasant state or occasion), *dukʹ-təklīf* ("sorrow and pain") (state full of sorrow), and *ʃadī -byah* ("wedding"). Note that in all these examples, one item is from Indic sources, the other from Perso-Arabic sources. This is extremely common, though not absolutely obligatory.

In Hindi–Urdu, the possessor normally precedes the possessed and the possessive postposition *kA* agrees with the possessed in number, gender, and case, for example *ləṛke kī kitab* ("the boy's book"), and *ləṛke ke sir pər* ("on the boy's head") [the postposition agrees with the second noun, namely "book" and "head," respectively]. High Urdu has an alternative construction where the possessed precedes the possessor following the convention of the ezafe-construction in Persian, for example *ʃer-e-kəʃmīr* ("the lion of Kashmir"), and *qəvaid-e-urdu* ("grammar of Urdu").

Verbal

Two most notable features about Hindi–Urdu verbs are their occurrence in morphologically related sets and in series. The first phenomenon is known as causal verbs and the second as compound verbs. Whereas the causative is inherited from Old Indo-Aryan, the development of compound verbs in New Indo-Aryan is recent – it became frequent only in the period between 600 and 1000 CE.

Some examples of causal verbs can be seen in the chart given here.

Causal verbs

Intr.	Tr.	Dbl.tr.	Caus.
uṭʹ "rise"	uṭʹɑ "raise"	- - - - -	uṭʹvɑ
kəṭ "be cut"	kɑṭ "cut"	- - - - -	kəṭvɑ
- - - - -	sun "hear"	sunɑ	sunvɑ
- - - - -	kʹɑ "eat"	kʹilɑ	kʹilvɑ

Examples of compound verbs are *gir jana* ("fall go = fall down"), *k'a lena* ("eat take = eat up"), *pəɽ' lena* ("read take = read to oneself"), and *pəɽ' dena* ("read give = read out loud to someone").

Hindi–Urdu verbs occur in the following forms: root, for example *soc* ("think"), *a* ("come"); imperfect stem, for example *soctA, atA*; perfect stem, for example *socA, ayA*; and infinitive, *socnA, anA*. The stems behave like adjectives in that they agree with some noun in the sentence in number and gender. The imperfect and perfect participles, which are made up of the imperfect and perfect stems followed by the perfect stem of the verb *ho* ("be"), that is, *huA*, agree in case also. This means that the stem final *-A* changes to *-e* or *-i* for agreement. Whereas the imperfect and perfect aspectual distinction is expressed by suffixation, the continuous aspect is indicated by an independent lexical item, *rəhA*. This marker follows the root and behaves like the imperfect and perfect stems with regard to gender and number agreement.

The tense distinction of present versus past is expressed with the forms of the auxiliary verb, the present auxiliary *hE* and the past auxiliary *t'A*. These are the present and past forms of the stative verb *honA* ("be"). As in all Indo-European languages, the verb "be" is irregular in Hindi. It has the following forms: root *ho*; imperfect stem *hotA*; perfect stem *huA*; infinitive *honA*; stative present *hE*; and stative past *t'A*. The stem-final -A changes to *-e,-i* or *-ĩ* for number and gender agreement and the final -E changes to various vowels to indicate person, number, and gender agreement. The forms of the verb *honA* in stative present are as follows: 1st person sg. *hū̃*, 2nd and 3rd person sg. *hε*, 2nd person pl. *ho*, and 1st and 3rd person pl. and 2nd hon. *hε̃*.

In addition to tense and aspect distinctions, the verbal forms express mood distinctions as well. There is no distinction made between indicative and interrogative, that is, in assertions as well as questions, the verbal forms are made up of the stems and auxiliaries described above. Historically, Old Indo-Aryan did not make a distinction between these two moods either. The moods in Old Indo-Aryan were indicative, imperative, optative, and subjunctive. In Hindi–Urdu, the optative forms are made up of the root and the following suffixes: 1st person sg. *-ũ*, 2nd and 3rd person sg. *-e*, 1st and 3rd pl. and 2nd honorific *-ẽ*, and 2nd pl. *-o*. The future tense is formed by adding the suffix -gA to the optative forms, for example *ja-ū̃-ga* ("I (m.) will go"), and *jaogī* ("you (f.) will go") The following are the imperative forms: root form of the verb (intimate or rude), 2nd pl. optative (familiar), root with the suffix *-iye* (honorific, polite), root with the suffix *-iye* followed by the suffix *-ga* (remote, therefore, extra polite) and the infinitive form of the verb (remote imperative, therefore even when used with second plural, polite). Thus, the imperative forms of the verb *soc* are (*tū*) *soc* ("you (intimate) think"), (*tum*) *soco* ("you (familiar) think"), (*ap*) *sociye* ("you (honorific) think"), (*ap*) *sociyega* ("you (honorific) please think (perhaps a little later?)"), and (*tum*) *socna* ("you (familiar, polite) think" or "you (familiar) think (perhaps a little later?)").

The paradigm of the verb *g′ūmna* ("to take a walk") illustrates the full range of the forms discussed above.

Paradigm of verb forms

Root:	g′ūm "take a walk"
Imperfect stem:	g′ūmtA
Perfect stem:	g′ūmA

Optative: g′ūmū̃ (1st sg.), g′ūmo (2nd pl.), g′ūme (2nd and 3rd sg.), g′ūmẽ (1st and 3rd pl., 2nd honorific)

Imperative: g′ūm (2nd sg., intimate/rude), g′ūmo (2nd pl., familiar), g′ūmiye (2nd honorific, polite), g′ūmiyegɑ (2nd honorific, extra polite)

Future

	1st		*2nd*		*3rd*	
	M.	F.	M.	F.	M.	F.
Sg.	g′ūmū̃gɑ	g′ūmū̃gī	g′ūmegɑ	g′ūmegī	g′ūmegɑ	g′ūmegī
Pl.	g′ūmẽge	g′ūmẽgī	g′ūmoge	g′ūmogī	g′ūmẽge	g′ūmẽgī
Hon.	-	-	g′ūmẽge	g′ūmẽgī	g′ūmẽge	g′ūmẽgī

Present imperfect

	Sg.	*Pl.*	*Hon.*
1st M.	g′ūmtɑ hū̃	g′ūmte hɛ̃	
1st F.	g′ūmtī hū̃	g′ūmti hɛ̃	
2nd M.	g′ūmtɑ hɛ	g′ūmte ho	g′ūmte hɛ̃
2nd F.	g′ūmtī hɛ	g′ūmtī ho	g′ūmtī hɛ̃
3rd M.	g′ūmtɑ hɛ	g′ūmte hɛ̃	
2nd F.	g′ūmtī hɛ	g′ūmtī hɛ̃	

The past forms are: Past imperfect: *g′ūmtɑ t′ɑ, g′ūmte t′e, g′ūmtī t′ī, g′ūmtī t′ī̃*, etc.; Present perfect: *g′ūmɑ hū̃, g′ūmī hū̃*, etc.; Past perfect: *g′ūmɑ t′ɑ, g′ūme t′e, g′ūmī t′ī̃*, etc.; Present continuous: *g′ūm rəha hɛ, g′ūm rəhe hɛ̃, g′ūm rəhī hɛ*, etc.; Past continuous: *g′ūm rəha t′ɑ, g′ūm rəhe t′e, g′ūm rəhī t′ī̃*, etc.

In general, Urdu speakers use the masculine plural form as undifferentiated for gender in the first person, e.g. *həm kəl kəlkətte ja rəhe hɛ̃* ("We (m./f.) are going to Calcutta tomorrow").

The contingent, past contingent, and presumptive tenses are formed with the imperfect and perfect stems and the continuous form followed by the auxiliaries *ho* ("contingent"), *hotA* ("past contingent"), and *hogA* ("presumptive").

Roughly, these three are translatable into English as follows: *pīta ho* ("(he) may be drinking"), *piya ho* ("(he) may have drunk"), *pīta hota* ("had (he) been drinking"), *piya hota* ("had (he) drunk"), *pīta hoga* ("(he) must be drinking"), and *piya hoga* ("(he) must have drunk").

Hindi–Urdu verbs are very regular, which means that once we know the infinitive form of the verb, we can isolate the root and derive the imperfect and perfect stems by suffixing *-tA* and *-A* respectively. Thus, from *hə̃sna* ("laugh"), we get the imperfect stem *hə̃stA* and perfect stem *hə̃sA*. Note that when the root ends in a vowel and the perfect stem-forming suffix -A is added to it, a semivowel is inserted to separate the two vowels. If the root ends in *ī*, *-a*, or *-o*, a *-y-* is inserted, if the root ends in *-ū*, a *-v-* is inserted, for example *ga* + *-A* = *gaya* ("sang (m.)"), *ro* + *-A* = *roya* ("cried (m.)"), *pī* + *-A* = *piya* ("drank (m.)"), *cʰū* + *-A* = *cʰuva* ("touched (m.)").

One verb, *cahiye, is* completely irregular in that it is invariable, that is, it occurs only in this form. It takes dative subject and means "to need" or "want". The following verbs have irregular perfect stems: *kər* ("do") *-kiya, le* ("take") *-liya, de* ("give") *-diya*, and *ja* ("go") *-gəya*. The following verbs have irregular polite imperative forms: *kər* ("do") = *kījiye, le* ("take") = *lījiye, de* ("give") = *dījiye*, and *pī* ("drink") = *pījiye*.

Hindi–Urdu has two types of compound verbs: those that involve verbs in a series and those that involve a nominal and a verbal. Some examples of the former have already been given (see the beginning of this section), a few examples of the latter are: *svīkar kərna* ("acceptance do") or ("to accept"), *pəsənd hona* ("liking be" or "to like") (nonvolitional), *pəsənd kərna* ("liking do" or "to like") (volitional), and *təng ana* ("torment come" or "to be fed up").

In the verbs-in-series type of compound verbs, usually the meaning of the whole is derived from the meaning of the first, or main, verb; the second, or explicator, verb performs the function of either restricting, or adding some specific shade of meaning to the meaning of the main verb. Additionally, the explicator verb (EV) necessarily expresses the meaning "a one-shot action or process." For instance, *marna* can mean either "hit" or "kill", *mar ḍalna* ("hit / kill pour") means only "kill;" *likʰna* means "write," *likʰ marna* "write hit" means "to dash off a few lines in a hurry/thoughtlessly;" *rəkʰna* means "keep, put," *rəkʰ cʰoṛna*, "keep leave" means "save." The main explicator verbs are the following and they roughly signify the meanings described below:

The EV *ana* ("come") occurs with intransitive verbs of motion and indicates that the action of the main verb is oriented toward a focal point which may be a person or which may be set in time or space; for example *vəh sīṛʰiyãcəṛʰ aī* ("she came up the steps") and *vəh sīṛʰiyã utər aī* ("she came down the steps").

The EV *jana* ("go") occurs with intransitive verbs of motion and other change-of-state verbs and indicates motion away from the focal point; with dative subject verbs, it indicates definitive meaning; and with transitive verbs, it indicates hurried, compulsive action; for example *vəh sīṛ'iyā̃ cəṛ' gəī* ("she went up the steps"), *rajū ko kitab mil gəī* ("Raju got the book"), and *vəh gusse mẽ jane kya kya lik' gəya* ("who knows what he dashed off in his anger").

The EV *lena* ("take") occurs with affective (transitive) verbs and indicates completive meaning; with other transitive verbs, it indicates a self-benefactive meaning; and with certain intransitive verbs, it indicates internal expression; for example *usne kam kər liya* ("(s)he completed (his/her) job"), and *mɛ̃ ne ṭ'īk soc liya hɛ* ("I have made a decision").

The EV *dena* ("give") occurs with transitive verbs other than affective verbs and indicates that the action is directed toward a beneficiary other than the agent of the action denoted by the main verb; and with intransitive verbs of expression, it indicates external expression; for example *usne sara rəhəsy bəta diya* ("he divulged the whole secret"), and *sīma zorõ se hə̃s dī* ("Sima laughed loudly").

The EV *uṭ'na* ("rise") occurs with intransitive and transitive verbs of punctual action and indicates suddenness; for example *vəh muj'he dek'te hī ro uṭ'ī* ("she suddenly began to cry when she saw me").

The EV *bɛṭ'na* ("sit") occurs with certain transitive verbs and indicates impudence; for example *vəh əpne 'bas' se ləṛ bɛṭ'a* ("he fought with his boss").

The EV *pəṛna* ("fall") occurs with intransitive change-of-state verbs, and certain verbs of expression, and indicates suddenness; for example *bəcca d'əmaka sun kər cɔ̃k pəṛa* ("the child was startled to hear the big noise").

The EV *ḍalna* ("pour") occurs with transitive verbs that express violent action, e.g., *mar*, 'hit', and reinforces the violence. With other transitive verbs such as *pəṛ*^{h} 'read', *lik*^{h} 'write', etc., it indicates action performed in a casual, off hand manner.

The EV *rək'na* ("keep") occurs with certain transitive verbs and indicates a temporary state resulting from the action of the main verb; for example *mɛ̃ ne kəmīzẽ d'o rək'ī hɛ̃*("I have washed (and kept ready) the shirts").

The EV *c'oṛna* ("leave") occurs with certain transitive verbs and indicates dissociation of the agent with the result of the action; for example *pitajī ne merī pəṛ'aī ke liye pɛse rək' c'oṛe hɛ̃* ("father has put aside money for my education").

The EV *marna* ("hit") occurs with very few verbs and indicates rash action; for example *kuc' b'ī lik' maro!* ("just write something!")

The EV *d'əməkna* ("thump") occurs with *ana* ("come") and *jana* ("go") and indicates unwelcome arrival; for example *vəh subəh-subəh a d'əmka, muj'e cay pīne tək tək ka mɔka nəhī̃ mila* ("he showed up very early, I did not even get a chance to have a cup of tea").

The EV *pəhũcna* ("arrive") occurs with *ana* ("come") and *jana* ("go") and indicates arrival rather than motion; for example *ʃyam dillī a pəhũca* ("Shyam arrived in Delhi").

The EV *nikəlna* ("emerge"): indicates sudden emergence from some enclosed space – real or imaginary; for example *uskī ãkʰõ se ãsū bəh nikle* ("Tears began to flow from her eyes").

There are verbs-in-series constructions in which the stem of the main verb is in a participial form; these, however, participate in the tense-aspect system in terms of their meaning. For instance, the following have inceptive, continuative, and frequentative import: *pita jī dəftər jane ləge* ("Father began to go to (his) office"); *ramū der tək gata rəha* ("Ramu continued to sing for a long time"); and *mīna əksər film dekʰne jaya kərti hɛ* ("Mina frequently goes to the movies"). See also Y. Kachru (2006).

Syntax

In this brief section on syntax, I will discuss mainly the verbal syntax of Hindi–Urdu after a few remarks on word order. The reason for this will become clearer as the discussion progresses.

Hindi–Urdu is a verb-final language, that is, the order of words in a sentence is subject, object, and verb. Actually, the position of the verb is relatively more fixed than the position of any other constituent. Since most grammatical functions of nouns are indicated by the postpositions following them, the nominal constituents can be moved around freely for thematic purposes. The position of the verb is changed only in poetic or extremely affective style. Historically, word order was relatively free in Old Indo-Aryan, but became more fixed in Middle Indo-Aryan between 200 and 600 CE.

In existential sentences, the locational/temporal adverbial comes first: *mez pər kitab hɛ* ("there is a book on the table"), *kəl bəɽī ʈʰənd tʰī* ("it was very cold yesterday"). The verb agrees with the unmarked noun in the sentence. In intransitive and nonperfective transitive sentences, where the subject is unmarked, the verb agrees with the subject, for example *ləɽke bɛʈʰe* ("the boys sat"), *ləɽkī səmacar sun rəhī hɛ* ("the girl is listening (f.) to the news (m.)"), *rajū cay pīta hoga* ("Raju (m.) must be drinking (m.) tea (f.)"). In transitive sentences in the perfective, where the subject is followed by the postposition *ne*, the verb does not agree with the subject. It agrees with the object if it is unmarked; if the object is followed by the postposition *ko*, the verb remains in its neutral form, that is, third person singular masculine: cf. *rajū ne kitab pəɽʰī* ("Raju (m.) read (f.) the book (f.)"), *əfsərõ ne əpnī pətniyõ ko bulaya* ("the officers called (3rd sg. m.) their Wives"). Not all transitive verbs require that their subjects be marked with the agentive postposition *ne*: for example *bolna* ("speak"), and *lana* ("bring") do not take *ne*, and *səməjʰna* ("understand") can occur either with or without *ne*: *mɛ̃ apkī bat nəhī̃ səmjʰa* ("I do not understand you"), and *ap ne kya səmj'a?* ("what did you understand?"). In the case of compound verbs, only if both the main and the explicator verbs require *ne* does the compound verb require *ne*: *ʃīla ne dūd' piya* ("Sheila drank the milk"), *ʃīla ne dūd' liya* ("Sheila took the milk"), *ʃīla ne dūd' pī liya* ("Sheila drank up the milk"), but *ʃīla dūd' pī gəī* ("Sheila drank up the milk") since the intransitive verb *ja* ("go") is not a *ne* verb.

Semantically, Hindi–Urdu makes a distinction between volitional versus non-volitional verbs and affective versus nonaffective verbs. A verb is volitional if it expresses an act that is performed by an actor/agent. A verb is affective if the act expressed by the verb is directed toward the actor/agent, that is, it is self-benefactive. Ingestive verbs such as *k'ana* ("eat"), *pīna* ("drink"), are good examples of affective verbs in that it is the actor/agent of eating, drinking, and so on who benefits from these acts. Verbs such as ("work"), and ("write") on the other hand may be either self-benefactive or directed toward some other beneficiary. Typically, the explicator verb *lena* ("take") occurs with an affective verb, the explicator *dena* ("give") does not, that is, sentences such as the following are ungrammatical in Hindi–Urdu: **usne k'ana k'a diya* ("he/she ate for someone else") because *k'ana* ("eat") is an ingestive verb whereas the explicator *dena* ("give") indicates that the beneficiary is someone other than the actor/agent of the main verb. Verbs such as *girna* ("fall"), and *jana* ("go") express self-directed actions, hence are affective. These distinctions are important for the verbal syntax of Hindi–Urdu. Transitivity, volitionality, and affectiveness do not necessarily coincide. For instance, *sona* ("sleep") is intransitive, volitional, and affective, *sīk'na* ("learn") is transitive, volitional, and affective, *girna* ("fall") is intransitive, nonvolitional, and affective, and *dena* ("give") is transitive, volitional and non-affective. Only the affective verbs participate in the compound verbal construction with *lena* ("take") as the explicator, only volitional verbs occur in the passive construction (Y. Kachru 1980, 1981b, 2006).

In many cases, verbs in Hindi–Urdu come in related forms so that the stative versus active and volitional versus nonvolitional meanings can be expressed by varying the syntactic constructions. For instance, the verb *milna* can mean both "to run into someone" (accidental meeting) or "to go see someone" (deliberate meeting). In the first case, the verb is used with a dative subject and the object of meeting is unmarked, in the second case, the subject is unmarked and the object is marked with a comitative postposition *se*, for example *kəl bazar jate hue muj'e ram mila t'a* ("yesterday while going to the market I ran into Ram"), and *kəl mẽ ram se uske dəftər mẽ mila t'a* ("yesterday I met Ram in his office"). In a large number of cases, the intransitive verb denotes nonvolitional action and if the actor is to be expressed, it is expressed with the instrumental postposition *se*, for example *apka ʃīʃa muj'se ṭūṭ gəya* ("your mirror got broken by me"). The deliberate action is expressed with the related transitive verb in the agentive construction, for example *is ʃərartī bəcce ne apka pyala toɽ ɖala* ("this naughty child broke your cup"). Most intransitive and all dative subject verbs are either stative or change-of-state verbs and are nonvolitional. Hindi–Urdu has sets of stative, change-of-state, and active verbs of the following types:

Stative	Change-of-state	Active
kʰula hona "be open"	*kʰulna*	*kʰolna*
kruddʰ hona "be angry"	*krodʰ ana*	*krodʰ kərna*
yad hona "remember"	*yad ana*	*yad kərna*
pəsənd hona "like"	*pəsənd ana*	*pəsənd kərna*

The stative verbs are usually made up of an adjective or past participle and the verb "be", the change-of-state verbs are either lexical verbs or compounds made up of a nominal and the verb "become" or "come," and the active is either a causal verb morphologically derived from the noncausal or a compound made up of a nominal and the verb "do" (or a set of other active transitive verbs).

This, however, does not mean that all intransitive verbs in Hindi are of the above types. There are active intransitive verbs such as the verbs of motion (*cəl* "move," *bʰag* "run," etc.), verbs of expression (*hə̃s* "laugh," *ro* "cry", etc.), and others. Verbal compounding is also exploited to reduce the volitionality of verbs, for example, *ro pəɽna* ("cry + fall = to burst out crying"), *bol uʈʰna* ("speak + rise = to blurt out"), and so on.

The nonvolitional intransitive sentence above (*apka ʃīʃa mujʰse ʈūʈ gəya* ("Your mirror got broken by me")) has been translated into English with the passive; it is, however, not a passive construction in Hindi–Urdu. The passive in Hindi–Urdu is formed by marking the agent of the active sentence, if retained, with the instrumental postposition *se* and using the perfect stem of the verb and the auxiliary *ja* ("go") which takes all the tense-aspect endings: for example *ram ne kʰana nəhĩ kʰaya* ("Ram did not eat") versus *ram se kʰana nəhĩ kʰaya gəya* ("Ram was not able to eat"). The translation equivalent of the Hindi–Urdu passive in English points to an interesting fact about this construction. If the agent is retained and marked with the instrumental postposition, the passive sentence is usually interpreted as a statement about the capability of the agent; if, however, the agent is deleted, the passive sentence has a meaning similar to that of English. That is, the sentence is interpreted as being about the object in the active sentence and the agent is either unknown or not important enough to be mentioned (Guru 1920; Y. Kachru 1980, 2006).

In addition to the present and past participles, there are two other participles in Hindi which are used a great deal: the conjunctive participle which is formed by adding the form *kər* to the root of the verb and the agentive participle which is formed by adding the suffix *-vala* to the oblique form of the verbal noun, for example *lik'nevala* ("writer"), *janevala* ("one who goes"), *sonevala* ("one who sleeps"), and *ugnevala* ("that which rises or grows"). This suffix has become a part of the English lexicon in the form *wallah* and is used extensively in Indian English and the native varieties of English, especially in the context of topics related to India. Forms such as *Congresswallah* ("one belonging to the Indian National Congress"), and *Bombaywallah* ("one from Bombay") are common in literature dealing with India.

The syntax of Hindi–Urdu differs from that of English most noticeably in the use of the participles. For instance, the preferred constructions for modifying nouns or conjoining clauses are the participles: the present, past, and agentive for modifying nouns and the conjunctive participle for conjoining clauses. Compare the following Hindi sentences with their English translations: *vah g'ər se bahər nikəltī huī ɔrtõ ko dekh raha t'a* ("he was observing the women (who were) coming out of the house"); *muj'e məhadevī jī kī lik'ī huī kəvitaẽ bəhut pəsənd hɛ̃* ("I like the poems written by Mahadevi ji very much"); *usko bat bat par ronewale bəcce bilkul əcc'e nəhĩ ləgte* ("he does not like children who cry at the smallest provocation"); and *vəh g'ər akər so gəya* ("he came home and went to sleep"). Both the present and the past participles are used adjectivally as well as adverbially, compare *mã ne rote hue bəcce ko god mẽ uʈ'a liya* ("(the) mother picked up the child who was crying") and *vəh rote hue b'ag gəya* ("he ran away, crying"), and *mɛ̃ vəhã bɛʈ'ī huī ləɽkī ko nəhĩ jantī* ("I don't know the girl seated over there") and *ləɽkī vəhã bɛʈ'ī (huī) pətr lik' rəhī hɛ* ("the girl is writing a letter sitting there"). The agentive participle is used both as an agentive noun, for example *(gaɽī) cəlanevala* ("driver (of a vehicle)") and as an adjective, for example *b'arət se anevale c'atr* ("the students who come from India"). The conjunctive participle is used to express the meanings of sequential action, related action, cause-effect relationship and purpose adverbial, for example *vəh hindī pəɽ' kər k'elne jaega* ("he will go to play after studying Hindi"), *vəh kūd kər ūpər a gəī* ("she jumped and came up"), *həm ne use pɛse de kər xuʃ kər liya* ("we pleased him by giving him money"), *jəldīse panī gərm kərke nəha lo* ("heat the water quickly and take a bath") (Y. Kachru 1980, 2006).

Although the participial constructions are preferred in Hindi–Urdu, there are linguistically determined environments where full relative and other types of subordinate and conjoined clauses are used. The relative clause, unlike in English, is not a constituent of the noun phrase. It may either precede or follow the main clause as in the following: *jo ɔrtẽ gana ga rəhī hɛ̃ ve merī səheliyã hɛ̃* or *ve ɔrtẽ merī səheliyã hɛ̃ jo gana ga rəhī hɛ̃* ("the women who are singing are my friends"). Note that, depending upon the order of the relative and the main clause, either the noun in the subordinate or the main clause is deleted, that is, the above are the results of deleting the noun in parentheses in the following: *jo ɔrtẽ gana ga rəhī hɛ̃ ve (ɔrtẽ) merī səheliyā̃ hɛ̃* or *ve ɔrtẽ merī səheliyā̃ hɛ̃ jo (ɔrtẽ) gana ga rəhī hɛ̃*. The relative marker *jo* (obl. sg. *jis*, obl. pl. *jin*, special forms with *ne* and *ko*, *jinhõne*, and *jinhẽ*) and the correlative marker *vəh*, which is identical to the remote demonstrative/third person pronoun, function like a determiner to their respective head nouns. Both the head nouns may be retained in the case of an emphatic construction; in normal speech/writing, however, the second instance is deleted. Under the influence of Persian and later, English, the relative clause is sometimes positioned following the head noun, for example *ve ɔrtẽ jo gana ga rəhī hɛ̃ merī səheliyā̃hɛ̃*; in this case, the second instance of the noun (following *jo*) must be deleted.

Earlier, it has been said that the nominal constituents of a sentence in Hindi–Urdu can be moved around freely for thematic purposes. Usually, the initial element in a sentence in Hindi coincides with the theme. The focus position in Hindi is identified with the position just before the main verb. In addition to manipulating the word order, heavy sentence stress and certain particles are used to indicate focus [heavy sentence stress indicated by capitalization], for example *RAM ne mohən ko pīṭa* ("it was Ram who hit Mohan"), *ʃīla ne hī yəh bat kəhī tʰī* ("it was Sheila who had said this"), *sīma to cəlī gəī* ("as for Sima, she has left"), where the item in capital letters in the first sentence and the item followed by the particle *hī* in the second is under focus. In addition to the initial position, the particle *to* indicates the theme, for example in the third sentence the item followed by *to* is thematic. As the initial position is not the favored device for indicating focus, the interrogative pronouns in Hindi–Urdu do not necessarily occur sentence-initially; compare the Hindi–Urdu sentences with their English equivalents: *ap kya pəṛʰ rəhe hɛ̃*? ("what are you reading?"), *vəh kəl kəhā̃ gəya tʰa?* ("where did he go yesterday?"), and *in mẽ se ap ko kɔn sī kitab pəsənd hɛ?* ("which of these books do you like?").

Conclusion

In conclusion, Hindi–Urdu differs from its European cousins typologically in several respects. Phonologically, aspiration, retroflexion, nasal vowels, and lack of distinctive stress mark Hindi–Urdu as very different from English. Morphologically, the gender and case distinctions and the devices of reduplication and echo-compounding exemplify the major differences between the two languages. Syntactically, the word order differences are striking. So is the fact that Hindi–Urdu makes certain semantic distinctions which are not made as clearly in English, namely volitionality and affectiveness. These distinctions result in a closer correspondence between semantic and syntactic grammatical roles that nominal constituents have in a sentence, for example all agentive (*-ne*-marked) subjects are agents, all dative (*ko*-marked) subjects are experiencers, and so on. Many of these characteristics of Hindi–Urdu are shared by not only the other Indo-Aryan but also the Dravidian and other languages of India.

Further reading

The following represent a small selection of resources on Hindi–Urdu: (1) Learning aids: Bhatia, Tej K. and Shakuntala Chandana (2002) and Shapiro, Michael (2003); (2) History of grammars: Bhatia, Tej K. (1987); (3) Syntactic description of Hindi: Y. Kachru (1966); (4) Semantics, grammar and lexis of Urdu: Chapter 14 of Hasan (forthcoming); and (5) Two recent grammars of Hindi: Montaut, Annie (2004) and Y. Kachru (2006).

4 Persian in South Asia

S. A. H. Abidi and Ravinder Gargesh

Introduction

South Asia is linguistically and culturally a pluralistic region where not only different languages of the region coexist and affect each other, but, more important, foreign languages also get acculturated. Persian and English are the two foreign languages that have got acculturated in South Asia at different points of time. Acculturation implies a process of Indianization of the foreign language. In this chapter the word India is used interchangeably with South Asia to refer to India, Pakistan, Bangladesh, Nepal, Bhutan, and Sri Lanka. B. Kachru (1983b, 1992c) has provided an in-depth study of the process of Indianization in the context of Indian English. According to him the process is not a superficial one but results in a linguistic system that reflects an identity and lends authenticity to the nativized variety (B. Kachru 2001: 25). The emergence of two nativized varieties, that is Indian Persian and Indian English, is unique to the subcontinent. Not only this, the process of Indianization of both the foreign languages is identical. The Persian experience, resulting in the development of Urdu and Hindustani, appears to be far more intense than that of English at present (see Abidi 1981, 1998, 2000). It, however, needs to be mentioned that while the spread of Persian has come full circle in its approximately eight hundred years of history in South Asia, English is still a dominant language and its circle is far from complete. The present chapter will briefly look at the spread of Persian in South Asia and then go on to look at the elements of Indianization of Persian and the Persianization of Indian languages in the region.

The spread of Persian in South Asia

Relations between Persian-speaking regions and India date back to pre-Islamic days; however, the beginning of the spread of Persian is generally linked to the time of Mahmud of Ghazni (1001–1026 CE), particularly after his conquest of the Punjab. Although Persian was not the mother tongue of the occupying rulers, yet it was so popular with them that they used it instead of Turkish in their courts (Marek 1968: 714). The shifting of the court from Ghazna to Lahore and the liberal patronage attracted men of letters from areas such as Khurasan, Transoxania, and even the then Afghanistan to India. In fact it was the patronage of the court that helped in the spread of Persian language and literature in South Asia. The first India-born poet who composed in Persian was Abu-'Abdu'llah Nuqati from Lahore. Localized talent further flourished in widely known poets like Masud-I-Sa'd-I-Salman Jurjani (1046–1121 CE) and Abu'l-Faraj Runi (d. at the beginning of the twelfth century). The early Persian literature that came to India already had the impact of mysticism as in Abu'l-Hasan 'Ali ibn 'Uthman al-Jullabi al-Hujviri's earliest treatise on the life and doctrine of the Sufis – *Kashfu'l-mahjuub* ("The Discovery of the Hidden") (Marek 1968: 714–15). After the Ghaznavid kings the center of literary activity shifted to Multan, ruled by Nasiru'd-din Qabacha from Sind, and to Delhi ruled by the "slave" king Qutbu'd-din-Aybak. It was in the early period of the "slave" kings (1206–1220) that major works like Muhammad Aufi's tadhkira *Lubaab-ul-Albaab* ("The Quintessence of the Hearts") and Hasan Nizami's *Taaj-ul-Ma'athir* ("The Crown of Exploits") were compiled. The former is considered to be the oldest biography of Persian poets and the latter a historical work in high-flown language which has been translated by Saroop (1998) into English. Up to the thirteenth century Persian panegyric poetry in the form of *qasida* was mainly written in India and it developed its "Indian style." The *qasidas* glorified the campaign and the heroic deeds of the patrons. The melodious *ghazal*, a more natural form, is reported to have been taken seriously by the end of the thirteenth century by Fakhru'l-Mulk Amidu 'd-din Lumaki in the time of Nasiru'd-din Mahmud (1246–1266) and Ghiyathud-din Balban (1266–1287) (Marek 1968: 717).

Brilliant literary activity flourished in the time of the Khiljis (1290–1320) and the Tughlaqs (1320–1413). Amir Khusrau, (1253–1325 CE) a very popular poet till today and rated highly even by the Persians, composed major works in the fourteenth century, works such as *Matla'ul-Anwaar* ("Rising of the Lights"), a didactic poem; the *Aain-e-Sikandari* ("The Laws of Sikander"), an epic poem; the *Hasht-Bihisht* ("The Eight Paradises"), which has several interwoven Indian tales; the *Qiranu's-Sadain* ("The Conjunction of the Two Lucky Stars"), dealing with the struggle for the throne and the ultimate reconciliation between the son Kay-Qubad and his father Bughra Khan; the *Miftaahul-Futuh* ("The Key to Victories"), *Ashiqeh* ("A Love Tale"), the *Nuh-Sipahr* ("Nine Skies") a patriotic poem; and *Tughlaqnaamah* ("The Book of Tughlaq"), a narrative poem detailing the events in the reign of Ghiyathud-din Tughlaq, and many other significant works. More important, the subject of Khusrau's poetry was the subcontinent – its climate, its flowers, its birds and animals, its language, and the people. Another major name at the time was that of Amir Khusrau's friend Najmu'd-din Hasan Sanjari (d. 1327).

The golden age of Persian language and literature in South Asia was the Mughal period, (1526–1707 CE) particularly the period from the reign of Akbar to the end of Shah Jahan's reign (1556–1659). In this period almost every ruler or his courtiers contributed to the spread and development of Persian language and literature. The influx of numerous Persian poets and scholars continued due to liberal patronage, and local talent began to emerge in greater numbers. Akbar's policy of *Sulh-e-kul*, that is of universal peace and toleration, won him many friends. Hindus who did not take kindly to Persian earlier began to work in the language after exhortation by Todar Mal to support the language of the court and that of the administration (Marek 1968: 723). Another very eminent personality who had an effect on the spread of Persian in India was Abdul Rahim Khanekhana who was fond of literary gatherings. He had an equally good command over Hindi, Persian, and Turkish. Khanekhana had translated Babur's *Tuzuk-e-Babari* ("Autobiography of Babur") from Turkish into Persian. Further, he used to reward both Hindi and Persian scholars and writers.

One of the elements that led toward hybridization of Indian Persian began through the translation process. Akbar had established a department of translation where a large number of Sanskrit texts were translated into Persian. As a result Mir Ghayasuddin Ali Qazveni translated the *Mahabharata* as *Razmnaamah* ("The Book of the Battles"), Girdhar Das translated the *Ramayana* into Persian in 1626 CE, and Makhan Lal also rendered it into Persian and named it *Jahaan-e-Zafar* ("The World of Success"). Amarnath presented an abridged account of the four *Vedas* into Persian. There were many other translations that were undertaken at this time.

Persian in India was bound to be strongly Indianized since by this time Persian was used to express typically Indian situations. Faizi composed *Nal Daman*, the Indian love story of Nal and Damayanti, amongst his many works, and Abu'l Fazl wrote the monumental *Akbarnaamah* ("The Book of Akbar"), and the *'Aain-e-Akbari* ("The Law of Akbar"). The two of them left their mark on *insha* literature (epistle writing) as well in the form of Faizi's *Latifa-e-Faizi* ("Subtleties of Faizi") and Abu'l Fazl's *Insha-e-Abu'l Fazl* ("Epistles of Abul Fazl").

Jahangir (1605–1627) was the most learned of all the Mughal rulers. His learning is revealed in his *Tuzuk-I-Jehaangiri* ("Autobiography of Jehangir"). The times were so congenial that Sa'ib, who was appointed the poet laureate of Persia after taking retirement from the service of Shah Jahan said that the patronage and literary atmosphere in India was definitely far superior to that of Persia:

niist dar iraan zamiin saamaane tahsile kamaal
taa niiamad suiye hindostaan hinaa rangiin nashud

There is not in the Persian land the requisite material for the perfection of art,
Until henna came to India it acquired no color (Cited in Rahman 1957: 17)

In addition to Turkish or Persian poets named above, Hindus, too, contributed immensely to the Persian language in India. Two notable histories written by them are Bhagwan Das's versified history *Shaahjahaannaamah* ("Book of Shah Jahan") and Munshi Hiraman Lal's *Gwaliornaamah* ("The Book of Gwalior") (1667 CE). The number of Hindu prose writers in other branches of learning was also sizable. For example, Rai Mannu Lal "Falsafi" was a philosopher, scientist and a poet. Some of his works are *Gulistaan-e-Aram* ("The Rose Garden of Aram") and *Bostan-e-heraat* ("The Orchard of Herat"). Birbal also wrote *Risaala-e-Najuum* ("Book on Astronomy").

There were many Hindus employed in the finance department of the Mughals. They displayed their talents in the writing of firmans (orders) and letters, which were collected and provided as examples to students in educational institutions. The *Munshaat-e-Brahman* ("Brahmans Letters"), *Insha-e-Madho Ram* ("The Letters of Madho Ram"), *Munshaat-e-Rawar Mal* ("Rawar Mal's Letters") and so on were works of this kind.

Another area in which the Indians excelled was lexicography (Anwar 1957, 1958). For example *Farhang-e-Jahaangiri* ("The Dictionary of Jahangir") by Azud-ud-Daulah (1018 CE) listed words of Persian origin along with appropriate quotations. *Farhang-e-Rashidi* ("The Dictionary of Rashidi") by Abdul Rashidi Tatavi was a critical dictionary of Persian, the *Burhaan-e-Qaati* ("Irrefutable Logic") compiled by Muhammad Hussain (1651 CE) was a dictionary of the Persian language which included words borrowed from Arabic and other languages. Siraj-ud-din Ali Khan Arzu was a linguist as well as a poet and a lexicographer. He set the tone of Indo-Persian lexicographical school in his *Muthmir* ("Fruit Providing") which was also a pioneer work in the field of Persian phonetics and phonology. His correspondence with Hazim Lahiji reveals his conviction in favor of strengthening the Indo-Persian language. He had a number of pupils who continued to follow his principles of lexicography. One of his students was Tek Chand Bahar. His *Bahaar-e-Ajam* ("The Persian Springtime") (1766 CE) is a poetical glossary consisting of words and phrases used by the modern poets of Iran. It needs to be mentioned that the largest dictionary of Persian, Arabic, and Turkish was produced in south India by Munshi Muhammad Badshah with the title *Farhang-e-Aanandraj* ("The Dictionary of Anandraj") named after his patron Maharaja Anand Gajapati Raj of Vijayanagar.

Another feature which indirectly may have led to the acceptance of Persian by the Hindus is the spread of Sufism in India. The *Bhakti* movement, which began in south India in the eighth century and after Ramanuja's period (1017–1137 CE), spread to the whole of north India by the fourteenth century. This resulted in the mingling of Hindu mysticism with Sufism (Sarkar 1985a, b). The mingling of these two streams also led to the mutual influence of Persian and the Indian languages.

After Shah Jahan, Aurangzeb overthrew his elder brother Dara Shikoh and became emperor. The traces of Indian ethos could be seen in the lyrical poems of *Mukhfi*, that is Zebunissa (d. 1702–1703 CE), Aurangzeb's daughter, who became a victim of the tyranny of her own father. Her poetry is the confluence of Hinduism, Islam, and Zoroastrianism (Marek 1968: 729).

The process of Indianization of Persian language as well as the absorption of Indian philosophical thought in Persian literature to a very great extent can be perceived in the literature of the seventeenth century and beyond. Mirza Abdul Qadir Bedil spanned the last phase of Aurangzeb and the early phase of Mohammad Shah. He excelled in presenting factual details. His *Chahaar Unsur* is a collection of poetry and prose, and he has composed many mathnavis as well. In Punjab, Guru Gobind Singh composed the *Zafarnaamah* ("The Book of Victory") in the rhyme and meter of Firdausi and it was a record of events between 1702 and 1704 when the Guru was engaged in battle against Aurangzeb (Rahman 1978).

After Aurangzeb there was an overall decline and India ceased to be a place of great patronage for Persian poets. By now Urdu as a language was taking root in the courts. Urdu had begun to be accepted as an important language of culture by the end of the eighteenth century. In fact Urdu writings began to eclipse Persian writings. Poets such as Sauda (1780 CE), Mir (1811 CE), Dard (1780 CE), and Soz (1798 CE) became the models for the literati. It may be added that Urdu writers freely borrowed words from classical Persian poets. The last Mughal King Bahadur Shah II with the pen name *Zafar* made Urdu the language of the court in 1835 CE. Poets who began to compose in Urdu, however, were composing in Persian as well. In mid-nineteenth century Mirza Asadullah Khan Ghalib (d. 1869 CE) came on the literary scene. He composed both in Urdu and Persian. His Persian poetry is rated highly. His *Gul-e-Ranaa* ("The Charming Rose") and *Kulliat-e-Nezaame-Faarsi* ("The Collection of Persian poems") are great poetical works in the Persian language.

In the twentieth century, poets like Har Gopal Taftah, Qadir Girami, and Shibli Noamani have composed poetry in Persian. However, the last bright star in the dying phase of Persian in India was Mohammad Iqbal. His Persian works the *Asraar-e-khudi* ("The Secrets of the Self"), *Rumez-e-Bikhudi* ("The Mysteries of Selflessness"), *Jaavednaamah* ("The Book of Eternity"), *Zabuur-e-Ajam* ("The Persian Psalms"), and the *Payaam-e-Mashriq* ("The Message from the East") reveal his love of humanity and skill.

In the context of the spread of Persian in other parts of India, a word needs to be said about Persian in Bengal, Kashmir, and south India (Ali 1985).

In Bengal, the influence of Persian was quite widespread just as in other parts of the country. Suniti Kumar Chatterji narrates that around 1350 CE a Muslim Sultan of Bengal invited Hafiz, the great lyric and mystic poet of Persia to

Bengal. Though Hafiz could not come, he appreciated the invitation and sent a couplet instead to the lovers of Persian poetry in Bengal:

shaakar shikan shavand hame tutian-e-Hind
ziin Qande paarsi ke beh bangaala mi ravand

Sugar nibbling is all the parrot of Ind, from the Persian candy that travels to Bengal. (Chatterji 1976: 114)

Chatterji tells us that from the time of the Mughal rule to the full establishment of the British rule the Persian language was adopted in Bengal by the Bengali elite as the language of administration and all higher culture outside the Sanskrit or native Indian orbit (see Chatterjee 1976, 1985). Raja Ram Mohan Roy, in order to propagate his views, started a journal, the *Miratul Akhbaar* ("Mirror of Happenings") in Persian from Calcutta in 1822. In addition, he left behind some books on Persian culture and language, too.

Kashmir had been a flourishing center of Persia studies since the thirteenth to fourteenth centuries when a number of Sayyids migrated there from Iran following the Timurid persecution. Sultan Zaimal Abedin (1420–1470) had instituted Persian as his court language. After a long rule of Muhammad Daughlat, a kinsman of Babur's father, Persian culture became more widespread. He was responsible for the translation of many Sanskrit works into Persian such as *Raajatrangini* by Kalhana (1148 CE) and the *Mahabharata*. Later in the Mughal period, especially in the age of Jahangir and Shah Jahan, the court of *Subedar* (Governor) Ahsan, the scholar-statesman, became a center of literary activities. He invited great Persian scholars including Sa'ib to his court. Persian continued to flourish even after the fall of the Mughals under the Afghans (1753–1819) and the Sikhs (1819–1846). In the context of Persian studies the work of G. L. Tikku in post-Independence India is noteworthy. In his learned work *Shu'ara-e-Kashmir* ("The Poets of Kashmir") he has presented poems as well as brief biographies of those eminent poets hailing from Kashmir who composed in Persian. These included poets such as Mirza Darab Beg Juya, Mirza Kamil, Aslam Salim, Ghani Kashmiri, Diwan Shah Azar, Mulla Ashraf, the eminent historian Khwaja Muhammad Azami, Bhawani Das Kachru, and Gopal Pandit (Tikku 1961).

Persian had made inroads in the Deccan in the fourteenth century with the formation of the Bahmani Kingdom. In fact before Timur's invasion (1398–1399 CE) there was a general decline and many scholars and poets fled from Delhi to smaller towns and even to places in the Deccan. The Muslim kings of the Deccan also kept Persian as the court language. Isami was a great poet of the Bahmani dynasty. He composed *Futuhu's-Salatin* ("The Conquest of Sultans") which is the first versified history in Persian of the Muslim conquest of India, narrating events from the advent of Islam up to the establishment of the

Bahmani dynasty. Sheikh Adhari of Isfarain compiled a verse chronicle of the Bahmanids titled *Bahmannaamah* ("The Book of Bahmans"), which was later completed by Naziri and other poets (Marek 1968: 720).

Later the court of Ibrahim Adil Shah II of Bijapur attracted a large number of poets and scholars from abroad. Most prominent among them was Zuhuri of Tarshez (d. 1615 CE) whose *Saaqiinaamah* ("Book of the Cup-Bearers") is a grand achievement in Persian poetry written on the model of Sa'di's *Gulistan* ("The Rose Garden").

Persian language lost its widespread roots with the promotion of English as the language of administration, science, and other intellectual activities particularly from 1837 onwards. At present there is a general lack of interest in Persian studies; its earlier position has been usurped by English, another foreign language. However, South Asia's interaction with the Persian language has been very intense resulting in the Indianization of Persian and Persianization of Indian languages.

Indianization of Persian

The subcontinent has a history of accepting a foreign language for intellectual activity and then nativizing it as per its cultural environment. The roughly eight hundred year span of Persian in India shows a process of increasing Indianization, a fact reminiscent of the "Indianization of English" in present times. It has been noted by Kachru that the Indianization of English reveals a process similar to that of the Indianization of Persian, and the case of English today is like a repetition of "the linguistic history of the sub-continent" (B. Kachru 1983b: 3). The Indianization of Persian is manifested not only through a large-scale borrowing of words from Indian languages but also from expressions that carry the emotional content and thought processes which are Indian. In addition, we find numerous instances of code mixing and code switching, of hybrid expressions and of semantic shift in the lexicon. Such changes have been conditioned by the influence of customs, creeds, legends, myths, romance, folklore, and languages of India. The widespread convergence of Persian with Indian languages was visible not only in the work of Indians but also in the works of Iranians who had come to India in search of better opportunities and recognition. By the time of Akbar and after, the impact of Indian culture and environment become so visible that the Indianized Persian was called *Sabk-e-Hindi* (the Indian style). The term has two connotations, first it was a flowery and an ornate style which made it different from the *Sabk-e-Khurasani* (the first school of Persian poetry represented by Rudaki, Unsuri, and Farrukhi in Khurasan) and the *Sabk-e-Iraqi* or *Irani;* and secondly, the occurrence of Indian words and expressions made the style distinct (Rasheed 1996). The contemporary Iranians did not consider Indianized Persian as a part of their national literature but "felt it to be an alien element" (Marek 1968: 713) although its masters were for the most part of Persian birth (Rypka 1968: 295). This style of writing flourished not only in India under the influence of poets like Urfi, Faizi, Sa'ib, Bedil, and others but it also found its way to Persia and Transoxania and especially to the Tajik people. An example of this ornate style can be taken from the poetry of Khusrau:

abr mi baarad-o-man mi shavam az yaar judaa
cun kunam dil becuniin ruuz dildaar judaa
abr baaraan-o-man-o-yaar sitaadeh be vidaa
man judaa girye kunaan, abr judaa, yaar judaa.

The clouds pour down their burden chill
While I from my loved one part,
How can I pray on such a day
From her severe my heart,
The rain doth fall while with sad hearts
We stand to bid farewell, the clouds do weep (Cited in Mirza 1974: 209)

The above lines reflect the impact of Indian poetical moods (*rasa*), like the falling of rain symbolizing both reconciliation as well as pangs of separation. The rainy season is widely used in Indian romantic poetry as a season which arouses feelings of both joy and sadness.

The use of Indian words in Persian by the time of Shah Jahan had become quite natural. Abidi (1960: 11–18) provides a list of 130 such words which were prevalent in some literary works in the reign of Shah Jahan. The words include common nouns such as *baan* ("arrow"), *baaNs* ("bamboo"), *paan* ("betel leaf"), *pakhaavaj* ("a drum"), *supaari* ("betelnut"), *giit* ("song"), and *maalaa* ("garland"); names of fragrant flowers such as *cameli* ("jasmine") and *campaa* ("flowers of Michelia Champacca"); and occupational groups like *dhobi* ("washerman"), *saahu* ("a moneylender"), and *kahaar* ("palanquin bearer"). To these are added various names of birds, animals, fruits, trees, seasons, festivals, and so on. The mixing of the lexicon not only provided local color but was also expressive of local cultural factors. Mixing also provides the lexicon to signal the sociocultural contexts. Below are given two examples, which are about a place Benaras (Varanasi). Binish Kashmiri in a mathnavi *Shori-e-Khayaal* ("The Upsurge of Thoughts") presents an interesting picture:

banaaras raa ajab aab-o-havai ast, baraai ishq baazi tarafe jaaye ast
brahman zaadgan fatana ain, cuu gul daarand dar bar jaame purciin
butaanesh az namak niiku sharastand, ke huuj saabzi baagh bahishtand
shudan ruzi ke Hindustaan gulistaan, (a)z sabzaan shud banaaras manbulistaan.

Benaras has a strange climate; it is an astonishing place for the game of love.
The sons of Brahmin rouse calamity, they don colorful garments, resembling the

flowers. The idols like damsels have selfish beauty, as if they were the waves of the vernal paradise. The day when India became a garden, Benaras became a hyacinth garden out of its flowers. (Cited in Umar 1979: 68).

Another example of Benaras from Shaikh Ali Hazin:

az banaaras ne revam ma'bad ilmast
har barhaman bacce lachman u pesare raam ast injaa

I cannot leave Benaras, it is a place of worship
Every Brahman is a child of Lachman or Ram here. (Cited in Umar 1979: 69)

The above two examples reveal not only the name of a place and a caste but attempt to express a subjective perception of Benaras in local terms. The simile in line 3 and the metaphor in line 4 of the first example give the lines a flourish or ornateness. The second example is expressive of obedience from a socioreligious perspective.

In a lighter vein Mulla Tughra Mashadi, the Munshi of Murad Baksh in the time of Shah Jahan, expresses the variety of beauty found in the different corners of the subcontinent:

'eshrat ghamza khuban gujaraati, wa 'esho butaan somnaati,
taluu's khurami mahbuuba agraa, wa tuuti kalaami
dilbar shodharaa, taazgi tan ra'naai Lahore wa
nazuk badani ziibaai jaunpuri, laaghar
miiyaanii shokh Bangala wa farba suriinii bat Ambaalaa.

Expressive eyes of Gujarat, and pleasures of Somnath, elegant (peacock like) walk of Agra, sweet talk of Shodhara, fair complexion of Lahore, and delicate limbs of Jaunpur, slim waist of Bengal, and the heavy hips of Ambala (Cited in Abidi 1960: 5–6)

The use of lexicon is an integral part of language use to express sociocultural contexts. For instance, Abidi cites two interesting pieces on Holi, the colorful Hindu festival, one by Tughra and the other from a manuscript by Mohammad Yusuf Nighat Burhanpuri. The following three lines are from a poem by Tughra:

kar diide mainaa-e-raagi khwaan rang-e-sadaa gashte 'iaan
waz naghma-e-'aab arghuwaan dar juuyi takraar aamde
shud vaqt-e-holi baakhtan baa rang-o-buu pardaakhtan

If one hears the Maina sing, colorful sound manifests itself.
And the song of the purple water repeatedly occurs,
At the time of Holi I lose myself in the colors and aroma (Cited in Abidi 1960: 6)

There are various descriptions of places, people, festivals, seasons, flora, fauna, and experiences which are Indian and not Iranian in Indian Persian poetry. The resulting Persian is bound to be quite foreign to Iranian ears in Iran. The Indian concepts of cremating the dead and ceremonies associated with it or the description of *Jauhar* (ladies voluntarily burning themselves rather then allowing themselves to be captured in times of war) are experiences quite foreign to the native Persian.

Persian reveals code mixing with Indian languages at various other levels of linguistic structure. Mixing occurs at the level of morphemes, at the level of phrases, and even clauses.

The following examples illustrate code mixing at the level of morphemes:

Hathnaalcian	elephant-gunners – gunners on elephants
baa paalki	with palanquin
be kahaar	without palanquin bearers
pickaarish	his sprinkler/syringe (Examples from text cited by Abidi 1960: 4, 7)

In the first example, *haathi* is a Hindi word for ("elephant") and *naal* for ("pipe"). The compound *hathnaal* means an ("elephant-gun") +*ci* and +*aan* are the agentive and plural suffixes respectively in Persian. In the other two examples, *paalki* and *kahaar* are Hindi words while *baa*+ and *be*+ are the positive and negative prefixes in Persian. In the fourth example *pickaari* in Hindi is a word with a fixed meaning but +*sh* is the third person singular possessive marker, hence ("his sprinkler") and so on.

Compound forms are also visible with one item from Persian and the other from Hindi. Some examples are *raag suraaiyaan* ("name of a raga of music") *raag khwaan* ("raga-singer") *raag basant* ("name of a raga") *paayii darshan* ("feet viewing/paying respects"), and *giit-khwaani* ("song singing") (examples drawn from texts cited by Abidi (1960: 5, 8, 10)). In the first three compounds the first word *raag* is from Hindi and the second word is from Persian. In the fourth example the first word is from Persian and the second one from Hindi, and in the fifth the order is reversed.

One also finds examples of the use of *izafe* and of the use of *vaw* (i.e. the use of *-e-* when using modifiers or *-o-* when coordinating words) involving Hindi words only or even Hindi and Persian words. See the following examples.

(1)	*baaNs-e-paalki*	palanquin of bamboo
	patkaa-e-patnii	sash of Patna
	tel-e-cambeli	oil of jasmine
(2)	*baasurkhi-e-Holi*	with redness of Holi
	huqm-e-barsaat	command of rains
	vaqt-e-holi	time of Holi
(3)	*darshan-e-lahutish*	Sighting of His Divinity
	har-e-gul	garland of flower
	malmal-e-surkh	red muslin

(4)	*piise-o-rupiie*	pices and rupees
	raag-o-rang	music and color
	chambeli-o-bel-e-nargis	jasmine and creeper of primrose
		From texts cited by Abidi (1960: 3, 5, 8, 10)

In set (1), the *izafe* joins two Hindi words, in set (2) a Persian and a Hindi word, and in set (3) a Hindi and a Persian word. The first two examples in set (4) show the joining of Hindi nouns and the third example shows the joining of two Hindi words with a Persian word. Thus, in Indian Persian, one finds a greater absorption of Indian words. One can even find examples of conjunct verb formations where the first word, a noun, is from Hindi and the verb from Persian. See for example *mantar kunad* ("to recite a mantra"), *cun supaari zamukht* ("lime and betel nut painted"), *shaastar khaanaan namikardad* ("reader did not perform") and *kev-raas pakhshad* ("sprinkles KevRa (a fragrant liquid)").

Some syntactic influence of Indian languages on Persian is shown by Sinha (1998: 53–64). He points out that in Indian Persian the number agreement of a plural inanimate subject with a verb is more acceptable than in traditional Persian because Indian languages generally have agreements between the subject and the verb. Thus, whereas it is correct to say:

iin darakhtaan kohne/gadiimn ast

These trees (plural) old is (singular)

But it is also possible to say:

iin darakhtaan kohne hastand

These tree (plural) old are (plural)

Sinha states that Persian, which is more like English in the formation of relative clauses, shows Indian influence because the relative clause has begun to show a different behavior, for example in English it is acceptable to say:

(1) The boy who came here yesterday is my friend
(2) The boy is my friend who came here yesterday

But the next sentence is unacceptable:

(3) That boy came here yesterday who is my friend

But Hindi has a correlative construction parallel to this:

(4)	*wo laRka*	*meraa*	*dost*	*hai*	*jo*	*kal*	*yahaaN*	*aayaa*	*thaa*
	That boy	my	friend	is	who	yesterday	here	come	had

The following Persian sentence is also acceptable:

(5) *aan pisar duste man ast ke diruuz injaa aamdeh buud*
That boy friend my is who yesterday here came

Code mixing/code switching in communicative situations also reveals a strong Indic influence. One finds numerous examples of code mixing/switching as in the following few lines ascribed to Amir Khusrau (fourteenth century).

zehaal-e miskin makul taghaaful, duraaye nainaaN banaaye batiyaaN
ki taab-e-hijraN nadaaram ay jaan, na leho kaahe lagaaye chatiyaaN
shabaan-e hijraaN daraaz chun zulf wa roz-e waslat cho umr kotah
sakhii piyaa ko jo maiN naa dekhuuN to kaise kaTuuN andheri ratiyaaN

Do not overlook my misery by hiding your eyes which wish to speak to me;
I cannot tolerate your separation, O sweetheart, why do you not take me to your bosom,
My nights have become longer like your long hair, and a day of meeting is like a short span of life,
Friend, if I do not see my lover how will I pass the dark nights (Persian text from www.alif-india.com/love.html)

The first half of the first two lines is in Persian and the second half in Hindi. Line 3 is in Persian and line 4 is code switched into Hindi. Such mixing/switching is part of the communicative strategy, which in this case is the expression of strong inner feelings.

Persianization of Indian languages

In a convergence situation spanning a number of centuries it is natural for the languages involved to affect each other. In the context of Persian in India one finds not only the process of Indianization of Persian but also that of Persianization of Indian languages. The latter process is quite similar to the "Englishization" of Indian languages in present times (B. Kachru 1983b: 196–8). Although for more than a hundred years Persian has ceased to be a dynamic language in India, its influence on the culture and linguistic profile of India can be distinctly perceived even today. Linguistically, the influence is seen in two areas: (1) widespread borrowings in Indian languages and (2) numerous localized adaptations. Both the processes can be seen to be at work in most languages of South Asia, namely Urdu, Hindi, Punjabi, Kashmiri, Sindhi, Marathi, Gujarati, Bengali, Assamese, and even Tamil. The significance and popularity of Persian can be gauged from the fact that Persian was used not only in regions under the control of Muslim kings in the north and in the Deccan but was also used along with regional languages in the non-Muslim Maratha state of Chatrapati Shivaji and in the Sikh state of Maharaja Ranjit Singh.

Borrowings from Persian into Indian languages

The influx of Persian vocabulary in India also included Arabic and Turkish words via Persian. With the Muslim rule in India came a new religion, a new polity, a new government, a new social structure, a new set of etiquettes, a new way of life, a new dress system, new food habits, new furniture, a new philosophy, and a new literature. All these facts, pertaining to all walks of life came to India through the Persian language and thence gradually entered the Indian languages. Some examples of borrowings, which may not have the same meanings as in Iranian Persian, pertaining to different areas of daily life can be seen below:

(1) *Proper names*: While Muslims use Persio-Arabic names in full; some Hindus too use them as the first name. For example:
Muslim names: *Akhtar Nawaz*, *Aftab*, *Dilshad*, *Shah Bano*, *Zarina*, etc.
Non-Muslim names: *Bahadur Shah*, *Chaman* Lal, *Iqbal* Singh, Lal *Bahadur*, *Roshan* Lal.

(2) Many *titles* bestowed earlier on eminent people were also of Persian origin, for example:
Khan Bahadur, *Rai Bahadur*, *Yavar Jung*, *Salaar Jung*.

(3) Many names of the parts of the human body have been borrowed from Persian:
jism "body," *khuun* "blood," *naakhuun* "nail" (finger and toe), *siinaa* "chest," *dil*, "heart," *gardan* "neck," *zabaan* "tongue," and *halaq* "throat".

(4) Some borrowed kinship terms:
daamaad "son-in-law," *baabaa* "father," *shauhar* "husband," and *biraadar* "brother".

(5) Items relating to food habits:
sabzii "vegetables," *naan* "bread," *kormaa* "curry," *kiimaa* "minced meat," and *tanduuri* "roasted".

(6) Words pertaining to dress:
paushaak "dress," *pajaamaa* "pyjamas," *kamiiz* "shirt" *jeb* "pocket," and *astar* "inner, lining".

(7) Names of places obtained by using/borrowing Persian suffixes:
+aabaad: *Ahmadaabaad, Hyderaabaad, Firozaabaad, Ghaaziabaad.*
+pur: *Mirzaapur, Burhaanpur, Ahmadpur, Miirpur*
+ganj: *Nawaabganj, Hazratganj, PahaaRganj*
+bagh: *Arambaagh, Karolbaagh*
+saraai: *Mughalsaraai, Lakhisaraai, Khatiasaraai*

(8) Places within a house:
gusalkhaanaa "bathroom," *paakhaanaa* "toilet," *baawarchiikhaanaa* "kitchen," *darwaazaa* "door," and *diwaar* "walk."

(9) Ornaments:
zewar "ornaments," *gulband* "necklace," *dastband* "bracelet," and *pazeb* "anklet."

(10) Fruits:
seb "apple," *anaar* "pomegranate," *anguur* "grapes," *naarangii* "tangerine," *baadaam* "almond."

(11) Names of animals and birds:
sher "lion," *khargosh* "rabbit," *bulbul* "nightingle," *baaz* "falcon," and *kabutar* "pigeon."

(12) Names of vegetables:
shalgam "turnip," *qadduu* "pumpkin," and *sakarqand* "sweet potato."

(13) Names of trees, plants, flowers:
cinaar "plane tree," *hinaa* "henna," *banafshaa* "pansy," *gulaab* "rose," *niilofar* "water lily," and *yaasmiin* "jasmine."

(14) Professions:
darzii "tailor," *hajjaam* "barber," *sabzii-farosh* "greengrocer" and *khaansaamaa* "cook."

(15) Relating to agriculture:
fasl "crop," *rabi* "spring," *khaariif* "autumn," *aabpashii* "watering," *nahar* "canal" and *zamiin* "land."

(16) Law: There are many Arabic terms but used in a Persian or Indian sense. For example:
adaalat "court," *qaanuun* "law," *muddai* "plaintiff," *vakiil* "lawyer" and *muakil* "client."

(17) Administration:
darbaar "court," *paadshah* "emperor," and *tehlsiildaar* "tax collector."

(18) Writing:
qalam "pen," *dawaat* "inkpot," *syaahi* "ink," and *kaagaz* "paper."

(19) Measurement:
gaz "yard," *miil* "a mile," *man* "a mound," *ser* "a seer," and *murabbaa* "square."

(20) Military:
sipaahii "soldier," *top* "gun/cannon," *topcii* "gunner," and *topkhaanaa* "artillery."

There is hardly any area of life which has remained untouched from Persian influence. Even colloquial expressions, either in original or in a translated form are part of everyday language, for example:

-*dilli duur ast* ("Delhi is far" implying that the job is far from completion.)
-*gurube kushtane ruuze awwal* ("kill the cat on the first day" – for an awesome impression).
-*qatra qatra dariyaa mi shavad* (drop drop make an ocean – "savings")
-*aab aab shudan* (water water become – "to be ashamed")

In addition to such semantic borrowings certain processes of compounding, prefixation, and suffixation have also been borrowed and one can see them applied to a word of the local stock. In compound formations one generally finds a Persian word following a native word, and +*khaanaa* (house) and +*kaar* (the doer) are the words found most often, for example *jelkhaanaa* "jail," *ḍaakkhaanaa* "post office," *kalaakaar* "artist," *patrakaar* "journalist," and *jaankaar* "one who knows." Some common prefixes borrowed are +*naa* "without" and *ghair* "non" examples, such as *naasamajh* "without understanding," *naakaaraa* "jobless," and *ghair zimedaari* "irresponsibility." Similarly, some common suffixes adopted are +*daar*, +*baaz*, examples, such as *phaldaar* "fruitbearing," *maaldaar* "rich," *dendaar* "debtor," *bhaagiidaar* "partner," *caalbaaz* "schemer," *patangbaaz* "kite flier," and *daghaabaaz* "deceiver."

Many words have been borrowed form Persian and their plurals are made according to the rules of our Indian languages, and many genderless Persian words have been supplied a gender in gender maintaining languages such as Hindi and Punjabi, for example, muslim (singular) – muslim*õ* (oblique plural), darwaazaa – darwaaz*e* (plural), darwaaz*õ* (oblique plural); taazaa "fresh" – taaz*aa* (masculine)/taz*ii* (feminine). In addition, a large number of function words such as adverbs like *bilkul* "just like/sure," prepositions like *qariib* "near," conjunctions like *magar* "but" and interjections like *shaabaash* "well done" are commonly used.

Further there are numerous words that have been borrowed but they have a different meaning in Indian languages because of semantic shift. For example:

Lexicon	Meaning in Hindi	Meaning in Persian
aavaaraa	bad character	homeless
kharaab	bad /defective	spoiled/ruined
hawaa	wind	weather
raftaar	speed	character/behavior
saazesh	conspiracy	accord

The changes in meaning have been listed in Naqvi (1962).

One last factor that needs to be mentioned is that most words from Persian entered not only Hindi–Urdu but the lexicon of most regional languages. The borrowed words reveal phonological approximations to local conditions. In most languages of South Asia the fricative sounds of south Persian, that is *q, kh, gh, z, f* tend to become *k, g, j,* and *ph* respectively, some examples are as below:

qaraar	= *karaar*	firmness
qarz	= *karj*	loan
kharc	= *kharc*	expenditure
khud	= *khud*	self
ghulaam	= *gulaam*	slave
ghulaal	= *gulel*	catapult
gaz	= *gaj*	yard
aazaad	= *aajaad*	independent
farmaanaa	= *pharmaanaa*	to say
daftar	= *daphtar*	office

Another major change is related to the *haa-e-mukhtafi* of Persian (P) words (i.e., words ending in ***h*** in the Persian written script) which changes to the **aa** sound in most Indian (I) languages. Examples are (P) *aaineh* – (I) *aainaa* ("mirror"), (P) *kinaareh* – (I) *kinaaraa* ("corner"), (P) *cehreh* – (I) *cehraa* ("face"), (P) *kaarkhaaneh* – (I) *kaarkhaanaa* ("factory"), and (P) *namuuneh* – (I) *namunaa* ("sample"). In fact sounds have been changed as per local phonological conditions. For example Persian *dabiir* ("secretary") and *ganjawar* ("treasurer") became *dibira* or *divira* and *ganjavara* in Kashmiri. In Punjabi the word *masjid* ("mosque") is colloquially called *masiit* and the Persian word *zan* ("woman") with plural form "*zanaan*" and the form *zanaanii* "some women" changes to *janaanii* "woman (singular)" and is pluralised as *janaaniyaaN* "women" and so on. The Persian *fardnavis* (a title) becomes *fadnis* in Marathi, the Persian word *amaanat* "deposit" undergoes metathesis in Gujarati and becomes *anaamat*, and diphthongs like *ai* and *au* become the mid vowels *e* and *o* respectively, thus *qaul* ("promise") becomes *kol* and *ghairat* ("zeal") becomes *gerat* and so on. Bangla and Oriya also show similar changes in the articulation of consonants as in Hindi–Urdu . In Assamese *ajab* ("strange") becomes *ajiib/ajiip*, *kaagaz* ("paper") becomes *kaakat* and so on. Some borrowings in Tamil: *qaidi* ("prisoner") becomes *kaidi*, *sifaarish* ("recommendation") becomes *shipaarsh*, and *khushi* ("happiness") becomes *gushi*. The Persian forms *darbaar* ("court") and *bazaar* ("market") become *darbaaru* and *bazaaru* in Kannada, and *amaanat* ("deposit") and *daftar* ("office") become *amaanatu* and *daphtramu* respectively in Telugu. Even the southernmost Malayalam speech shows forms like *darkhasa* for *darkhaast* ("petition") and others.

In the matter of script Sindhis were the first to be exposed to the Arabic script during the Arab invasion and conquest of Sindh in the eighth century. With the onset of Persian influence the use of this script got strengthened. In Kashmir the Sharda script gave way to the Persio-Arabic script. In the Punjab the Persio-Arabic script was adopted along with the Gurumukhi script. Under the influence of Persio-Arabic characters the script of Marathi was changed from Nagari to Modi and so on.

The large-scale influence of Persian forms enriched the Indian languages. Some of them began to reveal different styles of writing. Thus, in addition to KhaRiboli and Brajbhasha, a Persianized version now known as Urdu, came into existence. A poet like Dadu has exploited all the three language varieties in his poetic compositions (see Gargesh 1998: 85–6). Much literature in Urdu is modeled on Persian literature. The versification in couplet form became increasingly popular, as is evident from couplets such as the following from renowned nineteenth-century poet Mirza Asadullah Khan Ghalib (Kejariwal 2002: 182, 188).

muddat hui hai yaar ko mahmaaN kiye hue
joshe qadah se bazme caraaghaaN kiye hue.

It's been so long
Oh so long
That I've played host
To my friend and love
When wine flowed free
And the cup met cup
And the whole congregation
Came alive
And was full of light.

jii DhuuNDhataa hai phir vahii fursat, ki raat din
baiThe raheN tasavvure jaanaaN kiye hue.

Oh for those days
And those nights
Where one had little
On one's mind
Than to think
And to weave
Images of her
My love.

In the above the expressions *muddat* ("time/interval"), *yaar* ("friend/beloved"), *mahmãã* (*kiye hue*) ("having entertained/hosted"), *joshe-qadah* ("with cupfuls"), *bazme caraaghãã* ("ebullient/wonderful party"), *fursat* ("time/opportunity"), and *tasavvure janãã* (*kiye hue*) ("reminiscing about the beloved") are from Persian and they lend the language a new poetic vigor and freshness.

Conclusion

The process of Indianization of Persian and Persianization of Indian languages resulting from a prolonged South Asian contact with the Persian language shows the extent to which the latter had taken roots in South Asia. It was the language adopted by South Asians, both Muslims and Hindus, for intellectual and aesthetic discourses. No branch of knowledge, scientific or otherwise, was left untouched by it. All poetic forms found in the Persian language were explored, such as the didactic, the lyrical, the romantic, and the mystical.

The case of Persian in India has been unique where a foreign language is accepted and nativized and significant original contributions are made through it. The only comparable example is that of English, the current language with global dimensions. However, it is yet to be seen whether English would be accepted, adopted, mastered, and creatively used to the same extent as was Persian in South Asia.

5 Major regional languages

Tej K. Bhatia

Introduction

This chapter focuses on various facets of the major regional languages of South Asia (hereafter, SA) with special reference to their role in networking and communication (e.g. media, trade, multiple identities). It shows that the magnitude and scale of regional linguistic diversity and parameters of language use are often beyond the imagination of those who are accustomed to a monolinguistic view of language competence and use, and monolithic linguistic models. Whenever deemed necessary, historical background is provided to clarify the contemporary status and role of regional languages in the communicative and sociopolitical settings of SA. As the home to the largest number of major regional languages in SA, India receives greatest attention, though to give a comparative and contrastive perspective on the topic, Pakistan and Bangladesh are treated in some detail as well. Nepal is home to a great many languages, but little detailed information is available on their sociolinguistic situation. Nepali has gained the status of the national language with more ease in Nepal than Hindi, for example, as the linguistic symbol of the nation in India.

This chapter is divided into two sections: the first section presents a general account of regional languages, and the second section presents a case study of Punjabi and Bengali. The main reason for the selection of these two languages is that while the two languages are regional languages of India, they represent the international dimensions of the regional languages of SA. Punjabi is the dominant language in Pakistan, and Bengali is the national/official language of Bangladesh. This is not to claim that other languages, such as Gujarati or Tamil, have no international dimension. The Gujarati diaspora of Africa and the Tamil diaspora of Southeast Asia, for example, are centuries old. However, given the limitation of space, it is difficult to deal with all major SA languages in one chapter.

The discussion addresses the following key questions:

1. Why do regional languages persist even though the monolithic linguistic policies (one language, one script, one religion, and one nation) of some SA governments are not conducive to their promotion?

2. Why do they persist to varying degrees?
3. What criteria are used by a government to bestow the status of a regional language on some languages and not on others?
4. How do regional languages carve out their domains and functions in a multilingual society?
5. What are the effects of regional languages on national, societal, and individual bilingualism (multiple identities, language contact and change, and verbal repertoire)?

Regional languages: A profile

Defining a major regional language in SA is not an easy task. The discussion below explicates this claim. I start by identifying the major regional languages of India and other SA countries.

Rather than subscribing to a monolithic linguistic and cultural model (one language–one script, or one nation–one religion), the Indian constitution, which came into effect in 1950, recognizes India's religious and linguistic diversity and plurality by declaring India a secular democratic republic and recognizing eighteen "scheduled" or "national" languages, listed here in descending order of number of speakers: Hindi, Bengali, Telugu, Marathi, Tamil, Urdu, Gujarati, Kannada, Malayalam, Oriya, Punjabi, Assamese, Sindhi, Nepali, Konkani, Manipuri, Kashmiri, and Sanskrit (see Table 5.1 for the 1991 Census data on the number of speakers of these languages). From the table it becomes clear that several "national" languages are associated with linguistic regions/states, and in that respect these languages are regional languages. The congruence of linguistic and state boundaries is not a coincidence; rather, it is the result of the government's effort to reorganize state boundaries along linguistic lines in 1956 (see Krishnamurti 1995 and Chapters 6 and 15, this volume, for more details on the linguistic reorganization of states in India). For example, Madras Province was divided along linguistic lines into the Tamil-speaking Tamil Nadu and Telugu-speaking Andhra Pradesh. Although Hindi is a regional language spoken in the states in the so-called "Hindi-belt," it is also the "official" language of the Republic, with English being an "associate" official language. Hindi was adopted as the official language as it was recognized that it, along with the variety of Hindi known as Hindustani, was understood and spoken more widely than any other language of the Republic. Hindustani was used widely and consistently by the leadership of the Indian National Congress to gain public support for the freedom struggle, beginning in the 1920s when Mahatma Gandhi entered the scene in India. Thus, though regional in one sense, Hindi is also pan-Indian in character and in its functions as the official language (see Chapter 3 for more on Hindi–Urdu–Hindustani).

Table 5.1. *Languages in the Eighth Schedule of the Constitution*

Languages	Language family	State/spoken in	Number of mother-tongue speakers (1991 Census: Government of India)
Assamese	Indo-Aryan	Assam	13,079,696
Bengali	Indo-Aryan	Bengal	69,595,738
English[a]	Indo-European; Germanic	Meghalaya, Nagaland, Tripura	178,598
Gujarati	Indo-Aryan	Gujarat	40,673,814
Hindi	Indo-Aryan	Hindi belt: Bihar, Rajasthan, Haryana, Delhi, Himachal Pradesh Madhya Pradesh, Uttar Pradesh	337,272,114
Kannada	Dravidian	Karnataka	32,753,676
Kashmiri	Indo-Aryan	Jammu and Kashmir[b]	56,690
Konkani	Indo-Aryan	Goa	1,760,607
Malayalam	Dravidian	Kerala	30,377,176
Manipuri	Tibeto-Burman	Manipur	1,270,216
Marathi	Indo-Aryan	Maharashtra	62,481,681
Oriya	Indo-Aryan	Orissa	28,061,313
Punjabi	Indo-Aryan	Punjab	23,378,744
Sanskrit	Indo-Aryan	No state	49,736
Sindhi	Indo-Aryan	Metro areas of western India	2,122,848
Tamil	Dravidian	Tamil Nadu	53,006,368
Telugu	Dravidian	Andhra Pradesh	66,017,615
Urdu	Indo-Aryan	Jammu and Kashmir	43,406,932

[a] The number of mother-tongue speakers of English decreased in 1991. According to the 1981 census, the mother-tongue speakers of English numbered 202,000.
[b] These figures are not complete as no census was taken in Jammu and Kashmir in 1991.

Defining a regional language: Problems and perspectives

It is not possible for each language to have its own state since, according to the Government of India figures, there are more than 114 languages in India (in addition to 216 mother tongues, some of which are so-called dialects; not counting languages which have fewer than 10,000 speakers) (see Chapter 10 for details). The question naturally arises, what is so magical about the constitutional number eighteen? What was the motivation for this number and the selection process? The reasons for the selection of the eighteen languages in the Eighth Schedule of India's Constitution are varied: numeric strength, literary tradition, regional representation of the speakers of the major languages, political and ideological pressure groups (B. Kachru 1997; also see Krishnamurti 1995 for the criteria used). This list is by no means complete, and neither is the process of elevating other languages to the list of scheduled languages. The number of scheduled languages has now increased to twenty-two with the addition of Bodo, Dogri, Maithili, and Santali in 2003, and attempts are under way to add to this list languages such as Tulu, with speakers numbering more than one-and-a-half million (see Table 10.2 on page 224).

From the foregoing discussion, it becomes clear that the notion of a regional language in India is a dynamic one. The regions/states represented by regional languages are neither linguistically homogeneous nor spatially static (see Chapter 6). The main reason for this is that the language dominant in a particular region or state invariably coexists with other regional languages in that state. For instance, Andhra Pradesh is a Telugu-speaking state, but it has substantial numbers of minority-language speakers of Marathi, Oriya, Hindi–Urdu, and other languages. Language boundaries are not permanently fixed either. Before 1966, the state of Punjab included the present-day states of Haryana and Himachal Pradesh. Additionally, the question of language versus dialect is problematic. Konkani, for example, was considered a dialect of Marathi but now is treated as an independent language, as is Maithili, which was previously counted as a dialect of Hindi. Various manifestations of such conflicts are also witnessed in the Hindi-speaking area (see B. Kachru 1977; Y. Kachru and Bhatia 1978 for more details).

Regional languages and modes of communication

Regional languages play a critical role in the cultural, communicative, and ethnic network of pluralistic SA in general and India in particular. In this process, they carve out their sociolinguistic domains and perform sociopsychological functions in the inter- and intraregional communicative setting. Consequently, they serve as an important component of widespread bilingualism and provide a bridge between national languages (such as Hindi and English) and local vernaculars. Punjabi, for instance, provides a major link as a contact language between several languages and Hindi in the north, which in turn yields the Hindi–Hindustani–Urdu–Punjabi core/axis. This axis forms a giant speech community with direct links to Bengali in the east, Gujarati and Marathi in the west, and Telugu and Kannada in the south. As a result of contact with these languages and other regional varieties, Hindi has developed its own regional varieties, for example Punjabi Hindi (Delhi Hindi), Mumbai Hindi (Bombay Hindi, Bindi), Kalkatiya Hindi (Calcutta Hindi), and Madrasi Hindi (Madras, renamed Chennai, Hindi). The variety known as Dakhini Hindi (southern Hindi) has a very long history (see Sharma 1964). Regional languages are in turn colored by contact with regional varieties of Hindi and local varieties present in the region.

The most obvious linguistic vehicles for reaching rural India are either Hindi or the regional languages and their local vernaculars. The incidence of literacy in English is not significant in rural India. Owing to the literature of the past and popular media at present, the boundaries between rural vernaculars, regional languages, and Hindi have become very fluid. Historically, literature (e.g. in the devotional poetry tradition, of which poets such as Kabir [fifteenth century], Tulasidas [1532–1623], Surdas [1479–1586], and Meera Bai [1478–1540] are representative) played a major role in neutralizing such boundaries and bringing the influence of regional languages (from east to west and south to north, and vice versa) and rural varieties into Hindi and other regional languages. The consequence was a mixed speech, favored especially by Kabir and Meera bai termed *sadhukkaRī bhāshā* (the language of wandering saints free from any prescriptive norms). In short, convergence of regional languages has played and continues to play a vital role in the formation of India or SA as a linguistic or sociolinguistic area (see Emeneau 1956, 1980; Masica 1976; Pandit 1972, among others) and in the promotion of bilingualism grounded in regional languages.

In what follows I will focus on the important domains that regional languages have acquired in India.

Regional-language media

Regional-language identity is another very salient feature of SA and is one of the factors responsible for the vibrant and fiercely independent SA media. The number of languages used in print media in India is eighty-seven, in radio and broadcasting, seventy-one; and thirteen in films. Advertising in regional languages is quite widespread. For more details on the various facets of SA media, including regional-language media, see Chapter 19.

To demonstrate the formidable power and reach of the regional-language media, let me cite the case of the political campaign to elect the chief minister of the state of Haryana in 1987. For the first time in the electoral history of India, the electronic media were used by the opposition in a state election to match and outdo the power and reach of the ruling-party-controlled television network, Doordarshan.

In 1987, Devi Lal used the Video on Wheels (VOW) medium – a medium grounded heavily in regional language and culture – as a vehicle of political propaganda. Lagging in the polls, he decided to use this medium rather than Doordarshan. The new medium proved to be a boon for Devi Lal, who came from behind and secured a stunning victory over the ruling party. This revealed the unmatched power of VOW and regional languages in mobilizing rural India. The dramatic success of Devi Lal became the subject of numerous news stories within and outside India. For more details on the campaign, see Bhatia (2000: 71–6).

Education

The introduction of the Three Language Formula in education is yet another notable feature of national policy to promote regional languages. This formula calls for trilingualism or quadrilingualism in education. In addition to learning Hindi and English, students are expected to learn their native tongue (and, in case of minority language speakers, the regional language). In the Hindi–Urdu–Punjabi belt, students are expected to learn one of the four Dravidian languages (Tamil, Telugu, Kannada, and Malayalam; see Mallikarjun 2001 for details of the Three Language Formula and its implementation). Although debate concerning the effectiveness of the Three Language Formula continues, the underlying merit of this educational policy in the promotion of multilingualism is hardly questionable and best represents the multilingual character of the nation (see B. Kachru 1997).

The number of languages used as the medium of education in primary education is twenty four; in secondary school, twenty-two (these figures for 1990 are from Mallikarjun 2001). Some "minor" regional languages that represent tribal languages, such as Khasi, Santhali, Bodo, Manipuri, and Mizo, are also used as vehicles for primary and secondary school education. Although regional languages are used in undergraduate education, English takes precedence over regional languages at the graduate and post-graduate levels. For more on the role of regional languages and their hierarchical significance in education, see Chaturvedi and Singh (1981); for Pakistan, Rahman (2004).

In order to promote the teaching and learning of regional languages as second languages, the Central Institute of Indian Languages (CIIL) and its regional affiliates make notable efforts in teacher training, design of language curricula, and models of language evaluation. Similar notable institutions are the Central Institute of Hindi (Kendriya Hindi Sansthan), the National Council for Educational Research and Training (NCERT), and the Indian Institute of Language Studies, Patiala. However, these efforts have had a limited impact on the educational scene, where English, Hindi, and major regional languages continue to gain territory from the comparatively "weaker" languages, whether regional or tribal (Mallikarjun 2001).

Literature

The National Academy of Letters (the Sahitya Akademi) of the Government of India and its regional counterparts promote literary activities in the twenty-two languages they recognize. Prestigious annual awards are given for the best creative writing in these languages, including Indian English. In addtion, state counterparts of the National Academy (e.g. the Karnataka Sahitya Akademi) give literary recognition to selected majority and minority languages spoken in their respective territories.

Administration and modernization

At least thirteen regional languages of India are used in state-level administration. Government and non-government attempts to equip regional languages for education and modernization fall into the following eight categories: development of materials, creation of technical terms, technological application, information storage and dissemination, book publication, translation, staff development, and language promotion. See Annamalai (2001: 138–40) and Krishnamurti and Mukherjee (1984) for details on language modernization.

Having accounted for the main domains of regional languages, let me turn to the case of Punjabi and Bengali in SA.

Punjabi and Bengali: A case study

What is interesting is that some regional languages of India, such as Punjabi, Bengali, and Sindhi, have an international status in the overall context of SA. This is a direct consequence of the partition of India into India and Pakistan in 1947 and later the split of East Pakistan from West Pakistan leading to the birth of another nation, Bangladesh. Consequently, Punjabi and Bengali found homes in two nations – Punjabi became the majority language with no official status in the state of Punjab in Pakistan, and Bengali became the official language of Bangladesh. Bengali is ranked fifth in the world in terms of number of speakers, according to the *World Almanac* (2002: 447), and is the official language of the country, along with English. Bengali is spoken by more than 90 per cent of the population. Although the official language of Pakistan is Urdu, it is spoken as a native language by just 8 per cent of the population; the majority native language is Punjabi, spoken by approximately 60 per cent of the population. Punjabi is ranked among the top twenty languages in the world in terms of number of speakers.

In spite of the national divide, the Punjabi-speaking regions of India and Pakistan form a single (socio)linguistic area. The region is characterized by a multiplicity of religions, speech varieties, writing systems, literary traditions, and identities. Although Punjabis exhibit multiple identities at various levels (nationalities – Indian versus Pakistani, religions – Hindus, Sikhs, and Muslims; literary traditions – sufi versus nirgun; and sociocultural ethnicities – Gujar, Jats, Dogras, Multanis, and Jhangis, among others), they are united by a common heritage. This heritage manifests itself in many forms, such as folk dances, songs, art, literature (poetry, story tradition), highly Persianized proper names (Hindus, Sikhs, and Muslims), and belief systems, which form part of a unified mosaic called *Punjabiyat* ("Punjabiness") or *biradari* ("brotherhood") (Khubchandani 1997b: 83). In terms of discourse domains, Punjabi is a marker of intimacy, humor, and informality among Punjabis.

Consider the multiplicity of scripts. Punjabi is written in four scripts: Gurmukhi, Perso-Arabic (Shahmukhi), Devanagari, and the dying business script, LaNDa (see T. Bhatia 2003 for details about business and endangered scripts of Punjabi). Sikhs often write Punjabi in Gurmukhi, Hindus in Devanagari, and Muslims in Perso-Arabic. Punjabi – written in Gurmukhi – is the official language of the Indian state of Punjab. What is interesting is that the use of the three scripts plays a critical role in forging a common Punjabi identity among Punjabi speakers rather than splitting them along religious lines. This is a total reversal of what one witnesses in the case of Hindi–Urdu. Hindi and Urdu are mutually intelligible but are written in two different scripts – Hindi in the Devanagari script and Urdu in Perso-Arabic script. Hindi is associated with Hindus and Urdu with Muslims. The two scripts are the main reason for forging distinct religious identities rather than establishing a common linguistic bond. In addition to the two scripts, vocabulary is a source of distinct religious identities in Hindi–Urdu. While Urdu borrows its technical and learned vocabulary from Persian and Arabic, Hindi borrows such terms from Sanskrit. In order to assert their Punjabi identity, it is a common practice among Punjabis in Pakistan to dissociate themselves from Urdu and thus from Perso-Arabic vocabulary but not from the Perso-Arabic script. Urdu vocabulary is viewed as a threat to their Punjabi identity. Therefore, attempts have been made in the past two decades to cleanse Punjabi of the influence of Urdu, even at the cost of intelligibility and risk of being labeled anti-Islamic. See Table 5.2 in this regard.

A cursory examination of such attempts shows that they favor drawing vocabulary and morphology (e.g. reverse compounding) from indigenous Indic sources (from either Sanskrit or local vernaculars). The Punjabi daily *Sajjan* (1989–1990) employed many of these coinages in actual practice. In short, Pakistani Punjabis juggle their identities in the following fashion: Perso-Arabic script and Urdu for national and religious identity, and Indian and rural Punjabi vocabulary and morphology for Punjabi identity.

Although Pakistani Punjabis do have a linguistic identity, their language identity takes a back seat to their religious identity. The reverse is the case with Bengalis in SA. Cases in point are Bangladesh and West Bengal in India. Before Bangladesh became an independent nation in 1971, it was part of Pakistan (called East Pakistan). Although Islamic identity was the main reason that Bangladesh became part of Pakistan rather than India in 1947, the imposition of Urdu, the national language of Pakistan, on Bengalis was a major factor in the split between Pakistan and Bangladesh (for more details on the Bengali language movement, see Rahman 1996a: 79–102). In contrast, Punjabi Muslims' identity with their language is weaker than Bengalis' identification with theirs. Therefore, although Punjabi speakers form a majority in Pakistan, the imposition of Urdu on Punjabis did not lead to a separatist movement as it did in the case of the former East Pakistan. Among Muslims, Sikhs, and Hindus, Sikhs

Table 5.2. *Punjabi: Language purification attempts in Pakistan*

Words commonly used and meaning in Urdu and Punjabi	Punjabi coinage
lafz "word"	*akhar*
saalaanaa "yearly"	*varhe var*
bhejnaa "to send"	*ghalnaa*
aquaam-e-muttahidda "the United Nations"	*ik mukh qauman*

Source: Adapted from Rahman (1996a: 207).

have the greatest degree of loyalty to Punjabi, comparable to the Bengalis in Bangladesh. The stance of Punjabi Muslims is to divorce themselves consciously from Punjabi in order to assert their national and religious identity. In short, Punjabi in Pakistan exhibits a split linguistic identity, but this is not the case for Muslims in Bangladesh.

Because of its stronger association with Sikhs, Punjabi 'vanished as a university subject' soon after the creation of Pakistan (Shackle 1970: 243); the monolithic language policies of the state (one nation, one language, and one script) contributed further to the lack of promotion of Punjabi in Pakistan. Consequently, while Punjabi has flourished in India in spite of its minority status (one of the eighteen languages), it is still struggling in Pakistan even though Punjabi speakers, in addition to being in the majority, hold power in military and other arenas in Pakistan.

The struggle of Punjabi and the search for linguistic identity and language standardization continues in Pakistan (see Rahman 1996: 191–209 for the Punjabi language movement in Pakistan). Another manifestation of the Punjabi language movement is the Siraiki language movement in Pakistan. In addition to a separate Siraiki language identity, the center of the debate is the language versus dialect conflict in SA (see Rahman 1996a: 173–90; Shackle 1977 on the Siraiki language movement in Pakistan; Rahman 1996: 211–14 for Hindko, Pothohari). The Siraiki, Hindko, and Pothohari (also spelled/called Patohari, Pothwari, Putohari, Puthohari, Mirpuri Punjabi) movements assert that Siraiki, Hindko, and Pothohari are three separate languages in their own right rather than three dialects/varieties of Punjabi.[1] Siraiki is also called Lahanda or Multani. Other names used for this language, which Grierson classified as Western Punjabi, are Mazaffargarhi, Uchi, Riasati, Darewali, Hindko, Thalchari,

[1] Grierson classified Pothohari as a variety of Northern Lahanda. British diasporic Pothoharis/ Mirpuri Punjabis, however, seek a separate identity from Punjabis.

Jaghdali, Jatki, and Balochki (see T. Bhatia 1993 for more details). Punjabi no doubt is experiencing turbulence in forging its linguistic identity in Pakistan; it is not clear whether the Punjabi diaspora in Europe and North America is going to help in strengthening its case or further diluting its claim to be an important major language of the nation.

It is worth mentioning that language movements in Pakistan are not restricted to Punjabi and Siraiki; other language movements, such as Sindhi, Pushto, Khowari, Khohistani, Shina, and Hindko, are also gaining strength. It is interesting to note that Sindhi is recognized as a regional/national language of India, while it lacks any official status in Pakistan. In contrast, while the Indian state of Jammu and Kashmir chose Urdu over Kashmiri as its state language, a Kashmiri language movement is emerging in Pakistan (see Rahman 1996a for details).

Further dimensions of Punjabi

The language contact situation between Hindi–Urdu and Punjabi is notable for the emergence of a new variety of speech which is colorful in its own right and is called "Punjabi Hindustani." The tonal pattern of Punjabi renders a sing-song character to Hindi in Delhi and Urdu in Lahore. A notable grammatical characteristic of this variety is obligative constructions with the replacement of a dative subject with an ergative subject (e.g. *mãĩn ne jaanaa hai* "I need to go" instead of *mujh ko jaanaa hai*). The phenomenon of code mixing and code switching with other languages and language varieties of Punjabi is a natural part of the verbal behavior of Punjabis. It is often noticed that Punjabis interacting with bilinguals (e.g. Hindi–Urdu speakers) mix Punjabi verbs with the Hindi–Urdu tense-aspectual system (*andar vaRtaa hai* "he comes inside"; the verbal root, *vaR*, is from Punjabi, while the tense marking is from Hindi–Urdu). This type of verbal behavior makes Punjabis a subject of jokes in the Hindi–Urdu speech community.

In spite of language purification movements (e.g. purging of Urdu items from the language) Pakistani Punjabi diverges from Indian Punjabi primarily in terms of lexicon, thus mirroring the trend found in Hindi–Urdu (see Dulai 1989: 226). The implosive sounds of Western Punjabi and negativized copula represent yet other features of Pakistani Punjabi (see T. Bhatia 1993: 84).

Domains of Punjabi in India

The domains which Punjabi has acquired in India far exceed the domains of Punjabi in Pakistan. While domains such as the media (particularly radio and television) are accessible to Pakistani Punjabi, other domains such as administration and education remain a distant reality. Punjabi does not have the status of language of administration in the province of West Punjab in Pakistan.

Sociopsychological features common to Indian and Pakistani Punjabi in SA are rurality, openness, liveliness, and fun-lovingness. (For more details see the discussion of the treatment of Punjabi in advertising in Chapter 19, particularly Table 19.8). Advertising is not alone in making effective use of these features; the Indian film industry in general, and Hindi film in particular, has exploited them effectively by mixing Punjabi with Hindi in various genres (e.g. music, songs, dances, and story line). In fact, most popular Bollywood movies of recent years have a distinct "Punjabi flavor" to them.

Conclusion

In conclusion, regional languages and regional-language identities play a central role in the communicative and cultural setting of SA in general and India in particular. Government policies in India and Pakistan offer two contrasting and mutually exclusive approaches to the promotion of regional languages – the Indian policy embraces the multilingual and multicultural character of the nation, while the Pakistani policy largely adheres to a monolithic linguistic model of "one nation, one language." In spite of these differences, bilingualism/multilingualism based on regional languages is firmly rooted in the sociopsychological, historical, and attitudinal life of SA, particularly of India. Because of the multilingual policies of the Government of India, it is not surprising that regional languages have acquired many domains and functions which make their maintenance a natural aspect of the Indian way of life and communication. The preservation and promotion of regional languages is still an uphill battle in Pakistan and other SA countries. In spite of the differing national language policies and national visions, SA values its regional-language heritage to varying degrees; ruthless efforts to eradicate regional languages are viewed as counterintuitive in SA because of its long history of linguistic diversity and a multiethic, multireligious, and multicultural heritage.

6 Minority languages and their status

Rakesh M. Bhatt and Ahmar Mahboob

This chapter discusses the minority languages in South Asia, exploring the implications of their status in terms of various sociolinguistic processes. Although the empirical scope of this chapter is restricted mainly to India and Pakistan, the generalizations presented here can be extended to other South Asian countries, such as Nepal, Sri Lanka, and Bangladesh.

Minority languages: contexts of definition

A numerical definition of the term minority languages renders all the languages spoken in India "minority," since there is no language whose speakers constitute more than half of India's total population of roughly 1.1 billion. Hindi, the "official" language of India, has the highest number of speakers; yet they constitute less than 40 percent of the Indian population. Similarly, Urdu, one of the two official languages of Pakistan is spoken by less than 10 percent of the Pakistani population as a native language. In fact, according to the 2001 census, Urdu is the mother tongue of only 7.57 percent of the people in Pakistan (Census 2001: Table 2.7, cited in Rahman 2004: 2).

A sociological definition of the term, based on functional or ethnolinguistic vitality, turns "numerical" majority languages (at the state level) into minority languages. A good example of this is Kashmiri in the Indian state of Jammu and Kashmir. Although Kashmiri is spoken by a little over 53 percent of the total population of the state of Jammu and Kashmir, its functionality is severely restricted mainly to the home/family domains (Bhatt [Mohan] 1989; Kak 2001). Similarly, in Pakistan, while Punjabi is the majority language of Punjab (spoken by 44.15 percent of the population, according to Rahman 2004: 2) and is officially recognized, its functionality is restricted to domestic and informal domains. It is not taught in schools and no official work is carried out in this language (Mansoor 1993; the only regional language that is used in education, lower administration, and judiciary is Sindhi [Rahman 2004: 7]).

A related, demographic, definition of the term presents a division between autochthonous and immigrant populations. This distinction seems vital in the understanding of the phenomena of language retention and attrition. A political definition of the term invites interrelated issues of power (dominating/dominated), autonomy (language rights/movements), and space ("linguistic" states). An economic definition of the term introduces the notion of a language's role and its value in the global division of labor. English bilingualism in India (K. K. Sridhar 1989) and in Pakistan (Mahboob and Ahmar 2004), especially its role in the political economy of minority languages, is a case in point.

The issue of minority languages and their status is further complicated by the sociolinguistic dynamics of language contact, particularly as it relates to the politics of identity demographics, a classic illustration of which is provided by Srivastava (1984a). In an attempt to minimize the problems of linguistic minorities in India, the boundaries of certain states were redrawn on a linguistic basis in 1956 upon the recommendation of the State Reorganization Commission of India (see Chapter 15 in this volume). Accordingly, the Indian state of Punjab was divided in 1966 into two: Punjabi-speaking Punjabi Suba (area) and Hindi-speaking Haryana. However, as Srivastava (1984a) and Dua (1986) have argued, the division did not resolve the minority issues, primarily because those Hindus who reported Punjabi as their mother tongue before 1961 identified with Hindi after the linguistic division, creating a substantial Hindi-speaking minority in 1971 (over 20 percent of the population).

In contrast to India, in Pakistan, while suggestions were made to divide the provinces on linguistic/ethnic basis, these plans were never carried out. In India, the proposal to demarcate provinces on the basis of linguistic nationalities has been promoted since the 1920s. As early as 1928, the Motilal Nehru Committee of Indian National Congress had recommended reorganization of states in India on the basis of the "linguistic unity of the area concerned," noting that "[t]he [Indian] National Congress recognized this linguistic principle 8 years ago and since then, so far as the Congress machinery is concerned, India has been divided into linguistic provinces" (Thirumalai 2005). In India changes were made to the prevailing state boundaries to accommodate various linguistic groups after Independence, but this did not happen in Pakistan. The insensitivity to linguistic identities in Pakistan has led to problems. A number of ethnolinguistic groups have been demanding separate provinces. For example, Siraiki speakers in Punjab have been demanding a separate province for themselves. Siraiki is the majority language of the southern part of Punjab. However, this and such other proposals have never been seriously considered by the government. In his study of minority language movements in Pakistan, Rahman (1996a: 254) states that ethnic movements have been looked down upon in Pakistan and ideas of creating more provinces along linguistic lines suppressed because this "will harm the Punjab [the state of the ruling elite] the most . . . for one thing, it will not remain a large province and its weight in the legislature will be reduced considerably."

The other dimension of the dynamic of language contact has to do with the consequences of demographic politics, most clearly visible in the changing population profile of Tripura (cf. Chaklader 1987). The policy of the state of Tripura, ever since the rule of the "Rajas," actively encouraged immigration from neighboring states that transformed the status of tribal languages from a majority to a minority (See also Chapter 7). The essence of this transformation is captured in the fact that whereas the tribal population in the state was 57 percent of the total in 1874–1875 and 52.81 percent in 1901, it fell steadily through the decades to 28.44 percent in 1981 (Chaklader 1987). However, it has steadily risen since to 30.95 percent in 1991 and 31.05 percent in 2001, according to Lokpriy 2005 (Table 7: 14).

In dealing with the complexity of the demographic politics as outlined above, we follow Srivastava (1984a) in presenting the conceptualization of minority languages (see Table 6.1 below). The two important variables of this conceptualization, "Quantum" and "Power," interact to yield an informed typology of majority/minority languages: (1) languages that have both an official status and a numerical superiority (Cell A), for example Bengali in Bangladesh or Sinhala in Sri Lanka; (2) languages that have no official or functional power but have numerical superiority (Cell B), for example Kashmiri in the state of Jammu and Kashmir; (3) languages that have official or functional power, but do not have numerical superiority (Cell C), for example Urdu in Pakistan; and (4) languages that have neither official power nor numerical superiority (Cell D), for example most "minority" languages in South Asia fall under this category, such as Gujari or Gojari, in the state of Jammu and Kashmir, Brahui in Pakistan, Sunuwar in Nepal, and Santali in Bangladesh.

This chapter focuses on minority languages that belong mainly to types B and D in Table 6.1 below. The discussion of minority languages with reference to Table 6.1 has so far been somewhat simplified. In India, for example, the minority languages belonging to types B and D can be further empirically divided into two categories: major (scheduled) and minor (nonscheduled) languages.[1] The minority languages belonging to type B can be either major or minor languages that are a numerical majority, like Kashmiri (major-minority) in the state of Jammu and Kashmir or Bhili (minor-minority) in the Dadra and Nagar Haveli Union Territory of India. The minority languages in type D, on the other hand, are either major languages that enjoy the status of "official" language in another state where they also constitute a numerical majority or minor

[1] The Constitution of India originally singled out eighteen languages (subsequently expanded to twenty-two languages by constitutional amendments; See Table 10.1). They are termed "scheduled languages" since the original eighteen were listed under the VIII Schedule, Articles 343–351 of the Constitution. The "non scheduled languages" (for top twenty-two nonscheduled languages, see Table 10.2), referred to as "minority" languages, are those that are left out of the list.

Table 6.1. *Language types*

		Power	
Quantum		+	–
	+	(A) Majority	(B) Janta
	–	(C) Elite	(D) Minority

Source: Srivastava (1984a).

languages that do not have numerical superiority in any state or territory. An example of a major language is Tamil, a minority language in Andhra Pradesh but a majority and "official" language in the state of Tamil Nadu; an example of a minor language is Santali in Bihar.

Minority language in language planning

Languages in South Asia perform a surprising array of sociolinguistic roles, such as home language, regional language, medium of instruction, official regional (state) language, official (national) language, national language, link language, literary language, library language, classical language, liturgical language, and world language. Language planning in this role-oriented sociolinguistic system becomes a complex undertaking of planning privileges for a language in the domains of education, administration, court, civil services, and so on. Given the functionally unequal status of minority languages relative to the dominant regional languages, language planning for minority languages becomes critical for their survival. In South Asia, there have been several attempts at the state and national level to address the problems of minority languages.

The first effort toward macro language planning in multilingual India, made upon the recommendation of the States Reorganization Commission, was to redraw the boundaries of states on a linguistic basis, as mentioned above. Andhra Pradesh (Telugu majority) was created out of Madras, Maharashtra (Marathi majority) and Gujarat (Gujarati majority) were carved out of Maharashtra, Haryana (Hindi majority) emerged from Punjab (Punjabi majority), and Assam was divided into several states including Meghalaya, Manipur, Mizoram, Nagaland, and Arunachal Pradesh.

The principle of linguistic homogeneity played a key role in the determination of these states (cf. Gopal 1966). Where several minority languages coexisted within a geographic space, reflecting linguistic heterogeneity, a demand for a separate state was sometimes denied. Jharkhand is a case in point. It was denied a separate statehood by the States Reorganization Commission of India on the grounds of lack of viability of the area as a linguistic unit (Ghosh 1998;

Table 6.2. *Interstate distribution of some selected tribal languages in the Jharkhand area (1981)*

Languages	Speakers (thousands)	Speakers in states (%)			
		Bihar	West Bengal	Orissa	Madhya Pradesh
Munda					
Santali	4,208	50	37	13	
Ho	802	67		33	
Mundari	753	84	14	14	
Kharia	198	50	4	4	6
Bhumij	47	15	6	6	
Korwa	28	4			90
Dravidian					
Kurux	1,265	51	13	13	28
Parji	33				86

Source: Khubchandani (1992) and Abbi (1995).

cf. Munda 1989). The language scene of Jharkhand was complicated not only by the absence of either linguistic homogeneity or a common language for different tribal communities but also by the fact that the tribal communities were spread out among different states (see Table 6.2), where they came into contact with the local dominant languages (Hindi, Bengali, Oriya) and in most cases adopted these languages and their scripts. Later the protagonists of the Jharkhand movement rallied around Sadani (also called Sadari) as the official lingua franca of the state of Jharkhand as it is either the first or the second language of most of the tribal communities and is the mother tongue of the majority of nontribal Sadans (Keshari 1982). Finally, the Jharkhand state was carved out of Bihar in 2000.

However, as noted by Srivastava (1984a) and Dua (1986), the reorganization of states on a linguistic basis has changed the nature of noncompeting and nonconflicting bilingualism into a competing and conflicting type.[2] A quick look at Table 6.3 shows that in some states and union territories of India the percentage of minority language speakers far exceeds that of the single majority

2 The first prime minister of independent India, Pandit Jawahar Lal Nehru, a master language-strategist, never supported and in fact stalled the creation of linguistic provinces, arguing that such measures intensify provincial feelings and weaken the concept of a united India (Gopal 1980; King 1997; cf. Narasimhaiah 1969). Recognizing Indian multilingualism, he defended his antilinguistic reorganization of states position in the most insightful manner: "You must realize that while there are clearly marked linguistic regions there are also bilingual areas and even trilingual areas between such regions. And wherever you may draw your line, you do justice to one group and injustice to other" (Gopal 1980: 522).

Table 6.3. *Distribution of minority languages in selected states or union territories of India*

State/Union Territories	Single largest language and the percentage to total household population	Other minority languages
Above 50%		
Nagaland	Ao (13.94)	86.06
Arunachal Pradesh	Nissi/Dafla (23.59)	76.41
Andaman and Nicobar Islands	Bengali (24.68)	75.32
Meghalaya	Khasi (47.46)	52.34
Above 30%		
Jammu and Kashmir	Kashmiri (52.73)	47.27
Chandigarh	Hindi (55.11)	44.89
Goa, Daman, and Diu	Konkani (56.65)	43.35
Manipur	Manipuri (62.36)	37.64
Karnataka	Kannada (65.69)	34.31
Dadra and Nagar Haveli	Bhili/Bhilodi (68.69)	31.31
Tripura	Bengali (69.59)	30.41

Source: Adapted from the Census of India, 1981; Chaturvedi and Mohale (1976).

language speakers, whereas in many other states and union territories the minority language speakers are substantially large (see Appendix 6.1 for details).

Clearly, the changes in linguistic geography did little to solve the problem of minority languages or to promote their status vis-à-vis the regional languages. The States Reorganization Commission did acknowledge that even if the principle of linguistic homogeneity was followed rigidly, "the problem of linguistic minorities will, by no means, be solved" (*Report of the States Reorganization Commission* 1956: 205). The Commissioner for Linguistic Minorities, in his report on the constitutional safeguards for linguistic minorities, concluded:

> The division of the States on linguistic basis has given rise to the inevitable result that the regional language should gain prominence and should in course of time become the official Language of the State. The other languages which are the mother-tongue of the minority communities . . . naturally do not get equal prominence or status. The result is that those whose mother-tongue is the minority language have not only a sentimental grievance but certain practical difficulties and inconveniences from which they suffer (*First Report of the Commissioner of Linguistic Minorities*: 1957: 44).

As noted earlier, unlike India, Pakistan did not go through any linguistic reorganization of its provinces. Instead of accepting and developing policies to accommodate linguistic pluralism, the Pakistani government chose to foster a national identity by using Urdu as the sole national language. This choice of using a single national language led to a number of problems: the Urdu–Bengali conflict discussed below being the most significant.

At the time of Independence in 1947, Pakistan, like most other ex-colonial countries, was faced with the problem of developing a language policy. This problem was complicated by languages and language groups competing to be recognized as national languages, the two dominant native languages being Urdu and Bengali. Urdu was used as a symbol of Muslim identity and national unity. Bengali was the majority language of East Pakistan or East Bengal (modern Bangladesh). Bengal was the largest province of Pakistan. According to the 1951 census, Bengali speakers made up 54.6 percent of the total population of Pakistan, and Bengali thus was the majority language. Bengal also produced the most revenue. However, the prominent leaders of the Pakistan movement, including Muhammad Ali Jinnah (the first Governor General of Pakistan) and Liaquat Ali Khan (the first Prime Minister of Pakistan), were in favor of Urdu being the only national language. Jinnah, in a speech delivered in English in Bengal, said, "it is for you, the people of this Province, to decide what shall be the language of your Province. But let me make it very clear to you that the State Language of Pakistan is going to be Urdu and no other language. Anyone who tries to mislead you is really the enemy of Pakistan" (Jinnah 1948: 183). While this speech recognized Bengali as a regional language, it also made it clear that Bengali was not to be officially recognized as a national language. Furthermore, it labeled antistate those who wanted Bengali to be recognized as a national language. The Bengalis protested against this speech, and friction was created between East and West Pakistan. In trying to develop a national identity for Pakistan, the Urdu Committee, which was set up by the Advisory Board of Education to cultivate the Urdu language in Bengal, tried to introduce a uniform script for all languages spoken in Pakistan, further inflaming passions. The policy to promote Urdu and Perso-Arabic script was vigorously opposed by Bengalis and people of other linguistic groups who had their own scripts and literary traditions. The government policy toward Bengali was viewed as suppression of the Bengali culture and became a powerful symbol during the Bengali nationalist movement that eventually led to the secession of East Pakistan and formation of an independent Bangladesh in 1971. The genesis of the separatist movement and resultant continued violence in Sri Lanka is also attributable to the legislation in 1956 that made Sinhala the sole official language, thus marginalizing the Tamil-speaking minority (Stearns 2001).

The cases of Bengali and Tamil cited above show the complexity of language planning in South Asia and the profound political and social impact that such policies can have.

Constitutional safeguards

In India, the problems of linguistic minorities, anticipated and identified by the States Reorganization Commission, led to several constitutional safeguards to protect the interests of all linguistic minorities of India. Article 29 (1) of the Indian Constitution (1950) states: "Any section of the citizens residing in the territory of India or any part thereof having a distinct language, script or culture of its own shall have the right to conserve the same." This article allows for the preservation of special linguistic and cultural traditions of the minority which distinguish it from the dominant group. The first clause of Article 30 of the Indian Constitution states that all minorities, whether based on language or religion, shall have the right to establish and administer an educational institution of their choosing. The second clause of Article 30 says that the state shall not, in granting aid to educational institutions, discriminate against any educational institution on the grounds that it is under the management of a linguistic or religious minority. The second clause enables linguistic minorities to claim state aid for running their educational institutions.

Article 347 facilitates the use of minority languages for official purposes. For example, it declares that a state should be recognized as unilingual only where one language group constitutes about 70 percent or more of the entire population and that where there is substantial minority constituting 30 percent or more of the population, the state should be recognized as bilingual for administrative purposes; it further declares that the same principle should hold good at the district level. It is not uncommon in South Asia to find areas where minority languages locally reach a majority language position, such as in (1) Rajasthan-Bhili region, Khandesh and Northern Bihar, all having different varieties of Hindustani; (2) Himalayan region, with Pahari in Uttar Pradesh, Hindi in Himachal Pradesh, Hindi and Himalayish in Nepal, and Nepali in Sikkim, Darjeeling, and southwestern Bhutan; (3) south Assam, with Karbi and Dimasa in the Autonomous Districts and Bengali in Kachar; (4) north of Jammu and Kashmir, with Tibetan in Ladakh and Baltistan, and Shina and Burushaski in Gilgit; (5) northern North-West Frontier Province, with Khowar and Kohistani; and (6) Jammu, with Dogri and Hindko in eastern North-West Frontier Province (cf. Breton 1997).

Article 350(A), critical to the development of minority languages, stipulates that "[I]t shall be the endeavour of every State and of every local authority within the State to provide adequate facilities for instruction in the mother-tongue at the primary stage of education to children belonging to linguistic minority groups." Article 350(B) empowers the President of India to appoint a special officer for monitoring, investigating, and safeguarding the constitutional rights of linguistic minorities.

In sum, protection of the interests of minority language speakers in India includes establishment of facilities for learning the mother tongue, use in administration, and establishment, recognition, and promotion of minority educational institutions in general. According to the Twelfth Report of the Commissioner for Linguistic Minorities in India, facilities for instruction in minority languages at the primary education level exist in the following states and union territories: Andhra Pradesh; Bihar; Gujarat; Karnataka; Kerala; Maharashtra; Nagaland; Rajasthan; Tamil Nadu; Uttar Pradesh; West Bengal; Andaman and Nicobar Islands; Dadra and Nagar Haveli; Delhi; Goa, Daman, and Diu; and Pondicherry (Wadhwa 1975).

Minority language politics: The special case of Urdu in India

The case of the Urdu language vis-à-vis other minority languages is different, in fact special. In northern India, Hindustani was the language of the leaders and the masses in the struggle for Indian independence. Munshi (1971), for example, notes:

> In the early stages of the Constituent Assembly, the Sub-Committee on Fundamental Rights, following Gandhiji's lead, adopted the following formula: Hindustani, written either in Devanagari or the Persian script at the option of the citizen, shall, as the national language, be the first official language of the Union ... All official records of the Union shall be kept in Hindustani in both the scripts. (1971: 215)

In the aftermath of partition, however, Hindustani lost support (see Chapter 3 in this volume) and Urdu came to be viewed less favorably vis-à-vis Hindi due to its association with the Muslim League's religion-dominated politics, and also perhaps due to the fact that Urdu was made the official language of Pakistan (cf. Gopal 1966; Wadhwa 1975). The Constituent Assembly in 1949 adopted Hindi in Devanagari script as the official language of the Union.

The case of Urdu is interesting in terms of its demographic distribution and political status in different states and union territories. It is the mother tongue of a very large number of people, 43,406,932 (1991 Census) and is spoken by a significant minority in several states and union territories (see Table 6.4). It is also the official language of the state of Jammu and Kashmir, where its speakers constitute an insignificant minority (0.53 percent), and it is an additional official language in the states of Andhra Pradesh, Uttar Pradesh, and Bihar.

In response to the Urdu movement, spearheaded by the Anjuman-e-Taraqqi-e-Urdu, the Home Ministry at the center eventually issued a press note in 1958

Table 6.4. *Number of Urdu speakers in states and union territories: 1991 census data*

State or union territory	Total population (in millions)	Urdu-speaking population (in millions)	% of population
Andhra Pradesh	66.5	5.56	7.86
Bihar	64.52	7	10.42 (includes Jharkhand)
Delhi	9.42	0.51	5.91
Goa	1.16	0.04	2.81
Gujarat	41.3	0.55	1.89
Jharkhand	21.84	1.47	—
Maharashtra	78.94	5.73	7.3
Rajasthan	44	0.95	2.23
Uttar Pradesh	132	12	9.02 (includes Uttaranchal)
Uttaranchal	7	0.4	—

Source: A.R. Fatihi (2003).

dealing exclusively with Urdu and accepting its importance among minority languages. The press note addressed the issues as follows (Gopal 1966: 138–9):

(1) Facilities should be provided for instruction and examination in the Urdu language at the primary stage to all children whose mother tongue is declared by the parent or the guardian to be Urdu.
(2) Arrangements should be made for the training of teachers and for providing suitable textbooks in Urdu.
(3) Facilities for instruction in Urdu should be provided in the secondary stage of education.
(4) Documents in Urdu should be accepted by all courts and offices without the necessity of translation into any other language or script, and petitions and representations in Urdu should be accepted.
(5) Important laws, rules and regulations, and notifications should be issued in the Urdu language also in areas where this language is prevalent and which may be specified for this purpose.

According to the Twelfth Report of the Commissioner for Linguistic Minorities in India, facilities for teaching the Urdu language exist in the following states and union territories: Andaman and Nicobar; Andhra Pradesh; Bihar; Delhi; Goa, Daman, and Diu; Gujarat; Jammu and Kashmir; Madhya Pradesh; Maharashtra; Mysore (Karnataka); Punjab; Rajasthan; Uttar Pradesh; Tamil Nadu; and West Bengal (Wadhwa 1975).

Minority languages in education

A key measure in safeguarding primary education for linguistic minorities in India was provided by what is commonly known as the Three Language Formula. The formula was proposed to equalize the burden of language learning among the different linguistic regions and, at the same time, foster sociocultural integration. According to the formula, education would have to be provided in at least one language from each of the following three divisions (Mallikarjun 2001):

- The first language to be studied must be the mother tongue or the regional language.
- The second language:
  - In Hindi-speaking states the second language will be some other modern Indian language or English.
  - In non-Hindi speaking states the second language will be Hindi or English.
- The third language:
  - In Hindi-speaking states the third language will be English or a modern Indian language not studied as the second language.
  - In non-Hindi speaking states the third language will be English or a modern Indian language not studied as the second language.

These provisions for linguistic minorities notwithstanding, different states have responded differently to the implementation of the Three Language Formula: the government of Andhra Pradesh has elected to follow it faithfully, but not so the government of the state of Jammu and Kashmir. Furthermore, some states in India such as Tamil Nadu and Mizoram have in fact backed out from the compulsory provision of a *third* language, thus avoiding the teaching of Hindi.

In Pakistan, the situation is different. As a result of the emphasis on Urdu as a national language, schools have chosen to teach only Urdu and English at the expense of other local languages. Thus, in Punjab, Punjabi, even though it is officially recognized as the provincial language, is not taught in schools. Similarly, in the Northern Areas of Pakistan, where Shina, Balti, and Burushski are the regionally major language, these language are not taught in schools. One exception to this lack of vernacular language teaching is Sindhi. The emphasis on Sindhi in Sindh is a result of a strong Sindhi nationalistic movement (see Rahman 1996a: 103–32, for a detailed study).

Initiating literacy in multilingual contexts is complicated by the internal as well as the external ecology of language (Srivastava 1984b, 1987; Srivastava and Gupta 1983, 1990). Internal ecology refers to regional or sociolectal variation, of which the different lects of Hindi – High Hindi, High Urdu, and

Hindustani – provide a good illustration. The recognition of internal ecology raises an important question for initiating literacy in minority languages: which lect should be used? In the case of Tamil in Andhra Pradesh the question has to do with whether literacy should be initiated in literary Tamil or colloquial Tamil. These two varieties of Tamil, used in diglossic relationship (Britto 1986; cf. Ferguson 1959; Shanmugam Pillai 1960), pose an interesting challenge to the acquisition and spread of literacy among the Tamil minority in that region. As Shanmugam Pilliai (1960) has argued, the acquisition of reading and writing skills in literary Tamil is like learning a second language.

External ecology, on the other hand, refers to the attitudes and dispositions speakers have toward different languages/dialects of their verbal repertoire. This raises the question of whether literacy should be initiated in the mother tongue or the regional language, especially where attitude toward the mother tongue, a minority language, is unfavorable as evidenced by language shift to regional languages (Ishtiaq 1999). In the case of the state of Jammu and Kashmir, literacy is in fact initiated in a second language, Urdu or Hindi, for the majority of Kashmiri speakers. The negative consequences of initiating literacy in a second language are enumerated by Srivastava (1984b):

- it leaves many learners at the level of semi-literacy;
- it creates intellectual imbalance between standard language literacy and mass literacy;
- it downgrades the learner's mother tongue;
- it interferes with the channel for crosscultural communication that would serve as a bridge between oral and written culture;
- it generates a disharmonious relationship between functions of literacy (i.e. what literacy does for the learners) and uses of literacy (i.e. what learners do with literacy skills).

The case of Kashmiri as a minority language in literacy education is further confounded by the presence of two – Persianized and Sanskritized (B. Kachru 1981) – varieties of the language characterized by extreme digraphia: the Sanskritized variety is written in the Devanagari script from left to right, whereas the Persianized variety is written in the Perso-Arabic script from right to left. The two scripts for writing Kashmiri do not represent a freedom of choice but rather represent close ties to religious identities, as discussed by King (1997: 84): "Like it or not, the Urdu [Perso-Arabic] script *means* Muslim, the Devanagari script *means* Hindu" (emphasis original). Similar, if not the same, identity politics played a critical role in the introduction of the Roman script for the Konkani language to stress its identity as different from that of Marathi (K. S. Singh and Manoharan 1993).

The case of tribal (minor) minority languages involves additional difficulties for literacy education. In addition to the absence of a common language, the tribal communities also use different scripts in different states to write their languages. For instance, Santals use the Bengali script in West Bengal, Devanagari in Bihar, and Oriya in Orissa. Recently, due to increased consciousness regarding linguistic identity, there is an ongoing effort within the Santal community to use the Ol-Chiki script, developed by Pandit Raghunath Murmu, as a common script (Mahapatra 1989). However, as U. N. Singh (2001a) correctly notes, in such instances of multiscriptality, the development of a new set of characters for a language may not be a good option since it "may result in the obvious problem of turning all literate Santalis into illiterates overnight" (U. N. Singh 2001a: 65).

In addition to the problems associated with multiscriptality, there is also a problem with languages that have no scripts at all. For example, Shina, a major tribal language in the Northern Areas of Pakistan, has a rich oral tradition but was, until recently, not written. Recently, a few writing systems have been proposed, but there is as yet no sign of a single system acceptable to all Shina speakers. Other languages, such as Domaaki, another language spoken in the Northern Areas of Pakistan, do not have a script at all (not even in the making).

Mahapatra (1989) points out several problems in the learning and teaching of minority languages, particularly the tribal languages. The first problem pertains to geopolitical identity. Because speakers of minority/tribal languages like Bhili, Kurukh, Mundari, and Santali are spread over different states, they are unable to gain linguistic stability in terms of developing a standard. Kurukh speakers of Orissa, Mahapatra notes, insist upon an identity that is different from those living in Bihar. Similarly, Santalis are unable to convince members of their community in Orissa and West Bengal to adopt a standard uniform script. The second problem pertains to the predominantly rural character of these (tribal) minority languages: generally inaccessible and culturally closed. To quote Mahapatra (1989: 65): "In fact, the very presence of an outsider within a community is often sufficient reason to breed suspicion and hostility, infinitely more so when the mission is language learning, which demands intimate and prolonged contact, naïve intrusions, and probing interviews on subjects which the community might be hiding because of taboo, secrecy, shame, or discretion." The third problem pertains to the difference between the home language of the tribals and the school language (Pattanayak 1981). Even where the minority tribal community is bilingual in the dominant language, that language is invariably different from the standard variety which is the language of the books (ibid.: 89). Finally, there is the problem of the cultural context of learning: most minority language communities find insulated school language teaching programs an aberration, which contributes a great deal to their failure (Mahapatra 1989: 64).

The problems enumerated above present the difficulties in literacy education for minorities and, at the same time, give some understanding of the low literacy rates in minority language communities, especially the tribal communities where the literacy rate in 1971 was as low as 11.30 percent as compared to an overall literacy rate of 29.35 percent.

Minority language bilingualism

The complexity of societal multilingualism in India is best characterized in Pandit's (1977) sociolinguistic study of the Gujarati spice merchant settled in Bombay, who speaks Gujarati in his family domain, Marathi in the vegetable market, Hindi with the milkman, Kacchi and Konkani in trading circles, and (rarely) English on formal occasions. This paradigm example of South Asian multilingualism demonstrates how transplanted communities manage linguistic diversity. Srivastava (1988), quoted in K. S. Singh and Manoharan (1993: 20), captures the generalization of Indian multilingualism with reference to minority languages in the following manner:

> India as a region provides an exemplary instance of linguistic complexity ... We have lived in harmony even with split ethnicity. No wonder that the Khand tribes employ five Dravidian languages – Ko, Kuvi, Pengo, Manda, etc. and languages like Saurashtri. This came into existence through language contact situations between languages belonging to different language families (i.e., Indo-Aryan and Dravidian).

Srivastava's observation on multilingualism in India is demographically represented in Table 6.5. Notice that despite the efforts of the States Reorganization Commission, not a single state is monolingual.

The national bilingualism in India is slightly over 13 percent.[3] The rate of bilingualism among linguistic minorities is as high as 42 percent (U. N. Singh 2001a). In most cases, and especially in the case of tribal minority languages, the contact languages are mainly of the Indo-Aryan family of languages. Out of the 623 tribal communities taken up for analysis under the "People of India" (POI) project (K. S. Singh and Manoharan 1993), only 123 communities (19.74 percent) were monolingual and the remaining 500 (80.26 percent) were bilingual. For tribal minority languages, K. S. Singh and Manoharan (1993: 22) note that "[T]he second or third language may be either a minor language, a Scheduled language or even a regional language of the area in which they reside ... Apart from the official language of the State, regional languages like Chhattisgarhi, Halbi and Tulu are also spoken for intergroup communication by

[3] This figure according to Pattanayak and Khubchandani is substantially below what seems to them to be the existing multilingual realities of India.

Table 6.5. *Nature of multilingualism in the states of India (1971)*

State	Number of mother tongues reported	Percentage of minority language speakers
Andhra Pradesh	73	14.03
Assam	62	42.86
Bihar	48	55.70
Gujarat	37	9.50
Jammu and Kashmir	42	42.58
Kerala	55	4.96
Madhya Pradesh	58	21.93
Madras	70	16.83
Maharashtra	187	23.45
Mysore	87	34.83
Orissa	12	17.69
Punjab	60	44.36
Rajasthan	13	43.51
Uttar Pradesh	41	14.61
West Bengal	139	15.72

Source: Census of India.

tribal communities." The only exceptions to bilingualism among the communities in India are the Jarawa, Sentinelese, and Shompen communities of the Andaman and Nicobar islands (K. S. Singh and Manoharan 1993). Ishtiaq (1999), on the other hand, shows that the prevalence of linguistic diversity among the tribal minority language speakers as relative, from 0 percent among the Korkus in Mirpur village to 100 percent among the Korkus of Punasa, Richhi, and Udaipur villages of Khandwa Tehsil.

Language attitudes, language shift, and language attrition

Attitudes people have toward their own languages and the languages spoken around them are an essential tool to study the status of languages. In a survey of attitudes of college students conducted by one of the authors of this chapter in Pakistan in 1998, the researcher found that 56 percent of the respondents stated that they do not think it is important to study their first language (see Mahboob and Ahmar 2004, for details). Briefly, the results show that college students in Pakistan find English to be the most important language, followed by Urdu. The results also indicate that students are not supportive of their own mother tongues (other than Urdu). In their discussion of the reasons why they did not support their mother tongues, students stated that the function of these languages is restricted to what Nadkarni (1983: 153) has called "communication with people of the in-group", and therefore they do not play a large role in achieving the social and economic aspirations of the speakers. Participants in the study also feel that studying their languages in school is a waste of time because, as one student put it, "we can learn it at home."

Such attitudes toward local minority languages also signal a slow language shift of the people to major languages. The effects of such a shift can already be observed. For example, Domaaki, a language in the Northern Areas of Pakistan, has fewer than 500 speakers left. Domaaki speakers have shifted to Shina, one of the major regional languages. Another example of a language loss in progress is that of Gujarati in Pakistan. The transfer of this language from older generation to the younger generation is no longer effective. Most Gujarati speakers 30 and below can speak Gujarati, but can neither read nor write it. Another manifestation of the loss of Gujarati in Pakistan is that the number of daily newspapers in this language has decreased from four in the early 1990s to only one at present. In addition to Pakistan, the impact of language shift can be seen in Nepal and Sri Lanka, too. In the case of Nepal, Noonan (1996) states that at least four languages are on the verge of extinction. Of these, according to *Ethnologue*, one, Kusunda, is already extinct). In Sri Lanka, according to the same source, one language is already extinct and two are threatened.

Language attitudes of native speakers toward their minority language mother tongues are also leading to assimilation of minority language speakers to local dominant language groups in India (see Appendix 6.2), where language shift is more widespread in tribal minority languages. U. N. Singh (2001a: 66) notes that "although the total tribal population of India is 7.8 percent, speakers of tribal languages are only 4 percent, suggesting a language shift among the minorities." Breton (1997: 30–1) also argues that most tribes are involved in a general process of linguistic acculturation in favor of the regional language. The process of linguistic acculturation among minority language groups can be seen along a continuum, from those who have kept the tribal language as a second language and have adopted the regional language as their mother tongue to those who have become monolingual in the regional language (ibid.). Raza and Ahmad (1990) estimate that a little less than half of India's tribal population have already lost their linguistic identity and have adopted regional languages as their mother tongue. Ishtiaq (1999) claims that a positive valuation of factors such as urbanization, literacy, economy, and changes in traditional occupation and belief systems fosters language shift. Abbi (1995: 177) concurs:

> It is a sad fact that the Kurux and Kharia languages are quickly disappearing from most of the urbanized area of the Ranchi district . . . the urban tribals seldom consider it their privilege to speak their mother tongues . . . ignorance of the tribal languages is regarded as an enhancement of status and prestige. In speaking Hindi they feel superior in comparison to other fellow-tribals who cannot speak it.

Although there is overwhelming evidence of language shift among minority language groups, there are several minority ethnolinguistic groups such as Khasis, Nagas, Santals, and Khonds that show fierce language loyalty. In some cases, their language loyalties have found political expression as language movements (Ekka 1979; Mahapatra 1979). The Santali language movement is a case in point (Mahapatra 1979). In spite of a high incidence of Santali bilingualism with four state languages – in Assam 41.89 percent, Bihar 20.78 percent, Orissa 65.48 percent, and West Bengal 41.08 percent (1961 Census) – the Santalis show considerable ethnolinguistic identity and vitality. Beginning around 1938, they have mobilized to create a "great tradition" of their own rather than accept the one belonging to their neighbors (ibid.: 113), demanding, among other things, "establishment of a separate province for the aboriginal tribes of Chota Nagpur within the framework of the Government of India . . . and the introduction of Santali and other aboriginal languages as the media of instruction in schools" (ibid.: 112). The Santali language movement was thus meant to create and perpetuate new linguistic and cultural markers to defend the survival of the tribe against sociolinguistic assimilation, which ultimately succeeded in getting the language included among the scheduled languages.

Bangladesh, Nepal, and Sri Lanka

The focus of this chapter has been primarily on India and Pakistan. However, any chapter on South Asia cannot be complete without reference to Bangladesh, Nepal, and Sri Lanka.

Bangladesh, like the other South Asian countries is also a multilingual country. According to the *Ethnologue* there are thirty-eight living languages in Bangladesh belonging to four language families: Austro-Asiatic, Dravidian, Indo-European, and Sino-Tibetan. Of these, the Sino-Tibetan is the largest group with nineteen languages followed by the Indo-European family with twelve languages. However, there are more speakers of Indo-European languages than Sino-Tibetan languages.

In contrast to Pakistan, India, and Nepal, there is only one major language in Bangladesh: Bengali. Bengali, an Indo-European language, is spoken by approximately 98 percent of the population of Bangladesh. This implies that the speakers of the thirty-seven other languages spoken in Bangladesh add up to just about 2 percent of the total population of Bangladesh. In some ways, this makes the situation in Bangladesh simpler: there is only one major language and it is spoken by almost everyone as a native language (and by others as a second language). However, this overwhelming majority of one language puts the minority languages in Bangladesh in an even tighter position. Bengali is the only medium of instruction in schools in Bangladesh and no official efforts are underway to maintain or preserve other minority languages.

In contrast to India or Pakistan, where some of the minority languages are spoken by millions of people and therefore have numerical power, minority languages in Bangladesh are spoken by only small groups of people in rural areas and are therefore easily forgotten. In fact, in informal interviews conducted with ten Bangladeshis living in a campus town in the US Midwest, it was found that none of the Bengali speakers were aware of languages other than Bengali being spoken natively in Bangladesh. When some of the minority languages were named, these people either said that they had never heard the names of these languages, or that these languages were dialects of Bengali, or that they were spoken in border areas and therefore were not really languages of Bangladesh.

Nepal boasts of a linguistic treasure of 121 living languages belonging to four language families. However, a number of these languages are moribund. Noonan (1996) lists several languages as being on the verge of death, such as Chantyal, Majhi, Kumbale, Bayu, and Kusunda (according to *Ethnologue* this language is now extinct). In his study of the Chantyal people, a remote tribe of about 10,000 people in Myagdi District, Noonan states that only about 20 percent of the Chantyal people can speak their ethnic language.

Like Bangladesh, there is only one preferred medium of instruction in government schools in Nepal: Nepali. Eagle (2000) refers to a report by Shrestha and van den Hoek (1994: 46) who state that there were only two minority language schools (one for Newari and one for Magar) in Nepal in 1994. They also state that Newari used to be taught in all school in the Kathmandu Valley until 1972 when Newari (and all other languages) was replaced by Nepali as the sole medium of instruction. The 1990 Constitution of Nepal made some amends to this Nepali-only policy. It acknowledged all languages to be equal and primary education in mother tongue to be a fundamental right of every individual. According to the Ministry of Education and Sports Document dated October 27, 2004, Nepal is set to carry out the national Action Plan in primary education that will implement the three language policy between the years 2005–2007. The three languages identified are the local language, the national language (Nepali), and English (For a reconfirmation of this policy, see the following website accessed on September 7, 2005: www.moe.gov.np/documents/npad_chapter_three.php).

Sri Lanka is different from the other four countries discussed here in that there are only six living languages in Sri Lanka (one is extinct). Of these six languages, three are Indo-European, one Dravidian, and two are creole languages (one is Portuguese based and the other is Malay based). Sinhala is the official language of Sri Lanka and is spoken by approximately 72 percent of the population. Among the other languages, Tamil is the largest and is spoken by approximately three million people (approximately 16 percent of the total population).[4] The official policy is to encourage Sinhala and Tamil, the latter in

[4] The other languages are spoken by less than 100,000 people each.

its region, as media of education. English is not discouraged as a medium of instruction and has been recognized as a medium for imparting higher education.

Conclusion

All the minor languages of South Asia are facing unprecedented challenges in that increasing mobility and job-oriented life styles are making it difficult for minority-language-speaking groups to maintain their habitat and their linguistic heritage. The trend points to increasing contribution to statistics of language death, or at least significant language shift toward dominant languages from the region in spite of the pull of ethnic, religious, and other loyalties.

Further reading

The literature on minority languages in South Asia is surprisingly small, especially in the area of the sociology of minority languages (Paulston 1994): the perspective that allows us to ascertain whether and how the declining role of these languages is generally associated with issues of power and control, education and literacy, and demography, development, and planning. Two books deserve special mention: E. Annamalai's 1979 edited volume, *Language Movements in India*, and Tariq Rahman's 1996 book, *Language and Politics in Pakistan*. Both of these books, taken together, present evidence to claim, quite contrary to from the received wisdom on the fate of minority languages in the West (cf. Williams 1991), that minority languages in South Asia can become entirely free from the impediment of relative powerlessness. The authors are able to successfully show the resilience of minority languages in the context of assimilation to either the "official" or the "majority regional" language, that the minority languages become politicized as a group marker, expressed as "language movements" demanding legal recognition of their linguistic rights and representation in the sociopolitical processes.

Two papers of Srivastava (1984a, b) are excellent in terms of presenting a conceptualization of minority languages in India. These papers also discuss the literacy and educational problems of minority languages. In addition, Breton (1997) presents vital statistical and demographic data of the minority languages of South Asia. The data on bilingualism and language shift in minority (tribal) languages in India is skillfully presented in Ishtiaq (1999).

Among other useful texts: Wadhwa (1975) and Gopal (1966) are good introductions to the linguistic affairs of minority communities in India; Mansoor (1993) presents a detailed sociolinguistic investigation of Pakistan, whereas Baldauf Jr. and R. Kaplan (2000) present the linguistic situation of Nepal.

Appendix 6.1

Numerically significant minority languages in selected states and union territories of India

Andhra Pradesh			*Arunachal Pradesh*		
Telugu	56,375,755	84.8	Nissi/Daffla	172,149	19.9
Urdu	5,560,154	8.4	Nepali	81,176	9.4
Hindi	1,841,290	2.8	Bengali	70,771	8.2
Assam			*Bihar*		
Assamese	12,958,088	57.8	Hindi	69,845,979	80.9
Bengali	2,523,040	11.3	Urdu	8,542,463	9.9
Bodo/Boro	1,184,569	5.3	Santhali	2,546,655	2.9
Gujarat			*Karnataka*		
Gujarati	37,792,933	91.5	Kannada	29,785,004	66.2
Hindi	1,215,825	2.9	Urdu	4,480,038	10.0
Sindhi	704,088	1.7	Telugu	3,325,062	7.4
Madhya Pradesh			*Maharashtra*		
Hindi	56,619,090	85.6	Marathi	57,894,839	73.3
Bhili/Bhilodi	2,215,399	3.3	Hindi	6,168,941	7.8
Gondi	1,481,265	2.2	Urdu	5,734,468	7.3
Meghalaya			*Mizoram*		
Khasi	879,192	49.5	Lushai/Mizo	518,099	75.1
Garo	547,690	30.9	Bengali	59,092	8.6
Bengali	144,261	8.1	Lakher	22,938	3.3
Tamil Nadu			*Tripura*		
Tamil	48,434,744	86.7	Bengali	1,899,162	68.9
Telugu	3,975,561	7.1	Tripuri	647,847	23.5
Kannada	1,208,296	2.2	Hindi	45,803	1.7
Uttar Pradesh			*West Bengal*		
Hindi	125,348,492	90.1	Bengali	58,541,519	86.0
Urdu	12,492,927	9.0	Hindi	4,479,170	6.6
Punjabi	661,215	0.5	Urdu	1,455,649	2.1
Chandigarh			*Delhi*		
Hindi	392,054	61.1	Hindi	7,690,631	81.6
Punjabi	222,890	34.7	Punjabi	748,145	7.9
Tamil	5,318	0.8	Urdu	512,990	5.4

Source: Census of India 1991; excludes figures for Jammu and Kashmir.

Appendix 6.2

Language shift among tribal population

State/Union Territory	language shift (%)	Major tribal languages
Andhra Pradesh	64.25	Gadaba, Savara, Gondi, Khond, Koya, Kui
Arunachal Pradesh	< 1	Adi, Mishmi, Mopna, Nissi/Dafla, Nocte, Wancho
Assam	39.62	Bodo, Garo, Lushai/Mizo, Mikir, Miri/Mishing, Santali
Bihar	14.53	Kurukh/Oraon, Bhumji, Ho, Kharia, Mundari, Santali
Gujarat	92.86	Bhili/Bhilodi, Khandeshi
Himachal Pradesh	21.18	Bhotia, Kinnauri, Lahuli
Jammu and Kashmir	1.02	Balti, Ladakhi
Karnataka	74.21	Tulu, Coorgi/Kodagu
Kerala	98.31	Tulu
Madhya Pradesh	65.31	Bhili/Bhilodi, Halbi, Gondi, Kolami, Kurukh/Oraon, Korku
Maharashtra	68.78	Bhili/Bhilodi, Khandeshi, Halbi, Gondi, Korku
Manipur	< 1	Hmar, Kabui, Kacha Naga, Kuki, Mao, Paite, Tangkhul, Thado
Meghalaya	2.74	Bodo, Garo, Khasi
Mizoram	< 1	Lushai/Mizo, Tripuri
Nagaland	26.43	Ao, Angami, Chang, Lotha, Konyak, Phom, Sangtam, Sema
Orissa	49.66	Bhumij, Ho, Kharia, Mundari, Savara, Santali, Gondi, Kurukh/Oraon, Khond, Kisan, Kui, Koya
Rajasthan	29.68	Bhili/Bhilodi
Sikkim	< 1	Bhotia, Lepcha, Sherpa
Tamil Nadu	94.90	Coorgi/Kodagu, Tulu
Tripura	9.16	Mogh, Garo, Tripuri
West Bengal	20.71	Kurukh/Oraon, Bodo, Mundari, Santali
Andaman and Nicobar Islands	< 1	Kharia, Nicobarese
Dadra and Nagar Haveli	18.21	Bhili/Bhilodi
Lakshadweep	82.98	

Source: Ishtiaq (1999).

7 Tribal languages

Anvita Abbi

Introduction

It is an extremely difficult task to define what is a tribe or who is a tribal. The term "tribe" has been used since the British rulers introduced it in 1872 to describe a few select communities in India. A year earlier in 1871 they had identified supposedly "criminal" tribes by an act. This act was repealed by the Government of India in 1952, thereby denotifying these tribes. Ironically, denotifying the tribes has not removed the stigma attached to these communities, as Denotified Tribes (DNT) are still considered "criminal tribes."

Tribes or *Adivasis* in India, whether DNT or not, do not form a neat, homogenous sociocultural category. No one can demarcate a clear divide between the tribal and the nontribal in India. Yet "tribe" in India is a significant reality, characterized by a distinct way of life, rather than by virtue of forming a constituent part of the hierarchical structure of society as in the rest of India. They are outside the "caste," or "*jati*" system.

The term "tribe" is thus employed by the Constitution of India to refer to certain communities. These tribes are "scheduled" as per Article 342 of the Constitution by the President and the parliament. The concept of tribe in India is an administrative, judicial, and political concept, which is applied to sections of the population that are relatively isolated. These scheduled tribes constitute 623 varied communities (K. S. Singh and Manoharan 1993), but not even half of them speak a tribal mother tongue.

Languages spoken by these scheduled communities are considered "tribal languages." There is no linguistic definition of tribal language(s). "The tribal languages of India are not special kind of languages which could be linguistically characterized as a homogeneous group, except as languages of a special kind of people who are historically, geographically, politically, socially and culturally differentiated from other people" (Annamalai 1997b: 22).

The scholars who have provided me information on specific areas of Nepal and Pakistan have been identified in Acknowledgments (p. xvii of this volume).

Other than India and Bangladesh, no other country in South Asia uses the term "tribe" or "tribal language." Nepal uses the term "nationalities" for indigenous groups, and Pakistan uses "ethnic groups" to refer to the indigenous population of the country. Sri Lanka has no such indigenous population; Bhutan has a large number of Tibeto-Burman languages that are indigenous to the nation. I have, therefore, used the term "tribal" languages in case of India and Bangladesh, and "ethnic" languages for the other nations in the subcontinent.

Information on languages from different countries is not uniform in nature, nor are the census reports [where available] accurate. Yet I have tried to follow a somewhat uniform pattern to discuss the issues. I will discuss the status of tribal languages, the number of their speakers, their prominent speech areas and, if possible, also the areas of emerging convergence. This will be followed by the question of language shift and maintenance, which is intimately related to the inquiry into the forms and functions that these languages play in their respective societies. South Asia can indeed be conceptualized as one big continent with more similarities than differences among the countries that constitute it. However, as language policies differ from nation to nation, I will first discuss the case of India and then of Nepal, followed by Pakistan, Bangladesh, and Bhutan.

Language profile: India

The number of languages

According to the 1991 Census, 114 mother tongues are spoken by 800 million people (96.29 percent; in 1991 the Indian population was estimated to be 838,583,988). The Constitution of India recognizes only twenty two languages (generally termed "scheduled languages" as they are listed under VIII Schedule, Articles 343–351 of the Constitution and later amendments to the schedule) and the Indian states are broadly organized on linguistic basis. India represents basically five language families as listed below. The number of scheduled languages (SL) in each family is given in parenthesis.

Indo-Aryan	(scheduled languages 15)
Dravidian	(scheduled languages 4)
Austro-Asiatic	(scheduled languages 1)
Tibeto-Burman	(scheduled languages 2)
Andamanese	(scheduled languages 0)

Each of these families has its own tribal languages and its specific speech areas. Every tribal language shares a large number of linguistic features with other (nontribal) languages of the same family. Linguistically there is nothing distinct about tribal languages. Tibeto-Burman has the largest number of distinct tribal

Table 7.1. *Distribution of nonscheduled tribal languages spoken by more than a million persons in states and union territories* (1991)

Language	Number of speakers in India	States where spoken most	Number of speakers in various states
Bhili (Indo-Aryan)	5,572,308	Madhya Pradesh	2,215,399
		Rajasthan	2,258,721
		Dadra and Nagar Haveli	76,207
Bodo (Tibeto-Burman)	1,221,881	Arunachal Pradesh	1,184,569
Gondi (Dravidian)	2,124,852	Madhya Pradesh	1,481,265
		Maharashtra	441,203
Kurukh/Oraon (Dravidian)	1,426,618	Bihar	681,921
		Madhya Pradesh	393,825
		West Bengal	192,833
		Orissa	85,358
Munda/Mundari (Austro-Asiatic)	1,275,272	Assam	89,643
		Bihar	692,308
		Orissa	398,303
Santali (Austro-Asiatic)	5,216,325	Bihar	2,546,655
		Orissa	661,849
		West Bengal	1,858,010

Note: Bodo was not among the scheduled languages in 1991.
Source: Gordon, Raymond G., Jr. (ed.), 2005. *Ethnologue: Languages of the World* (15th edition). Dallas, Tex.: SIL International.

languages followed by Austro-Asiatic (Munda), Dravidian and Andamanese. The Indo-Aryan family has the least number of tribal languages in its fold.

Some of the nonscheduled tribal languages (those that are left out of the list of the twenty-two SLs mentioned above) are spoken by more than a million people (Table 7.1). Though spoken by such a large number of people, these languages in the Indian context are known as "minority" languages, because they are not included in the VIII Schedule of the Constitution.

The four-layered minority status (see Figure 7.1 below) accorded to various languages spoken by the Indian population, which is not reflective of their large communities, emerges from the flawed language policy. Out of ninety-six non-scheduled languages, ninety are tribal. This implies that tribal languages constitute almost 96 percent of total nonscheduled languages and around 28 percent of the total languages of India listed in the census.

These four-types of languages mentioned in Figure 7.1 have varying linguistic statuses in their communities, which directly correlate with the social and economic statuses of the respective speech communities. Though each language

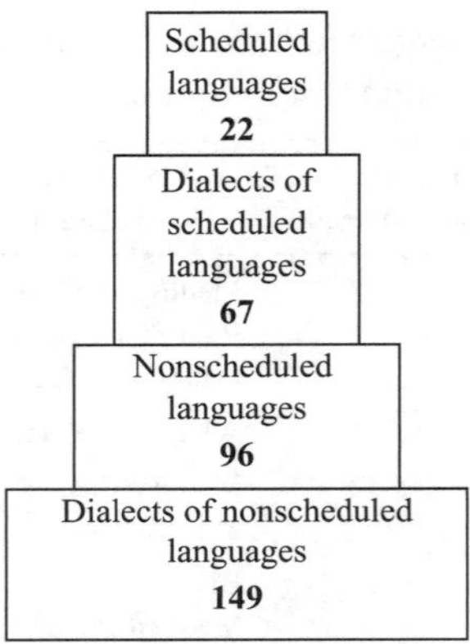

Figure 7.1. *Hierarchical status of 334 Indian languages.*

family has tribal languages as its members, at least one of the language families, Andamanese, has only tribal languages, and no scheduled language in its fold. Among the five language families of India, Tibeto-Burman has the largest number of distinct languages. In fact, this family contributes the greatest degree of linguistics diversity to the Indian scene. Only very recently, in 2003, Bodo, and a decade earlier in 1992, Meithei (or Manipuri) were given the status of an SL.

Speech areas (Geographical location)

Let us consider the geographical location and spread of the tribal languages from each of the families. See Map 7.1 on page 158.

Though tribal languages are found all over India, they are more common in some areas than others. While discussing the geographical locations and spread of these languages, it is worth mentioning (1) the density of the tribal population, (2) the percentage of tribals speaking their indigenous languages, and (3) coexistence/presence of the languages from other families creating high or low convergence areas. The last, we believe, will throw light on the nature of the "contact" of these tribal languages with other languages and their pattern of bilingualism.

The northeast

The most striking region of South Asia in terms of the area of high density of tribal languages is the northeast, represented by the Tibeto-Burman family. This area touches the border of Nepal and thus the two countries, India and Nepal, share the language family. Most of the population of this area is constituted of tribals. A large proportion of the tribal population speaks tribal languages and thus language maintenance is highest in this region as compared to other tribal areas. In the state of Meghalaya alone, language retention ratio (i.e. percentage of population speaking mother tongues) in 1981 was calculated as 99.9 percent. Between 88 and 100 percent of the population in most of the regions of the northeast retain their languages (Khubchandani 1997a: 81–2). Interestingly, languages of this region are not mutually intelligible. This has served as perhaps one of the reasons for high maintenance of the Tibeto-Burman languages. Tribal languages of this family fall into one of eight groups. Among them, nine languages of the Bodo subfamily constitute the largest group spoken by over half of the tribal population spread over the Brahmaputra valley, North Cachar hills in Assam, Mehgalaya, and Tripura (Khubchandani 1997a).

In the northeast, non-Tibeto-Burman languages are spoken only in small pockets. Thus the area of Tibeto-Burman languages does not show much convergence. Though the area of northeast includes Assam, which is an area where the Indo-Aryan language Assamese – an SL – is spoken, tribals in Assam prefer to maintain their respective languages. The entire region has contact only with English as the state language (the state of Assam is an exception), or with Hindi, which is used for intertribal communication (Abbi *et al.* 2000; K. S. Singh and Manoharan 1993). The northeast as a whole represents three major families: Tibeto-Burman, Indo-Aryan, and Mon Khmer (Austro-Asiatic). In addition to the northeast, Tibeto-Burman languages are spoken also in Himachal Pradesh. As they all are spoken in the Himalayan ranges they are popularly known as Himalayan languages.

In Nagaland alone, twenty-three indigenous linguistic communities, each speaking its respective indigenous language, are recognized by the government of Nagaland for the purpose of education. Though most of them do not have a distinct script, the Roman script is adopted for literacy and educational programs. Tibeto-Burman languages of the area also enjoy the status of being used in school at the primary level, after which the state language, English, is used for higher education. In general, people in this region are proud of their languages and cultures.

Jharkhand

The second region rich in tribal languages is the state of "Jharkhand". The area is inhabited by the tribals of the Munda and Dravidian language families as well as by speakers of SLs and their various dialects. Jharkhand was carved out of Southern Bihar in 2000 (see Map 7.2a on page 160).

However, Jharkhand as originally proposed, covered a wider area spread across four adjacent states, namely Bihar, Bengal, Orissa, and Madhya Pradesh (see Map 7.2b). Tribals belonging to the Munda group are believed to be among the original inhabitants of India.

In Jharkhand, as in the northeast, 70 to 100 percent of the tribals speak their mother tongues (mainly as a home language), a larger number maintaining their

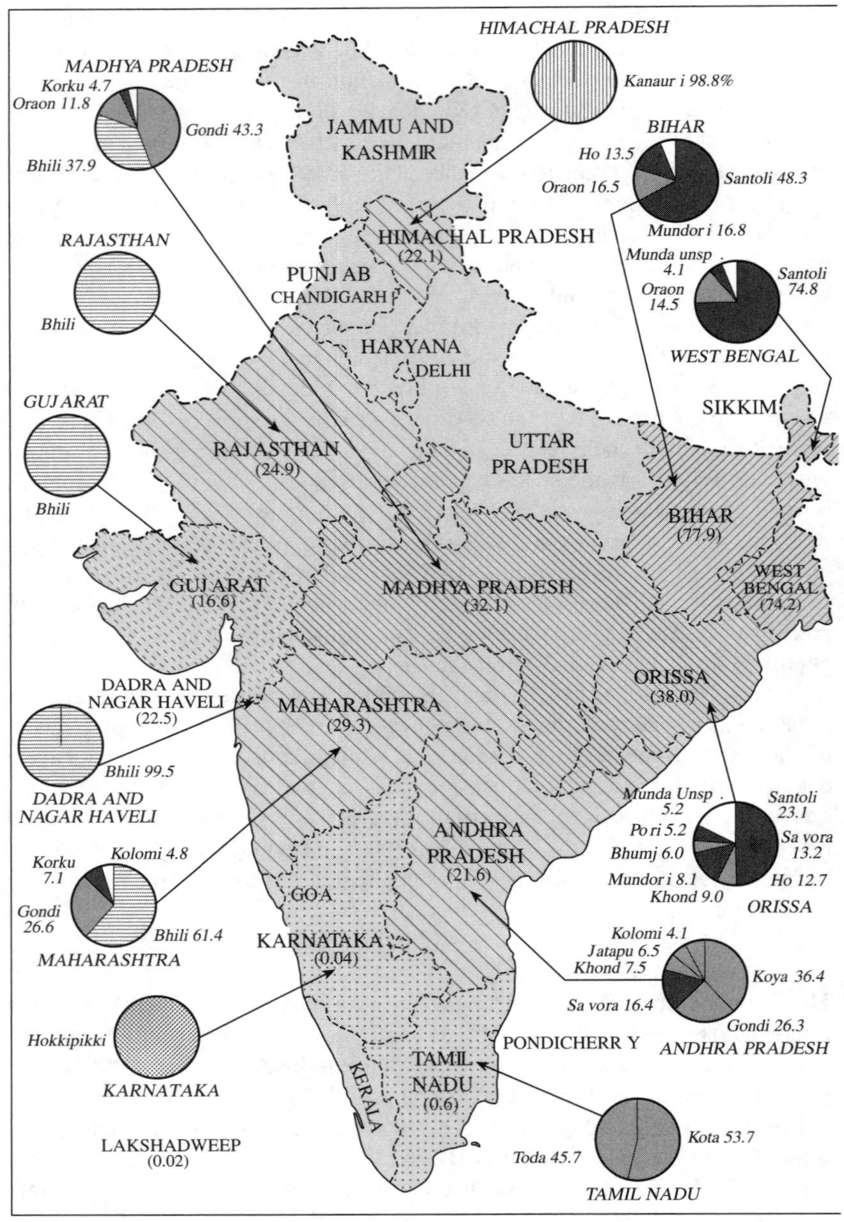

Map 7.1 *Distribution of tribal languages*. Distributed by *The Central Institute of Indian Languages, Mysore, India.*

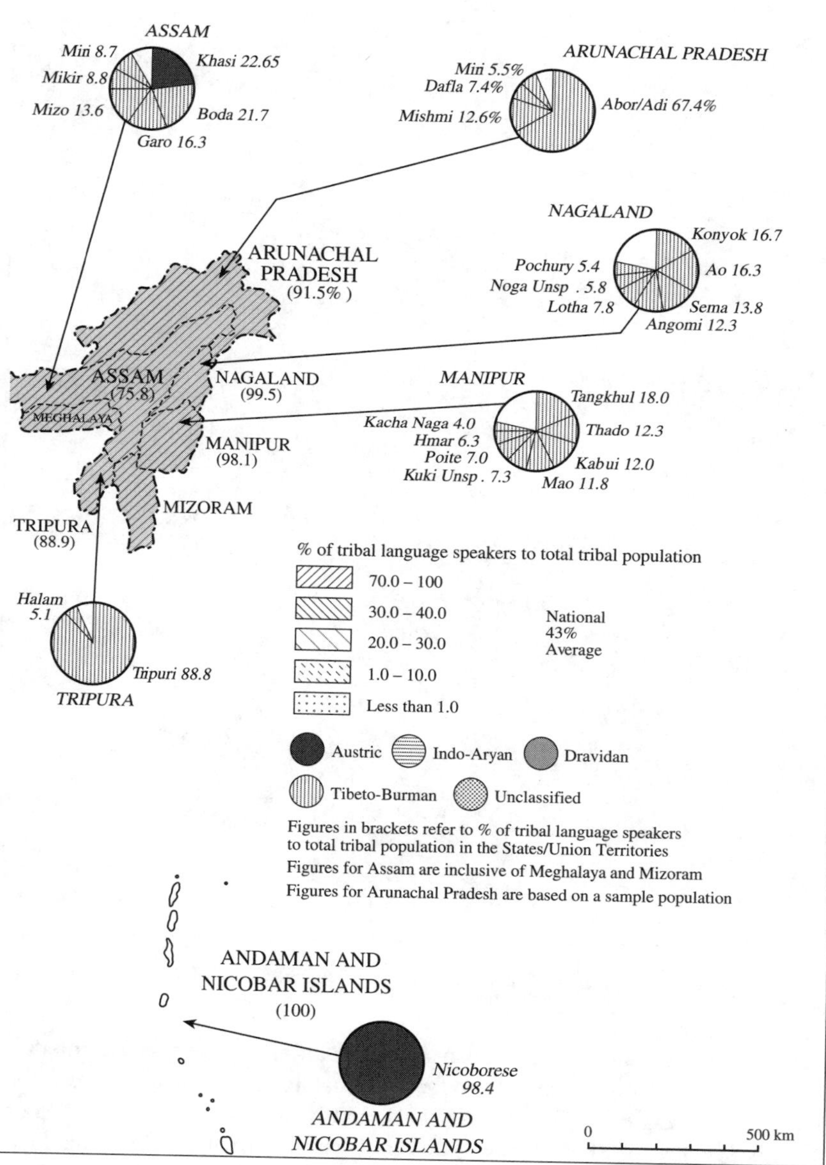
ASSAM
Miri 8.7
Mikir 8.8
Mizo 13.6
Khasi 22.65
Boda 21.7
Garo 16.3
ARUNACHAL PRADESH
Miri 5.5%
Dafla 7.4%
Mishmi 12.6%
Abor/Adi 67.4%
NAGALAND
Konyok 16.7
Pochury 5.4
Noga Unsp . 5.8
Lotha 7.8
Ao 16.3
Sema 13.8
Angomi 12.3
ARUNACHAL PRADESH (91.5%)
ASSAM (75.8)
MEGHALAYA
NAGALAND (99.5)
MANIPUR (98.1)
MIZORAM
TRIPURA (88.9)
MANIPUR
Tangkhul 18.0
Kacha Naga 4.0
Hmar 6.3
Poite 7.0
Kuki Unsp . 7.3
Thado 12.3
Kabui 12.0
Mao 11.8
% of tribal language speakers to total tribal population
70.0 – 100
30.0 – 40.0
20.0 – 30.0
1.0 – 10.0
Less than 1.0
National 43% Average
Halam 5.1
Tripuri 88.8
TRIPURA
Austric
Indo-Aryan
Dravidan
Tibeto-Burman
Unclassified
Figures in brackets refer to % of tribal language speakers to total tribal population in the States/Union Territories
Figures for Assam are inclusive of Meghalaya and Mizoram
Figures for Arunachal Pradesh are based on a sample population
ANDAMAN AND NICOBAR ISLANDS (100)
Nicoborese 98.4
ANDAMAN AND NICOBAR ISLANDS
0
500 km

Map 7.2a *Map of Jharkhand. 'Maps of India'* Govt. of India.

languages in rural areas than in urban areas. The difference between the tribals of the northeast and those of Jharkhand lies in the nature of the language *contact* and linguistic *convergence*. The tribals of Jharkhand are in contact in greater numbers with the speakers of other language families (such as those of Dravidian and Indo-Aryan) than those of the northeast. Intertribal contact among the people of Jharkhand has a history of more than 2,000 years leading to language change in

Map 7.2b *Map of proposed Jharkhand.* In *Tribal and Indigenous Languages of India: The Ethnic Space*. Edited by Anvita Abbi. Delhi: Motilal Benarsidass, 1997. p. 132.

the area of grammar (see Abbi 1995a). Consequently, language shift has taken place in larger numbers and at a faster pace here than in the northeast.

Lakshadweep

The area included in the small islands of Lakshadweep, formerly known as Laccadive and Minicoy Islands, is inhabited by speakers of an Indo-Aryan tribal language, Mahl, which is closer to Sinhalese than to any other Indo-Aryan language spoken in the region. The Mahls are multilinguals in Malayalam, Urdu, and Arabic. The educated Mahls know English as well. Mahls constitute the major population of the island and are proud to retain their language at home and outside it. Their language is used for education.

South India

The tribals of south India, largely concentrated in the Nilgiri Hills, speak different languages of the Dravidian family. The significant languages, such as Toda, Kota, Kurumba, and Paniya are surrounded by one or the other SL of the Dravidian family, leading to a high rate of bilingualism. The literacy rate of these tribals is higher than the literacy rate of the tribal people in the rest of the country. Yet, contrary to expectations, higher literacy does not always lead to language attrition. Todas and Kotas are known to maintain their languages both in urban and rural settings. Tribal languages in the rest of south India have been known to shift to other dominant languages easily. For instance, speakers of Gondi, a Dravidian language, spoken in the middle of the Dravidian speech community of Telugu, an SL, are known to shift to Telugu in high numbers. South India thus does not present a homogenous picture of language maintenance and language shift.

Western India

The other regions of India, such as western India, are represented by only 20 to 30 percent of the tribals speaking their indigenous languages. They are surrounded by the SLs and non-SLs of the same family and thus represent low convergence areas. For instance, Bhili, an Indo-Aryan tribal language, is surrounded by various dialects of Gujarati in Gujarat, Rajasthani in Rajasthan, and by Marathi in Maharashtra.

Andaman and Nicobar Islands

The last region to be discussed is the Andaman and Nicobar Islands in the Bay of Bengal. As the total numbers of speakers of these languages have been depleting very fast and now number no more than a few hundred, the Government of India does not even report them in the census as the government takes cognizance of only those languages that are spoken by 10,000 speakers or more. The languages of Nicobar Island are called Nicobarese and belong to the Austro-Asiatic family of the non-Munda branch. The Andamanese languages form a distinct family about which very little is known. The tribals of the Andaman Islands are of the Negrito group and have been living there for the last 20,000 years. They are the Great Andamanese (a generic term used for disparate groups living in Strait Island and speaking mutually intelligible languages), the Onge, the Jarawa, and the Sentinelese. Most of them have been victims of constant marginalization and colonization of various types. The Great Andamanese has been wiped out as a viable community. The community, which had an estimated 3,000 members about 150 years ago, is today left with only about thirty-six members. The Onges of Little Andaman (they call it Egubelong) today number only ninety-six. They lead an isolated life and there is a constant threat to their existence as they have been time and again deprived of their forests and land in the name of development. This area can be marked as a very high intensity maintenance area as almost all the tribals, no matter how small in number, maintain their languages. As the tribals live in government-marked reservation areas, contact with mainland dwellers is little, though some young male members of the society have acquired a variety of Hindi spoken in the area. An intensive study on these languages is urgently warranted. These languages are in the true sense endangered languages.

The 1981 Census recorded five tribes with a single speaker (s/he may not be there by now), seventeen tribes with a population of two to ten persons each, sixteen tribes with eleven to fifty persons each, nine tribes with fifty-one to hundred persons each, and seventeen tribes with 101 to 500 persons each. The 1991 Census found it convenient to ignore the whole issue.

The rural–urban divide

The divide between rural and urban tribals plays a role in language retention and shift. My earlier study (Abbi 1995a) shows that the urban tribals seldom consider it a privilege to speak their mother tongues. On the contrary, ignorance of the tribal languages is regarded as an enhancement of status and prestige. In speaking Hindi or the regional contact language, they feel superior in comparison to other fellow tribals who cannot speak it.

A very low percentage of urban tribals is monolingual in its use of ancestral languages. Ethnolinguistic minority status induces a negative attitude toward language loyalty. A gradual adoption of a nontribal language as mother tongue presents a classic case of language shift. Generally, these symptoms are diagnostic of potential language death.

"Mother tongues" and "foster mother tongues": Language loyalty and claimed identity

Discrepancy between what is claimed as a mother tongue and what really exists is wide. Claiming a language as mother tongue is different from actually using it as a mother tongue. A sense of inferiority, awareness of their lowly status in the society, and anxiety to be associated with the "superior" groups discourages people from declaring their traditional languages as mother tongues. In reality they speak and use their traditional languages in the home domain but refuse to admit it. This is especially true of many of the Munda and Dravidian tribes in general. Fieldwork reports reveal that even those tribes and communities who claim to have lost their traditional languages maintain them in home domains. This is true of tribals as well as of the migrant communities living in various states. It is the low prestige associated with their indigenous languages that motivates them to shift their *loyalty claim*. The "claimed mother tongues" that are reported in various census reports are at best *foster mother tongues*. Most of our rural tribals do not really fit into the molds of "terminal speakers" (Dressler 1991) or "semispeakers" (Dorian 1981). Instead, a large number of them may be considered "healthy speakers" or, particularly those in the northeast and Jharkhand, "thriving speakers."

Convergence areas

Because of such patterns in language shift and change in language loyalty, some areas of India are emerging as strong convergence areas, such as Maharashtra,

Jharkhand, Madhya Pradesh (North-Central), Bengal, Orissa, and Chattisgarh. These areas are marked by several tribal languages surrounded by nontribal languages and the motivation for the speakers of tribal languages to shift to any SL and its dialects is very strong.

Contact languages

Heterogeneity of languages is a significant part of tribal life. Tribals are multilingual and adapt to new languages without any qualms. Theirs is an oral culture and thus easily lends itself to the emergence of new languages. Several different tribal groups have evolved one common lingua franca or contact language for intertribal communication and are not concerned when this common language is named differently in different regions. For instance, the Mundas of Chotanagpur area (Santali, Mundari, Ho, Kharia speakers) communicate with Dravidian tribals (Kurux, Kui, Kisan) in Sadari/Sadani (an Indo-Aryan language) which is identified by different labels such as Nagpuria, Khortha, and Kurmali. A large section has adopted the language as their mother tongue. Similar is the case of Halbi – a hybrid of Gondi (Dravidian), and Chattisgarhi and Marathi (Indo-Aryan) languages of Madhya Pradesh and Maharashtra.

In Nagaland (northeast region) many contact languages have emerged despite several hostile language groups claiming separate identities. A new language Zeliangrong is a hybrid of Zemi (spoken in Nagaland), Liangmei (spoken in Manipur), and Rongmei (spoken in the Cacher district of Assam). The word "Zeliangrong" is an acronym derived by juxtaposing the first syllables from these three languages. Another contact language, called Chakesang, has emerged in Kohima from three distinct languages Chokri, Khezha, and Sangtam. What is most encouraging is that speakers speaking these languages also share a common identity. Such cultural and linguistic assimilation can only come from within the society.

Bilingualism, language shift, and language maintenance

Bilingualism among tribals is 50 percent more than the national average for bilingualism. Linguists generally maintain that group bilingualism is unusual (Paulston 2000: 30). They also believe that the road to language shift is by bilingualism, often with exogamy. However, this is not entirely true of the South Asian situation. South Asia has been multilingual for thousands of years without posing a great threat to any particular language or culture of a community. Language maintenance has been the rule and not an exception (Gumperz and Wilson 1971; Pandit 1972). This phenomenon can still be attested in the speech of the migrant communities within the country as well as those living outside the country.

The question arises as to why and how tribals and other minority communities manage to retain their languages when the forces of urbanization and bilingualism, labels of "minority" and "low status," must be operating as significant factors to encourage language shift. The answer lies in the nature of the multilingualism that prevails in India, lack of educational and other opportunities to climb the social ladder as well as in the cultural and psychological attitude that the speakers of these "minor" languages possess. The foremost factor among these is that South Asian multilingualism is of a coexisting and not of a competing nature, which allows a speaker to assign different domains to different languages. In other words, functional specialization of different languages has identified the role of the real mother tongue (the indigenous language) for intratribe communication (Gumperz and Wilson 1971). This factor certainly has helped people retain their languages even if they claim otherwise.

Second, literacy programs and other educational opportunities that are easily available to SL speakers are missing in the tribal regions. Ironically, this has served as a significant factor aiding mother-tongue maintenance.

Third, an important reason for mother-tongue retention has been the *cultural and psychological makeup* of the speakers toward their languages. More than an identity marker, the mother tongue has been seen as a "personal matter" satisfying a psychological need, something which is outside the bounds of external intervention. One's mother tongue is more like a way of life, which one does not change easily. Mother tongues are seen in the same light as one's food habits, one's religious beliefs, and one's living habits.

Adherence to mother tongue could also be due to political and economic gains. Language revivalism, not language loyalty or love of language, could be a contributing factor in mother-tongue retention (see below).

The bipolar pull of language retention and adoption of other languages without resistance has brought amazing contact-induced changes in the tribal mother tongues. Tribal languages have been found to restructure their grammars incorporating linguistic material from more than one language in contact.

However, South Asia is full of contradictions. We do observe heavy to modest language shift in some areas. Any language shift that we encounter as reported in Table 7.2 is an outcome of various factors, among which the following are significant.

(1) inferiority complex of the mother tongue speakers;
(2) economic benefits of learning the dominant language;
(3) facility to learn the dominant language as part of free schooling in the language concerned;
(4) low tolerance of the dominant language speakers toward the minority language speakers.

Table 7.2. *Language shift among Indian tribals in various Indian states*

Language shift (%)	Indian states
<1	Sikkim, Meghalaya, Arunachal Pradesh, Manipur, Mizoram, Nagaland, Andaman and Nicobar
1–10	Jammu and Kashmir
10–20	Bihar including Jharkhand
20–40	Himachal Pradesh, Rajasthan, West Bengal, Assam
40–80	Madhya Pradesh including Chattisgarh, Maharashtra, Orissa, Karnataka, Andhra Pradesh
>80	Gujarat, Kerala, Tamil Nadu, Lakshadweep, Uttar Pradesh, Goa, Diu, Daman

Source: Ishtiaq (1999).

According to one estimate, almost half of the tribal languages have ceased to be mother tongues. Eagerness to assimilate to the higher group in the social ladder has been the key factor for language shift.

Language endangerment has two manifestations. One is when the speech community itself starts dwindling. This is the case of the Andamanese. They are endangered tribes and so are their languages. The second is when speakers start shifting to some other language in large numbers, usually to the major regional language. This is a common factor operating in the Dravidian tribal languages. Dravidian tribal languages in south India are on the verge of endangerment because of very high percentage of language shift reported due to the likelihood of political and economic gains. Languages of Jharkhand, mainly those of the Munda family, are not in danger right now, but in the future, say in about one hundred or two hundred years, they will surely be so. At present they are spoken widely as home languages.

Languages start their journey to obsolescence and death when they cease to be used in homes. When either of the parents stops using their mother tongue with their children, it is a sure sign that the language has set on its path to death. This is what is happening at present among Kurux (Dravidian) speakers in urban areas of Jharkhand. Children are punished for speaking their mother tongues at home. Fortunately, all languages of Jharkhand are not in the same situation.

A redeeming factor is that not all tribal language speakers see their mother tongues as deprived languages. A case in point is Santali. Various movements of language loyalists in the past fifty years have revived this tribal language. It is used as a medium of instruction in villages at the primary level as well as for publication of magazines and journals. An independent script by the name of "Ol Chiki" has been created to write the language. Interestingly, Ol Chicki is now adopted by some other tribal languages in order to maintain a tribal

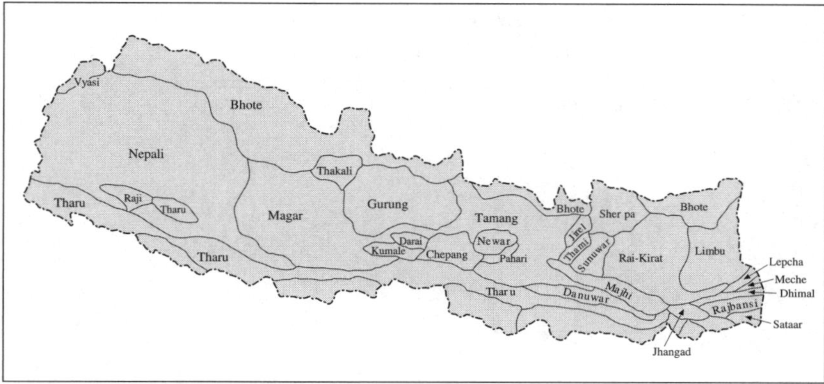

Map 7.3 *Ethnic languages of Nepal.* Based on *Nepal-Social Demography and Expression* by Hark Gurung. New ERA Kathmandu, Nepal 1998.

identity. Many schools in the Jharkhand area are known to use Ol Chiki for primary education despite the resistance from the tribals to learn their mother tongue in school domain. These conflicting behaviors by tribals indicate a common aspiration to be a part of the main stream and yet maintain their distinct identity and way of life.

Language profile: Nepal

Linguistically, the languages of Nepal represent four distinct language families, namely Dardic (Indo-Aryan, Indo-European), Bodish, Eastern Himalayan, Baric (Tibeto-Burman), Munda (Austro-Asiatic), and Dhangar and Kurux (North Dravidian).

The new Constitution of Nepal (1990) recognizes Nepali as the official language (*raashtra bhaashaa*) and all others as national languages (*raashtriiya bhaashaa*). It recognizes sixty-one diverse nationalities identified by "their own unique religions, languages, and dialects and their own outstanding and intriguing ways of life."[1] These nationalities are divided into four major groups according to the topographic distribution of each nationality (see Map 7.3 above). Thus, Himalayan nationalities include twenty-one groups (0.7 percent of the total population), Hill nationalities, twenty-three diverse groups (25.1 percent), Inner Madhesh region, seven groups (1.1 percent), and Terai, ten groups (7.9 percent). Nearly 43 percent of the population of Nepal constitutes these nationalities and is indigenous population. Out of these sixty-one nationalities the most prominent ones are given in Table 7.3.

[1] 'The Nationalities of Nepal' by Ukyab and Adhikari (2000).

Table 7.3. *Distribution of nationalities as a percentage of total population*

Nationalities	Percentage
Magars	7.2
Tharus	6.5
Newars	5.6
Tamangs	5.5
Rais	2.8
Gurungs	2.4
Limbus	1.6

The rest of the nationalities constitute less than 1 percent. For example, Raute is spoken by merely 2,878 speakers. Nepal thus identifies and recognizes the mother tongues of groups other than Nepali-speaking groups as national languages. The criterion used by National Language Policy Recommendations Commission for inclusion of a language is that the speakers constitute a minimum threshold of 1 percent of the total population of the country. Further, the recognition of various languages implies development of these languages for educational purposes as well as purportedly saving them from extinction. This task is undertaken in a planned manner. Table 7.4 indicates the status of various ethnic languages in Nepal.

Table 7.4. *Status of ethnic languages in Nepal*

Language	Stage of development	Availability of written tradition
Limbu	Most developed	Yes
Tharu, Tamang, Magar, Gurung, Rai (some dialects), Thakali, Sherpa, Rajbanshi	Less developed	In the process of developing written tradition
Chapang, Jirel, Rai (some dialects), and thirty odd languages	Least developed	No written tradition
Raute or Khamchi and Rai (some dialects)	Dying languages	

The government policy envisages preparing teaching materials in each of these (except the dying languages) so that mother tongues could be used for instructional purposes in schools.

The new Constitution recognizes Nepal as a multiethnic and multilingual country. Radio Nepal has been broadcasting programs in Tamang, Tharu, Rai-Bantawa, Limbu, Magar, and Gurung since 1994. This provides opportunities to various nationalities to develop their languages for education and radio broadcasting, urging audiences at times to establish an identity either on the basis of language or on the basis of an ethnic group. Examples are Tamangs and Tharus. Tamang speakers constitute 5 percent of the total population. Tamang is basically a mixture of a variety of Tibeto-Burman languages. Thus Tamangs are in search of an ethnic group to establish their own separate identity. Conversely, Tharus are one of the oldest identifiable ethnic groups in Nepal but do not speak a language separate from regional Indo-Aryan variants such as Maithili, Bhojpuri, and Awadhi. "The Tamangs and Tharus are each working on opposite ends equating language with ethnicity, an equation put into effect by Nepal's new language policy" (Sontaag 1995: 118).

Language shift and retention

According to Watters (2001), the languages of Nepal can be categorized into two broad divisions : "moribund" and "endangered." The former term refers to languages that have less than 1,000 speakers, such as Lingkhim, Chhintang, Chukwa (all three are nearly extinct), Raute, and Koi. Endangered languages, on the other hand, are those that have between 1,000 and 100,000 speakers. These are approximately 100 in number at present. Watters compares two important studies, one that was undertaken by Gurung (1997) and the other the Census of 1991, to study the language retention and shift among the "moribund" and "endangered" languages of Nepal. Unlike in the case of India, language retention is higher in Nepal among the ethnic communities. However, the highest rate of shift is around 80 percent in Bote-Majhi, followed by 52 percent in Kagate, Kumhali, Palpa, and others. Nationalities like Sherpa shift marginally (only 0.08 percent). see Table 7.5.

Table 7.5. *Average mother-tongue shift in major geographical regions of Nepal*

General Area	Average shift %
Average shift group	66.5
Central Hill group	52.4
Eastern Hill group	15.2
Terai group	14.2
Mountain group	5.6

Source: Based on Watters 2001.

Language profile: Pakistan

As the Census of 1991 for Pakistan is not available due to political reasons, the following figures and statements are based on 1981 Census and/or the Summer

Institute of Linguistics Publication, *Ethnologue* 1996. The major families that represent ethnic languages are Iranian (Indo-European), Dravidian, and Dardic (Indo-Aryan, Indo-European). Iranian ethnic languages that occupy the North-West Frontier Province (NWFP) are Dehwari, Baluchi, Ormuri (Western Iranian), Pushto (nontribal) Wantesi, Yidgha, and Wakhi. Among the Dravidian languages the prominent one is Brahui spoken by more than one million people, who constitute about 1.21 percent of the total population. As Pakistan makes no distinction between tribal and nontribal languages, we will restrict our discussion to known ethnic languages of the region. The major ethnic languages and their speakers (given in parenthesis), according to the *Ethnologue*, are Brahui (1,500,000), Khowar in its various dialects (188,000 to 222,800), Kalasha (2,900 to 5,700), Kohistani (220,000), Burushaski (55,000 to 60,000), Balti (270,000), and Shina (450,000 to 500,000) (see Map 7.4 below). These are discussed in their geographical order.

North

Shina, Balti, and Burushaski are the major languages of the north, while Wakhi (6,000 speakers) and Domaaki (only 500 speakers) are the minor ones. Shina is used mainly in local domains for intratribal communication or for political (election) purposes (Rahman 1996a: 217). Balti speakers, though they are willing to send their children to Balti schools, if available, are known to shift toward the dominant language, Burushaski or Urdu, for socioeconomic reasons. Similar is the fate of Wakhi and Domaaki (see Table 7.6 given below). Burushaski speakers, though bilingual, have a positive attitude toward their language. Efforts are being made to evolve a script for it so that it can be used for educational purposes. It is also used for radio broadcast. Its influence is seen on other minor neighboring languages such as Domaaki and Wakhi, whose speakers are shifting toward Burushaski.

Northwest

Another important language, or rather, mixture of mutually intelligible dialects with 90 percent shared vocabulary among them, is Kohistani, spoken by approximately 220,000 speakers in the northwestern part of Pakistan. Kohistani speakers are very proud of their language and want it to be used for education. Khowar[2] (*kho* "people" + *war* "language," i.e., language of the Kho people) is

[2] Khowar is the language in which British army officers were to acquire proficiency within three months before they were posted in Chitral district failing which they were denied the *gasht* allowance (i.e. the allowance given to officers for patrolling the area). Ironically, *gasht* allowance is still given to the officers posted in the area but the requirement of learning Khowar has been replaced by that of learning Pashto.

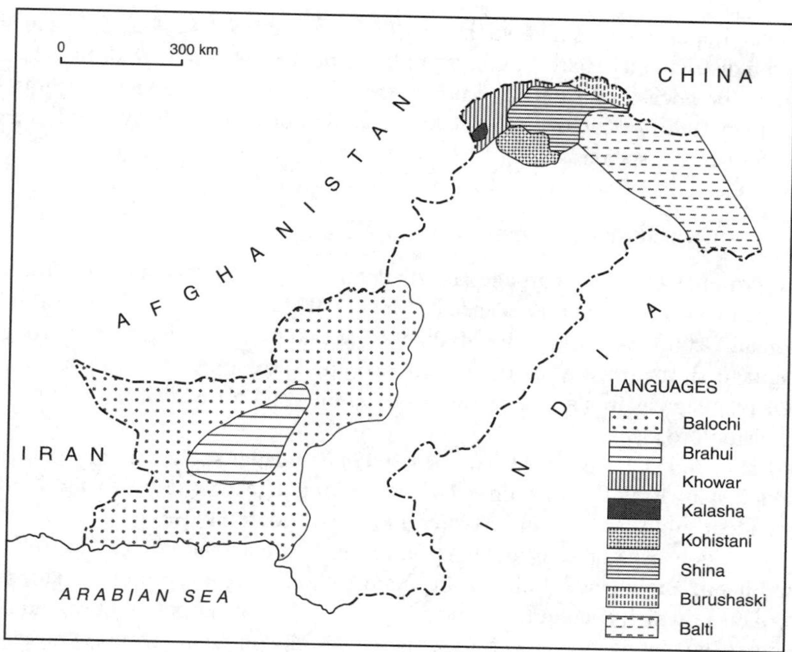

Map 7.4 *Ethnic languages of Pakistan.* Based on *Atlas of Pakistan.* By survey of Pakistan. Rawalpindi, 1985. p. 64. Note that it includes the disputed territories of the state of Jammu and Kashmir.

Table 7.6. *Ethnic languages and number of speakers (under 10,000)*

Languages	Number of speakers
Yidgha [Indo-Iranian]	5,000–6,000
Dameli [Indo-Aryan, Dardic]	5,000
Kati [Indo-Aryan, Nuristani]	3,700–5,100
Ormuri [Indo-Iranian]	3,000
Kalasha [Indo-Aryan, Dardic]	2,900–5,700
Ushojo [Indo-Aryan, Dardic]	2,000
Chilisso [Indo-Aryan, Dardic]	1,600–3,000
Kamviri [Indo-Aryan, Nuristani]	1,500–2,000
Gawar-Bati [Indo-Aryan, Dardic]	1,500
Domaaki [Indo-Aryan, Dardic]	500
Gawro [Indo-Aryan, Dardic]	200

another important language spoken in the extreme northwest of Pakistan in Chitral district and in parts of Gilgit. It is used for education and trade as well as in radio broadcasts. Written literature in the language is traced back to 1680 CE (Rahman 1996a). Language maintenance is high despite the heavily bilingual behavior of the speakers.

Central and Southern Pakistan

The prominent ethnic languages in the central region of Pakistan are Ormuri (Iranian: 3,000 speakers), Wanetsi (Iranian: 90,000 speakers), and Balochi (Iranian: 1,000,000). Ormuri and Wanetsi speakers are known to go through language shift in heavy numbers, whereas the speakers of Balochi maintain their language as it is a literary language and is used for education, radio, and television broadcasts.

Brahui and Dehwari are the two prominent languages spoken in the region of Baluchistan. Brahui is the only Dravidian language belonging to the North Dravidian group spoken in Pakistan and is considered close to its sister languages such as Kurux, spoken in India and Nepal, and Malto, spoken in Jharkhand. Brahui and Balochi are major ethnic languages of Pakistan, the speakers of which constitute around 5 percent of the total population. Brahui is a major tribal language spoken by 1.21 percent of the population and is known to be maintained by its speakers in various domains, such as in education, written literature, radio and television broadcasts, and publishing (newspapers and weeklies). Brahui is highly converged with Balochi yet it stands as an independent language.[3] Dehwari is an Iranian language, spoken by an estimated 10,000 speakers (the exact figure is not known) and is heavily influenced by Brahui.

Southwest

A language overlapping with one spoken in Afghanistan is Kati (spoken by 3,700 to 5,000 people) of the Nuristani family, considered an intermediate form between Iranian and Indo-Aryan. A larger group of speakers of this language is in Afghanistan.

The ethnic language speakers of Pakistan, excluding Brahui and Balochi, constitute no more than 3 percent of the population. Here, as in the case of India, social bilingualism has not led to language obsolescence or extinction. Language shift, though noted at several places, has not engulfed the whole community.

[3] Brahui (also spelt as Brahvi) and Balochi have been considered as one ethnic group speaking two different varieties of the same language by nationalists in the past. For details see Rahman (1996a).

Yet, in case of a few languages where mother tongues are retained as home languages, modernization and educational promotional measures have motivated a second language adoption (and in some cases, language shift).

Language profile: Bangladesh

The demographic figures for Bangladesh are not very accurate as the censuses after the independence of the nation in 1971 do not give a very clear picture. The projected estimate by Breton (1997) provides a somewhat plausible scenario. The official projection of 1981 Census lists 558,000 speakers (0.65 percent of total population) of tribal languages. The prominent languages and their projected number of speakers are Santali (135,000), Kurux or Oraon (110,000), and Garo (170,000). Many Tibeto-Burman languages such as Kokborok (75,000), Mru (18,000), Bom (7,000), Pankua (3,000), Chak (6,000), Khyang (2,000), Kumi (2,000), and Mizo (1,000) are minor languages that share their speech areas with India. Other than Indo-Aryan language speakers, who constitute 99.3 percent of the total population, Dravidian, Austro-Asiatic, and Tibeto-Burman languages each have their share of tribal languages spoken in the area. Due to lack of any substantial sociolinguistic research not much can be said about language shift and bilingualism patterns demonstrated by these tribal speakers. The fact that all these languages, despite being spoken by very small numbers, are used in home domain, is encouraging.

Language profile: Bhutan

As far as the situation of Bhutan is concerned, the nontribal major language Nepali represents the Indo-Aryan family and the ethnic language Dzongkha and its various dialects represent the Tibeto-Burman family in the region. Again, serious demographic studies of tribal languages and their bilingualism patterns are not available.

Conclusion

This review of tribal languages of South Asia reveals the following facts. The first is that most tribal languages are surrounded by nontribal languages. They are not isolated linguistically. Bilingualism, which appears to be a natural outcome, is higher in the tribal communities than in other communities of the various nations. However, Andamanese seems to be an exception.

The second is that tribal languages survive, and are maintained, in the subcontinent despite the absence of support factors, such as institutional status, because these languages provide two significant elements of vitality, namely, marking distinct identity and facilitation of intergroup communication.

The third is that contact with other languages has given rise to several lingua francas that the tribals use for intertribal communication.

The fourth is that though tribal languages in the case of India are maintained in the home domain, Hindi has emerged as a contact language in each tribal belt for intertribal and wider communication. This emergence is in addition to the lingua francas mentioned above.

The fifth is that language endangerment is higher in India than in any other nation in the subcontinent. The language policy of India, and a lack of will on the part of tribals to maintain their mother tongues are two significant factors contributing to the threat of extinction of such languages. In many South Asian countries it is observed that the will to disassociate from the indigenous language is stronger than the will to use it as an identity marker.

Finally, larger efforts are made in Nepal than in India and Pakistan to use these languages for literacy and educational programs. Many tribal languages, such as the various Tibeto-Burman languages of India and Nepal, Austro-Asiatic languages of India, and some Iranian languages of Pakistan, are used for radio broadcasts, publication of journals as well as primary education. The situation may appear to be encouraging but, considering the sheer number of speakers and the variety of the languages involved, these efforts are small and inadequate.

Part 3

Sanskrit and traditions of language study

8 Sanskrit in the South Asian sociolinguistic context*

Madhav M. Deshpande

Introduction

Sanskrit as a language has had a life span of more than thirty-five hundred years. Like the proverbial nine lives of a cat, Sanskrit has survived in changing circumstances, some of which we do not yet fully understand. Its manifestations range from its near-mother-tongue usage to its ritualized, technical, narrative, and poetic forms. Its changing geography extends from its original home in the northwestern corner of the Indian subcontinent to its use as a language of high social, literary, and political culture to a region extending from Central Asia to Cambodia and Vietnam, but most importantly surviving as the classical language of the Indian subcontinent. There must have been a time when a form of Sanskrit was a mother tongue of some Indo-Aryan group, and yet with all the sources available to us, we are today unable to recover that stage of Sanskrit. What we have is mostly a picture of Sanskrit embedded in a social context where it is a language of high prestige, but a language that must coexist and compete with other Indo-Aryan and non-Indo-Aryan languages. The sociolinguistic context of Sanskrit must be recovered from this massive literary, geographical, and social environment.

M. B. Emeneau remarks (Deshpande 1979b, foreword, 1):

> In the earliest period speakers of Indo-Aryan – Vedic and living Sanskrit – were concerned with neighboring languages, whether they were other varieties of Indo-Aryan or were non-Indo-Aryan; the historical dimension had hardly yet come into play. Thereafter, when Sanskrit was no longer a living language but was a language of high prestige that had ceased to be anyone's first language, the concern was essentially an evaluation of various vernaculars as against the classical language. The situation was complicated by the circumstance that some "Protestant" communities combined an adversary position on the language with an adversary stance against the religious and social doctrines and practices of Hinduism.

* This chapter is a revised version of Chapter 1 in Deshpande (1993).

Studies by this author have attempted to disentangle the complicated sociolinguistic factors involved in these different phases of the Indian linguistic history (see Deshpande 1978, 1979a, b, 1985a, b, 1991, 1992, 1993, 1994, 1996, 1999; Deshpande and Bronkhorst 1999; Deshpande and Hook 1979). The current discussion presents a brief account of these factors.

Sociolinguistic attitudes in Vedic India

The literary record of India begins with the Ṛgveda, a collection of hymns in praise of Aryan gods composed by various priests who served different Aryan clans and their kings. Certain Indo-Aryan speaking clans gradually migrated into the Indian subcontinent from the northwest around the middle of the second millennium BCE. The best guess is that they entered the Indian subcontinent at a time when the Indus Valley Civilization was at a decline. There was in all probability a long interaction of the Indo-Aryan speakers with the earlier populations represented by the Indus Valley Civilization as well as other communities. Unfortunately, our only linguistic source at this time is represented by the Vedic texts, and hence we know something about the attitudes of the Vedic peoples toward others, but we have no direct access to the attitudes of the non-Vedic peoples. The Vedic peoples seem to be dealing with non-Vedic indigenous people whom they called Dāsas and Dasyus. Though one must assume that the Vedic peoples had already coexisted with, and perhaps partially converged with, non-Aryan peoples in Iran, Afghanistan, and the regions now covered by the Bactria Margiana Archaeological Complex (to the north of Afghanistan), before reaching the northwestern regions of the Indian subcontinent, the Vedic texts indicate that they had a pervasive notion of their own ethnic "Arya" identity. They glorified their language as being divine and as being produced by the gods themselves.

Though there is enough evidence in the Vedic texts of occasional positive relations with the nonVedic chieftains who gave gifts (*dāna*) to Vedic poets, the Vedic Aryans generally looked at the mass of non-Aryans as substandard peoples, godless nonsacrificers, worshippers of dummy gods and phallic gods, and those whose language was obscure and unintelligible. The non-Vedic languages could not have pleased the Vedic gods and hence were held to be ritually inferior. As the Vedic Aryans gradually moved into the interior of India, they began adjusting themselves to the local scene. Through increasingly intense contacts and convergence with non-Aryan languages and through internal propensities of its own, the old Indo-Aryan language of the Vedic texts slowly became archaic and was in many domains of usage replaced by new vernacular forms of the Indo-Aryan and non-Aryan languages. These circumstances probably forced the Aryans to look at the sacred old Aryan language and their own current form of language more carefully, and this is the likely reason for the emergence of linguistic analysis in ancient India represented in the folk etymologies found in the Vedic texts as well in the formal traditions of phonetics, etymology, grammar, metrics, and ritual interpretation.

The high achievements of this stage are marked by the *Aṣṭādhyāyī* ("Grammar in Eight Chapters") of the great grammarian Pāṇini (about 500 BCE). Pāṇini calls what we call Sanskrit simply *bhāṣā* (language) and describes this *bhāṣā* with some regional and scholastic variation. It covers a north-Indian geography from Gāndhāra and Saurāṣṭra in the west to Madhyadeśa and Prācya in the east. A further distinction is made in his grammar between *bhāṣā* (the colloquial language) and *chandas* (the language of the Vedic texts). To be more specific, these two are viewed as being distinct subdomains of a unified Sanskrit language, which is explicitly considered to be eternal by Pāṇini's successors, Kātyāyana and Patañjali. While literally the term *bhāṣā* stands for "language," in fact, it actually refers to the upper-class language, in relation to which other forms of Indo-Aryan and non-Aryan languages were viewed as being substandard, as those peoples themselves were placed lower in the social hierarchy. Strictly speaking, Pāṇini seems to be describing the Sanskrit usage of non-śūdra males. While the śūdras and women seem to be outside the domain of "standard Sanskrit" (*śiṣṭa-prayoga*), the place of Kṣatriyas and Vaiśyas is equally marginal in this domain. Like the *Dharmaśāstra* texts, the Sanskrit grammar of Pāṇini is primarily a text addressed by a Brahmin male to an audience of Brahmin males describing the standards of their usage of Sanskrit. It is not clear whether these Brahmin males addressed by the grammar of Pāṇini spoke Sanskrit as their first language. With women as the speakers of standard Sanskrit being marginalized by the grammatical tradition, it is unlikely that many male Brahmin children could have learned standard Sanskrit from their mothers. It is more likely that Sanskrit was already an elite second language, though very widely used in many ritual and nonritual domains. It describes usages of Sanskrit directed at Śūdras and non-Śūdras (P. 8.2.83: *pratyabhivāde*' śūdre) and women (P. 8.4.48: *nādiny ākrośe putrasya*) but not usages of Śūdras and women, nor even usages that can be specifically attributed to Kṣatriyas and Vaiśyas.

Pāṇini's successors, Kātyāyana (third century BCE) and Patañjali (second century BCE) provide more detailed sociolinguistic information regarding Sanskrit. Kātyāyana raises the status of general standard Sanskrit to that of the Vedic texts and exhorts his audience to use proper Sanskrit rather than a non-Sanskrit language by suggesting that only the usage of Sanskrit produces religious merit. "Inability" is suggested as one of the reasons why certain people speak deformed speech, a reference to vernacular forms. While Patañjali basically continues the same account, he adds some further interesting details. While women in general could not speak proper Sanskrit, there were exceptional women studying Sanskrit Śāstras like *Mīmāṃsā* of Āpiśalī. Patañjali refers to sages called Yarvāṇastarvāṇa. These sages spoke proper Sanskrit during ritual, but elsewhere used the vernacular forms *yarvāṇa* and *tarvāṇa* for proper Sanskrit *yad vā naḥ* and *tad vā naḥ*. Patañjali says that these sages acted properly. This story goes to indicate the actual restricted domain of the use of proper Sanskrit. However, it also suggests that "improper" or vernacular forms of Sanskrit, more or less close to the known Prakrit languages, were quite common. Patañjali himself narrates the speech of a girl. The girl says *akṣīṇi me darśanīyāni* "my eyes are beautiful" and *pādā me sukumārāḥ* "my feet are delicate." Here, the girl uses plurals, instead of the proper duals, but the phonology and morphology is still that of Sanskrit, rather than Prakrit. The loss of duals in this vernacular usage is similar to what one finds in Prakrits. However, the Sanskritic phonology and morphology speaks of closeness to Sanskrit. But another girl, as reported by Patañjali, could not pronounce the proper Sanskrit *r̥taka* but said *l̥taka*. The use of *l* for *r* is suggestive of the environment of the Māgadhī Prakrit. Here, the phonology is also moving in the direction of Prakrits. The Buddhist Sanskrit usages like *bhikṣusya* for proper Sanskrit *bhikṣoḥ* indicate a similar situation where the surface phonology and morphology is that of Sanskrit, but the usage of *bhikṣusya* matches the Prakrit usage of *bhikkhussa*. Thus, Patañjali's work indicates the presence of a range of vernacular Sanskrit and Prakrit varieties in use among people, including members of Brahmin households. Besides these social details, Patañjali outlines a linguistic domain called Āryāvartta as the home of the most noteworthy usage of standard Sanskrit. This region lies to the east of the disappearance of Sarasvatī, to the west of the Kālaka forest, to the north of the Vindhyas, and to the south of the Himālayas. In this region, only the most selfless and learned Brahmins are looked upon as the elite speakers of Sanskrit. It is these exceptional people who speak proper Sanskrit without having to learn it from a grammar, and it is their usage that is supposed to be the object of a grammarian's description. The story of the Yarvāṇastarvāṇa indicates that even these exceptional people did not speak Sanskrit at all times and in all environments. They felt the need to speak proper Sanskrit only in the context of ritual. While the demons (*asura*) did not and could not speak proper Sanskrit even during ritual, the elite Brahmins did speak proper Sanskrit during ritual. Outside of ritual, they were free to speak the vernaculars.

Alternative sociolinguistic perspectives in India

I have outlined above the conservative view of Sanskrit as held by the Sanskrit grammarians for whom all linguistic usage other than proper Sanskrit is "deformed" usage. This view is referred to by Daṇḍin in his *Kāvyādarśa*, while bringing out an alternative view regarding the languages of literature: "In literature, (only) the languages of Ābhīras, etc., are considered to be Apabhraṃśa ('deformed'; the term is not applied to Prakrits). On the other hand, in the

(Brahmanical) sciences (such as Sanskrit grammar), anything other than Sanskrit is labeled Apabhraṃśa." Here we have a clear statement of the difference between the view held by traditionalists like Kātyāyana and Patañjali on the one hand and that held by the poeticians on the other. There is obviously a greater degree of puritanism among Sanskrit grammarians, which is also shared by the traditions of *Mīmāṃsā* and other orthodox philosophical systems.

But it would be inappropriate to assume that the low prestige for Prakrits was a universally acknowledged fact in ancient India. This is analogous to the question concerning the relative prestige of Brāhmaṇas and Kṣatriyas. Would it be appropriate to say that the Kṣatriyas of ancient India universally acknowledged the higher status of the Brāhmaṇas? There is clear evidence that the Brāhmaṇas and the Kṣatriyas upheld a parallel but opposite social hierarchy, each group placing itself at the top and lowering the other group to a second spot. Even in Brahmanical texts such as the *Śatapatha-Brāhmaṇa*, there is evidence for such a dual perception. One can clearly see in these texts two concurrent images fused together. The physical fact is that the Brāhmaṇa priest sat below the king in the ceremony of Rājasūya. This shows the true political/social hierarchy. However, the Brāhmaṇa priest, in his own theological speculation, raises himself above the king and derives the essence of kingship (*kṣatra*) from his own essence (*brahma*). The Buddhist and Jaina texts of the early period provide us a counterbalance to this Brahmanical perspective. They provide us the Kṣatriya perspective. A close study of these sources can give us a better sense of the differing perspectives held by the various social groups in ancient India.

Sociolinguistic attitudes relating to Sanskrit in Buddhism

All evidence points to the fact that the Buddha used his own Prakrit dialect to teach his doctrine. One of the obvious reasons is that he wanted to reach the masses, and he could have done this by using only the local dialect. He claimed that his doctrine was for the benefit of the masses (*bahu-jana-hitāya bahu-jana-sukhāya*). The *Araṇavibhaṅgasutta* of the *Majjhimanikāya* indicates the Buddha's preference for local dialects for preaching. However, this does not mean and should not be interpreted to mean that the Buddha used "lower" languages, which he would not have used otherwise, simply to reach the lower classes. Such a view would be quite misleading. The Buddha clearly claimed to represent the Aryan way of life, as can be seen from dozens of expressions in the Buddhist canonical texts. For example, in all cases such as *ariya dhamma* (the Aryan doctrine) and *ariya magga* (the Aryan path), the word Aryan may be generally translated as "noble," but it is a loaded word. It represents an attempt on the part of the Buddha to create and assert a new conception of Aryanhood, to combat the conservative concept held in the Brahmanical circles. On the higher philosophical plane, the Buddha totally rejected hereditary caste rank. But on the lower social plane, the Buddha asserted a social hierarchy different from that of the Brahmanical belief. He clearly asserted that Kṣatriyas were superior to Brāhmaṇas. Thus, far from its being an inferior dialect, the Buddha must have considered his own dialect to be superior to that of the Brāhmaṇas, as he considered his own Kṣatriya rank superior to theirs. The same may then be extended to the language used by the Buddha. The Prakrit, which he used to preach, was in all probability no lowly language in his own view. It must have been, in his own estimation, superior to the Sanskrit of the Brāhmaṇas.

The Buddha advises his monks that they should teach the doctrine in their own language (*sakāya niruttiyā*). However, it is reported in different Buddhist texts that monks who were of Brahmanical origin showed concern that the Prakrit-speaking monks of diverse origins would corrupt the sayings of the Buddha and that they asked his permission to render his words into Sanskrit. The Brāhmaṇa monks were worried that the non-Brāhmaṇa monks who made "mistakes" in the use of genders, numbers, and tenses, and in pronunciation, were sure to corrupt the words of the Buddha. If such pleas are historically true, they certainly indicate that Brāhmaṇas, even those who had been converted to Buddhism, could not leave behind many of their Brahmanical sociolinguistic attitudes. It is likely that this story is constructed by the early Buddhist monks, who thereby wanted to emphasize their fear that any attempts to render the Buddha's words into Sanskrit originate in Brahmanical intentions to subvert the Buddhist faith from within. The Buddha is said to have rejected these pleas and to have ordained that everyone should use his own particular dialect in reciting the sacred texts.

We may contrast this situation with the late traditions of Mahāyāna Buddhism. These viewed the Buddha as a Sanskrit speaker, and their canon is in mixed or pure Sanskrit. This shift may be explained on the basis of the sociolinguistic factor that almost all the major Mahāyāna teachers were Brāhmaṇas converted to Buddhism. Thus, in terms of language use and linguistic attitudes, one may safely conclude that the early Buddhism represented a distinct point of view of Kṣatriya superiority over Brāhmaṇas, whereas the late Buddhism of Sanskrit Hīnayāna and Mahāyāna texts represents importation of Brahmanical linguistic attitudes into Buddhist traditions. For this later Sanskrit Buddhism, the Buddha's Kṣatriya status has a somewhat different value. Interestingly, according to the later Buddhist traditions, which being in Sanskrit represent a different sociolinguistic point of view akin to that of the Brāhmaṇas, the Bodhisattvas are born either in Brāhmaṇa or Kṣatriya families, but never in Cāṇḍāla, Veṇukāra, Rathakāra, or Puṣkasa families. The *Lalitavistara* says that when Brāhmaṇas are prominent in the world, the Bodhisattva is born in a Brāhmaṇa family, and when the Kṣatriyas are prominent in the world, the

Bodhisattva is born in a Kṣatriya family. But the Bodhisattva is never born in a hīna (lower) family.

Sociolinguistic attitudes in Jainism

In choosing Prakrits for religious discourse, the Jainas had a motive quite similar to that of the early Buddhists. Mahāvīra was born in a Kṣatriya family, which from the Brahmanical point of view belonged to the mixed Aryanized population of northeastern India. His conflicts with the Brahmanical order were quite similar to the Buddha's. Just as everything Buddhist is emphatically labeled Aryan in the Buddhist canon, similarly the Jaina canon presents a distinctive notion of Aryanhood. It will be apparent by now that conceptions of the Aryan as a social entity vary widely and are heavily laden with hierarchical values.

The *Paṇṇavaṇāsutta*, dated about the first century BCE, has a long section describing the Jaina conceptions of "Aryan" and "Mleccha" or non-Aryan. These notions are discussed in detail to bring out their significance as an alternative social conception contrasting in every way with the corresponding Brahmanical conception. Here the discussion begins with a list of peoples whom the Jainas considered non-Aryan or Mleccha. The list includes Saga, Javaṇa, Cilāya, Babbara, Kāya, Muruṇḍa, Uḍḍa, Bhadaga, Niṇṇaga, Pakkaṇiya, Kulakkha, Goṇḍa, Siṃhala, Pārasa, Gondhoḍamba, Damila, Cillala, Pulinda, Meya, Palhava, Mālava, Gaggara, Ābhāsiya, Nakka, Cīna, Lhasiya, Khasa, Khāsiya Neḍura, Maṇḍha, Ḍombilaga, Lausa, Bausa, Kekkaya, Aravāga, Hūṇa, Romaga, Bharuga, Ruya, Gandhāhāraga, Ajjala, Pāsa, Malaya, and Mūyali. If we compare this list with the lists of Mlecchas from the Brāhmanical literature, we do find some agreement between the Jainas and Brāhmaṇas as to who the Mlecchas are, but the Brahmanical conception excludes several communities, which are considered to be Aryan by the Jainas.

Who are the Aryans? According to the *Paṇṇavaṇāsutta*, there are two kinds of Aryans: (1) iddhipattāriya = ṛddhiprāptārya (Exalted Aryans) and (2) aniḍḍhipattāriya = anṛddhiprāptārya (Nonexalted Aryans), or perhaps (Normal Aryans). The exalted Aryans, according to this text, include Arahanta, Cakkavaṭṭi, Baladeva, Vāsudeva, Cāraṇa, and Vijjāhara. Interestingly, it excludes Brāhmaṇas, and also Vaiśya and Śūdra groups. It includes Kṣatriya characters and religious figures. The conception of normal Aryans provides even more fascinating information. They are subdivided into nine different categories:

(1) Ārya by region (*khettāriya*);
(2) Ārya by birth (*jāti-ariya*);
(3) Ārya by clan (*kulāriya*);

(4) Ārya by function (*kammāriya*);
(5) Ārya by profession (*sippāriya*);
(6) Ārya by language (*bhāsāriya*);
(7) Ārya by wisdom (*ṇāṇāriya*);
(8) Ārya by realization (*daṃsaṇāriya*);
(9) Ārya by conduct (*carittāriya*).

The Jainas, at this stage, seem to claim that the peoples listed as Mlecchas were not Aryan, but on the other hand, there is an implicit claim that whoever is Aryan in terms of the listed features is Aryan in some sense. Thus, there must have been a large population that was Aryan from the Jaina point of view, and that regarded itself as Aryan, but whose claims to Aryanhood were denied by the Brāhmaṇas.

The first category of Aryans is "Aryan by region." Our text lists regions, which are Aryan in its opinion, and says that the exalted Aryans are born in these regions. The Jaina Aryan regions are Magadha, Aṅga, Vaṅga, Kaliṅga, Kāsī, Kosala, Kuru, Kusaṭṭa, Pañcāla, Jaṅgala, Suraṭṭha, Videha, Kosambī, Saṇḍilla, Malaya, Vaccha, Accha, Dasaṇṇa, Cedī, Sindhusovīra, Sūraseṇa, Bhaṅgī, Vaṭṭa, Kuṇāla, Lāḍhā, and Keyaiaḍḍha. This conception of Jaina Aryan lands must be closely compared and contrasted with the Brahmanical conception of Aryan lands. The Brahmanical conception as seen in Patañjali's Mahābhāṣya and in Dharmaśāstra texts claim that the Aryans mainly reside in the region of Āryāvarta, which lies to the east of the Ādarśa mountains, to the west of the Kālaka forest, to the south of the Himalayas, and to the north of the Vindhyas. The *Baudhāyanadharmaśāstra* (1.1.32 – 1.1.33) gives us a clear idea of how the Aryas of Āryāvarta viewed the mixed populations of the "outer regions": "The inhabitants of Ānarta, of Aṅga, of Magadha, of Surāṣṭra, of the Deccan, of Upavṛt, of Sindhu and Sauvīra, are of mixed origins. He who has visited the countries of the Āraṭṭas, Kāraskaras, Puṇḍras, Sauvīras, Vaṅgas, Kaliṅgas, or Pranūnas shall offer a Punastoma or a Sarvapṛṣṭhī sacrifice for purification." It is extremely important to note that seven of the eight regions here listed as "impure" are included in the Jaina list of Aryan lands. Many more of the Jaina Aryan regions would not be acknowledged as such by the Brahmanical Dharmaśāstras. This is indicated on Map 8.1. Thus, there was considerable tension between Brahmanical Aryans and the Jaina and Buddhist Aryans.

The *Paṇṇavaṇāsutta* lists six *jāti-ariyas* (Aryans by birth): Ambaṭṭha, Kalinda, Videha, Vedaga, Hariya, and Cuṃcuṇa. The Brāhmaṇas are not listed here at all. According to the Brahmanical sources, however, one of these six, the Ambaṭṭhas, are born of a Vaiśya mother and a Brāhmaṇa father (*Manusmṛti* 10.8); another, the Videhas, are born of a Brāhmaṇa mother and a Vaiśya father (*Manusmṛti* 10.10). The other four are not even mentioned in the Brahmanical

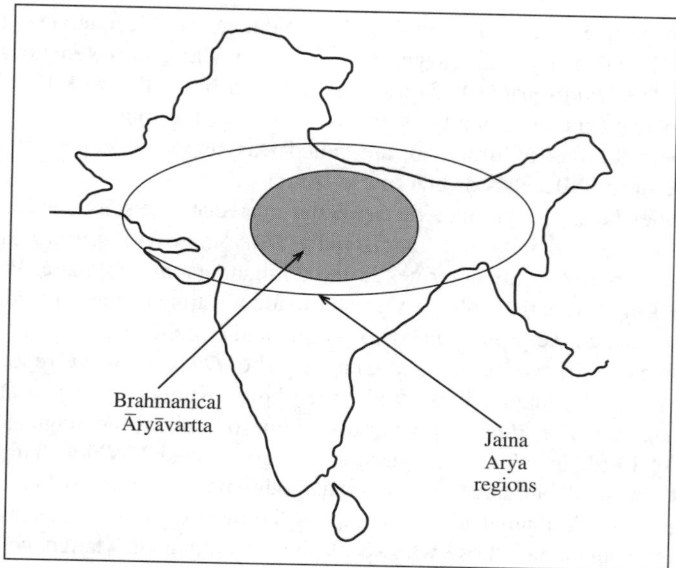

Map 8.1 *Brahmanical and Jaina Ārya regions.*

lists. This may indicate that the early Jainas defined their social prestige in term that were markedly non-Brahmanical.

As for the Aryans by clan, the *Paṇṇavaṇāsutta* lists six Aryan clans: Ugga (Ugra), Bhoga, Rāiṇṇa (Rājanya), Ikkhāga (Ikṣvāku), Ṇāta (Jñāta), and Koravva (Kauravya). Mahāvīra was born in one of these: the Nāta. The Buddha's Śākya clan is traditionally believed to be part of the Okkāka (= Ikkhāga, Ikṣvāku) line and is therefore included here. This includes a few clans that were of probably very low status from the Brahmanical point of view. Thus, the *Manusmṛti* (10.9) says: "From a Kṣatriya and the daughter of a Śūdra springs a being, called Ugra, resembling both a Kṣatriya and a Śūdra, ferocious in his manners, and delighting in cruelty." The conflict between these two conceptions is quite obvious.

Who are Aryans by their work? According to the *Paṇṇavaṇāsutta*, there are many kinds of Aryans, including merchants, pot sellers, bards, and bearers. The Aryans by profession include tailors, weavers, and makers of woolen straw footwear, bookmakers, makers of vehicles, and painters. If we compare these lists with the Brahmanical notions of castes and professions, we find that all of these must be subsumed in the two lower caste ranks, namely Vaiśyas and Śūdras. The agricultural profession is not included in the Jaina list.

According to the *Paṇṇavaṇāsutta*, the Aryans by language are those who speak Ardhamāgadhī and use the Brāhmī script. The Brahmanical tradition would of course regard any non-Sanskrit language as "degenerate," though they do admit that Aryan languages were spoken by those who were not Aryans socially. The *Manusmṛti* (10.45) says: "All those tribes in this world, which are excluded from the community of those born from the mouth, the arms, the thighs, and the feet of Brahman, are called Dasyus, whether they speak the language of the Mlecchas or that of the 'Aryans'."

With the above background, we can better appreciate the self-assertion of the Jaina texts, both socially and linguistically. The *Samavāyaṅgasutta* says that Mahāvīra expounded his doctrines in the Ardhamāgadhī language. While he was speaking Ardhamāgadhī, it was automatically transformed into different languages which were pleasant, wholesome, and beneficial to all the Aryans, non-Aryans, animals, birds, and snakes. The *Ovavāiyasutta* reports that Mahāvīra had conversations with the king Kūṇiya (=Ajātaśatru) in Ardhamāgadhī. The *Bhagavaisutta* raises a question about the language of the gods: "O Lord, in which language do the gods speak? Which language is the distinguished language? O Gotama, gods speak in this Ardhamāgadhī language. This Ardhamāgadhī language is the most distinguished language." For the ancient Jainas, those who speak the Ardhamāgadhī language are linguistically Aryan, speakers of the most distinguished language.

Political factors and sociolinguistic attitudes

Deshpande (1979b) discusses how political factors affect sociolinguistic attitudes. The current discussion briefly explores the connection between the political factors and the sociolinguistic attitudes expressed in the early Buddhist and Jaina texts. The Pali tradition calls the Pāli language by the name Māgadhī and claims that the Buddha spoke this language and that this language is the original language of all beings (*sabbasattānaṃ mūlabhāsā*). As quoted above, the Jaina texts make a similar claim on behalf of Ardhamāgadhī. Both of these are indeed varieties of Magadhan Prakrit and make the highest claims of prestige. We are not concerned here with the purely linguistic question of whether Pāli and Ardhamāgadhī, as we know them now, are truly Magadhan dialects or not. We are concerned about the origins of the sociolinguistic claims made on behalf of these languages.

K. R. Norman (1980) has extensively discussed these Buddhist and Jaina passages making a claim for Pāli and Ardhamāgadhī to be the original language of the canon and the original language of all beings, respectively. He suggests (67):

> I would suggest that the idea of languages developing from Māgadhī is a clear indication of the state of affairs in North India during the time of the Mauryan empire in the fourth and third centuries B.C., and I think that the idea of language development expressed in the Buddhist and Jain texts must have been arising during, and very probably because of,

that empire. During the Mauryan period Māgadhī, the language of Aśoka's capital Pāṭaliputra, was the administrative language of North India, and it, or a modified form of it, was inscribed all over India to make Aśoka's decrees known to his subjects. I would, therefore, suggest that Māgadhī sabbasattānaṃ mūlabhāsā was a (fairly) correct statement as far as North India was concerned in the fourth and third centuries B.C., and it was natural that a statement which Aśoka might have made about his administrative language should be adopted by the Buddhist missionaries when they went to Ceylon. A similar use for missionary purposes would doubtless account for the Jain adoption of the same phrase.

I fully agree with the political motivation that Norman finds in these Buddhist and Jaina assertions. However, as I have pointed out there are much deeper social reasons for the adoption of Prakrit, instead of Sanskrit, by these traditions, and the initial blossoming of these traditions obviously occurred in the region where Māgadhī was the dominant Prakrit.

Since the fall of the Mauryan Empire, however, things gradually changed, and Māgadhī, which was once the most prestigious language, later became a low-class language in Sanskrit dramas. This has to do with the loss of power to the region of Magadha and the rise of empires in other regions of India, more to the west and south of Magadha. Thus, the rise in the prestige of Mahārāṣṭrī Prakrit may indeed be connected with the rise of the Sātavāhana power. In later centuries, the overall political prestige of Sanskrit rose continuously in such a way that it eclipsed the earlier prestige of Prakrit in the Mauryan days. As Romila Thapar (1973: 51) points out, "the earliest Sanskrit inscription of any importance is that of the Śaka ruler Rudradāman, and dates to the second century A.D., the previous inscriptions having been composed in the Prakrits and the local languages, such as Aramaic and Tamil." The rise in the prestige of Sanskrit must have begun slowly after the fall of the Mauryas at the hands of the Brāhmaṇa Puṣyamitra Śuṅga, and it gradually continued to rise in such a way that the royal inscriptions in India gradually changed from Prakrit to Sanskrit. The Śaka rulers began using Sanskrit, which was also used extensively by the Gupta kings. While the early Vākāṭaka inscriptions are in Prakrit, they gradually change to Sanskrit across regions. Also, the early Pallava inscriptions are in Prakrit, the late Pallava inscriptions are in Sanskrit. Nowhere do we see a shift from Sanskrit to Prakrit in the history of Indian inscriptions.

This directionality is quite instructive. This loss of prestige for Prakrit resulted in a remarkably different picture in Sanskrit dramas where the king always speaks Sanskrit, while the thieves and rogues are given Māgadhī as their speech. It is not always clear whether those kings whose inscriptions are in Sanskrit ever spoke Sanskrit themselves, but certainly the ideal was a Sanskrit speaking king, as can be seen from the anguish of the Prakrit-speaking Sātavāhana, insulted by his Sanskrit-speaking wife, depicted in the famous story about the origins of the Kātantra grammar. Interestingly, while the later

Prakrit poets and Jaina authors continued to defend Prakrit against Sanskrit, as has been shown in detail in Deshpande 1979b, these defenses were based more on aesthetic grounds than that of social prestige. Even a poet such as Rājaśekhara who clearly has a soft corner for Prakrits, insists in his *Kāvyamīmāṃsā* that a good poet should have servants fluent in Apabhraṃśa and maidservants fluent in languages like Māgadhī. His wives should be fluent in Sanskrit and Prakrit. It is important to note that Prakrit for Rājaśekhara refers not to Māgadhī but to Mahārāṣṭrī. Thus, even those who loved Prakrits in later centuries could not defend their social prestige in terms of the then current state of affairs. This is what may have forced the reluctant Jaina traditions to use Sanskrit in later periods.

Conclusion

Sanskrit continued to be the language of high literary and ritual status as well as the language of most of the philosophical and technical/scientific writing right up to the coming of the British. The last efflorescence of Sanskrit literary and philosophical activity occurred during the period of the sixteenth and the seventeenth century CE, on the eve of colonialism in South Asia. The coming of the colonial rule gradually supplanted Sanskrit as the language of higher learning. English usurped that place. Gradually Sanskrit became more and more restricted to the domain of religious practice and inspiration. Within this domain, while Sanskrit continues to be used in Hindu rituals till today, its comprehension has steadily diminished, while the high respect for its sanctifying potency keeps its place in ritual assured for the foreseeable future. In modern times, Sanskrit survives in political, social, and economic competition with vernacular languages on the one hand, and with English, the language of business, science, and technology, on the other. On the one hand, its scope is ever diminishing, while on the other hand, there are increasing official efforts to keep it alive and to make it the core of the emerging Hindu nationalism in politics. Its future depends on the relative strength of these various forces pulling in diverse directions.

9 Traditions of language study in South Asia*

Ashok Aklujkar

We will focus in this chapter on two phenomena that are nothing short of extraordinary if one considers their antiquity, richness, precision, and significance to human thinking on language: Indian[1] engagement with language in general and the study of Sanskrit traceable in its roots to the grammar of Pāṇini in particular. The latter, as will be clear below, is a part of the former. However, it is a part that surpasses all other parts in its achievement, longevity, sustained vitality, and influence. Therefore, it deserves to be treated somewhat extensively in a space of its own. This is what the present chapter will do in its latter half.

Manifold interest in manifestations of language

The passion that educated Indians of the premodern period displayed for preserving information on speech forms, particularly of the languages of the Indo-Aryan family, is unmatched in world history.

Even minute differences in the pronunciation of words were preserved in a variety of ways: (a) in recensions of Vedic texts, (b) in works highlighting the peculiarities of Vedic recensions, (c) in discourses on the articulation aspect of phonetics, (d) in grammars, (e) in lexicons, (f) in treatises that sought to guide literary authors and the readers of *belles lettres*, (g) in monographs that discussed expressions suspected to be ungrammatical, (h) in booklets that listed different forms caused by alterations such as "b : v" or "ś : ṣ : s" of what was

* Dr. Mahes Raj Pant and Dr. Diwakar Acharya caught my oversights in the first draft of this chapter. Professors Tej K. Bhatia, Peter E. Hook, Madhav M. Deshpande, P.R. Subramanian, S. Sridhar, and Dr. James Nye supplied the necessary bibliographic information when the sources accessible to me proved to be inadequate. My thanks go to all these scholars.

1 The following discussion is confined to the pre-British and, to a large extent, to the pre-Muslim periods of South Asian history. In discussing these periods, it is common among specialists to think of "India" and "Indian" as synonyms of "South Asia" and "South Asian." Hence, in the following lines, the former pair of words has been used, which also has the advantage of being less cumbersome.

believed to be essentially the same word, and (i) in commentaries that explained literary texts abounding in puns.[2]

Many stories, some similar to jokes and some grimly instructive, were preserved in the tradition from very ancient times about the consequences of mispronunciation, ungrammatical speech, or ignorance of grammar texts.

Investing sentences of respectable texts, including those of grammar, with meanings their author could not have dreamt of, also seems to have been a favorite pastime of scholars over many generations.

A system of education that especially suited oral preservation of the scriptures was instituted by Brahmins. Modes of recitation (*krama*, etc.) that would magnify any deviation about to occur in the text to be preserved and thus resist the deviation's entry into the text were a part of this system. As a result, we find much less variation in the wording of the scriptures as they have been handed down than we should expect, given their large sizes and great antiquity.

The Jain copyists, probably more frequently than others, took the trouble of recording even the number of syllables which constituted a text.

The Buddhist monks too, had a tradition of memorizing the Buddha's sermons, or what they believed to be the Buddha's words, with exactitude. It

[2] (a) Sanskrit names for the types of literature referred to in (b) to (f) are, respectively: Prātiśākhya, Śikṣå, Vyākaraṇa, Kośa, and Alaṁkāra-śāstra (the last is also known as Kāvya-śāstra or Sāhitya-śāstra; it has a subbranch called Kavi-śikṣå).

Examples of the texts intended in (g) and (h) would be *Mukha-bhūṣaṇa (Sāhitya-kaṇṭakoddhāra*, etc.) and *Śabda-bheda-Prakāśa*.

Sanskrit has a huge commentarial literature showing much variety and taking care of the diverse needs of readers. Almost as a rule, the comments in this literature concern themselves with the expressions used in the commentandum. In the present context, therefore, the commentaries on all the text types listed in (a) to (h) are to be understood as included. What makes the commentaries mentioned in (i) worthy of a specific mention is the degree to which a specific kind of punning (*sabhaṅga śleṣa* "double or multiple meanings through different splittings of a sound sequence") has been cultivated in the Sanskrit tradition (and to some extent in the Prakrit and Apabhraṁśa traditions). A language like English may have a few expressions like "anicebox" that can, in their written form, be read either as "a nice box" or as "an ice box." Sanskrit authors came up with an overwhelming number of such concatenations. Several works narrating two or more stories with a shared syllable sequence are available. At least one work, Araśāṇipālai Veṅkaṭådhvarin's *Rāghava-yādavīya* or *Yādava-rāghavīya*, which narrates one story from its presumed beginning to its end and another story from its presumed end to its beginning is available. In explaining such works, the astoundingly learned and resourceful commentators must focus on even minute differences of pronunciation.

(b) While an endless series of examples may be produced as evidence of the great Indian interest in details of pronunciation, I will cite only two telling ones: (i) In his rule *udak ca vipāśaḥ*, Pāṇini (4.2.74) notes that the epithets of wells dug on the north side of the Vipāś river are accented differently from the epithets of those which are dug on the south side. (ii) Sometimes a lexicographer would come across a form of a word (e.g. that of *bhṛṅgāra)* that was corrupt due to faulty copying or physically damaged state of the manuscript. The meaning would be contextually clear but the form unusual. Even such forms were noted and associated with probable meanings by some compilers of lexicons.

is largely to this tradition that we owe our precious possession of the Pāli canon.[3]

A number of words that had acquired specific meanings (at least in certain contexts) or that did not have a structure easily relatable to the recurring or well-known morphemes were preserved in works like the *Nighaṇṭu* and the *Uṇādi* lists. This must have required much consistent and devoted attention to language as well as to the works of those who were studying it.

Lexicons that grouped words according to their meanings, according to the number of syllables, or according to what the suffix or phoneme at the end was were compiled with great care. Due to the vigor of the scholarly culture, this seems to have happened every few hundred years. The lexicons do not include dictionaries following the alphabetical sequence of lexeme initials, which is somewhat unexpected, given the attention paid in India to developing scientific alphabets at least from 400 BCE, but most of the lexicons offer the user a convenience difficult to imagine elsewhere: being metrical in nature, they facilitate memorization; consisting of groups of synonyms and homonyms, they function as thesauruses, come nearer to giving a sense of the whole language (especially by indicating mythological and other cultural associations), and reduce the possibility of being misled in interpretation by similarity of sound. Furthermore, adherence to alphabetical order *applied to the ends of stems* is noticed in a few of them, including a reverse application of the alphabetical order (cf. Cardona 1976: 171; Vogel 1979: 305). These lexicons, in effect, provide morpheme lists differing from each other in a predictable way (a certain sequence of the final sounds) and thus serve to sharpen grammatical awareness.

The only major deficiencies in early Indian bodies of linguistic information then seem to be that the information was generally not preserved in a form displaying historical sequence and that diachronic linguistics did not develop in an overt or impressive way.[4] However, despite the lack of historical orientation

[3] The Indian achievements in the oral preservation of texts are in keeping with the remarkable fascination with sound that we witness in the *mantra* phenomenon that pervades India's religious life and in the development of a very sophisticated theory of music in India's culture. In fact, it may not be an exaggeration to say that no other premodern culture studied and valued sound the way India did.

[4] The branch of learning called Nirukta, which is frequently explained as "etymology," is not primarily historical in orientation. It concentrates on deriving a word from one or more basic elements (the verbal roots are given primacy in these elements) in such a manner as to bring out its particular meaning in a given context. It does not usually pause to consider if the derivation or explanation suggested has parallels elsewhere or has the support of laws of phonetic and semantic change (Scharfe 1977: 78, 83–4, 122). It does in some cases yield historically sound or "true" etymologies, but frequently its results seem like those of folk etymologizing to a superficial reader.

The Nirukta failure to satisfy the expectations of historical linguistics has frequently been taken to point to a disjunction in the application of the very impressive skills in synchronic word derivation that the Indians developed. It is thought that they could not at all give a diachronic

in what has come down to us, it must be acknowledged that our knowledge of antiquity, particularly of Indo-European antiquity, would have been extremely poor if the Indian tradition had not invested so much energy in preserving the past in its own words – in many cases even to the extent of preserving the very accent with which the past spoke. The linguistic data that India made available have contributed to improvement in our understanding of classical languages of Europe and to development of diachronic and comparative linguistics, as they have, indirectly, to the emergence of comparative philosophy, comparative mythology, and comparative religion. Indian linguistic thinking, including development of phonetic scripts, had some influence on countries to the north and east of India (e.g. Tibet and Indonesia) as well (cf. Scharfe 1977: 79–80, 167).[5] This is so in spite of the fact that a huge quantity of literature that was obviously full of subtle and varied observations about Sanskrit in its various manifestations or that was replete with advanced discussions about the nature of language *(vāc)* in general has been lost. Most recensions, to which ancient authors refer, of early Vedic literature have also fallen prey to the ravages of time, despite what must have been greatly disciplined and self-sacrificing efforts to preserve them orally. Had they remained available, the Indian tradition would have provided an even sharper picture of antiquity.

The contribution that the ancient Indian tradition has made to the classification of sounds and to the scientific construction of scripts should also be noted in this context as a factor that contributed significantly to the emergence of phonetics as a science in the nineteenth- and twentieth-century West.

Situating branches of knowledge that deal with language

In the literature giving linguistic information that the preceding paragraphs describe, much is systematic and, of that systematic subgroup, much has been

theatre of operation to these skills. However, to look at the Nirukta tradition in this way is to ignore its context of Vedic ideology (particularly the *bandhutā* or "connectivity" aspect of *mantra* and ritual thinking). Moreover, the nonengagement of the Nirukta tradition with the historical side of language study should not be interpreted to mean that the Indians did not at all become aware of linguistic change or of the possibility of there being laws of sound change. In writing the grammars of Prakrit languages, they derived Prakrit words by assuming Sanskrit originals that were shown as undergoing certain definable sound changes. To this extent, they came close to realizing that words may be changing in definable ways, although the ways they identified did not apply to the same domain as the sound laws of modern historical-comparative linguists (the domain was more commonly the language of established texts – scriptures, plays, poems, and so on – not language at large) and were not viewed as not amenable to exception.

Despite this and despite contacts with the Greeks and Persians, with whose languages the Indians seem to have felt Sanskrit was similar, detailed discussions about how specific languages evolved are not to be found in their literary heritage. Consequently, the theoretical concepts and issues of historical linguistics are also absent in that heritage.

5 Scholars have sometimes wondered how advanced our knowledge would have been if materials of similar extent and quality had been furnished by the Greek and Roman traditions.

given recognition in the Indian tradition through class names indicating systematization. These class names are Vedāṅga ("Veda ancillary, a text or study branch that aids in the preservation and use of the Veda"), Smṛti ("traditionally remembered or preserved knowledge"), and *śāstra* ("means of instructing, oral or written texts that guide in theory or practice").

The Vedāṅgas constituting linguistic literature are Vyākaraṇa ("language analysis, grammar"), Nirukta ("context-supportive word derivation"), śikṣā ("phonetics") (see notes 4 and 9), and Chandas or Chandaḥ-śāstra ("metrics, prosody"). Like Chandas, the first three also have been thought of as *śāstra*. In addition, Vyākaraṇa and Nirukta have been thought of as Smṛti. The śikṣā and Chandaḥ-śāstra, although connected with the Veda in their origin as systematic inquiries and although a part of preserved knowledge, have a significant theoretical component which makes them atemporally and secularly applicable. This may be the reason why the designation Smṛti is not *strongly* associated with them.

Other systematic works primarily or directly concerned with language, from one point of view or another, belong to the branches Prātiśākhya, *kośa*, and Alaṁkāra-śāstra.[6] It should be noted in the case of the last, standing for "poetics," that its subject matter is not confined to poetic literature in metrical or verse form only but also includes prose or predominantly prose literature such as plays and romances.

In addition to the bodies of literature specified in the preceding two paragraphs, theorizing about language in general is found in the literature of many schools of philosophy developed in Sanskrit. The occasion for such theorizing is usually provided either by the issues of scriptural hermeneutics or by a school's getting involved in epistemological or psychological matters to defend its metaphysics (or sometimes even its opposition to metaphysics).[7]

There is some overlapping in the spheres of Prātiśākhya, śikṣā, Vyākaraṇa, and Nirukta. The tradition of Vyākaraṇa, by and large, presupposes the phonetic observations of the Prātiśākhyas and śikṣās; it does not *generally* get into a specification of how sounds are made or in which texts they occur. As it derives word, phrase, clause, and sentence forms, it simply begins to use notions

[6] The word *alaṁkāra* may not always figure in the titles of the works belonging to the Alaṁkāra-śāstra. They also carry names such as *Kāvya-lakṣaṇa*, *Kāvya-mīmāṁsā*, *Kāvya-prakāśa*, and *Sāhitya-darpaṇa*, and names such as *Sahṛdayāloka* (or *Dhvanyāloka*) and *Rasa-gaṅgādhara* based on important concepts of poetic theory.

[7] If the impressive collection of bibliographic information available at Karl H. Potter's website <http://faculty.washington.edu/kpotter/ckeyt/home.htm> is searched for titles containing words such as "etymology," "grammar," "grammarian," "language," "linguistic," "meaning," *śabda*, and *vāc*, it will be evident that languge has been one of the major concerns of Indian philosophers. In addition, introductions to linguistic–semantic notions and issues as discussed by specific traditions within Indian philosophy can be found in the *Encyclopedia of Indian Philosophies* volumes edited by the same scholar.

approximating the modern Western linguistic notions of phoneme (*varṇa*),[8] allophone, and so on as they apply to the object language as a whole. It shares with the Nirukta the methodology of deriving words from basic verbal roots (*dhātus*, mostly monosyllablic units conveying actions or states), but it is not as uncompromising in this respect as the Nirukta. At certain levels, it derives words from morphemes other than verbal roots and, in certain cases, it simply leaves the words underived. It departs from the Nirukta also in not making its derivations depend on specific contexts.[9]

The Prātiśākhyas, śikṣās, and, with isolated exceptions, Nirukta remained tools of study for the Vedas only[10] and thus were associated with a particular historical phase and with the religio-philosophical sphere of life, but Vyākaraṇa, even as a Vedāṅga, had certain generalizing tendencies that enabled it to flourish beyond a certain period. A similar observation applies, on a smaller scale, to the other discipline, Chandaḥ-śāstra ("prosody"), that had the basis for wider applicability. It too, like Vyākaraṇa, began as something specifically concerned with the Vedas, but soon transcended that limitation.

[8] The term "phoneme" has not meant the same thing in different traditions of linguistics. Likewise, *varṇa* has related but slightly divergent meanings as a technical term of language discussion in the Indian tradition.

In certain contexts, *akṣara* seems to have been used for the same theoretical notion as *varṇa*.

[9] A subbranch of Vyākaraṇa represented by various Uṇādi-sūtras resembles the Nirukta in that it derives words not derived by the "mainstream" grammar. This it does mainly by assuming additional suffixes, which the Nirukta is not seen as doing (at least explicitly; it may have inherited some suffixes, etc., from grammars not accessible to us). Furthermore, the words the Uṇādi-sūtras deal with are not necessarily Vedic words and they are not analyzed on the background of specific textual contexts. As regards their domain, the Uṇādi-sūtras thus have some affinity with the efforts made by grammarians like Hema-candra to account for regional *(deśya, deśin)* words not accounted for by their grammars for Sanskrit and (literary) Prakrits. The Uṇādi-sūtras come across as appendices would.

[10] (a) Nirukta, as a specific text ascribed to Yāska, should be distinguished from *nirukta, nirukti*, or *nirvacana* as a specific kind of derivation – as anhistorical etymologizing. The latter is typified by Yāska's work but is not confined to it. It occasionally surfaces in later religious traditions claiming proximity to the Veda as well as in the Buddhist and Jain traditions.

(b) Śikṣā must have begun as a discipline of general importance when a social apparatus for oral preservation of the Vedas developed. As its name "wish to be able, act of making oneself capable" implies, it was designed as a tool that gave the students the general phonetic knowledge (still mainly concerned with articulation) which would then help them in mastering the Vedas as configurations of sounds. Thus, in contrast to Prātiśākhya, Nirukta, and Vyākaraṇa, it was general in its initial impulse – in its seeking to be distinct from those parts of the Prātiśākhyas which dealt with the specifics of Veda texts, but its application remained limited. This may be due to the fact that (i) religious traditions other than that of Brahmanism attached less importance to the sound aspect of language (the notion of a sacred language appeared late in them; the languages that came close to claiming sacredness did not have accents of the Vedic type or an extensive *mantra* literature to preserve) and that (ii) a discipline like phonetics can progress only up to a certain point in the absence of continuing development of physical, physiological, and technological knowledge.

Grammar as a determinant of intellectual culture

It should be evident from the foregoing comments that, among the branches of learning based on or devoted to the study of language, grammar occupies a commanding position. Some scholars have even concluded that grammar is to India what mathematics is to the West in the development of systematic thought (Ruegg 1978 and Bronkhorst 2001 discuss this conclusion, among other things).

It has been suggested that the logical categories (substance, quality, action/motion, generality/universal, individuator, inherence, and absence), accepted in the ancient Vaiśeṣika system of philosophy and later adopted by Nyāya philosophy, ultimately owe their inspiration to the analysis in terms of substantives, adjectives, and verbs which the grammarians of Sanskrit made. The first three of the categories correspond to what must have been the early language analysts' word types. As the remaining categories logically depend on the first three, they too might have owed their identification indirectly to the theoretical notions developed by the language analysts.[11]

The fine sense of taxonomy that pervades all *śāstra* writing can also be traced to the intellectual discipline instilled by grammar. "Adhérer à la pansée indienne, c'est d'abord penser en grammairien" ("To bond with Indian thought means, first of all, to think like a grammarian"; Renou 1947: II.86) is thus a valid observation.

One also notices that the type of logical arguments and hermeneutical devices that dominates later Indian commentarial literature is at present attested for the first time in the *Mahābhāṣya* of Patañjali, a grammatical text belonging to the second century BCE, if not to an earlier century.

Thus, indirectly through abstract analyses of various kinds as well as directly through providing a particular kind of literature, grammar shaped the thinking of the largest number of students. The dominant way of thinking was that "As the face is the means for knowing a person, grammar is the means for knowing the other branches of learning", and grammar was viewed as the subject that all students had to study, usually from the very beginning of their formal education.

Prominent Sanskrit grammars and grammarians

Indian grammatical literature, particularly what survives of it in Sanskrit, forms a large body, despite great losses. It is customary to speak of it in terms of systems or schools, although the distinctions between what are usually

[11] The switch from "grammarians" to "language analysts" is done to indicate that the very early thinkers interested in generalizing about the nature of Sanskrit of whom we should be talking here (the Vaiśeṣika is an older system of philosophy) might not have been followers of a particular system of grammar. Compare Scharfe (1977: 120–1). For the relationship between the Pāṇinian system and other Indian systems in terms of terminology, and so on, see Cardona 1976: 230–2, 1999: 210–13.

considered to be different grammatical traditions do not always go very deep and some grammars have not attracted the following we would expect of schools. In the approximate chronological order, the grammarians whose grammars have survived and have noteworthy peculiarities or have generated noticeable scholarly activity are as follows:

Table 9.1. *Chronology of grammars*

Grammarian	Probable date	Grammar name
Pāṇini	Fifth century BCE or earlier	*Aṣṭādhyāyī*
Kumāralāta	First/second century CE?	*Kaumāralāta*
Śarva-varman	Second century CE?	*Kātantra/Kālāpa/Kalāpaka/ Kaumāra*
Candra-gomin	Fourth century CE?	*Cāndra*
Deva-nandin/Pūjya-pāda	Fourth/fifth century CE	*Jainendra*
Śākaṭāyana/Pālya-kīrti	Ninth century CE	*Śākaṭāyana*
Bhoja	Tenth to eleventh century CE	*Sarasvatī-kaṇṭhābharaṇa*
Hema-candra	Twelfth century CE	*Haima*
Vopa-deva	Thirteenth century CE	*Mugdha-bodha*
Kramadīśvara and Jumara-nandin	Thirteenth century CE	*Jaumāra/Rāsavata*
Padma-nābha-datta	Fourteenth century CE	*Saupadma*
Narendra or Anubhūti-sva-rūpa	Thirteenth to fifteenth century CE	*Sārasvata*
Nārāyaṇa-bhaṭṭa	Sixteenth to seventeenth century CE	*Prakriyā-sarvasva*

As can be seen from the above table, many of the names of grammars listed here are derived from the names or epithets of authors (historical or legendary), which indicates that there was a plurality of grammars in use at most of the times and authorship had to be mentioned to distinguish grammars. The respectable standing of the author may also have been responsible in some cases for the name that was used for his grammar.

Besides the ones noted above, we have manuscripts or editions of grammars under such author names or titles as *Buddhi-sāgara*, *Malaya-giri*, *Hari-nāmāmṛta*,[12] and *Prabodha-prakāśa* (cf. Scharfe 1977:162–9; Maurer 1981:18–26). Grammars or grammarians with the names Vāmana (author of *Viśrānta-vidyādhara*), Bhīma-sena, Jayotpala, *Muṣṭi-vyākaraṇa*, and Jaya-deva are also mentioned in our sources.

The appeal of some of the grammars mentioned here (e.g. *Jaumāra*, *Saupadma*) was confined to certain parts of India. They were either not known in other parts or were known only to specialists through their mention in literature or through manuscripts usually acquired with considerable effort.

[12] There are two different works which carry the title *Hari-nāmāmṛta*.

Some of the grammars appealed only to certain religions or sects. The *Kātantra* and *Cāndra* were considered to be their own by the Buddhists, although they may not originally have been written with only the Buddhists in mind. The *Jainendra*, *Śākaṭāyana*, and *Haima* were authored by Jains and remained largely confined to the Jain scholarly community. The *Mugdha-bodha* was a Brahmanical "devotee's grammar" in the examples it gave to illustrate its rules, whereas the two grammars named *Hari-nāmāmṛta* gave the devotees of Viṣṇu an even greater opportunity to be reminded of him; they used Viṣṇu's names as technical terms.

Abridgements or recasts of many grammars were made. In addition, a significant secondary stratum of grammars meant specifically for teaching Sanskrit, as distinct from describing it for scholars, existed (some of the ones mentioned above may also be associated with such a pedagogical stratum). Scores of ancillary texts on topics that were especially important to general learners of Sanskrit were also composed, as works such as the *Samāsa-cakra* (some of them available in various recensions) bear out. Furthermore, there were verse manuals written, like Halāyudha's *Kavi-rahasya*, highlighting the differences of grammatical elements in a particular category and facilitating the entry of students into a full-scale grammar. Works that ingeniously illustrated the derivations of grammar through the medium of poetry were written from a very early time, probably preceding that of Patañjali (second century BCE) but definitely from the sixth to the seventh centuries CE, to which the earliest available extensive specimens, *Rāvaṇārjunīya* (or *Arjuna-rāvaṇīya*) and *Rāvaṇa-vadha* (or *Bhaṭṭi-kāvya*) belong.

Grammars of Indian Languages Other than Sanskrit

In addition to this literature pertaining to Sanskrit, we have the grammars, lexicons, and poetics and prosody texts of Pāli,[13] of various Prakrit dialects, of Apabhraṁśa, of Dravidian languages and of the early phases of modern Indian vernaculars – even a few grammars of Persian such as *Pārasī-prakāśa* (Scharfe 1977: 191–9). Generally, premodern Indian scholars seem to have followed the policy of analyzing those languages which came to possess written literatures. Languages of culturally foreign groups seem to have received grammatical treatment at their hands only if those groups settled in India in large numbers for a long time and/or held political power.

[13] As is pointed out in Norman (1983: 1–7), von Hinüber (1994: 76–90), and others, "Pāli" is strictly speaking not a language name. Its use as a language name probably dates from the sixteenth to seventeenth century CE. A word meaning "a form of old Māgadhī reflected in the canon of the Thera-vādin Buddhists (but different from the Māgadhī Prakrit later described by the grammarians and from the language attested in many of Magadhan emperor Aśoka's inscriptions)" should substitute "Pāli." However, since such a word does not exist, since using "Māgadhī" in imitation of the Thera-vādin commentators will now be misleading and since "Pāli" can be used for a unique language without causing any serious misunderstanding, it is better to stick to the current usage as the specialists have.

Although Ardha-māgadhī is a very important Prakrit language variety because of its acceptance for the Jain canon and preservation of several old Prakritic features, it does not receive separate grammatical descriptions or lexicons until the twentieth century. One of its grammars attempted on traditional lines is Muni Ratna-candra's *Jaina-siddhānta-kaumudī* (*ardha-māgadhī-vyākaraṇa*), published around Vikrama-saṁvat 1982 (=1925/1926 CE).[14]

The situation of Apabhraṁśa is similar but probably for different reasons. No self-standing accounts of Apabhraṁśa words, prosody, or grammar seem to be available in the tradition. In the present state of knowledge, the traditional treatment of this language-and-literature complex is found only in the chapters or sections of some Prakrit and Sanskrit works. The Prakrit grammars of Hemacandra, Mārkaṇḍeya, and Trivikrama are especially helpful in informing us about the grammatical features of Apabhraṁśa.[15]

Of particular historical importance among the surviving non-Sanskrit grammars is *Tolkāppiyam*, a grammar (with a section on poetics), of the old Dravidian language Tamil. It is usually assigned to the early centuries of the Christian era. Preliminary information regarding *Tolkāppiyam* and other grammars, language-centred accounts, and so on of Dravidian languages can be found in Scharfe (1977: 178–86). Some of these other grammars are as follows:

Language	Author	Title
Kannada	Nṛpa-tuṅga	*Kavi-rāja-mārga*[a]
	Nāga-varma	*Kāvyāvalokana*[b]
	Nāga-varma	*Karṇāṭaka-bhāṣā-bhūṣaṇa*
	Keśi-rāja	*Śabda-maṇi-darpaṇa*
	Bhaṭṭa Akalaṅka-deva	*Karṇāṭaka-śabdānuśāsana*
	Kṛṣṇamācārya	*Hosagannaḍa nuḍigannaḍi*
Malayalam	Raja Raja Varma, A. R.	*Kerala-pāṇinīya*
	Author not known	*Līlā-tilaka*[c]
Tamil	Author not known	*Avinaya*
	Pavaṇanti	*Nannūl*
	Puttamittiran	*Vīracoḷiya-kkārikai*
	Kuṇavīra-paṇṭitar	*Nemināta*
	Cuppiramaṇīya-tīṭcitar	*Pirayoka-viveka*
	Vaittiyanāta Nāvalar	*Ilakkaṇa-vilakka*
Telugu	Nannaya(bhaṭṭu)	*Āndhra-śabda-cintā-maṇi*
	Mulaghatika Ketana	*Āndhra-bhāṣā-Bhūṣaṇa*

(continued)

[14] Reprint 1988 of Muni Ratna-candra's *Jaina-siddhānta-kaumudī* (*ardha-māgadhī-vyākaraṇa*) published by Bhāratīya Book Corporation in Delhi does not provide any details about the original edition.

[15] Modern scholars have, of course, treated the Apabhraṁśa language complex in separate monographs.

Language	Author	Title
Telugu	Atharvaṇācārya	*Vikṛti-viveka*[d]
	Atharvaṇācārya	*Triliṅga-śabdānuśāsana*
	Paravastu Chinnaya Sūri	*Bāla-vyākaraṇamu*
	B. Sītārāmācāryulu	*Prauḍha-vyākaraṇamu*[e]

Note:

[a] *Kavi-rāja-mārga* is primarily a text on poetics but has grammatical matter, too.

[b] The *śabda-smṛti* part of *Kāvyāvalokana* is devoted to grammatical considerations.

[c] *Līlā-tilaka* describes the Maṇi-pravālam variety, which, although mainly known in the case of Malayalam, could be extended to all linguistic expressions that combine Sanskrit with other languages.

[d] *Vikṛti-viveka* supplements the *Āndhra-śabda-cintāmaṇi*.

[e] Also known as *Triliṅga-lakṣaṇa-śeṣa*, the *Prauḍha-vyākaraṇa* forms a supplement to *Bāla-vyākaraṇa*.

The dates of the preceding language-centred treatises, to the extent specialists could determine them, give us the following approximate chronological sequence: *Avinaya* (fragments): pre-ninth century CE, *Kavi-rāja-mārga*: ninth century, *Vīracoḻiya-kkārikai*: eleventh century, *Āndhra-śabda-cintā-maṇi*: eleventh century, *Kāvyāvalokana*: twelfth century, *Āndhra-bhāṣā-bhūṣaṇa*: thirteenth century, *Nemināta*: thirteenth century, *Śabda-maṇi-darpaṇa*: thirteenth century, *Līlā-tilaka*: fourteenth century, *Vikṛti-viveka*: fourteenth century, *Karṇāṭaka-śabdānuśāsana*: seventeenth century, *Pirayoka-viveka*: seventeenth century, *Ilakkaṇa-vilakka*: seventeenth century, *Bāla-vyākaraṇa*: nineteenth century, *Hosagannaḍa nuḍigannaḍi* (also titled *Grammar of the Modern Canarese Language)*: nineteenth century, *Prauḍha-vyākaraṇa* (or *Triliṅga-lakṣaṇa-śeṣa*): nineteenth century.

This sequence indicates that a few examples of the grammars of the early phases of modern Indian vernaculars are contained in the list given above. Arjunavāḍakara (1992) and Bhatia (1987) furnish more examples of such grammars of Marathi and Hindi, respectively. In addition, *Kaśmīra-śabdāmṛta*, a Pāninian grammar of Kashmiri, exists.[16] Furthermore, the sequence indicates that, as we approach the nineteenth century, the bridging between traditional Indian grammars and the Western-style grammars of modern Indian languages begins to take place. Sanskrit is gradually given up as the medium for expressing the author's observations. The examples as well as the "rules" tend to appear increasingly in the regional languages.

[16] Professor Peter E. Hook's recollection is that a PhD dissertation on *Kaśmīra-śabdāmṛta* was completed at the University of Delhi sometime around the year 1980. According to recently acquired information, *Kaśmīra-śabdāmṛta* was published in 1898 C.E. More information about it will be available in a volume being edited by Mrinal Kaul and Ashok Aklujkar.

Further information about the works containing linguistic analysis mentioned in this section, as well as about the commentaries that elucidate and expand upon them, can easily and adequately be had from the introductions to the editions of the works and from the sources mentioned under "Suggestions for Further Reading" below. For this reason and also because most of the methodological, notional, and terminological features of the non-Sanskrit linguistic literature are the same as those of the corresponding literature in Sanskrit,[17] I shall now revert to the discussion of the Sanskrit grammatical tradition.

Pre-eminent position of Pāṇini's grammar

Even within the Sanskrit tradition, the non-Pāṇinian grammars of Sanskrit mentioned earlier differ from that of Pāṇini mainly in such *relatively* superficial respects as omission of observations pertaining to Vedic texts, inclusion of a grammar of Prakrits, addition of a few words or rules to cover new facts of Sanskrit or facts that escaped Pāṇini's attention, rewording of some *sūtras* to faciliate pronunciation and memorization, explicit discussion of syntax, use of different technical terms, and rearrangement of topics. The basic grammatical notions, their interrelations, and the procedure of derivation remain the same. This is true also of grammars and aids written for teaching Sanskrit.

In Pāṇini's immediate tradition, the changes noticed in the later grammatical literature are confined to addition of a few statements, alteration of the wording of some statements, and preference for a different order of statements for the sake of easy comprehension of the subject matter. Even if one were to maintain that some significant changes were made not to appear as changes by hiding them in Pāṇini's text, that is, by tampering with the *Aṣṭādhyāyī, Dhātu-pāṭha* ("catalog of verbal roots") and *Gaṇa-pāṭha* ("sets of language items meant to go with specific rules"), one would have to demonstrate convincingly that the original theoretical position or the functional mechanism of his grammar was altered. Such a demonstration as far as I am aware has not been offered.

Thus, Pāṇini's grammar, the *Aṣṭādhyāyī* ("Eight Study-units") or *Śabdānuśāsana* ("Instruction in Words or Linguistic Expressions")[18] has played the most significant role in shaping the Indian intellectual tradition.

[17] It has sometimes been said that the earliest available Tamil grammar *Tolkappiyam* does not contain Pāṇinian elements. Even if this statement were to be valid, the possibility that it draws on pre-Pāṇini sources, to which Pāṇini was close, cannot be ruled out, for it cannot be denied that there is considerable affinity between the *Tolkappiyam* and the early Sanskrit grammatical tradition. The *Tolkappiyam* is not a grammar that comes from an unrelated or entirely independent tradition.

[18] The word *śabda* has a wide range of meanings. It can refer to everything figuring in communication – from simple, isolated sounds to entire sentences. Usually, the title *Śabdānuśåsana* is glossed with "Instruction in Words." But this translation can be misleading if it is not clarified that "word" here does not stand only for the shortest free morphemes. Misconceptions such as "Pāṇini's grammar does not deal with syntax" or "Pāṇini's grammar is

Although composed in the context of the Vedic tradition and probably as an aid in furthering the activities that were considered especially important in that tradition, it did not remain confined in its use and appeal. Even Jain and Buddhist authors followed it, at least from the time they began to write scholarly commentaries on their sacred texts or from the time they began to use Sanskrit for systematic instructional *(śāstra)* writing. Although they eventually had grammars written by scholars belonging to their own religious tradition, it does not appear that those grammars replaced the *Aṣṭādhyāyī* completely, widely, or for a long time. Nor are most of those grammars or the grammars of Prakrits and other languages very different from the *Aṣṭādhyāyī* in the manner of presentation or in the basic technique of analysis. In short, unlike most other grammars, the *Aṣṭādhyāyī* became a truly pan-Indian grammar, known to almost all persons involved in the educational process. Pāṇini's commentators did not hesitate to give *ākumāraṁ yaśaḥ pāṇineḥ* ("Pāṇini's achievement is known even to boys") as an illustration for one of his own rules!

The process or derivation *(prakriyā)* aspect of the fascinating structure that Pāṇini erected for describing Sanskrit has, in particular, been assiduously studied by scholars in India for about 2,500 years – with significant creativity until the eighteenth century[19] and at least with ready mastery until the twentieth century. Even now there are scholars who devote their lifetime to the study of Pāṇini's work and contribute creatively to its understanding, but they are not as numerous or generally as well-prepared as they used to be. The decline of Sanskrit education or the growing anglicization or westernization of India has affected the field of Pāṇinian studies as it has many other.

Pāṇini has trained, disciplined, and challenged for centuries some of the sharpest minds the world has ever seen, has been a seminal influence in the traditional educational system,[20] has shaped the way practically all the surviving grammatical literature of pre-British India has been written, and has been declared to be to Indian intellectual tradition what Euclid was to the Classical European intellectual tradition.

Since the systematic study of Sanskrit by the Western world began in the eighteenth century, it is mainly Pāṇini's grammar that has exerted and continues to exert considerable influence on the development of language study in the West. The analytical details and techniques it contains have led, albeit

an 'item arrangement' grammar" can then take hold as they actually have. Hence I have pointed out the other possibility of rendering the title *Śabdānuśāsana.*

19 Nāgeśa or Nāgoji-bhaṭṭa, who died in 1755 CE, may be said to be the last author who is widely acknowledged to have made a truly original and wide-ranging contribution to the Pāṇinian system. There have been independent thinkers even after Nāgeśa. However, their works have not attracted the same degree of attention in the Pāṇinian tradition as Nāgeśa's.

20 Students used to memorize the *Aṣṭādhyāyī* at an early stage in the course of their studies. In some traditional schools, especially in the ones run by Ārya Samāj, they do so even now.

intermittently and sometimes quite indirectly, to the rise of phonetics as a science, refinement of the general technique of grammatical description, and enrichment of the theory of grammar in the West. The concepts of (a) ablaut, (b) division of Indo-European verbs into imperfect and perfect systems, and (c) rule ordering may be mentioned as examples in this context. Concepts in Pāṇini related to these are, respectively: (a) *guṇa : vr̥ddhi*, (b) *sārvadhātuka : ārdhadhātuka*, and (c) *asiddhatva*. Whorf (1940: 232) has thus rightly remarked: "Modern scientific linguistics dates from the rediscovery of Pāṇini by the Western world in the early nineteenth century." Scharfe's (1977: 115–16) observation that Western linguistics had to advance to a certain stage before it could appreciate certain features of Pāṇini's grammar also points in the same direction.

The preceding statement, however, should not be understood as implying that everything of significance in modern linguistics can be traced to Pāṇini. For example, as Cardona (1976: 232–7) and Sharma (1981: 44–5) point out, there are differences between Pāṇini's system and transformational linguistics. Further, the influence of Indian systematic philosophical works, including the ones in the line of Pāṇini, is yet to be prominently felt in the mainstream Western philosophical tradition. These works have much to share with disciplines such as semantics, textual hermeneutics, philosophy of language, theory of grammar, language-based approach to philosophical problems, literary criticism, and psychology. They have succeeded in engaging the minds of some Western specialists of these disciplines. Yet they cannot be said to have really penetrated the Western tradition.

The historical context of Pāṇini's grammar

Pāṇini's is the first full-scale surviving grammar in the Indian tradition. Incidental references to some morphological categories and use of some grammatical terminology are found in a few Brāhmaṇas, which are texts providing largely ritualistic and mythological comments on the earlier Veda collections known as the Saṁhitās. Some grammatical thought is preserved in Yāska's *Nirukta* and Śaunaka's *Br̥had-devatā* and *R̥gveda-prātiśākhya*, works most probably earlier than Pāṇini's *Aṣṭādhyāyī*. Śākalya's breakdown of the R̥gveda text into words, the *R̥gveda-pada-pāṭha*, can be used to reconstruct pre-Pāṇinian notions in grammar to some extent. The *Uṇādis* (word forms or suffixes, possibly *Sūtras)* referred to by Pāṇini could largely be there in the *Uṇādi-sūtras* associated at present with the *Aṣṭādhyāyī* (in their Pañca-padī version, not the Daśa-padī one). A Śikṣā attributed to Āpiśali and the *Phiṭ-sūtras* attributed to Śantanu or Śāntanava may antedate Pāṇini (See Cardona 1976: 146–53, 270–5 for conclusions that differ in some respects from the ones given here; also Scharfe 1977: 117–34 for differing views on the chronology of most of the works mentioned in the preceding lines). Kāśakr̥tsna's list of verbal roots that can be recovered from a much later Kannaḍa work may, in part, take us to a time before Pāṇini's. It is also possible that some post-Pāṇini grammars include or "recycle" statements from pre-Pāṇini grammars (Cardona 1976: 151). However, beyond a few citations, nothing from works that attempted to cover just about the same territory of linguistic usage as Pāṇini's *Aṣṭādhyāyī* and were composed before his time has come down to us.

Thus, the *Aṣṭādhyāyī* is like the Pyramids in that, while it impresses us, we have no accompanying explanation of the technique employed or real evidence of earlier attempts leading up to it; we have the finished product, but no statement from the author's time on how it was arrived at and no pointers in the form of earlier grammars. We are forced to infer the steps from Pāṇini's statements and often on the basis of commentaries in his tradition that put together the earlier and the later information (generally) without any indication of chronology or that try to derive later views from Pāṇini's much earlier statements in order to bestow authority on the views.

Pāṇini obviously had a large number of followers – followers endowed with critical acumen – not far removed from him in time. However, much of the literature they composed is unfortunately lost. We do not get a complete explanatory commentary on the *Aṣṭādhyāyī* until we come to the sixth to seventh century CE. This is when the *Kāśikā*, a work probably fashioned out of two originally independent commentaries by Jayāditya and Vāmana, was composed. What we have available for the more than one thousand years that passed since the time of Pāṇini are works rich and important in their own way but providing guidance only at specific points, more like lighthouses than steady beams of light showing the path from beginning to end.

These works are only four in number:

(a) the *Vārttika* ascribed to Kātyāyana or Vara-ruci (unlikely to be later than third century BCE) but containing the observations of many individuals;
(b) the *Mahābhāṣya* of Patañjali composed not later than the second century BCE;
(c) the *Mahābhāṣya-ṭīkā* or *Tripādī* (wrongly published under the title *Mahābhāṣya-dīpikā*) written by Bhartṛ-hari in the fifth century CE or earlier;
(d) the *Trikāṇḍī* or *Vākyapadīya* also written by Bhartṛ-hari in the same period as (c) above.

Among these (a) is preserved, as far as we know at present, only as a part of (b) and, derivately, as a part of the *Kāśikā*. No manuscripts giving an independent textual tradition of it have been reported. The voluminous text of approximately 1,500 printed pages, the *Mahābhāṣya* (b above), has been satisfactorily edited in the nineteenth century, but a critical edition of it utilizing manuscripts discovered later, particularly the manuscripts discovered in south India, is yet to be prepared. Its only early commentary, (c) above, survives in the form of a single, late, fragmentary, and badly written manuscript and has so far defied the attempts of scholars at a uniformly intelligible reconstruction. Finally, the fourth work, *Trikāṇḍī*, also survives in an incomplete state and bristles with textual problems, although in its present state it is much more extensive and helpful than (c) above.

The problems of understanding Pāṇini would seem insurmountable in this state of affairs, and there is no denying that they are difficult to tackle. However, the situation is not as bad as it seems at first. Much progress has been made, especially in recent times. The first helpful factor is the retentive tendency of the commentaries. As the direct and indirect commentators mentioned above tend to incorporate earlier explanations and readings, even if only to reject them, one can recover much of the thought of the intervening period and, on its basis and through a careful study of all available indications, form an idea of what Pāṇini is likely to have intended. Secondly, although much of the record of usage on which Pāṇini must have based his grammar has been lost, a relatively large record still survives in the form of various Vedic, Vedāṅga, and (early) Epic texts. This record is not in as clear a chronological order as we would have wished it to be, but it can nevertheless be pressed into service to determine the ground Pāṇini's statements probably tried to cover.

Theoretical frame of Pāṇini's grammar

Although Pāṇini's *Aṣṭādhyāyī* or *Śabdānuśāsana* is the earliest available grammar, it furnishes evidence of a very advanced awareness of what a grammar is supposed to achieve and of the tools and techniques it needs to achieve the goal. Its author must have had many predecessors in addition to the ten he refers to for specific purposes in different contexts; a grammar like it is very unlikely to be a sudden development brought about by ten or eleven persons. Secondly, there is some justification even to hold that Pāṇini was partly a redactor of the works of his predecessors. The few pieces of evidence that survive about the grammar of Āpiśali, one of the forerunners named by Pāṇini himself, indicate that Āpiśali had probably already employed some of the devices we associate with Pāṇini. Yet it cannot be denied that the *Aṣṭādhyāyī* embodies a theoretical vision that anyone thinking of human knowledge as progressing from crude to sophisticated or gross to subtle would hardly expect to have occurred so early in human history as the fifth century BCE, the latest time segment we can reasonably assign to Pāṇini's floruit.

Until about 1960, the most ambitious grammarians of Western languages understood the scope of their enterprise to be precise definitions or enumerations of items and exact formulation of rules regarding them, so that all the features of the language being described were captured. The scope of Pāṇini's enterprise is not exactly the same, but it is fairly close. In certain respects (e.g. in achieving a phonetic output to the extent of containing the right accents), it is even wider. It comes close to the expectations several Western linguists influenced by Noam Chomsky's views have entertained of grammar since the 1960s.

In the theory implicit in it, the final level of Pāṇini's grammar consists in formulation of sentences. What it does directly, however, in most of its statements is to show how the word forms *(padas)* leading to sentences can be derived (with no limit presupposed for the number of possible sentences). The assumption behind this derivation is that the basic elements necessary for the formulation of any sentence are already laid out; that is, it is presumed that the speaker already knows what is to be conveyed, what the constituents of what is to be conveyed are, and how the constituents are related (i.e. there is a semantic phase or level with an awareness of the syntactico-semantic nature of its constituents; the conceptual structure of the sentence is known). Different technical names are assigned to the constituents in accordance with the type of meaning they are expected to convey and how that meaning is related to other meanings.[21] In keeping with those names, the constituents, that is, the linguistic units expressing the constituents, take various verbal and nominal affixes, undergo further operations (mainly substitutions of or additions to affixes), if necessary, and appear in a phonetic form in which they are found in actual usage (see Cardona 1976: 182–7, 210–22, 1997: 7, 136–42 and Sharma 1981: 44–53 for explanation with examples). Keeping the sentence as the implicit context of his endeavor,[22] Pāṇini thus deals with syntax to the extent necessary, given the

[21] (a) The technical names are primarily *kriyā* "action (inclusive of state or condition)" and *kāraka* "participant in or deliverer of action." There are six divisions of the latter. As the later Pāṇinians clarify, the meanings of words eligible to take the designation *kāraka* have a stable, sequenceless, or "accomplished" (*siddha*) character. Those suitable for the *kriyā* designation convey meanings characterized by sequence – something that is "on the move" or is yet to be accomplished (*sādhya*).

(b) For the notions not covered by "participant in action" (e.g. the genitival meaning or possession in its various senses), which have a purely semantic relationship, as distinct from the syntactico-semantic one seen in the case of the *kārakas*, Pāṇini arranges for an assignment of case suffixes that depends directly on the occurrence of some other word forms and only indirectly, if necessary, on abstract notions such as the ones involved in the *kāraka* relations. His arrangement then is primarily morphological, not semantic.

(c) Pāṇini, in effect, makes do with only two parts of speech: *sub-anta* "nominal stem having a declensional affix" and *tiṅ-anta* "verb, a word having a conjugational affix." He does not need to recognize particles, adverbs, and adjectives as classes. They are all covered by his *sub-anta*, since he arranges for the deletion of declensional affixes at the appropriate stage in derivation wherever necessary (Cardona 1976: 222–4, 1997: 178–85). Several notional categories are thus merged into formal categories.

[22] (a) Pāṇini's general assumption is that, prior to the application of his grammar, discourse is broken down into sentences. He introduces the discourse level into his account only in so

nature of the language he was describing. He is generally not required to be concerned with the word order aspect of syntax, except in deriving compound or composite expressions, which he does in a masterly way.

While dealing with syntax in a generalized or abstract way, as indicated, Pāṇini treats within the frame provided by it the morphology and phonology of his object language. While his treatment of the former is nearly exhaustive, he is concerned with the latter only to the extent he needs it for constructing (accurate or efficient) morphological rules and to cover the changes the morphemes may undergo in the company of other morphemes or in the transition from the level of the word to that of the sentence.

As for phonetics, his work presupposes knowledge of it on the part of the user of his grammar (Cardona 1976: 206–10, 1983: 1–36, 1999: 180–7).

A similar observation can be made about gender and number distinctions. Pāṇini evinces interest in them only to the extent they are relevant to his derivational process. Otherwise, he assumes his user to be knowledgeable about them (Cardona 1997: 227–9; cf. Kiparsky 1979: 215–216, 224).

Thus, there is a well-defined direction to the *Aṣṭādhyāyī*. Pāṇini does not expand on an area of linguistic description simply because some components of that area figure in his grammar. The richness of detail is not achieved by departing from and making obscure the underlying objective or theory of the *Aṣṭādhyāyī*.

Operational domain of Pāṇini's grammar

Looking at the scope of Pāṇini's grammar in terms of its object language, as distinct from its scope in terms of the theoretical areas (phonology-morphophonemics, morphology, and syntax) it encompasses, one is struck by its breadth as well as beautiful balance between the actually attested language and the language that could conceivably come into being. Pāṇini includes in his presentation not only the language that was being spoken around him but also an older form of that language. In the former, he deals with (probably) the elite language of his part of northwestern India, the Gandhāra region around modern Lāhur or Attock, but does not fail to mention at least those dialectal peculiarities of the east and the north that seemed significant to him or that were known to him from the observations of others. Furthermore, while tying the rich and complex present of his object language to its past without departing from the synchronic stance of his statements, Pāṇini displays awareness of the fact that

far as it has a bearing on what he intends to derive, as, for example, in 1.4.40: *pratyāṅbhyāṁ śruvaḥ pūrvasya kartā*.

(b) Pāṇini does not define what a sentence is, nor is it clear that he should (Kiparsky 1979: 224–5). The *kāraka* procedure takes care of the syntax of simple sentences and of clauses in compound and complex sentences.

For a discussion of how Pāṇini deals with complex sentences see Cardona (1997: 139, 141–2, 167–78).

language continues to grow and that at least some of its molds are not exhausted by a grammarian's account, no matter how comprehensive he is in his coverage. For this anticipated creative use of the molds, Pāṇini provides (a) by not restricting his grammar only to the attested forms, (b) by leaving the extent of certain formations like compounds and sentences undefined, and (c) by adopting the devices such as *gaṇas* ("sets"), especially what his successors take to be *ākṛti-gaṇas* ("open sets/classes").

Because of the impressive scope of Pāṇini's grammar in the senses clarified above and because his successors thought of devices to make his statements accommodate later or missed linguistic facts, it has come to be widely believed that Pāṇini's grammar is a complete grammar – even to the extent of holding that whatever is not accounted for by his work, either directly or through the *Vārttika* and *Mahābhāṣya* comments, is not really Sanskrit.[23] The status of a seer *(ṛṣi* or *muni)* accorded to Pāṇini, due partly to his achievement and partly to the usual processes of myth formation, has served to strengthen this and similar views. However, it would be more justifiable to take the views as a well-deserved tribute to Pāṇini than to take them as absolutely or literally valid. Some linguistic facts of his time could have escaped Pāṇini, or he could have purposely kept them out of his grammar (Kiparsky 1979: 190–2). Similarly, his intention does not seem to have been to define Sanskrit for all time to come. Nevertheless, it is true that no other grammar known at present achieves as much as Pāṇini's and that his grammar is as close to a complete grammar that the world has ever come. "It describes, with the minutest detail, every inflection, derivation, and composition, and every syntactic usage of its author's speech. No other language, to this day, has been so perfectly described." (Bloomfield 1933: 11)

Pāṇini's technical devices

What is perhaps even more amazing is that Pāṇini's multifarious description is couched in only about 4,000 statements *(sūtras)*[24] of "utmost brevity and

[23] As an unintended extension of the latter kind of tribute Pāṇini has been accused of creating a stranglehold for Sanskrit – of regularizing Sanskrit to such an extent that it ceased to be a freely evolving language, could no longer express the changing needs and circumstances of people, and soon went out of currency as a living language. While it must be admitted that there is an ongoing dialectic between language and grammar, that grammars lend respectibility and power of social control to certain forms of language, and that Pāṇini's grammar did play a role in keeping Sanskrit *fundamentally* unchanged roughly after the beginning of the Christian era, it would be incorrect to attribute to it the intention of controlling the development of Sanskrit or to hold it responsible for Sanskrit's going out of common currency, regardless of what view one holds on the period or domain of Sanskrit as a living language.

[24] The exact number would depend on which *sūtras* one accepts as authentic and on how one splits some of the *sūtras*.

algebraic condensation" (Sharma 1981: 33).[25] True, these *sūtras* are supplemented by a list of roots, lists of language items (mostly nominal stems) attached to specific rules, and a phoneme list or sound catalog,[26] but even these accompanying texts are only moderately long.

The devices adopted by Pāṇini to achieve brevity are truly brilliant. Even if one were to see some of them as instances of clever reading or rearrangement of his text on the part of later scholars, there would still remain much that would make his grammar "one of the greatest monuments of human intelligence" (Bloomfield 1933: 11).

For example, Pāṇini presupposes a regrouping of the phonemes of Sanskrit in such a manner as would be convenient to him in composing grammatical rules. The phonemes were almost certainly arranged according to the places, processes, and features of articulation even before his time. They can be presumed to have had the following order: *a, ā, i, ī, u, ū* (simple vowels, short and long, back to front), *ṛ, ṝ, ḷ* (remaining simple vowels having consonant elements), *e, ai, o, au* (complex vowels), *k, kh, g, gh, ṅ, c, ch, j, jh, ñ, ṭ, ṭh, ḍ, ḍh, ṇ, t, th, d, dh, n, p, ph, b, bh, m* (stops from back to front; within each pentad a sequence of unvoiced unaspirate, unvoiced aspirate, voiced unaspirate, voiced aspirate, and nasal), *y, r, l, v* (semivowels), *ś, ṣ, s* (sibilants), and *h*. However, Pāṇini does not seem to have hesitated to reshape even this already convenient and scientific arrangement. How clearsighted he was about the purpose of his grammar and how consistent his procedure was is indicated by the fact that the sequence presupposed by him is as follows: *a i u Ṇ, ṛ ḷ K, e o Ṅ, ai au C, h[a] y[a] v[a] r[a] Ṭ, l[a] Ṇ, ñ[a] m[a] ṅ[a] ṇ[a] n[a] M[a], jh[a] bh[a] Ñ, gh[a] ḍh[a] dh[a] Ṣ, j[a] b[a] g[a]ḍ[a] d[a] Ś, kh[a] ph[a] ch[a] ṭh[a] th[a] c[a] ṭ[a] t[a] V, k[a], p[a] Y, ś[a] ṣ[a] s[a] R, h[a] L.* Here the vowel in brackets and the uppercase consonant letters are to be ignored in the actual process of derivation. The presence of the former is for ease in pronunciation and of the latter for formation of short forms. Thus, *aṆ* stands for *a i u*; *aC* for all vowels; *h[a]Ś* for *h*, all semivowels; all pentad or consonant class nasals, and all voiced consonants;

[25] A revealing saying current among Sanskrit scholars is *ardha-mātrā-lāghavena putrotsavaṁ manyante vaiyākaraṇāḥ* "If a grammarian can save as much as half a mora in the formulation of his rule, he rejoices as he would at the birth of a son." Cf. "To call these *sūtras* 'exceedingly brief' is, however, to indulge in the grossest understatement . . . even so laconic a document as a telegram would be prolix compared to a *sūtra*." Maurer 1981: 8–9.

[26] The *Dhātu-pāṭha*, *Gaṇa-pāṭha*, and *Akṣara-samāmnāya* are texts that Pāṇini's grammar clearly anticipates. For that reason, they must be deemed to be a part of it, despite the possibility that some items in the *Dhātu-pāṭha* and the *Gaṇa-pāṭha* may be later additions.

Other texts traditionally associated with the *Aṣṭādhyāyī* to a varying degree are *Uṇādi*, *Phiṭ-sūtra*, *(Pāṇinīya)-śikṣā*, and *Liṅgānuśāsana*. There is evidence to ascribe the first two to other authors. While Pāṇini may have presupposed their existence, there is no compelling reason why they should be viewed as a part of his grammar. Specialists have generally regarded the last two as post-Pāṇini works. In any case, the operation of his grammar does not depend on them. See Cardona (1976: 161–7, 170–82, 240–2, 1997: 85–135, 377); Scharfe (1977: 104–5).

and *h[a]L* for all consonants. The device of markers (shown here by capital letters) gives rise to a capacity for fashioning very short expressions resembling the formulae in chemistry. The order of phonemes that is adopted provides scope for convenient generalizations, especially in preparing rules of sound change. The savings are impressive in both departments.

In addition, Pāṇini achieves brevity of statement by employing monosyllabic artificial technical terms such as *ṭi* and *bha*, by using one-phoneme markers *(anubandhas)* to carry grammatical and procedural information, and by taking full advantage of the nominal sentence structure that is possible in Sanskrit. To explain the last first, Sanskrit does not require that a copula verb like "is" or "are" be physically present in a sentence; it is understood whenever a verb with a specific meaning is not employed by the speaker. Pāṇini not only dispenses with the prescriptive verbs that grammars (especially of standard or prestigious languages) and other *śāstras* tend to use but he also uses only *dṛśyate* ("is seen") and *dṛśyante* ("are seen") as predicates in nine *sūtras* and *anuprayujyate* in one.[27] As for the markers, they help Pāṇini in a variety of ways other than formation of abbreviations. With them, he indicates where a certain affix should be added, what the accent of the resultant morpheme would be, to which class certain items belong, and so on (see Cardona 1997: 47–50 for examples).

Making the statements short with the devices described above is one way of reducing the size of a grammar. Remarkable and probably revolutionary though the devices are for the time in which they were conceived, they turn out to be relatively elementary, given what Pāṇini has to offer further. He realizes that a grammar can be reduced in size by eliminating altogether the need for certain kinds of statements. If a grammar's rules can be viewed as automatically activating themselves whenever a certain string of phonemes is present or certain conditions (e.g. being eligible for a particular technical name) are met, the grammarian is not required to advise the reader about every step to be taken or not to be taken. By allowing interdependence or context-sharing among rules and by leaving room for them to refer to antecedents (cf. Sharma 1981: 33–41; Cardona 1997: 401–27), the grammarian can eliminate the need to guide the

27 (a) These *sūtras* have the form "*anyeṣv api / anyebhyo 'pi / anyeṣām api / chandasy api / bhūte 'pi/itarābhyo 'pi*" followed by *dṛśyate/dṛśyante*. They supplement or extend the preceding rules in an uncharacteristically nonspecific way and look like marginal notes that got interpolated into the text. So it is possible that there is only one real exception, *anuprayujyate* in rule 3.1.40, to Pāṇini's avoidance of verbs as predicates. If a good case is made for regarding rule 3.1.40 or the word *anuprayujyate* in it as an interpolation, Pāṇini may be said to have refrained from using a single finite verb in his statements.
(b) It is generally agreed that *sūtra* 1.2.55, in which the verb *syāt* is found is part of small group of interpolated *sūtras*.

user of his grammar through such advices as "Do Y after X" or "Don't do Y after X."

However, for such automatic application of rules to take place without generating unintended results, a particular sequence must be established among the rules, and provision must be made for cyclical application as well as blocking of some of the rules whenever it is desirable to do so. It is one of the amazing features of Pāṇini's grammar that he orders his rules and provides in very ingenious ways for their activation, reactivation, and nonactivation (Cardona 1976: 189–91).

To facilitate this computer-like working of the grammar, Pāṇini selectively allows a substitute to have the status of its substituend (thus to inherit a technical name needed for triggering an operation) and, using the zero morpheme device, and permits the effects of certain linguistic elements to linger even after the elements themselves disappear. Furthermore, he brilliantly provides that the results brought about by some rules will not be "known" to certain other rules, so that the question of these other rules becoming activated does not arise. The best example of the application of this device, known as *asiddhatva*, is the last three chapters of his eight-book grammar. What these chapters state or derive is considered to be nonexistent from the point of view of chapters 1.1–8.1. The situation of the preceding chapters is like that of a grandfather who did not witness his grandson's deeds and hence could not react to them. The results of chapters 8.2–8.4 remain impervious to the relevant operations stated in the preceding chapters, and unwanted transformations are blocked.

The ordering of rules, in turn, helps Pāṇini further in reducing the size of his individual rules. Conforming to a convention that can be inferred from the works of other *sūtra* authors but is not as impressively exploited as in his own work, he opts for *anuvṛtti* ("recurrence, dittoing"). If an expression occuring in rule R1 can be understood in rule R2, then Pāṇini does not employ it again in R2. The same for R3, R4, and so on, if possible. When this device is followed to assign a technical name to a class of elements, to continue an operation, or to institute an interpretion, an *anuvṛtti* of the *adhikāra*-type or "heading"-type results (Cardona 1997: 64–74; Sharma 1981: 33–7). It allows Pāṇini to create useful domains and subdomains within his grammar.

How could Pāṇini have achieved what he did?

It is suggested by the preceding sketch that Pāṇini went about constructing his grammar in four basic (long and demanding) steps. A conceptually helpful reconstruction of his major moves would be as follows, unless he was heavily indebted to a predecessor for the major structural decisions regarding the *Aṣṭādhyāyī*:

(a) Like any other competent and committed grammarian, he first arranged his findings[28] about the object language in logical groups,[29] composing as precise and unambiguous rules for each group as he could and creating convenient sets in the form of a sound catalog, a list of roots, and several lists of language items (primarily nominal stems) meant to be covered by specific rules.
(b) Then he brought about as much brevity among these rules as he could by employing devices such as abbreviations, markers, and *anuvṛtti* or *adhikāra*.
(c) Next was applied to the groups the machinery he had thought of to introduce automation. This application must have caused changes in the places of groups as well as in the internal sequences of groups (necessitating frequent reconsideration of *adhikāra* and *anuvṛtti* details) and also required a rearranging of the subsets within the *akṣara-samāmnāya*. Through a constant weighing of the implications or consequences of all such changes, Pāṇini must have "fine-tuned" his grammar *and* his descriptive devices.
(d) The final step probably was to add methodological statements (or, rather, the final versions of methodological statements) that he did not expect his reader to know or figure out precisely, including clarifications of terminology and of how automation was to work. Such statements disturb in some cases the continuity of the logical groups he must have established (at least as a preparatory step). This indicates that the statements' placing was not based only on the consideration that they belonged to a higher or metalevel. If that were the case, they *all* would

[28] It is assumed that such steps in the discovery procedure as collection of language data, application of the principle of binary opposition to determine the linguistic units causing difference of meaning, analysis of forms into smaller units, and determination of the grammatical meanings of certain morphemes have already been completed at this point. See Cardona (1997: 428–542) for a reconstruction of Pāṇini's discovery procedure.

The principle of binary opposition or the strategy of setting up minimal pairs is implicit in the method of *anvaya-vyatireka* well-known to Indian philosophers and explicitly accepted at an early date by the Pāṇinians.

[29] The topical division of the *Aṣṭādhyāyī* is roughly as follows (the first number stands for the book and the second for the chapter):

1.1–1.2: rules introducing technical terms and interpretive or methodological conventions;

1.3–2.4: cases or postnominal endings, compounds;

3.1–5.4: affixation for primary and secondary stem formation and for deriving sentence-usable words;

6.1–8.4: variations in nominal stems, roots, and suffixes; accents of compounds; sentence accents, morphophonological rules; rules of synthesis in general.

have been found together, probably at the very beginning of his grammar, as many of them indeed are.

The magnitude of the variables one must keep track of to bring about a result of the described kind is mind-boggling,[30] especially if one remembers (a) that the automation mentioned in this context must contend with blocking as well as reactivation, (b) that the number of affixes involved in a highly inflectional language like Sanskrit is large, and (c) that the possibility of Pāṇini having carried out his work in the absence of writing or extensive access to writing cannot yet be convincingly ruled out. Even if one were to assume that Pāṇini derived much help from his predecessors or that, enthralled as we are by the work of his successors, we are reading too much into his work, he would still remain a *ṛṣi*, a seer. "Only those who see the invisible can do the impossible" as a poster in a dentist's office once declared!

Pāṇini's grammar is remarkable also in terms of the awareness it displays of certain basic methodological principles.

He could have been concerned with the language of a particular stratum in the society, but this does not, as indicated above, impart a strong prescriptive or restrictive tone to his work. He still clearly accepts primacy of language over grammar.

If writing was known or was in common use in his time, then his empiricism must be said to be even more sophisticated. He must have then considered language in its spoken form as "more real" than written language (i.e. actual usage).

His descriptivism is not likely to have been of a secular sort in the sense that he could have viewed the use of grammatical speech as yielding something akin to religious merit (Cardona 1976: 242–3, 1997: 546–56). This is how his temporally close successors thought of the use of grammatical speech, and there is no reason to believe that his thought on the matter diverged radically from theirs. Yet the descriptivism does not result in a grammar meant to teach and spread the

[30] (a) It seems from the statements in a few early Pāṇinian works that in some cases even Pāṇini had second thoughts and reworded some of his rules subsequent to his work's gaining currency. He is spoken of as having given two versions to his students.
(b) Scharfe (1977: 91) thinks that some of the interpolations in the *Aṣṭādhyāyī* were made by Pāṇini himself.
(c) The difficult nature of Pāṇini's undertaking as an author can be judged also from the hard work his readers have to put in before they even begin to feel that they understand his work. To quote Scharfe's (1977: 91) witty comment, "To the uninitiated the first impression is one of organized chaos." Before one memorizes a significant part of the *Aṣṭādhyāyī*, one cannot really see where one is headed. The practice followed in traditional schools of Sanskrit was (and, to some extent, is) the sensible one of making the students memorize the *Aṣṭādhyāyī* at a young age and then explaining its application in appropriate installments.
The attempts to rearrange Pāṇini strictly in terms of topic and to eliminate or delimit the operation of the rule order factor begin at least as early as the fourth to fifth century CE. They gain in strength as we move ahead in time and are an index of how difficult Pāṇini's task must have been.

language he valued. His grammar is a grammarian's grammar. It assumes that the reader already knows the language.

His use of meaning as a tool of analysis and grammatical statement is also judicious. Meaning is used in his grammar only where it can initially or ultimately serve to distinguish forms and does not result in comparisons of one nebulous or slippery concept with another. He does not indulge in an exploration of how (what is felt to be) the same or similar meaning is articulated differently, although he does use synonymy and interrelatedness of meaning wherever he must or when they can provide him with an elegant descriptive tool.[31] To explore identity or similarity of meaning without some such constraints would have probably resulted in a never-ending exploration and brought no benefit to his grammar. Also, there is a distinct preference for formal definitions over notional definitions in his work.

Furthermore, as indicated above, he holds the view that the mission of a grammar is not complete until it generates instances of the spoken language (the surface structure).[32]

Another noteworthy feature of the *Aṣṭādhyāyī* is that Pāṇini maintains a distinction between object language and metalanguage (Scharfe 1971; Cardona 1976: 193–206). He states that the reference of words in his rules is to themselves, not to something external to them (what we normally call meaning,

[31] (a) Cardona (1976: 224–5); Kiparsky (1979: 217); P.S. Subrahmanyam's article in Joshi and Laddu (1983: 127–36).

(b) As examples of how Pāṇini avoids getting into possible semantic and philosophical problems, see his (1.4.105–1.4.107) definitions of first person and second person in terms of explicit or implict co-occurrence of the forms of *asmad* and *yuṣmad*, the first and second person pronouns.

One of the astute moves Pāṇini makes to avoid detailed or enumerative definitions of complex or vague areas is to follow a particular order in offering his definitions. For example, he (1.4.108) first defines the first and second persons and thus frees himself to make the simple declaration: "the remaining area is that of the third person." To think of such a sequence in defining is especially remarkable given the fact that the Sanskrit designation of (what English grammar calls) the third person known to Pāṇini was *prathama* "first." In many other situations also, Pāṇini uses this "remainder" or *śeṣe* strategy effectively.

[32] It has been debated whether Pāṇini does this out of necessity – writing was not known to him (contrast Scharfe 1977: 113) or was scarcely used in his community – or as an indication of the position (later expressed by his successors) that the written form of language is derivative and hence less real.

If Pāṇini indeed composed his grammar in an entirely or primarily oral culture, it would probably be the most complex achievement ever registered in an oral tradition.

There can, however, be little doubt that Pāṇini intended his grammar primarily to be taught and preserved orally. This is evident from his use of a particular type of *(svarita)* accent to mark the expressions that were to be understood with all the rules of specific sections as presiding terms *(adhikāra)*, from his use of nasalization to indicate the vowels that were not to form part of derivation, and from his use in the *Dhātu-pāṭha* of certain accents to indicate the kinds of endings the roots are to take; cf. Cardona (1976: 206); Scharfe (1977: 89–90).

sense, or thing meant) as in the language the rules describe.[33] He uses the object language's ablative, genitive, and locative cases with a metalinguistic value to indicate the contexts "to the right of," "to the left of," and "as a substitute for" that need to be specified in grammatical operations for the intended results. Also, there are many cases in the *Aṣṭādhyāyī* where the rules of *sandhi* or sound variation applicable to the object language are not applied to the rules themselves, because doing so would have made it difficult for the user to understand the intended linguistic units precisely and thus to understand the intent of the rules.

Above all, Pāṇini comes across as a person who does not lose sight of what his principal goal is. The criteria of brevity and securing maximum defensible generalization carry much weight for him. He does not hesitate to align the components of his (implicit) theory and technique differently within the limits of these criteria as the need may be. He does not maintain a separation between phonology, morphology, syntax, or discourse just because these concepts are applicable to units at different levels.[34] He would have probably maintained such a separation if he were to write a work on the theory of grammar or if he were to write an "item arrangement" grammar of the type commonly written for Western languages in the last few centuries, but his is, at the extremities, a grammar of transformation of concatenations, resorting, wherever it is convenient to do so, to item arrangement. He allows his statements in one area to be shaped by his needs in another, regardless of the theoretical–conceptual divisions. For example, his sound catalog given above does not list all semivowels or all voiced aspirates with one marker at the end. To group them so would have been conceptually consistent but would not have met his needs in the sphere of morphology and morphophonemics in an economical manner. So at these junctures in the sound catalog, he introduces the markers where they will give him abbreviations of greater use in morphology and morphophonemics, that is, more efficient devices for the larger needs of his grammar. Similarly, he treats case usage *(kāraka)*, compound formation *(samāsa* or *vṛtti)*, primary derivation *(kṛd-anta)*, and secondary derivation *(taddhita)* in mostly continuous sections, but he does not hesitate to go against the logical or conceptual associations (indicated by the labels *kāraka*, *samāsa*, *kṛd-anta*, and *taddhita*) and puts some of the statements

33 An exception to this general principle is carefully included in Pāṇini's statement 1.1.68. This *sūtra* contains a word meaning "except where the words in the rules are terms standing for linguistic units." Such terms could be words which by their very nature or ordinary language meaning stand for linguistic forms (e.g. *vākya* "sentence"). They could also be words which are defined to refer to certain forms (e.g. *guṇa* is defined to stand for "*a*," "*e*" and "*o*"). In the latter sense, they would be technical terms.

34 Although Pāṇini may not have had equivalent terms for "phonology," and so on, it is evident from his practice that he was aware that linguistic analysis takes place at levels analogous to our "phonological level," and so on.

having a bearing on the formations concerned (e.g. the statements about the phonetic features of formations) away from the sections which are primarily devoted to them. As the primary and explicit target of most of his statements is derivation of word forms, one notices the crisscrossing of phonological, syntactic, and discourse levels most in his morphology.

Successors of Pāṇini

In terms of form, a significant change in the later history of the *Aṣṭādhyāyī* was its recasting as a grammar arranged according to topics.

The trend, begun much earlier in what are considered to be non-Pāṇinian grammars, is first evidenced in Pāṇini's own tradition, as far as the available literature goes, in the *Rūpāvatāra* of Dharma-kīrti (tenth century CE). Through the *Prakriyā-kaumudī* of Rāma-candra (fifteenth century CE), it culminates in the *Siddhānta-kaumudī* of Bhaṭṭoji-dīkṣita (seventeenth century CE).

The difficulties of mastering the *Aṣṭādhyāyī* "machinery" and the changing social and educational conditions (especially of Brahmanism or older Hinduism) make this change understandable. The change also served to bring into focus some problems of interpreting the *Aṣṭādhyāyī*. Yet it is not a change in the *basic orientation* of the Pāṇinīyas. Earlier commentaries like the *Kāśikā* followed the sequence of Pāṇini's statements and, practically under each statement, provided indications of how the statement was connected to other statements – what its field of applicability *(pradeśa)* was, which types of forms it helped us to derive, and so on. They brought the topical arrangement to bear on the rules where the latter stood. Commentaries such as the *Siddhānta-kaumudī* mainly reverse the direction involved in the process. They bring topics (e.g. *sandhi* and derivation of case forms) to the forefront and allow considerations of rule sequence to intrude into the discussion of topics when necessary. That is about all the *major* difference there is between the earlier and later procedures – sometimes referred to as *Kāśikā* method and *Siddhānta-kaumudī* method after the most prominent examples. Proficient users had to be aware of both aspects – sequence of the text and underlying topical concerns – of Pāṇini's "machine" in any case. The difference pertained to what was felt to be more convenient for getting an entry into the system and learning to run the machine.

The increasing attention given to the order of the *Aṣṭādhyāyī* serves as testimony to the tremendous intellectual interest taken in its arrangement, in the way it was expected to function, and in the wording of its rules. Another testimony to this interest is furnished by a subbranch of Pāṇinian literature that particularly flourished in the later centuries. It consists of *paribhāṣā* works which devote themselves primarily to a study of the metarules or metalinguistic principles of Pāṇini's system (Cardona 1997: 52–64). Although many significant observations of these works are derived from Patañjali's *Mahābhāṣya* and although there is a *paribhāṣā* text said to have been written by as early an author as Vyāḍi (generally thought to have lived sometime between the time of Pāṇini and the time of Patañjali), it is mainly the scholars of the later period (eleventh to eighteenth centuries CE) who brought *paribhāṣā* study into prominence.

The distinctive contribution of Bhartṛ-hari

The most significant development of the Pāṇinian school as a whole, as distinct from formal studies of only the *Aṣṭādhyāyī* and its supplements, was in the direction of semantics, general theory of grammar, philosophy of language, and linguistic approach to philosophical and religious–spiritual issues. Through Bhartṛ-hari, the school made an unparalleled contribution to these areas. Several of Bhartṛ-hari's ideas were inspired by Kātyāyana and Patañjali and whatever had survived of a work called *Saṁgraha* (traditionally attributed to Vyāḍi). He was also clearly indebted to Vasu-rāta, whose works do not seem to have come down to us, and to the author of the so far undiscovered *Dhyāna-graha*. Yet one gets the feeling that Bhartṛ-hari was an extraordinarily original thinker with amazing mastery of and penetrating insight into many branches of learning, in addition to the technical side of Pāṇini's grammar.

To speak in terms of logical connections, the theoretical thought preserved in Bhartṛ-hari's work (not the text of the work itself) begins where sentence derivation begins in Pāṇini's grammar. However, this thought proceeds in the opposite direction and delves deeper into what Pāṇini assumes. We noted above that the underlying assumption for the mechanism of Pāṇini's grammar to operate is that the semantic constituents of the sentence to be derived are known and the user is aware of how they are related. The action *(kriyā)* is the most central constituent or principal denotatum among them, and the fashioners of action *(kārakas)* are organized around it. It is the nature of this *kriyā* and the *kārakas* that Bhartṛ-hari explores, among other things, and he does so in the light of many subtle contributions of his predecessors.

In its full form the exploration covers: word meaning, sentence meaning; lexical meaning, grammatical meaning; signification and cosignification (*dyotana*, signification in dependence on another linguistic element); difference between sense and reference;[35] situations in which expressions are used and situations in which

35 As can be anticipated from the *kāraka* discussion, the Pāṇinians do not seem to maintain a sharp distinction between sense and reference (or meaning and object/referent). According to them, if an expression can refer to something external or physical in a given context, then that external or physical thing is its meaning in that context. If this is not the case, then the meaning is conceptual or in the form of a mental construct.

Lexical meanings are convenient abstractions. Sentence meaning, which obtains in actual linguistic communication, is the reality. Therefore, there is no problem for the Pāṇinians in accepting a fluctuating word meaning.

they are mentioned or quoted; nature of linguistic units *(sphoṭa);* relationship between sound and language; paradoxes; processes of communication, linguistic abstraction, and systematization, and how a correct understanding of these processes on our part leads to a correct understanding of the concepts and phenomena specified earlier; relationship between language and the world; and the nature of language and mind or worldly self *(buddhi)*, and so on.

As a result of Bhartṛ-hari's unrelenting pursuit of these notions and issues, a whole philosophy arises which concludes, among other things, that sentence is the primary unit of language; that meaning has no separate existence; it is just linguistic expressions looked at from another point of view; that our experience of the world is infused with language; that we create a conceptual universe out of the interaction between language (or mind) and the physical world; and that spiritual liberation must consist in wiping out the traces of diversity from language (or mind).

There is much more to Bhartṛ-hari's work than the preceding outline would indicate. The text of his work actually begins roughly where the preceding paragraph ends. It gradually unfolds into what I state earlier in the same paragraph. He weaves his thinking into the rich texture formed by several lines of thinking such as (a) the technical details of Pāṇini's grammar, (b) the explicit and not so explicit remarks of Kātyāyana and Patañjali, (c) the philosophies expounded in such systems as Sāṁkhya, Vaiśeṣika, Mīmāṁsā, and Buddhism, (d) the general Brahmanical socio-religious philosophy, and (e) the speech mysticism of the Veda.[36]

He explains the theoretical and philosophical bases or implications of Pāṇini's grammar and Kātyāyana's and Patañjali's comments thereto as no other available work written before his time does.

[36] The relationship of the different components of the Pāṇini-Bhartṛ-hari tradition with other traditions of learning or other bodies of texts can be approximated as follows (in some cases words with overlapping meanings have been used here to give a clearer idea of the intended area or areas):

Mantra/Saṁhitā literature, certain Brāhmaṇas, a few Upaniṣads, works from the older phases of Yoga and Tantra (lost or incorporated as parts of surviving works) → general thinking on the role of language, psycho-metaphysics, religious-spiritual practice based on speech

Brāhmaṇas, Pada-pāṭha, Nirukta → general concepts of grammar (stem, affix, parts of speech, etc.), morphology;

Prātiśākhyas → sound variation, morphophonemics, *sandhi*;

Śikṣā → phonetics, phonology;

Nirukta, Mīmāṁsā, Buddhist philosophy → study of meaning at various levels, linguistic and philosophical semantics.

While the historical indebtedness and interaction between text bodies and domains or levels of linguistic thought suggested here by arrows should be noted, the possibility that many developments within the tradition of the grammarians from Pāṇini to Bhartṛ-hari could have taken place because of (a) internal dynamics and (b) the work of nonconforming grammarians should not be overlooked.

His linguistic dissolution of philosophical and spiritual–religious problems did not become the mainstream of Indian philosophy,[37] but it did leave its impact on a number of religio-philosophical schools and started or preserved a tradition of *artha-granthas* (texts on semantics), as distinct from *prakriyā-granthas* (derivation texts) in the line of Pāṇini.[38]

One particularly significant achievement made possible by this sustained attention to meaning was the development in second millenium CE of various theories of how the meanings of sentences should be expressed and how grammatical relations should be rendered explicit *(śābda-bodha).*

Language-based poetics

An outcome of the combined orientations of Pāṇini and Bhartṛ-hari can be seen in the development of poetics in India. While this discipline derives its psychological side mainly from the traditions of dramaturgy and religio-philosophical thinking in general, its treatment of literary works as text is largely shaped by the traditions of Pāṇinian grammar (inclusive of the thought of such theoreticians as Bhartṛ-hari) and Mīmāṁsā. It has sometimes even been described as *vyākaraṇasya puccham* ("the tail of grammar"). Its principal and quite remarkable achievement, which brings it fairly close to some aspects of stylistics in the West (Aklujkar 1972), is its constant effort to tie readers' reactions to literary texts to the linguistic facts of those texts. It does not speak in vague impressionistic terms, except where it must in such contexts as describing the states of mind that literature in general generates. These states can be brought within the grasp of the *śāstra* reader only through explicit or implicit metaphors, and to that extent it does use impressionistic language (e.g. it speaks of *druti* "liquidity" of mind as the nature of response to a particular type of literary piece). Otherwise, however, it seeks to establish a correlation between the literary meaning understood by the reader and the words used by the author.

37 The reasons given by the philosophers who express their opposition to Bhartṛ-hari's views boil down to refusal to erase the boundary between cognition and language, that is, to nonacceptance of the thesis that all worldly cognition is pervaded by language and is ultimately inseparable from it.

For theologians or philosophers with a religious bent of mind, the principal or additional reason for parting company with Bhartṛ-hari is his elevation of the most basic form of language to the status of *brahman*, the supreme truth or God of their own philosophies.

38 (a) Important Pāṇinian *artha-granthas* written as late as the seventeenth and eighteenth centuries are Koṇḍa-bhaṭṭa's/Kauṇḍa-bhaṭṭa's *Vaiyākaraṇa-bhūṣaṇa* and its shorter recast, Nāgeśa-bhaṭṭa's/Nāgojī-bhaṭṭa's *Vaiyākaraṇa-siddhānta-mañjūṣā* in three versions, and Parvatīya Viśveśvara-sūri's *Vyākaraṇa-siddhānta-sudhā-nidhi*.

(b) For more on Bhartṛ-hari and the authors who followed him, see Cardona (1976: 293–307), Scharfe (1977: 170–5).

This approach leads it to develop theories of signification[39] and to map out the various units, layers, and ways through which literary texts affect readers. Its analysis (a) of relationship between sound and literary effect and (b) of figures of speech is especially impressive.[40] The latter analysis is systematized with an exquisite awareness of subtle semantic distinctions, and – what is of special interest to us in the present context – it draws heavily upon grammar to determine the varieties and subvarieties of poetic figures (Chari 1990; Dhayagude 1981; Gerow 1977).

Suggestions for further reading

Earlier publications about which information can be gathered from the following list are not separately specified. Secondly, somewhat in the manner of Pāṇini's *adhikāra* or *anuvṛtti* technique, what appears earlier in the suggestions is to be understood in the subsequent suggestions. The reader is expected to move, from the general to the specific or from a publications group aiming at wider coverage to a publications group concentrating on in-depth coverage of narrower study areas. If a publication primarily focuses on something other than a tradition of language study in India, the reader's attention is drawn to the immediately relevant pages.

1. To complete one's understanding of the literature of linguistic interest that may be surviving in the Indian tradition, one ultimately needs to go to manuscript collections, public and private, and their catalogs, accession lists and so on. However, one can prepare a nearly comprehensive list of such literature, especially of what is published, if one consults the following sources, the scope of each of which is indicated by the words preceding the entry: (a) Most Indian literary languages: Pattanayak (1973); Scharfe (1977); (b) Sanskrit, Pāli, and Prakrit: Banerji (1996); (c) Sanskrit: Cardona (1976) (pp. 139–41 list histories, including those of non-Pāṇinian schools of Sanskrit grammar, bibliographies, and earlier surveys of research, which, in turn, can inform one further about authors and their works); Chakrabarti (1996); Verhagen (1994); Cardona (1999); (d) Pāli: Law (1933: 630–8); Norman (1983: 163–8), Hazra (1994: 751–7); Pind (1989, 1990, 1995), 1997; (e) Prakrit and Apabhraṁśa: Jaina (1965: 26–41); (f) Prakrit: Nitti-Dolci (1938); Jaina (1961: 636–55); Upadhye (1975: 7–9); (g) Apabhraṁśa: Tagare

[39] The culmination of these theories may be seen in the *Dhvanyāloka* or *Sahṛdayāloka* of Ānandavardhana, ninth century CE.

[40] The logically most rigorous and helpful texts in this respect are Mammaṭa's *Kāvya-prakāśa*, Ruyyaka's *Alaṁkāra-sarvasva*, Śobhākara's *Alaṁkāra-ratnākara*, and Jagannātha's *Rasagaṅgādhara*.

(1948: 1–7). (h) Dravidian languages: Agesthialingom and Sakthivel (1973); Andronov (1966); (i) Tamil: Zvelebil (1973: 131–54; Tolkāppiyam, 1995: 705–9), (j) Kannada: Kulli (1991); (k) Marathi, early phases: Arjunavāḍakara (1992); and (l) Hindi, early phases: Bhatia (1987).

Besides surveying what are available as premodern texts in Indian languages, most of these sources specify the editions and translations of such texts and their studies carried out by modern and premodern scholars – the latter generally in the form of commentaries known by such designations as *vivaraṇa*, *vyākhyā*, *vyākhyāna*, *ṭīkā*, *paddhati*, *pañcikā*, *pañjikā*, *vṛtti*, *vārttika*, and *bhāṣya*.

2. A consideration of India's contribution to thought on language and to methods of language study, along with a consideration of what some other traditions have contributed in the same areas, can be found in Auroux (2000); Emeneau (1955); Itkonen (1991); Koerner and Asher (1995: 66b–68a, 69b–70a, 59–65, 66–71, 72–7, 77–9, 188–91); and Van Bekkum (1997).
3. Discussion of the features and accomplishments of individual grammars should particularly be read in Agesthialingom and Kumaraswami Raja (1975); Scharfe (1977); Maurer (1981); Sharma (1981); Cardona (1983); Sharma (1987); Kulli (1991); Cardona (1997); Pind (1997); and Bhatia (2001a).
4. Mukherji (1976) traces the evolution of Sanskrit prosody.
5. Vogel (1979) is a masterly survey of known Sanskrit lexicons carried out with superb attention to bibliographic detail.
6. For further information about Sanskrit poetics, one should consult: Raghavan and Nagendra (1970); Gerow (1971); Aklujkar (1972); Warder (1972); Dhadphale (1975); Gerow (1977); Dhayagude (1981: v–vi mentioning earlier comparative treatments); Chari (1990); (p. 218 fn. 2 lists earlier histories and surveys which are not intended to be replaced by Gerow's own work).
7. An attempt to unravel the connections between Bhartṛ-hari's linguistic and philosophical thought is made in Aklujkar (2001).

Part 4

Multilingualism, contact, and convergence

10 Contexts of multilingualism

E. Annamalai

Introduction

This chapter primarily presents the contexts of multilingualism in one major South Asian country, India. However, most of the observations made about India are applicable to multilingual contexts of other South Asian countries such as Pakistan, Bangladesh, Sri Lanka, and Nepal. India has been a multilingual country from the time of its recorded history and before. It was not a country in the geopolitical sense of being under one political authority but in the geocultural sense of having, through interaction between cultures over time, a superordinate synthetic culture with shared mythologies and beliefs that guide life. It is the plurality of cultures and the languages that codify them that define India throughout its history. It is the same plurality that continues to be the defining factor in making India into a nation in the modern period. It is a nation with no one language designated to define its nationhood. India has been functioning always, as a country in the past and as a nation in the present, in a multilingual context.

As with most countries, migration from outside was one reason for the many languages found in India, which added themselves to the languages already present. When the migrants (and invaders) became settlers, their language came to stay in the country. The new languages during historic times came in the earliest historical period from the west Asian region, in the medieval period, from the central Asian region, and in the modern, from Western Europe. Some of the migrated languages like that of the Zoroastrians and the Portuguese were lost, while some, such as Sanskrit and English, remained primarily as a second language, even though their native speakers were lost. Some native languages like the language of the Indus valley were lost with their speakers, while some linguistic communities shifted their language to one or other of the migrants' languages. Though the multilingual composition of the country has changed over time, multilingualism has remained constant. At no time in the history of India have the changes led to monolingualism in any region of the country.

Another reason for the multiplicity of languages is the emergence of new languages from the old. There is recorded evidence for language birth when the languages have written literature. Such births for oral languages could only be hypothesized by comparative linguistic reconstruction. There was a spurt of new languages in the medieval period. Most of the contemporary Indo-Aryan languages came to have autonomous status during this period, and in the Dravidian south of India, Malayalam became a separate language in this period. These new languages came into existence due to sociopolitical and cultural, primarily literary, happenings (Pollock 1998). New languages arose also due to contact between languages when communication was necessary. Sadari in Bihar, Halbi in Madhya Pradesh, Desia in Orissa, and Nagamese in Nagaland are examples of languages that evolved for interlanguage communication. These languages do not have social prestige and are often denied grammatical autonomy by their speakers. New languages also came into existence to serve the purpose of political identity, which get a differentiating name without having an autonomous grammar. Urdu, as distinct from Hindi, is an example.

Demographic context

To count the languages of a country is more than a statistical exercise. It invokes the linguistic problem of measuring mutual intelligibility based on grammar used to establish language status to a speech form as opposed to dialect status and the sociopolitical problem of perceiving and constructing separateness of one speech form from another based on the identity of the speech community. The first count of the languages was undertaken by the British colonial government (as it did the counting of the flora, fauna, castes, and tribes of the country to gain knowledge for controlling and governing it). It produced the Linguistic Survey of India, carried out in the 1930s under the superintendence of the British officer, George Grierson. Though the survey did not cover the whole country equally comprehensively, for the first time it identified, named, and classified languages from outside the perceptions of the linguistic communities and became the benchmark for future surveys. The decennial census, beginning in 1801, enumerates mother tongues of people as reported by them, which are markers of social identity rather than of grammatical autonomy, and abstracts them into languages based on grammatical and political considerations. There is also a survey of People of India, which includes self-reported information on languages collected from the communities surveyed (K. S. Singh and Manoharan 1993). As could be expected, the number of languages in different surveys does not tally.

The Linguistic Survey of India identified over one hundred languages and the survey of People of India, 191 (this survey does not distinguish between mother tongue and language, as the census does). The figure varies from census to census because of political and administrative decisions on the criteria for the inclusion of languages based on the number of speakers and the criteria for the

Table 10.1 *Scheduled languages in descending order of strength*

Language	Number (%)	Language	Number (%)
Hindi	337,272,114 (39.85)	Oriya	28,061,313 (3.32)
Bengali	69,595,738 (8,22)	Punjabi	23,378,744 (2.76)
Telugu	66,017,615 (7.80)	Assamese	13,079,696 (1.55)
Marathi	62,481,681 (7.38)	Sindhi	2,122,848 (0.25)
Tamil	53,006,368 (6.26)	Nepali	2,076,645 (0.25)
Urdu	43,406,932 (5.13)	Konkani	1,760,607 (0.21)
Gujarati	40,673,814 (4.81)	Manipuri	1,270,216 (0.15)
Kannada	32,753,676 (3.87)	Sanskrit	49,736 (0.01)
Malayalam	30,377,176 (3.59)		

Source: www.censusindia.net/results/eci11_page5.html, accessed August 21, 2005.

classification of mother tongues into languages. According to the 1961 Census, which is the most inclusive and exhaustive, there are 1,652 mother tongues classified into 193 languages (Government of India 1964; Nigam 1972). The number of languages in the 1991 Census came down to 114 (out of 216 mother tongues) not counting mother tongues/languages with less than 10,000 speakers (Government of India 1997). The speakers of eighteen languages listed in VIII Schedule of the Constitution, which get the lion's share of the resources of the states, constituted 87.13 percent of the population in 1961 and 95.58 percent, in 1981, because of reclassification of mother tongues into languages. The number of scheduled languages has now increased to twenty-two with the addition of Bodo, Dogri , Maithili, and Santali in 2003. The number of persons who claim one of the scheduled languages as their mother tongue (including the mother tongues claimed by the government as belonging to them) in 1991, in descending order of size, is given in Table 10.1 There are other languages that have a sizeable number of speakers that do not appear in the list of scheduled languages; these are listed in Table 10.2.

A map of languages giving their geographic context can be seen in Breton (1997).

It may be noted that no language is a majority language in India in the sense of having more than 50 percent of the population. Hindi, which has the largest number of mother tongues under it, is claimed to be the language of about 40 percent of the population. The situation is different in the states. The boundaries of the states were redrawn after Independence to coincide with language boundaries in order for the states to have a majority language. All states do not have a majority language; there are tribal states, such as Arunachal Pradesh, Jharkhand, and Nagaland that do not have any language in the majority. No state is monolingual; each has linguistic minorities whose strength varies from 4 percent in Kerala to 37 percent in Manipur. About a half of the

Table 10.2 *Top twenty nonscheduled languages in descending order of strength*

Language	Number (%)	Language	Number (%)
Bhili/Bhilodi	5,572,308 (0.66)	Tripuri	694,940 (0.08)
Santali	5,216,325 (0.62)	Garo	675,642 (0.08)
Gondi	2,124,852 (0.25)	Kui	641,662 (0.07)
Tulu	1,552,259 (0.18)	Lushai/Mizo	538,842 (0.06)
Kurukh/Oraon	1,426,618 (0.17)	Halabi	534,313 (0.06)
Bodo/Boro	1,221,881 (0.14)	Korku	466,073 (0.05)
Khandeshi	973,709 (0.11)	Munda	413,894 (0.04)
Ho	949,216 (0.11)	Miri/Mishing	390,583 (0.04)
Khasi	912,283 (0.10)	Karbi/Mikir	366,229 (0.04)
Mundari	861,378 (0.10)	Savara	273,168 (0.03)

Source: www.censusindia.net/results/eci11_page5.html, accessed August 21, 2005.

country's districts have 20 percent or more of the district's population who speak a minority language.

It should be expected that all languages do not have equal status. The scheduled languages listed in the Constitution have already been mentioned. The majority languages of the states are called regional languages. Languages spoken by the tribal communities are termed tribal languages. (see also Chapter 7). Of the 193 languages in 1961, 101 (abstracted from 204 mother tongues) are designated tribal, which are spoken by 613 tribal communities (Government of India 1978), who constitute 6.9 percent of the population.[1] The speakers of tribal languages, however, are only a little more than half of this population (57 percent in 1961). The tribal languages in 1981 number sixty five, excluding those with less than 10,000 speakers. They vary vastly in population size from under thirty speakers (Andamanese) to over four million (Bhili 4.5 million, Santali 4.2, Gondi 2.0, Kurukh 1.3, and Mundari 1.1 in the 1981 Census) and in status from being a preliterate language to being the official language of a state (Mizo, Khasi).

The languages of India belong genetically to four language families, namely Indo-European (Indo-Aryan and Iranian), Dravidian, Austro-Asiatic (Munda and Mon-Khmer), and Sino-Tibetan (Tibeto-Burman and Thai). Fifty-four languages are Indo-European (27 percent of the languages in the 1961 Census), twenty, Dravidian (10 percent), twenty, Austro-Asiatic (10 percent), and eighty-four, Sino-Tibetan (42 percent); the rest are foreign and unclassified languages. The tribal languages are spread over all four families, but differentially. One language of the Indo-European family, nine

[1] The survey of People of India identifies 432 tribal communities, who speak 191 languages.

of the Dravidian, nineteen of the Austro-Asiatic, and sixty-three of the Sino-Tibetan are tribal; the rest of the tribal languages are linguistically unclassified (Nigam 1972).

Communicative context

The geographic unit of communication is the entire country only for the elite. For the rest, it is the state or a subregion within the state or even a village. Communication has two aspects: transmission of knowledge (of all kinds, including cultural knowledge) and transaction between people (of all kinds, including cultural performance or practice). Plurality of languages has not been a problem traditionally with regard to both these aspects, which intersect each other. Cultural knowledge transmission was through oral performance in various languages. The spread of epics and the mythologies codified in an elite language such as Sanskrit and through folk performances in the local languages of the performers is a typical example of this. Though the spread took place also through translation of epics in literate languages, lack of literacy was not a barrier for the transmission of cultural knowledge. Scientific knowledge, however, was not so open. It was restricted to Sanskrit in much of India, which was acquired through formal learning by the upper castes and was kept from contributing to the practical knowledge of artisans, who made tools and other productive goods. The artisans were forbidden access to Sanskrit, in which scientific knowledge was created and stored, and so there was a barrier in the communication of the scientific knowledge.

Such elite control and restriction of scientific knowledge transmission through the languages of the common people is more pronounced in the modern period when English is the repository of such knowledge. Its transmission is only through translation into major Indian languages, whose contrived style is incomprehensible even to highly literate persons. There is no oral transmission of scientific knowledge except in mass campaigns to create scientific awareness about problems of health, hygiene, environmental degradation, and so on, which may use traditional folk performances and theater in addition to public lectures. The preferred way of acquiring the knowledge codified in English, unlike Sanskrit, however is to learn that language instead of transmitting the knowledge through the native languages. This is true of cultural knowledge also that pertains to popular culture among the urban youth. But access to English is only through formal education, which is not availed by all. This is a new development in the spread of knowledge in the multilingual situation of India.

Communication for transaction between people for trade, travel, political participation, bureaucratic dealings, and social interaction takes place in many languages and the languages vary at different levels. At higher levels, the language of communication is English followed by Hindi for the country as a whole. At middle levels, it is Hindi and English in that order, and at lower levels, it is Hindi. The language of communication at higher levels in the states is the majority language of the state and English, at middle levels it is the majority language of the state and less English, and at the lower levels it is the majority language and the minority languages. The language use in communication is not categorical level-wise as the above description may suggest. The choice of language is motivated by factors other then the level, which fall broadly in the axes of relation of power and solidarity between the interlocutors. It is not categorical code-wise either. There will be mixing and switching between codes in a single communication event (B. Kachru 1978a; S. N. Sridhar 1978). There is also diglossic use in which the first language in the pair is used in writing and the second, in speaking, for the same content of communication.

There is an important point about communication in the multilingual setting of India, which is the transparency and fluidity of boundaries between languages (Khubchandani 1997b). The problem of communication in having to use two autonomous codes is reduced when their grammatical boundaries are fluid. This helps people to glide from one language to another defined as different externally by others but perceived as a continuum internally by the speakers. Using the fluidity for communicative advantage is not constrained in informal interactions by normative requirements to use standard varieties. Due to intensive and extensive contact, languages have converged grammatically and pragmatically. There is greater convergence in the periphery of language territories than in their core. Convergence to the extent of one system and two expressions makes communication easy. In the linguistic border areas, interlingual communication is the norm, and convergence makes that communication less problematic. The same thing is true of linguistic minorities living in the midst of a majority community. Bilingual communication is less demanding when the parameters of language competence are determined situationally by the communicative needs and not centrally by the school system. To be a bilingual for most communicative purposes does not mean to have the linguistic competence of native speakers in the two languages. These are the features that do not hinder communication for the ordinary people to carry on their daily lives. The elite have different norms of communication and they learn the norms through education to successfully meet their needs of communication. The elite choice of languages for interlingual communication at the national level, however, is spreading downwards to linguistically mixed neighborhoods and families (Dua and Sharma 1977).

Though communication takes place using the language of one of the interlocutors or using each other's language, there are also contact languages, which are a third language different from the languages of the interlocutors. The contact language may be a language learned formally or derived from one or both languages of the interlocutors. English exclusively and Hindi predominantly belong to the category of formally learnt contact languages.[2] The contact languages produced as a result of contact are very few. They are restricted to specific regions, as mentioned above (Sreedhar 1988).

In short, the manner in which the problem of many languages in communication is handled in India (when the solution is not planned with emphasis on standards and teaching those standards) is through functional determination of language competence and convergence of grammars. The solution is not sought in monolingualism but in "mono-grammar" for, and variable competence in, the various languages!

Functional context

Multilingualism is more than the presence of many languages in a person, in a community, and in a country. It is the functional relationship between the languages in the repertoire of each of these three units of multilingualism. The functions may be the use of language in the public domain, where the use is normally legislated and the use in the private domain, where the use is by social contract. Language use in the public domain, which includes public administration, law and justice enforcement, and education, reflects the power equations of the linguistic communities. Language use in the private domain, which includes home, neighborhood, entertainment, and religion, reflects social solidarity and cultural identity. India has been functionally multilingual by not assigning the functions in the public domain to only one language and by allowing freedom of choice of language in the private domain.

India is noted for maintaining the home language across generations even when the population migrates to another linguistic area (Pandit 1979) and for having the largest number of home languages. Though different social groups,

[2] Of the bilinguals in the country (9.7 percent of the population in 1961), those who report English as the second language form 26 percent, Hindi, 22 percent, and regional languages (the majority languages of the states), 50 percent (Khubchandani 1978; of the 13.34 percent of the bilingual population in 1981, the second language speakers of Hindi went up to 56 percent and English went down to 4.6 percent inexplicably). Among the bilinguals in Hindi in 1961, a little more than half may be estimated to have learnt it in the school (Annamalai 2001: 42–55). Note, however, that the percentage of bilinguals has been going up steadily. According to Mallikarjun (2004), the national average has climbed progressively to 13.04 percent in 1971, 13.34 percent in 1981, and 19.44 percent in 1991. In case of major language speakers, 18.72 percent are bilinguals and 7.22 percent are trilinguals, and the bilinguals among minor language speakers are 38.14 percent and trilinguals, 8.28 percent. There is no estimate about the percentage of bilinguals in the regional languages who use them as a contact language in their communication with another minority linguistic community as against using them in communication with the majority linguistic community. The tribal communities report overwhelmingly the majority language of the state they live in as their second language (Annamalai 2001: 56–66), but the census does not give information on whether the majority language is used for intertribal communication also. The necessity of a contact language for intertribal communication is high given the high density of linguistic diversity among the tribes (Itagi *et al.* 1986).

that include castes and linguistic communities, traditionally cluster together in a living space, homes speaking different languages are now common in neighborhoods, particularly in the urban landscape, and so a neighborhood has more than one home language. Many languages are used in the local market between the shopkeepers and their customers to signal friendly relationship. While priests use Sanskrit in the Hindu temples of great tradition for liturgical purposes and worshippers use any language with devotional hymns for singing, any local language is used for oblations in the temples of little tradition. Punjabi is used for recitation in Gurudwaras, and Arabic is used for recitation and the local languages for Friday sermons in mosques. English and many major and minor languages, including tribal languages, are used for sermons in Churches. Movies are made in about fifteen languages and there are commercial television channels in as many languages. Radio, which is now less under the control of the government, broadcasts songs and other entertainment programs in many, including minor, languages. Popular magazines and newspapers or tabloids are published in all major languages and in many minor languages. Books of fiction and general information are read in all major languages. Reading habits of the people are restricted to their home language and/or the state language and they extend only to English among the two languages of national communication (unlike movie and television watching, which is also in Hindi).

In the public domain, there are two official languages of the Union, namely Hindi and English. There are fourteen other languages, making a total of sixteen official languages in the states. Some states have a second official language for all or parts of the state for all or specified functions and they number four. The courts at the district level use the state official language and English for arguments and judgments. Witnessing and cross examining are in either of these two languages depending on the knowledge of the person in the box. It is left to the advocate to translate from a minority language when the person in the box does not know any of these two languages and to transmit the proceedings to the court. The courts at the state and national levels use predominantly English, though the law provides for the use of the state official language and Hindi at these two levels, respectively. In education, forty-three languages are offered as medium of instruction at the primary level, and forty-four are taught as language at that level (NCERT 1992). They are about the quarter of the languages of the country, or about half, if languages with less than 10,000 speakers are excluded. Their number is reduced in the higher levels of education. At the level of general and professional education at the university level, English is the dominant medium, though parallel medium in the state official languages is offered, which is opted by scholastically and economically poor students. English and the state official language are taught as languages at the undergraduate level in general education, but only English is taught in professional education. At the graduate level no language is taught.

The functional arrangement of languages in the public domain has a pyramidal structure with many languages at the bottom and fewer at the top. Since the languages at the top have greater status and power, distributing opportunities unequally to speakers of other languages, this structure has the potential for language conflict. Language conflicts do take place and they are expressed through political action by the people and sometimes through legal action. Some are resolved by making changes in the functional distribution of languages like recognition of second official language, granting of a higher status or role to the state language, and greater role for minority languages in education. This shows that the functionally distributed multilingualism is not static but is stable in the sense that the principle of functional distribution of languages is constant when the languages in the distribution change.

Political context

The functional relationship of languages derives from the political equations of the communities speaking the languages. The communities constantly strive to improve their position in the power spectrum. Various means are used to achieve this, and they mostly fall into the political and legal arena. There are different kinds of political action. One is political campaign by interest groups to increase the demographic size of a language. This campaign becomes active before decennial censuses and it exhorts people to report a particular language to census enumerators as their mother tongue. It has political objectives, which reflect the political currents of the time. Wide variations in the number of speakers of mother tongues between censuses are indicative of this campaign. The communal politics, which accentuates differentiation through identifying markers including language, made the Muslims declare Urdu as their mother tongue. There was a huge increase in Urdu speakers in the Hindi belt in the 1981 Census; even in Tamil Nadu, where Muslims speak Tamil from birth, there was an increase of 32 percent in Urdu speakers. To force a division of Punjab into two states, one Punjabi speaking and another Hindi speaking, a political campaign persuaded a section of the people of Punjab to shift their mother tongue from Punjabi or Urdu to Hindi in the 1971 Census. The fluidity of language boundaries mentioned earlier makes this shift seamless to the speakers. As the mother tongue is a label of social identity rather than a measure of linguistic competence, the variation in the number of speakers signifies an identity shift rather than a language shift.

Another political decision is to submerge a language into another language as its dialect to gain the status of the amalgamating language and the ensuing benefits, or to win a political battle with the upper caste that controls the submerging language. This happened with Maithili, Bhojpuri, Avadhi in Bihar and Uttar Pradesh and a few others, which have their grammatical differences and literary traditions, but merged themselves with Hindi based on Khariboli spoken around Delhi (Brass 1974). The case of Maithili, which had a population of 50 million in the 1961 Census and is genetically closer to Bengali is unique; it denied itself its linguistic autonomous status but retained its literary autonomous status. The Government of India also accepted this split status of Maithili and recognized it as a language for national literary award but not as a language different from Hindi, till 2003. A similar but different process is to create a common name for related (even unrelated) languages and claim one linguistic identity in order to have an enlarged population base. The Pahadi language of Himachal Pradesh is an example of such a political creation of a language. Another example is found in Nagaland in the northeast where two or three smaller languages take a combined name like Chekesang or Zelionrong to make political bargains.

Such erasure of language identity by 'dialectizing' languages is legitimized by the government through the census by a process called language classification of mother tongues. This helps the government to obliquely reduce linguistic heterogeneity and to promote major languages. As already mentioned, Hindi has the largest number of mother tongues under it and reclassification of mother tongues under Hindi in subsequent censuses increases the mother tongue population of Hindi, which helps legitimize its status as the official language of the country. The speakers of Hindi were 29 percent of the total population of the country in 1961 and they became 39 percent in 1971 and 41 percent in 1981. Badaga in the Nilgiri Hills in the south is recognized as a separate language by Dravidianists but is made a dialect of Kannada in the 1971 Census.

The linguistic reorganization of the states in India mentioned earlier, to give a "homeland" for the major languages, gave rise to coalescing of the language of the majority and the language of power. In the historically earlier periods, the language of power, such as Sanskrit, Persian, and English, was not the native language of the population, which made the political and demographic strengths of languages disparate.[3] Such separation made the majority language less threatening to the minority languages. Both suffered from the dominance of the language in power. The emergence of the majority language as the dominant language was perceived as a threat by the linguistic minorities and they sought to check it. English was chosen as a weapon for this purpose and the minorities used the schools established under the right given to them by the Constitution for their children to have education through English medium and avoid majority language medium mandated by the state (Annamalai 2001: 152–67). In a comparable political use of English, the non-Hindi speakers, particularly in

[3] In the kingdoms in the historically earlier periods, the majority language of the region had royal patronage and was used even for some official purposes, but the nonnative languages mentioned above had superordinate power over the ruling elite.

Tamil Nadu and West Bengal, succeeded in changing the official language policy of the Union from one language (Hindi) to two languages (Hindi and English).

Languages in a multilingual country use the political system to improve their status through government's formulation of a particular language policy. The policy is shaped, or the formulated policy is changed, by the political action of linguistic communities. The communities that do not have enough political muscle to flex have to take recourse to demanding their linguistic rights granted by national laws and international covenants. Indian courts have deliberated and decided on ensuring that there is no discrimination in the equal treatment given to speakers of different languages and that there is no denial of opportunities to anyone because of the language they speak (Annamalai 1998). This gives legal protection to distributed functions of languages and survival of multilingualism.

Cultural context

Whether a language has political power or not, it is a vehicle of culture that codifies and transmits to the succeeding generations of the linguistic community its beliefs, values, and practices. The language shapes the community's worldview and the way of life of its members. It defines the speakers' network of kinship and their kin roles, which provide the sense of security. The community inherits its cultural heritage through its language and thus connects with its past. It gets its cultural identity from its language, whether it has a political use for it or not. The cultural value of the language is a crucial factor in its maintenance irrespective of how powerless the language is.

Indian culture is not monolithic; it is a collective whole of plurality of cultures represented by India's many languages. Multiculturalism in India is coterminous with multilingualism. It means that multiplicity of languages will continue to be maintained as long as multiplicity of cultures is. Culture being in the private domain, there is no role for the State to regulate it and the language used to express it. The cultural content and context of a language will help it survive, even if it is politically and economically marginalized.

Cultural distinctiveness is a defining feature of ethnicity. Language being a critical feature of cultural distinctiveness, it defines ethnicity as well, though language and ethnicity are not coterminous. There are, for example, 315 tribal communities out of 432, which are heterolingual, that is one tribal community is divided between more than one language (K. S. Singh and Manoharan 1993). Nevertheless, when ethnicity plays a role in the political game, language comes to the fore. Ethnic communities are treated as linguistic communities and ethnic minorities are equated with linguistic minorities. Thus language comes to play a political role through ethnicity with regard to minority languages. The political role is to obtain for the minority languages a place in the functional network of languages in the country.

Conclusion

The different contexts in which multilingualism manifests in India show that it is continuously evolving and adapting to changes in the social, political, and economic systems in which it is embedded. The number of languages may change, but the network of languages will sustain itself. It may be hoped that Indian multilingualism will survive, as it has through the historical changes in the past, in the current globalizing economic context as well.

11 Language contact and convergence in South Asia*

S. N. Sridhar

Introduction

It is often remarked that South Asia has a genius for assimilating foreign influences without losing its essential character. Nowhere is this resilience demonstrated more clearly than in the way the Dravidian languages have absorbed what, by any count, must be regarded as massive Indo-Aryan influence and yet retained their essential Dravidian character.[1]

In discussing the Indo-Aryanization of Dravidian languages, we are talking about an ongoing phenomenon that must have started more than about 3,500 years ago. The presence of linguistic features of possibly Dravidian origin in the Rig Veda[2] (e.g. retroflex consonants) suggests Aryan contact with the Dravidian-speaking peoples as several hundred years before the composition of the Rig Veda (at least 1500 BCE). This possibility is confirmed by the geographical distribution of the Dravidian languages, for example Brahui in Balochistan (Pakistan); Gondi in Madhya Pradesh, Maharashtra, Orissa, and Andhra Pradesh; Malto in Bihar and West Bengal, among others. Ignoring the possibility of reverse migration, this scatter suggests the presence of Dravidian-speaking people over most of South Asia at one time and their gradual recession before the advancing Aryans or language shift to Indo-Aryan over many generations (see Chapter 1). However, our recorded history of Dravidian contact with Indo-Aryan goes back only to the early centuries BCE.

* I am grateful to Professors Braj Kachru and Hans Henrich Hock for commenting on an earlier version of this chapter.

[1] The last part of this claim is not strictly correct. Burrow and Bhattacharya (1970: ix) note that in many areas, the Pengos have lost their own language and have become Indo-Aryan speakers. The authors cite the example of the agricultural tract west of Nowrangpur and adjoining the Bastar border, "where the Pengos no longer speak their own language, though they are aware of its one-time existence." Nevertheless, in so far as the basic character and identity of a language resides in its morphology and syntax (apparently basic vocabulary is less impregnable than commonly assumed if the Dravidian case is any proof [see section on Vocabulary below]), Dravidian languages may be said to be still pretty much intact.

[2] For a cautious questioning of this traditionally accepted position, see Hock (1975).

Language contact and convergence in South Asia may be – and has been – studied from many points of view. In this chapter, I will discuss this topic with reference to one major and extensive aspect, namely the Indo-Aryanization of Dravidian languages (S. N. Sridhar 1981). Of course, the Dravidianization of Indo-Aryan and the mutual impact of all the language families on one another also need to be studied extensively, but my present delimitation of the topic is necessitated first by the limitation of space but more importantly by the limits of expertise of the author. I have, however, made extensive references in the body of the paper to other aspects of this complex phenomenon.

Traditionally, the discussion to date has concentrated on the phonetic and semantic modifications undergone by Indo-Aryan words in Dravidian languages. However, there is much more to the topic than that. In this chapter, my aim is to present an overall picture of the many facets of Indo-Aryanization of Dravidian. Following this introduction, the next section discusses the reasons, sources, and mechanisms of Indo-Aryan borrowings, the section on the Variation in the extent of Indo-Aryanization provides an outline of the variation; section on Indo-Aryanization on various levels is a survey of the Indo-Aryan influence on Dravidian at various levels; section on nativization is devoted to various aspects of nativization; section on Sociolinguistic implications of language contact discusses the sociolinguistic implications of Indo-Aryanization; and the final section comprises the conclusion. Before proceeding further, I would like to point out that what follows is more in the nature of a bird's eye view than a microscopic examination of minutiae. Due to paucity of materials and my own limitations, I have not been able to do equal justice to all the languages involved. Yet, I hope the following discussion may serve at least as a programmatic sketch for a much needed booklength treatment of this important topic.

The reasons and sources of borrowing

The reasons for the prodigious influx of Indo-Aryan features into Dravidian are well known. First, Sanskrit has traditionally occupied an exalted position as the language of the elite in India, a position analogous to that of Latin in Europe until a few centuries ago. Sanskrit was not only the language of the scriptures, the epics, and classical literature; it was also the repository of a vast body of philosophical, scientific, and technical literature in every field (see Krishnamurthy 1997, and Chapter 8 in this volume). It enjoyed royal patronage, and the prevalence of Sanskrit-based education largely under the control of the Brahmans reinforced its prestige. All this led to the creation of a vast body of literature in the Dravidian languages, composed often in conscious imitation of the Sanskrit models, bringing in its wake a veritable flood of Sanskrit words. While many of these words were introduced to meet the technical needs of specialized language-types (or "registers," for example, in grammar) and often to suit the demands of intricate versification (for example, *ādiprāsa* and *antaprāsa*), a large number must have been introduced simply because it was prestigious to do so (Pillai 1924).

Secondly, Prakrit played a crucial role in the Indo-Aryanization process. In some languages (e.g. Tamil), the words that came in via Prakrit far outnumber those borrowed directly from Sanskrit. There are two major reasons for this Prakrit influence. It was the court language during some periods in the Dravidian south, for example, during the Śātavāhana and the early Pallava periods. Also, the south, especially Karnataka, was the haven of refuge for the Jainas, and a large number of very prominent authors in the Dravidian languages were Jainas who were proficient in Prakrit and often composed in Prakrit as well (e.g. Nēmichandra). Conversely, many prominent Prakrit authors also wrote in Dravidian languages, for example, Pushpadanta, Trivikrama, and Shākatāyana, who wrote in Kannada. Many of the Indo-Aryan loanwords in the nonliterary languages are also traceable to Prakrit forms.

The next major category of Indo-Aryan loanwords in Dravidian comes from modern Indo-Aryan, especially Hindi–Urdu and Marathi in the literary languages of the south as well as Oriya in Pengo and Kui, Sindhi in Brahui, Marathi in Kolami, Hindi in Kurukh, and so forth.

Parts of south India came under Muslim rule in various periods, especially during the reign of the Bahamani kings in Andhra Pradesh and north Karnataka, and that of Hyder Ali and Tippu Sultan in south Karnataka. During the latter period (eighteenth century), Persian was the official language of the princely state of Mysore, with official records being kept in that language (Kedilaya 1970). The prolonged Muslim rule has contributed a large number of words in the field of law, administration, and land-management, as well as provided us with Islamic culture (see S. N. Sridhar 1975b). This is true to an even greater extent, of Andhra Pradesh, parts of which were ruled by the Nizam of Hyderabad and the sultans of the Bahamani kingdoms for several centuries. Next, the increased commerce between the north and south since the beginning of the Independence movement has resulted in the introduction of more Hindi words (e.g. *kālāpānī*, *ghērāo, bandh, čarkhā*, etc.) and this has increased steadily with the greater role and acceptance of Hindi as the official language and the popularity of Hindi film and television.

As for the influence of Marathi on Dravidian, both geography and politics have been contributing factors. Maharashtra shares borders with both Karnataka and Andhra Pradesh, and there is intensive code mixing in these border areas (cf. Gumperz and Wilson 1971; Upadhyaya 1971). Politically, much of north Karnataka came under the Bombay Presidency until the reorganization of the states in 1956, and the administrative language as well as the language of education in this region was Marathi. Further south, the Tanjore or Thanjavur area in Tamil Nadu was under Maratha rule for nearly two centuries until 1800 CE (Subramoniam and Ganeshasundaram 1954) The Dēśastha Mādhwa brahmins in the south have traditionally been bilingual in Marathi and Kannada, Telugu, or Tamil.

The nonliterary languages of the south (Toḍa, Koṭa, Koḍagu, Baḍaga, etc.) also have numerous Indo-Aryan borrowings in them, but these seem to have resulted from diffusion from their literary neighbors (Emeneau and Burrow 1962). As for the nonliterary Dravidian languages outside the major Dravidian belt, their language contact with Indo-Aryan needs no explanation. Speakers of these languages often indulge in such occupations as wood gathering, and basket weaving, and perform menial jobs, and in general are crucially dependent on their Indo-Aryan neighbors for economic survival. Bilingualism in the dominant language of the region is for them a cardinal necessity. It comes as no surprise that some of these languages show much more radical changes in response to Indo-Aryan influence than their literary sisters.

The preceding discussion assumes, following the long recognized theory, that the main locus and agency responsible for the transfer of traits in a language-contact situation is the bilingual individual. Several sociolinguistic studies of language use in bilingual communities (e.g. Gumperz and Wilson 1971, and Upadhyaya 1971, in the Maharashtra–Karnataka border; Nadkarni 1975 in the Konkani–Kannada contact areas of south Kanara) give us insights into the processes by which the present-day convergence of features in Indian languages must have come about. B. Kachru (1978b) and S. N. Sridhar (1978, 1992) have argued that intrasentential code switching or code mixing may be a crucial factor in the kind of language change we have been discussing. S. N. Sridhar (1992) has documented specific ethnolinguistic examples of language contact and convergence in the individual speakers.

Variation in the extent of Indo-Aryanization

The Dravidian languages show a great deal of interlanguage and intralanguage variation in the extent of Indo-Aryan influence. The nonliterary Dravidian languages spoken in the Indo-Aryan region seem to have undergone a greater amount of structural (morphological, syntactic) influence (see sections on Phonology and Morphology), whereas the literary languages of the south have been influenced predominantly on the lexical level. Second, the nonliterary languages contain few unassimilated Sanskrit lexical items, while this category plays an important role in the lexicons of the literary languages, especially Kannada, Malayalam, and Telugu. Third, it is suggested (Andronov 1964) that the dialectal dissolution of Dravidian was already well under way before Indo-Aryan began to exert its influence. If this is correct,[3] then that fact could readily

[3] However, the reliability of the method of glottochronology on which Andronov's claim is presumably based, has been called into question; see for example Bergsland and Vogt 1962; also note Hock 1976.

account for the variation. Finally, the extent to which a given language has been influenced by Indo-Aryan also depends on the language attitudes of its speakers. For example, Tamil has traditionally been more conservative than its neighbors in this regard – a fact commonly attributed to the fierce loyalty of Tamilians to their language and their desire to preserve its "purity" (see section on Indo-Aryanization and language attitudes for a detailed discussion). In contrast, consider Bhattacharya's observation that speakers of Ollari (a nonliterary Dravidian language spoken in the Koraput district of Orissa) disclaim proficiency in their mother tongue (Bhattacharya 1957).

There is also a great deal of intralanguage variation with regard to the extent of Indo-Aryan influence. In this respect, the chief variables involved are (1) style, (2) caste, and (3) topic of discourse. Dravidian languages show more Indo-Aryan features in writing than in speech, and within the written style, perhaps more in poetry than in prose. It is well known that at various periods in the history of Dravidian literature, a style of writing characterized by heavy Sanskrit borrowings, often together with the original Sanskrit declensions and long compounds (e.g. Telugu *dharmanivahanōdyōgamummunaku)* became fashionable (see Kunjunni Raja 1972). This style, commonly referred to as *Maṇipravāḷa* ("combination of gems and corals") reached its peak in Malayalam (e.g. *Chandrōtsava)*, but it is seen in the other three literary languages as well (e.g. the inscriptions of Rāja Rāja Chōḷa and in the Jaina and Vaiṣṇava philosophical literature in Tamil, in the work of Nannaya and Pōtana in Telugu, and to give a modern example, Kuvempu's *Rāmāyanadarśana* in Kannada). Like the epic style of Milton, although it made for dramatic literary effect when used judiciously, *Maṇipravāḷa* never found universal favor and is largely a literary and linguistic curiosity now, being used marginally in orthodox Brāhman doctrinaire tracts, if at all.

The extent of Indo-Aryan features also varies according to the caste of the speaker (writer). Bright (1960), Bright and Ramanujan (1964), and Ramanujan (1968), among others, have observed that one of the variables distinguishing the Brahman dialects[4] in Tamil and Kannada from the non-Brahman is the presence of Sanskrit phonemes (e.g. aspirated stops) and clusters and vocabulary. Here we see what the renowned anthropologist M. N. Srinivas calls "Sanskritization" (Srinivas 1966) operating in a literal sense, the Sanskritic features serving as a symbol of caste identity and distinctness. The emergence of hypercorrect forms with unnecessary aspiration (commonly observed in the spelling errors of neoliterates) may also be regarded as a manifestation of this phenomenon.

[4] The author is aware that the use of the term "caste dialects" has been criticized recently, on the basis of the observation that education rather than caste is the relevant variable. However, if we recall that until recently, the term "educated" could be used interchangeably with "Brahman," much of the ground for objection disappears. Moreover, sociolinguistic stereotypes are not always commensurate with sociological reality.

The third parameter of variation is the topic of discourse: Indo-Aryan features are more likely to be present in the discussion of certain topics than in others. For instance, religious discourses, in particular explications of scriptures, known as *upanyāsas* in the south, contain extremely heavy Sanskrit borrowing, as do texts and oral discourses on poetics, aesthetics, philosophy, and sciences, in general. By the same token, one finds extensive use of Hindi–Urdu words (ultimately of Perso-Arabic origin) in discussions of law, land revenue, Hindustani (or north Indian) music, horseriding, and wrestling (for a detailed discussion of this register-oriented code mixing and its social meanings, see S. N. Sridhar 1975b and 1978). In modern times, Sanskrit has been serving as the principal source of new coining in all the scientific and technical fields (see Chapter 16). Tamil is, once again, an exception to this statement, the emphasis there being on the exploitation of native resources.

The foregoing discussion of variation in the extent of Indo-Aryanization should make clear that any facile generalization about Indo-Aryanization of Dravidian languages, and especially the nonliterary ones, is likely to prove wrong. One can only note here some general tendencies, always keeping in mind the complex inter- and intralanguage variation. With this caveat, let us now turn to an examination of the influence of Indo-Aryan on various levels.

Indo-Aryanization at various levels

Vocabulary

Anyone who looks at the dictionaries of Dravidian languages cannot but be struck by the extravagant proportion of Indo-Aryan words in general and Sanskrit words in particular, contained in them. Emeneau and Burrow (1962) rightly attribute this to "the tendency for all four of the Dravidian literary languages in the South to make literary use of the total Sanskrit lexicon indiscriminately" (1). Even in the colloquial language, so many words of Indo-Aryan origin have found their way and been assimilated that it is hard to speak even a few sentences without using some of these words. It was no doubt partly because of this high proportion of Sanskritic elements (and the similarity in the sound values of the graphemes in the scripts [counting the *grantha* script in Tamil]) that, until just over a century ago, it was generally believed that the Dravidian languages were descended from Sanskrit. Western scholars like Pope, Colebrooke, Carey, and Wilkins also subscribed to this view. Caldwell (1903) spends a considerable part of his classic work dispelling this misconception.

It is impossible to give a list of borrowings in Dravidian (for a partial list,[5] see Emeneau and Burrow 1962) or even to specify the conceptual fields they

[5] This list is limited to those borrowings from Indo-Aryan which have either (1) undergone extensions of meanings or far-reaching phonetic changes or both, or (2) penetrated into

denote, for there is no field of activity which has not been influenced by them. In many cases, the native terms have been replaced by the borrowed items, even in the areas generally regarded as part of the basic vocabulary. A case in point is the set of direction terms in Kannada, where the native words *mūḍal, paḍuval, baḍagal*, and *tenkal* have been replaced by the Sanskrit *pūrva, paścima, uttara, dakṣiṇa* (east, west, north, south, respectively) even in everyday colloquial use (Sreekantaiya 1956). Sjoberg and Sjoberg (1956) estimate that about 20 percent of the "non-cultural" part of the basic vocabulary in literary Dravidian now consists of loanwords from Indo-Aryan, creating problems for glottochronology (see Sjoberg and Sjoberg 1956), and the proportion of borrowings in those areas that are more prone to cultural influence is, obviously, much higher, probably as much as 50 to 60 percent. Among the nonliterary languages, Emeneau (1962a: 20) estimates that the vocabulary of Kolami (Wardha dialect) contains approximately 35 percent of words with Marathi etymologies. The case of other nonliterary languages is perhaps not much different.

Certain salient features of the Indo-Aryan loanwords in Dravidian may be noted. First, the loans are not restricted to any one register or set of registers; they are everywhere – in basic as well as technical vocabulary, in the written and the spoken language, in the language of intimate conversations and personal letters as well as that of newspapers and public speeches. Second, the loans are not restricted to content words but include a large number of function words, such as, quantifiers (*kēvala, bahaḷa, alpa*), intensifiers (*atyanta, mātra*), adverbial conjunctions (*akasmāt, bahuśah*), and so on, as well as bound morphemes of various kinds (see next section). Third, a large number of Sanskrit words have been borrowed both in their root form (e.g. *jīva*) and in their derived forms (e.g. *jīvanta;* cf. also, *śaktiyuta, aprakaṭita, tāratamya*, etc.). Fourth, the Dravidian languages, especially the South Dravidian languages, have a substantial number of Indo-Aryan loanwords in common (e.g. *nadi* "river," *čandra* "moon," *rātri* "night," *bhūmi* "earth") and these words often undergo similar phonetic and semantic changes in these languages (e.g. *anumāna(m) (u)* "suspicion" [< Skt. id. "inference, guess"]; however, see section on semantic changes below). Fifth, all the literary languages have sets of two forms, one taken from Sanskrit and employed with minimal modification and the other either borrowed from Prakrit or modified in the borrowing language, or both. Often these pairs are distributed in a diglossic fashion (see discussion in section on Diglossia). Finally, the majority of Indo-Aryan loans undergo various kinds of phonetic and semantic changes, some of which are common to all the Dravidian languages while some are language specific (see section on Nativization for details).

nonliterary languages, whether or not special meanings are found (Emeneau and Burrow 1962: Preface).

Phonology

This large-scale infiltration of Indo-Aryan words has resulted in the introduction of several phonemes alien to the Dravidian phonological structure. Among these, the most important are the aspirated stops (*kh, ch, th, th, ph*, and their voiced counterparts) as in, for example, Ka. *khāra* "spicy hot," *čhatri* "umbrella," *ṭhāṇe* "station," *kathe* "story," *phala* "fruit," *ghante* "bell, hour," *jhari* "centipede," *mūḍha* "fool," *nidhāna* "slow," and *bhāra* "heavy." Other Indo-Aryan introductions are the distinction between s, ś, and ṣ as in *saśeṣha* "yet to be finished," and the diphthong *au* as in *gauḍa* "village chief." The scripts of all the literary languages except Tamil now possess characters for the full complement of Sanskrit phonemes. Even in Tamil the *grantha* script accommodates these phonemes.

The Indo-Aryan loanwords have also resulted in the loss or violation of some positional constraints in Dravidian. Thus, the presence of voiced consonants in the word-initial position as in *gamaka*, initial consonant clusters and nonhomorganic plosive clusters as in *prārabdha*, word-final obstruents, as in *tākat* (< H–U), among others, may be attributed to Indo-Aryan influence.

However, it is important to note that these nonnative phonemes and consonant clusters are not found in all speakers and in all styles (see Fowler 1954; Sjoberg 1962). As already noted, these features mark certain styles and their presence is determined by sociolinguistic variables (see section on caste dialect for further discussion).

The nonliterary languages have also adopted many phonological features from Indo-Aryan. For example, Brahui and Kurukh have developed nasal vowels of the Indo-Aryan type. Brahui has also lost the short *e* and *o* characteristic of Dravidian (Emeneau 1962a). Similarly, Pengo (another nonliterary Dravidian language spoken in Orissa) has lost the distinction between *j* and *z* that it inherited from Proto-Central Dravidian, presumably under the influence of Oriya, which lacks that distinction. Pengo has also developed the feature of aspiration, although it is confined mostly to loanwords from Oriya and used sporadically even there (Burrow and Bhattacharya 1970).

Morphology

On the morphological level, the most striking characteristic is the productive use of a large number of Indo-Aryan derivational affixes. Sanskrit suffixes such as *-anta, -iṣṭha, -kāra* are freely used (e.g. Ka. *haṇavanta* "rich," Te. *kopisṭhi* "irascible," Ma. *vasaḷkāram* "imprecation"), as are the Hindi–Urdu ones, such as *-dār* (Ka. *pattēdāra* "detective"), *-khōr* (Te. *lančakōru* "corrupt man"), *-vālā* (Ka. *mīsevāla* "the moustached man"), and *-giri* (Ka., Te. *gumāstagiri* "clerk-ship").

The employment of prefixation as a productive word-forming device in Dravidian must be attributed to the Indo-Aryan impact and is seen in the large number of forms involving, for example, Sanskrit *apa-, ava-, ati-, su-, pari-*, as well as the Hindi–Urdu prefixes, *bē-, māji-*, and *gair-*. Consider, for example, the following Ka. *apakīrti* "ignominy," Te. *apadūru* "insinuation," Ka., Te. *aparūpa(m)* "rare," Ka. *ati mātu* "garrulousness," Ka. *sulōčana* "eye-glasses," Ka. *pari vīkśaṇe* "survey," Ka. *pratiobba* "each one," as well as Ka., Te. *bēniyat(tu)* "disloyalty," *gairuhājari* "absence," and *māji adhyaksa* "ex-president". Most of these affixes freely collocate with native roots as well, although it is more common to attach them to other borrowed words and use them in a sense not attested in the source language (as in the case of the Ka. *pattēdāra)*.

In a different strain, Andronov (1964) has observed that the gradual loss of many negative-incorporated forms in the major Dravidian languages and the use of analytical modes of expressing negation by means of a positive verb followed by a negative word may be due to the influence of Indo-Aryan. Thus, in Kannada, for example, forms such as *hōga, māḍa* have gone out of use, having been replaced by *hōgōd-illa* and *māḍōd-illa*.

Turning to the nonliterary languages, Bloch (1954) has pointed out that the infinitive suffix *-na* in Gondi is indubitably borrowed from Hindi–Urdu. Another infinitive suffix *-le* in the same language is attributed to the influence of eastern Marathi. Pengo occasionally employs the Oriya genitive morpheme in *-r* as in *rājar kuvar* "king's courtyard" and *kumrar ar* "potter's wife." In Pengo one also finds a marginal occurrence of the Oriya locative suffix *-ne* as in *barhane* "in the rain." More regular and widespread is the use of a number of Oriya postpositions, such as the instrumental *huduŋ, saŋ* "with," the dative *kajiŋ* "for the sake of," and the locative *bitre* "in," *tarento* "beneath" (Burrow and Bhattacharya 1970: 41 ff.).

Emeneau (1962b) has brought to light an interesting case of morphological borrowing in Brahui, namely the allomorphs *kar* and *kam* ("to do, make") from Sindhi and Balochi, respectively, on the lines of the established Brahui irregular structure with *-nn* and *-r*. Brahui has undergone several other significant morphological changes not attested elsewhere in Dravidian, but these changes, as Emeneau rightly suggests, are probably directly traceable to the influence of Balochi rather than of the Indo-Aryan Sindhi.

Syntax

The influence of Indo-Aryan is least pronounced on the level of syntax. Although a number of syntactic patterns modeled on those of Sanskrit were introduced by various authors from time to time,[6] by and large, few syntactic

[6] One can cite numerous examples of this tendency. Sekhar (1969: 161) has observed that Malayalam inscriptions of the eleventh and twelfth centuries contain examples of concord between modifiers and substantives. This phenomenon seems to have existed in Telugu as well

traits in contemporary Dravidian can be traced to Indo-Aryan influence. There are a few notable exceptions, however. Modes of compounding such as the *avyayībhāva* (where the first component carries the major semantic burden, e.g. *yatha śakti* "according to one's ability") seem to go against the general Dravidian tendency to place the determiner before the determined and are probably due to the influence of Sanskrit. Similarly, the passive construction, for example, Ka, *huḍugiyinda bāgilu tereyal-paṭṭitu* (girl-instr. door-nom, open-infin.-experienced) "the door was opened by the girl," seldom used as it is, is also likely to have developed under the influence of Sanskrit. The passive, however, is enjoying a greater frequency of use in modern times, a tendency further reinforced by the influence of English. The third major syntactic trait in Dravidian traceable to the impact of Indo-Aryan is the clausal mode of relative-clause formation described below, which is widely attested in all the literary Dravidian languages.

As is well known, the preferred mode of relative-clause formation in Dravidian is by turning the main verb into a participle and deleting the coreferential noun, as in Ka. *hasiru sīre uṭṭiruva hengasu nanna heṇḍati* "green-saree-wearing-woman (is) my-wife." In addition to this construction, we now find another construction, closely modeled on the Indo-Aryan, for example, Ka., *yāva hengasu hasiru sīre uṭṭiddāḷo avaḷu nanna heṇḍati* (which-woman-green-saree-is-wearing + indefinitizer-she (is) my-wife) "The woman who is wearing a green saree is my wife." It may be noted that this construction presents one of the few cases in Dravidian where the main verb in a subordinate clause is not changed into a nonfinite form, and a coreferential subject is not deleted. Nadkarni (1970, 1975) convincingly argues for the Indo-Aryan origin of this construction.

The nonliterary languages in day-to-day contact with Indo-Aryan show greater receptivity to syntactic influence. For example, Brahui has developed enclitic pronouns which occur suffixed to verbs and nouns (Emeneau 1962a: 64). Brahui has also lost the inherited Dravidian system of natural gender in the demonstrative pronouns. Both of these traits are, once again, probably due to Balochi influence. However, a third trait, the use of *ki* as a complementizer may be attributed as much to Sindhi as Balochi influence. Pengo has borrowed the morpheme *ki* from Oriya, which is used as an interrogative particle appended to the end of the sentence, as in *venvatay ki* "did you not hear?" *Ki* is also used in the sense of "or." Pengo also employs the Oriya conjunctive particles *ar*, *are* ("and," "again") (Burrow and Bhattacharya 1970: 61). Gondi has also lost the

(Sastri 1969: 271). According to Sekhar, *Līlātilakam*, the fourteenth century grammar disapproves of such imitations of Sanskrit syntax in Malayalam. The highly respected thirteenth-century grammar of Kannada, *Śabdamaṇidarpaṇa* contains an "extrapolated" (anukta) sūtra in which it is claimed that even intransitive verbs can be passivized in Kannada.

relative participle typical of Dravidian and has adopted the Hindi relative pronoun (Caldwell 1903: 50).

The preceding characterization is by no means intended to be exhaustive. It is merely illustrative of the kind of influence Indo-Aryan has had on Dravidian.

Nativization

There has been a long tradition, in the native grammatical literature, of distinguishing two broad classes of borrowings from Indo-Aryan, namely *tatsama* ("same as") or words which undergo little (final vowel or consonant) or no modification and *tadbhava* ("derived from") or words which have been nativized or assimilated. For example, Kannada has both the unassimilated *pakṣi* (< Skt. *pakṣin* "bird") and the assimilated *hakki*. In this context, "assimilation" refers only to phonological modification and does not include semantic changes that the Indo-Aryan loans undergo in Dravidian.

Phonetic adaptations

Some sound changes in borrowed words are common to all four major Dravidian languages. For example, the doubling of the final obstruent followed by the addition of the enunciative *-u* (e.g. *sampattu* "wealth," *hukummu* "order," *tējassu* "halo"), the substitution of unaspirated stops for aspirated ones (e.g. *parike* "broomstick" [< Skt. *parikhā*]), the dropping of a final consonant, for example, *rāja* "king" (< Skt. *rājan)*, the substitution *s* for *ś* and, *ṣ* (Ka. *hasu* [< Skt. *paśu* "cattle"]), simplification of consonant clusters by anaptyxis (e.g. Ma. *kāriya* [< Skt. *kārya* "work"]), intervocalic voicing of voiceless plosives (Ta. *vigaḍan* [< Skt. *vikaṭa*]), and so on. Many of the changes are, however, language specific. In Kannada, for example, the final *-ā* of loanwords changes to *-e* (e.g. *mātā* > *māte, ilākhā* > *ilākhe*, etc.) while in Telugu, such a change occurs only marginally. Similarly, Malayalam speakers substitute *l* and *ḷ* for the Sanskrit *t (d)* and *ṭ (ḍ)* in certain contexts, for example when followed by a plosive (*tālparyam, taḷbhavam; vaśaḷkāram, khaḷgam*, etc.), whereas Tamil substitutes an *r* (Aiyar 1973). Similarly, the regular substitution in Tamil of voiceless consonants for the voiced ones in Sanskrit (e.g. *cinkāram* < Skt. *sringāra)* occurs much less frequently in other languages.

By and large, most of the phonemic substitutions in Dravidian follow the regular phonological rules of the languages concerned. This adaptation, together with the fact that a majority of Indo-Aryan loans commonly used in Dravidian have come via Prakrit, makes some forms hardly recognizable as originating from Sanskrit. A case in point is Ka. *habba* "festival" (Skt. *parva)* which comes from Pkt. *pavva* (or *pabba*?) and, with the mutation of *v* and *b* in Kannada, enters as *pabba* in Old Kannada, and with the change of initial *p* to *h* which took place around the tenth century, becomes *habba* in Middle and Modern Kannada.

At this point, it is worth mentioning that this tendency to regularize loanwords to make them conform to the native phonological structure operates more strongly in Tamil than in the other literary Dravidian languages. As a result, Tamil has fewer unassimilated Sanskrit words than the others. At least two reasons may be advanced to account for this. One is the influential injunction in the ancient Tamil grammar *Tolkāppiam* (Sutras 397, 401–2) according to which only those Sanskrit words could be used that either had letters common to Tamil and Sanskrit or had been modified in such a way that they could readily be represented in the Tamil script. This rule was scrupulously adhered to for about 1,500 years until the great influx of Sanskrit words (including *tatsamas*) during the Vijayanagar period (fourteenth to sixteenth centuries). Note that the other literary languages have been more lax in this regard and have moved in the opposite direction, extending their phonemic (and graphemic) inventory to accommodate the foreign sounds.

Semantic changes

Many of the loanwords from Indo-Aryan undergo various kinds of meaning change when used in Dravidian. Some of these changes are common to South Dravidian as a whole, while others are innovations peculiar to one or two languages. Table 11.1, based on Aiyar 1934–1935, illustrates some common semantic developments.

Both Aiyar (1934–1935) and Emeneau and Burrow (1962) contain many more examples of this phenomenon, traceable probably to diffusion within South Dravidian. Similar changes may be noticed in Hindi–Urdu borrowings as well, for example Ka. Te. *khāyam* (< id. "stand erect") "permanent," *dubāra (i)* (< id. "twice") "excess, wastage," and so on.

On the other hand, cases in which the same Sanskrit word has developed different meanings in the Dravidian languages are more frequent. For example, *ārambham* in Telugu has the meanings, "pride" and "killing" (literary) as well as the original Sanskrit meaning of "beginning." The same word in Kannada means "cultivation" (i.e. farming) as well as "beginning." Similarly, *āmōdamu* in Telugu means "dalliance" as well as "fragrance"; in Kannada, the word is used only in its Sanskrit meaning of "enjoyment," *piramātam* in Tamil means "excessive" as well as "excellence"; the derivative of the same source in Kannada, *pramāda*, has the meaning of "blunder." The Malayalam word *gōṣṭhi* means "prank, contortions, gesture," while in Kannada and Telugu the same word has the original Sanskrit meaning of "assembly."

The semantic changes that take place in Indo-Aryan words when used in Dravidian comprise of virtually every known type of deviation discussed in the

Table 11.1. *Semantic shift in Sanskrit loanwords in Dravidian*

Source word	Meaning in Sanskrit	Meaning in Dravidian
anumānam	inference; guess	suspicion
antahstah	in the middle state	storey of a building; high rank
asahya	unbearable	loathsome
avasthā	state	miserable condition
pāpam	sin, evil	sin, pity

linguistic literature. There is, for example, restriction of meaning in S. Dr. *udyōga* "employment" (< Skt. "work"), extension in Ka. *anubhāva* "mystical experience" (< Skt. ibid.), specialization in Ka. *jangama* "a Viraśaiva saint" (< Skt. "mobile"), amelioration in Te. *ālaya* "temple," (< Skt. id. "house"), deterioration in Ka. *adhvāna*, Te. *adhvānamu*, Ta. *attuvānam* (< Skt. *adhvan* "path, way") "destruction, disarray," and so on. Similarly, Hindi–Urdu and Marathi words also change their meaning in various ways, for example Ka. *čāḍi* (< Ma. *čahad* "treachery") "petty complaint, informing on someone," Te., Ka. *ustād* (< H–U *ustād* "teacher") "wrestler, gymnastics or music teacher," Ta. *attāvanai* (Ma. *aṭhavana* "recollection") "index, ledger," and T., Ka. *śarā* (< H–U *śart* "condition") "postscript."

Sociolinguistic implications of language contact

It was remarked earlier that all the Dravidian languages are not uniformly Indo-Aryanized, nor are all varieties in a given language influenced to the same degree. This variation is sociolinguistically conditioned to a large extent, and, in turn, contributes to an already complex sociolinguistic situation in the Dravidian languages. In this section we shall briefly examine this aspect.

Caste dialect

The existence of caste-related differences in Dravidian languages has long been recognized. In particular, sharp differences are noted between the Brahman and non-Brahman dialects on the levels of phonology, morphology, and lexicon. While many of these differences have nothing to do with borrowing (e.g. Kannada *ide* (B) versus *aite* (NB) for "to be" 3rd sing. neut.), quite a few of the variables involve elements introduced in the process of Indo-Aryanization, in particular, Sanskritization. The most important of these variables is aspiration in loanwords from Sanskrit (and other Indo-Aryan languages). Until recently, it was not uncommon to find Brahman parents and teachers upbraiding an unaspirating speaker for "speaking like a śūdra." Another important variable is the existence of separate sets of lexical items in the Brahman and non-Brahman dialects. As Aiyar (1932) has pointed out with reference to Tulu, words borrowed directly from Sanskrit are far more numerous in the Brahman dialects, while words borrowed or adapted from Middle Indo-Aryan (Jaina Prakrit or Pali) are common to both Brahman and non-Brahman dialects (e.g. Tu. *upavāsa* (B) vs. *nompu* (NB) "fast"; Ta. *tīrthõī* (B) vs. *tanni* (NB) "water"). Even when the same Indo-Aryan word has been borrowed into both dialects, it undergoes different modifications: (Tu. *sāvira* (B) vs. *sāra* (NB) "thousand"; Ka. *bahaḷa* (B) vs. *bāḷa* (NB) "much, very").

The reasons for this conservatism[7] of Brahman dialects are not hard to find. The preservation of Sanskrit features in their speech gives Brahmans a social identity which their insignificant number denies them. As a byproduct of the elitist position of Sanskrit in India, this feature gives them prestige as well. Moreover, as Ramanujan (1968) correctly points out, part of the reason may also be the high premium placed in that community on the accurate rendering of the texts and their conservative outlook toward cultural innovations in general.

The symbolic value of Sanskritic features in the Dravidian sociolinguistic context has also led to the inevitable phenomenon of hypercorrection. Thus, we find scores of native Dravidian words restructured to incorporate prestige features such as aspiration. Kannada offers many examples of this sort: *bhatta* "paddy," *chaḷi* "cold," *jhari* "centipede," and so on (cf. also, Te. *iddharu* "two persons"). These hypercorrections are manifestations, in a literal as well as in the sociological sense in which M. N. Srinivas (1966) employs the term, of Sanskritization.

Diglossia

Indo-Aryanization – in particular, Sanskritization – has also contributed to the age-old cleavage in Dravidian languages between the literary and the colloquial styles. In this context, the term "literary style" is used in its broad sense, to refer to all styles of institutionalized use of language including that of the public platform and is not restricted to the written form. There have been a number of studies of diglossia in Dravidian (e.g. Britto 1986; Caldwell 1903: 78ff.; Nayak 1967; Radhakrishna 1971; Shanmugam Pillai 1960), all of which point out that one of the distinguishing characteristics of the "High" style is the preponderance of Sanskritic features. The "High" style is characterized by the

[7] "Conservatism" as applied to Brahman dialects in Dravidian may be confusing. It is true that the Brahman dialects have traditionally been innovative in acquiring nonnative phonology, lexis, and so on. However, in so far as the borrowed elements do not undergo the processes of nativization that apply generally in their respective languages, the Brahman dialects are relatively more conservative (see Bright and Ramanujan 1964, and the references cited in that work for further discussion).

presence of non-Dravidian features such as aspiration, and the use of unassimilated borrowings, as well as structures such as the passive construction and the clausal mode of relative clause formation. This penchant for mixing non-native elements in the literary style gives it a rather artificial and stilted character when carried to an extreme, as in the *Maṇipravāḷa* style, and often becomes unintelligible to the uninitiated layman. It is not surprising, therefore, that from time to time there have been movements, in all the literary languages, to bring the literary style closer to the language of the common people, and a recurrent theme in these programs has been a call for reducing the Sanskritic component in the literary style (see next section).

The association of Sanskrit with the High style in Dravidian has resulted in an interesting phenomenon: the diglossic distribution of multiple derivatives of the borrowed words. Dravidian languages provide many instances of two forms of the same Indo-Aryan loanword being used in different senses: one, typically the unassimilated Sanskrit word, retaining its original meaning or undergoing amelioration, and the other, typically the form borrowed or adapted from Prakrit, undergoing deterioration. The following examples from Kannada are relevant: *samsthe* "organization," *sante* "weekly village market"; *pariṣattu* "institution," *parise* "annual fair"; *dhana* "wealth," *dana* "cattle"; *ārya* "respected person, an Aryan," *ajja* "grandfather, an old man"; *vandhye* "infertile woman," *banje* "id. (pej.)."

Mention must also be made here of the resort to Sanskrit terms for euphemisms in polite conversation and writing. Thus, the preference for terms like *jaghana* "thighs," *kuča* "breasts," *s'iṣna* "penis," *yōnī* "vagina," *sambhōga* "intercourse," *mardana* "manipulation of breasts," *rati* "sexual intercourse," *āsana* "erotic position," and so on makes even erotic manuals read like learned treatises. Sanskrit also comes to the rescue in discussing previously taboo topics such as homosexuality "*salinga kāma.*" Turning to a sombre vein, terms like *vidhave* "widow," *nidhana* "death," *śivaikya* "death," *divangata* "demised" are generally preferred, in writing and formal speech at least, to their native-language counterparts.

Indo-Aryanization and language attitudes

As pointed out earlier, the large-scale importation of Indo-Aryan features into the Dravidian languages has not gone unopposed, even in the literary languages. However, the reasons for the opposition, its intensity, and scope vary from language to language.

In Tamil Nadu, it has turned out to be an emotional issue. Even from the dawn of Dravidian history, the attitude of Tamilians to this issue has been different from that of the speakers of other literary languages. It will be recalled (section on phonetic adaptations) that *Tōḷkāppiam* sanctions the borrowing of only those words that fit into the phonological structure of Tamil. This restriction is not met with in the grammars of the other three literary languages, which have traditionally adopted a more liberal attitude to loanwords, welcoming *tatsamas* and *tadbhavas* alike, often asserting that the aspirated sounds (*mahāprāṇaś*) are integral to their language, and expanding their scripts to incorporate nonnative sounds. All of these grammars, however, do recognize the distinction between native and foreign (*dēśya* and *anyadēśya*) words and enumerate elaborate rules for deriving the native forms of the loanwords, but they do not proscribe the use of *tatsamas*. In fact, they even go one step further and implicitly encourage the use of Sanskrit compounds when they criticize the employment of hybrid compounds (called *arisāmāsa* in Kannada and *vairisamāsa* in Telugu). Further, some grammarians even go out of their way to show the similarity between the native language and Sanskrit by concocting examples of constructions never used in the language. These grammars are also unlike *Tōḷkāppiam* in their adoption of the Paninian model and terminology. (Some of these grammars are, in fact, written in Sanskrit.)

While the Andhras, the Kannadigas, and the Malayalis have welcomed Indo-Aryan borrowings in principle, they have often reacted to the indiscriminate use of these loans. As noted earlier, the *Maṇipravāḷa* style never found general grassroots appeal. On the contrary, there arose a number of countermovements seeking to bring the literary language closer to the common colloquial idiom. In Kannada, for example, there have been at least three such movements. Āndayya (*c.* thirteenth century) composed his *Kabbigara Kāva* using only native words and assimilated loans; the Vīraśaiva protest (twelfth century) against the tyranny of Brahmanism found its literary counterpart in the *vačanas* (prose lyrics) whose language is relatively free from Sanskrit borrowings (see Ramanujan 1973). In modern times, there has been a sharp reaction against the Sanskritized style of Kuvempu and others, and a call to eschew unfamiliar Sanskrit words. Similar trends are found in Telugu and Malayalam as well, for example, in the work of Somanatha (who advocated *jānu Telugu* "pure Telugu") and Ezhuttacan (a contemporary Malayalam poet).

The target of these movements, however, is only the *excessive* use of Sanskritic elements – unfamiliar words, long compounds, and so on – but the forms already present in common parlance – both assimilated and unassimilated – are accepted as a proper part of their respective languages. Thus their attitude toward Indo-Aryanization is essentially rooted in considerations of general intelligibility rather than any philosophical objection to borrowing per se. The latter attitude, however, has played an increasingly important role in Tamilian glossopolitics in this century.

In his excellent discussion of the purism movement in Tamil, Annamalai (1980) observes that the movement was fostered by several factors: the desire to assert the identity of Tamils following the Independence movement which stressed national unity, the discovery of the antiquity of Tamil and its self-sufficiency as demonstrated in the ancient Sangam literature, and the change of power structure from the domination of Brahmans to that of non-Brahmans, among others (Annamalai 2001).

The scope of the "Pure Tamil" movement was quite comprehensive. It covered all styles of language, and affected the script, the vocabulary, and even proper names. Most of the borrowed words (including assimilated words) were excised and native Tamil words from the early literature revived to take their place. An informal estimate (quoted in Annamalai 1980) is that the Sanskrit words in use in Tamil writing have come down from 50 to 20 percent in the last fifty years (Annamalai 2001). However, there do seem to be more Sanskrit words used in the spoken Tamil. This situation is similar to Early Modern Icelandic, but we know where Icelandic has gone.

Conclusion

As we conclude this broad survey of the influence of Indo-Aryan languages on Dravidian, it may not be out of place to step back, as it were, and ask, what in the final analysis has been the role of this process of Indo-Aryanization in the history of Dravidian. This is a very difficult question, not only because it can quickly get transformed into an emotional question but also because the process is an ongoing one. However, trying to steer clear of value judgments, one may attempt a partial answer.

First, there is no denying the fact that the impact of Indo-Aryan has been both profound and widespread. There is no Dravidian language that has not been touched by this influence, nor is there any department of a given language. The Dravidian languages have stood to gain from this process in many ways – their vocabularies have been enriched and their style-range widened. They have developed countless new registers and added to their metrical repertoire. It should not be forgotten that many of the Indo-Aryan words were first introduced by way of literary compositions, some of which are among the very finest in Dravidian and world literature. The Indo-Aryan influence came at a time when the Dravidian languages were beginning to assert their separate identities and aided them in this process. It may be noted that Indo-Aryanization was probably the key factor in the separation of Malayalam from Old Tamil, the former having adopted a more liberal attitude toward the importation of Indo-Aryan features (Vaidyanathan 1971 discusses Indo-Aryan loanwords in Old Tamil).

Yet one does not have to be a purist to concede that Indo-Aryanization has not been an unmixed blessing. Among what in some quarters may be regarded as not quite wholesome effects of this process are the following: the creation of an elite variety based on the incorporation of foreign elements; the emergence of a pedantic literary style based on the same principle; widespread linguistic slavery manifested in the preference for borrowings over exploitation of native resources, the disappearance of scores of perfectly adequate and expressive native terms under the onslaught of the borrowings, and so on.

Granted, the tendency to borrow has, at times, been excessive and indiscriminate, it may still be maintained that Indo-Aryanization per se need not take all the blame for this phenomena. Socially defined variation is an integral feature of language, whether borrowed features serve as the relevant variables or not; variety in literary style is also equally inherent in the medium. Literature would be of little interest any other way; words do change their meaning, fall into desuetude, and their place is not always taken by borrowed items. The question, then, is, would the Dravidian languages have developed the variety of registers that they now have, without the benefit of Indo-Aryanization? Probably yes, but the more relevant question is, whatever be our language policy for developing technical terms to serve in contemporary registers, must we get rid of the terms that are already in use, just because they did not once belong to our language? The Tamilians say yes, the other Dravidians say no. So each group goes its own way, the former resorting to ancient Tamil, the latter to classical Sanskrit, but the two have one thing in common – they are both attempting to blow new life into antique forms, while history repeats itself with new actors – this time English and to a lesser extent, Hindi.

12 Pidgins, Creoles, and Bazaar Hindi

Ian Smith

Introduction

This chapter focuses on one of the more exciting results of contact between groups speaking different languages: the birth of new languages to serve the need for intergroup communication. Typically, such languages draw most of their vocabulary from a single lexifier, but their grammar is a result of compromise among the speakers of the lexifier and substrate languages.[1]

With its history as a cultural crossroads, South Asia has naturally provided the types of situations in which new languages might be expected to develop. Very few are reported, however, possibly because they actually do develop rarely, but also because they have traditionally been viewed as marginal phenomena – "bastardized" or "corrupt" versions of language, hence not worthy of study. The known new languages of South Asia, with the exception of Bazaar Hindi, are found around the fringes of the subcontinent and represent contacts with languages beyond the Indo-Aryan and Dravidian dominated heartland. A brief survey of the known new languages follows; later in this chapter, we will look at their linguistic characteristics.

Nagamese

The mountainous terrain of Nagaland (See Maps 12.1 and 12.2 on pp. 267, 268) has led, as in Papua New Guinea, to a large number of languages in a small area – a "choṭaasaa kintu bahubhaaṣii pradeʃ" (Kumar 1978: 1).[2] Just as the people of Papua New Guinea embraced Tok Pisin, the Nagas have adopted Nagamese, an Assamese-lexified pidgin, as the chief lingua franca of their state, and it has become creolized as the mother tongue of the (non-Naga) Kachari

[1] In some cases, such as Russenorsk, the vocabulary is also a compromise (Fox 1973, cited by Holm 1989: 621). The current term substrate will be used throughout this chapter, even though it implies an unequal relationship among the lexifier and the background languages which does not always obtain.

[2] Phonemic transcriptions follow IPA usage, except that in accordance with established South Asianist practice, *c* and *j* represent prepalatal affricates and *y* represents a palatal approximant.

community. Although the existence of Nagamese was first reported only in 1921 (Hutton, cited in Sreedhar 1976a: 372), it is not known when it first came into being. Lt Briggs' 1841 diary entry, "on arrival at the Lotha Naga Hills, about 70 Nagas came down, many of them knowing Assamese" (cited in Sreedhar 1974: 38), refers in all likelihood to Nagamese. The Nagas have a long history of trade with neighboring areas of Assam which likely provided the original context in which Nagamese developed (Sreedhar 1974: 38).

Bazaar Hindi

Bazaar Hindi is a simplified form of Hindi/Urdu found in major Indian cities outside the Hindi/Urdu-speaking region. Published reports exist of Bombay Bazaar Hindi (Apte 1974a; Chernyshev 1971) and Calcutta Bazaar Hindi (Chatterji 1931). Both varieties exhibit influence from the dominant local languages, Marathi and Bangla, respectively, but also have traits in common which may be pan-Indian. While Bazaar Hindi is a pidgin broadly speaking, it has a number of characteristics that make it an atypical one.

Indo-Portuguese

As in other parts of the world, European colonial expansion led to the creation of contact languages with European lexifiers. The colonial period in South Asia began in 1498, when Portuguese ships appeared at Kozhikode. In the following years, the Portuguese established trading bases at numerous ports around the coast of India and in Sri Lanka. A pidginized variety of their language had already developed in West Africa and this likely formed the basis of the pidginized Portuguese that emerged as a lingua franca in South Asia – even in areas which had never been in Portuguese hands. Moreover, the Portuguese policy of encouraging intermarriage resulted in communities which spoke creole Portuguese as a mother tongue. Europeans who came subsequently to South Asia used Indo-Portuguese in their early contacts, and stable pidginized varieties of other European languages appear not to have developed. In Sri Lanka, for example, Indo-Portuguese served as a lingua franca for about a century and a half after the Portuguese lost control of the island (Smith 1998: 16). Indo-Portuguese creoles continue to be spoken in Korlai near Bombay (Clements 1988) and Daman and Diu in India (Clements personal communication) and in Batticaloa and Trincomalee in Sri Lanka (Smith 2005).

Sri Lanka Malay

The Dutch, who first gained a foothold in Sri Lanka in 1638, brought annual contingents of troops to the island recruited in Java and their other possessions in the Indonesian archipelago. The Dutch also used Sri Lanka as a place of exile for troublesome notables from their eastern empire. The British, who took possession of the island in 1796, continued to recruit Malay troops from the Malayan Peninsula and elsewhere for the Ceylon Rifle Regiment until it was disbanded in 1873 (Hussainmiya 1987). Despite the heterogeneous origins of the Sri Lanka "Malays," a common language developed among them, based on Vehicular Malay and creolized when many of the soldiers found wives among the island's existing Tamil-speaking Muslim community (Smith and Paauw 2006).

Others

Because pidgins and creoles have both a linguistic and a social side to their definitions (see below) and because similar processes and the resulting linguistic characteristics can be seen in other language contact phenomena (language death, second language learning, convergence in the context of language maintenance, etc.), it is often difficult to decide whether a particular language is (or was) a *pidgin* or *creole*. The language spoken by the aboriginal community of Sri Lanka, the Veddas, has been claimed by Dharmadasa (1974) following deSilva (1972) to be a creolized version of a Sinhala-lexified pidgin. Although neither the circumstances whereby the Veddas acquired their current language, nor of the linguistic characteristics of their previous language are known, Vedda does have a number of linguistic traits that accord with a pidgin origin. Dharmadasa places the development of a creole somewhere between the tenth and the sixteenth centuries, from the preservation in Vedda of lexicon now lost in Sinhala. Similarly, Southworth's (1971) theory that a pidginized/creolized form of Indo-Aryan played a role in the development of Marathi is plausible, but cannot be substantiated on the basis of current knowledge. Certainly Marathi itself could not be classed as a creole. Another marginal candidate is "Butler English" (Hosali 2000; Hosali and Aitchison 1986), the English of poorly educated service workers. A range of other disparaging terms, such as "Kitchen English," "Babu English" refer to similar phenomena (B. Kachru 1983b: 25). Butler English has a few pidgin-like structural characteristics, but in general its instability and the fact that it is mostly used in dealing with English-speaking customers, employers, and so on make it more like an interlanguage or a prepidgin.

Pidgin and creole as archetypes

Scholars have not been able to agree on definitions for the terms *pidgin* and *creole*. It is useful to take them as archetypes around which individual contact languages may cluster, rather than as entities with sharply defined boundaries. This allows us to see the relationships among various types of contact languages and to classify intermediate forms that are troublesome in a world of discrete categories. In the linguistics of contact languages, recognition of the interdependence of sociolinguistic and structural aspects of language is vitally important (Sebba 1997). The following sections discuss the archetypal characteristics of pidgins and creoles using South Asian languages as examples.

Sociolinguistic characteristics of *pidgins* and *creoles*

First and foremost, pidgins and creoles develop in informal contexts in which groups are unable (or unwilling) to learn the lexifier in the form spoken by its mother-tongue speakers. In Bombay for example, Bazaar Hindi is spoken by "persons who are not well educated, come from the low socio-economic strata of the population, and either have such non-white-collar jobs as porter, taxi-driver, hawker, waiter, servant, etc., or are petty shop-keepers" (Apte 1974a: 23), while more educated individuals, who have had the opportunity to study Hindi–Urdu formally, speak a variety that is closer to standard. (Apte 1974a: 22–3). Often the major lines of communication are between speakers of languages other than the lexifier (Whinnom 1971). Certainly this is true in the case of Bazaar Hindi. In Bombay, for example, the dominant language, Marathi, is spoken by less than 50 percent of the urban population, the city's other main mother tongues being Gujarati, Hindi–Urdu, Konkani, Tamil, Telugu, Kannada, Malayalam, and Punjabi; but since Hindi–Urdu speakers constitute less than 10 percent of the population, much of the use of Bazaar Hindi is between speakers whose mother tongues are languages other than Hindi–Urdu.

Pidgins have three additional characteristics not shared by creoles. First, at least in their early life, they are used only in restricted contexts (or *domains*), usually associated with trade or work. Bazaar Hindi conforms to the archetype in being used primarily for petty commerce and in nonwhite-collar employment. Second, they are the mother tongue of no one, and again Bazaar Hindi has this characteristic. Third, communication in early pidgins is focused on message content at the expense of social and discourse information (Halliday's ideational as opposed to interpersonal and textual information, 1970: 143). Over time, of course, pidgins may extend their range of use to more and more domains and may begin to mark social and discourse information. Such extended pidgins may also attain mother-tongue status; Nagamese, as noted above, is an extended pidgin for the majority of its speakers, but a creole for the Kacharis. Continued contact with the lexifier may cause creoles and extended pidgins to develop a range of sociostylistic varieties known as acrolect (most like the lexifier), basilect (least like the lexifier), and mesolects (intermediate). Nagamese has continued to borrow from Assamese, extending its range of pronouns, for example, and adding complex numeral morphology. In time, the spectrum of variants may shrink toward the acrolect, a process known as decreolization.

Most of the well-studied pidgins and creoles have developed as a result of western colonialism. These languages result from contact between a high-status lexifier, the colonial language, and lower-status substrate languages spoken by the colonized and enslaved; typically the lexifier is unrelated to and radically different from the lower-status languages in phonology, grammar, and lexicon. Bazaar Hindi atypically developed from contact among languages of more equal status and those that are more closely related to one another.

While pidgins have special status as auxiliary languages, derived from the fact that they are not the primary language of any group, creoles do function as the mother tongue of a community; they are thus languages like any other, differentiated only by the historical circumstances of their birth. They are used in all of the domains that their communities require, and they routinely convey social and discourse information. Obviously, creoles may develop from pidgins that have acquired mother-tongue status; in fact this was the only way they were thought to arise in the life-cycle model (Bloomfield 1933) canonized in Hall (1966). However, Alleyne (1971) argued that many creoles have developed directly from the contact situation without passing first through a pidgin stage; Thomason and Kaufman (1988) have termed this process abrupt creolization. Most likely, the creole Nagamese of the Kacharis developed from a (more or less) stable pidgin, while Indo-Portuguese and Sri Lanka Malay are abrupt creoles.

Structural characteristics of pidgins and creoles

The structural characteristics of contact languages have their basis in the sociolinguistics of the contact situation. Pidgins must be easy to learn, because they must be acquired as a second language in informal circumstances where access to the structure of the lexifier is restricted; they also have reduced communicative possibilities, particularly in their early stages, because they are used only in limited domains. Finally they exhibit the influence of the different primary languages of their speakers. In Bazaar Hindi the constraints are attenuated because the substrate languages are similar to the lexifier. Creoles, by virtue of their mother-tongue status, have none of these restrictions, but they may still carry marks of the circumstances of their birth. Because of their radical restructuring, pidgins and creoles are generally not mutually intelligible with their lexifiers; Bazaar Hindi, however, is an exception to this rule.

Small vocabulary

Because of their limited communicative needs, pidgins can get by with a smaller stock of words than "full" languages. This in turn makes them easier to learn. Parsimony in the word stock is partially accomplished through polysemy, circumlocution, and transparent derivation. For example, the Nagamese plural

Table 12.1. *Assamese and Nagamese personal pronouns*

		Assamese		Nagamese	
Person	Status	Singular	Plural	Singular	Plural
I		*mɒi*	*ami*	*moy*	*moy-khan*
II	[−hon]	*tɒi*	*tɒ-hɒ̃t*	*əpuni*	*əpuni-khan*
			toma-lok		
		tumi	*apona-lok*		
	[+hon]		*apona-xɒkɒl*		
		apuni			
III	[−hon] (m/f)	*xi /tai*	*xi-hɒ̃/ta-hɒ̃t*	*tay*	*tay-khan*
		tẽɒ̃			*tay-bilək*
		tekhet	*tẽɒ̃-lok*		
	[+hon]		*tei-bilak*		
			texet-x t		
			tɒkɒl		

pronouns are formed by adding a suffix to the singular forms, as seen in Table 12.1. Assamese has this pattern in the third person only, with separate words for the first and second plural forms.[3] Dharmadasa (1974: 88–9) cites the large number of circumlocutions in Vedda as evidence for its pidgin origins: for example *uḍatanin mandovena diyaraaccaa* (above-from falling water) "rain," cf. Sinhala *væssa*. Chatterji's characterization of Bazaar Hindi as having "the ABSOLUTE MINIMUM OF COMMON WORDS OF AN ELEMENTARY AND NON-TECHNICAL CHARACTER, AND OF COMMON IDIOMS AND EXPRESSIONS" (1931: 14, emphasis original) shows that it too features a parsimonious word stock. But the rule may not be as strict if the substrate languages are similar to the lexifier, as Apte notes of Bombay Bazaar Hindi: "There is a significant percentage of vocabulary common between Hindi–Urdu and Marathi, or for that matter between Hindi–Urdu and other Indian languages . . . As a result, non-Hindi-Urdu speakers, especially Marathi speakers, feel comfortable in using Marathi words in their Hindi–Urdu speech since it is thought that any Marathi word can also be a Hindi–Urdu word." As a pidgin expands to new domains its vocabulary must grow. Creoles, of course, suffer no vocabulary restrictions at all, but traces of the early stages of the lexicon may often still be discerned. In Sri Lanka Portuguese, for example, the word *buskaa* "search;

[3] Assamese data in this chapter from B. Das Gupta (1966), Goswami (1978), Masica (1991), and Sommer (1991). Nagamese data from Borua (1993) and Sreedhar (1974, 1976a, 1985). Bazaar Hindi data from Apte (1974a) and Chatterji (1931). Sri Lanka Portuguese data from the author's own field notes.

earn" is polysemous (cf. Ptg. *buscar* "search," *ganhar* "earn," Tamil *ṭeeṭu* "search"; *compaaṭi* "earn."); *kaatru kaantu* "square" (lit. "four corners") is a circumlocution (cf. Ptg. *quadrado*) calqued on Tamil *naat-canṭi* "four-junction."

Lexicalization influenced by substrate languages

Where the lexifier is of high status and unrelated to the substrate languages, it normally provides the bulk of the lexicon for the pidgin or creole. For example, the few Sri Lanka Portuguese words of Tamil or Sinhala origin mostly concern local flora, fauna, or cultural phenomena for which there was no equivalent Portuguese term, for example, *suura* "toddy" < Si. *sura* "toddy," *baannḍu* "weevil" < Ta. *vanḍu* "weevil." The reason is that the lexifier is a target language for the substrate language speakers, who may not even realize that a difference exists between the lexifier and the pidgin or creole (Romaine 1988: 15). When the lexifier and the substrate languages are closer in prestige and genetic affiliation, lexicon from the substrate languages may have a greater presence in the pidgin or creole, as the passage from Apte (1974a), cited in the last section, demonstrates for Bombay Bazaar Hindi. Although the substrate languages may make little contribution to the actual vocabulary items, their effect may nevertheless be felt in the lexicalization patterns, that is, in the structure of derived and idiomatic forms and in the mapping between form and meaning. In Sri Lanka Portuguese, for example, the expression *aav botaa* "get drunk," literally "water put," is calqued on the Tamil expression of the same meaning, *taṇṇi pooṭu*, and the meaning of *værgɔɔɲa* (<Ptg. *vergonha* "shame") covers the range "shame, shyness" as does the corresponding Tamil word *vekkam*.

Phonological influence of substrate languages

Mühlhäusler notes that "pronunciation and phonology remain the least stable in stabilized pidgins . . . pronunciation and phonological rules can differ quite significantly from group to group and speaker to speaker" (1986: 148). South Asian pidgins are no exception. Chatterji observes that the phonology of Calcutta Bazaar Hindi varies with the speaker's own language (1931: 19). Similarly, Sreedhar lists variations in the phonology of Nagamese, which "can be attributed to the influence of the phonology of the mother tongue of the Naga community concerned" (Sreedhar 1974: 88). For example, in the Nagamese spoken by the Semas, dentals *s, z,* and n, but not *t* or *d*, are palatalized before a front vowel as in Sema (Sreedhar 1974: 76, 1976b: 41–54; the processes differ slightly in their details). Creoles are more stable but may reflect earlier phonological influence of substrate languages. Contact languages may exhibit fewer phonemic oppositions than the lexifier, since oppositions not found in the substrate languages of the majority of speakers may be collapsed. For example,

Table 12.2. *Assamese subject–verb agreement and Nagamese*

Assamese	Gloss	Nagamese
ahi-m	come–fut:1st pers.	*əhibo*
ahi-bi	come–fut:2nd pers. [−honorific]	
ahi-ba	come–fut:2nd pers.	
ahi-bɒ	come–fut:3rd pers./2nd pers. [+honorific]	

Sri Lanka Portuguese lacks the opposition between nasalized and nonnasalized vowels found in Standard Portuguese; this opposition is similarly absent from Tamil and Sinhala. By contrast, nasal vowels exist in Korlai Portuguese, just as they do in the substrate language, Marathi (Clements 1988: 60–1).

Minimal structure

Because they are learned informally as second languages by all their speakers, pidgins must avoid structural complexity in order to be easy to acquire. Structural aspects of the lexifier that are not necessary for basic communication do not usually find their way into the pidgin. Apte notes this characteristic in Bazaar Hindi: "Since people in this group depend extensively for their occupational security on the ability to communicate with others of different linguistic backgrounds, there is a greater emphasis on communication than on grammatical 'niceties'." Agreement morphology, for example, is usually absent from pidgins. As the examples in Table 12.2 demonstrate, Nagamese lacks subject–verb agreement, even though its lexifier, Assamese, has such agreement. In the future forms shown, the Assamese third person form is generalized for all persons in Nagamese. The same pattern is seen in Bazaar Hindi (Table 12.3), where the third person singular masculine form is generalized.

Similarly, arbitrary lexical categories such as grammatical gender are usually absent from pidgins and creoles. Indo-Portuguese, for example, lacks grammatical gender even in areas such as Korlai where the substrate languages have it.

Reduced number of grammatical categories

In keeping with their minimal structure and their minimal communicative functions, pidgins generally have fewer grammatical categories than their lexifiers. For example the range of honorific and familiar second and third person pronouns found in Assamese is not present in Nagamese (Table 12.1);[4] similarly only a single second person pronoun *tum* is in general use in Bombay Bazaar

[4] The more recent work of Borua (1993) reports a familiar/honorific distinction in the second person (*tumi, tumikhaan vs. aapuni, aapunikhaan*) and a masc./fem. distinction in the third

Table 12.3. *Hindi subject–verb agreement and Bazaar Hindi*

Hindi	Gloss	Bazaar Hindi	
		Calcutta	Bombay
jaa-ũũgaa/-ũũgii	go–FUT:1sg. masc./fem.		
jaa-oge	go–FUT:2sg.	*jaa-egaa*	*jaa-ygaa*
jaa-egaa/-egii	go–FUT:2sg. & 3sg. [−hon] masc./fem.		
jaa-ẽge	go–FUT:pl & 2nd pers. [+hon]		

Hindi uses while its lexifier, Hindi, has three: *tuu*, *tum*, and *aap; tuu* is also absent in Calcutta Bazaar Hindi, though *aap* is used according to Chatterji (1931: 33–4).

Avoidance of morphology

Morphology is generally harder to learn than syntax; *pidgin* and *creole* languages are therefore thought to eschew morphology in their early stages. New morphology may develop as a pidgin expands or as a creole develops. In Sri Lanka Portuguese, for example, the complex tense and agreement morphology of Standard Portuguese is nowhere to be found; however, auxiliaries and adverbs have developed into tense-marking prefixes, thus *jaa-* "past" (< Ptg. *ja* "already"), *ta-* "pres" (< Ptg. *está* "is," 3sg. pres. of the progressive auxiliary), and *lo-* "fut" (< Ptg. *logo* "soon"). For example, *jaa-oyaa* "saw," *ta-oyaa* "sees," *lo-oyaa* "will see" (Ptg. *olha, olhou, olhará*, respectively[5]). Occasionally, lexifier morphology that is regular, easy to analyze (and hence to learn), and unifunctional may get carried over into a pidgin or creole. For example Korlai Portuguese preserves the Standard Portuguese past suffix *-o*, e.g., *(j-)ulyo* "saw."[6] Both Bazaar Hindi and Nagamese exhibit surprising amounts of lexifier morphology. Bombay Bazaar Hindi verb morphology includes the participle suffix *-taa*, the future suffix*-(e)gaa*, the past suffix *-aa*, the imperative suffix*-o/-w*, and the oblique infinitive marker*-ne* (e.g., *rah-taa* "staying," *aay-gaa* "will come," *dekh-aa* "saw" and *dekh-ne kaa* "to see"); the verbal morphology of Calcutta Bazaar Hindi is similar. It is likely that such morphology is possible because of similar morphosyntactic patterns in the substrate languages.

The Nagamese situation is complicated by both the great amount of variation and the continuing contact with Assamese. All varieties of Nagamese have case

person (*taai, taaikhaan vs. taar, taarkhaan*). It is likely that these have developed as part of the expansion of the language.

5 The Standard Portuguese examples are third person singular forms; Sri Lanka Portuguese has no subject–verb agreement.

6 Korlai Portuguese has no subject–verb agreement and has generalized the most common allomorph of the Std. Portuguese third person singular suffix to all verbs.

Table 12.4. *Case suffixes versus syntactic expressions in Nagamese*

Function and gloss	Case suffix example	Syntactic example
ACCUSATIVE "I saw a boy."	*moy lora-k ekta dikhi-se* I boy-ACC a see-NONFUT	*moy lora ekta dikhi-se* I boy a see-NONFUT
GENITIVE "the boy's book"	*chokra-r kitab* boy-GEN book	*chokra (laga) kitab* boy (of) book
INSTRUMENTAL "Rita was beaten with a stick."	*rita-k lathi-di mari-se* Rita-ACC stick-INST beat-NONFUT	*rita lathi pora mari-se* Rita stick from beat-NONFUT
DATIVE "I gave the boy a book."	*moy ekta kitab lora-ke di-se* I a book boy-DAT give-NONFUT	*moy ekta kitab lora di-se* I a book boy give-NONFUT

suffixes derived from Assamese, but the number, distribution, and form of the affixes vary somewhat from community to community. Some, such as the Phom and Yimchungur have only a locative case suffix. Alternative syntactic expressions using parataxis or postpositions are found, as shown in Table 12.4. A likely interpretation of these data is that early Nagamese had no case morphology and it is now developing differently in different communities through continued contact with Assamese. Even if case morphology was present in early Nagamese, the varieties with only one case demonstrate the tendency for pidgins to avoid it.

Considerably more uniformity is seen in basic verb morphology: all varieties have the following suffixes from Assamese: *-bi* (imperative), *-bo* (future), *-ise* (nonfuture), and *-ile* (conditional), and there is no reason to believe that they were not present in early pidgin. While the morphology of Bazaar Hindi and Nagamese verbs is much simpler and more regular than that of Hindi and Assamese (see for example Table 12.2 and Table 12.3 on pages 260, 261), it nonetheless shows that lexifier morphology is not completely prohibited from pidgins and creoles. More work is needed to investigate the types of morphology that can survive pidginization and creolization and the kinds of social situations and substrate language typology that make its survival possible.

Structural regularity

For ease of learning, early *pidgins* and *creoles* tend to have a regular structure, though irregularity may creep back into creoles as they change over time. We have noted above that lexifier morphology tends not to survive in *pidgins* and *creoles*; when it does, there is a tendency to level out any allomorphy that is not the result of automatic phonetic processes. For example, a few Hindi verbs have unpredictable stems in the imperative, thus *de-naa* "give-infinitive," *d-o* "give-imperative," which are regularized in Bombay Bazaar Hindi, thus *de-w* "give-imperative." Contrary to this tendency, unpredictable allomorphy in very common words often finds its way into a pidgin or creole. In Hindi, for example, *jaa-naa* "to go" has a perfect stem *ga-* and this alternation is carried into Bombay Bazaar Hindi *jaa-ygaa* "go-fut" vs. *gay-aa* "go-past." Similarly, Sri Lanka Portuguese preserves Portuguese suppletive allomorphy in *andaa* "go" vs. *jaa-foy* "past-go" and Nagamese reflects Assamese allomorphy in *moy* "I" vs. *mu-k* "I-acc, me."

Structural influence of substrate languages

Learners of a second language have a strong tendency to view its structure in terms of their primary language, unconsciously assuming it has the same sound system, grammar, lexical semantics, pragmatics, and so on. Pidgins, being second languages par excellence, are under constant pressure from the primary languages of their speakers. If these primary languages are diverse in their structure, and if the speakers of no primary language are numerically dominant, then their individual influences may cancel one another. On the other hand, if the speakers of one primary language or a group of structurally similar primary languages predominate, then the structure of the dominant language(s) is likely to influence the structure of the pidgin. Creoles, whether abrupt creoles or those that develop from extended pidgins are obviously subject to the same kinds of pressures in their early stages. Once established, they take their own path of development, but may still be influenced by other languages if there is considerable bilingualism. South Asian pidgins and creoles exhibit clear influence of substrate languages, whether of one dominant language or a group of similar languages.[7] For example, in Assamese adjective phrases precede their head noun, but in Nagamese an alternative N-AdjP word order exists, under the influence of Naga language patterns (Sreedhar 1974: 88). The two alternative patterns and their counterparts in Assamese and Naga (as represented by Sema) are shown in 1 (Sema examples from Sreedhar 1974: 88):

1. "two good girls" / "a white horse" – lexifier pattern

Nagamese	*b*^{h}*al*	*duy*	*suali*	Assamese	*eʈa*	*b*^{h}*ɒg*	*g*^{h}*õra*
Gloss	two	good	girls	Gloss	DET a	white	horse

"two good girls" / "good house" – substrate language pattern

Nagamese	*b*^{h}*al*	*suali*	*duy*	Sema	*əki*	*kivi*
Gloss	two	girl	good	Gloss	house	good

[7] As noted, the substrate is not known in the case of Vedda.

Similarly, Sri Lanka Malay has left-branching structures like Tamil and Sinhala rather than right-branching structures like Malay and Bazaar Malay. For example (2) shows SOV order in Sri Lanka Malay and Sri Lanka Muslim Tamil but SVO order in Bazaar Malay.

2. "I gave him the money."[a]

SL Malay	*(see)*	*dedaŋ*	*duvit-na*	*ayŋ-kasi*		
SLM Tamil	*(naan)*	*avan-ukku*	*calli-ja*	*kuʈu-tt-an*		
Bazaar Malay	*(saja)*			*kasi*	*dia*	*duit*
Gloss	I	him: DAT	money: ACC	give: PAST	him	money

Note: [a] The author is grateful to B.A. Hussainmiya for the Sri Lanka Muslim Tamil and Sri Lanka Malay data and to Sonny Lim for the Bazaar Malay data.

Lack of stylistic and social levels

In the early stages of pidgins and abrupt creoles, the focus is on the communication of basic cognitive information. Thus stylistic and social "niceties" tend to be lacking at this stage, though they would normally redevelop in creoles and as part of the expansion process in extended pidgins. The smaller number of second-person pronouns in Nagamese and Bazaar Hindi vis-à-vis their lexifiers (see above) is an example of such stylistic minimalism.

Variability

All languages exhibit variability marking social and stylistic differences and as part of the process of language change. In pidgins and early creoles, variability is due more to the language learning process than to social and stylistic factors. Such initial variability subsides somewhat as a more stable norm emerges. In extended pidgins and creoles, new variability may be introduced from three sources: the development of social and stylistic levels, continued contact with the lexifier, and continued bilingualism in the substrate languages.

In Sri Lanka Portuguese, continued contact with Tamil in the Batticaloa community has introduced a new habilitative construction calqued on the Tamil pattern. This new pattern, which is used only in the negative, competes with the older construction derived from Portuguese. Both patterns are seen in 3.

3. (You) can't give money to him.

SLP:old	*eli*	*-pa*	*diɲeeru*	*naa-poy*	*daa*		
SLP:new	*eli*	*-pa*	*diɲeeru*			*pa-daa*	*naa-poy*
Tamil	*avan*	*-ukku*	*calli*			*kuʈukk-a*	*eel-aatu*
Gloss	him	DAT	money	HABIL:NEG	give	give:INFIN	HABIL:NEG

Table 12.5. *Occurrence of pidgin "universals" in Bazaar Hindi and Nagamese*

		Bazaar Hindi	Nagamese
(1)	SVO word order	–	–
(2)	Invariant word order for questions, commands, statements	+	+
(3)	Propositional clause qualifiers (such as negative) external to the qualified clause	–	(+??)/–[a]
(4)	Lack of number distinction in nouns	+	–
(5)	Minimal pronoun systems	+	+
(6)	Very few prepositions [/postpositions]	–	–
(7)	Lack of derivational depth/few grammatical rules/scarcity of complex sentences	–	–
(8)	WH-question words are analytic (e.g., what-place? = "where")	–	–
(9)	Anaphoric pronouns that may eventually become generalized predicate introducers	–	–

Note: [a] Both final (postverbal) and preverbal negatives are found: *moj moNso lhajn nəj* "I did not eat meat,"*moj moNso nə khaj* "I am not eating meat" (Sreedhar 1974: 148–9. In SOV languages, however, a postverbal negative is not necessarily to be constructed as clause external.

Multiple causation

The characteristics cataloged above are not all mutually exclusive and often more than one of them is reflected in a particular feature of a *pidgin* or *creole*. The lack of subject–verb agreement in Nagamese and Bazaar Hindi was listed under the rubric of minimal structure, but it could equally be considered an instance of reduced number of grammatical categories or avoidance of morphology.

Conclusion: The significance of South Asian contact languages

South Asian pidgins and creoles do not feature prominently in the general literature on pidgins and creoles, yet they have some important contributions to make to our understanding of these phenomena. First, South Asian contact languages in general demonstrate the importance of substrate languages as opposed to rather specific "universals," largely because they have formed through contact between a lexifier and either a single substrate language or a number of structurally similar substrate languages. For example, Mühlhäusler enumerates nine "syntactic properties that have figured prominently in recent discussion of pidgin universals" (1986: 154 ff.), but as Table 12.5 shows, neither Bazaar Hindi nor Nagamese conforms to the expected profile. Both languages are extended pidgins, however, and it may be argued that features such as (7) as well as possibly (4) in Nagamese were earlier present but have been obliterated by the expansion process; just as (5) is in the process of being lost in Nagamese (see Note 4).

In a similar vein, Smith 1979 demonstrates that Sri Lanka Portuguese does not conform to the profiles of creole characteristics proposed by Taylor (1971: 294) or Bickerton (1977: 58–60).

Finally, Bazaar Hindi itself poses a challenge to a narrow definition of pidgins. Several characteristics differentiate it from archetypal pidgins:[8]

1 a less unequal social relationship between speakers of the lexifier and speakers of the substrate languages;
2 mutual intelligibility with its lexifier;
3 relatively little visible restructuring;[9]
4 less radical simplification;
5 less radical reduction;
6 a less parsimonious lexicon;
7 a lexicon more open to imports from substrate languages.

On the basis of point (2) alone, some would say Bazaar Hindi is not a pidgin. Nida and Fehderau (1970), for example, regard this as a defining distinction between pidgin and koiné. More recent work, however, restricts the latter term to the product of dialect contact (Kerswill 2004; Siegel 2001). Siegel highlights several characteristics of koineization that distinguish it from pidginization:

1 continuous transmission (in the sense of Thomason and Kaufman 1988);[10]
2 no second language learning; no "target" variety and no distinction between lexifier and substrate languages;
3 intimate social interaction between speakers of the different varieties in contact;
4 structural continuity with the contributing varieties.

Since Bazaar Hindi results from imperfect learning of a target and is not the result of dialect contact, it lies in the constellation of pidgins rather than that of koinés. Its deviations from the pidgin archetype mostly result from the

[8] This discussion has benefited from email correspondence with Jeff Siegel. Remaining deficiencies are the author's own.

[9] That is to say, the structures created by speakers of the substrate languages because of their imperfect access to the lexifier happen to coincide with lexifier structures.

[10] Kerswill (2004) points out, however, that "a community using a koine is likely not to have the 'normal' contact with earlier generations' speech."

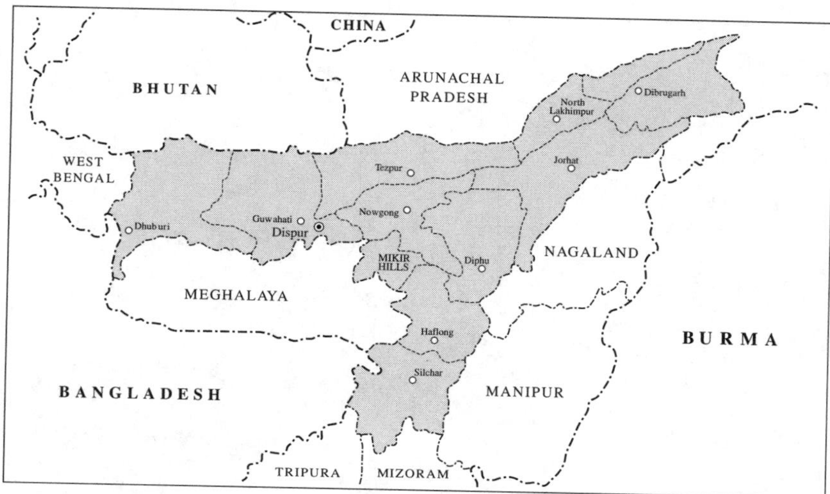

Map 12.1. *Map of Assam.*
Source: http://freeindia.org:8088/india_maps/statemaps/images/assam.gif (accessed September 6, 2005).

similarity of the substrate languages and the lexifier.[11] Thus, the main importance of Bazaar Hindi is that it demonstrates how certain variations in the input conditions to pidginization correlate with differences in the end product, and this ultimately leads to a clearer picture of the relationships between pidginization and creolization and other types of language contact.

11 If this view is correct, we should expect to find languages that are intermediate between Bazaar Hindi and the pidgin archetype. A possible candidate is Kituba (Nida and Fehderau, 1970), a KiKongo-based lingua franca of the Lower Congo that developed as a lingua franca among the BaKongo. It exhibits perhaps more simplification and reduction than Bazaar Hindi and is not mutually intelligible with the Manianga dialect of KiKongo (to which it is most closely related), but neither is it minimal: it has, for example, nine tense-aspect distinctions (as opposed to seventeen in KiManianga) and four noun classes (as opposed to six in KiManianga).

Map 12.2. *Map of Nagaland, office of the Registrar General of India.*
Source: www.censusindia/net/results/2001 maps/nagaland 01.html (accessed September 6, 2005).

Part 5

Orality, literacy, and writing systems

13 Orality and literacy

*Rama Kant Agnihotri**

Introduction

If we focus our attention on the ways in which we constantly fine-tune our linguistic and cultural behavior in response to changes in interactional situations, we will immediately realize that multilinguality (and attendant multiplicity of cultures) must be, as it were, constitutive of an individual's identity and a community's intra- and intergroup dynamics. With the progress made both in the sociolinguistic analysis of variability and the sociology of language, the multilingual nature of several societies has been carefully documented. Even the myth of "one nation–one religion–one language" that had gained considerable supremacy during the colonial and post world-wars period was seriously questioned and it became obvious that the countries hitherto regarded as the ultimate examples of monolinguality such as the United States, the United Kingdom, and various European countries were essentially multilingual. Even when "a language" was associated with "a community," it was obvious that the range of variability in terms of region, age, sex, and socioeconomic status was so substantial as to merit different linguistic labels. In fact, it is extremely difficult to define "language" and "community" with any clarity and precision; their definitions actually tend to be circular generally. Our multilinguality is of course built on a shared Universal Grammar that informs all linguistic behavior at some abstract level. We need this multilinguality not only to negotiate our day-to-day encounters that multiply exponentially in complexity as persons, places, and topics of conversation change, but also to construct, transmit, and continuously enrich our culture. This multilinguality subsumes not only the oral, but also the written and the performative (i.e. "performance-oriented such as dance, music, visual effects, and spatial arrangements"), including an intense dialogic interaction among them. It is extremely difficult to draw clear boundaries between them. The moment we try to say that here the oral or the

* There have been several scholars from the University of Delhi and other universities in India who have provided insightful suggestions and with whom I have had helpful discussions. I have identified them in Acknowledgments (see p. xvii of this volume).

performative ends and the written begins, we get into serious problems. Consider, for example, the dynamics of all the three in the reading, recitation, and performance of the *Ramayana*, not just in a variety of languages in India, but also in Nepal, Burma, Malaysia, Indonesia, Thailand, Laos, Sri Lanka, and so on (see Iyengar 1983; Raghavan 1980).

Even historically, it has not been possible to clearly define these boundaries, though the received wisdom suggests that "speech" begins around 30,000 BCE, and "writing" around 10,000 BCE. It was only, it is claimed, in the later Old Stone Age, that there was an outburst of graphic forms in France, Africa, and North America (Goody 1987: 4). In the case of South Asia, the relationship between speech and writing has always remained rather mysterious, partly because of the privileged status accorded to the oral tradition and partly because of the perishable materials used for writing. During the long period of 2,000 years between the largely undeciphered Harappan script of the first half of the third millennium BCE and the Brahmi and Kharoshti scripts of the third century BCE, there is hardly any trace of a writing system (Bright 1990: 132–3). But human societies and cultures are much older than speech and writing as known to us and there must have been efficient systems of transmission in place whether oral, graphic, performative, or various complex combinations of these in prehistorical times. If our present is any reliable indicator of our past, then that indeed seems to be the case. There are always processes at work that freeze the oral into a written text or a performative skill; similarly, the written and the performative get constantly modified by the continuously changing oral traditions. In between, of course, there are texts that are generally orally transmitted and recited and do not change for centuries just as there are oral recitations and performative renditions that are not controlled by any canonized text and vary almost infinitely in relation to performers, places, and audience. It is because of this dialogic relationship that the South Asian heritage in all its glory and plurality has survived all kinds of orthodoxy and destruction. Several "Vijayangars"[1] have been destroyed but not their languages and cultures. As Warder (1972: 213) says, "every centre of freedom was capable of generating others without end and replenishing the land. Much was obliterated, but more was created, so that the heritage is still with us."

Perspectives on orality and literacy

The question of the relationship between orality and literacy may be examined from two different perspectives (for an insightful discussion of the autonomous,

[1] The Vijayanagar Empire (1336–1565 CE) was established on a humble note to resist Muslim invasion but in less than fifty years became one of the most powerful kingdoms in south India. Hampi ruins in Karnataka still preserve the glory of that empire. It took a joint army of four Muslim rulers to destroy it (see Verghese 2002).

critical, and social models of literacy, see Street 1997). We may call the first perspective "pedagogical," where the focus is on making the "illiterate" oral societies "literate." It is assumed that there are levels of cognitive development that are possible only with literacy and that oral societies can at best have a limited storehouse of knowledge, which, it is claimed, is largely unscientific in nature. This perspective is further plagued by the manner in which "literacy" has been conceptualized in the modern society. Across the developing world, where literacy levels are extremely low, a farcical distinction is made between education and literacy (cf. Agnihotri 2002a), and literacy is measured in terms of *minimum* Levels of Learning or just the ability to count, say, upto 100 and the ability to read a few words and write one's name. Such a view of literacy is indeed an insult to human intelligence. In this perspective, a strong correlation is seen between poverty, disease, underdevelopment, and illiteracy, and it is assumed that the growth of "minimal literacy" will automatically solve all problems. That this can never be so should be clear from the case of Sri Lanka where though the literacy is above 87 percent (SIL International 2002), the levels of poverty are very high and there is hardly any industrial development. Nor has this high literacy rate helped in any way in the resolution of the conflicts arising out of the diglossia that separates literary Sinhala from its colloquial counterpart (Dharmadasa 1977). Literacy programs in all the South Asian countries, such as India, Nepal, Bangladesh, Sri Lanka, and Pakistan, generally assume that illiteracy is the root cause of all evil and that universalization of minimal literacy will automatically solve all problems. For example, according to the UNESCO (1984a: 3) report on Bangladesh, "overwhelming illiteracy is the most formidable obstacle to the modernization process." In the case of India, we are told, "literacy is an essential prerequisite as well as an obligation of a democratic government for bringing about large scale and informed participation of people in the process of democratic functioning of the Government and decentralization of tasks and responsibilities" (UNESCO 1984b: 33). But that literacy we know will at best consist of making people "read with understanding road signs, posters, simple instructions, newspapers for neo-literates etc.," "writing independently short letters, applications, filling up cheques, forms etc.," and having some "idea of percentage, interest, proportion and area *not involving fractions*" (ibid.: 24–5, emphasis added). How can people with such abysmally low levels of literacy actively and critically participate in a democracy and take on responsibilities? The fact is that when literacy figures are generally collected during the census or literacy programs are evaluated to estimate their success, these minimum levels are allowed to fall further and anybody who can write his or her name is counted as literate. How can programs that start with objectives that are so fundamentally insulting to human intelligence ever hope to provide common people access to the knowledge encapsulated in the written mode?

It should not surprise anyone that literacy levels in South Asia remain so low in spite of all the national and international noise that is made in the name of "education for all." Nobody is really serious about the issue. The budgetary allocation for education rarely exceeds 5 to 6 percent of the Gross Domestic Product (GDP). Those in power never really wish that the masses should get access to the knowledge that ensures their control on social institutions. The literacy programs and schools (for the poor, especially rural, children rarely have either teachers or rooms or books) completely ignore the languages and cultures of children. When in 1859, the then prime minister of the Rana regime opened several vernacular schools for the children of Nepal, he was promptly dismissed and all the schools were closed. In 1951, Nepal had only eleven secondary schools and only 2 percent of its population was literate (UNESCO 1984c). Even in the case of India where tall claims are made in connection with literacy, the 1991 Census showed that the literacy rate in the seven plus age group was only 52 percent, female literacy 39 percent, rural literacy 45 percent, and the drop out rate from Class I to Class V approximately 50 percent (National Institute of Adult Education 1993). This indeed is a dismal picture. According to SIL International (2002) estimates, the literacy rate in Bangladesh is 25 percent, in Nepal, 29 percent; in Pakistan, 26 percent; and in India, 52 percent. The orality, literacy, and education debate provides a space where we can reexamine the whole issue afresh. Lankshear (1987: 216) makes a distinction between proper and improper literacies, where proper literacy comprises education that enables people to make rational judgments "enabling them to identify, understand and act to transform social relations and practices in which power is structured unequally." Sustaining local literacies and oral traditions must be an integral part of proper literacy (see Agnihotri 1994, 1997; Barton 1994; Street 1994). In the context of India, the Central Institute of Indian Languages (CIIL), Mysore, has made an attempt in terms of the Bilingual Transfer Model where one starts with 80 percent mother tongue but ends up with almost no mother tongue by Class IV because the child "should be able to compete with non-tribal student without any difficulty in his school language" (Narayan 1997: 19). It is indeed difficult to understand the logic of the transfer model in the context of multilingual countries.

We may call the second perspective on orality and literacy "cognitive and cultural." In this case, the focus is not on literacy skills. Here one is concerned more with understanding the cognitive and cultural differences between the oral and literate societies. The oral societies are generally regarded rather primitive as far as cognitive skills and cultural sophistication are concerned. In the case of literate societies, fairly high levels of education in the modern sense are subsumed and it is often argued that the kind of abstract and complex knowledge that is possible in such literate societies is almost inconceivable in oral societies. Scholars such as Ong (1967), Goody (1968), and Oxenham (1980), have associated empirical analysis, logical thinking, and sustained reflective introspection with the invention of script literacy by the Greeks. The cognitively rich oral traditions, such as the ancient Indian Vedic tradition, pose a serious problem for such a view of orality and literacy. The Vedic texts are said to have all those features that are generally associated exclusively with writing, including technical information, moral judgment, universal definition, Kantian imperative, mathematical relationship, epistemology, and logic (cf. Havelock 1963), and, of course, the latter part of the Vedas, the Upanishads, are considered supreme examples of "sustained reflective introspection" and we know for sure that for centuries these texts have been orally transmitted. Yet Goody (1987: chapter 4, 110–22) makes considerable effort to show us that the Vedic texts must have been written even though orally transmitted as is actually the case today. He suggests that the written texts may be inaccessible for three reasons: the first is technological – it is expensive and difficult to make copies when there is no printing technology available; secondly, the process of oral teaching means that pupils can ask questions and learn better, and thirdly, owning the only available text ensures your job and endows you with unique power. There is no doubt that the possession of written codified knowledge has long been associated with sociopolitical power but Goody's arguments are weak because they proffer explanations of a general and conjectural nature, while discounting the tremendous emphasis placed in the Indian (Vedic) tradition on phonetic accuracy, absolute memorized command of the oral text as a criterion of scholarship, and the importance of sustained face-to-face interaction for proper understanding of the texts (see chapter 9 among others). Moreover, we are familiar with a variety of fairly complex and rich oral traditions across the world. These may include long folk tales, poems, songs, and plays accompanied with a variety of complex rituals. In fact, as Bright (1990: 131) points out, the complexity of relationship between the oral and the written in South Asia has caused serious problems to structural linguists for whom the orality–literacy divide was so obvious as not to demand any serious attention; Bloomfieldians focused on the spoken, while the Chomskians, on the idealized sentences of a native speaker–hearer (which were obviously as close to the written as possible, the actual speech being seen as vitiated by all kinds of performance variables). In India, it is not just that the Vedic and classical texts are orally transmitted; even in everyday life, the spoken word is considered far more reliable than the written one. Further, it is not just that one script, for example, Devanagari is used to write a variety of languages, such as Sanskrit, Hindi, Marathi, and Nepali, but also that the same language, for example, Sanskrit may be written in a variety of scripts, such as Devanagari, Grantha, Malayalam, Telugu, Bhoti, Sharda, and Bengali.

It would appear that the divide between orality and literacy and also the divide between the two perspectives on their relationship is untenable and is only sociopolitically motivated. The oral and the written, like the verbal and the graphic or like dance and sculpture, constantly flow into each other. Even in terms of language acquisition, Vygotsky (1978) showed how children develop their own systems of writing much before they start speaking coherently. The dots and lines they make at specific points of a piece of paper often represent for them the characters and events of the verbal stories they have heard from their parents.

In the pedagogical perspective, it is difficult to understand why nations, which consider "education for all" their constitutional responsibility, should make a distinction between education and literacy where education is clearly for the rich and literacy for the underprivileged. Similarly, in the cognitive perspective, it is difficult to understand why scholars who constantly harp on the specific intellectual abilities associated with writing do not see the dynamic relationship between orality and literacy and their complementarity. Denny (1991) has argued that orality and literacy cannot be distinguished on the basis of logic and abstract and rational thought; they can be distinguished to some extent on the basis of contextualization and differentiation. Features such as logic, abstract thinking, and interpretation are found in hunter–gatherer and agricultural groups; it is only a high order of decontextualization that distinguishes highly literate cultures. After all, "what matters is what people do with literacy, not what literacy does to people" (Olson 1985: 15). And in most cases what those in power have done with literacy is to use it to consolidate their power and to restrict its dissemination in such a way that the underprivileged do not get any access to higher forms of literate knowledge.

Multilingual South Asia

All the South Asian countries are multilingual both at the individual and the societal levels. According to the SIL International (2002) *Ethnologue* database, a small country like Nepal uses 121 languages. It has two official languages, namely Nepali and Gurung. Languages belonging to such diverse language families as Indo-Aryan, Tibeto-Burman, and Austro-Asiatic families are spoken by sizeable number of speakers. The situation in other countries, such as Sri Lanka, Bangladesh, Pakistan, and India, is not very different. Though it is a small island, Sri Lanka uses eight languages. These include the Indo-Aryan Sinhala, the official language, Indo-European English, Dravidian Tamil, Indo-Aryan Veddah, and two Creoles, one Portuguese based and the other Malay based. In Bangladesh once again several Tibeto-Burman, Indo-Aryan, and Austro-Asiatic languages are spoken. There are over thirty-eight languages used in Bangladesh including Bengali, which is spoken by over 100,000,000 people, Chittagonian (14,000,000), Sylhetti (5,000,000), Santali (157,000), Sadri (84,000), Meitei (92,800), Khasi (85,088), Garo (102,000), and Arakanese (185,000), among others. Pakistan uses sixty-nine languages and has three national or official languages, namely, Urdu, Sindhi, and English. As in other

South Asian countries, languages belonging to Indo-Aryan, Dravidian, and Tibeto-Burman families are spoken by substantial number of speakers here. A sizeable number of people (over 55,000) also speak Burushaski, a language isolate (see SIL International 2002). The paradigm example of multilingualism beyond doubt is indeed India. In spite of Grierson's remarkable *Linguistic Survey of India* and several census surveys, it has not been possible to exactly determine the number of languages spoken in India. This must really be the case for all multilingual countries for what is counted as a language (and not, for example, as a dialect, pidgin, or mixed code) is not a neutral linguistic question, but is decided by a variety of social, historical, and ideological factors. According to the 1961 Census, India had 1,652 languages belonging to five different language families: Indo-Aryan, Dravidian, Tibeto-Burman, Austro-Asiatic, and Andamanese; it also indicated that eighty-seven languages were used in the print media; seventy-one, on the radio, and forty-one, in the schools. The 1991 Census showed that there were 10,400 mother tongues used by the people of India. Through a sustained exercise of "thorough linguistic scrutiny, editing and rationalization," these mother tongues were reduced to 216 only and of these eight-five were subsumed under the eighteen scheduled languages of the Constitution. Major languages, often with long histories and a respectable literary tradition, such as Awadhi, Bhojpuri, Bundeli, Chattisgarhi, Maghai, Mewari, and Rajasthani (in fact over fifty languages), were subsumed under the rubric of Hindi. Bhojpuri alone is claimed as a mother tongue by over 23,000,000 people. In fact languages like Awadhi and Bhojpuri should be treated as the parents rather than the dialects of Hindi. For example, it is not just that Tulsidas' (1534–1623 CE) famous rendering of the story of Ram and Sita in the *Ramcaritmanas* is not in Sanskrit or Hindi but in Awadhi, but also even today there is an extremely rich and vibrant oral and literary tradition in Awadhi. Why then is Awadhi not regarded as a language? Why is it given the status of only a dialect of Hindi? Hindi is the official language of India; in fact many protagonists of Hindi mistakenly treat it as India's national language. In addition to English, it is the language associated with social mobility and power; for politicians of the northern belt it is convenient to project Hindi as *the* language of the north and subsume several full-blown languages like Awadhi and Bhojpuri under it. Away from the arena of political power games, the multilingual fabric of India, as of other countries, is sustained by functional differentiation as well as continuous convergence of different languages. It is not just in metropolises such as Mumbai, Chennai, Delhi, or Kolkata or in their ever multiplying urban slums that we find rich and complex multilingual behavior; even a remote village in Himachal Pradesh, Kerala, Manipur, or Gujarat would use several languages simultaneously. A school boy in, say, a small town, Mandi, of Himachal Pradesh in the north, may speak Mandayali at home, Hindi and English at school and a mixed variety among his friends. Such variability in linguistic behavior, as Pandit (1969, 1972) argued, facilitates rather than obstructs communication. Domains of behavior have to be seen on a linguistic continuum; at the extremes of these domains, linguistic behavior may display stability and language differentiation; that is, each extreme may be associated with an identifiable stable language in terms of structure and norms (thus constructed largely by the linguist), but in the areas where these domains flow into each other, linguistic behavior may be far less stable and normative and may be characterized by code mixing, code switching, convergence, and the emergence of new languages. The norm in India, as perhaps in the whole of the South Asian region, is language maintenance rather than language loss, though very few of the languages in each country may have written forms. As Abbi (Chapter 7) shows, in the relatively isolated tribal ethnic groups, the rate of bilingualism is higher than in other communities and despite the absence of political and institutional support, these languages have not only survived but have also developed several lingua francas. In some cases, it is perhaps true that languages die. In Pakistan, all the sixty-nine languages are living; in Sri Lanka, only one language, Pali, is extinct; in Nepal, of the 121 languages, only Kusunda, is extinct (see SIL International 2002). SIL lists 398 languages for India of which it seems eleven are extinct. Most of them however are spoken in the geographically isolated areas, for example, Andamanese and Greater Andamanese, including languages such as Aka-Bea, Aka-Bo, Aka-Jeru, and Aka-Kol. However, what is not noted in such surveys is the fact that even as some languages disappear new ones are created, and the overall architecture of the multilingual society is not destroyed. The emergence of new mixed codes in several Indian urban cities is now well attested. It is said that even in the Andaman region the incidence of intermarriage among different groups such as the Aka-Kol or Aka-Bea marrying into the Aka-Jeru group is very high and the children born of such marriages speak mixed languages (Anvita Abbi, personal communication). As shown in Agnihotri (2001a), even though India was divided into federal units on the basis of language, there is not a single unit that may legitimately be called monolingual. In several states, such as Andhra in the south, Haryana in the north, West Bengal in the east, Maharashtra in the west, and Uttar Pradesh in central India, all the eighteen scheduled languages are represented. The linguistic diversity is paralleled by a diversity in scripts, though all of them (except the Perso-Arabic-Urdu script) originate from the Brahmi script (see Chapter 14). India uses twenty-five scripts (K. S. Singh and Manoharan 1993: 28) and several educated people use more than one script. Over a period of time script (hence also oral tradition that may in due course get codified) has become a marker of group identity and a site for political struggle. "Many languages spoken in the North-East India which earlier used the Bengali script have now adopted either the Roman or the Devanagari script" (K. S. Singh and Manoharan 1993: 28); comparable changes have taken place in the case of Tamil and Konkani. Then there are languages such as Santhali, the language of the emergent Santals spread over several states of India, which uses several scripts including Roman, Bengali, Devanagari, and Ol Chiki.

Oral, written, and the performative

In this multilingual fabric of the South Asian societies, there is no line that clearly divides the oral, visual, performative, or the written. Consider, for example, the case of the *barahmasa* (twelve months) in Bengal; it is in fact a pan-Indian form variably realized in Rajasthan, Bihar, Uttar Pradesh, and Gujarat. It is known by a variety of names, such as *baramashi*, *baramasiya*, *barmasha*, *varamasi*, and *baromashsho*, and has a variety of forms and types, including *caumasa* (four months), *chaymasis* (six months), and *ashTamasis* (eight months). It could either be just a peasant calendar, or a religious song, or as is more often the case, it could be a *virah-barahmasa* (song of separation). As Madan (1986: v) points out, "these songs are a well-known and well-developed component of folk culture all over north India, from Bengal in the east, to Gujarat in the west. They are simple rustic songs describing the cycle and moods of the seasons, but doing so in terms of deep personal feelings, whether these be associated with foods and drinks, the agricultural cycle, the observance of religious festivals, or the experience of the agonized longing of the wife for reunion with her lover-husband." Several *barahmasas* will, of course, do all these simultaneously. I owe the following to Rimli Bhattacharya, who herself heard it from somebody who recollected it from his memory. She has now turned it into a written text for children, who in turn will transform it into a variety of oral, written, and performative forms (transcription in broad IPA; capitals for retroflex consonants; Capital N for vowel nasalization):

baromashsho

boishakh mashe pushechilam ekTi shalik chana
April–May month in brought up one bird small

joishTho mashe uThlo tar choTTo duTi Dana.
May–June month in came out its small two wings

ashaRh mashe baRlo or gaer palokguli
June–July month in increased his body's feathers

srabon mashe phuTlo mukhe dui carTi buli.
July–August month in came out mouth from two four utterances

bhadro mashe ghuMur kine dilam tar pae
August–September month in anklets bought his feet

ashshinete	naiedilam	holud	die	gae.
September–October	bathed	turmeric	applying	body

kartik	mashe	shikhlo	pakhi	daNRer	upOr	dola
October–November	month in	learnt	bird	perch	on	to swing

oghran	mashe	Ekebare	holo	she	hOrbola.
November–December	month in	totally	became	he	mimic

poush	mashe	thakto	khola	khaNcar	duTi	dar
December–January	month in	used to stay	free	cage of	two	doors

magh	mashe	khelte jeto	icche jOto	tar.
January–February	month in	would go to play	as much as wanted	he

phagun	mashe	dushTubuddhi	jaglo	tar	mone
February–March	month in	naughtiness	woke up	his	mind

coitro	mashe	phuRut	kore	palie gElo	bone.
March–April	month in	phurphur	having done	went away	in the forest

(I brought up a small *shalik*, a small yellow-beaked singing bird of the mynah group, in the month of April–May; it grew its two wings in May–June; its feathers developed during June–July and in July–August it started speaking a few words; in August–September, I bought a pair of anklets for it and in September–October I bathed it with turmeric; in October–November, it learnt to swing on the perch and by November–December, it had become a perfect mimic like a professional hunter; in December–January the doors of the cage were kept open and in January–February, it would go to play as much as it desired; in February–March a naughty idea got into its head and in March–April, it flew away swiftly to the forest.)

According to Madan (1986: vi), *barahmasa* perhaps encapsulates one of South Asia's typical ways of reckoning time. Time here is not measured in terms of a clock but in diverse other ways including the movement of heavenly bodies, waiting for rains which is generally associated with waiting for the separated lover, watching the ripening grains in the field and so on. The above *barahmasa* shows the complex relationship between man and nature, the joy associated with bringing up a bird and watching it grow and sing and dance; it also shows the *virah* associated with the separation from the bird. As Vaudeville (1986: 7) tells us, this form is "not a by-product or a rough imitation of an older, more refined literary type, in Sanskrit, Prakrit or Literary Apabhramsha." It is rather rooted in the oral folklore associated with seasonal and agricultural cycle, nature in general, and the complex relationship between man, woman, and nature. In such folk forms, it is impossible to separate oral, written, musical, and performative forms. The oral forms may get codified in written symbols often set to music and/or dance; the codified forms may then flow back into the oral tradition and get modified in a variety of ways. No sequence is involved here. The path may equally well be music and writing followed by recitation or all the three may happen simultaneously. Traditionally, a distinction has been made between the "Great Tradition" (elite, Vedic, written in Sanskrit, etc.) and the "Little Traditions" (popular, oral, folk, etc.). But as Ramanujan (1993: xviii) says, we need "to see all these cultural performances as a transitive series, a 'scale of forms' responding to one another, engaged in continuous and dynamic dialogic relations. Past and present, what's 'pan-Indian' and what's local, the written and the oral, the verbal and the nonverbal – all these are engaged in reworking and redefining relevant others. What are distinguished as 'the classical', 'the folk', and 'the popular', as different modes in Indian culture, will be seen as part of an interacting continuum. Texts, then are also contexts and pretexts for other texts."

Throughout the South Asian history such folk forms have also provided critical spaces for dissent, protest, and subversion (see, for example, Kumar 1994; Satchidanandan 2001). In Agnihotri (2002b), the author shows how the poets of the Bhaktikal (1350–1650 CE) in north India, such as Kabir, Surdas, Jayasi, Mirabai, Tulsidas, and Rahim, subverted the mainstream linguistic space writing in a "language" that defied all linguistic and geographical boundaries. Satchidanandan (2001) discusses forms, such as *vacanas*, *warkari*, *chandayan*, and *lallesvari*, and makes a distinction between the *sramana* and the *brahmana* traditions, the former being associated with protest and innovative heresy and the latter with the Vedic hegemony and power, though, echoing Ramanujan, he believes that the two streams "have not always remained in conflict but have also had dialogues and interactions so that they are often found interwoven in the history of our thought and literature" (35). He shows how these alternative forms of poetry, music, and dance emphasized the similarities rather than the differences among different religions, rejected the caste system, problematized the institution of priesthood, gave up Sanskrit and other standard languages to compose in the local and mixed languages, privileged the oral against the written, ignored the traditional barriers between the physical and the metaphysical, and developed a system of symbols that juxtaposed the natural, divine, and human symbols with the ordinary symbols from the world of home and hearth. He says, "while the Brahmanic ideology believes in the monopolization of knowledge, mystification of spirituality and the employment of the languages of the elite, the *Sramans* believe in democratizing knowledge, extending spirituality to the subaltern castes and classes and speaking in the people's tongues" (38). In Tamil Nadu, the Bhakti movement had started in the sixth century and included in its Siddha tradition are not only the Hindu saints and Tantrics but also the Muslim Sufis and Pirs. These poets came not only from different parts of India but also from Arabia and China. There are several cult sites across South Asia where the graves and tombs of Muslim sufis coexist with the shrines of Hindu saints and Siddhas. The Siddhas revolted against the hegemonic Vedic tradition and rejected even such powerful aspects of the canon as the transmigration of soul and rebirth. Satchidanandan (42) quotes a translated verse from Chivakkiyar, a Tamil poet who lived around 10th century CE:

Milk does not return to the udder
Likewise butter can never become buttermilk;
The sound of the conch does not exist once it is broken;
The blown flower, the fallen fruit, do not go back to the tree;
The dead are never born again, never!

The *vachan*, *warkari*, *chandayan*, and *lallesvari* traditions, like the Siddha tradition, revolted against the accepted elite aesthetic, cultural, and linguistic norms. For the Vachankaras of Kannada, art was essentially personal and oral, sometimes even occult and esoteric. They used pan-Indian symbols creating a distinct counterstructure where the "metre is not syllabic but syntactic; the regularities and returning units are not usually units of sound, but units of syntax and semantics" (*ibid*: 51); see also Ramanujan 1973, introduction. The most accessible and best description of the Warkari tradition of Maharashtra included not only the traditional forms like *puraNa* and *pravachan* but also the creative literary forms like *abhanga*, *pada*, *bhupali* and *Krishnaleela*, musical–dramatic forms like, *rupak*, *bhedik*, *lalit* and *shej arati*; *mantra*, *namasmaran* and *haripath* for individual worship and a variety of forms for collective performance where the audience played an active role such as *katha*, *saptah*, *kala*, *palakhi*, *bhajan* and *kirtan*. Notice how blurred are the lines that are supposed to separate the oral, the written, and the performative. Also notice how the oral–written continuum creates spaces for revolt and subversion. Warkaris included not only the outcasted Brahmins, such as Jnandev and Eknath, but also the low-caste shudras, such as Namdev and Tukaram. Kabir, the fifteenth century Hindi poet, raised a voice of protest against all religions that divided human beings. Bly (1971) has translated several of Kabir's ecstatic poems. One of them reads:

Are you looking for me? I am in the next seat.
My shoulder is against yours.
You will not find me in the stupas, not in Indian shrine
rooms, nor in synagogues, nor in cathedrals:
not in masses, nor kirtans, not in legs winding
around your own neck, nor in eating nothing but
vegetables.
When you really look for me, you will see me
instantly –
you will find me in the tiniest house of time.
Kabir says: Student, tell me, what is God?
He is the breath inside the breath. (http://www.allspirit.co.uk/kabir.html#looking [accessed on Feb 28, 2007])

Mirabai, the Hindi saint–poet, defied all the norms of the feudal Rajput society, refused to accept the King of Chittor as her husband, and through her devotional songs that could be interpreted on multiple levels, forged a community of skinners, dyers, leather workers, spinners, and weavers. According to Mukta (1994: 84), "these peasant communities appear to have taken to Mira precisely because she appeared as an antithetical figure to Rajput feudal power." The contribution of poets like Kabir and Mira in breaking the barriers of religion, language, and caste must have been immense. Mulla Daud's fourteenth century *Chandayan* is another illustration of how both the Hindu and Muslim poets shared a common language and culture. For both, love was the only path for understanding divinity. Both rejected the object–subject differentiation; both emphasized the similarities among different religions. The legend of Lalleshwari of Kashmir (fourteenth century) is reminiscent of Mirabai (sixteenth century) in the north. Lalleshwari, who was tortured by her mother-in-law, fell in love with Lord Shiva and left home to sing His praise. Satchidanandan (2001) concludes his insightful enquiry of these traditions by saying: "What made the Bhakti movement revolutionary was that it created a universal, non-hierarchical religion, a human, simple life-style, and egalitarian counter-communities along with a subaltern poetry and poetics of spiritual dissent. The Bhakti poets belong not merely to our past; they are our present as their agony and revolt continue to inspire the poetic movement of our own time" (78). In more recent times, the struggles of the masses against feudal hegemony as well as the dynamic relationship between orality and literacy may be seen in such works as Hardiman (1987) and Amin (1995). Amin tries to capture the peasant protest movement of Chauri Chaura against the British Raj in the "moment of its recall" and shows how the hegemonic master narratives condition the local oral narratives.

We may note that in these alternative traditions, South Asian women, such as Akka Mahadevi, Mirabai, and Lalleshwari, succeeded in creating a space for themselves in a completely patriarchal, male-dominated society. The traditional songs, dances, and proverbs used at the time of birth, wedding, and annual festivals often make visible cracks in the oppressive and normative male social order. For once, women have the liberty to abuse men, even men who have come to marry their daughter. Even though these folklore forms may appear to be fossilized in a male-dominated society, they are "rituals of rebellion which have meaning, not only for the dominant ideology but also for the subordinated women" (Kumar 1994: 18). The diverse perspectives that these songs and proverbs provide on kinship relationships and the contradictions inherent in them shows that women may to some extent undermine "the script of patriliny as their speech practices sketch a plural rather than monolithic moral discourse" (Raheja 1994: 74).

We may also note that in these "little traditions," the audience generally played a very active role. It is for this reason that the spaces created by these performances could be used for revolt and rebellion against exploitation. Folk songs and narratives constantly drew their inspiration from the audience and "the great heritage of popular stories contributed alongside (the Great) Tradition to the content of *kaavya*, and to the art of narrative, including realism. Since its origin *kaavya*, has absorbed many languages, expanding its resources of expression" (Warder 1972: 200).

Conclusion

We do not in any way wish to underestimate the significance of writing. There are obviously certain kinds of knowledge that will perhaps not be possible without writing such as the problems in complex mathematics or physics or a sustained interpretation and critique of a text. By virtue of a "fixed written text, suitable for rescanning, comparison, commentary, and analysis, the literate tradition has evolved an elaborate set of speech-act and mental-state verbs useful for legal, scholarly, and literary discourse" (Olson 1991: 266). In the modern world, there are additional kinds of literacy such as "computer literacy" or "legal literacy" which may have to be made an integral part of our educational curriculum. As Olson (1985) points out, though "no serious arguments have been advanced to indicate that civilization is tied to literacy" (1), scholars from fields as diverse as linguistics, psychology, anthropology, sociology, education, and history have come to appreciate the central role played by writing in human society (see Olson *et al.* 1985). Yet as shown in this chapter, orality is an essential part of human culture. It is not just that South Asian countries have had a very rich oral tradition. What is important is that orality and literacy constitute a continuum, constantly feeding into each other in human multilinguality at the individual and societal levels. Along with other resources such as land, water, and labor, those in power have used literacy also to consolidate their power. The masses have used orality, sometimes along with literacy, to create spaces for social rebellion.

14 Writing systems of major and minor languages*

Peter T. Daniels

Introduction

South Asia has been home to a nearly unique variety of writing systems over the past four millennia and more, comprising: one of a handful, worldwide, of script inventions out of nothing; two highly sophisticated adaptations of phonetic writing, grounded in preexisting linguistic theory; a plethora of paleographic, epigraphic, and typographic descendants; two successive adoptions of world scripts from the West; and a number of inventions of local scripts for local languages.

Indus script

Little can be said about the writing system that appears to have originated on South Asian soil, the so-called "Indus Valley" script, or Harappan (for the site where it was first found, in 1872–1873), because it has not yet been deciphered. One difficulty is that the inscriptions, virtually all of which are on small seals, are very short; another is that the language they record is not surely identified (though a form of Dravidian is the most likely candidate). Even the number of discrete characters is uncertain, since we cannot be sure which variants represent distinct signs, which might represent modifications of base forms, and which might simply represent scribal/artistic freedom.

The inscribed Indus seals date from about 2500 BCE on and have been found throughout the Indus Valley region; a few have even turned up in Persian Gulf lands and Mesopotamia. They went out of use around 2000 BCE, when their cities seem to have been abandoned due to climate change (rather than to invading Aryans, who appear on the scene perhaps half a millennium later).

A reason for supposing that the Indus script was devised for Dravidian is that the morphemes of Proto-Dravidian, as reconstructed, seem to have been primarily monosyllabic; in all the other known examples of independent script invention – Sumerian in Mesopotamia; Chinese; Mayan in Mexico – the

* Rich Salomon and the late Bill Bright provided useful commentary on this chapter. I thank them for their advice.

languages have that same property (I).[1] In contrast, writing was not invented in other complex societies, notably the Inca of Peru, ancient Egypt (where the invention of hieroglyphics appears to have been stimulated by acquaintance with Sumerian writing), or anywhere in the Indo-European–speaking realm.

Indic scripts

In particular, no script was invented for any ancient Indo-Aryan language. Instead, adaptations were made from the existing Aramaic script. Aramaic script reached the borders of India with the periodic expeditions of the Achemenid (Persian) Empire, which used Aramaic language (which belongs to the Semitic family, like Hebrew and Arabic) and script in the imperial administration. This script explicitly records only consonants (using twenty-two letters, those familiar from Hebrew); long vowels could be shown using the letters for similar-sounding semivowels – ⟨y⟩ for *i* and *e*, ⟨w⟩ for *u* and *o*. The vowel *a* would rarely be indicated except at the end of a word (and then with ⟨h⟩ or ⟨'⟩).

Kharoṣṭhi

This system was an adequate basis, however, for whoever adapted it to write in Prakrit (in Gandhāra?) (II). Like Aramaic, the resulting Kharoṣṭhi script is written from right to left; the number of letters is expanded greatly to accommodate the extensive Indic consonant inventory. Table 14.1 shows them in the phonetically organized order that later became the standard for all the Indic scripts. An alternative order is known in Buddhist tradition (variants omitted): *a ra pa ca na la da ba ḍa ṣa va ta ya ṣṭa ka sa ma ga tha ja śva dha śa kha kṣa sta jña rtha bha cha sma hva tsa gha ṭha ṇa pha ska ysa śca ṭa ḍha*.

Table 14.1 *Kharoṣṭhi akṣaras*

𐨀 a				
𐨐 k	𐨑 kh	𐨒 g	𐨓 gh	
𐨕 c	𐨖 ch	𐨗 j	jh	𐨙 ñ
𐨚 ṭ	𐨛 ṭh	𐨜 ḍ	𐨝 ḍh	𐨞 ṇ
𐨟 t	𐨠 th	𐨡 d	𐨢 dh	𐨣 n
𐨤 p	𐨥 ph	𐨦 b	𐨧 bh	𐨨 m
𐨩 y	𐨪 r	𐨫 l	𐨬 v	
𐨭 ś	𐨮 ṣ	𐨯 s		𐨱 h

The Aramaic consonantal script provided for eight ordinary stop consonants in three series (voiced, voiceless, "emphatic"), two nasals, four sibilants, two resonants, two

[1] Roman numerals refer to paragraphs in the Excursus on a Theory of Writing at the end of the chapter.

semivowels, and four "laryngeals." Prakrits involved thirty-two consonants, so for any sort of adequacy, the number of letters needed to be increased considerably. Of the various devices that have been used for doing so, including diacritics (as in Polish *ć*, *ś*, *ż*), varying letters (*G* based on *C*, or *W* on *V*), digraphs (the English solution, as in *ch*, *sh*, *th*), or inventing completely new ones, Kharoṣṭhi uses the first two: compare 𐨓 *gha* with 𐨒 *ga*, or 𐨢 *dha* with 𐨡 *da*.

It is difficult to make a match with any specific spatio-temporal variety of Aramaic script as the exact model for the creation of Kharoṣṭhi, but the family resemblance is undeniable. A. H. Dani goes too far in connecting every one of the twenty-two Aramaic letters with a supposed Kharoṣṭhi offshoot (1963/1986: 257–9) – in particular, the cross inside a circle of early forms of *Ṭet* cannot underlie the cross of + *tha*, because that form of *Ṭet* had long passed out of use and could not have been known to the creators of Kharoṣṭhi.

On the whole, though, the similarity in both form and sound between many of the Aramaic letters and the more unmarked Kharoṣṭhi letters is convincing – in particular the resemblance of 𐨡 *d* and 𐨪 *r* persists (see Figure 14.1).

The earliest texts in the Kharoṣṭhi script already display the almost uniquely Indian way of adding vowels to a consonantal script, and the system appears nearly fully worked out in the earliest texts. Each vowel, except *a*, is denoted by a mark – a *mātrā* – added to consonant shapes; the plain (inherited or adapted) consonant shape represents the consonant with *a* (III). Thus taking *ka* as the example, the possible syllables are 𐨐 *ka*, 𐨐𐨁 *ki*, 𐨐𐨂 *ku*, 𐨐𐨃 *kṛ*, 𐨐𐨅 *ke*, 𐨐𐨆 *ko*. If a word begins with a vowel, the letter 𐨀 *a* is used, or modified for 𐨀𐨁 *i*, 𐨀𐨂 *u*, 𐨀𐨅 *e*, 𐨀𐨆 *o*. Any consonant letter plus any vowel mātrā is called an *akṣara* "letter." There was little need in Prakrit to notate consonants not followed by a vowel, as consonant clusters were rare and most words ended with a vowel (IV). The two devices that became common centuries later for writing vowelless Sanskrit consonants can be found in traces already, though.

Salomon (2005) has discovered the standard ancient order of the vowels as *(a) e i o u*. He observes that this might reflect influence of the Greek alphabet, and that it also represents decreasing height above the line of the vowel mātrās.

Kharoṣṭhi inscriptions have principally been found in northwestern South Asia, around the locus of most frequent contact with the Achemenids. Recently, fragments of manuscripts bearing Kharoṣṭhi script have been recovered from arid regions along the ancient Silk Road, far to the north; this suggests a considerably wider use of the script than appears from surviving materials. Kharoṣṭhi was used, decreasingly, between about 250 BCE and 350 CE.

Brāhmī

Historically far more important was what was called the Brāhmī script (Table 14.2), which first appears throughout the subcontinent, almost fully worked out, during the reign of Aśoka (273–232 BCE). This script too has clear

Aramaic		Kharoṣṭhi		
phonetic value	5th–3rd centuries	Taken over	phonetic value	New formations
'			*a*	*i* *u* *e* *o*
b			*ba*	*bha*
g			*ga*	*gha*
d			*da*	*dha* *ḍa* *ḍha*
h			*ha*	
w			*va*	
z			*ǵa*	*ǵha*
ḥ			*śa*	
j			*ya*	
k			*ka*	
l			*la*	
m			*ma*	
n			*na*	*ṇa* *ña*
s			*sa*	
p			*pa*	*pha*
ṣ			*ča*	*čha*
q			*kha*	
r			*ra*	
š			*ṣa*	
t			*ta*	*ṭa* *tha* *ṭha*

Figure 14.1. *Suggested Aramaic Sources of Kharoṣṭhi*. Source: Jensen 1969: 365, fig. 339, which clarifies and updates Bühler's 1904: 39.

affinities with a Semitic, presumably Aramaic, forebear (see Figure 14.2); but because of its geometric regularity (and because it is written from left to right), the relationship is less striking, and it has been conjectured to be an independent

Table 14.2. *Brahmi akṣaras*

𑀅 a	𑀆 ā	𑀇 i	𑀈 ī	𑀉 u	𑀊 ū
		𑀏 e	𑀐 ai	𑀑 o	— au
𑀁 ṃ					
𑀓 k	𑀔 kh	𑀕 g	𑀖 gh	𑀗 ṅ	
𑀘 c	𑀙 ch	𑀚 j	𑀛 jh	𑀜 ñ	
𑀝 ṭ	𑀞 ṭh	𑀟 ḍ	𑀠 ḍh	𑀡 ṇ	
𑀢 t	𑀣 th	𑀤 d	𑀥 dh	𑀦 n	
𑀧 p	𑀨 ph	𑀩 b	𑀪 bh	𑀫 m	
𑀬 y	𑀭 r	𑀮 l	𑀯 v		
𑀰 ś	𑀱 ṣ	𑀲 s		𑀳 h	

invention. In that case, though, the *similarities* to Aramaic and Kharoṣṭhi would be difficult to explain! As with Kharoṣṭhi, vowels (other than *a*) are indicated by supplementary marks, but long vowels (including *ā*) and diphthongs are included as well. Taking 𑀓 *ka* as the example, the mātrās are 𑀓𑀸 *kā*, 𑀓𑀺 *ki*, 𑀓𑀻 *kī*, 𑀓𑀼 *ku*, 𑀓𑀽 *kū*, 𑀓𑁂 *ke*, 𑀓𑁃 *kai*, 𑀓𑁄 *ko*, 𑀓𑁅 *kau*. As Dani (1963/1986: 47) notes, the systematicity of relationships among these markings and their correspondence to the teachings of Pāṇini and his ilk demonstrate the dependency of the script on classical linguistics (and not vice versa).[2]

It would still be some five hundred years before writing Sanskrit was no longer taboo, and during that time, regional varieties of Brāhmī had begun to develop. So had the means of indicating vowelless consonants: very old was a stroke or a dot at the end of a word, *virāma*, to "kill" the word's final vowel. To denote word-internal vowelless consonants, one or another of the consonant forms receives a reduced shape, and the mātrā (if any) accompanies the resulting combination (see below). (If the mātrā is one that stands to the left of the consonant, then it appears at the far left of the whole group.) These strings of consonants are not necessarily consonant clusters, because even if the earlier consonant(s) end the first syllable and the later consonant(s) begin the next one, thus not entering into what we would consider a cluster, they are still written as and considered to be a single akṣara.

The basic principles of orthography remained the same almost without exception as the various regional styles of writing developed. Different-appearing scripts became associated with the regional Prakrits that grew up over time; and once it became licit to write Sanskrit, it would not have its own script, but it would use the script of the local language. Some of the epigraphic scripts of India are quite beautiful, and it sometimes happened that the decorative

[2] New doubts about the recency of the invention of Brāhmī (Salomon 1998: 12 at n. 21) appear to be based on ostraca recently excavated in distant Sri Lanka, dated only by the strata in which they were found. Such dating is archeologically not immensely reliable.

Old north-Semitic		Brāhmī script		
phonetic value	Sign	Sign taken over	phonetic value	newly formed signs
ʾ			*a*	*ā*
b			*ba*	*bha*
g			*ga*	*gha*
d			*dha*	*da* *ḍa* *ḍha*
h			*ha*	
w			*va*	*u* *ū* *o*
z			*ǰa*	*ǰha*
ḥ			*gha*	
ṭ			*tha*	*ṭha* *ṭa*
j			*ya*	
k			*ka*	
l			*la*	*ḷa*
m			*ma*	*-ṃ*
n			*na*	*ña* *ṇa* *na*
s			*sa, ṣa*	*sa* *ṣa*
ʿ			*e*	*ai* *i* *ī*
p			*pa*	*pha*
ṣ			*ča*	*čha*
q			*kha*	
r			*ra*	
š			*śa*	
t			*ta*	

Figure 14.2. *Suggested Semitic Sources of Brahmi. Source:* Jensen 1969: 367, fig. 343, which clarifies and updates Bühler's 1904: 26.

portions of the letters overwhelmed the parts that carry the identification of the consonant. Only with the advent of the British and the perceived need for typesetting languages of South Asia did the graphic diversity crystallize into standards – six for Indic languages and four for Dravidian (though the Telugu and Kannada scripts scarcely differ).

The lines of descent of the various standard scripts appear to be as follows (note that they do not particularly correspond with the genealogical relations of the languages concerned). This classification is taken from Masica 1991: 143 f., which is almost fully in accord with Salomon 1998: 37–42, based in turn on the lifework of D. C. Sircar. This analysis supersedes that of Bühler (1904), which has generally been followed in handbooks such as those by Diringer (1948: 301–4, 328–441) and Jensen (1969: 361–406). A. H. Dani's analysis relates only to the early centuries of Brāhmī and its regional varieties and does not directly concern the scripts listed here.

- Kharoṣṭhī
- Brāhmī
    - Northern
        - Gupta (fourth to fifth century)
            - Sharda (*śāradā*) (northwest, Kashmir)
                - Ṭākrī
                    - Camĕālī
                    - Ḍogrī
                - Lahṇḍa (Punjab, Sind)
                    - **Gurmukhī** (sixteenth century)
            - Kuṭila (*siddhamātṛka*) (center)
                - Early Nāgarī
                    - Modern Nāgarī (= **Devanāgarī**)
                    - Kaithi (Bihar, Uttar Pradesh)
                    - **Gujarātī** (nineteenth century)
                    - Modī (seventeenth century Marathi)
                - Proto-Bengali (Gaudi) (tenth to fourteenth century)
                    - Maithilī
                    - Modern **Bengali** (seventeenth century)
                        - Assamese (nineteenth century)
                    - **Oriya**
                    - Newarī/Manipurī
            - *Tibetan* (seventh century)
    - Southern
        - **Kannada/Telugu**
        - **Sinhalese**
        - Pallava
            - Grantha
            - **Malayalam**
            - **Tamil**
                - Vaṭṭeḻuttu
            - Southeast Asian
                - *Mon/Burmese*
                - *Khmer*
                    - Chakma Bengali
                - *Thai/Lao*
                - Javanese/Balinese/Celebes/Sumatra

The modern scripts

The modern standard scripts (bold in the outline above; standard scripts beyond South Asia are italicized) are presented below in the order they appear in the

Table 14.3. *Devanagari akṣaras*

अ	a	आ	ā	इ	i	ई	ī	उ	u	ऊ	ū
ऋ	r̥	ॠ	r̥̄	ए	e	ऐ	ai	ओ	o	औ	au
–ं (–ँ)	ṃ	–ः	h								
क	k	ख	kh	ग	g	घ	gh	ङ	ṇ		
च	c	छ	ch	ज	j	झ	jh	ञ	ñ		
ट	ṭ	ठ	ṭh	ड	ḍ	ढ	ḍh	ण	ṇ		
त	t	थ	th	द	d	ध	dh	न	n		
प	p	फ	ph	ब	b	भ	bh	म	m		
य	y	र	r	ल	l	व	v				
श	ś	ष	ṣ	स	s			ह	h	ळ	ḷ
क़	q	ख़	x	ग़	gh	ज़	z	ड़	ṛ	ढ़	ṛh

Note: The bottom row contains the additional akṣaras used in Hindi.

outline, except that the discussion of Gurmukhī is postponed because it differs idiosyncratically from the norm. Matters of present-day pronunciation of the languages written with these scripts are generally not considered in this chapter.

The script most familiar outside South Asia, because it is now generally used for Sanskrit, is Devanagari (Table 14.3). Since with slight modifications it serves also for Hindi and Marathi (and less popular languages as well), it is the most widely used script in India. Like its distant ancestor Brāhmī, it has separate akṣaras for each possible initial vowel. (Between the vowel and consonant akṣaras come the *anusvāra*, marking nasalization or a homorganic nasal, and the *visarga*, [h].) The mātrās that denote vowels other than *a* have forms that resonate throughout the Indic scripts (Table 14.4): *ā* is a vertical to the right; *i* is a curve above with a vertical to the left, and *ī* its mirror image. *U* is a curve below, and *ū* its inversion. *R̥* is a hook below and *r̥̄* its doubling. *E* is a curve above, doubled for *ai*, and combined with the *a* symbol for *o* and *au*. Absence of a vowel after a single consonant is marked by *virāma* –्. (The formation of compound akṣaras is postponed here so that conjuncts in all the scripts can be considered together.)

The Gujarati script (Table 14.5) is very similar to the Devanagari, only without the horizontal bar connecting the tops of the letters in a word.

Gurmukhi, too, perfected by the second Guru of the Sikhs for the Punjabi language, is very similar to Devanagari (Table 14.6), with two innovations. Instead of a separate akṣara for each initial vowel, it uses three "vowel-bearers" (which cannot stand alone) to which the mātrās are added: *u* ਉ, *ū* ਊ, *o* ਓ, *a* ਅ, *ā* ਆ, *ai* ਐ, *au* ਔ, *i* ਇ, *ī* ਈ, *e* ਏ; and the akṣaras that historically represent voiced

Table 14.4. *Vowels mātrās and virāma*

	k	ka	kā	ki	kī	ku	kū	kṛ	kṝ	ke	kē	kai	ko	kō	kau	kæ	kǣ
Devanagari	क्	क	का	कि	की	कु	कू	कृ	कॄ	के		कै	को		कौ		
Gujarati	ક્	ક	કા	કિ	કી	કુ	કૂ	કૃ		કે		કૈ	કો		કૌ		
Gurmukhi		ਕ	ਕਾ	ਕਿ	ਕੀ	ਕੁ	ਕੂ	ਕ੍		ਕੇ		ਕੈ	ਕੋ		ਕੌ		
Bengali	ক্	ক	কা	কি	কী	কু	কূ	কৃ		কে		কৈ	কো		কৌ		
Oriya	କ୍	କ	କା	କି	କୀ	କୁ	କୂ	କୃ		କେ		କୈ	କୋ		କୌ		
Kannada	ಕ್	ಕ	ಕಾ	ಕಿ	ಕೀ	ಕು	ಕೂ	ಕೃ	ಕೄ	ಕೆ	ಕೇ	ಕೈ	ಕೊ	ಕೋ	ಕೌ		
Telugu	క్	క	కా	కి	కీ	కు	కూ	కృ	కౄ	కె	కే	కై	కొ	కో	కౌ		
Sinhalese	ක්	ක	කා	කි	කී	කු	කූ	කෘ	කෲ	කෙ	කේ	කෛ	කො	කෝ	කෞ	කැ	කෑ
Malayalam		ക	കാ	കി	കീ	കു	കൂ	കൃ	കൄ	കെ	കേ	കൈ	കൊ	കോ	കൌ		
Tamil	க்	க	கா	கி	கீ	கு	கூ			கெ	கே	கை	கொ	கோ	கௌ		

Table 14.5. *Gujarati akṣaras*

અ	a	આ	ā	ઇ	i	ઈ	ī	ઉ	u	ઊ	ū
ઋ	r̥			એ	e	ઐ	ai	ઓ	o	ઔ	au
ં	ṃ	ઃ	h[a]								
ક	k	ખ	kh	ગ	g	ઘ	gh	ઙ	ṅ[a]		
ચ	c	છ	ch	જ	j	ઝ	jh				
ટ	ṭ	ઠ	ṭh	ડ	ḍ	ઢ	ḍh	ણ	ṇ		
ત	t	થ	th	દ	d	ધ	dh	ન	n		
પ	p	ફ	ph	બ	b	ભ	bh	મ	m		
ય	y	ર	r	લ	l	વ	v				
શ	ś	ષ	ṣ	સ	s			હ	h	ળ	ḷ
ક્ષ	kṣ	જ્ઞ	jñ								

a. Only in Sanskrit words.

Table 14.6. *Gurmukhi akṣaras*

ੳ	(back)	ਅ	(low)	ੲ	(front)	ਸ	s	ਹ	h		
ਕ	k	ਖ	kh	ਗ	g	ਘ	gh	ਙ	ṅ		
ਚ	c	ਛ	ch	ਜ	j	ਝ	jh	ਞ	ñ		
ਟ	ṭ	ਠ	ṭh	ਡ	ḍ	ਢ	ḍh	ਣ	ṇ		
ਤ	t	ਥ	th	ਦ	d	ਧ	dh	ਨ	n		
ਪ	p	ਫ	ph	ਬ	b	ਭ	bh	ਮ	m		
ਯ	y	ਰ	r	ਲ	l	ਵ	w	ੜ	ṛ		
ਸ਼	š	ਜ਼	z	ਫ਼	f	ਖ਼	x	ਗ਼	ɣ	ਲ਼	ḷ

aspirated stops now indicate the three-way tonal consonant of Punjabi. There are very few conjuncts (see below), but a diacritic, *addak* ੱ, has been introduced to mark gemination – placed not on, but before the doubled consonant: ਪੱਕੀ *pakkī* "ripe" (examples throughout are drawn from Daniels and Bright 1996).

Even Bengali script (Table 14.7), though more distantly related to Devanagari, exhibits its kinship. Aside from its calligraphic exuberance it displays no peculiarities that do not relate to historical sound changes in the Bengali language.

Table 14.7. *Bengali akṣaras*

অ	a	আ	ā	ই	i	ঈ	ī	উ	u	ঊ	ū
ঋ	r̥			এ	e	ঐ	ai	ও	o	ঔ	au
ক	k	খ	kh	গ	g	ঘ	gh	ঙ	ṅ		
চ	c	ছ	ch	জ	j	ঝ	jh	ঞ	ñ		
ট	ṭ	ঠ	ṭh	ড	ḍ	ঢ	ḍh	ণ	ṇ		
ত	t	থ	th	দ	d	ধ	dh	ন	n		
প	p	ফ	ph	ব	b	ভ	bh	ম	m		
য	ẏ	র	r	ল	l	ব	v			য়	y
শ	ś	ষ	ṣ	স	s			হ	h		

Table 14.8. *Oriya akṣaras*

ଅ	a	ଆ	ā	ଇ	i	ଈ	ī	ଉ	u	ଊ	ū
ଋ	r̥			ଏ	e	ଓ	o	ଐ	ai	ଔ	au
କ	k	ଖ	kh	ଗ	g	ଘ	gh	ଙ	ṅ		
ଚ	c	ଛ	ch	ଜ	j	ଝ	jh	ଞ	ñ		
ଟ	ṭ	ଠ	ṭh	ଡ	ḍ	ଢ	ḍh	ଣ	ṇ		
ତ	t	ଥ	th	ଦ	d	ଧ	dh	ନ	n		
ପ	p	ଫ	ph	ବ	b	ଭ	bh	ମ	m		
ଯ	j′	ୟ	y	ର	r	ଳ	ḷ	ଲ	l	ୱ	v
ଶ	ś			ଷ	ṣ			ସ	s	ହ	h

Oriya (Table 14.8) gives the impression of considerable divergence from its sister script Bengali, but this is due to a difference in writing materials: in the southern area the favored material was palm leaves, where curved strokes were necessary to avoid tearing. Oriya is a script of northern descent that developed farther south. It is the first of several scripts where vowel mātrās can cursively fuse with the consonant bases.

A diagnostic characteristic of the northern group identified by Bühler (1904: 64) that persists in the modern scripts is the knob at the lower left corner of *ma*; a similarly diagnostic feature of the southern group is mātrā *r̥* with a curled curve on the left (1904:80).

Kannada (Table 14.9) is characterized by a heavy bar at the top of many letters. It is replaced by the *i* and *ī* mātrās; the others extend (or do not affect) it. Like the other Dravidian languages, Kannada has *ē* and *ō* as well as *ai* and *au* and builds their mātrās from others in the script.

Table 14.9. *Kannada akṣaras*

ಅ	a	ಆ	ā	ಇ	i	ಈ	ī	ಉ	u	ಊ	ū
ಋ	ṛ	ೠ	ṝ	ಎ e	ಏ ē	ಐ	ai	ಒ o	ಓ ō	ಔ	au
ಂ	ṃ	ಃ	ḥ								
ಕ	k	ಖ	kh	ಗ	g	ಘ	gh	ಙ	ṅ		
ಚ	c	ಛ	ch	ಜ	j	ಝ	jh	ಞ	ñ		
ಟ	ṭ	ಠ	ṭh	ಡ	ḍ	ಢ	ḍh	ಣ	ṇ		
ತ	t	ಥ	th	ದ	d	ಧ	dh	ನ	n		
ಪ	p	ಫ	ph	ಬ	b	ಭ	bh	ಮ	m		
ಯ	y	ರ	r	ಲ	l	ವ	v				
ಶ	ś	ಷ	ṣ	ಸ	s			ಹ	h	ಳ	ḷ

Table 14.10. *Telugu akṣaras*

అ	a	ఆ	ā	ఇ	i	ఈ	ī	ఉ	u	ఊ	ū
ఋ	ṛ	ౠ	ṝ	ఎ e	ఏ ē	ఐ	ai	ఒ o	ఓ ō	ఔ	au
ం	ṃ	ః	ḥ								
క	k	ఖ	kh	గ	g	ఘ	gh	ఙ	ṅ		
చ	c	ఛ	ch	జ	j	ఝ	jh	ఞ	ñ		
ట	ṭ	ఠ	ṭh	డ	ḍ	ఢ	ḍh	ణ	ṇ		
త	t	థ	th	ద	d	ధ	dh	న	n		
ప	p	ఫ	ph	బ	b	భ	bh	మ	m		
య	y	ర	r	ల	l	వ	v				
శ	ś	ష	ṣ	స	s			హ	h	ళ	ḷ

Telugu (Table 14.10) has a "check-mark" where Kannada has the bar; in fact this check-mark can almost be considered an *a*-mātrā because it is replaced by the *virāmamu*.

Sinhalese (Table 14.11) adds yet another pair of vowels, æ/ǣ, with characters based on *a*. It also has a series of "half-nasals," prenasalized stops derived from the corresponding stop signs.

Malayalam script (Table 14.12) rivals Sinhalese in loopy elaboration. It has two special characteristics: First, rather than a diacritic to mark word-final vowellessness, five resonants have distinctive final forms: *ṇ* ണ, *n* ന, *r* ര, *l* ല, and *ḷ* ള become ൺ, ൻ, ർ, ൽ, ൾ, respectively.

Table 14.11 *Sinhalese akṣaras*

අ a ආ	ā	ඇ æ ඈ	ǣ	ඉ	i	ඊ	ī	උ	u	ඌ	ū
ඍ	ṛ	ඎ	ṝ	එ e ඒ	ē	ඓ	ai	ඔ o ඕ	ō	ඖ	au
–ං	ṃ	–ඃ	h								
ක	k	ඛ	kh	ග	g	ඝ	gh	ඞ	ṅ	ඟ	n̆g
ච	c	ඡ	ch	ජ	j	ඣ	jh	ඤ	ñ		
ට	ṭ	ඨ	ṭh	ඩ	ḍ	ඪ	ḍh	ණ	ṇ	ඬ	n̆ḍ
ත	t	ථ	th	ද	d	ධ	dh	න	n	ඳ	n̆d
ප	p	ඵ	ph	බ	b	භ	bh	ම	m	ඹ	n̆b
ය	y	ර	r	ල	l	ව	v				
ශ	ś	ෂ	ṣ	ස	s			හ	h	ළ	ḷ

Table 14.12. *Malayalam akṣaras*

അ	a	ആ	ā	ഇ	i	ഈ	ī	ഉ	u	ഊ	ū
ഋ	ṛ	ൠ	ṝ	എ e	ഏ ē	ഐ	ai	ഒ o	ഓ ō	ഔ	au
–ം	ṃ	–ഃ	h								
ക	k	ഖ	kh	ഗ	g	ഘ	gh	ങ	ṅ		
ച	c	ഛ	ch	ജ	j	ഝ	jh	ഞ	ñ		
ട	ṭ	ഠ	ṭh	ഡ	ḍ	ഢ	ḍh	ണ	ṇ		
ത	t	ഥ	th	ദ	d	ധ	dh	ന	n		
പ	p	ഫ	ph	ബ	b	ഭ	bh	മ	m		
യ	y	ര	r	ല	l	വ	v				
ശ	ś	ഷ	ṣ	സ	s	ഹ	h				
ള	ḷ	ക്ഷ	kṣ	ഴ	ḻ	റ	ṟ				

Second, several strides have been made toward simplifying the printing of Malayalam: instead of a plethora of idiosyncratic forms for ◌ു -*u* and ◌ൂ *ū* (രു രൂ, ഗു ഗൂ, നു നൂ illustrate the varieties, with *r*, *g*, and *n*), there are now separate mātrās for them (രു രൂ ഗു ഗൂ നു നൂ); and in clusters, the abovementioned final forms of resonants are used as well as consonants marked with ◌് (which otherwise is an additional mātrā for ə) rather than conjuncts.

The last of the Indic scripts, Tamil (Table 14.13), has done away with conjuncts entirely, placing a dot above a letter to mark it as vowelless: இந்த *inta* "this." It also has a highly reduced inventory of consonant letters but considerable variety in attaching vowels (றா *ṟā*, கு *ku*, சூ *cū*, ணை *ṇai*).

Some sets of numerals are shown in Table 14.14.

Table 14.13. *Tamil akṣaras*

அ	a	ஆ	ā	இ	i	ஈ	ī	உ	u	ஊ	ū
எ	e	ஏ	ē	ஐ	ai	ஒ	o	ஓ	ō	ஔ	au
க	k	ங	ṅ	ச	c	ஞ	ñ	ட	ṭ	ண	ṇ
த	t	ந	n	ப	p	ம	m				
ய	y	ர	r	ல	l	வ	v				
ழ	ḻ	ள	ḷ	ற	ṟ	ன	ṉ				
ஜ	j	ஷ	ṣ	ஸ	s	ஹ	h	க்ஷ	kṣ		

Note: The bottom row contains the "Grantha" letters, which are used for Sanskrit (and English) loan words.

Table 14.14. *Numerals*

	1	2	3	4	5	6	7	8	9	0
Devanagari	१	२	३	४	५	६	७	८	९	०
Gujarati	૧	૨	૩	૪	૫	૬	૭	૮	૯	૦
Gurmukhi	੧	੨	੩	੪	੫	੬	੭	੮	੯	੦
Bengali	১	২	৩	৪	৫	৬	৭	৮	৯	০
Kannada	೧	೨	೩	೪	೫	೬	೭	೮	೯	೦
Telugu	౧	౨	౩	౪	౫	౬	౭	౮	౯	౦
Malayalam	൧	൨	൩	൪	൫	൬	൭	൮	൯	൦
Arabic	١	٢	٣	٤	٥	٦	٧	٨	٩	٠

Conjunct Formation

The topic of conjuncts can be introduced gradually, beginning with the script where only a few are still in use: Gurmukhi has ੍ਹ *h*, ੍ਰ *r* (Symbols for *r* as either the first of second member of a cluster tend to be idiosyncratic: Table 14.15), ੍ਵ *w*, and ੍ਯ *y* to represent the second member of a cluster with these reduced forms. Sinhalese does the same for ්‍ය *y*, and Kannada uses ್ಕ *k*, ್ತ *t*, ್ನ *n*, ್ಮ *m*, ್ಯ *y*, ್ಲ *l*, Telugu ్క *k*, ్త *t*, ్న *n*, ్మ *m*, ్య *y*, ్ల *l*. Malayalam has "diacritics" for ്യ *y*, ്ല *l*; and for the doubling of some consonant letters with a right angle at the right side ്: ച്ച *cc*, ബ്ബ *bb*, വ്വ *vv* (but പ്പ *pp*, ല്ല *ll*).

Aside from these "diacritic" conjunct forms, the usual way of writing consonant clusters – or rather, sequences of consonants, since syllable boundaries are disregarded – is to employ reduced forms of the letters. The earliest examples, found already in Brāhmī, show the second consonant subordinate to the first; *kta* 𑀓𑁆𑀢 ← 𑀓𑀢 *kata*, *mha* 𑀫𑁆𑀳 ← 𑀫𑀳 *maha*. This technique persists in

Table 14.15. *Forms of ⟨r⟩*

	full, *ra*	before ⟨k⟩, *rka*	after ⟨k⟩, *kra*
Devanagari	र	र्क	क्र
Gujarati	ર	ર્ક	ક્ર
Bengali	র	র্ক	ক্র
Oriya	ର	ର୍କ	କ୍ର
Kannada	ರ	ರ್ಕ	ಕ್ರ
Telugu	ర	ర్క	క్ర
Sinhala	ර	ර්ක	ක්‍ර
Malayalam	ര	ർക	ക്ര

Kannada (ಗ್ಗ *gga*, ಚ್ಚ *cca*, ದ್ಘ *dgha*, ಬ್ಧ *bdha*, ಲ್ಪ *lpa*), Telugu (స్ఖ *skha*, ష్ట *ṣṭa*, ట్ఠ *ṭṭha*), Malayalam (ല്ക *lka*, ജ്ജ *jja*, ട്ണ *ṭṇa*), though Malayalam also uses a number of horizontal ligatures where adjacent portions of letters can merge (ത + ത = ത്ത *tta*, ന + ന = ന്ന *nna*, ഞ + ഞ = ഞ്ഞ *ñña*; ക + ത = ക്ത *kta*, ശ + ച = ശ്ച *śca*, ണ + ട = ണ്ട *ṇṭa*; ട + ട = ട്ട *ṭṭa*).

Bengali's exuberant calligraphy emerges in its conjuncts, and it is rather unpredictable which components of a letter will enter into compound akṣaras. Most conjuncts are vertical, with some horizontal ones (ক + ক = ক্ক *kka*, ঙ + ক = ঙ্ক *ṅka*, ক + ত = ক্ত *kta*, ত + ত = ত্ত *tta*; শ + চ = শ্চ *śca*).

Devanagari and Gujarati, conversely, reduce the first consonant(s) of a cluster (प + य = प्य *pya*, त + क = त्क *tka*; द + व = द्व *dva*, ह + य = ह्य *hya*; त + त = त्त *tta*, त्त + व = त्त्व *ttva*, क + ष = क्ष *kṣa*, क्ष + म = क्ष्म *kṣma*. પ + ય = પ્ય *pya*, શ + લ = શ્લ *śla*; હ + મ = હ્મ *hma*, દ + વ = દ્વ *dva*, દ + દ = દ્દ *dda*). When several vowelless consonants appear in sequence, as can happen in Sanskrit, it is the last of them that retains its full form. (The longest attested sequence gathers no fewer than five consonants *-rtsnya*.) Oriya can reduce either the later or the earlier member, or use an idiosyncratic mélange (ଷ + ପ = ଷ୍ପ *spa*, ଣ + ଠ = ଣ୍ଠ *ṇṭha*; ବ + ଦ = ବ୍ଦ *bda*, ଦ + ଭ = ଦ୍ଭ *dbha*, ଙ + କ = ଙ୍କ *ṅka*; କ + ଷ = କ୍ଷ *kṣa*, ନ + ଦ = ନ୍ଦ *nda*).

Further Dissemination

Meanwhile, script follows religion – Buddhist missionaries set out from various regions of India at various times for Tibet and Southeast Asia, bringing their scriptures and their scripts. In these neighboring areas they encountered languages that were very different from their own, and right away in some cases, over centuries in others, the rich resources of Indic writing were adapted to monosyllabically structured languages like Tibetan and Burmese, to the notation of tone and/or extraordinary ranges of vowel quality and register as in Thai and Khmer respectively, or even to the simplicity of Austronesian sound systems like that of Javanese.

Table 14.16. *The principal Arabic-derived scripts of South Asia, with their forebears*

LC [IPA]	Arabic	Persian	Urdu	Sindhi	Kashmiri	LC [IPA]	Arabic	Persian	Urdu	Sindhi	Kashmiri
–	ا	ا	ا	ا		z	ز	ز	ز	ز	ز
b	ب	ب	ب	ب	ب	zh [ʒ]		ژ	ژ		ژ [ts]
ḅ [ɓ]				ٻ		s	س	س	س	س	س
bh			بھ	ڀ		sh [ʃ]	ش	ش	ش	ش	ش
p		پ	پ		پ	ṣ	ص	ص	ص	ص	ص
ph			پھ			ẓ	ض	ض	ض	ض	ض
t	ت	ت	ت	ت	ت	ṭ	ط	ط	ط	ط	ط
th			تھ	ٿ		ẓ	ظ	ظ	ظ	ظ	ظ
ṭ [ʈ]			ٹ	ٽ	ٹ	ʿ	ع	ع	ع	ع	ع
ṭh			ڈھ	ٺ		gh	غ	غ	غ	غ	غ
s̱	ث [θ]	ث	ث	ث	ث	f	ف	ف	ف	ف	ف
p				پ		ph				ڦ	
j [ʤ]	ج	ج	ج	ج	ج	q	ق	ق	ق	ق	ق
j̆ [ɟ]				ڄ		k	ك	ك	ك	ك	ك
jh			جھ	جھ		kh			کھ	کھ	
ñ [ɲ]				ڃ		g [g]		گ	گ	گ	گ

c [ʧ]		چ	چ	چ	چ
ch			چھ	چھ	
ḥ	ح	ح	ح	ح	ح
kh̲ [x]	خ	خ	خ	خ	خ
d	د	د	د	د	د
dh			دھ	ڌ	
ḍ [ɗ]				ڏ	
ḍ [ɖ]			ڈ	ڊ	ڈ
ḍh			ڈھ	ڍ	
z̲	ذ [ð]	ذ	ذ	ذ	ذ
r	ر	ر	ر	ر	ر
ṛ [ɽ]			ڑ	ڙ	ڑ
ṛh			ڑھ		

g̈ [ɠ]				ڳ	
gh			گھ	گھ, کھ	
ṅ [ŋ]				ڱ	
l	ل	ل	ل	ل	ل
m	م	م	م	م	م
n	ن	ن	ن	ن	ن
ṇ [ɳ]				ڻ	
n̲ [˜]			ں		
v	و [w]	و	و	و	و
h	ه	ه	ه	ه	ھ
t			ة		
y	ي	ى	ى	ي	ے

Notes: The first column gives the Library of Congress transliteration of the South Asian scripts. The transliteration differs somewhat for Arabic and Persian. Phonetic values are given where needed; phonetic values in the Arabic column note sounds that do not occur in the South Asian languages (or Persian).

An alternative source for the Sindhi script places ڦ *ph* after پ *p* instead of ف *f*, and ڱ *ṅ* after ن *n* instead of کھ *ng*.

When a Brāhmī-derived script was adapted to write Tibetan, it encountered a language considerably different in typology from the Indic languages it fitted so well. Tibetan, distantly related to Chinese, is monosyllabically organized. The scholars who devised the script realized that writing all sequences of consonants as single akṣaras could be confusing; in Tibetan it was important to be able to see the division into syllables. Thus only a handful of conjunct forms are used; the letters for consonants in clusters, both before and after the vowel, are mostly written on the line; and a dot is written after the last letter of every syllable. Tibetan writes fewer vowels than Indic languages. The *a* is still unnotated, and *i, e, o,* and *u* are marked above or below their syllable. The Lepcha script of Sikkim is in turn derived from Tibetan.

In Southeast Asia, Hindu missionaries figured too; from the script with which they wrote Sanskrit, there eventually developed those of Khmer in Cambodia, and Javanese (and many other varieties) in Indonesia. The Sinhala Buddhist missionaries from Ceylon brought the Pali language and scripts that eventually turned into Burmese, Thai, and Lao scripts. Khmer, Burmese, and Thai scripts all retain the full inventory of Indic letters, for historical spelling of Sanskrit loanwords. Khmer, though, also uses the (historical) voiceless/voiced series of letters (a feature neutralized in Khmer phonology) to distinguish between two sets of vowels: those following the (former) voiced consonants are raised or monophthongized. Burmese differs from Indic scripts in using the conjunct technique only for clusters in borrowed words (and for four sonorants in native words); additionally it adds diacritics for tones. Thai uses combinations of consonant letter class, vowel symbols, and tone marks to notate its tones; Lao is simpler only in having abandoned nearly half the inherited consonant letters. A subset of Javanese letters have forms like "capitals": appearing anywhere in a word, they mark it as distinctive.

Imported scripts

Perso-Arabic

The assimilation of two scripts from the West was also, in part at least, due to the missionary impulse. Classical Persian script (an adaptation of Arabic script, itself like Kharoṣṭhi and Brāhmī a descendant of an Aramaic script) arrived in the thirteenth century; it was in turn adapted for Urdu – and Sindhi, Kashmiri, and other languages of the subcontinent – by taking advantage of the unusual base + differentiator nature of this script family (Table 14.16).

The letters that Classical Arabic inherited (as the Indic scripts had) from an Aramaic precursor, Nabatean, are (in the same order their ancestors are shown in, in Figures 14.1 and 14.2) ʾ ا, *b* ب, *g* ج, *d* د, *h* ه, *w* و, *z* ز, *ḥ* ح, *ṭ* ط, *y* ي, *k* ك, *l* ل, *m* م, *n* ن, *s* س, ʿ ع, *f* ف, *ṣ* ص, *q* ق, *r* ر, *š* ش, *t* ت. Note that over the centuries some of the letters had taken on shapes that were indistinguishable, or nearly so; in Arabic, they are differentiated with dots: *b* ب, *t* ت, *n* ن, *y* ي is one such set. (This is particularly important because when letters are combined, they are reduced to only their distinctive parts. Without the dots, the Arabic word تتثبتين *tataṯabbatīna* "you (f.pl.) ascertain" would appear as سسس!) It happens that a number of sounds merged in Aramaic that had remained distinct in Arabic, such as /d/ and /ð/, /t/ and /θ/, so that Nabatean provided fewer letters than Arabic needed. It must have been on the basis of etymological awareness that new letters were created by an extension of the dotting device – so that ð ذ is a dotted *d* د (and not, say, a dotting of the phonetically similar *z* ز), θ ث is a dotted *t* ت, and so on for six sets in all. This practice was then available as Arabic script came to be applied to many languages throughout the Islamic world. (The standard order of Arabic brings together the letters of the same basic shape, inserting them into the framework of the inherited order.) Note that only long vowels are required to be written (using ⟨'⟩ ا for *ā*, ⟨w⟩ و for *ū*, ⟨y⟩ ي for *ī*); marks exist for the short vowels (*a* ـَ, *i* ـِ, *u* ـُ, as in تَشْفِين), but they see only limited use.

The Arabic script spread to many other languages of Asia not so much with the initial Arab expansion of the seventh century CE, but with Persian political and intellectual hegemony some time later; thus the letters added for Persian became part of the heritage of Muslim languages of (in particular) South Asia: *p* پ, *č* چ, *ž* ژ, *g* گ. Persian and Urdu, being (rather closely related) Indo-European languages, lack a number of the consonants used in Arabic; but as it was customary to write all words borrowed from Arabic in their original spelling (even when the pronunciation differed considerably – for example, ð ذ, θ ث are generally pronounced as *z*, *s*), the Persian, Urdu, etc., sign inventories must retain all those letters and cannot even reuse some of them for their own idiosyncrasies (as was done in Southeast Asia with Indic-origin scripts). Urdu adds three letters for the retroflex series, using the Arabic letter ط in place of the dot: *ṭ* ٹ, ḍ ڈ, *ṛ* ڑ. It also exploits what in Arabic is a mere allographic distinction between two forms of *h* in the middle of a word: the form ﮨ is used for the independent consonant (initially ہ or ﮨ) and the form ﮭ (or ھ) to note the aspirated consonant series (these diagraphs do not however count as separate letters). Sindhi, however, takes the dot system as far as is feasible for retroflexion, implosion, and aspiration. (Even so, it resorts to the ﮭ-addition in several cases.)

Notwithstanding, unlike the much earlier adaptation of a Semitic script to Indic use, no provision was made for recording short vowels obligatorily. The Dardic language Kashmiri dispenses with nearly all the additional letters needed for the Indo-Aryan languages, but unlike nearly all Arabic-derived scripts, it requires the notation of all short vowels, and additional vowel markings and combinations have been created for the purpose (Table 14.17).

Persian and Urdu manuscripts, especially at wealthy courts, participated in the general Islamic delight in calligraphy, even going so far as to relax the prohibition on depicting the human form. Calligraphy was not a similar institution among Indic-script users, but the beauty of formal manuscripts cannot be denied.

Another instance of Arabic script influence is found in the Maldives, where it is not the letters but the numbers that became the first nine letters of the Dhivehī script (which is written right to left). An earlier set of numbers became the tenth through eighteenth letters, and six additional letters, appearing mainly in loanwords, come from other letters or from Persian. Yet another dozen letters

Table 14.17. *Kashmiri vowels*

LC	[IPA]	Kashmiri	LC	[IPA]	Kashmiri	LC	[IPA]	Kashmiri
a	[a]	اَ	u’	[ɨː]	اٟ	ọ	[ɔ]	اۆ
ā	[aː]	آ	ū’	[ɨ]	اٟ	ọ̄	[ɔː]	آوٚ
ạ	[ə]	أ	u	[uː]	اُ	e	[e]	ےٚ
ạ̄	[əː]	ٲ	ū	[ʊ]	اۆ	ē	[eː]	ے
i	[iː]	اِ	o	[oː]	اۄ	ẏ	[ʲ]	ےٕ
ī	[I]	اَی	ō	[o]	او			

Table 14.18. *The Dhivehi alphabet*

	Translit.	Official	[IPA]		Translit.	Official	[IPA]		Arabic	Translit.
ހ	h	h	[h]	ތ	t	th	[t̪]	ޙ	ح	ḥ
ށ	ṣ	sh	[ʂ]	ލ	l	l	[l]	ޚ	خ	x
ނ	n	n	[n]	ގ	g	g	[g]	ޢ	ع	ʻ
ރ	r	r	[r]	ޏ	ñ	gn	[ɲ]	ޣ	غ	g
ބ	b	b	[b]	ސ	s	s	[s]	ޥ	و	w
ޅ	ḷ	lh	[ɭ]	ޑ	ḍ	d	[ɖ]	ޛ	ذ	d̲
ކ	k	k	[k]	ޒ	z	z	[z]	ޘ	ث	t̲
އ	–		Ø	ޓ	ṭ	t	[ʈ]	ޠ	ط	ṭ
ވ	v	v	[v]	ޔ	y	y	[j]	ޤ	ق	q
މ	m	m	[m]	ޕ	p	p	[p]	ޝ	ش	š
ފ	f	f	[f]	ޖ	j	j	[ɟ]	ޞ	ص	ṣ
ދ	d	dh	[d̪]	ޗ	c	ch	[c]	ޟ	ض	ḍ
ަ	a	a		ު	u	u		ޮ	o	o
ާ	ā	aa		ޫ	ū	uu		ޯ	ō	oa
ި	i	i		ެ	e	e		ް	(no vowel)	
ީ	ī	ii		ޭ	ē	ee				

are used only in Arabic loanwords (Table 14.18). Unlike in Arabic, the vowel indicators are obligatory.

Roman

It was Christian missionaries, arriving with the Portuguese at Goa and elsewhere, that brought the Roman alphabet to India; a Roman orthography for Konkani has been in use for some five hundred years. Masica describes it as follows:

> Retroflexes are indicated by doubling the consonant (/māḷo/ “floor” = *mallo*), final nasal vowels by V + *m* (as partly in Portuguese): /pitā̃/ ‘I drink’ = *pitam*. This necessitates

ṅa	ga	ka
ña	ja	ca
ṇa	ḍa	ṭa
na	da	ta
ma	ba	pa
ha	la	ṛa
ra	ṣa	sa

Figure 14.3. *The consonants of Varang Kshiti, the Ho script. Source:* Zide in Daniels and Bright 1996: 616 [corrected].

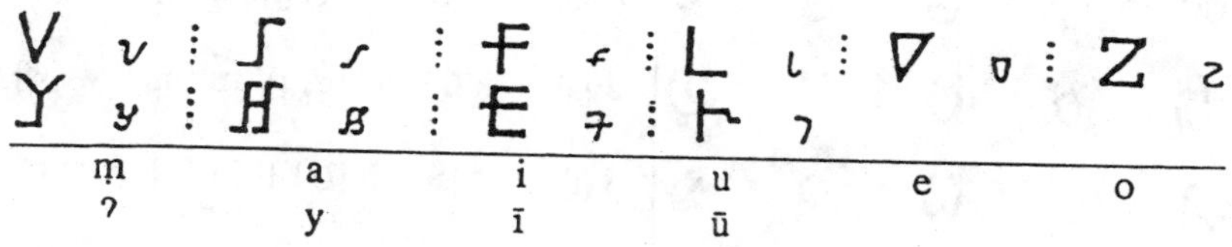

Figure 14.4. *The vowels of Varang Kshiti. Source:* Zide in Daniels and Bright 1996: 617.

> the use of a hyphen to indicate geminates (/māllo/ "beaten" = *mal-lo*, /kāḷḷo/ "took" = *kal-llo*, and of a double *-mm* to indicate final /-m/. . . . There is no indication of vowel quantity. A characteristic mark of Roman Konkani is the use of the letter *x* to indicate a hush sibilant /ʃ/, as in Portuguese. . . . Aspirates are written as C + *h*. (1991: 153)

Roman scripts developed by missionaries are used for many tribal languages. During the British Raj and since Independence, knowledge of and literacy in English became highly desirable.

Modern script inventions

In reaction to the dominance of both English and official state languages (specifically Oriya) and their scripts, a number of Munda-speaking scholars within the last century have devised scripts for their languages – scripts for Ho (Figures 14.3, 14.4), Sora (Figure 14.5), and Santali (Figure 14.6) have become known to scholarship. In those for Ho and Sora, the operating principle is the same as for the descendants of Brāhmī, while that for Santali is an alphabet. In all three, the shapes of the letters are innovative. The Santali alphabet, at least, seems to have achieved a measure of popular acceptance and has been promoted for use by other tribal languages, both Munda and Dravidian.

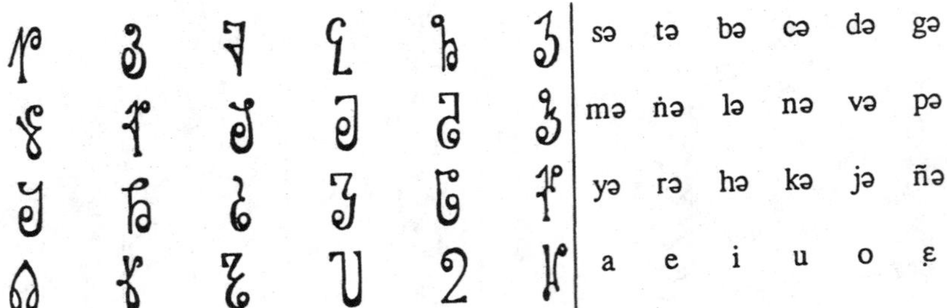

Figure 14.5. *The characters of Sorang Sampeng, the Sora Script. Source:* Zide in Daniels and Bright 1996: 613.

ọ [ɔ]	t [t]	k' [k', g]	ṅ [ŋ]	l [l]
a [a]	k [k]	c' [c', ɟ]	m [m]	w [w]
i [i]	s [s]	h [ʔ, h]	ñ [ɲ]	r [r]
u [u]	c [c]	t' [t', d]	ṇ [ɳ]	y [j]
e [e]	p [p]	ḍ [ɖ]	n [n]	ṛ [ɽ]
o [o]	ṭ [ʈ]	p' [p', b]	w̃ [w̃]	(C)h [ʰ]

Figure 14.6. *The Letters of Ol Cemet', the Santali alphabet. Source:* Zide in Daniels and Bright 1996: 614.

Epilogue

No account of the scripts of South Asia would be complete without a mention of James Prinsep (1799–1840), who deciphered Brāhmī in 1837. By 1834 he had compiled a consonant versus vowel matrix of all the akṣaras found on Aśoka's pillar at Allahabad, and he notes that if his knowledge of Sanskrit had been deeper, he would have been able to read the inscriptions that much sooner, since even at that point in time fairly old inscriptions could still be read by some pandits. Prinsep also made major contributions to the decipherment of Kharoṣṭhī, but that accomplishment was more of a communal effort.

Excursus on a Theory of Writing

(I) The explanation for the monosyllabic origin of writing appears to be as follows: It is not at all unusual for concepts to be recorded in the form of stylized pictures ("pictograms"); but unless the actual wording for the concepts can be recovered, they do not constitute writing, and to do so, the sounds of the language must be captured as such. The single syllable is the most salient unit of the stream of speech; when it coincides with an entire unit of meaning – that is, a monosyllabic morpheme – it becomes possible, and nearly inevitable, for a sign depicting some object to be reconceptualized as referring to the sound of its name, so that it can be used to notate a word with the same or a very similar sound that has an unrelated meaning for which devising a picture would be more challenging. A suggestion for the Indus script is that the fish, Proto-Dravidian **mīn*, also stands for **mīn* "star."

(II) Note that there is no question of Indo-European languages "needing" to write vowels, as is often said about the earlier important adaptation of a Semitic script to an Indo-European language, in that case Phonecian script to write Greek (*c.* 800 BCE): Aramaic scripts, in the guise of Pahlavi, served adequately for Middle Persian languages (used by the successors of the Achemenid Empire) for centuries (*c.* 50 BCE–650 CE). And, as we have seen in the text, Arabic script has been used for Classical Persian for many more centuries (*c.* 700 CE–present).

(III) The Indic method of indicating vowels cannot be called a syllabary, because both the vowel portion and the consonant portion of each syllable are identified in the writing system, whereas true syllabaries use signs for syllables that show no resemblance corresponding to phonetic similarity of the syllables denoted; and the method cannot be called an alphabet, because the symbols for vowels and for consonants differ in kind. In fact, this is a "type" of writing system distinct from both of those. The term "alphasyllabary," which seems to have been devised by William Bright and appears in work influenced by him, is unsatisfactory because it suggest a hybrid rather than an independent status for the type (and his conceptualization in fact differs from this author's; see Bright 2000). Other terms that have been used (neosyllabary, pseudo-alphabet) are similarly problematic; the author uses "abugida," from the name of the Ethiopic variety of this type – which arose in the fourth century CE probably through influence from some script of India – as a parallel to "alphabet" and to "abjad," an Arabic word that the author uses for the Arabic type script (described in the text).

(IV) We might venture a suggestion of the impetus for the invention of the abugida type of writing system. Over time, Aramaic scripts used the device of notating vowels with semivowel letters more and more; in some varieties of Aramaic, this came to be done for short vowels too. But *ă* was often still omitted. It is thus possible that the would-be Prakrit scribe could have gotten the impression from the Aramaic scribe that what the letters were *supposed* to represent was *Ca*; and made the improvement of not forcing the letters to do double duty as both consonants and vowels, but devised the mātrā system (Dani 1963/1986: 46 suggests that the forms of the Brāhmī mātrās derive from the corresponding initial vowel akṣaras).

Further Reading

Possehl 1996 collects the facts about the Indus script and evaluates the many attempts at decipherment. Parpola 1994 is a minutely detailed presentation of the linguistic and cultural materials relevant to a decipherment and makes a persuasive case for the Dravidian solution. The best brief overview of Indic scripts in English is Chapter 6, pp. 133–53, in Masica 1991. Salomon 2003 appeared long after this chapter was written. For Kharoṣṭhi, see Das Gupta 1958. Bright 1998 provides charts of all the consonant-vowel akṣaras in the four Dravidian scripts. The latest full treatment, Salomon 1998, deals with all aspects of South Asian inscriptions (but not manuscripts), but explicitly does not go into detail on the history of the shapes of the letters, for which the two earlier standard works, Bühler 1904 and Dani 1963/1986, remain reliable (though, as mentioned in the text, Bühler's account of the history of the script has been somewhat updated). Nearly 200 scripts of South and Southeast Asia are fully illustrated in Holle 1877 (which has now been reprinted with an English translation of the prefatory essay). A groundbreaking treatment that still bears consultation is Taylor 1883 (for an appreciation of Taylor as scholar of writing systems, see Daniels 2002). Among more recent general books on writing systems, those by Diringer (1948) and Jensen (1969) include fairly extensive historical accounts of the topic; for brief descriptive treatments of the standard scripts with specialized bibliography, see the articles by twenty contributors in Daniels and Bright 1996: 165–71, 371–484, 564–68, 612–18, and 743–62. Illustrations of additional scripts can be found in Coulmas 1996. Useful diagrams of the sequence of strokes used in writing Indic akṣaras, and extensive charts of conjunct combinations, are found in the "National Integration Language Series" (called *Learn X in 30 Days* on the front cover and *Learn X through English* on the spine). At least ten of these booklets (including Sanskrit, Hindi, and Marathi separately) are surprisingly widely available. Sinhala, not being a language of India, is excluded. For Indic-script calligraphy, see Anderson 1969: 311–16, Desai 1996, and Sander 1996. A clear and comprehensive account of the decipherments of Brāhmī and Kharoṣṭhi appears in Salomon 1998: 203–15.

Part 6

Language conflicts

15 Language politics and conflicts in South Asia

Robert D. King

Introduction

It is assumed here that South Asia consists of the seven sovereign nations of the subcontinent belonging to the loosely grouped organization SAARC (South Asian Association for Regional Cooperation): Bangladesh, Bhutan, India, the Maldives, Nepal, Pakistan, and Sri Lanka (Breton 1997: 16). Afghanistan is a special case, sitting squarely astride the divide between the Middle East and South Asia and drawing in about equal measure from each in culture and history, and I have chosen to leave it out of consideration here for space reasons. (For wide-ranging theoretical discussions of the problems involved in defining such concepts as "South Asia" and "India," see Emeneau 1980; Masica 1976; Roy 1985; and Sopher 1980).

It is useful to begin this chapter by asking the question: what are the ingredients that lead to language conflicts and language as a political concern? Obviously we cannot identify precisely those specifics about countries or regions that are necessary and sufficient conditions for language to become a political issue, for language politics is not an exact science. However, it is not difficult to identify recurrent factors for predicting language conflict in a country or region.

First, there should be more than one language (or dialect) competing for political, economic, and cultural "space." The larger the number of languages, the greater the likelihood that language will become a worrisome political issue. This is particularly true of countries that have become independent out of a condition of subservience (usually, since the Second World War, colonialism), where there is frequently the question of what the national language should be.

Second, there must be social differences that correlate with language. The term "social differences" is chosen intentionally for its vagueness: it includes religion, "class" in general and economic class in particular, caste, and perhaps most generally "ethnicity" – in contemporary usage an elastic and convenient cover term for anything that identifies one segment of society as apart, as the Other. When language is linked to that Otherness as a badge of iconic identification, then we have located a potential focal point of linguistic conflict.

Third, economic prosperity often keeps bad things from getting worse, and language is no different. While well-to-do countries like Belgium can have major language problems (R. King 1997: x, 24), normally the generalization holds that the better-off the country, the greater the likelihood that language will not be a major political problem. Conversely, widespread poverty bodes ill for language tranquility.

Fourth, history and awareness of history are peculiarly relevant to the probability of linguistic conflict. If a culture is inclined to "remember" slights from the past, those slights easily grow into language grievances. Every Quebec automobile license plate bears the foreboding *Je me souviens* "I remember."

These generalizations about the preconditions for language conflict are, of course, sweeping and superficial. Nevertheless, they are helpful in establishing one point that I wish to make about South Asia: that while by every measure South Asia should be in a condition of eternal linguistic strife, it is not. Measured against every one of the four indices enumerated above, South Asia should not pass a day without language turmoil.

Take the first point, that "there must be more than one language (or dialect) competing for political, economic, and cultural 'space.'" The monumental *Linguistic Survey of India* begun by George Grierson in the nineteenth century and completed in the twentieth listed 179 languages and 544 dialects (Grierson 1967–1968; S. Varma 1972–1976). (When Grierson did his fieldwork "India" subsumed what are today Bangladesh, India, and Pakistan.) The number of major languages of South Asia is of course much smaller. The Eighth Schedule of the Indian Constitution names eighteen languages: Assamese, Bengali, Gujarati, Hindi, Kannada, Kashmiri, Konkani, Malayalam, Manipuri, Marathi, Nepali, Oriya, Punjabi, Sanskrit, Sindhi, Tamil, Telugu, and Urdu (Mallikarjun 2001). These are the eighteen major ("scheduled") languages of India that, together with English, make up the nineteen languages of India having in some sense official status (see, however, the expansion of the list of scheduled languages discussed in Chapter 10 in this volume). The official language of Pakistan is Urdu, but Urdu is a minority language there (just over 7 percent of the population have it as their home language), being outnumbered by speakers of Punjabi, Sindhi, and Pushto (Breton 1997: 198). The principal languages of Sri Lanka are Sinhala and Tamil, with Sinhala outnumbering Tamil almost three to one (Breton 1997: 199). Bangladesh is the one large country in South Asia that is almost monolingual; it is Bengali-speaking overwhelmingly (Breton 1997: 191, See also Chapter 6 in this volume).

The first condition listed as favoring linguistic conflict is therefore abundantly fulfilled in South Asia – it has many languages. The other three conditions too are met, profusely. Social, religious, class, caste, and ethnic differences abound on the subcontinent. And there is usually very little of a physical barrier between the different castes (*varnas, jatis*), religions, classes, and ethnicities that might isolate the grievances of one language group from that of another. And on the issue of economics, speaking generally, the subcontinent is a poor region. If economic prosperity favors linguistic tranquility, its opposite favors linguistic conflict.

Finally, there is what I called "history and awareness of history" as factors in linguistic unrest. History's hand lies heavy on the present in South Asia. Conflicts between Hindus and Muslims in India and Pakistan regularly make newspaper headlines today. They disfigured public life in India long before the English came on the scene (Wolpert 1993: 149–86). Caste antagonisms played an important role in the linguistic battles that accompanied the division of India into linguistic states following Independence (R. King 1997: 70–3). (One must remember that caste, though Hindu, has spread into the societal structures of every other religion on the subcontinent, even those that preach equality, see Thapar 1966: 300-1). Awareness of history is a fact of South Asian linguistic life: old sins cast long shadows in the hot sun of the subcontinent.

There is one other significant fact about language on the subcontinent that enlarges its role as mischief maker in South Asia. What is alluded to here is what one might call the spiritual importance of language in South Asia. R. King (1997) states:

> Linguistics in ancient India was the core of the intellectual and scientific tradition. It possessed an intellectual centrality and scholarly hegemony that beggars belief today ... Linguistics was suffused with the light of sanctity, endowed with religious purpose. (6–7)

There is hardly any force in human society more tricky than religion. If language is perceived in the folk consciousness to be "endowed with religious purpose," then language becomes a force that touches people in secret and dangerous places. This quasi-religious role of language easily turns what could be a rational, unemotional discussion about, say, whether newly independent India should be divided into linguistic states into a bitter, protracted, and tormented struggle (Annamalai 1979; Gopal 1966; R. King 1997: 52–73; Kluyev 1981; Krishna 1991; *Report of the States Reorganization Commission* 1955; Schwartzberg 1985).

Language conflict from the Aryan invasion to the classical age of Hinduism

We know there must have been language conflict and therefore, in the broadest sense, language politics in South Asia at all periods, but most of what we know about earlier history is inferential and derivative. The texts tell us little directly of language conflict. (The method of "language paleology" is often useful here, cf. Polomé 1982, for resurrecting evidence of language conflict.)

We do not know precisely when the Aryan (Indo-European) invaders descended on a largely Dravidian and Austro-Asiatic linguistic subcontinent, but the date 1500 BCE is often taken as approximately correct. Sanskrit was the language of the Aryan conquerors (Burrow 1965; Cardona 1987) and became the language of the Vedic and Hindu sacred texts, commentaries, rituals, and literature. The spread of Sanskrit came at the expense of the autochthonous languages of the subcontinent, which were, we assume, mostly of the Dravidian family, a term that today means essentially "south Indian." There was a smaller sprinkling of Austro-Asiatic languages, never large, many of which have become the "tribal" languages of today (Wolpert 1993: 8). By 400 BCE or thereabouts the Aryans were in control of most of northern India, and their language had begun to differentiate itself regionally. These regional variants of Sanskrit, called the Prakrits, were the foundation of the modern Indo-European languages of Pakistan, northern India, and Bangladesh such as Hindi, Urdu, Bengali, Marathi, Gujarati, and Oriya (Deshpande 1993).

What we know of language conflict comes from offhand references in the literature of the time. Thus, in northern India, where Aryan control maintained itself longest, the process of Aryanization – the imposition of the Sanskrit language and Aryan religious and cultural practices – was carried out through the use of Sanskrit and Prakrit rather than the local dialect, which was referred to contemptuously as a "goblin language" (Thapar 1966: 122). In Sanskrit plays of the classical period characters of high social standing speak Sanskrit, while the lower-class actors and all women characters speak Prakrit (Thapar 1966: 157). Such observations betoken language conflict, but we know nothing about this directly.

Language conflict during Islamic rule

There is no evidence of major language conflict during the rule of the great Mughal (Muslim) emperors. The everyday language of the Mughal Empire was Urdu, a fusion of native Hindi dialects with Persian and Arabic, but its official and administrative language was Persian. That the use of Persian for official purposes and Urdu for oral and written purposes came at the expense of the vernacular languages is clear. That there must have been resentments and language conflicts is no less clear. But Mughal hegemony in northern and central India was virtually absolute, and illiteracy was widespread. Hindus who wished to rise in the Mughal bureaucracy learned Persian. Hindu pandits continued to use Sanskrit (Thapar 1966: 316–20), but these were elites. The common people adapted as best they could to Mughal rule, linguistically as well as culturally. The vernacular languages continued to develop, but there was no political consciousness behind them, and because they were not in competition with Urdu or Persian, language use settled into a stable situation of parallel usage.

Language conflict during the colonial period

The degree of interest in native languages among the more urbane and enlightened British overlords during the early colonial period of Indian history is astonishing by later standards. Sir William Jones, an early Western scholar of both Persian and Sanskrit, often considered the father of comparative linguistics, founded the Asiatic Society in 1784 partly in order to document his and others' interest in language (R. King 1997: 13).

With the influx of utilitarian liberalism during the governor-generalship of William Bentinck (1829–1835) the notion that the British had a higher responsibility to "improve" the natives gained control of public policy, and the new Mughals, the British, made a move that was fateful for the future linguistic dispensation of India, choosing English rather than Persian, the vernaculars, or Sanskrit as the language of instruction in schools and in the maintenance of official records. Today, it can scarcely be imagined that so momentous a move could be made without provoking major unrest. At the time its impact was confined to Indian elites, and elite opinion was divided on the issue. A large part of the impetus for the decision in favor of English came from middle- and upper-middle class Indians themselves, many of them guided by the desire for "jobs for the boys" (Frykenberg 1988; Kulke and Rothermund 1991: 251).

The freedom movement

Nationalism came late to the subcontinent. The waves of national feeling that began with the French Revolution and gained momentum as the nineteenth century unrolled began to lap up on the shores of the subcontinent only in the 1880s. The seeds of national feeling – and therefore the need to communicate effectively to the masses in languages they could understand – grew in the wake of the Sepoy Mutiny and with the formation of the Indian National Congress ("Congress") in 1885. "Local" patriotism was anciently present on the subcontinent but had intensified with the emergence of regional identity linked to national feeling that followed the growth of the Congress movement. Peoples, such as the Bengalis, the Marathis, and the Tamils, for whom language had always been closely identified with ethnic identity were powerfully fortified and found new political awareness in political events – the Partition of Bengal in 1905, for example (R. King 1997: 57–9).

Nationalism in Europe became increasingly attached to language as the nineteenth century came to an end. Of this development Arnold Toynbee wrote, disapprovingly: "The growing consciousness of Nationality had attached itself neither to traditional frontiers nor to new geographical associations but almost exclusively to the mother-tongues" (Toynbee 1927: 18). The crowning triumph of the new desideratum was the Treaty of Versailles, when the allied victors of the First World War redrew the map of Central and Eastern Europe according to nationality ("self-determination") as best as they could. Because language isoglosses are easier to locate and draw than lines of self-determination, the reorganization of the Austro-Hungarian Empire was actually carried out as much as possible along *linguistic* lines. Self-determination was thought of as a matter of "nationality," of what today we would be more likely to call "ethnicity"; but language was simpler to identify than nationality or ethnicity, so language became almost by default the supreme defining characteristic of nationality.

Independence and its aftermath

India

This heady mixture of language and nationalism and freedom and self-determination came to British India as the twentieth century dawned. The Indian freedom movement was almost from its beginnings concerned about language. (The story is told in detail in R. King 1997: Chapter 3. See also J. Das Gupta 1970; Dua 1985; Nayar 1969). One issue was the national language – what the national language of India (meaning today's India plus Pakistan and Bangladesh) should be once the British were gone. English, the language of the despised colonial ruler, obviously was unacceptable, and there emerged a general consensus that the national language of free and independent India would be "Hindustani," meaning Hindi/Urdu, essentially digraphic variants of the same spoken language, cf. C. King (1994) and R. King (2001). Hindi is written in Devanagari script and Urdu in a derivative of the Persian script, itself a derivative of Arabic. (Script conflict has also been an issue in the Punjabi language, which is written in Devanagari, a Persian–Arabic script, and a third script, Gurumukhi or, Gurmukhi, which was used for the religious writings of the Sikh religion.)

The other issue, which was to arouse just as much conflict as the question of the national language, was that of the "linguistic states" or "linguistic provinces." The British had carved up the map of those parts of India under British control not according to logical principles of any kind but by happenstance, history, imperfect geographical knowledge, and administrative convenience – by everything *but* language and ethnicity. For administrative convenience British India was divided up into an assortment of units: the Bombay and Madras Presidencies, Bengal, the United Provinces, the Punjab, the Central Provinces, Sind, and so on. Of these only Bengal, the Punjab, and Sind had any claim to historical organicity based on culture, language, land use, and ethnography. The hereditary princely states were no better. The textbook example was the huge Deccan state of Hyderabad with a largely Telugu-speaking Hindu populace ruled by an Urdu-speaking Muslim Nizam and a largely Muslim bureaucracy.

Hodgepodge as the map of India was, hardly anyone regarded it as peculiar until the 1920s. After all, the Austro-Hungarian and Ottoman Empires had existed for centuries without regard for language and ethnicity in the drawing of their internal boundaries. As early as 1891 the Maratha nationalist B. G. Tilak, an early leader of the Congress radical wing, had argued for redrawing the boundaries of a free and independent India according to linguistic lines (Kluyev 1981: 120–1). In 1920, Gandhi announced his support for linguistic provinces (overcoming earlier reservations that such divisions might weaken the freedom movement), and so they became a stock part of the Congress agenda down to Independence in 1947.

By 1947, the British, weakened by the Second World War, realized that they could no longer hold on to India, and they announced their withdrawal to take place August 15 of that year. Years of intense and bitter communal (Muslim–Hindu) tension forced Partition: the division of British India into a Muslim Pakistan and a secular but 80 percent Hindu India. The basis of the division was political of course, but essentially religious. Pakistan was formed out of two noncontiguous parts: East Pakistan, formerly East Bengal, and West Pakistan, formerly part of the Punjab, Sind, and the North-West Frontier Provinces.

When Independence arrived the general assumption was that Jawaharlal Nehru, the first prime minister of India, would move as rapidly as possible to put in place the two major language policies of a half century of the freedom movement: linguistic provinces, and Hindi as the national language. He did neither. He hesitated, he temporized, he pleaded for time. He argued that other issues had far greater priority: economic stability, resolution of conflict with Pakistan, world politics. This is often taken as weakness in the Hamlet-like Nehru. Rather, we believe that it demonstrated unusual linguistic sophistication on his part to recognize the potential linguistic issues had for the national polity, and by dawdling he gained for India almost ten years' time to unify the country before proceeding to divide it again on language lines (This is the principal thesis of the author's book *Nehru and the Language Politics of India*, R. King 1997).

Nehru came to recognize that beneath the demand for linguistic states lay ethnic and caste conflicts: between Tamil and Telugu, between Mayar Dalits ("untouchables") in Marathi-speaking regions, between Gujaratis and Marathis for control of Bombay:

> After Independence Nehru, though with few of the other leaders of India alongside him, was quickly to become attuned to the subtleties of caste-class-communalism in the frantic drive to put in place the linguistic provinces. It gave him pause and more than

pause . . . Within three months of Independence the dark side of the linguistic states movement quelled altogether whatever enthusiasm he may have once had to redraw the boundaries of India. (R. King 1997: 73)

Nehru's hand was forced by the fast to death of a revered Gandhian leader of the movement for a Telugu-speaking state, Sri Potti Sriramulu, in 1952. With this Nehru threw in his hand, and the division of India along linguistic-state lines proceeded apace: Andhra Pradesh (Telugu), West Bengal (Bengali), Orissa (Oriya), Bihar (Hindi), Kerala (Malayalam), Karnataka (Kannada), Tamil Nadu (Tamil), Madhya Pradesh (Hindi), Rajasthan (Hindi, Rajasthani – there are arguments whether they are separate languages or separate dialects of Hindi), Uttar Pradesh (Hindi), Assam (Assamese), Jammu and Kashmir (Kashmiri, also Punjabi), Maharashtra (Marathi), Gujarat (Gujarati), Haryana (Hindi), the Punjab (Punjabi).

"Perfect" linguistic states are never possible in the real world. Hardly any state or province is ethnically monolithic. Modern India has done an extraordinarily efficient job of drawing its state boundaries in such a way as to bring down the percentage of speakers of minority languages in its component states to an irreducible minimum. This is shown nicely in Schwartzberg (1985), whose maps tell the tale of fitting state lines to language isoglosses. (The maps in Breton 1997 are also very informative.) Even so, there will always remain linguistic minorities, in India or anywhere, however the lines are drawn – and therefore grounds for future linguistic grievances.

On the other great issue of language conflict, that of the national language, what had appeared so clear and so desirable during all those years of British rule lost its allure not long after India's first Constitution in 1950 proclaimed Hindi the national language of India. English was to exist until 1965 as an official language, but then it was to be banned for official uses. The trouble was that Hindi was a minority language in India, being spoken by some 35 percent of the population, and it had a very strong north Indian identification. It was assumed that nonspeakers of Hindi would have fifteen years to learn the language, that their children would willingly learn it, that the other vernaculars would willingly sacrifice themselves on the altar of national unity, and that English would no longer be needed to run the country's affairs.

Wishful thinking that. As 1965 approached major opposition to Hindi developed, especially in Tamil Nadu, and there were widespread language riots as the date for the abolition of English as an official language drew near. In July 1960, headlines in the international press read: "LANGUAGE RIOTS! SCORES KILLED! 40,000 FLEE!" Madras, the capital of Tamil Nadu, had terrible scenes of rioting against Hindi even as late as 1965.

Nehru again took the lead in contriving a constitutional formula that would enable English to coexist alongside Hindi for the foreseeable future. In his last great parliamentary address in the Lok Sabha in 1963 he argued forcibly and successfully for the continuation of English alongside Hindi:

> With the passage of the Official Language Act, Nehru rendered his last service to the cause of progressive language policy in India – and a very great service it was. By delaying the execution of linguistic states and by securing the place of English in India indefinitely into the future, Nehru guaranteed a foundation for progress that will always remain one of his most enduring bequests. (R. King 1997: 222)

I viewed what Nehru did favorably in 1998 and I do so now. This is a minority opinion. There are others, all of them critical of Nehru and the position of English in India. Postmodern theorizing has made almost anything a Western linguist says in favor of English odious, but I stand by my opinion as expressed above. If India wishes to rid itself of English, so be it. I shall shed no tears – or but one or two tears for the passing of a great tradition. But I also think it is unlikely in the extreme that I will have to. English has become simply one more Indian language, the language used by a minority, true – but a very important and articulate Indian elite minority – and by many writers with vast international sales and readers. That, I think, is not likely to change.

The present language situation in India is one of almost stasis. The linguistic states are in place and there is little trouble with them. The "Down with English" demands are heard now mostly at election time and then decrease in volume thereafter. A Hindu-based party (the BJP) has ruled India for most of the past ten years. The imposition of Hindi and the removal or lessening of the role of English is a staple of the party platform. But decisive action so far has not been taken. English remains the only pan-Indian language.

True, language will never *not* be a problem in India. That is a simple fact of life. There were ghastly scenes of communal rioting in the north Indian town of Badaun on September 28, 1989, sadly reminiscent of the partition death trains of 1947, that followed the decision of the Uttar Pradesh government to make Urdu the second official language of the state. Hindi remained the official language of Uttar Pradesh, as it always had been, but Muslims had fought for greater official recognition of their language, which was Urdu. There were similar scenes in Bihar in 1967, and there the violence cost at least seventy lives (J. Das Gupta 1970: 149).

But language conflict and its concomitant, language politics, in present-day India are altogether different from the tinderbox situation of the 1950s and 1960s. There are occasional language troubles, but they remain localized, or at least have so far.

Pakistan and Bangladesh

The principal languages of West Pakistan were Punjabi (64 percent), Sindhi (12 percent), Pashtu (8 percent), and Urdu (7 percent); of the remaining 9 percent

Baluchi is the largest with about 3 percent. (These are recent statistics, but they have remained fairly constant since 1947, cf. Breton 1997: 198; *Pakistan Languages* 2002.)

Muhammad Ali Jinnah, the "Father of Pakistan," spoke only English, having been educated in English and having had a very successful legal career in England and Bombay before joining the freedom movement. However, the Urdu language had been closely identified with the Pakistan movement from its inception in the 1930s. The great Urdu poet Muhammad Iqbal had first proposed a northwest Indian state as "the final destiny of the Muslims"; this proto-Pakistan did not contain the Muslim sections of Bengal (Wolpert 1993: 316–17). The Urdu language indeed had become virtually an icon of the idea of a Muslim Pakistan sheared off from a "Hindu" India – and so at Independence Jinnah resolved to make Urdu the sole national language of Pakistan, this in spite of the fact that very few East Pakistanis spoke Urdu and that even in West Pakistan Urdu was the native language of only about 7 percent of the population (and many of those 7 percent were refugees from India, where Urdu had been the major language of the Indian Muslims).

Ideology yielded to politics, and so both Urdu and Bengali were named as "state" languages of Pakistan while English was to remain the official language for twenty-five years, with the situation to be reviewed at the end of that period. Bilingual education in both Urdu and Bengali were supposed to be required in the schools of both East and West Pakistan. In practice very little Urdu was taught in the East, and very little Bengali was taught in the West.

The cultural, not to mention the linguistic and geographic, differences between West and East Pakistan were immense; the two sections had only a shared religion, and that was not enough for success. This unnatural nation construct was bound to fail, as it did when civil war erupted in 1971. After bitter fighting and intervention by India, the independent nation of Bangladesh was announced. Henceforward the linguistic conflicts were lessened: Urdu for West Pakistan, Bengali for Bangladesh. English continued in both countries as an elite and official or quasi-official language. Bengali–English bilingualism is common among Bangladeshi elites.

The linguistic uniformity of Bangladesh is extraordinary for a South Asian country, with Bengali spoken by virtually 100 percent of the population (Breton 1997: 191; U. Varma 1983). It says a great deal about the iconic value of language in the region that the name *Bangladesh* is composed of *Bangla* plus *desa* "country." The term *bangla* refers not to the Bengali people or the territory of (East) Bengal but specifically to the Bengali language (Klaiman 1987: 492).

In Pakistan, the former West Pakistan, several factors contributed to the selection and continuation of Urdu as the national language. One, Urdu was, as mentioned above, implicit in the concept of a Pakistan. Even today it continues to have something of the "founder aura" about it. Second, though Punjabi is spoken by a majority of the population (64 percent), the Punjabi language has a strongly "Sikh" association. Very few Sikhs remained in Pakistan after Partition, and the founders of Pakistan had no wish to take as the national language a language almost synonymous in the folk mind with another religion, Sikhism, and a major section, the northwest, of a neighboring country, India (Chaudhry 1977; Mansoor 1993).

The imposition of a minority language, Urdu, on (West) Pakistan has not been without its problems. Some of its "success" is doubtless due to the fact that Pakistan has often been under authoritarian, often military rule, so that a frank and open discussion of language disputes has usually been limited. There were, however, language riots in Sind during the 1970s on behalf of the Sindhi language as a school language. The normal state of affairs in Pakistan is bilingualism – Punjabi-Urdu or Sindhi-Urdu – but among the educated classes trilingualism (English fills out the triad) is the rule. Recently, with the ease of publication made possible by the Internet (Web), one encounters frequent criticism of the domination of Urdu and of English (Geocities 2002). That English is resented is of course understandable, but all efforts to prohibit its use have so far come to naught. As a means of communication in a multilingual country desiring to keep its hand in play in world and regional affairs, English, people find, cannot be wished away (Rahman 1996b).

After Partition the Hindi of official India and the Urdu of official Pakistan began inevitably to diverge. Freed now of the need to accommodate each other's sensitivities, lexically Hindi drew more and more heavily from Sanskrit and other Indo-Aryan languages, and Urdu – especially the Urdu of Pakistan – drew more from Arabic and Persian. In their highest forms the two can be virtually mutually incomprehensible (C. King 1994: 51–4).

Sri Lanka

Ceylon (now Sri Lanka) became independent in 1948, a year after the partition of India and Pakistan. Most of Sri Lanka's approximately seventeen million inhabitants are Sinhala-speaking Buddhists who came from north India some 2,500 years ago and settled in the south and southwest parts of the island. Tamil-speaking Hindus came to Sri Lanka in an early and a late wave, the majority coming in the late nineteenth and early twentieth centuries to work on the tea plantations for which the island is famous, and settled around Jaffna in the north. Prior to 1948 relations between the two ethnic/linguistic groups were on the whole reasonably calm, but the situation deteriorated badly after the British withdrawal (Wolpert 1993: 429).

At the outset Sinhala was named the official language, but soon thereafter Tamil was decreed, grudgingly by the Sinhalese majority, a second official language. Each ethnicity had separate school systems, and physical separation – Tamils in the north and northeast, Sinhalese in the south and southwest – did little to foster bilingualism or much in the way of bicultural mixing. Things went violently downhill after the governing Sinhalese majority in 1956 decreed a "Sinhala-only" Official Language Act. By the 1970s the violent conflict between Sinhalese and Tamils convulsed the country to a degree that it requires more scholarly aloofness to the real world than I possess to speak of "language conflict" in the Sri Lankan context. Suffice it to say that language conflict in Sri Lanka is the extension of communal antagonism so deep and profound that language is the least of it. Religion, economics, class, power politics, a deep sense of historical injustices, and the involvement of a large and powerful country a few miles away (India) all reduce the language conflict in Sri Lanka to a sad iconic reification of a great war.

As in all parts of what had been British India English has continued an often precarious position as a quasi-official language. The pressure to avoid or to prohibit English for official purposes has perhaps been stronger in Sri Lanka than in any of the other parts of formerly British India, but English continues to thrive as the second language of Sri Lankan elites. (For a variety of theoretical points of view about language in Sri Lanka, see Dharmadasa 1992; Dharmadasa 1996; Parakrama 1995; Theva Rajan 1995.)

The yawning gap

No reference is made here to the smaller countries of the SAARC – Bhutan, the Maldives, Nepal – primarily in order to conserve space for discussing language conflicts in the larger states of South Asia. But such an omission is made possible only because the smaller countries have been less troubled by language conflicts. (Some references for Nepal are Baldauf and Kaplan 2000 and Malla 1977.) There are a growing number of websites dealing with language problems throughout the world, including the smaller countries of South Asia, and these may be located in the usual ways.

The "yawning gap" of this subsection refers not to the smaller countries but rather to a huge missing part of the discussion that has been presented here: language conflicts and language politics in the *vernacular languages* of the subcontinent. Hand in hand with the growth of English domination in the language arena after the 1830s went a renewal and rebirth of the Indian vernacular languages, long dormant under the weight of Sanskrit and Persian.

One problem all the vernaculars had to come to grips with was the degree to which they had become Sanskritized, meaning mainly that they had borrowed extensively from the Sanskrit lexicon. It was the written, and, therefore, more artificial forms of these languages that were so heavily Sanskritized. The spoken languages were quite different, as spoken languages always are, and they had absorbed much less in the way of Sanskrit lexical items.

The nineteenth century witnessed the steady evolution of the vernaculars as literary vehicles. Journalism played a role here, as did in general the development of prose style. India produced many masters of English prose: Rabindranath Tagore, Arabindo Ghose, Sarvepalli Radhakrishnan and his historian son, Sarvepalli Gopal, and Nehru. But English prose mastery carried with it the seeds of the perfection of prose style in the vernaculars, and as printing of newspapers and journals in these languages grew and spread in the nineteenth century, so did the use and suppleness of the vernaculars. The vernaculars were on the move. The twentieth century would come to belong to them.

That there is a story here of huge linguistic importance is clear. But I am not the one to tell it. Very few scholars, South Asian or Western, know more than one or two of the vernaculars of the subcontinent. A team effort would be needed to write the history of language conflict and language politics in the development of the vernaculars. For present purposes the interested reader is refered to a handful of sources found useful and reliable: Annamalai 1979, Apte 1976, Chatterji 1973, Kishore 1987, Majumdar *et al.* 1961. In general the publications of the CIIL (Central Institute of Indian Languages) in Mysore provide useful points of entry to the vernacular issues.

Conclusion

Most of the conflicts over language that there are, South Asia has had. What should be the national language? What to do about English? Since the principle of linguistic states ("one nation = one language") is now so widely accepted as to be an assumption usually not questioned, how do we draw political boundaries? And how do we deal with the inevitable language-minority problems that are left behind when the boundaries have been drawn? How "authentic" is a language when it has extensive borrowings from another language?

As said at the beginning, by every reasonable standard, by everything we know about language conflict and language politics, some part of South Asia should be in linguistic turmoil almost any given day. But that is not the case. One wishes one could say with conviction that that is because South Asia is a triumph of good linguistic planning. But that is not the case either. What one can say is that by and large the countries of South Asia have done a pretty good job of sorting things out linguistically in ways that permit them to function. Minor problems remain, yes; problems occasionally that are worse than minor, yes. What Plato said of war in general – that only the dead have seen the end of it – is no less true of language "war" in South Asia. No one has seen the end of language "war" in countries as multilingual as those of South Asia. Language rises and falls as a source of political discontent – in Pakistan, in India, in Sri Lanka – but it has ceased to be a threat to national stability and national unity.

Tolerance is always and everywhere a commodity in limited supply. But South Asia has more tolerance than it is frequently given credit for today, when "conflict" is writ large across contemporary South Asian affairs: Pakistan versus India, Muslims and Hindus and Sikhs, caste and religion rivalries in India, Sinhalese versus Tamils in Sri Lanka. I would like to end by paraphrasing something I wrote earlier (R. King 1986: 141):

> The unique genius of South Asia, probably its greatest legacy from Vedic values, is the ability to absorb conflicting ideas and create harmony out of opposing views . . . These countries live every day with a degree of diversity unknown in the countries of the West. Language conflicts go against the grain of this tradition of tolerance. They are, as it were, the spiritual legacy of Aurangzeb (the most intolerant of Mughal emperors) rather than of Akbar (a model of tolerance).

I believe, though often in the face of sad evidence to the contrary, that the South Asian genius for reconciling dualities will prevail in language as well as in other matters. If this is true, then I do not think we will need to spend too much time worrying about language conflicts in the South Asia of the twenty-first century. The linguistic "marketplace," together with a little luck and a generous measure of traditional regional tolerance, will solve most of the problems.

Part 7

Language and modernization

16 Language modernization in Kannada

S. N. Sridhar

Introduction

In this chapter, which continues and complements S. N. Sridhar (1988), I analyze the effects of modernization on Kannada, with special reference to the structure of the lexicon, syntax, and style repertoire.[1]

Background

Kannada has a long and rich literary tradition, going back to at least the ninth century. The literature is primarily poetic, though there is relatively more prose than in many other literary languages of South Asia. The long cultivation of the language for literary purposes, together with a liberal attitude toward borrowing, has resulted in the formation of a rich and supple idiom. However, Kannada has but a sketchy (though ancient) tradition of scientific discourse (see Bhardwaja 1949 for an overview). For centuries, Sanskrit enjoyed hegemony as the premier language of intellectual discourse; Persian and Arabic dominated the spheres of law and administration during the eighteenth century, and the prestige and power of English led to a neglect of Kannada in the education system in the nineteenth century and the first half of the twentieth century. As a result, when Kannada intellectuals began to think of modernization toward the end of the nineteenth century, they found a language with a lopsided development: rich in the idiom of the humanities, but ill-equipped to serve as the

[1] The data for this chapter comes from a wide range of sources, including issues of the newspaper *Praja:va:Ni*, the magazines *Sudha:* and *Lankesh Patrike*, the journals *Rujuva:tu* and *Sa:kSi*, numerous books, fiction and nonfiction, and observations of casual conversations in buses, restaurants, and parties. My fieldwork in Bangalore, Mysore, and Shimoga was supported by a Senior Research Fellowship of the American Institute of Indian Studies. Research on this topic was also supported in part by a grant from the National Science Foundation. Earlier versions of this chapter were presented at seminars at the University of Illinois at Urbana-Champaign, the Central Institute of Indian Languages, Mysore, and Osmania University (1983), and as a S. S. Malavada Endowment Lecture at Bangalore University in 1987. The author wishes to thank E. Annamalai, Mark Aronoff, Bh. Krishnamurti, K. Marula Siddappa, K. V. Narayana, and Ki Ram Nagaraja for helpful comments.

vehicle of contemporary, Western-influenced intellectual, scientific, and technological discourse.

The beginning of the modernization[2] movement in Kannada may be traced to the founding of the *Karnataka Bha:sho:jji:vini: Sabha:* (1886) under the auspices of the then Maharaja of Mysore, Sri Chamaraja Wodeyar. (In a sense, 1843, the year of founding of the first Kannada newspaper, could be regarded as the beginning of modernization, cf. Havanur 1989.) The Kannada Academy of Letters, *Kannada Sa:hitya Parishat*, was formed in 1915. The first major academic journal in Kannada, *Prabuddha Karnataka*, began its illustrious publishing history in 1919. Science teaching through the medium of Kannada was introduced in selected schools in the 1920s. The university centers in Mysore, Bangalore, and Dharwar played an influential role in the renaissance of Kannada. The *Mysore University English–Kannada Dictionary* was completed in 1946. The Kannada Sahitya Parishat's monumental *Kannada Dictionary* (on historical principles, modeled after the *Oxford English Dictionary*) was initiated in 1941 and completed recently. The long awaited reunification of the Kannada-speaking people was achieved in 1956 with the reorganization of states on linguistic principles. The introduction of Kannada medium (optional) at the college level in the 1960s, the publication of a large number of textbooks prepared by the universities of Mysore, Bangalore, and Karnataka, as well as the State Directorate of Textbooks, the adoption of Kannada as the official language of the state of Karnataka (and its accelerated implementation over the last decade or so), and the growth of print journalism have been instrumental in the slow but steady expansion of the use of Kannada in a range of modern functions (Rao 1984). Nevertheless, it must be noted that modernization in Kannada has been primarily a product of informal or semiformal planning. The institutions mentioned above have helped but not controlled the process – the government or semigovernmental agencies have been but one participant, though a major one, in the essentially laissez-faire process.

Modernization in Kannada and South Asian languages

We start with a few general observations on the nature of modernization in Kannada.[3] First, the principal agency of modernization in Kannada, as indeed in

[2] I use the term "language modernization" in the sense of Ferguson (1968): "The modernization of a language may be thought of as a process of its becoming the equal of other developed languages as a medium of communication; it is in a sense the process of joining the world community of increasingly intertranslatable languages recognized as appropriate vehicles of modern forms of discourse." See also Fishman (1973).

[3] Modernization of Kannada has been discussed in Chidanandamurthy (1984), Shastri (1986), and S. N. Sridhar (1984, 1988). For discussion of modernization of Indian languages, see Shanmugan (1975), D'souza (1986), and Krishnamurti and Mukherji (1984).

other South Asian languages, has been bilingualism (Pandit 1977; Tamil may be a partial exception, see Shanmugan 1975). Second, modernization has involved Sanskritization of the lexicon and Englishization of syntax and discourse structure (cf. Y. Kachru 1989 for Hindi). Third, in terms of content, modernization is virtually synonymous with Westernization though it has involved, to a small extent, the rediscovery and reinterpretation of indigenous resources. Fourth, modernization in Kannada is marked by (1) unprecedented lexical expansion; (2) productive use of nonnative structural devices; (3) pervasive, though subtle, lexico-syntactic modification brought about by grafting English structural patterns onto Kannada (or Sanskritized Kannada) lexical material; (4) relaxation of prescriptive grammatical rules; (5) importation of colloquial language patterns into the written mode; (6) coexistence of alternative lexical resources resulting in greater style choice; (7) use of mixed codes, especially English-mixed Kannada (cf. S. N. Sridhar 1978); and (8) breakdown, and paradoxically, simultaneous reinforcement, on a different basis, of traditional diglossic patterns (S. N. Sridhar 1980), among other features.[4]

The following linguistic processes involved in modernization are particularly interesting from the structural point of view: (1) compounding, including stem compounds, genitive compounds, explicator compounds, and multilingual compounds; (2) affixation, including prefixation and hybrid word formation; (3) strengthening of the once marginal category of adjective through importation of Sanskrit (and English) words; (4) calquing, with English models and Sanskrit or Kannada lexical stock; and (5) the introduction of a number of new syntactic patterns modeled on English. These are discussed in detail below.

Effects of modernization at different linguistic levels

Morphology and lexicon

The Kannada lexicon has received a massive influx of new words – numbering no doubt in the tens of thousands – in this century. These words have been introduced primarily through three mechanisms: (1) borrowing; (2) derivation from native and nonnative sources; and (3) revival and reinterpretation of native words. Borrowing has been mainly from Sanskrit and English, with Hindi–Urdu playing a smaller role. As we shall see presently, it is not easy to distinguish borrowing from derivation when it comes to the thousands of recent Sanskrit-based words in Kannada. In the following selective discussion, my focus is on certain processes that indicate the coexistence of productive

[4] A more rigorous study of modernization than has been attempted in any of the studies of language modernization so far would make a systematic comparative analysis of roughly comparable texts from the premodern and modern periods. For Kannada, that would be approximately 1900 CE and the present.

linguistic processes from different languages. No attempt is made here to survey lexical expansion in general.

Traditional reliance on Sanskrit

In South Asia, being educated has always meant becoming a bilingual or multilingual, the other tongue being Sanskrit until recently; Persian and Arabic in a restricted sense in north India or English for the last two centuries. Sanskrit has traditionally served as the ultimate "High" language in South Asia's polyglossia before it was replaced by English in most fields over the last two centuries. Its association with Indic religions, its rich and diversified intellectual tradition, its role as the pan-South Asian lingua franca of the educated classes, and not the least, its derivational flexibility (cf. Srivastava and Kalra 1984) has made Sanskrit a favorite source of new words, phrases, and idioms in almost all the languages of South Asia (see Krishnamurti and Mukherji 1984).

Sanskrit words have been borrowed into Kannada from the earliest times – the very first document in Kannada, the Halmidi inscription of *c.* 450 CE, contains a large number of Sanskrit words (see S. N. Sridhar 1975a and Chapter 11 in this volume). Kannada writers have always treated the entire Sanskrit lexicon as an extension of the Kannada lexicon (cf. Emeneau and Burrow 1962: 1). And indeed, the influence of Sanskrit has not been confined to the borrowing of single lexical items; many writers have employed long nominal compounds and complicated syntactic expressions, creating a Sanskritized style known as *Manipravа:La* (see Chidanandamurthy 1984). From time to time, there have been writers who protested "excessive" reliance on Sanskrit and insisted on writing in "pure Kannada" (for example, Andayya, twelfth to thirteenth century). However, for the most part, Kannada writers have used a style that is a creative and judicious blend of Kannada and Sanskrit: for example, Kumaravyasa (*c.* fifteenth century). Among the thousands of Sanskrit words in Kannada, many have been used for hundreds of years as an integral part of the ordinary language and have been thoroughly assimilated. In fact, it is no exaggeration to say that it is almost impossible to talk or write in Kannada without using at least some words of Sanskritic origin. The new wave of Sanskrit words therefore continues a longstanding practice rather than a new trend.

Sanskritic lexical items in Kannada, which number in the tens of thousands, consist of several classes: outright borrowings (assimilated and unassimilated to the phonological system of Kannada); the class which I shall call "neo-Sanskritic lexicon" resulting from the productive use of Sanskrit derivational processes (see Ananthanarayana 1975) applied to etymologically Sanskrit stems, leading to the creation of expressions not attested in Sanskrit (e.g., *śikSake:tara* "nonteaching," as in "nonteaching staff"); Sanskritic derivational affixes applied to native Kannada or assimilated loan stems (e.g., *ka:nu:nuba:hira* "extra-legal or illegal," *isla:mi:karaNa* "Islamization"); and basically Sanskritic stem compounds, among others. Of these, the most interesting from the structural point of view is the class of neo-Sanskritic words.

Sanskritic derivational morphology active in Kannada

Sanskrit words are not only borrowed into Kannada, they are often *created* in Kannada, by combining Sanskrit stems and derivational affixes. This class of words cannot be described as borrowings because (1) they are often created and used by monolingual Kannada speakers who never studied Sanskrit but internalized its rules of word formation as part of Kannada morphology; (2) these words represent clearly contemporary meanings and are not attested with these or any other meanings in Sanskrit. The following are illustrative cases in point:

vike:ndri:karaNa	"decentralization"
anili:karaNa	"gasification"
vidyunma:nava	"electrical man"
vidyucchakti	"electricity"
vidyudvyavasthe	"electrical system"
stari:kruta	"stratified"
bahiSkruta	"banned"
udde:śita	"proposed"
sanghaTita	"united"
sa:mprada:yika	"traditional"
bhautika	"physical"
vayphalya	"failure"
ma:linya	"pollution"
spardha:tmaka	"competitive"
pra:gji:ve:tiha:saka:ra	"paleontologist"

The above examples illustrate several derivational and morphophonological processes that are not native to the Dravidian structure. These include the various types of assimilation process in the derivatives of *vidyut* ablaut, and discontinuous morphemes, among others. Sanskrit derivational morphology is, therefore, active and productive in Kannada. Thus, the linguistic competence of the modern educated Kannada speaker is best described in terms of coexisting morphological systems, those of Sanskrit and Kannada (cf. Emeneau 1951 for a simialr situation in Vietnamese).

It is true that the Sanskrit-based words of Kannada are created using derivational processes that apply primarily (though not exclusively) to Sanskrit words. In this respect, they are like certain Latin rules that apply only to "learned" words in English derivational morphology. However, there are a number of Sanskrit processes that apply to Kannada stems as well (see below).

Development of Prefixation as a Derivational Process

One of the results of the massive importation of Sanskrit words has been the development of prefixation as a productive derivational process. In an earlier work (Aronoff and S. N. Sridhar 1988), we have argued that prefixation – though marginal in Dravidian languages – has to be recognized as a productive derivational process in Kannada. The following examples are relevant.

asaha:yaka	"helpless"
ahindu:	"non-Hindu"
aniva:si	"nonresident"
avitaraNe	"nondistribution"
apratinidhita	"unrepresented"
ana:Nyi:karaNa	"demonetisation"
punarne:maka	"reappointment"
punarpariś'i:lane	"reexamination"
punarma:pane	"reevaluation"
svasaha:ya	"self-help"
svaśikSaNa	"self-study"
durbaLake	"misappropriation"
upacaraNDi	"underground sewage"
upajilla:dhika:ri	"deputy district commissioner"

In these examples, Sanskrit prefix *a-*, *punar-*, *sva-*, *dur-*, and *upa-* are used to create new words. Several of the above examples involve non-Sanskrit stems (e.g., *caraNdi* "sewage," *jille* "district," *baLake* "use," and *na:Nya* "coin").

Not only are Sanskrit prefixes used with Sanskrit and Kannada stems, certain native words are used as prefixes very productively in modern Kannada. Cases in point are *me:l* "above," *mun-* "pre-," and *hin-* "back-," as in the following illustrative examples.

me:lja:ti	"upper caste"
me:lmanavi	"appeal"
me:lkaTTaDa	"superstructure"
me:lcalane	"upward mobility"
me:lvarga	"upper class"
me:lpa:ya kSe:tra	"carpet area"
mumbayake	"anticipation"
mumba:laka	"advance guard"

mungo:De	"front wall"
munja:garu:kate	"precaution"
himbaDti	"demotion"
himbaraha	"endorsement"

Word class membership

The existence of a lexical category called adjectives is a controversial issue in Dravidian linguistics (see Nadkarni 1970; S. N. Sridhar 1990). It is clear, however, that such a category, if it exists, would have only a small number of native Dravidian words. The recent influx of Sanskrit, Hindi–Urdu, and English words has changed this situation. There can be no doubt that modern Kannada has a rich class of adjectives, populated mostly with borrowed words. English words such as *brilliant*, *stupid*, *wonderful*, *crazy*, *great*, *ordinary*, and *routine* are routinely used in Kannada. Sanskrit adjectives include frequently used words such as *sundara* "beautiful," *amu:lya* "invaluable," and *sabhya* "decent." A large number of Sanskrit adjectives are participles, for example *sanghaTita* "united" and *utpre:kSita* "exaggerated." The *–i:ya* suffix is also widely used: *gaNani:ya*, *ma:nani:ya* "honorable," *sambhavani:ya* "possible." So is *–ika*, as in *sa:rvaka:lika* "eternal, timeless" and *ra:sa:yanika* "chemical." Other adjectivalizing suffixes frequently found are given below (see S. N. Sridhar 1990 for detailed discussion):

-arha	*śikSa:rha*	"punishable"
-a:tmaka	*varNana:tmaka*	"descriptive"
-a:spada	*sande:ha:spada*	"suspicious"
-a:ti:ta	*pakSa:ti:ta*	"nonpartisan"
-ba:hira	*ka:nu:nuba:hira*	"illegal"
-e:tara	*śikkSake:tara*	"nonteaching"
-janaka	*cinta:janaka*	"critical"
-kara	*a:ro:gyakara*	"healthy"
-maya	*sne:hamaya*	"friendly"
-pu:rNa	*satvapu:rNa*	"substantive"
-pu:rvaka	*udde:śapu:rvaka*	"deliberate"
-yuta	*śaktiyuta*	"powerful"

Compounding

There has been a huge increase in nominal and verbal compounds. Nominal compounds reflect the highly nominalized style of English academic discourse, while verbal compounds have come into being to accommodate English borrowings.

kavana sankalana	"poetry collection" (anthology)
kruti caurya	"work theft" (plagiarism)
cuccu maddu	"prick medicine" (injection)
karaDu oppanda	"draft agreement"
saspenD ma:Du	"suspend"
adjasT ma:Du	"adjust" (accommodate)
fe:l a:gu	"fail"
impres a:gu	"be impressed"

In addition, stem compounds, hybrid compounds, loan compounds, and explicator compounds are all used to translate English expressions.

A large number of compounds represent calques on English terms.

aśru va:yu	"tear gas"
ra:tri ji:vana	"night life"
samu:ha ma:dhyama	"mass media"
niyantrita ma:rukaTTe	"regulated market"
sa:ma:jika me:lcalane	"upward social mobility"

In order to make English borrowings readily comprehensible, Kannada writers frequently employ what I shall call "hyponymous compounds," that is, compound nouns where the first element is a loanword and the second word, which designates the semantic category of the loanword, is a familiar Kannada word. For example,

ka:lara: ro:ga	"cholera disease"
Disko: nrutya	"disco dance"
a:spirin ma:tre	"aspirin tablet"

Hybrid or bilingual compounds, that is compounds in which all the elements do not belong to the same language, were proscribed by traditional Kannada grammarians (e.g., Ke:śiraja 1260 CE), who considered such mixing uncouth ("like mixing ghee and oil"). However, contemporary Kannada has thrown this injunction to the winds. It is not uncommon to find compounds in which elements come from three different languages. Consider the following bilingual and multilingual compounds:

taDeya:gne	"stop order"
bampar bahuma:na	"bumper prize"
sankSipta ja:hi:ra:tu	"brief advertisement"
riT arji	"writ petition"

sa:pta:hika la:Tari	"weekly lottery"
nya:ya:nga kasTaDi	"judicial custody"
ucita ho:m Delivari vyavasthe	"free home delivery service"

Modern Kannada abounds in compound nouns in which the first element, usually a loanword from Sanskrit, (but potentially also from Hindi–Urdu), ends in *a:* although it would appear in its unassimilated form with a final *e* when used independently (i.e., not in a compound in Kannada, see S. N. Sridhar 1990).

patrika: go:SThi	"press conference"
samata: va:da	"egalitarianism"
jilla: pariSattu	"district academy"

The usage of this class of what I will call "stem compounds" is slightly unstable: in some cases, the first word of the compound is used in its assimilated form (e.g., *patrike he:Like* versus *patrika: he:Like* "press statement"). In any case, this compound type is restricted to loanwords.

Stratification of loanwords from different sources

It is interesting to note that Kannada grammar makes a three-way stratification among loanwords in terms of phonological and morphological assimilation. Loans from Sanskrit, Hindi–Urdu, and English form a descending hierarchy in terms of their undergoing various grammatical processes.

Kannada does not have word-final *a:*. The final *a:* of loanwords regularly gets changed to *e*. This works without exception in Sanskrit words, as illustrated below:

katha:	*kathe*	"story"
samstha:	*samsthe*	"institution"
va:rta:	*va:rte*	"news"

In Hindi–Urdu words of Perso-Arabic origin, the rule is lexically conditioned – some words undergo the change, others do not, in yet others the rule applies optionally.

kha:ta:	*kha:te*	"account"
galla:	*galla:/galle*	"cash box"
raja:	*raja:/raje*	"holiday"
jumla:	**jumle*	"balance"
niga:	**nige*	"care"

manna:	**manne*	"grant"
daga:	**dage*	"deceit"

English words, however, never change:

go:rilla:	**go:rille*	"gorilla"
kya:mara:	**kya:mare*	"camera"
a:lji:bra:	**a:lji:bre*	"algebra"
ko:Ta:	**ko:Te*	"quota"
ayDiya:	**ayDiye*	"idea"
Dra:ma:	**Dra:me*	"drama"

A comparable stratification is found in verb morphology as well. Sanskrit words readily undergo verbalization with the Kannada verbalizing suffix *–isu*.

prakaTisu	"publish"
ś o:dhisu	"discover/purify"
uttarisu	"answer"

Hindi–Urdu words or Perso-Arabic origin variably undergo this affixation.

cha:pisu	"print"
ghe:ra:yisu	"surround"
dowDa:yisu	"run away"
rava:nisu	"dispatch"
**go:lma:lisu*	"misappropriate"

When English words are verbalized with *–isu* the effect is that of self-conscious or facetious wordplay.

Taypisu	"type"
proTekTisu	"protect"

Instead, a periphrastic mode involving the omnibus verbs *ma:Du* "do, make" and *a:gu* "become" are used to form transitive and intransitive verbs respectively.

saspenD ma:Du	"suspend"	
filTar ma:Du	"filter"	
aDjast ma:Du	"adjust"	
fe:l a:gu	"fail"	
Sa:k a:gu	"shock"	(intransitive)

Phonology

Nonnative phonological features such as aspiration, and clusters such as [str] have become a part of Standard or educated Kannada as a result of the impact of Sanskrit. The impact of English has led to the regular use of sounds such as [f], [z], and [æ], in educated Kannada.

The increased use of Sanskrit has intensified the old debate as to whether the sounds and clusters introduced as a result of Sanskrit borrowings should be regarded as part of the native phonology. This is an important point, since the distinction between standard and nonstandard pronunciation in Kannada is based crucially on the "correct" pronunciation of these sounds, for example aspirated consonants, distinctions among sibilants, and initial consonant clusters.

Syntax

The effect of modernization on Kannada syntax has been quite extensive, though this topic has not been studied at all (see S. N. Sridhar 1988 for a preliminary account). The following observations are, therefore, offered as starting points for a systematic study.[5]

As noted earlier, modernization in Kannada has involved recreation of English modes of conceptualization using Kannada, Sanskrit, and Hindi–Urdu lexical stock. This has inevitably resulted in the creation of new sentence patterns, relaxation of restrictions on others, and revival of marginal structures. The following are worth noting.

Passive

The passive construction is mentioned in classical Kannada grammars going back to at least the thirteenth century, though there are very few attestations in texts. It is hardly ever used in the spoken language. However, with the influence of Sanskrit and, more important and recently, English, the passive has come to be used quite frequently in Kannada writing, especially in the academic and journalistic registers.

vo:Tu ma:Duva hakku iddu: adarinda vancisalpaTTe.
vote doing right being it-from deceive-INF-PASS-PST-1S
"Although I had the right to vote, I was cheated of it."

[5] Some of the syntactic effects noted here are those found in other South Asian languages as well, cf., for example, Ramarao and Ramakrishna Reddy (1984) for Telugu and Y. Kachru (1989) for Hindi.

a:dare	*i:*	*geluvu*	*he:ge*	*sa:dhisalpaTTitu?*
but	this	victory	how	achieve-INF-PASS-be-PST-3SN

"But how was this victory achieved?"

Two observations are in order here. The agentless passive is more common than the full passive. The passive morphology is more widely, and according to some, more felicitously used as participial modifiers in relative clauses. The functions of the passive in Kannada are discussed in great detail in Tirumalesh (1979).

Impersonal passive

In the impersonal passive construction (see S. N. Sridhar 1979b), the agent is obligatorily absent, the object occurs sentence initially with an accusative marker, and the verb has an unmarked (third person, singular, neuter) agreement pattern. This construction has come to function as a popular equivalent of the English passive in contexts of agent suppression.

ve:davati	*avarannu*	*cikitsega:gi*	*a:spatrege*	*se:risala:gide.*
Vedavati	hon-ACC	treatment-for	hospital-DAT	admit-INF-be-PST-3SN

"Vedavati has been admitted to the hospital for treatment."

Complement fronting

The foregrounding of the content of quoted speech in news writing has led to the heavy use of a syntactic structure in which the quoted material, syntactically a complement, appears in the sentence-initial position, and the subject is placed next to the verb.

[. . .]	*endu*	*balla*	*mu:lagaLu*	*tiLisive*
[. . .]	quote	knowledgeable	sources	said-have

"Knowledgeable sources have indicated that . . . "

A psycholinguistic explanation of this structure is that it is apparently motivated by a concern to reduce the processing load imposed by the length and complexity of the quoted material, which would, in a canonical order, intervene between the subject and the verb.

Coordinate use of nonrestrictive relativization

Following the English pattern, modern Kannada employs relative clauses in a nonrestrictive function to add supplementary information about the relativized noun phrase.

gaDira:jyadalliya	*prakSubda*	*paristhitiyu*	*ra:STravannu*
border state-in	tense	situation	nation-ACC
durbalagoLisuttide	*emba*	*sangatiyannu*	*jna:pakadalliTTira-*
weakening-is	that	fact-ACC	remember-
be:kenda		*pradhani*	*avaru . . .*
must-said-REL.PTPL.		Prime Minister-hon	

"The Prime Minister, who said that we must remember that the tense situation in the border state is weakening the nation, . . . "

Nominal style

With the increased cerebralization of the language, there has developed a noticeable tendency to express actions and processes as abstract concepts, leading to the use of highly compressed noun phrases with multiple modifiers. The following items are illustrative.

bas	*sanca:ra*	*pra:rambhadalli*	*taDava:dudakke*	*kSame*
bus	*movement*	*beginning-in*	*delay-becoming-DAT*	*forgiveness*
ke:Lidda:re.				
asked-has				

"[The minister] has asked [the public's] forgiveness for the delay in the resumption of bus services."

kruSi	*varama:na*	*terige*	*vina:yati*	*masu:de*
farm	income	tax	exemption	bill

"farm income tax exemption bill."

Relaxation of selection restrictions

The influence of English is also seen in the relaxation of syntactic restrictions on lexical items. Nouns such as *be:saragaLu* "frustrations" and *ottaDagaLu* "pressures," show the syntactic change brought about by subtle semantic shifts.

New collocations

The influence of English is more pervasive than it may appear on the basis of overt borrowing or mixing. English collocations and idioms are freely translated into Kannada. Such widespread calquing has led to the superimposition of English collocational patterns on Kannada. Consider the following examples:

gambhi:rava:gi tegeduko:	"take seriously"
ku:dalu si:Luva	"splitting hairs"
krama kaygoLLu	"take action"

ti:rma:nakke ba:	"come to a decision"
rajeya me:le ho:gu	"go on leave"
eraDu dinagaLa bhe:Tiya me:le	"on a two-day visit"

This covert influence, which has not been studied in Kannada, is possibly as important in giving modern Kannada its tone and idiom as the more noticeable borrowings.

Style

In this section, three major stylistic trends in modern Kannada are discussed. These may be called (1) empowering the common language (2) classicization, and (3) code mixing.

In contemporary Kannada, one notices a tension between – or at least a parallel cultivation of – two potentially polarizing trends. One is the trend to cultivate a style that is in touch with the spoken language. One sees this in the work of, say, P. Lankesh, in the articles in the immensely popular tabloid *Lankesh Patrike*, and in the work of the *Dalit* writers, such as Devanuru Mahadeva. This style avoids pretentious Sanskrit expressions and abstractions wherever possible and favors racy, colloquial, idiomatic, and often rural expressions, for example *ta:kattu* instead of *śakti* or *sa:marthya* "strength," and the use of expression like *hucca:paTTe*, *yadwa:tadwa:*, and *yarra:birri*, all meaning "crazy." Although this type of aggressively iconoclastic, egalitarian style cannot be said to be characteristic of a very large proportion of Kannada writers, it has, nevertheless, challenged the decorous norms of Standard (largely middle class, largely Brahminical) Kannada, and may well result in an "opening up" of the language. This phenomenon may be called "empowering" of the common language.

This trend turns counter to what is called "classicization," the general tendency in the modernization of Kannada, namely resorting to borrowing from or creating words out of Sanskrit. Modern academic or formal Kannada, with a few notable exceptions, such as in the psychological writings of Dr. R. Sivaram, is highly Sanskritized in its vocabulary. A good case in point is the register of literary criticism, which is replete with words such as *svo:pagnate* "creativity." This classicization obtains in varying degrees even in semiformal writings, such as feature articles and book reviews in newspapers and magazines.

The third major stylistic tendency is mixing with English or codemixing. Codemixing with English is all-pervasive among the urban and semiurban educated population. It is used in technical contexts (e.g., in classroom lectures and technical writings) often out of necessity, that is, because Kannada equivalents of English technical terms and expressions are either not available or, being too new or neo-Sanskritic, are too opaque. Codemixing is also used in informal contexts, such as family get-togethers, business and official transactions, and conversations among friends or colleagues. The prevalence of codemixing is reflected in creative literature (e.g., in fiction, drama, and satire, albeit less in poetry) and the media. The mixed style performs important and specific sociolinguistic functions in the bilingual's repertoire (see S. N. Sridhar 1978). Because of the association of English with domains of power and prestige (administration, judiciary, big business, and academia), mobility (all-India and, indeed, worldwide mobility), and glamour (up-to-date, Westernized entertainment and fashion), the use of codemixing with English enjoys highly positive connotations. It is thus a versatile and powerful resource in the style repertoire of the urban, upwardly mobile, middle-class population.

Codemixing is context restricted, attitude restricted, and medium restricted. In some "standardizing" contexts, such as in textbooks and reference books, or when the author is a committed proponent of "pure" Kannada, it is avoided. It is not used, of course, in contexts such as religious discourses, or when the addressee has an insufficient knowledge of English. It is also more common in informal speech than in formal speech or writing.

Conclusion

Modernization of Kannada is, of course, an ongoing process. The observations made above are, therefore, to be interpreted only as an interim report. Many of the tendencies noted in this chapter are constantly being reevaluated and the language is truly in a state of flux – much more so, perhaps, than at any other period in its history.

Nevertheless, I believe that there is enough evidence involving the coexistence and interaction of linguistic systems – only a sample of which is provided here – to suggest that the study of the modernization of languages like Kannada can be of great interest in constructing models of language change and multilingual competence. Such a study might contribute to the modernization of linguistic theory to truly address language form and function in multilingual societies such as those of South Asia.

Part 8

Language and discourse

17 Language in social and ethnic interaction

Yamuna Kachru

Introduction

All social and ethnic groups operate within a cultural context, and as such, culture becomes a relevant parameter in any discussion of social and ethnic interaction. Before discussing the role of language in interaction in South Asia, it is necessary to briefly examine what is meant by culture and what aspects of culture are relevant to this discussion.

As Halliday (1993: 11) observes, the relationship between language and culture is not deterministic. Rather, "culture and language co-evolve in the same relationship as that in which, within language, meaning and expression co-evolve." What I attempt to do in this chapter is to look at the interaction of language and culture as it manifests itself in strategies of oral and written interaction in South Asia.

The chapter is organized as follows: the first section discusses the interface of the relevant aspects of culture and language in social interaction in the South Asian context, the second section focuses on the general conventions of verbal interaction, and the third section concentrates on the traditions and constraints that operate in academic discourse in South Asia. The conclusion presents a summary of the discussion and points to areas of research that need attention.

The cultural context of language

First, "culture" is not an easy concept to define. It has been defined in many different ways in the anthropological literature. One way of defining culture may be to suggest that culture is "the pattern of meanings embodied in symbolic forms, including actions, utterances and meaningful objects of various kinds, by virtue of which individuals communicate with one another and share their experiences, conceptions and beliefs" (Thompson 1990: 132). Obviously, not all aspects of culture in this sense are immediately relevant to the interaction between language and culture. For instance, not all human behavior and activities, or artifacts that humans use in their lives, involve language. It may be argued that all human activities, behavior, and artifacts are expressed in language (e.g., every activity, behavior, and artifact has a name) and are, therefore, relevant to the interplay of language and culture. Nevertheless, there are certain aspects of culture that are more immediately relevant for *verbal* communication and sharing of experiences within a culture and across cultures. It is helpful to discuss in some detail which aspects of culture figure in any discussion of language and social and ethnic linguistic interaction.

The aspects of culture that are relevant and provide a context for language in verbal interaction for the purposes of this discussion are the following: socialization, belief systems, "face" considerations, and conventions of language usage and use. Socialization takes place in the institutions of family, community, education system, group, and network; these are the sites within which an individual is initiated into becoming a social being. Belief systems are involved in that language reflects our notions of self in relation to family and community. "Face" considerations dictate what is considered polite or impolite in interaction and how people treat each other in linguistic interaction. Finally, successful verbal interaction requires a shared grammar and conventions of language use in terms of who can speak when, with whom, and under what conditions. The rules and conventions that apply to speaking operate in the context of writing as well with necessary adjustments to the channel.

Socialization

The most important institution for socialization in South Asia is still the family (Kakar 1981: especially 113–39). Schools and peer groups play their roles, no doubt, but the belief systems and interactional strategies are still largely based on the explicit or implicit acts and attitudes shared by the family. Family includes not only the nuclear family of parents and children, but also the extended family of grandparents, uncles, aunts, cousins, and their kin by marriage. That is to say, the extended family stretches out on both the patriarchal and matriarchal sides. There are, of course, exceptions to the general rule where in metropolitan urban areas, families may shrink to nuclear families or a much reduced extended family, but the vast majority of children are still socialized in a much larger family setting than the one familiar in the Western European – North American context.

The family, in turn, shares the belief systems and attitudes of the larger community or caste (*jati*) group to which it belongs (Kakar 1979, 1981; Srinivas 1976). There are well-defined codes of conduct for every caste and subcaste, and families in general follow them in matters of food, dress, rituals, marriage alliances, and professions. In short, they follow these codes of conduct in all aspects of life. No doubt this is changing because of urbanization, education, and political awareness. A majority of South Asian families, nevertheless, are still rooted in their caste loyalties and derive their strength from caste groupings (Kakar 1981; Srinivas 1976, 1997).[1]

After family and caste come educational institutions, professional groups, and networking of various other kinds. Educational institutions are not as effective in socializing children in India as they are, for instance, in the United States. They, however, create awareness among children from different families belonging to different caste groups of common interests, rights, and obligations. Friendships formed at educational institutions go a long way toward forming extended networks which are relied upon to achieve certain objectives. (For an example of such an event, see Srinivas 1989: 152.)

Belief systems

Beliefs about self and family that develop as a result of the kind of socialization discussed above have several characteristics. The Indian sense of self is not that of an individualized self; rather, it comprises "three overarching or supraordinate organizations of the self: the familial self, the individualized self, and the spiritual self, as well as an expanding self" (Roland 1988: 6).[2] The psychological organization of familial self "enables Indians [and I would suggest South Asians in general] to function well within the hierarchical intimacy relationships of the extended family, community and other groups" (Roland 1988: 7). The individualized self is characterized by inner representational organizations that emphasize an individualistic "I-ness," competitive individualism and self-actualization, and strong orientation toward rationalism, self-reflection, efficiency, mobility, and adaptability to extrafamilial relationships. The spiritual self is the inner spiritual reality within everyone. It is psychologically deeply engraved in the preconscious of all Indians, even if they make no effort to

[1] The following from Davidar (2002: 214–15) provides testimony to the power of caste identity in South Asian society irrespective of religious affiliation. The context is that of the protagonist, Daniel Andavar, returning to his ancestral village and establishing a settlement of the entire extended Andavar [a caste name] family. Daniel proposes removing all traces of caste from the family in a meeting of the committee of elders. 'Christianity does not recognize caste, and we have all seen the dangers of caste conflict,' he said. 'I would like to suggest that all of us drop caste names and only retain the birth, marriage and death rituals of our caste.' He didn't find a single supporter for the idea and even Ramdoss [Daniel's brother-in-law and his right hand in establishing the settlement] demurred. 'It's all very well to abolish caste in the community anna [big brother],' he said, 'but we are also part of society at large. It gives us our identity. You can not change the entire world.'

[2] Although Roland's research sites were in India and therefore his generalizations are based on Indian subjects, it is safe to conclude that they extend to South Asia as a whole. His subjects in India did include practitioners of different religions and speakers of different languages.

realize it, and it is usually confined to a highly private self (Roland 1988: 7–9). The expanding self is posited to represent "a growing individuation of self" (Roland 1988: 6) with its attendant conflicts generated by the processes of modernization/Westernization.[3]

One's family, community, and group loyalties, as opposed to any other external network related to education, profession, and so on play a significant role in defining the perceptions of *one's own* (e.g., the concept of *əpna* in Hindi and Urdu) versus *the other* (e.g., the concept of *pəraya* in Hindi and Urdu).[4] These perceptions in turn define the parameters of politeness in verbal interaction in the Indian sociocultural context.

"Face" considerations in the context of *one's own* versus *the other* differ subtly but significantly and lead to varying choices in politeness strategies. Interacting with these considerations are notions of social hierarchy that in turn link up with concepts of power and status. In South Asia, determination of relative power, status, and social distance or intimacy of participants in any verbal interaction is based on a complex web of factors. For instance, within the domain of *one's own*, intimacy may take precedence over relative status and power, except when the verbal interaction is in public, and demonstration of intimacy is "inappropriate" according to community norms. One exponent of this constraint is the use of the familiar pronoun between wife and husband in private domains in the Hindi-speaking region, but the use of honorific forms for referring to one's wife or husband in the public domain. Within the domain of *the other*, however, the interlocutor's status and power are to be given exaggerated consideration for projecting one's own "sophisticated" and "cultured" upbringing when the occasion demands. An example of this is the use of expressions such as "*What is your command?*" to mean "*What can I do for you?*" in interaction with an acquaintance, knowing full well that the addressee is not superior or equal in status.[5] Thus, predictability of choices in verbal strategies, including those of politeness, does not depend on a simple weighting of PDR (Power, Distance, and Ranking of Imposition) factors, which refer to the power relationship, social distance in term of intimacy, and ranking of imposition on the speaker or addressee in verbal interaction between participants

3 In the case of India, it is possible to hyphenate modernization/Westernization, as this author, following Roland (1988: xxi–xxii), has done above. However, it would be a mistake to equate modernization, as defined in Singer (1972), with Westernization, as defined in Srinivas (1966). As Roland (1988: xxii) observes, in the case of India, "Westernization and modernization are . . . intertwined in highly varying complex ways and cannot be easily or readily separated" (For a detailed discussion, see, among others, Singer (1972), Srinivas (1966), and Y. Kachru (1994: 339–40)).

4 The convention of transliteration followed in this chapter is based on the IPA symbols for representing vowel quality and length, nasalization of vowels, retroflexion, aspiration, and so on.

5 The translation equivalent in Hindi for the English question is "*kyā āgyā̃//huqm hɛ?*" (literally, "What is (your) command?").

(Brown and Levinson 1987: 15).[6] These characteristics are discussed in greater detail in the section "General conventions of verbal interaction" below.

Conventions of language use and usage

All languages have redundant features. Conventions of usage, or grammar, provide a number of choices among these redundancies. Conventions of use exploit the redundancy of language and the choices provided by the grammar for various specific purposes. South Asian language use provides interesting examples of this phenomenon. An example from an Indo-Aryan language – Hindi – and a Dravidian language – Kannada – may make this interface of usage and use clear.

For reasons of space constraints, the following is a partial description of the phenomenon. Hindi has a distinct second person pronoun marked [+honorific]– *ap*–which is used for elders, new acquaintances, and anyone considered worthy of respect. It takes plural agreement even when it refers to one individual. The plural first and third person pronouns are used in the honorific sense, and as usual, control the plural agreement. There is a honorific particle, *jī*, which is used with names to denote respect, for example *gand^{h}ī jī* "Gandhi [+honorific]," *indira jī* "Indira [+honorific]." The imperative verb has the following forms:

(1) root form of the verb for example, *lik^{h}*! "write!"
(2) verb + familiar second person agreement marker, for example *lik^{h}o*!
(3) verb + infinitive marker, for example *lik^{h}na*! "write!" (implies, when convenient)
(4) verb + second person [+honorific] marker, for example *lik^{h}iye!* "Please write down!"
(5) verb + second person [+honorific] marker+optative marker+plural agreement, for example *lik^{h}ẽ*! "Please write!"
(6) verb + second person [+honorific] marker+optative marker+future marker, for example *lik^{h}iyega!* "please write!" (implies, when convenient)

The pronoun *ap* "you [+honorific]" can co-occur with the forms in (1–6) whereas the other pronouns cannot co-occur with them.

In addition to these grammatical markers, there are lexical items and expressions which are marked for politeness and respect. Just a few examples

[6] Brown and Levinson (1987: 15–17, 74–84) claim that the gross weight of factors PDR (Power, Distance, and Ranking of Imposition) predict the choice of politeness strategies in verbal interaction. Their discussion of politeness strategies crucially depends on the notion that every speech act potentially threatens the face, or self image, of the hearer, that is, it is a face threatening act (FTA). The PDR factors represent the relative Power of hearer over speaker, the social Distance between speaker and hearer, and the Ranking of imposition on the hearer as calculated by the speaker in performing the FTA.

are given here. The item *zəra* "a little" used with the imperative forms in (1–3) softens the command. Any kinship term used with the imperative forms has the same effect. So does the expression *kripa kərke* or *mehərbanī kərke* "being kindly" along with *zəra* "a little" with the forms in (1–6). In some contexts, in several parts of the Hindi region, the use of passive is more polite than the active, for example *əb cəla jae* "let's leave now," uttered when the interlocutors know that the speaker is not accompanying the addressee, and it is urgent that the addressee leave (so that, say, she does not miss her flight), is more polite than the direct imperative, "*ap əb jaiye/cəliye, jaẽ/cəlẽ*" "please leave now" or, even *əb apko jana/cəlna cahiye* "you should leave now," as Pandharipande (1979) argues and contrary to what Srivastava and Pandit (1988) claim.

In Kannada, according to S. N. Sridhar (1990: 203), there are two second person pronouns, singular *niinu* and plural *niivu*. In addition, the reflexive plural pronoun *taavu* is used as an ultra honorific second person plural pronoun in markedly formal contexts (124). The plural forms of the second and third person pronouns are used as honorifics. In imperatives, the suffixes *–i* and *–ri* indicate politeness. The polite form of the vocative attention-getter is *enri* "what," which is commonly used by wives to get their husband's attention (149, 179). There are several forms of the information question word *eenu* "what" used with a number of clitics that functions as a vocative. The clitic *–ē* is attached to a profession name (doctor, teacher, etc.) or to a proper noun augmented by the respect-marking morphemes *avaru* "he/she honorific plural" or *–gaḷu*, the plural marker, as in *ramaNNanavarē* "Sir, Mr. Ramanna!" or *mantrigalē* "Sir/Madam Minister" (180). Thus, honorific forms occur in several parts of the Kannada grammar.

A language with a complicated system of honorific marking is Maithili, an Indo-Aryan language spoken in northeast Bihar. It has been described in detail in U. N. Singh (1989). See also Krishnamurti (1992) for a discussion of politeness in Telugu, Shah (1994) for Shina and Burushaski, and Van de Walle (1993) for Sanskrit.

One of the relevant parameters for conventionalization of verbal behavior in South Asia, in addition to age, gender, and other social variables, is caste. Terms of address, greetings, patterns of interaction are all determined by the caste of the speaker and the addressee (Mehrotra 1985: 97–102). For instance, certain forms of greetings in the Hindi region, such as *palagən məharaj* "I touch your feet, Sir" are uttered only by non-Brahmins when greeting a Brahmin (Mehrotra 1985: 98–9). Terms of address such as *pəṇḍit jī*, *ʃastrī jī*, and *acary məhodəy* are reserved for Brahmins; *ṭʰakur saheb, raja saheb, and ray saheb* are for the Kshatriyas (warriors); and *lala jī, and Seṭʰ jī* are for the Vaishyas (traders). Although these terms of address are undergoing change in the cosmopolitan culture of the metropolises, they are still prevalent in urban areas and quite common in nonurban settings. For details of the effect of caste on language use and usage in South Asia, see, among others, Bright (1960), Ferguson and Gumperz (1960), McCormack (1960),

Mehrotra (1985), Nair (1971), Pandit (1963), Ramanujan (1968), Shanmugham Pillai (1965), and Shapiro and Schiffman (1981).

Oral and literate traditions of language use

Unlike the Anglo-American tradition of "essay-text literacy," characterized by a heavy emphasis on explicit, decontextualized, impersonal language (Gee 1986), Indian tradition continues to exhibit an interesting interdependence of orality and literacy. There are oral textual genres that later transform themselves to written texts and written texts that have the characteristics of oral texts. Thus, the dividing line between orality and literacy in South Asia is not sharp. Features of oral genres permeate the written, and the characteristics of the written show up in the oral texts. One good example of the former is the medieval devotional poetry that was composed for oral recitation or singing, and later became a significant part of the literary canon in Indian languages from Kashmir in the Himalayan region to Kanyakumari at the southernmost tip of the Deccan Plateau. The reverse is true of the genre of traditional personal letters in Hindi. Letters do not have neat subparts of salutations, body, and signature. Instead the first line of the letter usually contains both the salutation and the signature. The closest English translation is something like: "May to the [attributes] addressee the writer's greetings [a variety of expressions depending upon the age, sex and relationship to the addressee] reach."[7] This is like the verbal greeting upon meeting someone: "(Term of address) I bow to you/touch your feet," and so on. The term of address is optional in face-to-face greeting, but is obligatory in written letters for obvious reasons: the addressee and the writer cannot see each other and the writer has to identify herself/himself in terms of his/her relationship to the addressee (for a further discussion of orality/literacy in South Asian languages, see Chapter 13).

Popular versus high literature

Throughout the known history of South Asia, the boundaries of folk versus high literature have been permeable. The epics, *Rāmāyaṇa* and *Mahābhārata*, the Buddhist *jātaka* stories, the tales of *Panchatantra*, and the medieval saint poetry are good examples of this. All these works represent later compilations of earlier oral texts. The *Mahābhārata* probably began around 500 BCE as a narrative poem about the rivalry between the descendants of two royal brothers, Kauravas and Pāṇḍavas. Through the centuries it absorbed many philosophical ideas and around 400 CE was compiled into a work of 107,000 octameter couplets – seven

[7] The Modern Standard Hindi sentence that represents this traditional opening of a letter may read as follows: *pūjyə pitajī ko unkī beṭī sujata ka prəṇam pahũce* "May the respectful greeting of his daughter Sujata reach worthy-of-worship father."

times the length of the *Iliad* and *Odyssey* combined. It contains one of the most important philosophical treatises of India, the *Bhagvadgīta*, as well as treatises on staecraft (Shānti Parva) and numerous subnarratives. The *Rāmāyaṇa* is the story of the legendary *Rāma*, a brief epic that grew to its present form by accretion from the third century BCE to second century CE. The *jātaka* stories (fifth century CE) contain narratives depicting the Buddha's earlier lives. *Panchatantra* (500 CE) is the source of fables that later spread to the Middle East and possibly from there to Europe. Although there are legends about who the authors of these works were, it is difficult to establish authentic authorships and accurate dates for them. They seem to have begun as oral epics/narratives and were told and retold through the centuries. Each telling resulted in additions reflecting the imagination of the storyteller, and the final product was eventually systematized and committed to writing. Once written down, they became works of High or elite literature.

General conventions of verbal interaction

The general account given above needs to be modified in several respects in view of the fact that South Asia is extremely pluralistic. Many different languages, subcultures, and literary traditions live and interact with each other in the region. The four language families, though exhibiting numerous features of convergence, still show characteristic patterns of linguistic behavior in both usage and use. There are several major traditions of literary creativity, with their origin in Buddhist, Jain, Sanskrit, Tamil, and much later, Perso-Arabic and Anglo-European traditions. Each major language of the region has its own tradition of literature, though there have been crosscurrents of influence between regions and languages throughout the history. The entire region has shared philosophical thought, religious practices, and social organization, which justifies treating South Asia as a linguistic, sociolinguistic, and literary area (D'souza 1987; Emeneau 1956; B. Kachru 1992a; Masica 1976; Pandit 1972).[8]

[8] The shared philosophical ideas across Buddhism, Hinduism, Jainism, and Sikhism include the notions of *karma*, cycles of birth and death, the ultimate goal of escaping from this cycle through spiritual quest, especially devotion to (a personal) God or to an abstract entity without attributes. The medieval literature in Indian languages shows a remarkable coalescence of ideas in the devotional compositions of Hindu, Buddhist, Jain, Sikh, and Sufi saints.

The shared social organization is reflected in the notions of family and caste. For a discussion of caste across religions, see Gupta (1991), Ahmad (1978), H. Singh (1977), Raj and Raj (1993), and Bannerjee (1997). H. Singh (1977) is a brief introduction to caste distinctions in various religions in different parts of India; Ahmad (1978) discusses caste distinctions among Muslims and the efforts by communities to establish Arab, Iranian, Moghul, or Afghan lineages to distance themselves from common converts of Indian origin to Islam; and Bannerjee (1997) is an appraisal of the caste distinctions prevalent in Christian churches and communities in India.

Verbal interaction between a speaker and an addressee has been viewed in terms of *ritual* (Goffman 1967) and *politeness* (Brown and Levinson 1987). The sociologist, Goffman, observes (1967: 44–5):

> [S]ocieties everywhere, if they are to be societies, must mobilize their members as self-regulating participants in social encounters. One way of mobilizing the individual for this purpose is through ritual; he is taught to be perceptive, to have feelings attached to self and a self expressed through face, to have pride, honor, and dignity, to have considerateness, to have tact and a certain amount of poise . . . The general capacity to be bound by moral rules may well belong to the individual, but the particular set of rules which transform him into a human being derives from requirements established in the ritual organization of social encounters. And if a particular person or group or society seems to have a unique character all its own, it is because its standard set of human-nature element is pitched and combined in a particular way.

Brown and Levinson (1987) base their definition of politeness on the notion of face in Goffman (1967: 5) "an image of self delineated in terms of approved social attributes." They identify two aspects of politeness in verbal interaction: positive face and negative face. Positive face refers to a want or need to be desirable to others, therefore, it functions as a strategy of friendliness or camaraderie. Negative face refers to a want or need not to be imposed on or impeded by others; therefore, it functions as a distancing strategy of formality. Brown and Levinson (1987) further describe a number of strategies and their linguistic realizations that maintain and enhance positive and negative face of interlocutors in conversation. Their data are drawn from multiple languages of the world.

The difficulty with this view of verbal behavior is that any linguistic exchange between participants is viewed as face threatening. It also requires that all utterances be analyzed in terms of their relation to the positive or negative self-image of the speaker or hearer. Research based on interaction in African, Asian, and Latin American contexts, however, raises serious issues with the concepts of *face* and *politeness* as conceived in the works mentioned above (see Y. Kachru 2003).

The main problem is that the South Asian concept of self is not that of an individual self, as was pointed out above (see Y. Kachru 1994; Roland 1988). This becomes clear as we look at the concepts of face and polite behavior in South Asia.

It is impossible to cite the lexical items expressing these concepts in each language of the region. The examples here will be drawn from Modern Standard Hindi, one of the most widely known languages of the subcontinent. The concept of face in the Hindi-speaking region of India, for example, has some distinct properties. The word *mũh* "face" refers both to the physical part of the body, and the social face of the person, but does not necessarily include the person's name, status, or fame in society. The person's name, status, fame, or reputation is referred to as *nam* "name" (the corresponding concept in Kannada is *māna*). Thus, to lose one's face is *mũh kala hona* "for one's face to be blackened," and to lose one's name, status, reputation, or fame is *nam miṭṭī mẽ milna* "for the name to be in the dust" or *nam ḍūbna* "for the name to drown."

There is no single equivalent for politeness in the major languages of South Asia. Social interaction is governed by notions of *məryada* "decorum, propriety of conduct" and *lihaj* "considerateness, deference."[9] Protection of each participant's face and name is essential for maintaining decorum and deference in all social interactions. One crucial property of both *mũh* and *nam* is that the concepts do not exclusively refer to individual face and name; rather, they refer inclusively to the face and name of the group that is relevant for interaction in the specific communicative situation. The relevant group may be the family (*pərivar* or *kul* or *xandan*), the caste (*jati*), the village (*gãv*), the institution one is associated with, or whatever is germane to the context of situation. An undesirable action perpetrated by an individual or directed toward an individual may result in blackening the face of an entire community or drowning the name of an entire group. Therefore, all actions have to be weighed according to the notions of *məryada* and *lihaj*.

An essential component of the notions of *məryada* and *lihaj* is "humility," which is reflected in overstating the addressee's status and downgrading one's own in verbal interaction to demonstrate one's civilized, cultured upbringing referred to above.

The concepts of *məryada* and *lihaj* together subsume the notions of "discernment" and "deference" discussed in works on linguistic interaction in Japanese (Ide 1989) and Korean (Hwang 1990), respectively. Discernment refers to "the almost automatic observation of socially-agreed-upon rules" (Hill *et al.* 1986) that characterizes Japanese verbal and nonverbal behavior. Deference has been defined as "power as a social fact, established a priori by the differential positions of individuals or groups within the social structure" (Treichler *et al.* 1984: 65). Although the two concepts are defined differently, one in social behavioral terms and the other in ideological terms, their linguistic manifestations take the same form: grammaticization of honorific forms. South Asian languages have distinct honorific forms at all grammatical levels and at the level of discourse, as do Japanese and Korean (see the examples of Hindi and Kannada given above).

Considerations of *məryada* "decorum" and *lihaj* "deference" combined with the notions of *əpna* "one's own" versus *pəraya* "the other" have resulted in

[9] The original literal meaning of *məryada* is "limit, bounds," later extended to mean "bounds or limits of morality or propriety" (Monier-Williams 1899 [1990]).

distinct strategies of verbal exchange in South Asia. For instance, the younger in age greet the elders first by saying "I bow to you", "I touch your feet," or equivalent expressions in a majority of languages (see Krishan 1990). The elders normally reply "May you live long" or "May you be happy." Equals may greet each other by invoking the name of a deity such as "*ram, ram*" or "*jɛ ram jī kī*" in a large part of the Hindi-speaking region (Krishan 1990). In interaction between interlocutors belonging to different religious communities, it is usual for people to switch to a mode of greeting of the addressee to show solidarity. Thus, a Hindu may greet a Muslim with *adab ərz* or *səlam* "salutation" and a Sikh with *sət srī əkal* "true + hon. + Timelss, or The One Without Attributes is True" [comparable to "God is Great" in theistic terms], or a Muslim or Sikh may greet a Hindu with *nəməste*. Among the educated professionals, the English greetings, such as the casual "hi," "hello," or the more formal "good morning," are replacing the traditional greetings in inter-community interactions. Similarly, a "good bye" obviates the necessity to choose between *xuda hafiz* "may Allah protect you", *sət srī əkal*, and *nəməste* at leave taking.

Other conventions of interaction specify that in assemblies, where all age groups are together, younger people may not speak unless spoken to. Silence is a way of showing respect, not of defiance, so in most cases of requests or criticisms from elders, the younger interlocutors observe silence as a mark of their acceptance of the request/criticism. Verbal expression and demonstration of love between parents and children, husband and wife, or other kin, remarks on the physical appearance (good looks, weight, height, etc.) of individuals, enthusiastic reaction to anyone or anything is considered crossing the boundaries of *məryada*. Expression of personal sentiments are expected to be muted. The more these constraints are observed by someone, the more respect s/he gets as a "serious" (*gəmb*^{h}*īr*) and "sophisticated" (*susə̃skrit*) person.

In South Asian languages, speech acts such as making requests, paying compliments, voicing criticism, and others employ strategies that are very different from what is common in Anglo-American English. For instance, indirect requests such as "Could you open the door?" is not used for polite requests. In fact, direct requests, such as imperatives, are considered more polite (Y. Kachru 1998; K. K. Sridhar 1991). This is not as strange as it may seem, since Indian languages have various devices to make imperatives polite and respectful. Some such devices are the use of kinship terms to address the interlocutor, using honorific endings on verbs (see above), the use of special particles that transform the direct imperative into a respectful request, and the use of expressions such as "a little," as has been mentioned above (see D'souza 1988; Ferguson 1976; Srivastava and Pandit 1988 for a more detailed account). In fact the utterance that would be most polite depends on, in addition to the age, gender and status of interlocutors, the role relationship between the speaker and the addressee, directionality of the benefit of the act referred to in the propositional content of the utterance, and implicit assumptions about the social context of discourse (Srivastava and Pandit 1988).

It may be useful here to digress a little and make clear that it is necessary to keep the concepts of status, rank, and role quite separate in discussing the relationship between interlocutors in South Asia (Y. Kachru 1998, 2001) instead of conflating them under social distance, as in Brown and Levinson (1987).

According to E. Goody (1978), status is "hierarchy and position in a system of rules." Status is a given in the social system by birth, by age, by gender, by economic, educational, or other relevant variables. As Cicourel (1972) states, "status relationships are based upon norms (external to immediate interaction) that have a broad consensus by third parties in ego and alters' social networks or some larger community."

Rank is hierarchically organized with reference to a social institution, for example the principal of a school or the commander of an army. In an environment where rank takes precedence over all other considerations in determining speech levels, as in military organizations, there will usually by no ambiguity. In everyday social life, however, rank may be negotiable.

Cultures vary as to which relationships are treated as rank relationships and which ones are treated as status relationships. For instance, in some cultures, a teacher not only commands respect by virtue of his/her rank, he/she also has a high status. This explains why in South Asia, it is unthinkable to address one's teacher by his/her first name. This is true of most Asian and African cultures as opposed to, say, the contemporary American or British culture.

Role refers to the less institutionalized position one assumes in some interaction. Examples are host/guest, captain of the team/players in sport, and so on. Even a lower status person in the role of guest deserves markedly polite treatment in South Asia.

The interplay of the concepts discussed above in characterizing politeness in South Asia is reflected in strategies such as the following (the data are from Hindi):

(1) Welcoming status-equal guests to one's home: *əpna hī g^hər səmə$\dot{j}^h$iye* "Please think of this as self's + emphatic particle home," that is, "Consider this your own home." The reflexive pronoun *self* refers to the guest, the second person pronominal subject of the verb *think*, and not to the host.
(2) Introducing one's children to the guests: *ye apke bəcce hɛ̃* "These are your children."

(3) Addressing one's older colleagues in notes or letters as "Respected name + honorific particle."
(4) A long opening paragraph asking about the well-being of the recipient and his/her family before coming to the point of the business letters, that is letters of request for off prints, information, and so on.
(5) Mixing of languages to achieve various goals (B. Kachru 1978a, 1982a). An example of such mixing with English is presented below.

The traditional ways of verbal interaction, however, are undergoing change, as a result of modernization/Westernization, as has been mentioned above in the context of greetings and leave taking. One further illustration of this change can be seen in the following example.

Consider the speech act of apology.[10] There are no exact translation equivalents in Hindi for "apology," "apologize," or "sorry" just as there are no expressions comparable to "thank you" of English (Apte 1974b). One expresses one's apology about an unwanted situation by saying something like the following:

*mujʰe bəhut kʰ*ed/ *əfsos hɛ* ... "I am very distressed ... "
bəɽe dukʰ/əfsos kī bat hɛ ... "It is a matter of pain/sorrow ... "

One apologizes for a perceived transgression by asking for forgiveness by using the lexical items *kʂəma* (S) or *mafī* (P-A).

The item *kʰed hona* is enough to express regret at minor inconveniences suffered by an interlocutor; there is no implication of the speaker being responsible for them, however. More serious matters, such as any reporting of serious illness or death by an interlocutor, require *dukʰ hona* "to feel pain/ sorrow." The semantic range of *əfsos hona* encompasses both these meanings. None of these involve or imply responsibility on the part of the one expressing distress, or sorrow. In contrast, one indicates acceptance of some responsibility for some transgression when one asks for forgiveness with *kʂəma* or *mafī mãgna*.

The social convention is that in intimate circles (i.e., between friends, among siblings, etc.) one does not apologize for minor lapses except for saying some thing like *gəltī/bʰūl ho gəī* "mistake happened" (Hindi), which makes it quite clear that it was unintentional and more like an oversight. That, however, is changing as a result of linguistic and cultural contact with English.

Among educated speakers, code mixing with English is very common (B. Kachru 1978a, 1982a). In the code-mixed variety, the contexts in which

[10] Bilingualism in English and the resultant changes in speech acts are discussed in greater detail in Y. Kachru (1995b) on which this account of apology is based.

apology is expressed, and the devices by which this speech act is realized are different from the traditional ways of expressing regret or asking for forgiveness. The following example occurs in a recent Hindi short story, where a friend is apologizing in English for becoming lost in thought and not paying attention to the car, which is making a strange noise:

"*əjīb hɛ tū īva, itnī der se gaṛī avaz kər rəhī hɛ ɔr tū jane kəhā̃ gum hɛ. bəs, tera ʃərīr yəhā̃ pər hɛ, tuj^he kuc^h sunaī nəhĩ deta na.*"

"*hā̃ suna nəhĩ* . . . I am sorry Kiran." Ansal 1990: 98

"You are strange, Eva; the car has been making this noise for such a long time and you are lost God knows where. You are here just in your body. You aren't able to hear a thing, are you?"

"No [lit. yes], I didn't hear it . . . *I am sorry, Kiran.*"

Speech acts related to expressing gratitude, paying compliments, voicing criticism, and so on also show the impact of bilingualism in English so that one hears the expressions *thanks, thank you* very often even in the intimate domain.

Academic and scientific writing

The discussion of language in social interaction must include language use in academic and scientific–technological fields. Traditional Indian discourse used the genre of poetry, that is, verse form, for all discourse including philosophical, scientific, and technological discourse. The verse form is easier to commit to memory and since knowledge was transmitted orally, the verse form was a suitable vehicle.

Although prose was not unknown, the development of different registers and genres in prose is a relatively recent phenomenon in South Asia, going back to approximately three centuries, after contact with the West began.[11] Academic and scientific–technological prose genres in modern South Asian languages are a relatively recent phenomenon and show influence of the

11 The term "register" (Halliday and Hasan 1976) refers to the specialized language that is used in texts that embody three types of information: what is being talked about (i.e., the topic), what is the relationship of the participants in the discourse (speaker-audience as in formal lectures, reporter–readers as in news reports or academic reports), and which channel is used in the discourse (speaking versus writing). One can thus talk of scientific register, journalistic register, and so on. Genre (V. Bhatia 1993) refers to specialized language use with a communicative purpose and a highly structured and conventionalized text form. The purpose, the conventions, and the constraints on what counts as contribution to the particular genre are shared by a professional or academic community. Thus, we can identify the genres of poetry, literary criticism, scientific reports, academic papers in specific disciplines, and so on.

English language. However they still reflect the Indian cultural values, as recent research has shown (see Y. Kachru 1988, 1992, 1995a, 1996, 1997, and 2003).

The tradition of philosophical debate in South Asia, though intense, still projected the value of *saṃvāda* "dialogue, discussion", instead of that of *vivāda* "dispute, argument." According to Heimann (1964: 170–1):

> The method applied in Indian epistemology is that of gaining higher knowledge through discussion. One standpoint is first pronounced, and then confronted and denounced by a second, a third and further *pakṣas* "wings" or "viewpoints." Finally the highest, or at any rate the at present no-more-refutable notion is reached. The Indian textbook of philosophical systems, the *Sarva-daršana-saṃgraha*, "the compilation of all viewpoints," is so arranged that the first mentioned is the worst, and the last the best, from the *Vedāntic* standpoint which is here proclaimed. It is divergency which helps to elucidate the comparatively higher, i.e., wider grasp of the problem in hand. *Saṃvāda*, "discussion," instead of *vivāda*, "dispute," is the methodical means of gathering all the different facets of the truth, which is only indirectly and gradually approachable.

The same values are echoed in modern instructions to writers. A standard textbook on grammar and composition published by the National Council of Educational Research and Training, India (Vyas *et al.* 1972: 209), mentions the following categories of essays: descriptive (*vərṇənatmək*), narrative (*vivrəṇatmək*), deliberative (*vicaratmək*), explanatory (*vyak^{h}yatmək*), and imaginative (*kəlpənatmək*). These are further regrouped into three: descriptive (including narrative), deliberative (including explanatory), and imaginative. Argumentation is one subtype of deliberation or explanation; it is not a distinct category. The "deliberative" is not necessarily equivalent to the Anglo-American "argumentative" essay. In an argumentative text the goal is to convince the audience that the view put forward in the text is right and that all competing opinions lead to undesirable consequences. In the deliberative text, on the other hand, the points in favor as well as those opposed to a particular position are put forward so that the audience is informed on all facets of an issue, and the decision as to which one of the positions presented is right or wrong is left to them. The advice given to students in Vyas *et al.* (1972) is as follows: "[F]or elaboration (*prəsar*) [i.e., the body of the essay], material should be categorized carefully to facilitate the sequential presentation of points. Everything that is said must be proved (*prəmaṇit*) by arguments (*tərk*), facts (*tət^{h}y*), events (*g^{h}əṭna*) or quotation (*udd^{h}ərəṇ*) [citing authority] and they should be arranged in such a form that *readers can easily arrive at the conclusion desired by the writer*" (emphasis added). The purpose is not to *provide solutions* and *convince* the audience of their rightness, rather, it is to *lead* the readers to find the right solutions. Thus, deliberative essays are indirect by design. The instruction to students conforms to the Indian tradition.

The indirectness referred to above is encountered in academic writing by South Asians and has caused much anxiety in the Western academic institutions. It has led to the erroneous assumption that South Asian scholars have insufficient command of the English language. It is only recently that inquiry into traditions of literacy has begun and culturally preferred styles of writing have been recognized by researchers (see Ferdman *et al.* 1994).

In addition to indirectness, academic discourse in South Asia displays some or all of the following characteristics. Unlike in the West, and like the Chinese scientific writing (Taylor and Chen 1991), few argumentative texts carry a detailed critical evaluation of earlier research. Instead, earlier research is mentioned as a background to current research in order to place it in the same tradition. More digressions are included and tolerated. A "high style" with rhetorical flourishes is not considered unsuitable (Y. Kachru 1992). Citing authority is considered one kind of proof or evidence (Y. Kachru 1997).

Conclusion

Language both reflects and gives shape to social and ethnic interaction in South Asia. Many of the traditional patterns of interaction are undergoing changes as global influences permeate the local society and culture. In turn, the global language, English, as used in South Asia is absorbing the social and cultural values of the region and is becoming the medium of South Asian cultural experiences. This interaction of language and regional sociocultural conventions is a vast area of research that is waiting for a more sustained research effort.

18 Language and the legal system

Vijay K. Bhatia and Rajesh Sharma

Introduction

In South Asia, law and language are inextricably intertwined not only in the construction and consumption of sociolegal relationships and in the authorization of sociopolitical and individual actions but also in the creation of social structures, the nurturing and shaping of political ideologies, and the negotiation of social and individual identities. In order to have a comprehensive understanding of the role and function of language in legal systems, it is necessary to specify the complexity of interpretations of some of the terms and issues arising from this dynamic relationship, especially in the contexts of multilingual and multicultural contexts.

First, although legal systems are invariably influenced by religion and culture, they have an inseparable relationship with language, which is typically used as an instrument of legal expression, both in spoken and written forms. We are more familiar with the use of written language as a vehicle for the communication of legal content in modern times, but the use of speech in legal settings was common in ancient times. The ancient Indian legal systems provide good examples of such uses of speech in legal contexts. The legal system during the Vedic period created social norms to regulate human behavior, but there were no facilities to record these rules and regulations in the written form. The social code embodied in the *Shruti* was memorized and handed down from one generation to another. One may argue that this did not represent a legal system in the modern sense of the term; however, in a more general sense, it was a system based on morals to regulate human behavior, which is the main function of any legal system. The concept of Dharma, referred to as *Dhamma* in Buddhist texts, was nothing but a moral code of conduct. The legal world has now recognized Dharma (*Dhamma*) as a form of the "rule of law."

Second, in modern legal systems, language is not just a means of communication or expression, but is also a right and a privilege. Language represents the culture of a group of people or country, and as such, cultural rights are protected by recognizing and protecting the language used by such groups. Legal documents such as the International Covenants of Cultural and Political

Rights (ICCPR), Human Rights Act, Fundamental Rights, and Bill of Rights have all included language as a right, ensuring that no one is discriminated on the basis of language. Minority languages have often been given special treatment. Thus, language is not simply a mode of expression in legal systems; it is also one of the important components of any legal system, and Constitutions in various countries often explicitly recognize the status and use of languages in various contexts. The language used in the Constitution itself reflects the importance of that language in a particular country. Language thus serves as a mark of national identity in the legal system. The authoritative text of the Constitution is an important indicator in this regard. A Constitution may also include terminology, such as "national language," "official language," and "recognized language." These descriptors, among other factors, are also constrained by religious and cultural influences. In general, one may see that a multicultural and multilingual country often uses the term "official language," as in the case of India and Sri Lanka, whereas a nation aspiring to promote a single culture, such as Pakistan, invariably uses "national language" to show the supremacy of one language and culture in that country. The Eighth Schedule of the Indian Constitution lists eighteen languages (later extended to twenty two) that are designated as "recognized languages." These languages recognize the cultural traditions of particular groups of people (see Chapter 7).

Languages used in courts, on the other hand, may not necessarily be representative of a country's political, cultural, and religious philosophy as such. For example, in the Indian context, the use of English as the language of the Supreme Court and state high courts is largely determined by the use of the British Common Law system in the country. In the Indian Constitution, however, there is an element of flexibility allowed to high courts in the use of languages other than English, depending upon the seat of the high court and the official language adopted by that state legislature. At present, in some high courts, regional languages have been allowed in court proceedings but judgments are still being written in English. The Supreme Court, however, does not allow such flexibility.

Another important issue arising from the context in which language and legal systems are explored is the diversity in the region. South Asia is a medley of diverse, though geographically as well as historically related, countries that offer an interesting landscape for the study of the use of language in the legal systems. Among India, Pakistan, Sri Lanka, Nepal, and Bangladesh, all except one have had long-term historical links with Britain; they were British colonies at one time, and have thus inherited a common law system. However, over the years they have drifted in various directions, creating their individual blends of common law systems. The differences, in spite of an overwhelming presence of common British heritage, are distinctly visible in their use of language, especially in the context of law, and also in their distinct sociopolitical ideologies and dominant religious practices, which play a significant role in the construction and consumption of legal discourse in each of these countries.

This chapter investigates the historical development of legal systems in South Asia, with a focus on the use of language. It begins with a brief account of the sociopolitical and legal systems in South Asia, which will focus on historical development, and identify distinctive relationship between language use and legal systems. We will then take up more recent provisions for language use in each of these countries and analyze them for their typical use of linguistic variants in different legal contexts, especially in legislation and judiciary at various levels.

Historical development

The historical development of legal systems in South Asia, especially from the point of view of language use, can be seen in terms of three major influences: those of Indic (Hindu) philosophy, including Buddhism; the Moghul rule; and finally the British colonial rule.

The origin of the ancient legal system may be traced back to the Vedic period. Although these were not written down at that time, they were memorized and passed on from one generation to another. The spoken language of that period was Sanskrit, and hence it could be regarded as the language of the law (code of human behavior). The most authoritative and influential text of ancient Indian laws is found in the Laws of Manu, known as *Manu Samhita* or *Manava Dharma Shastra*, which dates back to about the beginning of the Common Era (see Doniger 1991; Lingat 1998). The Laws of Manu codifies the sacred laws of each of the four chief classes or *varnas*. In a technical sense, the Law of Manu was not law as such, but a moral code governing human behavior. Jurisprudentially one of the purposes of law is to regulate human behavior, which is not very different from the function of the legal code in the modern sense. In this context it is interesting to note that the great Indian epic, the *Ramayana*, may also be seen as a body of law. Widely representing the Hindu values and way of life, the story of *Ramayana*, like the Laws of Manu, incorporates a code for the rights and duties of a king toward his subjects. It embodies a code of conduct for people in sociopolitical contexts even today. *Ramayana* is available in hundreds of versions, in all the major languages of South Asia, the original being *Valmiki Ramayana* in Sanskrit and perhaps the best known one the *Tulsidas Ramayana* in Awadhi/Hindi.

Among the earlier codes of law, the first code found in written form and deciphered were the edicts of King Ashoka (304–232 BCE). The edicts of Ashoka survive to this day because they were carved on stones. They were found at several places in India, Nepal, Pakistan, and Afghanistan. Most of them were written in the Brāhmī script. The language used in the edicts found in the eastern part of India is a type of Māgadhī, the official language during the period of Ashoka. The language found in the western part of India is closer to Sanskrit. One bilingual edict in Afghanistan is written in Aramaic and Greek.

Ashoka's edicts explained "state morality" and "private individual morality." Both these types of morality were based on the Buddhist values of compassion, moderation, tolerance, and respect for life (Dhammika 1993). Ashoka also adopted the foreign policy of "peaceful coexistence." The judicial system was fair, less harsh, less open to abuse, and the introduction of the appeal system was one of its landmarks. The principle of *Dhamma* based on the Buddhist philosophy was the guiding principle. Modern legal scholars have rightly accepted *Dhamma* as a form of the "rule of law." *Dhamma* includes no evil, much good, kindness, generosity, truthfulness, and purity, all of which were used to develop state and individual morality.

After Ashoka, the second most famous Indian polity or legal system has been associated with Kautilya, better known as Chanakya (*c.*350–*c.*275 BCE). He was the prime minister of Chandragupta Maurya of the Maurya Dynasty, which dates back to the fourth century BCE. Kautilya's famous treatise, *Arthashastra*, depicted the political role of the king, which included the treatment of the poor, the slaves, and the women. His ruthless approach to practical politics has often drawn comparison with Machiavellian Prince (Brians *et al.* 1999). Although Magadhi was the official language of the kingdom, the treatise was written in Sanskrit.

After this period several kings ruled in different parts of India. The bedrock of these rulers' policies was religion. Initially, the rulers were Indian and the governments and the judicial systems were all influenced by philosophy indigenous to the country. In this respect, the Moghul period was the turning point, as by then, a language (Persian) and religion transplanted (Islam) became part of the Indian social fabric, which continue to play an important role in Indian society even today. The legal system of India made some advancement particularly in the sixteenth century, when Akbar (1542–1605) introduced Urdu as the official language of the court. Although the political and judicial systems were largely based on the Shariya, he promoted a secular thinking by showing respect for other cultures. His state was not secular, yet one may see in it the precursor of the secular system, which India adopted in the Constitution after it became independent.

During the period of Aurengzeb (1658–1707), this religious and cultural tolerance gave way to a strong imposition of Islam as the state religion. Hindu temples were pulled down to make way for mosques. Such religious intolerance created social unrest, which led Shivaji, a Maratha ruler of that period, to establish and assert Hindu rule. To restore the language, religion, and culture, he started using Sanskrit as his official language as a reaction to the imposition of Islam. During his rule an effective judicial system was established, but it was primarily confined to his kingdom in the Maharashtra region. The judicial system of Aurengzeb based on Shariya, on the other hand, continued to dominate most of India.

The next major impact on the Indian legal system came from the British occupation of the country. It brought common law tradition to India, which became an integral part of the court system. The English language and the English law both found a significant place in the Indian legal system. The British changed the system gradually, first by implementing the Warren Hastings Judicial Plan of 1772 in Bengal, Bihar, and Orissa. The system was called the *Adalat System*. The technical terms used in the courts were all in Urdu, such as *moffusil, faujdari*, and *dewani*. Personal laws dealing with marriage and inheritance were based on religion. For Muslims the "laws of Quran" and for Hindus the "Laws of Shastras" (the law books) were used. The judicial plan also included courts of appeal, which were called *Sadar Nizamat Adalat* and *Sadar Diwani Adalat*. In 1780 another change was made in which *Dewani Adalat* was presided by an English Judge, who was assisted by native law officers, when disputes involved a Hindu or a Muslim. When a dispute was not related to personal laws, the guiding principle was "justice, equity and good conscience" (M. P. Singh 1997).

The Regulating Act of 1773 created the Supreme Court of Calcutta and the judges were barristers from England or Ireland. It was not clear which law the Supreme Court had to apply. Although, it mostly applied English law, there was no clearly stated policy on this issue. It was not clear whether Indians were always governed by the English law. In criminal matters, the court applied the law of England, which was unfamiliar to the local public, and thus created a number of problems (See Raja Nandkumar case (1775) and Patna case (1777) for the problems created by this system).

As the local people could not go to the Supreme Court in Calcutta (now Kolkata), the British Government created circuit courts under their judicial plan of 1790. These were like the moving courts of England, in that the magistrate was often assisted in the case of Islamic law by a *Kazi* and a *Mufti*, to decide on the issue of *Fatwa* (rulings). These religious people always assisted the local courts in the administration of justice. They were locals and had better knowledge of local customs, circumstances, and languages.

Lord Cornwallis, the governor general, made a provision in 1793, that every regulation had to have a preamble and title by which the nature and purpose of the regulation could be clearly and easily ascertained. The regulations were to be produced in the form of sections and clauses to be numbered serially. Each section was to have marginal notes to show the subject given within it. Regulations of each year were to be recorded properly, printed, published, and circulated regularly. Such detailed specifications were meant to make laws more accessible to the general public, which has always been a concern in legal discourse. This collection of regulations is called the *Cornwallis Code*. Cornwallis also made possible the appointment of local people as law officers, as they had better understanding of the local languages and local problems. Before this, it was common to find no shared language between the law officers and the accused. Lord Warren Hastings (1732–1818) extended this policy by appointing Indian judges to try criminal cases, which was not possible before his time, although they were not empowered to hear cases involving a British national. The English judges had all the powers but had neither the language nor any understanding of the local culture, which often led to widespread dissatisfaction among the local people. Around this time, the names of the courts were changed to reflect the English nomenclature, such as "court of commissioner," "district court," and "sessions court".

Language in legal systems in modern South Asia

In spite of geographical proximity, considerable intercultural and sociopolitical overlap, and common historical developments, most of the South Asian countries have developed into very different sociopolitical entities. Today these countries display significant diversity in their constitutional provisions for the use of languages in specific contexts.

South Asian countries use a variety of labels to legislate the use of language in different functional domains and contexts. These include "official language," "national language," "associate language," and "regional language." Language use in legal system functions primarily in written mode as a vehicle for the expression of legislative intentions, in forms such as statutory provisions, ordinances, rules and regulations, and by-laws. Language also functions somewhat differently, though again in the written mode, in genres such as cases and judgments, legal opinions, and court proceedings for record purposes in various courts – in particular, the Supreme Court, the high courts, and the district courts. In the courts it also functions primarily in spoken form to negotiate justice as part of the adversarial system. In addition to these contexts, the use of language in parliamentary and other legislative contexts is specified in the Constitutions. Closely related to this is the use of language in government affairs, especially in the written mode. If law provides an interesting and complex setting for various functions of language, South Asia provides a rich multilingual and multicultural setting for the use of a number of different languages, some ancient and indigenous, others more universal. For this study, we will focus on three major aspects of language in legal systems: languages used in legislative contexts, languages recognized by the Constitutions in each of the South Asian countries as a mark of sociopolitical identity, and languages prescribed in the Constitutions for use in the parliament or legislative contexts. We will now consider some of the issues emerging from the diversity in the provision and use of languages.

People's Republic of Bangladesh

The People's Republic of Bangladesh came in to existence in 1971 and comprises territories formerly known as East Pakistan. Although Bangladesh broke away from Islamic Pakistan, it has retained its essential Islamic character in its Constitution. It has, however, replaced Urdu by Bangla (Bengali) which is "the state language of the Republic." Section 41 of the constitution provides for freedom of religion. However, there is no specific provision for the use of any language other than Bangla in every day sociopolitical, bureaucratic, and legal contexts.

The Republic of India

In the case of India, the situation is much more complex for a number of reasons. First, it has enormous diversity in the use of languages, cultures, religions, and sociopolitical beliefs and ideologies. India is a multilingual, multicultural, and secular nation. Although the Constitution of India, which came into effect in 1950, designated "Hindi in Devanagri script" as the official language of the country, it also provided for the use of English for all official purposes of the Union for an initial period of fifteen years. As Austin (1999: 266) points out, this policy was essentially an effort to bring together a diversity of several languages, cultures, and sociopolitical beliefs to foster national unity by adopting a common language. Although framers of the Indian Constitution carefully avoided giving one of the regional languages the status of the "national language," they could not help "using a tactful euphemism" to promote Hindi as the "official language of the Union." There was considerable opposition to this provision from the non-Hindi speaking states, and for this reason, the Constitution provided for the parliament to legislate continuation of English after the period of fifteen years. There was also a clear provision in the Constitution for the use of regional languages within individual states. Article 345 clearly stated that the legislature of a state may by law adopt any one or more of the languages in use in the state or Hindi as the language or languages to be used for all or any of the official purposes of that state. Article 351 provided for the promotion of Hindi as the official language of the Union, so that it could serve as a medium of expression for all the elements of "the composite culture of India" (Austin 1999), and to secure its enrichment by drawing on Sanskrit and other regional languages.[1] Article 344 of the Constitution provided for the appointment of a commission to report on the progressive use of Hindi as the official language and restrictions on the use of English for communication between the

[1] In this context, it is interesting to note that the Supreme Court in 1976 disapproved a scheme by the Government of Tamil Nadu to pay pension to anti-Hindi agitators as it was seen as violating the provisions of Article 351.

Union and a state or between one state and another. The Official Languages Act of 1963 provided for English to be used for purposes of communication between the Union and a state that had not adopted Hindi as its official language. It also provided that where Hindi is used for purposes of communication between one state that has adopted Hindi as its official language and another state that has not adopted Hindi as its official language, such communication in Hindi shall be accompanied by a translation of the same in the English language. (See Sridhar 1987 for a detailed analysis of the issues and politics involved in the spread of Hindi in India.)

Language of the courts

The Indian Constitution provides for all the proceedings in the Supreme Court and the high courts, and the authoritative texts, which include bills and amendments and acts passed by either house of parliament or either house of the legislature of a state, the ordinances promulgated by the president or the governor of a state, and the orders, rules, regulations, and by-laws, to be in the English language. The governor of a state, however, is empowered, with the previous consent of the president, to authorize the use of Hindi, or any other language used for any official purposes of the state, including the proceedings in the high court that has its principal seat in that state. The Official Languages Act of 1963 also empowers the state governor to provide for the optional use of Hindi or other official language in any judgment, decree, or order passed or made by the high court in that state. In all such cases, whether it is the bills, ordinances, or acts passed by the state legislature or judgments, decrees, or orders passed by the high court, it is mandatory to provide a translation of these documents in English, which are considered to be the authoritative versions. However, English continues to be the only official language used in the Supreme Court. In this context, M. P. Singh (1994: 837) refers to an interesting case, *Madhu Limaye v. Ved Murti* (1970, 3 SCC, 738: AIR 1971 SC 2481), in which one of the interveners insisted on arguing in Hindi, which was objected to by the counsel on the opposite side on the basis that he could not follow Hindi. The Supreme Court suggested three alternatives to the intervener: (1) to argue in English, (2) to allow the Counsel to represent his case, or (3) to give written argument in English, none of which was acceptable to him. This gave no option to the Supreme Court but to cancel his intervention, as the language of the court was English.

In this context, it is interesting to note that in spite of strong support from leaders like Mohandas K. Gandhi and India's first Prime Minister Jawaharlal Nehru, the use of Hindustani as the official language did not find favor in the Constitution, although the leadership of the most important political party, the Indian National Congress, had adopted Hindustani as the language of the Independence movement, as it was seen as bridging the widening gulf between

Hindus and Muslims (see S. N. Sridhar 1987). History reveals that although the British introduced English to India, they continued using Urdu for official purposes. But nationalist Hindus wanted to change the official language from Urdu to Hindi, which is written in an Indian script. This debate between Hindus and Muslims continued right up to the Independence of India. To promote a commonly used variety, Nehru and Gandhi supported the idea of one Hindustani language, which "drew its vocabulary from both Sanskrit and Arabic–Persian roots" (Austin 1999: 273) and which could be written in either Devanagari or Perso-Arabic script. But when the British divided India into two countries, India and Pakistan, Muslims who primarily comprised the population of Pakistan opted for Urdu as their official language and Indians opted for Hindi, in Devanagari script, as India's official language. However, Hindustani has survived as the language spoken in the courts, especially in the district and other subordinate courts. It is seen as the language of the masses, and is very common in the negotiation of justice in the lower courts, especially in the Hindi-speaking states. Common expressions from various Indian languages and English are often mixed with the formal use of Hindi in lower courts and remind one of the popularity of Hindustani as the court language. These expressions are part of the mixed code, which is illustrated in items such as the following: *Dafa 302* (Section 302), *Taje Rate Hind* (Indian Penal Code), *muwakkil* (client), *vakalatnamah* (lawyer's form), *halafnama* (affidavit), *banam* (versus), *vald* (son of), *muddaiya* (plaintiff), *Muddailaya* (defendant), and *patwari muharrir* (government officers).

The Kingdom of Nepal

Historically, Nepal has always been an absolute monarchy, with the *panchayat* system of courts at the lower level. However, in recent years, widespread pro-democracy protests toppled the *panchayat* system to bring in democratic values. The Constitution, broadly based on British practice, is the fundamental law of Nepal. It vests sovereignty in the people and declares Nepal a multiethnic, multilingual, democratic, independent, indivisible, sovereign, and constitutional monarchical kingdom. The Constitution of the Kingdom of Nepal follows the adversary legal tradition. Establishment of an independent and competent system of justice was one of the basic objectives of the Constitution.

The constitutional safeguards include the right to conserve and promote one's language, script, and culture and the right to education in the student's mother tongue. The right to receive information about matters of public importance and the right to secrecy and inviolability of one's person, residence, property, documents, letters, and other information also are guaranteed.

Part three of the Constitution provides for the fundamental rights of citizens. Although some elements of fundamental rights guaranteed in the 1962

Constitution are reflected in the 1990 Constitution, the latter provides new safeguards.

In addition, sections on fundamental rights provide for, among other rights, freedom of thought and expression. Prior censorship of publications is prohibited, and free press and printing are guaranteed. Unfettered cultural and educational rights are also guaranteed.

Article 6 of the new Constitution assigns the Nepali language in the Devanagari script the status of the national and also the official language. In addition, it provides for the use of all the other languages spoken as the mother tongue in the various parts of Nepal as the national languages of Nepal. Although Nepal is officially regarded as a Hindu kingdom, the Constitution also gives religious and cultural freedom to other religious groups, such as Buddhists, Muslims, and Christians. All laws, rules, and regulations issued by or on behalf of the government are in Nepali. It is the language in which most of the official transactions are undertaken. Professional facility in the use of language depends not only on superior skill in reading and writing the Nepali language but also upon the development of special skill in the use of the language which is peculiar to the law. Most of the research works in law targeted at Nepalese lawpersons are done and published in Nepali. Those authors who want to reach a wider audience, however, prefer to write in English.

Islamic Republic of Pakistan

Pakistan was born in 1947, as a result of the struggle by a section of Muslims in the British occupied India for a separate homeland. Urdu enabled the Muslim community, during the period of its ascendancy, to preserve its separate identity in the subcontinent. Muslim identity had already become a serious issue as the Muslim power started to decline in the region, and the British had conceded separate electorates in the Government of India Act of 1909, which confirmed the Muslim League's position as an all-India party. The demand for a separate Muslim State became popular during the Second World War under the banner of the All-India Muslim League.

The legal system in Pakistan is primarily based on English common law, combined with elements of the Sharia, the Islamic legal code. Commercial law is almost entirely English, with English case law having much persuasive authority. Ultimate judicial power rests with the Supreme Court. There is a high court in each of the four provinces. The Sharia Court has eight Muslim judges, including the chief justice; four of the judges are qualified to be high court judges and three members of the Ulema (scholars versed in Islamic law). Other courts exercise civil and criminal jurisdiction. Special courts and tribunals deal with specific types of cases, such as drugs offences, income tax appeals, and traffic offences.

The Constitution of Pakistan provides for the use of Urdu as the national language, although it further provides for the use of English for official purposes so long as the arrangements for the use of Urdu are not adequate. Similar to India, Pakistan also initially specified this period as fifteen years. Section 251 of the Constitution provides that the national language of Pakistan is Urdu, and arrangements shall be made for its being used for official and other purposes within fifteen years from the commencing day or until arrangements are made for its replacement by Urdu. It further empowers the provincial Assembly to prescribe measures for the teaching, promotion and use of a provincial language in addition to the national language.

The Republic of Sri Lanka

Sri Lanka was subject to domination by a number of foreign powers, including the Portuguese, Dutch, and British. From the time of Independence in 1948, the legal system of Sri Lanka has developed into a complex mixture of English common law and Roman–Dutch, Sinhalese, Muslim, and customary law. Under Dutch rule in the late eighteenth century, the colonial administrators codified the rules of inheritance, marriage, and divorce law in order to facilitate the application of Muslim family law. Preference was given to customary usage and the provisions of the "Mohammedan Code" over classical legal treatises. These special laws were preserved and adapted after the British defeated the Dutch in 1799. The Code was initially applicable to Muslims but was later extended in late nineteenth century to others.

Although Sri Lanka has a Buddhist majority, the 1978 Constitution does not establish Buddhism as the state religion. It gives Buddhism the "foremost place," imposing a duty on the state to protect and foster Buddhism, while assuring every person freedom of thought, conscience, and religion, including the freedom to profess or adopt a religion or belief of his or her choice, and guaranteeing all citizens the freedom to manifest their religious beliefs in worship, observance, practice, and teaching.

The Constitution of Sri Lanka clearly declares Sinhala and Tamil the official languages of the country (Section 32), whereas in the list of national languages, English is added (Section 33). Section 39 allows all the three national language to be used for legislation, so that the laws are written in all the three national languages, and Section 39(2) gives equal authority to all the three versions, if any dispute arises from interpretations of different versions. Similarly, in court proceedings, all the three languages are permitted (Section 43). The Constitution of Sri Lanka contains very detailed provisions for language use in various public, sociopolitical, and legal contexts. Every citizen, for instance, is entitled, alone or in association with others, to enjoy and promote his or her own culture and language. The Constitution also forbids any restrictions to be placed on the exercise of this right, except those prescribed by law as are necessary in a democratic society.

The Sri Lankan Constitution seems to be very comprehensive in its recognition and specification of languages in the country for various purposes. As mentioned above, the official languages of the Republic are legislated to be Sinhala and Tamil. In addition, three languages are recognized as national languages: Sinhala, Tamil, and English. In the parliament, a member is entitled to use any of the national languages. Similarly, Sinhala and Tamil are given the status of languages of the administration throughout the Republic. Sinhala is used for the maintenance of public records by national and regional public institutions and local authorities in the capital territory and all the regions except some where Tamil is used. Section 36 of the Constitution also allows the use of Tamil or English in any area where Sinhala is used as a language for the maintenance of public records. A person is entitled to receive communication from, and to communicate and transact business with, any official in his or her official capacity, in either Tamil or English and to receive a response to such communication from such official in the language in which the person communicated. The person is also allowed to obtain copies of documents related to official records in either Tamil or English. Similarly, in any area where Tamil is used as a language for the maintenance of public records, a person is entitled to exercise the rights and to obtain the services in Sinhala or English.

As far as legislation is concerned, Section 39 of the Sri Lankan Constitution explicitly provides that all Acts of Parliament, Statutes of Regional Councils, and subordinate legislation shall be enacted in Sinhala, Tamil, and English, and in the event of any inconsistency between any two texts, each such text shall be regarded as equally authoritative. The languages of the courts are legislated to be Sinhala and Tamil throughout the Republic. The language of record and court proceedings is also Sinhala in the courts situated in all the areas of the Republic except in some regions where Tamil is used. Similarly, court proceedings can be initiated and pleadings submitted in any of the national languages, that is Sinhala, Tamil, or English. However, if the judge, juror, party, or applicant is not conversant with the language of the court, he or she is provided by the State interpretation and translation into Sinhala, Tamil, or English, to enable him or her to understand and participate in the proceedings.

Section 45 empowers the minister in charge of Justice to issue directions permitting the use of English in the records and proceedings in any court for all purposes and every judge is bound to implement such directions. Similarly, a judge may, at the request of the parties to any proceedings, use English in relation to the records and proceedings where the use of such language would facilitate the expeditious conclusion of proceedings. The medium of instruction is either Sinhala or Tamil, and if facilities are available, English. At the university level also, wherever reasonably possible, a person is entitled to be instructed in any course, department, or faculty of any university in any of the national languages. As we see, Sri Lanka, with the exception of India, has the most comprehensive and explicitly stated language policy in the Constitution.

Language, law, and religion

Apart from language, the second most important influence on the legal system of any country is that of religion. The situation in South Asia is quite revealing in this respect. Even a surface level analysis of the Preambles to the Constitutions of the five nations in the region shows interesting contrasts. India and Sri Lanka are secular and democratic, whereas Pakistan and Bangladesh are Islamic countries. Bangladesh is also a democracy. Nepal is a Hindu State, with a constitutional monarchy. It is interesting to see how these characteristics are reflected in the construction and interpretation of the laws from these countries.

Constitutional Preambles are highly conventionalized and standardized performatives. They have important communicative functions to perform and often take highly formulaic formats. One of the most typical syntactic patterns used for Preambles is, "We, the people of (Name of the Country), do hereby give ourselves this Constitution." All the Preambles from these five countries conform to this general syntactic pattern, though they all show considerable variation in terms of length, lexico-grammatical realizations, and substance. Although they are often ignored when one considers applications of laws, and thus attract least attention, they often are extremely revealing in the way they are written. In the context of the five countries in the South Asian region, these Preambles to respective Constitutions are different in length. Preambles to Indian and Sri Lankan Constitutions are relatively brief, whereas that of Pakistan is very long. In fact, we have two different Preambles, one from Pakistan Constitution and the other from Sharia Law, and the two are very different in character. Preambles from Nepal and Bangladesh are somewhere between the two extremes. In terms of style, most of them have typical legal style, with each brief paragraph beginning with either "whereas" or "wherein," except in the case of India, which is written in a more modern style, starting off with "We, the people of India, having solemnly resolved to constitute India into a sovereign socialist secular democratic republic . . . do hereby adopt, enact and give to ourselves this constitution." In the case of Sri Lanka, it begins with a conventional whereas clause, "WHEREAS it is the will of the people of Sri Lanka to establish a stable legal order . . . NOW THEREFORE, WE THE PEOPLE OF SRI LANKA . . . do hereby give unto ourselves this CONSTITUTION." In terms of the style differences between the two, the one from India uses more modern plain language, and the other from Sri Lanka uses more conventional and obsolete expressions, such as the "whereas" and "do hereby give unto ourselves." This assumes more significance as we look at the dates of these constructions; the Indian Constitution was enacted in 1950, whereas the Sri Lankan Constitution is more recently enacted in August 2000. However, both these Preambles have a number of other aspects in common, especially the principles on which the Constitutions are based, such as those of democratic values of justice, equality, and liberty. Although the two countries have somewhat different religious provisions, in that Sri Lanka gives to Buddhism the foremost place, while at the same time, giving adequate protection to all religions and guaranteeing to every person the rights and freedoms to follow their own religious beliefs, whereas India has more open secular policies, the two are very similar in their democratic pronouncements.

The other three countries Nepal, Bangladesh, and Pakistan seem to have strong religious commitments. Nepal is a Hindu State, whereas both Bangladesh and Pakistan are Islamic nations, and their respective Preambles indicate these commitments, except in the case of Nepal. Pakistan, as indicated earlier, has two sets of laws, the Constitution and the Sharia Law. The Preamble to the Constitution is written in a very traditional style with a number of clauses beginning with the conventional "Whereas," "Wherein," and "Therein." However, the most striking element of the Preamble is the reference to Islamic values and traditions. It begins with "Whereas sovereignty over the entire Universe belongs to Almighty Allah alone, and the authority to be exercised by the people of Pakistan within the limits prescribed by Him is a sacred trust," positioning Islam above everything else. Although there is a commitment to democratic principles and values, to freedom, equality, tolerance, and social justice, as in democracies like India and Sri Lanka, these principles and values are defined within the boundaries of Islam. One invariably gets the impression that the requirements of Islamic values as set out in the Holy Quran and Sunnah are supreme. In the enacting section also religion plays a predominant role:

Now, therefore, we, the people of Pakistan,
Cognisant of our responsibility before Almighty Allah and men;
Congnisant of the sacrifices made by the people in the cause of Pakistan;

Faithful to the declaration made by the Founder of Pakistan, Quaid-i-Azam Mohammad Ali Jinnah, that Pakistan would be a democratic State based on Islamic principles of social justice;

Dedicated to the preservation of democracy achieved by the unremitting struggle of the people against oppression and tyranny;

Inspired by the resolve to protect our national and political unity and solidarity by creating an egalitarian society through a new order;

Do hereby, through our representatives in the National Assembly, adopt, enact and give to ourselves, this Constitution.

As we can see, Islam, sacrifices of the people, faithfulness to the Founder of Pakistan, preservation of democracy, protection of national and political unity, and creation of egalitarian society appear in that order of importance. It is interesting to note that politics and religion have always been mixed in Islam. The history of Islam shows religion and governance have been treated as one. According to Islam, the purpose of a good government is to provide an environment for the practice of their religion. In 1977 Zulfiqar Ali Bhutto made some superficial changes by outlawing alcohol and changing the weekly holiday from Sunday to Friday, without any substantive Islamic reforms. General Zia introduced an Islamization program in 1979, introducing new measures based on Islamic principles of justice. He introduced a welfare and taxation system based on *zakat* and a profit-and-loss banking system based on Islamic prohibitions against usury. He relied on a strong policy grounded in Islam, which gave rise to factionalism between Sunnis and Shias, caused ethnic disturbances in Karachi between Pakhtuns and *muhajirs*, increased animosity toward Ahmadiyyas, and revived Punjab–Sindh tensions. More profoundly, he also advocated an ideal image of women in Islamic society, which was antithetical to that existing in everyday life. A major development in the Islamization program was the passing of the Shariat Bill in 1991, which required all laws in the country to conform to Islamic values. It is clear, therefore, that Islamic principles and values play a dominant role in Preamble to the Constitution of Pakistan.

Sri Lanka, which also provides for Buddhism as the dominant national religion, has no mention of religion in the Preamble, and the prioritized order is establishing "supreme law to strengthen institutions of governance," "wider sharing of power," enshrining "democratic values, social justice and human rights," facilitating "economic, social and cultural advancement," and promoting "peace, ethnic harmony and good governance." Nepal, which again is proclaimed as a Hindu State, has no mention of religion in the Preamble to the Constitution. Though this also begins with the conventional "Whereas" clauses, it focuses more on the role of the will of the people in the governance of the country. The main functions of the Constitution seem to be to reduce the role of absolute "Monarchy" to a "constitutional monarchy;" to consolidate "adult franchise," 'The parliamentary system of government," and "the system of multi party democracy;" to promote "liberty and equality;" and "to establish an independent and competent system of justice."

In the case of Bangladesh, which once again is an Islamic nation, the Preamble, on the surface, begins with the conventional religious incantation, that is *bismillah-ar-rahiman-ar-rahim*, that is "In the name of Allah, the Beneficent, the Merciful." However, unlike Pakistan there is no elaborate attempt to make democratic functioning of the government subservient to the principles and values of Islam, except a general acknowledgment of "the high ideals of absolute trust and faith in the Almighty Allah." The dominant principles and values of "nationalism, democracy, and socialism meaning economic and social justice" are emphasized as "the fundamental principles of the Constitution." The priority is "to realise through the democratic process a socialist society, free from exploitation – a society in which the rule of law, fundamental human rights and freedom, equality and justice, political, economic and social, will be secured for all citizens."

This brief account of the Preambles from the five South Asian countries shows how different countries make use of the same standardized syntactic pattern to create documents that are very different in terms of their "communicative intentions" in order to respond to very different rhetorical contexts. The Preambles to the Constitutions from India, Sri Lanka, and Nepal largely share their concerns for upholding democratic principles and values, whereas the one from Pakistan puts Islamic principles and values above those of democracy. The Preamble from Bangladesh appears to be closer to the first three, but with some obvious influence of the Islamic values. In another respect, the Preamble from Nepal is somewhat unique in emphasizing the role of the constitutional monarchy as the authority for enactment of constitutional provisions.

Conclusion

In this chapter we have made an attempt to offer a brief overview of language use in legal systems in South Asia, emphasizing specifically the historical development of legal systems and language use in ancient India, through the periods of Moghul and British occupations, to modern times. We have attempted to show the common heritage in the region in terms of democratic values, freedom of expression, language use, and religious practices. We have also been able to show that these countries, in spite of the common geographical and sociocultural influences, have drifted in different directions in terms of their use of languages, religious practices, and legal systems. The present-day South Asia is thus a complex mix of democratic values, varying religious beliefs and practices, sociopolitical affiliations, and linguistic traditions.

19 Language in the media and advertising

Tej K. Bhatia and Robert J. Baumgardner

Introduction

The function of language in South Asian media is multifaceted, colorful, and distinct in a number of ways. These characteristics are the direct consequence of the complex linguistic, social, political, historical, and economic situation in the subcontinent. What might appear to be graffiti to an uninitiated Western eye may in fact turn out to be wall paintings whose evolution can be traced back to rock paintings of the sixth century BCE. Wall painting in its present form makes an integral and distinct part of the South Asian media scene and symbolizes the economic and developmental vibrancy of the region. Other manifestations of this vibrancy are popular films by Bollywood (Bombay+Hollywood) cinema. Not only do they offer unique appeal in terms of cinematic techniques, dance, drama, and music, but they also offer a viable marketing alternative to Hollywood in the world of entertainment. Similarly, Hindi–Urdu music is notable for making inroads into the popular music of the youth of North America and other parts of the world. The reach of South Asian media indeed extends well beyond the one-third of the world's population that inhabits South Asia.

The scope of the topic at hand is quite vast in terms of its geographical and linguistic variants, media types, and their intrinsic manifestations. However, the focus of the chapter is to address the main issues that confront contemporary South Asian media. In the process of answering the questions raised, this chapter will identity innovative aspects of South Asian media together with a rich array of its conventional and nonconventional forms found in South Asian media; assess the present state of South Asian media in terms of its linguistic diversity; and examine textual characteristics of South Asian media discourse. For the purpose of isolating textual characteristics, the chapter focuses on the written advertising discourse present in two media modalities: wall paintings and print media. The generalizations drawn from such an analysis are, to a large extent, valid for written South Asian media discourse in the region, and to a lesser extent for spoken discourse. A number of topics and issues, such as production, reception (intelligibility), effectiveness, the influence of various media forms on each other, and sociocultural history, are beyond the scope of this chapter (see T. Bhatia 2000 for treatment of these topics).

Major issues

Having remained unchanged for centuries, rural populations constitute the heart of South Asia. According to the 1991 Census, for instance, most of India (about 77–78 percent of the total population) lives in more than half a million (total 627,000) villages and speaks in numerous languages. The same is true to some degree for other South Asian countries of the region as well. The dispersion phenomenon poses a twofold challenge to advertisers and mass communicators wishing to reach rural audiences:

- *Geographic dispersion*: Rural audiences are scattered over many small villages, many of which are still beyond the reach of conventional media, and corporate giants and champions of rural marketing, such as Hindustan Lever (see McDonald 1993–1994: 47), are struggling to reach them.
- *Linguistic dispersion*: South Asia is a multilingual subcontinent with dozens of major languages and hundreds of dialects/varieties (see Chapter 10 for details).

The question of language and dialect choices together with spatial dispersal makes the task of reaching the rural audience an even more daunting one. There are other variables too, such as income disparity, social stratification, and gender scatter, that can complicate the already nightmarish problem. However, they are not as fundamental and immediate as the issues of geographical and linguistic dispersion. Therefore, the following are the most urgent concerns of mass communicators, advertisers, and marketers.

1 How do media planners, advertisers, and marketers reach the unreachable with the most suitable media to ensure maximal spatial reach?
2 How can the consumers be reached linguistically and effectively?
3 Assuming that one can reach rural masses, then the critical problem still remains: how to mobilize villagers to the point of sale or the focal point of action (e.g. for developmental campaigns such as family planning)?

Media: terms and classification

In South Asia media are broadly classified into two groups: conventional and nonconventional. The term "conventional" refers to electronic media forms, such as television, radio, and print, whereas the term "nonconventional" denotes "wall" and "video-van" advertising. This usage is in agreement with typical usage by experts in South Asian media in general and Indian advertising and the mass-media industry in particular.

The major question therefore is how to reach the unreachable?

The easiest solution would be to reach rural population by means of the conventional electronic media (radio and TV). Following are the limitations of the conventional media forms:

- TV
  - TV is beyond the reach of rural South Asia. Electricity is not yet accessible to many if not most people living in rural areas. According to the Indian Readership Survey, 1995, the national TV network, Doordarshan's penetration in rural areas was 28.8 percent and that of cable and satellite TV was 2.7 percent. Remote rural areas are still inaccessible to this powerful medium;
  - more than half the reach of TV is created through secondary viewing programs such as community viewing;
  - reach and frequency of regional language and vernacular programming is still limited;
  - the ownership of color TV sets is extremely low. This in turn places severe limitations on the artistic delivery of the message;
  - viewers' low involvement with advertised messages is another weakness.

- Radio
  - has maximum reach but is still under a lot of government control;
  - program options are limited;
  - no visual content;
  - Like TV, low involvement with ad messages on the part of listeners.

- Cinema
  - experiencing downward trend in viewership;
  - popular primarily with young males only;
  - not free.

- Print media
  - low level of literacy and lack of availability at the right time and right place are still problems.

Nonconventional media forms: Innovation and reach

According to one estimate, approximately 238 million adults in India are still beyond the reach of the conventional media. In order to overcome the problems posed by the limitations of electronic media, the media have devised the following strategies:

- go where rural India lives and go where villagers go;
- tailor the message according to rural viewing tastes and linguistic preferences;
- bring interactivity with the message, which is usually lacking within the conventional media;
- bring state-of-the art narrowcast and broadcast viewing to rural audiences.

This strategic planning led media innovators and entrepreneurs to develop the idea of mobile video vans. Dr. J. K. Jain's Video on Wheels (VOW) was credited for the pioneering attempt in this area. Virtually unknown until 1987, VOW has transformed and modernized rural media and advertising. Launched initially for political campaigns, it has found its niche in every communicative aspect of rural India. VOW takes advertisers' messages from urban centers to rural areas via electronically equipped vans with capabilities of both narrowcasting and state-of-the art broadcasting. The success of the video vans has enabled media planners to emulate the act of VOW in India and outside India. These vans include point-of-purchase video displays, which enable advertisers to screen their commercials and noncommercial messages in busy rural markets and communicate with villagers by means of live performances in a language/dialect variety appropriate for the region, unlike network television advertising, which is primarily in national languages, such as Hindi, Urdu, or English. Furthermore, these video vans are capable of building into their programs the interactional capacity that national TV and satellite networks lack. The success and power of video vans to send political, commercial, and social/developmental messages are so overwhelming that Indian video vans (both governmental and commercial) have become the subject of national and international media attention (e.g. BBC, CNN, and Japan's national TV (NHK) have done stories on this uniquely Indian medium).

The video van media can be termed "hybrid." This hybrid medium utilizes a mix of conventional and nonconventional forms coupled with old and new media. Though some of the limitations still persist, the solution is unorthodox and innovative in nature. Therefore, it is not surprising that video van media form is considered "an excellent model" for third-world advertising and media reach.

In addition to video-van media, wall advertising presents another alternative to advertisers and media planners to reach inaccessible areas and tailor their messages specifically to the needs of rural audiences. These two media forms constitute a unique and striking feature of the modern rural landscape and market as well as social communication. They are viewed as the most far-reaching, economical, effective (in terms of audience recall), artistic, innovative, and indigenous way of sending messages to both the literate and illiterate rural audiences.

Conventional media: From print to the Internet

Let us now turn to the state of conventional media in South Asia. The first newspapers in South Asia were published in English for the local British expatriate population; the first South Asian language newspaper appeared in Bengali in 1818 (Robinson 1989: 489). South Asian newspapers are now published in both print and electronic editions in a wide variety of indigenous languages as well as in English.

Table 19.1 gives a summary of print media in the five countries of South Asia where newspapers and periodicals appear in fewer than three indigenous languages. In Bangladesh print media appears either in Bengali or in English. Of the 192 daily newspapers published in Bangladesh, nine are major English dailies (*Europa World Year Book* 2000). Bhutan has one weekly newspaper published in Dzongkha, English, and Nepali editions and one monthly English publication. The Maldives has three dailies that appear in both Dhivehi and English, and ten government periodicals. There are 166 daily newspapers published in Nepal, the majority of which are in Nepali; among the 166 are four major English-language dailies and one Hindi daily. In Sri Lanka, newspapers and periodicals appear in Sinhala, Tamil, and English. The majority of publications are in Sinhala; there are two major Tamil-language dailies and four English-language dailies (including Sunday editions).

Tables 19.2 and 19.3 give a language-wise summary of publications in India and Pakistan, respectively, where newspapers and periodicals appear in numerous languages. In India, major dailies are published in more than twenty languages. Some of the "other" languages in Table 19.2 include Assamese and Nepali. Pakistan publishes daily newspapers in eleven languages; Robinson (1989: 491) also includes a Turkish daily.

South Asian print media is also well represented on the Internet. Bangladesh has nine newspapers on the Web: five in Bengali and four in English. Bhutan has one newspaper in English. Multilingual India has fifty-three newspapers in eleven different languages: English, twenty-two; Gujarati, three; Hindi, five; Tamil, three; Bangla, one; Telugu, two; Malayalam, six; Malayalam–English,

Table 19.1. *South Asian newspapers and periodicals*

	Daily	Biweekly	Weekly	Fortnightly	Monthly	Miscellaneous
Bangladesh	192	—	—	—	—	235
Bhutan	—	—	1	—	1	—
Maldives	3	—	2	2	3	3
Nepal	166	3	814	—	—	—
Sri Lanka	9	—	43	—	—	—

Only for some countries is a complete breakdown of daily, weekly, and other periodical publications given.
Source: Turner (2001).

Table 19.2. *Indian newspapers and periodicals by language*

Languages	Daily newspapers	Total periodicals
Assamese	14	207
Bengali	93	2,333
English	338	6,227
Gujarati	99	1,272
Hindi	2,118	16,864
Kannada	279	1,424
Kashmiri	0	1
Konkani	0	5
Malayalam	209	1,268
Manipuri	12	38
Marathi	283	1,896
Oriya	63	625
Punjabi	104	796
Sanskrit	3	48
Sindhi	8	97
Tamil	341	1,698
Telugu	126	976
Urdu	495	2,670
Other (Nepali, etc.)	56	396
Bilingual	63	2,409
Multilingual	15	455
Total	**4,719**	**41,705**

Source: Bhatia (2000: 48–9).

one; Urdu, three; Hindi–Urdu, one; Oriya–English, one; Kannada, two; Kannada–English, one; and Marathi, two. The Maldives has one paper each in English and Dhivehi, and Nepal has two papers, one in English and one in Nepali. Pakistan has sixteen: English, nine; Sindhi, two; Urdu, four; and English–Urdu,

Table 19.3. *Pakistan newspapers and periodicals by language*

	Urdu	English	Sindhi	Pashto	Punjabi	Saraiki	Gujrati	Balochi	Brahvi	Persian	Arabic	Total
Dailies	209	41	17	2	—	—	4	—	—	—	—	273
Biweeklies	2	2	—	—	—	—	—	—	—	—	—	4
Weeklies	341	65	42	4	1	—	2	1	1	—	—	457
Fortnightlies	57	34	2	—	—	—	1	—	—	—	—	94
Monthlies	598	237	17	5	1	2	5	7	—	3	1	876
Bimonthlies	3	11	—	—	—	—	—	—	—	—	—	14
Quarterlies	75	136	1	—	—	—	3	—	—	—	—	215
Biannual	59	83	—	—	—	—	—	—	—	—	—	142
Annuals	119	127	—	2	—	—	—	2	2	—	—	252
All	1,463	736	79	13	2	2	15	10	3	3	1	2,327

Source: Rahman (1996a).

one. Sri Lanka is represented by four English newspapers.[1] The legacy of English in South Asia is easily seen in the number of English newspapers on the Internet: Bhutan's only paper is in English, and four out of five of Bangladesh's Internet publications are in English. Fifty percent of India's Web offerings are either partially or totally in English; the Maldives and Nepal each have two papers – one of which is in English. The majority of Pakistan's World Wide Web newspaper publications are in English, and all of Sri Lanka's electronic press is in English.

Radio and television

Electronic media has made great strides since British colonial times in reaching the masses in South Asia. Table 19.4 gives country-by-country figures for the proliferation of radio and television receivers during the period 1996–1997. Cable television is also making inroads throughout the subcontinent. The government-controlled radio and television stations in each country broadcast daily Home Services in a variety of languages and dialects. Bhutan broadcasts in Dzongkha, Sharchopkha, Nepali, and English on the radio and in Dzongkha and English on the television; Bangladesh in Arabic, Bengali, English, Hindi, Nepali, and Urdu on the radio; Nepal in Nepali and English on the radio and Nepali, English, and Hindi/Urdu on the television; the Maldives, in Dhivehi and English on the radio and television; and Sri Lanka in Sinhala, Tamil and English on the radio and television.

Table 19.4. *Radio and TV receivers in South Asia*

	Bhutan	Bangladesh	India	Maldives	Nepal	Pakistan	Sri Lanka
Radio	0.035m	6 m	99 m	0.032m	0.81m	12.9 m	1.7 m
Television	0.0115m	0.85m	66 m	0.0101m	0.079m	9 m	3.8 m

Note: m = millions
Source: Turner (2001).

India and Pakistan radio and television broadcast in multiple languages: India's Home Services broadcast in seventy-two languages and dialects (*Europa World Year Book* 2000), and Pakistan's, in twenty-two languages (see Table 19.5). Most South Asian countries also have radio External Services; The Sri Lankan Broadcasting Corporation, for example, provides External Service in Sinhala, Tamil, English, Hindi, Kannada, Malayalam, Nepali, and Telugu (*Europa World Year Book* 2000). India's External Services broadcast in twenty-two languages and Pakistan's, in seventeen. The

[1] One Tamil-language newspaper can also be found on the Internet (*Europa World Year Book* 2000).

Table 19.5. *Language-wise Radio Pakistan Broadcasting*

Sites	Broadcast in Languages
Abbottabad	Urdu, Hindko
Bahawalpur	Urdu, Saraiki
Chitral	Urdu, Chitrali
Dera Ismail Khan	Urdu, Saraiki, Pushto
Faisalabad	Urdu, Punjabi
Gilgit	Urdu, Shina, Brushishki, Wakhi
Hyderabad	Urdu, Sindhi
Islamabad	Urdu, Balti, Shina, English
Karachi	Urdu, Sindhi, Gujrati, English
Khairpur	Urdu, Sindhi
Lahore	Urdu, Punjabi, English
Larkana	Urdu, Sindhi
Loralai	Urdu, Pushto
Multan	Urdu, Saraiki, Punjabi
Peshawar	Urdu, Pushto, Hindko, Chitrali, Kohistani, Gojri
Quetta	Urdu, Pushto, Balochi, Brahvi, Hazargi
Rawalpindi	Urdu, Punjabi, Kashmiri, Gojri, Pahari, Potohari, English
Skardu	Urdu, Balti
Turbat	Urdu, Balochi
Zhob	Urdu, Pashto

Source: PBC.

Pakistan Broadcasting Corporation also broadcasts World Services in Urdu for overseas Pakistanis (*Pakistan Broadcasting Corporation*).[2] The prominent place of English can again be seen in the above data: all South Asian countries have both radio and television broadcasts in English.[3] According to B. Kachru (1992b: 958), "English-language announcers generally use the educated form of the local variety." While the prominence of English in South Asian media is self-evident, the diversity and the power of the regional-language media can hardly be underestimated. In the aftermath of the September 11 terrorist attack, South Asian regional-language media gained a new significance and relevance.

Table 19.6 gives the rich array of media forms employed in South Asia together with their strengths and characteristics.

[2] The officials who provided materials for Pakistan and Sri Lanka are listed in the Acknowledgment (see p. xvii of this volume).

[3] For links to the various South Asian radio and television corporations on the World Wide Web, go to the website of the Asia-Pacific Broadcasting Union (www.abu.org.my; accessed on 5/15/2000).

Table 19.6. *Media typology: Intrinsic characteristics*

Media form	Reach	Audience involvement	Type: urban versus rural	Accessibility time/place	Viewing cost	Audiencee exposure
TV	Mass	Low	Urban	Limited in rural area	No	Transient
Cable	Mass	Low	Urban	Limited in rural area	Yes	Transient
Radio	Mass	Highest in mass media	Urban	Highest in mass media category	No	More lasting than TV
Print	Mass	No	Largely urban	High	No	Permanent
Cinema	Mass	Higher than TV	Mixed	Limited in rural area	Yes	Transient
Video *raths/ vans*	Personal – customized	Very high (always there)	Mixed	Highest/ but not mass media/ reaches where mass media can't reach	No	More lasting than TV
Wall paintings	Personal – customized	High	Rural	Highest in rural area	No	Lasting
Calendar Art	Less than print	No	Mixed	Limited in rural area	Yes	Lasting
haats/oral sales calls	Personal – customized	Highest (hands-on demonstrations)	Rural	Highest/but not mass media/ reaches where mass media can't reach	No	More lasting than conventional media

Source: Bhatia (2000).

Advertising media discourse

The structure of South Asian advertising discourse is a series of complex mixes – mix of media forms on the one hand and languages and their regional, social, and genderlects together with various scripts on the other. Not just bilingual-language mixing but also multiple-language mixing is the rule and the hallmark of South Asian advertising discourse (T. Bhatia 1988, 1992). The qualitative and quantitative aspects of mixing is subject to the following factors: media modality (e.g. wall advertising versus print), degree and the nature of language contact, and domain and functional allocation of languages, among other things.

Media modalities: Wall versus print advertising

Consider the degree and the nature of language or script mixing in wall and print advertising. The incidence of language mixing is much higher in print advertising than in wall advertising. Wall advertising is different from print advertising in the sense that it usually avoids the body-copy or main-text component of the print ads. This is a natural consequence of wall advertising, which prefers conciseness to elaborate explanation about the properties of the product. This gap is filled by means of providing an evaluative statement about the product. In short, wall advertising comes close to the banner type of advertising witnessed in sport arenas in the West, rather than the elaborate print advertising in magazines. The only difference is that wall advertising contains invitational closing structure that often gives information about the availability of the product and its distributor. While such structural units are invariably absent from the banner ads, they are present in print ads.

Color schemes and the physical properties of a wall are usually exploited (un)consciously and systematically to impose a structure on an ad and distinguish at the same time its different structural properties (for more details on the structural properties of print advertising, see T. Bhatia 2000: 132–5 and for wall advertising, see T. Bhatia 2000: 142–3). Consider, for example, the tea ad for *Taaza* in Figure 19.1.

The ad carries a Hindi–Urdu attention-getter in the Roman script. The attention-getter turns out to be product name, which is prominently displayed on the package. A subheader, *daane daar caay* "the grainy tea" is from Hindi and is written in the Devanagari script. The third structural property, slogan (*kamaal kii taazgii* "incredible freshness"; *lipTan taazaa* "Lipton Taazaa"), is written in Urdu with Perso-Arabic script. This wall ad best captures the multiple language and script mixing which is the hallmark of advertising discourse in India (see Table 19.7).

Table 19.7. *Multiple language/script mixing: Domain allocation*

Languages	Structural domain	Functional domain
English in Roman	Attention-getter	Product name/company name
Hindi in Devanagari	Subheader	Product type
Urdu in Perso-Arabic	Slogan	Product quality/evaluation company's name

Figure 19.1 *Wall advertising.*

One witnesses a different qualitative and quantitative pattern in Sri Lanka.[4] Although Sri Lanka is a multilingual country, bilingual mixing pattern is more predominant than the multiple mixing. This is true of print advertising in which the conditions for multiple mixing are more favorable than, for example, in wall advertising. Consider a print ad for an STC digger. The text size of the ad is twice the size of a wall advertising text. The ad is a mixture of English and

[4] See fn. 2.

Sinhala languages and their respective scripts. Mixing with Tamil is rare. The text of the ad is given below:

(1) STC (in the Sinhalese script)

goDa	polaavat	*mud* (in Sinhalese script)	kuumbuura-Ta
dry	ground	mud	field-for
no-dainii	ega-Ta	keTeii yaasa-Ta	
neg-feel	body-for	to dig well-for	
STC (in the Sihalese script)		STC	udiala
STC		STC	digger

"STC. For (converting) a dry ground into mud (soft). (And) to dig well effortlessly. STC digger."

Notice the use of English is restricted to the brand name, that is STC.

English and structural domains

Mixing with English is the unifying and integral feature of South Asian advertising discourse. The use of English is particularly favored in the following structural domains of an ad. It is important to observe that English is assigned these domains neither randomly nor symmetrically.

Product naming: The most favorite and most easily accessible domains to English are product naming and company naming. T. Bhatia (1988) analyzed more than 1,200 advertisements of Hindi that were printed between 1975 and 1985. The study revealed that more than 90 percent of these ads carried a product name for a wide variety of product types in English, for example, Trigger, Signal-2, Mustang, Click-IV, Freedom Mealmaker, VIP, Travel-light, Fair and Lovely, Protein Conditioner Shampoo, Clinical Special, High Power Surf, and Oriental Stereo Recorded Cassettes. Not only this, both durable and nondurable products produced by domestic companies aimed at indigenous populations are also named in English (e.g. Mohan's Gold Coin Apple Juice). Meraj (1993: 224) shows a similar trend in Urdu advertising in Pakistan. Her sample reveals that English product names account for 70 percent of the ads while only 9 percent of product names were drawn from Urdu . The remaining 21 percent were mixed product names (English+Urdu) such as Chanda Battery Cell, Good Luck Haleem, and National Kheer.

Company's name/logo: Next to product names, company names show preference for English. Both local and global business tend to favor English in this domain. Names which are not from English are given the appearance of English by writing them in the Roman script.

Slogans: English is gradually gaining prominence in this domain in South Asian advertising. Slogans expressing changing or new value systems, democratic values, choices, progress, and prosperity are not subjected to translation in South Asian languages (e.g. Freedom is my birth right).

Main body: Since the product description and explanations about the utility of the product are given in the main body of an advertisement, it is not surprising that this structural domain departs from the other domains in terms of its preference for a sentence-like structure. In this domain, however, native languages are usually preferred over English. Needless to say, English is conquering this last barrier by capitalizing on those domains that are within its easy reach such as product names and lexicon associated with product types, for example computer, technology, and fashion. New technologies such as the Internet and multimedia have provided a special boost to English usage. The discussion of futuristic themes and developments is often carried out by means of key words which are drawn from English. Numbers, graphs, and figures are presented in English.

Headers and subheaders: As is the case with English in the body of the advertisement, English takes a back seat in headers. This domain is occupied by native South Asian languages. The English-only Roman text as a header usually appears in the form of a product name being employed as a header as in example (3) below. The English-only structures are often nominal or phrasal as in examples (2) and (3) below. If a header goes beyond the phrasal-level (i.e. either a sentence or conjunct sentence), the use of English is discouraged. Nevertheless, like slogans, this domain is gradually surrendering to English. Similarly, the use of English in headers is expanding to subheaders. In a mixed structure, English forms either a subject or an object argument of the sentence, as exemplified in (5) or as occuring in a topic-comment structure as in example (4). The following attention-getters illustrate the generalizations drawn here.

(2) Phrasal

a feast of elegance

Expanding frontiers of telecommunication

(3) Nominal

Golden moments. McDowell moments.

The cotton collection

Cooking

(4) Mixed: Topic-Comment

Kancan, mixer grinders	aur	nonstick cookwares
Kancan,	and	

(5) Mixed: object argument

super champion	baniye.
	become

"Be a super champion."

On the basis of the generalizations drawn about the pattern of English use in advertising worldwide, T. Bhatia (2001b: 206–7) postulates a structural hierarchy of English in global advertising (see Figure 19.2). This hierarchy is valid for English in South Asian language advertising as well. The hierarchy, represented in a staircase fashion, claims that in order to reach the highest step of the staircase, English must pass through all those steps, which precede it. When English manages to reach the step of product naming, then other, more difficult steps, such as company name become available to English. However, if the use of English is restricted to product naming, the probability of it being used in the body of the advertisement is not guaranteed. If one finds the use of English in the main body of an ad, one can predict that all the domains of advertisement for that product are within the reach of English. The real test of the presence of English in the body of an advertisement is when it begins to appear, as in slogans, with verbs coded with English tense-aspectual information. In addition to predicting structural dependencies, this hierarchy also predicts the process by which English gains currency in global advertising. The onset of English penetration begins with naming and then spreads to other domains. The reversal of this process is not plausible.

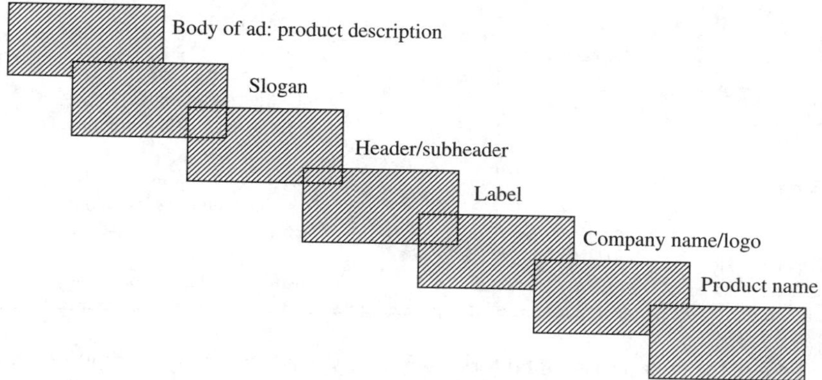

Figure 19.2 *English – the structural dependency hierarchy.*

"Mixers" and "mixing"

The underlying reasons for mixing English and other languages are invisible sociopsychological effects that these languages are capable of delivering in advertising discourse. T. Bhatia (2001b) attempts to analyze and classify these features into the threshold (seedlike) sociopsychological features, which can best be characterized as general but critical features. Once these threshold features are acquired, the floodgates to proximity zones are opened, which leads to a domino effect. Proximity zones can be characterized as subcategorical or subsets of threshold features. The threshold features and the proximity zones posited here are presented in Table 19.8. An analogy will further clarify the point we are making here. Similar to a door threshold giving access to different zones in a house or building, threshold categories provide access to proximate zones, which in turn can lead the way to other related zones.

Table 19.8. *Sociopsychological motivations for multiple mixing*

Languages	Threshold trigger	Proximity zones
English	Future and innovation	Vision, foresightedness, advancement, betterment
	American or English culture	Limited Westernization, Christianity, values such as independence, freedom, modernization
	Internationalism and standardization	Certification, standards of measure, authenticity
	Rationality and objectivity	Scientific appeal, problem solving
	Competence	Efficiency, organization, quality, safety, protection, functionality, pragmatism
	Sophistication	Elegance, style, rarity
	Physical fitness	Self-improvement
Hindi	Pragmatic	Utility, no-nonsense
Sanskrit	Indian culture	Deep-rooted Hindu tradition, reliability
Punjabi	Rurality	Lively, fun-loving, charitability (kindness)
	Sikh culture	Bravery and social justice
Persian–Urdu	Islamic culture	Brotherhood, etc.
	Luxury	Royal (medieval), physical

While the features specified for English are shared uniformly by South Asian media, it is not the case with South Asian languages. English is best suited to convey American or British culture. Sports images and physical fitness themes dominate the globe in order to market products, such as Nike shoes, through English. To best convey standardization, technical information is provided in the form of abbreviations, graphs, tables, and acronyms rendered in English.

The features specification for South Asian languages, on the other hand, is sensitive to the pattern of bilingualism/multilingualism specific to the region. For example, the multiple language mixing of Sanskrit, Punjabi, and Persian–Urdu is the salient feature of advertising in the Hindi-speaking regions of India. However, this is not the case either in Sri Lanka or in Pakistan. In Pakistan,

Urdu clones those features represented by Hindi in India, and the use of Sanskrit may be negligible.

Globalization and marketization

While the discussion in this section is focused on South Asian language advertising, we hasten to add that the English-language advertising aimed largely at the urban population is quite vigorous and widespread in South Asia (e.g. see Kemper 2001). The new world economy rests largely on global bazaars, the global shopping mall, the global workplace, and the global financial network (Barnet and Cavanagh 1994: 15). English is no doubt the chosen language in these four aspects of the new economic order. English is the leading linguistic cause of the homogenization of global advertising discourse. English-language advertising in South Asia is no exception in this regard; see T. Bhatia 2001b: 207–13 for more details. A cursory analysis of English-language advertising in South Asia reveals absolute linguistic and nonlinguistic homogenization which, in turn, often makes South Asian ads indistinguishable from American or British ads. This conclusion is further supported by Griffin *et al.*'s (1944) comparative cross-cultural study involving Indian and US advertising. Griffin *et al.* contend that the diffusion of global marketing and advertising render striking similarities in gender advertising in the United States and India.[5]

Globalization or glocalization?

From the discussion in the immediately preceding paragraph, one should not arrive at the conclusion that English is leading to complete homogenization of advertising discourse in the region. As van Elteren (1996: 58) rightly points out, globalization should be viewed as the "organization of diversity," rather than the "replication of uniformity," despite the homogenization of English-advertising discourse on a global basis. The process of localization of English parallels the process of globalization. The primary carriers of localization are undoubtedly the native languages of regions that have been exposed to English. However, the other notable aspect of localization is the local adaptation of English. A case in point is a very popular facial cream, "Fair and Lovely." The product name at first glance shows no overt signs of localization. However, the term *fair* refers to "light skin," a usage which is not predominant either in American or British English. For more details on the South Asianization of English see T. Bhatia (1988, 2001b) for advertising discourse and B. Kachru

[5] Their cross-cultural study is based on gender depiction in ads drawn from *Life* and *Newsweek* (the United States) and *Illustrated Weekly* and *India Today* (India).

(1990). This dual role of English may appear paradoxical at first sight, but it is a natural consequence of the globalization of English.

Conclusion

In order to meet the formidable challenge of reaching more than one billion inhabitants, scattered in approximately 750,000 villages, South Asian media experts and planners have not only pioneered new media forms, but also have mastered the art of crafting messages customized to effectively meet their audiences' regional sensibilities and tastes. The dazzling array of both conventional and nonconventional media forms together with programming in dozens of major and scores of minor languages of the region adds distinction and color to the media scene of South Asia. While multiple-language mixing is the most distinctive feature of advertising discourse, mixing with English represents its unifying feature. These features render various manifestations of creativity in media discourse. With the arrival of satellite TV, the appetite for media is growing at a faster rate than ever witnessed before, so are creativity and diversity in media.

20 Language in cinema

Wimal Dissanayake

Introduction

We normally tend to think of cinema as essentially a visual medium in which language plays only a subsidiary and inconsequential role, lending support to the ambitions of the visual images displayed on the screen. However, as modern film scholars, through their carefully conceived and nuanced analyses, have demonstrated, language and the soundtrack fulfill far more significant roles in film diegesis than such common assumptions would have us believe. A work like *The Voice in Cinema* by Michel Chion (1999) underscores the fact that the human voice is of pivotal importance in the experience of cinema and that the relationship that exists between the voice and the image is complex and many sided, and serves to foreground the complex ontology of this technology-based medium of entertainment. Thus, various aspects of language are increasingly attracting the attention of film scholars with commendable results.

Language fulfills many important functions in cinema, which are significantly linked to questions of narrative discourse, content, form, and styles of presentation. It facilitates the forward movement of the narrative, reinforces the intent of the image, opens up psychological depths in characters, and guides the viewer through the cinematic diegesis. These can be termed the positive functions of language in cinema. One has only to examine any popular Hollywood film to realize the positive ways in which language functions in cinema. On the other hand, language can function in a negative way, challenging, counterpointing, and subverting the imperatives of the image as is evidenced in some of the innovative films of Jean-Luc Godard. Hence, one can justifiably say that the function of language in cinema is complex and multifaceted, dispelling the widely held notion that language is of secondary importance in the cinematic experience.

The relationship between language and cinema varies from one cultural geography to another, thereby underlining the nature of cinema as a significant social practice that brings together economics, politics, ideology, technology, the weight of tradition, and so on into fruitful conversation. In the case of

South Asian cinema, language is of crucial importance in the constitution and communication of the filmic experience, enabling the propulsion of the narrative in culture-specific ways. Unlike the standard Hollywood film, which positively valorizes linear development, tightness of structure and unified narrative trajectories, South Asian films by and large tend to privilege circular development of plots, loosely combined segments with independent lives of their own, and constant detours, preferring a digressive and nonlinear mode of narrative discourse. Within such a narrative strategy, language, as is indicated later, plays a crucial role.

In South Asian films, like those produced in India and Sri Lanka, song and dance sequences, fight episodes, dialogues and moral exhortations, comedy, and so on while tenuously connected to the flow of the narrative also have an autonomous life of their own. For example, dialogues play a crucial role in the cinematic experience textualized in South Asian film, and very often they are enjoyed and appreciated as independent and self-contained segments. The dialogues and declamations of Shivaji Ganeshan in *Parashakti* (1946) or Amjad Khan in *Sholay* (1975) – two highly popular movies made in south and north India, respectively – are often played on public address systems at fairs and other public gatherings, much to the joy and uplift of the listeners. Such dialogues are applauded in the theaters. Just as much as there is a star system in operation among actors and actresses, there is a star system in operation among dialogue writers, suggesting the importance of this area of activity. K. A. Abbas, M. Karunanidhi, and Salim–Javed in India and Hugo Fernando and Sirisena Wimalaweera in Sri Lanka are good examples of writers who earned a national reputation as writers of memorably powerful dialogue. This general predilection for, and investment in, dialogues has deep implications for the question of language in South Asian cinema.

The languages of South Asian cinema

This chapter focuses on language in films produced in India and Sri Lanka in relation to the questions of narrative and politics, which are deeply imbricated with the role of language. The conclusion focuses on certain areas related to this topic that merit further sustained study.

India presents us with one of the most complex, and at times confusing, linguistic landscapes found in any country in the world. The government has officially recognized eighteen languages (now twenty-two), and English as an associate official language. These "scheduled" languages are Assamese, Bengali, Bodo, Dogri, Gujarati, Hindi, Kannada, Kashmiri, Konkani, Maithili, Malayalam, Marathi, Manipuri, Nepali, Oriya, Punjabi, Sanskrit, Santali, Sindhi, Tamil, Telugu, and Urdu. According to the *Linguistic Survey of India*, there are 179 languages and 544 dialects that can be divided into four distinct groups – Indo-Aryan, Dravidian, Austro-Asiatic, and Tibeto-Chinese. Some others maintain that there are around 3,000 (in 1961 Census) to 10,000 (in 1991 Census) mother tongues in India (see Chapters 5, 6, and 10 for latest data and discussion of language in India). This complex linguistic landscape, understandably enough, has generated many conflicts, at times extremely ferocious, as for example between the advocates of English and Hindi as national languages and Tamil and Hindi in the south. In the case of Sri Lanka there are three main languages, Sinhalese, Tamil, and English, and the current civil war occurring in the island between the Sinhalese and Tamils is largely language based. Although narrative film have been made in most of the officially recognized languages in India, the languages that have and continue to dominate Indian cinema are Hindi, Bengali, Malayalam, Tamil, Kannada, and Telugu. Similarly, although feature films have been made in all three languages prevalent in Sri Lanka, the number of movies made in Tamil and English is negligible.

The situation of language-based cinema in India becomes more complicated when we realize that movies are sometimes made simultaneously in different languages and are continually dubbed from one language to another. For example in the studio era of the 1930s, identical takes were made of each shot in different languages, very often with different actors and actresses, but with the same music and crew of technicians. V. Shantaram's *Kunku* (Marathi) and *Duniya Na Mane* (Hindi) made in 1937 are cases in point. Hence, the easy move to identify Indian film in terms of language has to be tempered by the knowledge that there are complex processes at work.

Formative influences

A useful way of approaching the issue of language and Indian cinema – the complex ways in which language has inflected the growth of Indian cinema – is to explore it in terms of the formative influences that shaped Indian movies. Among these influences, classical Sanskrit theater, the folk theater, the Parsi theater, and the Hollywood musical are, to my mind, important and allow us to attain a better understanding of the complexities of the situation. Classical Sanskrit theater (see Barnouw and Krishnaswamy 1963) inspired the imagination of early Indian filmmakers who were also attracted by the power of the two epics, the *Ramayana* and the *Mahabharata*, with which it is vitally connected. One of the noteworthy features of the Sanskrit theater was the linguistic hierarchy and exclusivities of enunciatory positions. Sanskrit was used by kings and courtiers and Brahmins, and various form of Prakrit were employed by women and people belonging to the lower rungs of the social ladder (see Chapter 8; Hock and Pandharipande 1978; Krishnamurthy 1997).

Hence language as a reflector and enforcer of social divisions was central to the classical Indian theatrical experience, and this linguistic desire to preserve the social hierarchy seems to have animated the early India filmmakers as well.

Since the decline of the Sanskrit theater somewhere around the twelfth century or so, owing to a variety of social and religious causes, various regional theaters, which can be regarded as lineal descendants of the Sanskrit theater, emerged in India. In many of the regional folk theaters, such as Yatra, Ram Lila, Bhagavata Mela, Yakshagana, and Terukkuttu, we find the same linguistic hierarchization that characterized Sanskrit stage plays. In addition, many of the comic episodes, which were impromptu, held up to ridicule some topical event or occurrence, and once again linguistic diversity was used to good effect. This aspect of the folk theater had an impact on the imagination of the early Indian film directors.

The most dominant influence on the formation of popular Indian cinema was the Parsi theater that came into prominence, and began to gain international recognition, in the nineteenth century. The Parsi theatre influenced the theatrical imagination of vast numbers of theater goers not only in India but also in neighboring countries like Sri Lanka. The Parsi theatre represented a tradition of melodrama that combined realism and stylization in equal measure to dramatize both social and historical experiences. And the use of language in these plays is extremely interesting in that there was an attempt made to combine the power of rhetoric, the vigor of colloquial speech and grandiloquence to communicate experiences that would appeal to the generality of the masses.

Finally, the impact of the Hollywood musicals of the 1940s on the growth of Indian popular cinema is important in that they served as an object lesson for Indian film directors to make musicals based on contemporary experiences using colloquial speech. Here again the use of language both for dramatic and musical purposes merits close study. Thus, what we find is that the various formative influences on Indian cinema that served to infuse it with its characteristic stylistic features and narrative strategies were vitally imbricated with questions of language.

Linguistic structure

The linguistic structure that undergirds Indian and Sri Lankan films and the diverse linguistic styles that operate in them invite closer analysis. Sinhalese films are of course largely modeled on Indian film. There are a number of linguistic styles in operation that give the Sri Lankan films their recognizable character: elitist language; urban language; anglicized middle-class language; rural language; language as spoken by linguistic minorities like Tamils and Muslims; classically inspired language as found in the lyrics; and so on. Each of these styles has its own distinctive lexicon, syntax, idioms, and intonation. In addition, just like popular Indian films, Sinhalese films are replete with melodious songs that contribute significantly to their popularity. These songs contain very sophisticated lyrics, very often composed by highly talented lyricists of the caliber of Mahagama Sekera, Chandraratne Manavasinghe, Madawala Ratnayake, and Sunil Ariyaratne. Interestingly, these highly literary and ornate lyrics do not relate directly to the social background and the linguistic styles that are normally associated with the different characters. These lyrics seem to occupy a kind of transcendental space with their own recognizable conventions and codes of composition. Speaking about Hindi film songs, Madhav Prasad (1998) observes that,

> the lyrics are written in a language which has its own set repertoire of images and tropes for themes like romantic love, separation, rejection, maternal love, marriage etc. The songs adopt a literary style which has a predilection for certain recurrent metaphors: "*mehfil*, *shama/parwana*, *chaman*, *bahar*, *nazaare* and so on."

As remarked by many commentators, these images and tropes are largely inspired by Urdu poetry. Songs, which are "de rigeur" in Indian and Sinhalese popular films, occupy an independent space, and they are memorable for catchy tunes as well as romantic imagery. Let me give two examples from Sinhalese cinema. The first is a love song and the second, a "philosophical" rumination. They are taken from the two films *Sujatha* (1953) and *Asoka* (1955), respectively.

Love's glow has faded
You have departed leaving behind your image in my heart
Will a fallen flower reattach to the branch?
Just so, our love was severed.

We are born singly
We die singly
In this brief period
Why be frolicsome?
Why should we feast and dress up showily?
Where will we take our body after death?

Similarly, Hindi films are replete with songs containing romantic imagery and "philosophical" thought. Let me illustrate this point with an excerpt from a song from one of Raj Kapoor's films, *Satyam, Shivam, Sundaram* (1978).

They say, where even the sun cannot reach, the poet can
But neither sun nor poet can reach you, my beautiful
For even as I stretch my arms, you fly away,
As though on angel wings, my love

Narrative structure

One cannot understand the nature and significance of language in Indian and Sri Lankan films without paying adequate attention to the narrative structure of these works. Broadly speaking, these films can be characterized as romantic musical melodramas that set in motion the interplay of the good and the evil and demonstrate the ultimate triumph of the good over the evil. Their narrative structure is loose, episodic, and circular, and each of the loosely connected segments, like music and dance, action, humor, and dialogue are relatively autonomous. In seeking to understand the role of language in Indian and Sri Lankan cinema, we need to explore the manifold ways in which audiences respond to and valorize dialogues, songs, and comic episodes. Dialogue writing in Indian and Sri Lankan popular films is an art form by itself with its own recognizable conventions, linguistic registers, tropes, and idioms. Dialogue, rather that being an ancillary adjunct, which serves to carry forward the plot of the film, as in most Hollywood films, takes on a life of its own as an independent entity. Consequently, language in Indian and Sri Lankan popular films assumes a very important and recognizable role in the cinematic experience both as a propeller of the narrative and as an independent entity in its own right. Popular cinema in South Asia operates against a background of consumer culture and capitalist modernity, and the role of language in cinema has to be understood in terms of the discursive regimes of consumer culture. These observations are mostly relevant to the popular cinemas of India and Sri Lanka. In the art cinemas as represented by the works of such film directors as Satyajit Ray, Mrinal Sen, and Adoor Gopalakrishnan in India and Lester James Peries, and Prasanna Vithanage in Sri Lanka, dialogue functions far less independently than in the popular commercial films.

Politics of language

Another area that merits attention is the politics of language in South Asia. More than most other national cinemas, Indian cinema presents a convoluted relationship between the politics of language and the desires of cinema. Let us consider the question of Hindi or better still Hindustani. Indian popular cinema has played a pivotal role in the dissemination of Hindustani as a lingua franca not only in India but in some of the neighboring countries as well where Indian films enjoy a wide popularity. Nearly 45 percent of the population speaks Hindustani in India and the Bombay-based commercial cinema has contributed immeasurably to this dissemination. The gap between Hindustani and Urdu spoken by the Muslims in India is negligible despite the religious nuances. For example, growing up in Sri Lanka where Hindi movies were extremely popular, avid filmgoers picked up not only words and phrases of Hindi but rudiments of the language as well. This is also true for countries such as Burma (Myanmar), Malaysia, and Indonesia. This popularity of Hindustani has to be understood against the efforts of the government and various state institutions to popularize a highly Sanskritized Hindi. This so-called "pure" Hindi, which was largely a hothouse product, was put into circulation by government radio broadcast, academic writings, and state-run institutions, but the popular Hindi propagated by the commercial cinema is clearly outpacing the so-called "pure" Hindi (see S. N. Sridhar 1987)

The vexed question of politics of language in Indian cinema has many sides to it related to issues of nationhood, regionalism, art, and entertainment. As was stated earlier popular Indian cinema played a crucial role in the dissemination of Hindi as a vital lingua franca. However there were other developments taking place within Indian cinema that had a direct bearing on the question of politics of language. Since the 1960s with the rise of the so-called "New Indian cinema" more and more artistic films based on regional languages were being made. The state, through the National Film Development Corporation, contributed significantly to the growth of the New Indian cinema. Films based in Bengal and Kerala had the most profound effect. Before long, interesting, and artistically significant films were being made in such languages as Assamese, Oriya, and Marathi. The rise of the regional cinema and the international recognition and legitimacy granted to it had the effect of focusing more and more attention on these films. This trend served to enforce the constitutionally accepted notion of a multilingual and multiracial India. Interestingly, the rise of the regional cinema and the increasing attention directed to the new cinema as represented by the works of such filmmakers as Mrinal Sen, Adoor Gopalakrishnan, Aravindan, Buddhadeb Dasgupta, Gautam Ghose, and Ketan Mehta had the effect of reinforcing the hegemony of the Indian nation-state.

While interesting developments were taking place in the domain of art cinema, consequential transformation was also occurring in the sphere of popular cinema. In the 1960s and 1970s, Bombay (now Mumbai) was the capital of Indian popular cinema, and Hindi films exerted a deep and pervasive influence on the thought and imagination of the generality of moviegoers. However, by the 1980s, popular films in Tamil Nadu, Andhra Pradesh, Karnataka, and Kerala, made in Tamil, Telugu, Kannada, and Malayalam, respectively, began to be produced in large numbers, and these challenged the supremacy of the Bombay-based Hindi commercial films. Now popular cinema became pluricentric and some of these films made in south Indian languages began to appeal to the diasporic communities spread throughout the world, just as much as the Hindi films had done earlier. This linguistic picture is complicated by the fact that popular films made in one language get dubbed in another language, as for example Mani Ratnam's films that were originally made in Tamil and later dubbed in Hindi.

When discussing the politics of language reflected in and fashioned by Indian cinema one cannot ignore the indissoluble link between language and cinema in Tamil Nadu. Powerful politicians like C. N. Annadurai and M. Karunanidhi cannot be separated from their popularity in cinema and the power of the Dravida Munnetra Kazagam. The Dravida Munnetra Kazagam films with their desire to challenge the power of the Congress party and the Brahmanical religious authority, and with their desire to propagate Tamil as a language with a hoary past are vitally connected to the question of politics of language in cinema. A film like *Parashakti*, which gained wide popularity not only in India but also in countries like Sri Lanka, illustrates this admirably. It valorized Dravidian heritage in defiantly prideful terms. M. S. Pandian (1992) who has done considerable work on this topic discusses the manner in which the dialogues contained in *Parashakti* had a galvanizing impact on Tamil audiences stirring their deepest passions and enabling the spread of Dravidian culture.

Mixing languages

Any discussion of the role of language in Indian and Sri Lankan cinema should lead to a nexus of issues of indubitable interest to linguists as well as scholars of communication. For example, let us consider the question of code switching and code mixing that we frequently find in Indian films representative of both the popular and artistic tradition. A person who speaks two or more languages is often confronted with the choice of using one or the other in different situations and this choice involves code switching. Code mixing is more subtle in the sense that a word or phrase or locution that is associated with one language is injected into a discussion conducted in another (B. Kachru 1978a; S. N. Sridhar 1978; S. N. Sridhar and K. K. Sridhar 1980). This is extremely common in Indian cinema as, indeed, in South Asian society in general, prompting us to raise such questions as when code switching occurs, under what circumstances, and what the cultural and communicational implications of this phenomenon are. For example in Satyajit Ray's films, which deal with middle-class experiences, there is frequent code mixing between Bengali and English. Similarly in the movies of a Sri Lankan filmmaker such as Lester James Peries we find frequent code-mixing of Sinhalese and English. The communicative and linguistic import of these phenomena need to be explored more fully in order to understand the complex dynamics of language and cinema in South Asia (see Dissanayake and Ratnavibhushana 2000).

Humor is another fruitful area of inquiry. In Indian and Sri Lankan films much of the humor is generated through language-linguistic misunderstanding.

For example, in popular Sinhalese films until very recent times the way Tamil speakers of Sinhalese mispronounced and misunderstood the language formed a vital part of humor. Similarly, characters who sought to speak in English or use English phrases with less than satisfactory results became the butt of humor. Hence linguistic humor in South Asian cinema is a topic that can yield valuable results in the hands of sensitive researchers.

Earlier on in this chapter, the interplay of diverse linguistic registers in South Asian films was discussed. The author wishes to suggest that this phenomenon can be most productively comprehended in relation to the concept of heteroglossia formulated by Bakhtin. Although his focus of interest is the novel, it appears that this concept could be used with equal profit and validity in the domains of drama and film. For Bakhtin (1981) the world is constituted by a plurality of language each of which possesses its own specific formal characteristics. However, these characteristics are never solely formal and each is imbricated with social values, visions, and formations. The concept of heteroglossia enables Bakhtin to identify a locus within which the unifying and fissiparous forces that inflect discourses converge. This provides a framework with which to study the interplay of diverse linguistic registers in Hindi, Bengali, or Sinhalese films, thereby focusing on questions of ideology in the construction of linguistic subjectivity as well as the polyphonicity associated with the national space.

The use of English expressions and locutions in Indian and Sri Lankan cinema, is another topic that can prove to be extremely significant in our understanding of language, cinema, and cultural discourse in South Asia. Let us, for example, consider the English expression, "I love you," that has become widely popular in Indian films in recent times. As Prasad (1998) points out, it is becoming increasingly clear that in Hindi commercial films as well as in south Indian films, songs and dialogues are animated by this English expression. This is, of course, vitally connected with consumer culture of which Indian cinema is a powerful representation. Prasad goes on to say that,

> but beyond this consumerist function, the utopian aspiration to social transformation that the concept of love embodies also finds itself invoking a certain state-form as its true ground. A striking illustration of this intersection of consumerism, romantic love in its congealed form as an English expression, and the modern nation-state is provided by Mani Ratnam's highly popular Tamil film "Roja."

He quotes the following lines from the film to establish his point:

> Hey, village girl, if I say something to you in English, will you be able to understand it?
> Say it, let's see
> I love you

This exchange takes place between a married couple holidaying in Kashmir. As is customary in popular Indian films, after the couple cavorts around in the hotel room they get into bed. Although the husband is from Madras (Chennai) and the wife is from the hinterland in Tamil Nadu, they choose to use the English expression as a way of creating an intimate space. Similarly, in Sinhalese films English locutions are pressed into service to discuss abstract concepts, intimate feelings, urbanized values, and so on.

South Asian cinema, then, becomes a useful terrain in which diverse linguistic conflicts and tensions are played out. As B. Kachru (1982b) observes:

> In India only Sanskrit, English, Hindi, and to some extent Persian, have acquired pan-Indian intranational functions. The domains of Sanskrit are restricted, and the proficiency in it limited, except in the case of pandits. The cause of Hindi was not helped by the controversy between Hindi, Urdu, and Hindustani. Support for Hindustani almost ended with independence; after the death of its ardent and influential supporter, Gandhi, very little was heard about it. The enthusiasm and near euphoria of the supporters of Hindi were not channeled in a constructive (and realistic) direction, especially after the 1940s. The result is that English continues to be a language both of power and prestige.

(See S. N. Sridhar 1987 for a detailed analysis of this controversy.) B. Kachru's (1982b) statement enables us to put the developments in Indian cinema in relation to language in an interesting perspective.

Conclusion

In order to map the true dimensions of language issues inscribed in South Asian cinema, one has to see them in relation to the power exercised as well as the challenges encountered by the nation-state. Formations of the nation-state and cultural production are inextricably linked, one feeding the other in interesting and complex ways, and generating a complex of issues related to the topic of ideology, nationhood, cultural identity, and cinematic representation. Language and cinema in South Asia can be most productively explored in terms of the concept of nationhood that serves to focus our attention on conjunctures of regionalism, state formation, and globalization. Nationhood comprises a plurality of intersecting discourses, and one that is of particular relevance in the present context is that of symbolism, including topics of construction of meaning, consciousness, problematic of cinematic representation, and cinema lover's pleasure. How a nation chooses to tell its putatively coherent and unified story to its citizens as a way of relegitimization is of fundamental importance in the understanding of nationhood. In modern times, it need hardly be stressed that cinema has come to play a crucial role in this effort. Benedict Anderson (1983) has underlined the importance of print capitalism in engendering notions of nationhood and the deep horizontal comradeship it entails. It is his view that newspapers and novels dealing with nationalistic themes are mainly responsible for the formation of a sense of nationhood. In times before the advent of cinema, print media and novels were successful in coordinating time and space in a way that was conducive to addressing the nation that he saw as an imagined community. In more modern times, cinema has come to occupy a central role in the construction of this imagined community. David Harvey (1990) has drawn attention to the power of cinema in capturing the complex relationship between space and time in a way that the earlier media could not and underlining the significance of cinema as a field of force. The foregoing issues related to language and cinema that have been discussed gain depth of perspective and definition by being measured against the imperatives and compulsions of nationhood.

I have already focused on the issues of regionalism and the function of language in cinema in the reconfigured space of deterritorialization and nation-state; in a similar manner, we need to understand the issue of language in relation to globalization and transnational diasporic audiences as well. During the last decade or so, the diasporic audience has come to occupy a central place in the calculations of film producers as the global market has generated more dependable returns than the local market. It is the Hindi-language films, followed by Tamil-language films that have attracted the greatest diasporic audiences. In the past decades, Bombay-based commercial melodramas such as *Hum Aapke Hain Kaun* (Who Am I To You), *Dilwale Dulhania Le Jayange* (Brave of Heart Wins The Bride*), Pardes* (Foreign Land) and *Kuch Kuch Hota Hai* (A Certain Feeling) have enjoyed wide popularity among audiences in the United Kingdom, United States, Canada, and Australia. The role of language in Indian cinema and the diasporic experience merits closer study.

Finally, I wish to raise a question of a more theoretical nature regarding this topic that would have a resonance with film scholars. The interplay between language and cinema has been studied by various theorists from diverse angles and vantage points. For example, it was Jean Mitry's (2000) considered judgment that cinema is not analogous to language, in contradiction to the views of Christian Metz (1982) and that it was more productive to think of cinematic language in a more philosophical sense. For him the meaning in cinema is generated by images moving across time and space, and hence editing was of fundamental importance in cinematic narrativity. The well-known Italian poet, filmmaker, and thinker Pasolini (1978) thinks of language of cinema not in terms of grammar, as Metz and others have done, but in terms of images that lend a certain generic quality to cinema. For Pasolini, cinema is constructed out of prelinguistic images and not from verbal language. However, one can well raise the question whether in Indian and Sri Lankan popular films, as opposed to art films, the reverse is sometimes not the case – whether verbal language shapes and determines the flow of visual images. If this is indeed the case, then the study of popular South Asian cinema would lead to the opening up of a line of inquiry that is theoretically compelling and empirically productive. How language functions in the ever-evolving techno-aesthetic space of cinema is a problem of continual interest.

21 Language of religion

Rajeshwari V. Pandharipande

Introduction

In South Asia including Tibet, the indigenous religions, Hinduism, Buddhism, Sikhism, and Jainism, and the extraneous religions, Islam, Christianity, Judaism, and Zoroastrianism, currently coexist with various tribal religious systems. One of the striking features of the language of religion in this region is that there is no fixed equation of one linguistic form with one religion. Many languages are used to express one religion and one language is used to express many religions. For example, Christianity is expressed through English (in India, Pakistan, Bangladesh, and Sri Lanka), Portuguese/Konkani (in Goa), Tamil (in Tamil Nadu), Hindi (in India), Sinhala (in Sri Lanka), Urdu (in Pakistan), and Bengali (in West Bengal and Bangladesh). Similarly, Hindi is used to express not only Hinduism, but also Buddhism, Christianity, and Jainism. Within the same religious community, diverse languages are used to perform different religious functions, thereby producing a diglossic situation. For example, Sanskrit is used for major rituals of Hinduism, while for household rituals, modern Indian languages are used. Adding to this variation are various registers of regional religious languages such as Sanskritized, Arabicized, Persianized Hindi, Marathi, and so forth.

The emergence, sustenance, and change in the patterns of variation in the use of linguistic codes (languages or language varieties) for expressing religions in South Asia has not been systematically and adequately studied. There are individual studies that explain the variation based on the historical events. For example, the religious movements of the mystics and saints in the medieval period (1500 CE) across South Asia, which were instrumental in promoting the use of the regional as opposed to the classical languages as religious codes, are discussed in, among others, Gaeffke (1978), Ranade (1933), Shapiro and Schiffman (1981), Tulpule (1979), and Zvelebil (1974). Similarly, the role of Bible translation (from English into regional Indian languages) in the use of modern South Asian (SA) vernacular codes for Christianity is discussed in Hooper (1963) and Shackle (2001). However, the studies fail to provide answers to the following questions: (1) why is there variation in the language of religion? Why are several languages used for one religion? (2) if the choice is not random, what are the determinants of language choice? (3) what mechanism causes change across time? (4) when a new religious code is introduced to carry out the function of the earlier religious code, what happens to the earlier code and the reasons for their coexistence? (5) which authority implements/authenticates the change? (6) whether the authority remains constant across time and space or undergoes change? and, finally, (7) when one religious code is replaced by another, what changes occur in the linguistic code and religious content? The following discussion addresses the above questions and attempts to present possible answers. However, in order to do so, it is necessary to briefly describe the constituents of language of religion. A linguistic code is labeled as language of religion on the basis of its three components – its form or linguistic structure, its religious content, and its function. The combination of these three varies across religions. Even within the same religion, it changes across time. The following discussion points out that the patterns of variation in the choice of codes across time and space can be explained in a straightforward fashion within the framework of ideology and hierarchy of power of languages.

In South Asia different languages are perceived as powerful in different domains. Even within the same domain of religion, not all languages are perceived as equally powerful. At any given point in time, there is a hierarchy of power of linguistic codes to express a particular religion. The choice of the code for expressing a particular religion is determined by the degree of power of the code. The power of a code to express a religion as well as the hierarchy is determined by the ideology of the religious communities. The ideology is implemented by the "authority," which serves as the medium or mechanism through which the choice of the codes for particular religions is institutionalized.

The ideology and authority change across time and space due to which the power hierarchy of the codes is restructured. The use of one code for many religions and the use of many codes expressing one religion have an impact on the structure of the codes as well as on the religious content.

Languages of religions in South Asia

The population in South Asia is extremely diverse. However, the degree of concentration of different religions varies across different regions. The breakdown according to religion is as follows according to Census 2001 data: Hindus, over 80 percent; Muslims, over 13 percent; Christians, about 3 percent; Sikhs, about 2 percent; Buddhists 0.75 percent; Jains less than 0.5 percent; other religions less than 0.5 percent (Source: http://hinduism.about.com/library/weekly/extra/bl-population2.htm, accessed October 9, 2005). In contrast,

Pakistan and Bangladesh have a relatively larger concentration of Muslims and significantly less percentage of the Hindus and other religious communities. Sri Lanka has a larger Buddhist community compared to India and Pakistan. Similarly, the distribution of languages varies significantly across South Asia (see Chapter 1). While a major concentration of Indo-Aryan languages is observed in north India, Pakistan, Bangladesh, Nepal, and Sri Lanka, the Dravidian languages are primarily concentrated in south India and Sri Lanka. Tibeto-Burman languages are dominant in the eastern regions in South Asia (India, Nepal, Tibet, and Bangladesh). The focus here is on the issue of the pattern of choice/use of religious language(s) to express different religions and not on the issue of the distribution of the religious languages across the region.

Distribution of languages across religions

The current distribution of languages across religions is given as follows: Hinduism uses Sanskrit, Sanskritized varieties of Modern South Asian (MSA, henceforth) languages, current local, non-Sanskrit codes, and English, but not Arabic or Persian.[1] The languages of Islam are Arabic, Persian, Urdu, and Arabicized/Persianized varieties of MSA languages. Buddhism uses Pali, Hybrid Sanskrit, and MSA languages. The language of old Jain scriptures is Ardhamāgadhī (Middle Indo-Aryan). However, its use is largely replaced by the MSA languages. A large body of Jain literature exists in Kannada and Hindi (and, to a lesser extent, in other MSA languages). Portuguese, Latin, English, and MSA languages are vehicles of Christanity. The language of the Sikh scripture (*Guru Granth Sahab*) is a combinaiton of Old Punjabi (Lahanda) and Khaṛi Boli, and modern Punjabi is readily used for religious discourses in current South Asia.

The choice of a language for a religion is not random. Although more than one language is used for Hinduism, Islam, Buddhism, and Christianity, some languages are typically excluded from the list of options. Furthermore, the pattern of languages mentioned above has not been constant through the history of these religions. For example, the use of MSA languages for these religions is relatively recent (approximately, after 1200 CE, except in the case of Kannada for Jainism). Also, an interesting fact about the current situation in South Asia is that the use of Sanskrit and Arabic, the classical languages of Hinduism and Islam, respectively, which was more restricted in the medieval period, is on the rise in contemporary South Asia. The use of English for Hinduism has a history

[1] This description has no implication for writing systems, for example, the Persian script was used for the Sanskrit religious texts in Kashmir by the Hindu Pandits (see Pushp and Warikoo 1996) though neither Arabic nor Persian was a language of Hindu religion.

of almost two hundred years.[2] Another fact to be noted is that two remarkably different varieties of MSA languages (i.e. highly Sansritized versus highly Arabicized/ Persianized varieties) are used to express their corresponding religions (i.e., Hindusim and Islam). It is instructive to look at the historical events that have been instrumental in propagating the use of many languages for one religion.

Many languages, one religion: Historical evolution

The medieval period (after 1200 CE) marked a major shift in the pattern of languages used to express religions. Before this period, the status "language of religion" was enjoyed by one language for one religion. For example, the classical languages such as Sanskrit (for Hinduism), Arabic/Persian (for Islam), Pali/Hybrid Sanskrit (for Buddhism), Ardhamāgadhī (for Jain), and Latin (for Christianity) were considered to be the linguistic codes endowed with the "power" to express their corresponding religions. Other SA languages were excluded from the domain of religion. During the period 1200 CE to 1700 CE, mystics and saints from the above religions in various parts of India, such as Basavaṇṇa (twelfth century CE) in Karnataka, Jñāneśwar (thirteenth century CE) in Maharashtra, the Āḷvars and Nammāḷvār in Tamil Nadu (fourteenth and fifteenth centuries CE), Mīrābāī and Tulsīdās in the north (fifteenth century CE), and Nānak and Kabīr (sixteenth century CE), independently argued for the legitimacy of nonclassical /vernacular languages. They composed their religious poetry in vernacular regional languages, such as Kannada, Marathi, Tamil, Rajasthani, Awadhi, and Khaṛi Boli/Old Hindi. The mystics and saints were the integrators (see e.g. Ramanujan 1973; Ranade 1933) who, on the one hand, liberated the religions from the constraint of the linguistic form of their expression, and elevated the status of the vernacular languages on the other (for further discussion on the medieval Bhakti movements, see Dwivedi 1964; Nagendra 1973; Shukla 1929; Varma 1947). The classical languages had become virtually inaccessible to the common people by this period. The use of MSA languages for religions brought the scriptures to the common people in their own languages.

The other major historical development during the medieval period was the translations of the scriptures (which were in the classical languages), into MSA/

[2] The use of English for the religious discourse of Hinduism was enhanced by the English discourses of Vivekānanda (nineteenth century CE) as well as by the mystic–saints such as Aurobindo (twentieth century CE). Moreover, the English translations of the Vedas (Max Müller in particular) propogated understanding of the Hindu texts in the West. The term Hinduism (the Persian word "Hindu" with the English suffix) was legitimized during the nineteenth century. An active exchange of concepts and lexicon between Sanskrit and English is observed during this time. However, the use of English was largely restricted to the philosophcical/religious discourse, and the use of Sanskrit and regional languages in the ritual performances of Hinduism was common.

vernacular languages. The impetus for translation came from the following facts: (1) the common people needed access to the scriptures and religion, and (2) the Syrian, Roman Catholic, and the Protestant missionary activities in the colonial era included conversion of the SA population to Christianity (except for Syrian Christians, who have a long history in India). To facilitate such missionary activities the need to translate the Bible into local SA languages became necessary. The first Bible translation in the local (Konkani) language is *Doutrina Crista* (1622 CE) by the English Jesuite Thomas Stephens. Large-scale conversions to Christianity continued through the British rule after the eighteenth century CE (see Hooper 1963), which resulted in translations of the Bible in MSA languages. Thus, the use of languages other than the original languages of religion became prominent after the medieval period. The need for translation was also because of other factors: (3) Buddhist texts that were translated into Tibetan in the seventh century CE began to be used as the Buddhist canonical texts in the medieval period and (4) although Arabic continued to occupy the central place in the orthodox mosque, several versified, bilingual glossaries (of Arabic and local languages) termed *Khaliq bari* or Sufi poetic romances and hymns were composed in MSA languages (Schimmel 1973). The Qur'an was first translated into Persian in 1737 and later into several Urdu versions, which inspired translations in numerous SA languages (Tamil 1873, Gujarati 1879, Telugu 1938, and Kannada 1949). It is important to note that the language of Buddhism in Sri Lanka and India remained the same, that is Pali and Hybrid Sanskrit (a Sanskritized variety of Middle Indo-Aryan), while the language of Sikhism, a mixture of Old Punjabi and Lahanda, was supplemented by modern Punjabi. Translations of Jain scriptures into Kannada and Hindi (in addition to other MSA languages) allowed the use of many languages for the religion.

These historical events provide a background for understanding the use of the MSA languages for their corresponding religions. However, in order to better understand (1) the rationale for the coexistence of the earlier/classical languages and the MSA languages as the religious codes; (2) why Hinduism, Buddhism, Christianity, and Jainism allowed the use of more than one language for their expression while Islam did not; and (3) why classical languages as well as the MSA languages are used in both the secular and religious domains, it is essential to go beyond the historical facts to the framework of ideology essential to answer the above questions.

Ideology and power hierarchy: The ancient and the medieval period

Variation and change in the pattern of the choice of languages for expressing religions is determined by ideologies about language of religion at different points in time in different religious systems. The hierarchy of power of languages to express a religion is based on the ideology which licenses power to different languages. The change in ideology changes the power hierarchy and consequently the choice of the language.

Current research on language ideology and power (Bourdieu 1991; Fairclough 1989; Fowler *et al.* 1997; Hodge and Kress 1988; Silverstein 1979, among others) has shown beyond doubt that ideology, which is a system of beliefs, practices, and representations in the interest of an identifiable class in the society, creates linguistic power hierarchies. In the context of language of religion, ideology may be defined as a system of beliefs about (1) the linguistic form, (2) the religious content, and (3) the function of language of religion at a given point in time within a community. It is a system of beliefs about the interrelationship among the three components, that is the form, conent, and function/use of the religious language. Ideology provides a rationale for the choice of a particular language/linguistic form for expressing a particular religion. This approach to ideology does not treat ideology exclusively as "a distortion in perception of social and economic relations" (Luke 1998: 366); rather, the underlying ideology forms the basis for variability in each of these components of the language of religion. It allows the possibility of coexistence of ideologies of diverse groups within the society, provides a mechanism to identify diachronic changes in the ideology and thereby in language choice, and explains variation in the language choice across religions.

First, let us look at the power hierarchy of religious languages in the ancient period (2000 BCE – the medieval period) in South Asia. As mentioned earlier, Sanskrit was considered to be the only legitimate language of Hinduism. No other languages (Indo-Aryan or Dravidian) were viewed as appropriate to express Hinduism. The ideology, which sanctioned this power hierarchy viewed the language of religion, Sanskrit, as the divine code (*devavāṇī*), which alone was endowed with the power or efficacy of expressing the ultimate truth (*satya*). The Vedas, the ancient Sanskrit texts, were viewed as the first "revelations" of the early sages (*ṛṣis*) that were orally transmitted to the subsequent generations as the truths about the phenomenal reality as well as its foundation in the higher reality which lies beyond human conceptualization and thought. The term *mantra*, literally, "that which protects when meditated upon," had multiple meanings such as, "the sacred formula (the Vedic hymns addressed to the deities)," "verses recited at the Vedic rituals," and so forth.

The Vedic theologies of sound attributed the origin of the universe to the phonic sound and claimed that the language of the Vedas had the power of creation. When uttered flawlessly, it was assumed, the *mantras* had the power to bring about the intended results for the sacrificer (the performer of the Vedic ritual; for further discussion on *mantra*, see Staal 1989). The purity of the language was assumed to be a prerequisite for the success of the ritual. Thus, the religious language was defined on the basis of both its linguistic form as well as its content. Similarly, a few centuries later (but before the medieval period), Islam treated Arabic alone as the language of religion. Qur'an was believed to be the literal word of God revealed through his Prophet Muhammad. Pali and Hybrid Sanskrit remained the languages of Buddhism, and Ardhamāgadhī was considered to be the language of Jainism. Christianity was expressed exclusively through Syriac (in Kerala) and Latin (in the Roman Catholic churches in the southern, mostly western coast of India). In general, the language of the scripture(s) was viewed as the only appropriate form for expressing the corresponding religion. Similarly, the scriptural content was the only source of the legitimate religious beliefs, and the function of the religious language was to express, promote, and follow the religious beliefs presented in the scriptures. There was no variation allowed in the form, content, and the religious function of the language. This ideology gave enormous power to the classical languages, while the regional languages were left totally powerless.

The medieval period marked a major change in the ideology as well as the power hierarchy of religious languages. The mystics and the saints as well as the religious communities under their influence claimed primacy of religious content over linguistic form. It was the religious content which was considered to be the differentia of the religious language, and all languages, including Sanskrit and MSA languages, were viewed as equally powerful to express the religious content. The plea of Jñāneśwar (thirteenth century CE), who argued for the equality of all linguistic codes, was for legitimizing the MSA languages as languages of Hinduism (for further discussion, see Ranade 1933).[3] This ideology can be called "sacralization of secular codes." It granted power to nonclassical regional Indian languages to express Hinduism. Moreover, it sanctioned the use of more than one language (regional languages) for this purpose.

The process of sacralization of MSA languages was expressed through two major trends – one that marked Sanskritization of MSA languages, thereby approximating them to Sanskrit by borrowing linguistic features of Sanskrit, and the second and opposite movement, their de-Sanskritization. Although both emphasized the legitimatization of the MSA languages in the religious domain, their assumptions and impact significantly differed from each other. The first, Sanskritization, implicitly assumed superiority of Sanskrit over MSA codes, and resulted in the development of a commonly shared Sanskritized register of MSA languages, thereby promoting their convergence. In contrast, the

[3] Jñāneśwar, who used Marathi, as opposed to Sanskrit, for his commentary on the *Bhagavadgītā*, claimed that Marathi, a regional language, would win over the people with its power as it is clear from the following quote from *Jñāneśwarī* 6.14: *madzā maraṭhītSi bolu kautuke*, *parīamṛtātehī paidzā djinke*, *aisī akṣare rasike*, *meḷawīna*. "My speech is Marathi indeed, but my composition for the connoisseurs will be so effective that it will surpass even ambrosia."

deliberate de-Sanskritization of the MSA languages asserted the legitimacy of MSA codes as well as the regional (Hindu) religious identity of their users. Wherever this trend took hold, Sanskrit became powerless since it did not express any regional variety of Hinduism; it simply signaled pan-SA Hinduism (see Pandharipande 2001)

The simultaneous maintenance of Sanskrit and MSA languages as religious codes was possible because the community was diglossic in religious practices as in other social domains. While Sanskrit was used in pan-SA rituals (sacrifices, weddings, funerals, etc.), regional languages were used in the household rituals and personal or regional rituals or worship ceremonies.

In the case of Christianity, Bible translations allowed the use of MSA languages for church service, and so on. Latin and Syriac continued to be used as the languages of Roman Catholic and Syrian Christianity, and the use of Potuguese, English, and MSA languages became prevalent in Catholic and Protestant Churches. Diglossia was introduced whereby Latin, Syriac, Portuguese, and English were used by the elite and the MSA languages were used by the new converts from the lower classes (see Brown 1980; Shackle 2001). The ideology was similar to the one for Hinduism. It was the religious content which gave the identity as religious language to a code. The linguistic structure by itself was not viewed as endowed with particular efficacy.

In contrast to Hinduism and Christianity, Islam did not recognize MSA languages as legitimate codes for Islam. Arabic continued to occupy the central position as language of Islam, despite the fact that some local MSA languages had developed their Arabicized varieties. While those varieties marked the religious identity of the Muslim community in social domains, they were excluded from rituals in the mosque. The ideology that justified this exclusion was based on the understanding that the Qur'an is God's word transmitted to human beings through the Prophet Muhammad. Therefore, the proper language of Islam had to be Arabic though in Pakistan Urdu is the language of examination of the madrassas affiliated to Central Board such as the Deobandis, the Barelvis, the Ahl-i-Hadith and the Shias (see Rahman 1999a: Chapter 5). Thus, diglossia of Arabic and MSA languages marked the language of Islam as well. In the case of Buddhism, MSA languages (including Tibetan in Tibet) were accepted as the religious codes, though Pali and Hybrid Sanskrit remained major languages of the Buddhist canon (Ekvall 1964; Williams 2001). Underlying ideology thus gave rise to diverse power hierarchies, allowed use of many languages for one religion, and was responsible for the emergence of diglossia as a strategy of maintenance of more than one code in the same religious domain. An interesting note of worth is that while MSA languages were used for Hinduism, Christianity, Islam (to some extent), and Buddhism, the use of the classical languages (Arabic, Latin) and "foreign" languages (Persian, Portuguese), and to a large extent English, was restricted to their corresponding religions, namely Islam and Christianity.

Sanskrit continued to be used in more than one religion, namely Hinduism, Buddhism, and Jainism in the medieval period.

Ideology, power hierarchy, and language choice in contemporary South Asia

Although the patterns of language choice in medieval and the contemporary period in South Asia look similar, they are not the same. The most striking difference between the two patterns is that the domain-related diglossia which existed in the medieval period seems to be breaking down in modern South Asia. The languages are crossing over their earlier domains. In fact, two (at least) apparently contradictory processes seem to be currently operating in South Asia. MSA languages are more readily used in domains where earlier classical languages (Sanskrit for Hinduism, Arabic for Islam, Latin/Syriac for Christianity, Pali for Buddhism, etc.) were used exclusively, for example in stable ritualistic contexts, such as wedding, funeral, and naming ceremony. Religious sermons and discourses are readily given in the MSA languages mixed with the classical languages. This process is accelerating sacralization of MSA languages. In contrast, classical languages such as Sanskrit and Arabic are being revived in some secular context in contemporary South Asia. This process can be called the "secularization of the sacred languages." An interesting choice is that of the English language, which, earlier excluded from the domain of Hinduism, is readily acceptable within the Hindu community for philosophical discussions, sermons, and theological discourses. Mixing MSA languages with English is seen as a strategy to popularize religious beliefs (of Christianity, Hinduism, neo-Buddhism, and Islam) among the diverse groups which use mutually unintelligible languages.

In contemporary South Asia, the choice of a language for a particular religion is not determined by the sociocultural domain but by its function, that is the socioreligious identity which it symbolizes. In contemporary South Asia, religion is one of the major symbols of social identity. The SA society is largely divided on the basis of religion. Thus, Hinduism, Islam, Christianity, Sikhism, and so on, mark not only religious groups, but also social groups. Embedded within the same religious/social group, there are other identities, such as pan-South Asian religious/social group, and regional religious/social group etc. Additionally, the regional groups are further divided along ethnic lines such as Aryan and Dravidian. Each language expresses a particular type of religious/social group identity. The choice of a language is determined by the intended identity and the power of the language to express it.

The correspondence here is not necessarily between the social domain and the linguistic code, rather, it is between code and identity, a "heteroglossia of identities." The connection between the codes and the identities is shown in

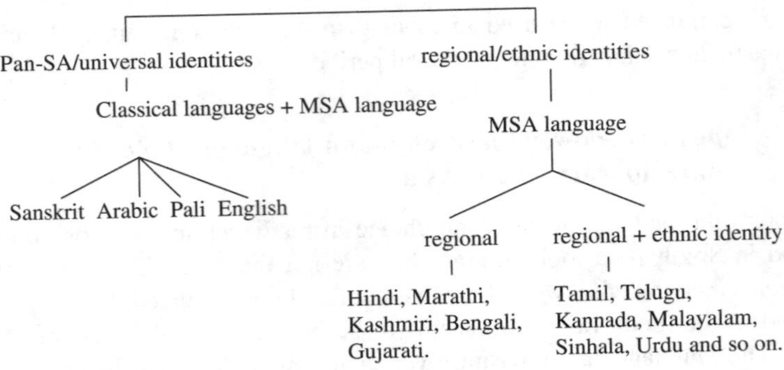

Figure 21.1 *Heteroglossia of identities.*

Figure 21.1. The classical languages Sanskrit, Arabic, Pali, and English symbolize the larger, pan-SA or Hindu, Muslim, Buddhist, Christian universal identities (religious as well as social), respectively. In contrast to this, MSA languages express the regional religious/social identities. For example, the use of Hindi for Christianity, Bengali for Islam, and Tamil for Hinduism as religious codes express the regional version of their corresponding religions. It should be noted here that the use of English for Christianity is similar to the use of classical languages. However, the use of Syriac and Latin is also marginally maintained in some churches in Kerala.

The heteroglossia of identities include microlevel identities in many cases. The regional languages (similar to the medieval period) use one of the two registers: one which shows the influence of the corresponding classical language and the other without it. For example, the use of Sanskritized Hindi or non-Sanskritized Hindi can be readily used to express regional religious/social identity. Additionally, various dialects of Hindi are also used to express Hinduism. The choice of a language in this case is determined by the religious theme[4] (for a discussion of thematic diglossia, see Pandharipande 1992a). However, especially in Tamil Nadu, the use of the regional languages, devoid of any Sanskrit influence, indicates intentional dissociation from the Indo-Aryan Hindu tradition and assertion of the Dravidian identity (Hart 1976; Narayanan 1994; Peterson 1989; Zvelebil 1974).

[4] In the northeastern part of India, Sanskrit is used for the Vedic rituals and chants, while for non-Vedic regional rituals MSA languages are used. Language of recitation /chanting is determined by the theme of worship of a particular deity. For example, for the worship of the god Rāma, the language is generally Awadhī while for the worship of Krishna, the language is generally Braj. This choice is based on the languages of the sacred texts for the respective deities. While the *Rāmcharitmānas*, a sacred text for Rāma is in Awadhī (a north eastern 'dialect' of Hindi), the texts for Krishna are in Braj (a northwestern 'dialect' old Hindi).

The use of English (as opposed to Latin, Syriac, and Portuguese) for pan-SA Christianity is becoming more common as the knowledge of the traditional languages for Christianity is rapidly decreasing.

Modernization, composite identities, and the ideology of language mixing

The ideology of heteroglossia is a consequence of modernization, a phenomenon characterized by globalization as well as localization at the same time (Appadurai 1996; Robertson 1992; Stuart Hall 1996). While globalization (marked by technologization, Englishization, and homogenization) results in undermining, and, at times, obliterating differences within and across societies, it also causes emergence of local identities expressed by age-old symbols. While Sanskrit, Arabic, and Pali express the pan-SA or universal Hindu, Muslim, and Buddhist identities, respectively, they diffuse those regional/ethnic differences that are embedded within the broad labels of Hinduism, Islam, and Buddhism. The increased awareness of the "particular" or "local" identities is symbolized and expressed by the use of regional languages.

A phenomenon that has not received attention in current research on language of religion is of mixing languages within the same event. For example, in a typical wedding ritual (in Maharashtra state in India), the priest conducts the ritual in Sanskrit, while the concluding ritual of blessing the newly wedded couple (*mangalāṣṭaka* "the eight auspicious verses") is in Marathi. The social act, wedding invitation card, can be in English. Another typical example of mixing of languages is the popular religious sermons delivered to the public on the television or in an "open air theater." The local language (for example, Hindi, Marathi, or Gujarati) is the primary language of the sermon. However, the use of Sanskrit quotations from the Hindu scriptures is abundant. English items are also mixed with the primary language of communication.

The construction or make-up of the contemporary SA identity is complex. The identities (universal and local) do not exist mutually exclusively; they exist simultaneously. The SA multilingual community consists of multiple identities, each relevant for an individual function. Language can symbolize a particular identity. The use of Sanskrit in the wedding event indicates the pan-South Asian/universal Hindu identity of the group, the use of Marathi articulates the regional identity, and the use of English allows communication with the larger group with many mutually unintelligible languages. The use of English items in the public (popular) religious sermon is a strategy to express religion in common people's language which contains a *large* body of English items, such as *station, car, TV, table, fast, slow, traffic, and post office.*

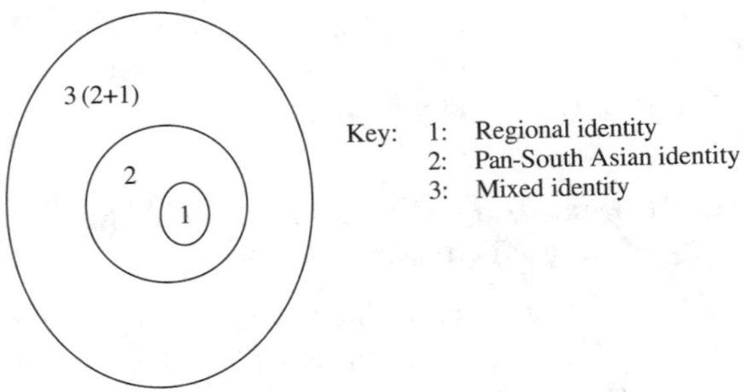

Figure 21.2 *Overlapping identities.*

Mixing occurs in secular domains, too. Sanskrit, the classical language of Hinduism, is mixed with other SA languages in most secular contexts. For example, the logo of the life insurance company owned by the Government of India (Life Insurance Corporation of India, LIC, or Bharatāya Bīmā Company) is in Sanskrit. It is a direct quote from one of the most prominent scriptures of Hindus (*Bhagavadgītā* 9:22) *yōgakṣēmam vahāmyaham*, "I take care of their needs /I provide them security (who depend on me)." In the original text of the *Bhagavadgītā*, the God Krishna advises Arjuna, his friend and devotee, to trust him because God always takes care of those who depend on Him. This quote encourages people to have faith in the insurance company. In this advertisement, the quote occurs in Sanskrit while the rest of the text is in various SA languages.

Another example of a Sanskrit quote from *Bṛhadāraṇyakopaniṣad* (1.3:28) *tamaso mā jyotirgamaya*, "Lead me from the darkness to light," a prayer to God to remove ignorance and bestow knowledge on the person offering the prayer, is used as the caption in an advertisement for fabric for men's suiting. The intended meaning seems to be, "Let the knowledge dawn that this fabric is indeed the best. Let the ignorance about the quality of the fabric be dispelled." The phenomenon of using religious language for promoting commercial products is fairly common in South Asia (see Chapter 19). This process exemplifies "secularization of the religious language."

The ideology that justifies such cases is based on the following assumptions about religious language: (1) religious language symbolizes religious as well as secular/social identity, and (2) the identity of the SA community at large is a composite one which allows use of multiple languages to express these overlapping identities (Figure 21.2).

While the innermost circle (1) in figure 21.2 expresses the local /regional religious/social identity, the circle in the middle (2) expresses a broader, pan-SA religious/social identity. The outer circle (3) expresses the composite identity of the religious community which encompasses the other two identities.

Impact of multiple linkage on the structure of the languages

A language does undergo change when it is used for different religions, that is it develops different registers (Pandahripande 1992a, 2001). For example, when Hindi is used for Hinduism, Christianity, Buddhism, and Islam, it develops Hindu, Christian, Buddhist and Islamic registers, respectively. These registers differ from one another primarily in the religious vocabulary, which varies across religions. When one language is used for many religions, its vocabulary (which was previously shared in common by different religions) comes to acquire contextually determined meanings. For example, the term *Iśvar* is interpreted differently in different religious systems, as shown in Figure 21.3 below.

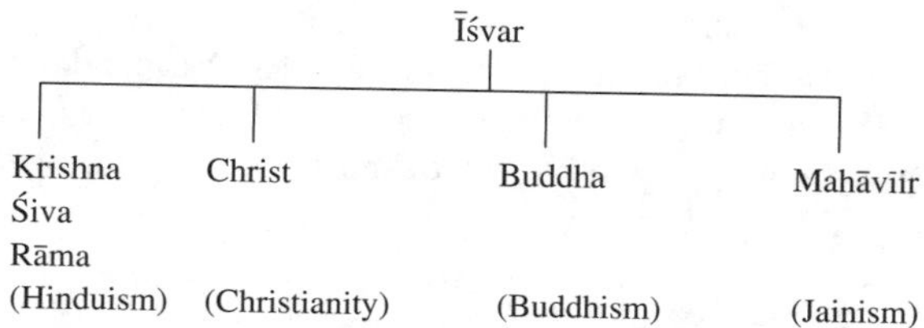

Figure 21.3 *Interpretation of Īśvar in different religions.*

An additional impact of the use of SA languages for many religions is seen in their convergence. Each of the major SA languages developed similar varieties, such as Sanskritized (for Hinduism), Arabicized/Persianized (for Islam), and Englishized (for Christianity), which share linguistic features (mainly religious themes and vocabulary). Note the Sanskritized Hindi (1) and (2) and Tamil (3) in the following examples:
Hindi: Tulsïdās' (fifteenth century CE) *Vinay Patrikā* (*pad* : 43). The italicized portion is in Sanskrit.[5]

(1) *vedabodhita-karma-dharma-dharaṇī-dhenu-vipra-sevaka-sadhumodakari*
Veda-instructed-action-duty-earth cows-Brahmins-servants-saints-joy giver
He makes the whole world (earth), cows, Brahmins, and servants happy by performing actions, (religious) duties which are instructed by the Vedas.

The following example illustrates modern religious prayer in Hindi:

(2) *jay jagadīś hare, svāmī jay jagadīś hare*
bhaktajanõ ke *sankaṭa* pal mẽ dūr kare

[5] See, *Vinaypatrika: Tulsi Das Letter to Sri Ram.* (compiled by Camille Bulcke, presented by "Khristanath"). Patna: Navjyoti Niketan, 1988.

Victory to you Hari, who is the lord of the world. O Hari, you are the controller, the lord of the world. You instantaneously remove the troubles of your devotees.

Tamil: The following example is from Thirugnanasambandhan (1992: 119)

(3) muttukkḷalum *iva* naṟpavalannaḷāum
kōttukkalanta tamiḷḷ *api samskṛtena*
ettikkilum *bhavatu hāralateva baddhā*
puttikku *matkṛtir iyam sudṛśam vaibhava.*

May my composition where Tamil and Sanskrit are mixed and strung together like pearls and excellent corals mixed and strung together in a garland be an embellishment for the intellect everywhere.

See Chapter 11 for a discussion of *maṇipravālam* style.

The use of different languages had an impact on the religious content as well. As the medium changed, the message did too (Pandharipande 1992a, 1999). The use of MSA languages included metaphors, narratives, and religious themes which were not necessarily part of the earlier scriptures in their corresponding classical languages.

Genres of religious discourse

The other major impact of the multiple linkage of religious languages is seen in the emergence of an intricate network of genres of religious discourse which determine language choice in particular contexts. Over a period of time, new genres were introduced, which coexisted with the old ones and with one another, and were at times, replaced. The languages chosen for those genres also went through changes. Although it is difficult to provide here a comprehensive survey of the entire range of the genres for each religion, a brief sketch is presented by way of illustration of the genres in Hindu religious discourse. The ancient genre of Vedic hymns, rituals, and *mantras* were in Sanskrit poetry, while the philosophical as well as theological discourses/teachings/dialogues of the Upaniṣads, and the Sūtra literture were in Sanskrit prose. The enormous body of critical scholarly commentaries, the expository discourse, was also in Sanskrit prose. A large body of *Stotra* (literally, prayers in praise of deities) literature in the post-Vedic period was in a stylized form of poetry. However, after the seventh to eighth centuries CE, MSA/regional languages began to be used for the transcreation of the Sanskrit classics, for example *Jñāneśvarī* (thirteenth century CE), a commentary/transcreation of the *Bhagavadgitā* in Marathi, Villiputtur Āḷvār's Tamil *Mahābhārata* (1400 CE), Kamban's Tamil version of the *Rāmāyaṇa*, *Rāmāvatāram* "The descent of Rāma," Kumara vyāsa's *Mahābhārata* in Kannada (fifteenth century), and Tulsīdās's Awadhi version of the *Rāmāyaṇa*, *Rāmcaritmānas* (sixteenth century CE). Moreover, extremely popular and powerful devotional literature in the premedieval and medieval period was primarily composed in poetry in the regional languages. The *Vacanas* (in Kannada), *Kirtanas*, and *Padas* of Purandara Dasa and other saint–poets, and *Dohe* and *Padas* (in Old Hindi and Rajasthani), and so on, are examples of this genre. Additionally, *Kīrtan* and *Bhajan* established some of the new genres of devotional poetry in regional languages.

A Śaivite woman mystic–saint Lalleshwari from Kashmir composed her devotional poetry in the Kashmiri language (B. Kachru 1981: 15) in the native form of the meter called *Vīk*, while Akka Mahadevī, Basavaṇṇa, and others evoked a poetic prose genre in the *Vacanas* of Kannada (twelfth century, see Ramanujan 1972).

The question of functional transparency

A question that arises in this context, is that while MSA languages are readily used for different religions, why are classical languages (Sanskrit, Arabic, Persian, and Pali) restricted to their corresponding religions? The reason seems to be that these are the languages of ancient scriptures and therefore of their corresponding religions. Their affinity with the respective religions is viewed as almost exclusive and self-evident. By contrast, the MSA languages came on the scene much later and their identification with a particular religion is relatively less transparent and more flexible. In the medieval period, they were chosen for transcreating Hindu texts, for Bible translations as well as for the translations of the Qur'an.

Authority

Traditionally, mystics, saints, institutions, and institutional officials have been perceived as authorities in determining the choice of religious language for religions. However, their perception of religious language changes across time. Thus, while the ancient mystics and saints did not allow the use of MSA languages, those in the medieval period did. In contemporary South Asia, the mystics and saints use a mixture of many languages. Such mixture of languages is more readily allowed in the oral discourse about religion than in the religious rituals and written discourse.

Although the traditional authority of saints and mystics continues to play a role in authenticating the choice of a code appropriate for the religious in contemporary South Asia, the "social magic" (Bourdieu 1991) is the media which constructs, communicates, and promotes religious languages as symbols of religious/social identities. More specifically, the visual (TV) and audio programs on and about religion play a major role in the communication and authentication of religious languages as identity symbols.

In addition to symbolization, the languages used in the programs get authenticated and gradually institutionalized as religious languages. For example, the languages used by the saints in the religious discourse on the TV or in the movies based on religious epics are accepted as authentic languages of religion. The most interesting case is that of the Hindu epics, the *Rāmāyaṇa* and the *Mahābhārata*, enacted serially on the TV. The language of the epics is Hindi mixed with Sanskrit. However, the genre is new. The vocabulary, syntax, and the symbols depict a novel composite form which is intentionally produced to recreate the ambience of the ancient period. Although this genre has no precedents in history, it is well accepted as an authentic religious code of Hinduism. Just as the use of the MSA languages was authenticated by the religious scriptures composed by the mystics in the MSA languages in the medieval period, the use of the Sanskrit-mixed Hindi (or Sanskrit–MSA language mixing in the secular advertisements) is authenticated and institutionalized by their presentation on TV or in the print media.

Script as a determinant of religious language

Similar to the multiple linkage of languages and religions, some SA languages of religions are written in more than one script. For example, Punjabi and Sindhi are written in both Devanagari and Perso-Arabic scripts; Kashmiri has four scripts (Sharada, Devanagari, Perso-Arabic, and Roman); Maithili has two scripts – Devanagari and Kaithi; and Konkani has four scripts – Devanagari, Roman, Malayalam and Kannada. This situation raises the question about the choice of the script for a particular religious language.

Although there does not always exist a definite correlation between a script and religion in South Asia, some correspondence is generally observed. Devanagari, due to its historical connection with Sanskrit, the language of the ancient Hindu scriptures, is traditionally associated with Hinduism. However, it is important to note that neither is it used exclusively for Hinduism nor is it the only script used for the language of Hinduism. Many translations of the Bible in Devanagari are currently used in Christian churches. Moreover, the scripts of MSA languages (Tamil, Malayalam, Telugu, Bengali, Kannada, Gujarati) are used extensively to express Hinduism. Though Devanagari is usually selected for Hinduism, Pushp and Warikoo (1996: 22) point out that the Hindu religious texts such as the Upaniṣads and the epics (the *Rāmāyaṇa*, and the *Mahābhārata*) were rendered in the Persian script in Kashmir.

In contemporary South Asia, distinction between Hindi and Urdu is to a large extent based on the difference in the scripts. While Hindi in the Devanagari script is the marker of Hinduism, Urdu with the Perso-Arabic script has become the pan-SA symbol of Islam. Similarly, the Devanagari script differentiates

Hindu Konkani from Christian Konkani in Goa which uses the Roman script (see Miranda 1978).

The script of the languages of Sikhism is the Gurumukhi script and not a particular language which is the differentia of the religious literature. While the *Ādi Granth* (the oldest scripture of Sikhism) is in Punjabi–old-Hindi mixed language, and the Sikh religious literature from the seventeenth to the nineteenth centuries is in Braj Bhāṣā, modern Punjabi is becoming the language of contemporary Sikhism. Despite the diversity of langugaes, Sikh literature (in all of the above languages) is typically recorded in Gurumukhi script.

While Perso-Arabic script is generally associated with Islam, the correlation between the two is not invariable. Muslims in Bengal prefer to use Bengali script more than Perso-Arabic to write Bengali. Similarly, the Ismāilī Muslims use Gujarati (language and the script) which has replaced the earlier script derived from Sindhi. While the Devanagari script is accepted as the script of the canonical Buddhist scriptures in India, Sri Lanka, and Tibet, the use of Tibetan script is most common in Tibet. Similarly, while the Devanagari script is well accepted for Jainism, other scripts such as Kannada and Telugu are very commonly used as well.

Conclusion

In a multilingual and multireligious region such as South Asia, the choice of language of religion is determined by the ideology about the function of the religious language and the relative power of the language(s) to carry out that function. The ideology changes across time, which restructures the hierarchy of power of languages, and consequently, affects the choice of languages for religions. Further, the ideology is implemented through two mechanisms, one, the authority, and second, the degree of functional transparency of the language. Therefore, ideology, authority, and functional transparency should be treated as mechanisms of change in the structure and function of religious languages in particular, and languages in general. Furthermore, the same ideology can be expressed in two mutually exclusive and apparently opposite processes. For example, the ideology of using MSA languages for religious expression (in the medieval period) was expressed in the two linguistic processes of Sanskritization and de-Sanskritization. This challenges the current theory of ideology, which assumes that an ideology promotes only one structural realization. Also, authority is not static. Moreover, even if the authority remains the same, it licenses different ideologies at different points in time.

When one language is used for different religions, its linguistic form changes (recall the various registers of Hindi). Similarly, when one religion is expressed in many languages, the religious content changes as well. The use of the MSA languages to express religion has promoted convergence of SA languages across language families through the development of shared religious registers. Similar convergence of MSA languages is seen in their Englishization (in contemporary South Asia) and the emergence of Englishized registers of MSA languages. The concept of heteroglossia explains language choice in modern South Asia better than diglossia because the choice of codes is determined not only by the social domain of language use but also by the identity (religious/ social) which is intended to be expressed. Finally, sociolinguistic conditions (ideology, authority, and functional transparency of the code) that determine a code as "language of religion" undergo change at different points in time as is exemplified in South Asia. In the first period, the form, content, and function were viewed as invariable since the languages chosen for expressing religions at this time were the classical languages or the languages of the scriptures. In the medieval period, the ideology changed, allowing variation in form while the content was perceived as invariable. As long as the religious content was maintained, the form which expressed that content was perceived as religious. The function of the religious language also remained the same as before. Diglossia was the mechanism that allowed maintenance of both – the classical as well as the MSA languages. In the contemporary period, with greater mobility, the choice of the language for expressing a religion is determined by the identity of the religion/ community across state and national boundaries. The form, content, and function are variable, thus allowing languages to transcend the religions as well as the boundaries of the secular and the sacred.

Further reading

The literature on language of religion in South Asia is diverse in its scope, language, and religion. It covers its philosophical, theological, mythological, literary, and social dimensions over a long period of over a thousand years. Moreover, literature on each religion is available in different languages. It is difficult to find a systematic analysis of languages and religions in South Asia in a single text. The following recommended readings are selected on the basis of their contributions to the study of languages of religions in South Asia.

A comprehensive review of religious literature of Hinduism, Jainism, Christianity, and Buddhism in each of the major languages of India, is covered in the series, *A History of Indian Literature*, edited by Jan Gonda published by Otto Harrassowitz, Wiesbaden. Each of the volume in the series includes excellent discussion on the religious literatures and languages. *The Concise Encyclopedia of Language and Religion* edited by John F. A. Sawyer and J. M. Simpson (2001) includes a valuable collection of entries on languages of religions in South Asia.

For special topics, some important texts are (1) *Mantra*, edited by Harvey P. Alper (1989), which is a collection of articles on the analysis of *mantra* and the Vedic language within the traditional Hindu as well as modern linguistic frameworks and (2) *The Word and the World* by Matilal (1991), which is an excellent analysis of the language of Hinduism within the philosophical tradition of India. For various aspects of the languages of Christianity in South Asia, the following works are valuable: *Bible Translation in India, Pakistan, and Ceylon* (now Sri Lanka) by J. S. M. Hooper (1963), and R. V. Miranda (1978). The latter provides an excellent discussion on the controversy over languages and script of the Christian dialect in Goa.

A. Schimmel's (1973) text, *Islamic Literatures of India*, and C. Shackle's *Encyclopedia of Islam* provide an excellent source for the history, structure, and function(s) of the languages of Islam in South Asia. T. Rahman's (1999) book, *Language and Politics in Pakistan* as well as A. Rai's (1984) *A House Divided* cover the issues related to the language of Islam and Hinduism in South Asia. An excellent source for the early Buddhist tradition in India is H. Bechert's (1980) text, *The Language of the Earliest Buddhist Tradition*. A brief historical survey of Indian Buddhism is Collins (2001) in *Concise Encyclopedia of Language and Religion* edited by Sawyer and Simpson. For the language of Sikhism, and social and political issues surrounding it, the following sources are notable: C. Shackle's (1983) *An Introduction to the Sacred Language of the Sikhs*, P. R. Brass's (1974) *Language, Religion, and Politics in North India*, and H. Singh's (1995–1998) *The Encyclopedia of Sikhism*.

For a comprehensive discussion on the structure, philosophy and attitudes toward the language of Jainism, the following sources are of significant importance: P. S. Jaini's (1979) *The Jain Path of Purification* and S. Jain's (1989) *Jaina Philosophy of Language*.

For a discussion of Bible translation in MSA languages, for example for Hindi, see McGregor (1974).

Part 9

Language and identity

22 Language and gender

Tamara M. Valentine

Introduction

Over the past thirty to forty years, issues related to the study of language and gender have been examined, described, interpreted, explained, revised, and revisited by linguists, sociologists, psychologists, educators, feminist scholars, and others primarily within the contexts of the middle-class, white, monolingual, heterosexual, Western societies and cultures, generalizing the findings to all populations of the world. A major criticism of the work done in this area has been that language and gender scholarship has taken positions that are fundamentally ideological and political, forcing scholars to take a stand on one side of an issue or the other. When tracing the history of writings on language and gender from early anthropological accounts that touched on sex differences in non-European languages to the frequently cited scholarly works and popular readings influencing the prominent models used to study language and gender today, we see that this perspective certainly holds true. As a result, criticized for being motivated by feminist politics and personal interests, gender studies has been marginalized as an "unscientific" academic discipline by mainstream linguists and shunned by women and men of Asia, Africa, Latin America and other regions of the developing world (Kishwar 2000; Schirmer 1989).

A further challenge to scholars of language and gender research is the essentialist principle of "gender is difference," a persistent theme that runs through early language studies. Within the essential feminity of women and masculinity of men, early researchers assumed that the language differences found between women and men reflect underlying biological differences. Accepting this premise, a long history of work assumes that there is one single way of being female and being male, ignoring the many different cultural systems, speech communities, and expressions of feminism that exist in the world. And finally, not only has language and gender research been faced with the ideological challenges, but it has been criticized for assuming that women

I am grateful to the American Institute of Indian Studies and National Endowment for the Humanities for providing me with the support to conduct my field research on language and gender in India during the 2000–2001 academic year.

across the world share a collective identity. A review of the literature shows that traditionally, scholars have concentrated on the study of the language of speech communities in the Western world contexts, that in Asia, Africa, and Latin America (Mohanty 1984); as a result, a leveling of the multiple gender identities that exist in other speech communities has taken place. For too long the position taken has been that gender means the same across communities, and women cross-culturally and intraculturally speak as a single homogeneous social group.

To understand the central issues that surround language and gender research in recent years, this chapter examines some of the ideological conditions that have taken place and that have laid the groundwork for making universalistic claims about gender as a global category. For the most part, the direction of study in gender research has been driven by Western ideologies, theories, and writings, as examples from South Asian languages will show. In addition, in response to the charge that the gap has widened between Western elite feminist research and nonelite feminist research, this chapter discusses the "rethinking" currently taking place in language and gender research (Bergvall *et al.* 1996). The focus has shifted from viewing gender as an unchanging natural fact to investigating the unfolding of gender in the "local" contexts and examining women as active members of their particular speech communities. First-world gender politics of "global, generic, and feminist" has heard the words of third-world gender politics: "practical, local, and particularistic." Illustrated with examples from the languages of South Asia, this chapter examines these issues as they relate to the study of language and gender within the contexts of traditional South Asian societies.

Rethinking the ideology of biological sex

Rethinking the study of language and gender means departing from the mainstream notions and cultural assumptions about gender differences. Rethinking means approaching the world in terms other than dualisms, oppositions, dichotomies, and conflict (Tannen 1998). Rethinking means expanding the boundaries when defining gender and uncommitting ourselves to polarizing the sexes and to ascribing women and men as opposite sexes.

One of the basic assumptions held by specialists and nonspecialists alike is that the male and female genders are categorically and fundamentally different based on their natural sex determined at birth. For the most part, Western science and thought have led the world in the assumption of biological essentialism: one's gender is identical to one's sex. Based on socially agreed upon characteristics rooted in biology, such as chromosomal factors (XX female and XY male), genetic explanations, reproductive capacity, genital appearance, and hormonal differences, humans are assigned the label of either *female* or *male* at birth. Although there is no standard legal or medical definition of the term, *sex* has retained its original meaning of "either of the two divisions of organic beings distinguished as male and female respectively" (Oxford English Dictionary). And its users in compliance have accepted the natural bipolarity of human beings.

In the mid-1970s, with the advent of feminist scholarly work, Western feminists strongly criticized the essentialist definition on the grounds that *sex* is associated with characteristics that are narrowly defined and strictly grounded in biology, disregarding social and cultural factors that may shape an individual's sense of reality and identity (Anselmi and Law 1998; Cameron 1992; Romaine 1999). To destabilize gender binaries the interests of Western feminists turned to making a distinction between socially acquired behavior and biologically innate categories. The term *gender*, then, was infused with a sociocultural dimension to refer to the social arrangement of the relationship between the sexes (Oakley 1981): a "social, cultural, and psychological phenomena attached to sex" (McConnell-Ginet 1988). A conscious effort was made to distinguish the two terms: one's sex is based on biological factors; one's gender on social factors. Sex is natural, biological, and fixed; gender is sociocultural and variable. According to Western society, then, biological *sex* becomes the organizing principle of social structure which determines *gender*, one's social roles and behaviors. Obscuring the distinction between the two terms, its users for the most part have come to use them interchangeably, collapsing gender and sex.

Translating *gender* and *sex* into the languages of South Asia is somewhat problematic. Most South Asian languages have one word for both sex and gender: *linga*, one's sex, is identified as either *strii linga* or *pu(ṃ) linga*. To distinguish biological from social sex, descriptors are used: *praakritik linga* for "natural/biological sex" and *saamaajik linga* for "cultural/social gender." As with English users, the distinction between *praakritik linga* and *saamaajik linga* remains fuzzy to its users.

But herein lies a dilemma: depending on the approach, training, and social leaning, a researcher operates from a set of "commonsense" assumptions and a framework of experiences and expectations, which cannot be separated from shaping his/her work, defining his/her terms, and formulating his/her questions. The way the scientist approaches the problem reflects the epistemological framework or system of beliefs and values that he/she and the field of academic study share and accept. To the extent that ideologies and cultural values and beliefs about sex and gender inform and reinforce scientific thinking, science can be said to be gendered, in contradiction to scientists' beliefs in objectivism and impartiality. Therefore, when using specific terms such as sex and gender, the researcher reveals his/her epistemological perspective as well as his/her political and ideological positions on gender differences. "Sex difference findings never enter the scientific discourse neutrally. Rather, they are reinterpreted within the context of deeply held beliefs about women's natures. In accounting for their results, researchers cannot avoid being influenced by the sociocultural discourse of gender, because "facts" about sex differences have no meaning outside that discourse" (Crawford 1995: 32).

By accepting the essentialist view of only two distinct biological categories, language and gender study has fallen into the trap of searching for sex differences and hastily jumping to the conclusion that gender *is* difference: men and women *are* essentially and fundamentally different; therefore, the difference is reflected in language use. The status of this gender ideology has become a battleground associating feminity with femaleness and masculinity with maleness – the basis for a *natural* division of society by sex. As will be discussed later, unfortunately, this ideology has influenced the thinking on gender differences in non-Western cultures where being male and female is not necessarily viewed in such absolute dichotomous ways.

Early language and gender accounts

Emphasis on fundamental sex differences had serious consequences on the scholarly direction that language and gender research took. The essentialist view that gender is inextricably linked to an individual's biological sex influenced the kind of questions asked in the early investigations on language variation and gender. From the assorted anthropological accounts describing "primitive" peoples of the seventeenth century to the fieldwork surveys of European languages by the traditional dialectologists of the twentieth century, observers made note of the differences between male and female speech patterns. In general, the body of ethnographic literature on culture identified "male" and "female" variation in language as *gender exclusive* and *gender preferential*. In languages with gender-exclusive differences, women and men used different words for the same thing, different grammatical or lexical morphologies, or different pronunciations. In contrast, in languages with gender-preferential differences, women and men used the same linguistic forms but in different frequencies.

In such American Indian societies as the Yana in California (Sapir 1949) and the Koasati in Louisiana (Haas 1944), or in the traditional African and South Asian cultures, where the behaviors and activities of women and men were clearly dictated by rigidly defined social, moral, and linguistic codes, anthropologists identified gender-exclusive languages, embracing the widespread androcentric belief of male linguistic superiority. One explanation for separate gendered languages was the societal observance of linguistic taboos. Certain forms of "proper" linguistic behavior were prescribed for each sex, emphasized more often for women than for men. Numerous sociolinguistic studies on Indian languages (Chandrasekhar 1970 in Malayalam; Das 1968 in Bengali; Koul 1984 in Kashmiri; Koul and Bala 1989 in Punjabi; Mehrotra 1981, 1985 in Hindi; Valentine 1983; and Vatuk 1969 in north India) have described the forms of address and reference, pronominal usage, modes of greeting, and the naming practices of speakers in the family, social, and professional contexts of South Asia. Dhanesh Jain (1973), for example, illustrates the power associated with linguistic taboos and the cultural significance of naming avoidance in a traditional Hindu household revealing the importance of older males and the power of the husband's family. To show respect and deference a wife avoids uttering the name of her husband or the names of her husband's father, husband's brothers, and other male family members. This taboo extends to any words or syllables similar sounding to the forbidden male name. For example, a wife avoids the Hindi word *dhaniyaa* "coriander" or any word phonetically similar to it because her husband's elder brother is named *dhanii raam*. Instead of *dhaniya* the wife substitutes the common phrase *harii botal waalaa masaalaa* ("the spice in the green glass bottle") to erase any sound association between the brother's name *dhanii raam* and the spice *dhaniyaa*.

The strength of the naming avoidance principle in South Asian languages is reflected in the cultural belief that a wife's verbalization of her husband's name shortens his life. For example, to attract the attention of her husband a wife replaces his personal name with evocatives and interjections such as *are* in Hindi, *aaho* in Marathi, and *ajii* in Bangla, with respect forms such as *saahab* ("master"), *suno jii* ("please listen"), and *pati dev* ("honorific husband"), and third person plural pronominal forms to address or refer to him – forms not reciprocally returned. Commonly used to emphasize the unequal subordinate status, in Tamil for example, husbands may address their wives as *kalutai* ("donkey.") Proverbs and sayings from the cultural past, too, act as mechanisms to sanction traditional truths and linguistic taboos by teaching young girls and boys proper social etiquette and correct conduct. To illustrate, Indian proverbs instruct young wives to respect their husbands and honor their sons: *apne patiyõ ke naam to praaya sabhii striyãã jaantii hãĩ, kintu ve unhẽ sabodhit kartii hãĩ "he he" kar ke* ("All women know the names of their husbands, but would never utter their names. They would simply refer to them by saying 'he he'); *put parale sapuut* ("You beget a son by good luck".) Not confined to English or Western cultures, cross-cultural and cross-linguistic studies provide sufficient evidence demonstrating that the unconscious bias embedded in language reflects the pervasiveness of patriarchy and the difficulty in changing the established cultural attitudes that challenge the fundamental belief systems of traditional societies.

In contrast, in the "advanced" European societies where women and men engage in less rigidly sexually segregated activities, anthropologists identified languages in terms of gender-preferential differentiation. Terms and expressions in these languages were not exclusive to one gender; rather men and women simply favored certain linguistic forms over others. These societies were considered to be more egalitarian and less tied to traditional ways, so their language systems were assumed to reflect less gender discrimination. Clearly anthropologists were expressing their Anglo-European male ethnocentric bias when defining their terms.

Well into the nineteenth and twentieth centuries, language specialists continued to perpetuate the view that women's speech did not measure up to the male standard. Although sensitive to gender differences in European languages, traditional dialectologists, too, revealed their male bias, singling out women's speech as deviating from the male norm. In their fieldwork investigations, they rejected women as informants because women and their speech posed the problems of being too conservative, too innovative, or too deviant. The highly respected Danish grammarian Otto Jespersen in his 1922 chapter "The Woman" only fueled the fire, contributing to the view of gender as difference by making cross-cultural claims that women's language was inferior to men's and a byproduct of biological sex, using the Indian languages Pali and Sanskrit as supporting evidence. The androcentric sentiments of Jespersen suggested that women used more standard speech forms than men because women were just plain conservative in nature and men naturally innovative. Women were deficient, so the language of women was deficient. Influenced by Jespersen, Sukumar Sen (1979) examines the standard colloquial dialect of women in Western Bengal, ascribing women's dialect as pejorative and vulgar, specialized in meaning, and "archaic both in pronunciation and vocabulary." The beginnings of the "women's language as deficit" model provided the basis for the many stereotypes and negative attitudes associated with women that existed and persist in the world today.

Second wave of linguistic feminism

The tradition of gender as fundamental difference continued well into the 1970s. Committed to discovering and eliminating social inequities, sociolinguistics in general and women's studies in particular raised speakers' awareness of how language shaped the understanding of their world and their place within it. Into the decade, linguists sympathetic to the Anglo-American women's movements undertook efforts to debunk the political agenda of "keeping women in their place" by exposing gender bias and male domination in the form and function of language.

Blazing new sociolinguistic territory, linguist Robin Lakoff in her pioneering work *Language and Women's Place* (1975) hypothesized that a woman's recognizably *peculiar* style of speaking reinforced women's subordinate status in English, and by using this style, in collusion she helps maintain male dominance and female subordinate status in society. Her description of two socially and linguistically distinct gender groups led to a proliferation of studies assuming a direct relationship between women and their use of particular linguistic forms. It was during this time that the idea that women and men speak different languages began to gain attention, giving rise to the notions of a *woman's language* (Lakoff 1975), *genderlects* (Kramarae 1981), and a *female register* (Crosby and Nyquist 1977). Although this view helped to further establish two separate gendered languages, it suggested that women were the users who were socialized to be skilled in both styles to function as mothers and wives in the family, as professionals in the "real" world, and as powerless speakers in interpersonal communication. Albeit endorsing *essential feminism,* Lakoff's approach offered possibilities to finding new direction for understanding male domination and to building an egalitarian society through language change.

Lakoff's work generated further exploration into the sexist content and structure of the English language and the need for adopting guidelines for language reform. Socially concerned linguists considered it their social and moral responsibility to examine how language was male constructed to exclude, demean, limit, degrade, deprecate, and dehumanize females making them and their actions invisible, underrepresented, misrepresented, and nameless (Spender 1980; Vetterling-Braggin 1981). Her work encouraged countless studies, both in Western and non-Western languages, demonstrating the widespread sexist ideologies reflected in the structure of language with evidence of gender stereotypes, markedness of women, sexual asymmetries in the lexicons, and other sex-linked linguistic forms (Brown 1980 in Mayan; Keenan 1974 in Malagasy; Lee 1976 and Peng *et al.* 1981 in Japanese; Nagamma Reddy 1991 in Telugu; Sreedevi 1991 in Malayalam; Valentine 1983, 1985b, 1987 in Hindi; Vasanthakumari 1991 in Tamil; and Weil 1983 in Hebrew). To illustrate the ways that dominant gender-based ideologies were reflected in non-European languages, discussions centered on lexical analyses, nonreciprocal naming practices, and cultural proverbs to uncover the deep-rooted and negative beliefs about women and the sexist ideologies prevalent in the cultures. In South Asian languages, as in other languages (Schulz 1975), for example, male terms often acquire a universal meaning inclusive of both sexes, whereas female terms acquire a narrow sex-specific meaning, often pejorative in reference. Lexical items in Hindi, too, reflect the strictly defined gender roles and rigidly regulated Indian family system and represent the importance of kin groups, male relationships, and hierarchies based on age and gender. Hindi masculine terms such as *beTaa* ("boy, son"), *puutaa* ("son"), and *bhaaii* ("brother") are spoken by both sexes to address females and males; according to Indian tradition, using a masculine term for a girl or daughter shows deep affection. The use of the honorific masculine term *saahab* ("sir") universalizes to names and titles of females: *memsaahab* ("lady, madam"), *DaakTar sahab* ("doctor sir"), and *profesar saahab* ("professor sir"). To show surprise, references to male terms and male deities are invoked: *are baap re/baap re baap* ("Oh brother!") *Raam Raam* ("Lord Ram! Goodness!"), *Raam kaa naam lo* ("Take the name of Ram! Oh my god"). In Hindi only women are *juThii strii* ("defiled"), *baazaaru aurat* ("available in the market"), and *gaman strii* ("promiscuous"), only a wife with a living husband can enjoy *sadaasuhaagin*, *ahivaat*, and *suhaag* ("the protection and good fortune of a husband"). Because only men are given social license to marry a second time, there exists only the term *sautelii mãã* ("stepmother") but not *sautelaa baap* ("stepfather"). And the pejorative terms *saalaa* ("wife's brother/son of a bitch") and *saalii* ("wife's sister/bitch") are unique to females and their relatives. This phenomenon is not exclusive to the north Indian languages. Essential femininity of women is marked in the Dravidian languages as well. Vasanthakumari (1991) illustrates the socially approved female conduct of wifehood, widowhood, and maidenhood in Tamil.

The patriarchal ideology of *pitrsattaa* in Hindi, *pidarshaahii* in Urdu, and *pitritontro* in Bangla is illustrated in the inordinate number of proverbs and sayings expressing cultural truisms about the misfortune and unluckiness associated with the birth of girls or the death of a husband, the subordinate position of females in the society, and the uncontrollable, dangerous nature of women (Narawane 1978).

a. *vyaaparii ko narm, raaja ko garm, strii ko sharm waalii honaa caahiye*
   A businessman ought to be humble, a king hot-tempered and a woman shy
b. *pããch vars ke baalak ke saamne pacaas varsh kii strii ko apnaa pair moRnaa paRegaa*
   A woman of fifty must bend her knees before a boy of five
c. *purwaiyaa ke baadal aa rããD ke rowal baav na jaaye*
   When there is east wind, the result is rain and when a widow cries, the result is an evil happening
d. *beTii jaatii re jagannaath! HeTai aayo haath*
   His prestige is lowered, who has a daughter born
e. *joruu kaa marnaa aur juutii kaa TuuTnaa baraabar hai*
   A dead wife is like a torn shoe (replaceable)

Whatever the society, sexist language became a political matter, and there was a call for action to eliminate all forms of gender hierarchies in language.

A scientific alternative to the folklinguistic beliefs and anecdotal evidence of the past were the quantitative sociolinguistic studies of the variationists, most notably sociolinguists William Labov (1972) and Peter Trudgill (1972), who attempted to quantify selected linguistic features and correlate them with the social categories of class, ethnicity, age, and sex, markers of speech designating a speaker's membership in different social groups. They, too, operating under the assumption of "gender as difference," treated sex as a given and relatively fixed variable. Their conclusions on the use of prestige and stigmatized forms were merely based on stereotypes recounted in earlier reports: women's language reflected her conservative nature, status consciousness, linguistic insecurity, and hypersensitivity to social norms (Cameron and Coates 1988). Not immune from making general statements about the speech of women, subsequent comparative linguistic studies further reinforced the general universal linguistic claim that "women are more likely to be favorably disposed towards prestigious varieties than are men"(Edwards 1985: 72). A few quantitative sociolinguistic studies make some mention of gender-specific language variation in South Asia. R. S. Pathak's (1985) study on Hindi–English code switching in north India shows that women, especially those from the upper- and upper-middle-class families, are more self-conscious and careful in their speech. Women's extensive use of English, widespread code switching, and tendency toward hypercorrect phonetic and grammatical forms lend support to the argument that women's speech reflects "linguistic insecurity." R. K. Agnihotri and Anju Sahgal's (1986) sociolinguistic study finds that in the urban setting of Delhi, women use a higher proportion of prestige variants than do men. They explain women's overuse of prestigious forms as evidence of their insecure social and linguistic status within the male dominated society. In contrast, Farhat Khan's (1991) study on consonant cluster simplification in Indian English indicates that the speech of female speakers in the traditional Muslim culture of Aligarh (Uttar Pradesh) in northern India shows a higher proportion of reduced clusters and nonprestigeous forms than in the speech of male speakers, which shows a greater proportion of unreduced clusters. Where Agnihotri and Sahgal's study suggests that women are susceptible to Western influences, Khan's study suggests that women in traditional cultures do not conform to the linguistic norms of the dominant male culture.

To their credit, the works of Lakoff and the variationists at the time were motivated by doing socially relevant linguistics and the results heightened attention on sex as a legitimate sociolinguistic variable. But the view of gender as static and fixed across time and communities was accepted as the standard sociolinguistic course. These and related studies and discussions still presupposed that men and women were essentially and fundamentally different, and one of these differences was reflected in language, an assumption that the succeeding two influential models in language and gender do not shake.

The dominance versus differences debate

By the 1980s, the stage for the next act in language and gender study was set: investigating language in natural spoken interactions and the different linguistic choices speakers make in cross-sex conversation. Moving from tallying individual linguistic features and testing Lakoff's claims of a woman's language, research on gendered language behavior entered a phase of moving beyond the sentence level to examining pragmatic features in ordinary cross-sex conversations.

Counting the number of interruptions, questions, attention beginnings, back channels, topic choices, and violations of conversational space used by women and men became the prevailing fashion of the decade (James and Clarke 1993; James and Drakich 1993). The natural progression shifted from the philosophy of "women's language as inferior to men's" to "language styles as reflective of the inequitable power distribution between the sexes."

The **dominance** approach, as it became known, proposed that the cluster of linguistic and pragmatic features that typified women's language was a function of the existing power relationship between women and men: men's dominance in conversation paralleled men's dominance in society. Supporters of the power approach argued that "verbal interaction helps to construct and maintain the hierarchical relations between men and women" (Fishman 1983: 89). Men's speech is a vehicle for male displays of power (Zimmerman and West 1975). This perspective claimed that the male speaker dominated talk in cross-sex conversation by using the noncooperative strategies of interruptions, silence, delayed responses, topic control, and selective verbosity, among other conversational infringements.

Research on the relationship between language and power in South Asian language communities, supports the dominance approach. The language strategies used by women and men in informal spoken discourse illustrates how talk is constructed within and across gender groups (Valentine 1985b). This paper examines the language strategies used by women and men in informal spoken discourse and how talk is constructed within and across gender groups (Valentine 1985a). The following English exchange between two Indian friends, a female and a male, illustrates the controlling tactics of interruptions, overlaps, disagreements, and changing topic by the male speaker. It supports the dominance view that like most female speakers of the world, Indian women too, are not equal partners in conversations nor are they granted equal speaking rights in mixed sex discourse.

F: They [Indian women] like these things because from a very young age the condition is such a way that they have to like it. It's not something they do actively something that grows in them this fondness for housework and

M: I mean I think it can be explained from a very simple analogy. For example you have South Indian pundits who don't who vomit at the sight of seeing pig and I love to eat pig. So it's social conditioning. I think everything is social condition. Now if I say that I am forced to like pig I mean it would be hypocritical because I love it.

F: This totally different between eating pork and

M: No, I am saying social conditioning is there ...

In a challenge to the politically charged power-based views of the dominance approach and the deficit learning theory of Lakoff, by the mid-1980s a less threatening and an apolitical (Tröemel-Plöetz 1991) perspective known as the **differences** or **two cultures model** emerged. De-emphasizing the androcentric bias and devaluation of women's speech, this approach put a positive spin on women's interactional style and faulted neither women nor men for conversational discord. It proposed that women and men come from different sociolinguistic subcultures and so observe different styles of friendly conversation, follow different rules of discourse, and interpret different ways of meaning (Maltz and Borker 1982). Extending the cross-cultural interethnic sociolinguistic framework of John Gumperz to an American model of gender, Deborah Tannen (1990, 1993, 1994, 1998) explained the two cultures in terms of different and equally valid styles of talk: "women speak and hear a language of connection and intimacy, while men speak and hear a language of status and independence" (Tannen 1990). According to Tannen, the stylistic dichotomy between adult women and men inevitably leads to miscommunication, and each gender wrongly interprets the other's cues based on each gender's own set of rules and linguistic norms acquired in play activities when young girls and boys.

The differences approach argued that the sexes speak and hear two different conversational styles. In the Indian interpersonal contexts as well, this argument appears to hold true. The conversational style of Indian women in Hindi shares similar characteristics with the style of American women in English (Valentine 1985a, 1986). In the following conversation (Valentine 1988), the style of the two female Hindi speakers signals gender solidarity and establishes community. Their talk shows a liberal exchange of cooperative discourse strategies, which convey a woman's style of mutual understanding, involvement, and agreement: topical coherence, exchange of personal stories, building of turns, rephrasals, repetitions, back channeling, interactive synchrony among other devices of linguistic cooperation. It supports the differences view that like other women of the world, Indian women too, share a conversational style of community and connection.

F1: *mãĩ bhii shaayad na jaaũũ kyõki mujhe uskaa point of view maaluum hai [hm hm] uh mujhe . . . mãĩ usko jaantii hũũ ki [hm hm] vo kyaa kahegii [hm hm] kyõki ek baar pahale bhii mãĩ uskii sun cukii hũũ.*

I too may not go because I know her point of view. I know what she will say because I have heard her once before.

F2: *mãĩ bhii ek baar pahale sun cukii hũũ [hãã] jab tum sab saath the na. (both laugh) vaise mãĩ pataa nahĩĩ, mujhe lagaa ki zyaadaa extreme feminism [hm] ho rahii thii wahãã [hãã]*

It doesn't agree with what I feel like.
I too have heard her once before, when you were all together remember? (laugh) and you know I don't know I felt that there was too much extreme feminism going on there.
It doesn't agree with what I feel.

F1: *wahãã tum ne dekhaa thaa, mãĩ jo thii, sab se maailD thii mãĩ?*

Did you see that I was milder than all the rest?

F2: *hãã mujhe bhii wahii lagaa.*

Yes I felt that way too

F1: *mere baat . . . vo phir vo . . . kyõki mãĩ vo . . . bilkul radical feminism mẽ believe nahĩĩ kartii=*

. . . I do not believe in absolute radical feminism.

F2: *=mãĩ bhii*

me too

The differences approach has certainly struck a chord with the ever-popular cultural belief in a communicative gender gap: relationships break up because communication between women and men break down. Not speaking a common language, men and women fail to understand each other because they lack an awareness of the differing gender styles in communication. Popularizing this position is the American bestselling series *Men Are from Mars and Women Are from Venus* written by pop psychologist Dr John Gray (1992). In circulation in India, these books are sold as pirated copies at book stalls and have found their way on Indian self-help book shelves. Being snatched up by young married and unmarried women in India, such books offer a guide to the modern Indian women to improve communication with their husbands and boyfriends. The Western ideology of miscommunication between the sexes has not only penetrated into the Indian way of thinking but has also led to a new genre for the self-improvement industry in India.

For the most part, interests in language and gender study have shown to be primarily a Western intellectual endeavor established on the deeply held belief that there are two biological sexes, and social gender is rooted in this dichotomy of sex. The limited number of linguistic studies that were done on non-Western cultures, my work included, were merely cookie cuttings of those studies on Western languages. These studies helped to spread the belief that the language differences found between women and men reflected underlying essential differences. Therefore, the ideology of gender differentiation in language styles only strengthened the socially constructed fiction of the binary categories of biological females and males. Mixing the ingredients of "real" biological sex differences and "believed" gender differences led to a research community sorting the population into two categories and asking the loaded question: how do men and women use language differently?

Fluidity of gender

If biology alone were the sole determiner of sex and predictor of behavior patterns, then we would not find such great cultural diversity and fluidity of gender in the world. Western culture typically classifies humans as either male or female at birth for his/her entire lifetime, but this dichotomy and permanency throughout one's life does not capture the experiences of individuals in all social arrangements (Unger and Crawford 1996). Being male or female is done differently in different cultures. Many cultural systems recognize more than two genders and accept a person's ability to change his/her sex/gender within a lifetime. For example, the ambiguous gender roles of the Xanith in Oman of Saudi Arabia, the Berdache of northwestern American Indian societies (Williams 1986), and the Mahu of Tahiti are often cited as alternative sex and gender roles institutionalized and sanctioned within their cultural systems (Nanda 1990). Margaret Mead's (1949) work in Papua New Guinea describes both Arapesh men and women as displaying "feminine" behaviors by Western standards. Clifford Geertz (1995) describes Balinese society as "unisex" and "egalitarian." Examples of multiple gender systems abound in the societies around the world.

Within the context of South Asia, in Indian mythology, literature, art, and music, other categories of sex are recognized and accepted as alternative, necessary gender roles. "The interchange of male and female qualities, transformations of sex and gender and alternative sex and gender roles, both among deities and humans, are meaningful and positive themes" (Nanda 1990: 375). For Hinduism in general holds that all human beings contain within themselves both male and female principles. Vedic scholar Wendy Doniger (1999) provides ample evidence from early Indian myths to illustrate overlapping and contradictory gender identities: males acting like females, females acting as males, females transforming into males, transsexual deities, androgynous beings, doubling and splitting women and men and so on. She states that "Myths are stories about the way the world is about the ambiguity of all existence" even gender distinctions (295). Earliest Hindu texts, too, mention a third sex divided into four categories: the "waterless" male eunuch who has desiccated testes; the "testicle voided" male eunuch who has been castrated; the hermaphrodite; and the "not woman" or female eunuch, that is, a woman who does not menstruate" (Nanda 1990). Drawing evidence from early medical texts as well, social historian Ashis Nandy points out that in precolonial Asian Indian communities, gender identities and ideologies were more fluid (1983, 1988); it was only after Victorian moral and cultural codes were imposed did gender become more rigid and fixed. In fact, the construction of a third sex or gender category in India dates back to the late Vedic period. According to Leonard Zwelling and Michael Sweet (2000), by 8–6 BCE there was the emergence of the acceptance of a tripartite sex model in India: female, male, and the third sex *napumsaka* ("neither female or male"), which later comes to refer to natural gender. Although there were "rigid conceptions of dimorphic sex and gender roles, based on the primacy of reproductive function; at the same time, it accepts a third sex" (123).

Treating gender as a unitary, natural fact does not capture the shifting gender positions in contemporary Indian society either, such as among the socially recognized, religious community of *hijras* (hijRaa in Hindi): communes of castrated males who assume the ritualized role of a divine power by imitating the dress, manners, and voices of women. The difficulty in translating the sexually ambiguous notion *hijra* into Western terms illustrates how uncompromising the pervasive female–male binary system is, for *hijra* is widely rendered as "eunuchs or men who have emasculated themselves, intersexed people, men and women with genital malfunction, hermaphrodites, persons with indeterminate sexual organs, impotent men, male homosexuals, and even effeminate men who are hijra impostors" (Sawhney 1997). Primarily in north India, these male performers, themselves, describe their gender as "neither man nor woman" (Nanda 1990), "neither here nor there" (Sawhney 1997), and "'deficiently' masculine and 'incompletely' feminine" (Hall and O'Donovan 1996). As an expression of an alternative gender, the Indian *hijras* adopt both masculine and feminine linguistic behaviors. Studies on the speech styles of the *hijras* reveal that the speakers overtly mark their language by identifying themselves as women, taking female names, exchanging female kinship terms ("sister," "aunty," "grandmother"), adopting feminized expressions and intonations, and using either the masculine language forms to signal social distance from, or the feminine language forms to signal solidarity to, the referent (Hall and O'Donovan 1996). Living outside the traditional gender norms of contemporary India, *hijras* have the distinctive linguistic status of having control of both masculine and feminine grammatical markers, thus constructing a "new" gender. The community of *hijras* has socially and linguistically created an alternate existence within the female–male binary system (Hall and O'Donovan 1996).

These cross-cultural studies show that a wide variety of attributes of masculine and feminine roles and characteristics exists in different societies as myth and as reality and that the boundaries of gender vary from society to society, challenging the traditional pervasiveness of the bimorphic ideas about gender and sex. South Asian cultures illustrate that there are alternative gender systems to the Western dualist notion of masculine and feminine where the world is not so neatly divided into opposition but allows overlapping, ambiguity, contradiction, and transforming categories. And these alternate gender systems find expression in language.

Gender viewed locally

Tracing the history of the study of language and gender, we see that for the most part the research community assumed the position of gender as a unitary, fundamental fact, as meaning the same across communities, and as context free. Too much emphasis had been placed on difference and treating women and men as global categories. In response, language and gender study has taken a second look at the fundamental assumptions of sex/gender, incorporating the diversity that exists across and within genders and considering the shifting of social identities within and across communities. In order to understand women and men as language users in their speech communities, focus has been diverted from examining gender as located within the individual to examining gender as an ongoing, changing process constructed in communities of practice (Eckert and McConnell-Ginet 1992). For women across world communities construct identities differently from each other.

Only in the last decade has language and gender study applied an interdisciplinary perspective, drawing methods and approaches from a variety of disciplines: sociolinguistics, ethnography, social theory, discourse analysis, and feminist studies. By using a variety of techniques, ethnosociolinguistic feminists have turned the page in language and gender research. Focus has moved from thinking of things in twos to examining the fluidity of social identity. Rather than viewing gender as something fixed, given, and readymade, gender is viewed as a unified collection of social identities existing in individuals; language is action oriented, jointly producing the many identities that speakers possess. Gender identity is no longer viewed as static or unidimensional but as a process, created and recreated as the cues change, the situation arises, and the relationships are negotiated in the social activities of the speech community.

More important, rather than talking globally, in order to act more inclusively, this approach thinks practically and looks locally (Eckert and McConnell-Ginet 1992). It constructs a speaker's identity within a community of practice, the collection of activities speakers engage in to construct identities of themselves. A community of practice is an aggregate "of people who come together around mutual engagement in some common endeavor." It is "defined simultaneously by its membership and by the practice in which that membership engages (for a mutual enterprise) . . . it is the practices of the community and members' differentiated participation in them that structures the community socially" (Eckert and McConnell-Ginet 1992). Adopting such an approach allows us to describe world speech communities and women's practices that have gone unnoticed by the mainstream approaches. Focusing on the culture of women, in the early 1980s, Pat Nichols (1980:140) proposed taking such an approach to examining language and women. She argued that a speech community should be the primary focus when doing language and gender research: women's experiences have much in common throughout the world to be sure. And it is possible that we may identify certain common patterns in women's lives and women's speech. But women are members first and foremost of their speech communities, and it is in the daily context of their lives as speaking members of a larger group that their language must be examined.

The cross-cultural studies that examine women in their speech communities take an ethnolinguistic approach to gender differentiation in language. Carrying out fieldwork in the natural local contexts, they help to illustrate how gender identity is constructed through language in the particular social activities that women regularly engage in: how women reconstruct their gender identities in their speech communities by developing culturally specific speech genres to express their femalehood. This increased interest in feminist oral history has led scholars to examining the words of women in local contexts (Gluck and Patai 1991). In India, for example, women shape their lives and their communities' practices by performing several of the linguistic traditions such as ritualized storytelling, devotional singing, and chanting (Wadley 1986); tuneful weeping (Tiwary 1978) and nonprofessional tale-telling (Ramanujan 1990, 1999). These social and religious forces in ritualized speech events enculturate Indian women into the appropriate social and family roles of wife, mother, and adolescent girl, speech rituals carried over to nonnative contexts as well (Remlinger 1994). Observed at an early age, Leela Dube (1988) notes that young girls of north India learn to modify their style of speech to be unlike that of males. "While they learn that great circumspection is necessary in using words that reveal the tensions in their expression of kinship relations, or words that undermine the authority of the official discourses of patriliny, they also learn that there are ways in which resistance to those discourses may be communicated" (Raheja 1994: 52). Upon approaching puberty, girls develop an auxiliary style of nonverbal gestures and speech intonations, and the capability of reading subtle metamessages in ordinary language to communicate their resistance to the male-dominant discourses. Gloria Goodwin Raheja (1994), too, shows that the community of women in rural north India constructs their gender when they chant ritual songs and proverbs. They also have developed an effective gendered speech genre in direct contradiction to the dominant hierarchical kinship and gender ideologies of their community. And Viv Edwards and Savita Katbamna's (1988) investigation of the community of Hindu Gujarati women in Great Britain illustrates the construction of Gujarati womanhood through the social practices of singing wedding songs. Their continued use of the mother tongue for singing songs of solidarity, of insult, and of conciliation acts as a means for Gujarati women to strengthen natal family ties and express emotional freedom from the familial orthodoxy to which women must conform. The use of language as ritual provides an outlet for Gujarati women to validate their native identity in the non-Indian setting of Britain but perpetuates the dominant ideology of the traditional family and social roles and expectations embedded in these songs and rituals.

To further illustrate the range of ways that language use constructs gender in everyday talk, other cross-cultural studies provide a glimpse into how women act as agents of language change, influencing the linguistic landscape of their local communities in South Asia. Stella Mascarenhas-Keyes (1994) finds that Catholic

Goan women play a major role in the marginalization and displacement of the mother tongue Konkani and in promoting the dominant Western languages of Portuguese and English. The legacy of Portuguese colonialism and the modern-day emphasis on women's social roles as teachers, writers, and progressive mothers have propelled women to act more favorably toward the prestigious Western languages and varieties. As mothers and as advocates for education, these women are reshaping the linguistic face of their Goan families and community by furthering the spread of non-Indian languages at the possible loss of the minority regional Indian languages. In contrast, in the Indian village of Totagadde in Karnataka (Ullrich 1992), maintaining the vernacular caste dialect, Havyaka, is the sole domain of the women who speak the variety amongst themselves in the community and transmit it to their children. Although the women consider themselves "linguistically limited," they understand the economic and social advantage of being multilingual in English, Hindi, or Kannada. By promoting multilingualism, these women offer greater opportunities to their children as well as enhance their own self-image and strengthen their social standing in the community.

Women as conversationalists co-construct their gender identities through the stories they tell about themselves (Valentine 1993). A longer version of a previous conversation between two 25 year-old Hindi-speaking women is provided below, adopting a discoursal approach to illustrate how gender is being constructed between women in spoken discourse. Displaying their shared gender and ethnic identities, these speakers negotiate femaleness and other aspects of their identity through the language they use, the stories they tell, and other social practices that they engage in.

(1) S: *yahãã pe matlab vo aaj tumhẽ maaluum hai ki vo R.D. yaa vo kuch presentation kar rahii hai [mm] shaam ko kuch Indian movement pe, jaantii ho? tum [Indian] jaanevaalii ho udhar?*

Do you know that R.D. is giving a presentation here today in the evening on the Indian movement, do you know? Are you going there?

(2) N: *pataa nahĩĩ. shaayad na jaaũũ*

I don't know. Maybe I won't go.

(3) S: *mãĩ bhii shaayad na jaaũũ kyõki mujhe uskaa point of view maaluum hai [mm] uh mujhe . . . mãĩ usko jaanti hũũ ki [mm] vo kyaa kahegii [mm] kyõki ek baar pahale bhii mãĩ uskii sun cukii hũũ.*

I too may not go because I know her point of view. I know what she will say because I have heard her once before.

(4) N: *mãĩ bhii ek baar pahale sun cukii hũũ [hãã] jab tum sab saath the na. (both laugh) Vise mãĩ pataa nahĩĩ, mujhe lagaa ki zyaadaa extreme feminism [hm] ho rahii thii wahãã [hãã]*

It doesn't agree with what I feel like

I too have heard her once before, when you were all together remember? (laugh) and you know I don't know I felt that there was too much extreme feminism going on there.
It doesn't agree with what I feel like.

(5) S: *wahãã tum ne dekhaa thaa, mãĩ jo thii, sab se maailD thii mãĩ?*

Did you see that I was milder than all the rest?

(6) N: *hãã mujhe bhii wahii lagaa*

Yes I felt that way too.

(7) S: *mere baat ... vo phir vo ... kyõki mãĩ vo ... bilkul radical feminism mẽ believe nahĩĩ kartii.*

I do not believe in absolute radical feminism.

(8) N: *mãĩ bhii*

me too.

(9) S: *mãĩ nahĩĩ soctii ki auratõ ko aadmiyõ ke against honaa caahiye.*

I don't think that women should oppose men.

(10) N: *hãa, it's very strange.*

(11) S: Yes, it's very strange.

(12) N: *inkii jo feminism [hãã] hai, agar kuch karnaa hai, to bas [mm] duniyaa ke aage laRo.*

The feminism that they believe in, if you want to do something then fight against the world.

(13) S: *hãã LaRo ... right aur ye nahĩĩ soctii hãi ki, auratẽ ki yahãã baiThe ... ki yahãã baiThke ye nahĩĩ soctii hãĩ ki aise nahĩĩ badalaa jaa saktaa [bilkul] ki hamẽ hamaare hamaarii jo tradition mẽ [mm] hamaare jo hindustaanii tradition mẽ hameshaa aisii rahaa hai, ki compromise karnaa [hm], compromise matlab, compromise ko do taraf se dekhaa [mm] jaa saktaa hai. [mm] ek taraf se dekhaa jaa saktaa hai ki hãã, you give in [um] vaise us tariike se nahĩĩ [mm] lekin compromise karnaa [um] ek tarah se acchaa hai, hamaare liye [mm] aur hamaare saare system mẽ, education system mẽ ham wahii koshish karte hãĩ ki [bilkul] compromise karnaa, compromise matlab ki jo chiizẽ hãĩ [mm] ki unko completely tum reject to kar nahĩĩ sakte [mm] agar tum unko completely reject karne kii koshish karo [mm] to tum tumhaare vo jo bhii tum karne kii koshish karo [mm] to tum you know, usmẽ yashasvii nahĩĩ hoge.*

Yes fight. Right and they don't think that the women that sit, that they don't sit and think that things can change [absolutely] that in our Indian tradition it was always like this that we must compromise. Compromise means, compromise can be looked at from two sides. From one side you give in. I don't see it like this but compromise can be good, for us and in our entire educational system we compromise, compromise means that you cannot reject everything if you try to reject everything completely then you, you know, will not be successful.

(14) N: *acchaa, phir pataa hai kyaa huaa? us din mujhe lag rahaa thaa ki vo jo kuch bol rahe hãĩ, aise aise speed dene ke liye bol rahe hãi, agar vo [hãã] khud aise karnaa paRe unko to mujhe nahĩĩ lagtaa [mm] ki vo karẽge.*

Okay, then you know what happened? That day I was thinking that what they were saying we must do things with speed they were saying, if they had to do it themselves I don't think it would have been possible to do so.

(15) S: *hãã, hãa. nahĩĩ, nahĩi vo nahĩi karẽge.*

Yes, yes. No, no they wouldn't do it.

(16) N: *duusre logõ [mm] ko kahane ke liye bahut aasaan hai, par khud karnaa [right] kaafii mushkil hai.*

It's very easy to tell others, but it is quite difficult to do it yourself.

The above conversation is a jointly produced, coordinated exchange of ideas between two Indian females. Centering on the heated issue of Western feminism, of which speakers S and N are hypercritical, the exchange begins (turn 1) with S asking N whether N is attending an advertised university event addressing the Indian women's movement. Raising this topic leads into a collaborative discussion of their aversion toward *absolute extreme feminism*, then by association, their contempt for the participants who attend, namely the communist women who smoke in public and casually display themselves in front of others, "feminist" behaviors S and N do not consider to be proper and ladylike.

In this highly charged exchange the two friends, S and N, sustain cooperative talk by using a number of different strategies. A feminine discourse expressing solidarity is realized through overlapping turns, expressions of agreement, repetition of ideas, and the joint advancing and building of text. For example, from the initial series of questions asked by S in turn 1, the synchronized hearer support cues from N (*mm, hm, bilkul* ("absolutely")), the personal involvement markers (*mãĩ bhii* ("I too"), *pataa hai* ("I know"), the repetitions and rephrasals (turns 10–11), the discourse markers in both Hindi and English (*I don't know, I mean, you know, pataa hai* ("I know,") hedges, etc.), to the building across of turns (turns 12–13), both speakers share ways of engaging in the linguistic activity of condemning feminism: they share stories, background information, and personal experiences as illustrated in turn 4 when speakers N and S remember a particular incident, then share an embarrassed laugh.

Their switching from Hindi to English reveals S and N's attitude toward the topic of feminism introduced early in their conversation (turn 4). Their shifts to English indicate their unfavorable opinion of feminism: *zyaadaa extreme feminism* (4) ... *It doesn't agree with what I feel like* (4), *bilkul radical feminism* (7). Conspiratorially, each speaker readily agrees with the other. Both associate the notion of feminism with American activism and with the "extreme" women's (liberation) movement: being radical, opposing men, fighting the male system, rejecting dominance and oppression, and acting and reacting to social change with unnecessary speed. Their antagonistic trade of barbs firmly establishes their negative personal position on Western feminism but at the same time aligns themselves with the collective beliefs held by the women of India: "compromise" and weighing both sides of an issue. Because the sentiments of S and N are in contrast to the feminist position, they linguistically create themselves as nonfeminists by shifting from Hindi to English again and again: (*I was milder than all the rest* (5), *I don't think women should oppose men* (9), *it's very strange* (10–11), and *compromise* (13)). Not only lexical items but strings of English sentences convey their discontent, for example *It doesn't agree with what I feel like, it lost all touch of reality*. Both express their disapproval of "academic communists" and "intellectual" feminism, creating a distance between themselves and the behavior of Western activists. Code shifting by these two women signals their allegiance to the ideology of the *Hindustani tradition*, which emphasizes "compromise" and nonopposition and their resistance to Western *extreme feminism*. Since both females share the same view on the subject they play off one another, building across turns, restating utterances, and reinforcing with acknowledgments and agreements, sometimes adopting the same English terminology and phrases – collaborating on their construction of what constitutes Indian womanhood. Speakers S and N talk about issues connected with femininity, presenting themselves as different kinds of women and co-constructing a shared image of what it means to be a woman according to their belief system.

As these ethnolinguistic studies and examples show, there is no single unified way of doing femininity or of being a female or of doing gender, especially if we take into account the many different cultures, speech communities, and expressions of femininity that exist in the world. Whether by creating a "new" gender as the community of *hijras* [hijRaa] have done, by constructing femininity in institutionalized gender-specific speech events, or by negotiating a shared image of womanhood among adult friends these language users, like all speakers, are involved in the never-ending struggle to define their identity. The diversity of gender and other social identities that exist across and within speech communities helps us better understand the dynamics of social practices across local cultures.

Conclusion

Language and gender research has taken a number of tumbles and turns in its past few decades of existence, and scholars are only now looking back to see what lessons can be learned and what lessons need to be unlearned. The review of the literature from the earliest travels of anthropologists to the most recent interdisciplinary approaches recommended by language and gender researchers shows that we are only now beginning to ask the probing questions necessary to account for the multiplicity of gender (social) identities constructed in the natural language practices of women and men as they engage in the activities of their speech communities across the multilingual, multicultural landscape. Moving beyond the "essential" woman, binary discourse, deficit/dominance/difference debates, gender stereotypes, and generic gender identity has led language and gender scholarship into a new phase of making connections and expanding boundaries to include multiple gender and linguistic identities, local social practices, and all world communities.

Moving toward a more flexible and accommodating approach is more sensible, practical, and appealing. Such an approach combines and blends perspectives to reflect and respect the complexity of linguistic and gender experiences: one that can account for both the hierarchical social levels in India yet the tolerance for diversity and group mobility, one that accounts for the differences that diversify women as well as the traditional ideologies that bind them, one that accommodates a range of language choices and expressions of language in multilingual experiences, one that examines women as products of linguistic imperialism and patriarchy, one that can account for the attitudinal differences in language choice, and one that can account for the relativity of discourse strategies and styles with regard to situational context and linguistic genres.

Where dominance and difference frameworks approach language with Western notions of universals, context-free rules, fixed, unconnected forms, and contradictions, a more fluid, accepting model is needed to account for context-sensitive cultures such as India (Ramanujan 1989). In place of the linear, two-dimensional, bipolar Western approaches, a multidimensional model shows embeddedness of forms, a continual, constant movement from one level to the next, a means to expand and contract as the context changes, and a continuum of forms. Such an approach is concerned with elements of historical processes and experiences, the functions of language use in social and cultural practices, the ways in which different linguistic genres are related to the local contexts, and the different ways of doing gender within speech communities. A model such as this takes into consideration the multilingual settings of South Asia and Africa, gender differences as well as similarities, varying strengths and frequencies of linguistic strategies, and individual repertoires as well as social networks. A model such as this confirms that the study of language and speech cannot be investigated outside the local interactional contexts in which gender and other social identities are constructed. For if the study of language and research does not adopt a more inclusive model, we will exclude a good portion of the speech communities of the world.

23 Dalit literature, language, and identity

Eleanor Zelliot

Introduction

In 1972 a new literary movement burst on the Marathi language scene, Dalit Sahitya (literature of the oppressed), accompanied by a militant group who called themselves Dalit Panthers.[1] Now a thirty-year-old phenomenon that is still in a creative and growing phase, the Dalit Sahitya movement has spread to half the states in India. The poets and writers of the movement added a term to the all-India vocabulary; the word "Dalit" is used now in most publications. It replaces the descriptive name of Untouchable or ex-Untouchable (now that the practice of untouchability is illegal); Gandhi's compassionate but patronizing appellation, Harijan (Children of God); and, when appropriate, the official term of Scheduled Caste.[2] Dalit is a self chosen word derived from the Sanskrit and Marathi word for ground down, broken, that is oppressed, but Dalit is used to indicate that untouchability is imposed by others, not a result of inherent pollution. It is also used to be inclusive of all the deprived and oppressed of India.

Although it seemed new to the English speaking world in the 1970s, Dalit literature began to appear in the 1950s and 1960s as part of the movement led by Dr B. R. Ambedkar (1891–1956), undisputed leader of India's Untouchables. The newspapers of Dr Ambedkars time published some Dalit stories and poems during the 1940s and 1950s most importantly the short stories of Bandhu Madhav. In the late 1950s and 1960s, five important writers were being published in Maharashtra. The stories of Bandhu Madhav and Shankarrao Kharat tended to be fairly gentle accusations of injustice. Kharat's *Bara Balutedar* (1959) told of the lives of all twelve village servants, including the untouchable Mahar. Baburao Bagul's work, *Jewha Mi Jat Corli Hoti* (1963) (When I Hid My Caste) and *Maran Swast Hot Ahe* (1969) (Death is Getting Cheaper), however,

[1] The name comes from the American militant group called the Black Panthers.

[2] Four hundred castes were placed on a schedule or list in 1935 by the Government of India to receive representation. Later special benefits aided them in gaining education, government employment and political representation. The term applied at that time was "Depressed Classes," to indicate their social and economic deprivation. Dr B. R. Ambedkar used "Dalit" as a translation in Marathi writing. The term Dalit often includes any group that sees itself as oppressed.

was a harsh look at the reality of slum life in Bombay (see Bhagwat 1995 for the role of Bombay in Dalit literature). Bandhu Madhav, Kharat, and Bagul were Buddhist converts from a Mahar background. Annubhau Sathe, a Mang and a Communist, created a heroic Dalit figure of resistance against the British, and Narayan Surve, a casteless orphan and also a Communist, wrote of the "university" of the Bombay slums and streets. The published material became so important that a prestigious Marathi journal in Aurangabad, *Marathwada*, brought out an issue on "Dalit Sahitya" in 1969 (see also Mahar 1972).

Wider recognition of the term Dalit and the idea of a new school of literature from the lower classes, however, did not come until 1972, and then with the explosive arrival of the Dalit Panthers and the poetry of the young radicals: chiefly Namdeo Dhasal, J. V. Pawar, Arun Kamble, Prahlad Chendwankar, Umakant Randeer, Daya Pawar, and Waman Nimbalkar, together with the art of Raja Dhale (see *Bulletin of Concerned Asian Scholars* 1978). Later several dozen other Dalit writers began to be published, Keshav Meshram, Yeshwant Manohar, and Trymbak Sapkale, among them, with Loknath and a number of women since the 1980s. The phenomenon was recognized early on by Dilip Padgaonkar of the *Times of India* who edited a supplement (November 25, 1973) that was an excellent collection of early Dalit poetry, short stories, and essays translated by other poets into English (Padgaonkar 1973; see also Jaawara 2001).

The major collection of Dalit literature translated into English is Arjun Dangle's (1992) *Poisoned Bread: Translations from Modern Marathi Dalit Literature.*[3] It contains the work of forty-six poets, ten short story writers, excerpts from nine autobiographies, and an excellent selection of essays and speeches by seven Dalits and one higher caste scholar of Black and Dalit literature. A supplement to the newspaper, *The Pioneer*, in January 2000 featured Dalit literature translations and the Dalit art of Savi Sawarkar. Other collections from Marathi are in the *Journal of South Asia Literature* (Zelliot and Engblom 1982, Deo and Zelliot 1994) and *Vagartha* (1976). Dalit literature in Maharashtra is now so important that it is included in the syllabi in all school levels up to the PhD, and there is an optional paper at the postgraduate level in Marathi departments.

The best-known figure in Marathi Dalit literature continues to be Namdeo Dhasal, the political maverick and always creative poet, and one of the founders of the Dalit Panthers and the Dalit Sahitya school (Hovell 1991). His first collection of poems, published when he was 23 was titled *Golpitha* (1972) a red light area in Mumbai. The book together with its lengthy introduction by Maharashtra's premier playwright, Vijay Tendulkar, (who found twenty-seven Marathi words and phrases he did not know) was an instant sensation. The poet

[3] Mulk Raj Anand and Eleanor Zelliot produced *An Anthology of Dalit Literature (Poems)*, New Delhi: Gyan Publishing House, 1992, but it contains many typographical errors, some of which change the meaning of the poetry.

Dilip Chitre, translator of Dhasal (2007), currently completing a biography of Dhasal, claims that "*Golpitha* occupies a position equal to that of T. S. Eliot's *The Waste Land* not only in Marathi but in pan-Indian poetry and it could have been written only by a Dalit." Dhasal's poetry is often scatological, at times impenetrable, filled with references to religion, slum life, Ambedkar's life, and wide-ranging world history. Dhasal went to Germany to the Berlin International Literature Festival in June 2001, and a book of his poetry has appeared in German, together with photographs of the Bombay he so vividly describes.[4] Most Dalit poets are college graduates, often from Ambedkar's colleges, but Dhasal, the most sophisticated of all of them, has only a high school education. He received the prestigious lifetime achievement award of the Sahitya Akademi in 2004.

The reasons for the origins of Dalit literature in the Marathi-speaking area of Maharashtra are easy to identify (Zelliot 1992). First, it is the homeland of Ambedkar, a Mahar himself before his conversion to Buddhism in 1956. Ambedkar's work in education, social reform, and politics led him not only to the leadership of Untouchables but to high positions in both British and Independent Indian governments. His inspiration by example and the colleges and institutions he founded produced a group of young followers determined to change the face of their country. The Marathi-speaking area had other advantages: it had an industrial base which allowed for some caste mobility, a history of social reform, a press which was open to new movements (perhaps most important, the innovative *Granthali*), a tradition of literature as a prime social value, and it had a critical mass of Dalit intellectuals, including editor Gangadhar Pantawane, who has kept the Marathi Dalit journal *Asmitadarsh* (Mirror of Identity) in circulation for over thirty years (see also Deo 1996, Dharwadkar 1994).

The meaning of Dalit

While many writers (and the press, in general) have found the word Dalit meaningful, some highly educated Marathi speakers have rejected it as demeaning to their independent and confident status. J. V. Pawar expresses this in an English collection of his poems, arguing that "Phuley-Ambedkarite literature" would be a better name since "We [in Maharashtra] are no more Dalits."[5] The author agrees, however, with Gangadhar Pantawane, who says:

4 Henning Stegmuller, Dilip Chitre, Namdeo Dhasal, with Lothar Lutze, *Bombay Mumbai*: Bilder einere Mega Stadt. Munich: a-1-verl., 1996. Dhasal also achieved fame with his interview in V. S. Naipaul's *India: A Million Mutinies Now*, 1990. He is represented in most Indian poetry anthologies.

5 Introductory statement in *Blockade*, poems from *Nakebandi* (1976) with translations by V. D. Chandanshive. Mumbai: Sanjana Publication, 1999, 11. The term "Phuley" refers to Jotirao Phule, the nineteenth century writer and reformer from the Mali caste who articulated an anticaste anti Brahmanical-oppression stance that is still meaningful.

What is Dalit? To me, Dalit is not a caste. Dalit is a symbol of change and revolution. The Dalit believes in humanism ... He represents the exploited men in his country ... Dalitness is essentially a means towards achieving a sense of cultural identity. The inferiority complex based on "to be Dalit" has now disappeared" (Pantawane 1986: 79).

The term "Phule-Ambedkar literature" is limited in its use, and cannot, for instance, be a descriptive word for the important school of Dalit Christian theology, literature, and art. In contrast, "Dalit" binds together those who still suffer violent oppression with those who are the educated spokesmen for a new and just society.

Work in the neglected field of aesthetics, as well as a substantial study of Dalit literature by one of its own writers, became available in English in 2001 and 2003. Sharankumar Limbale's work on aesthetics, translated by Alok Mukherjee, has been published in Hyderabad by Orient Longmans (see Limbale 2003a and Jaawara 2001).

Autobiography

With the publication of two autobiographies, Daya Pawar's *Balut* (1978) and Laxman Mane's *Upara* (1997), a rich new field was opened for Marathi writing. Mane, a Kaikadi (nomadic tribe), and Pawar, a Mahar before conversion to Buddhism, were joined later by several other writers. Laxman Gaikwad's *The Branded* (1998) reveals the life of the Berads, called a "criminal tribe" by the British. Kishore Shantabai Kale penned *Against All Odds* (2000), revealing the difficult life of the son of a Kolhati dancer and her sponsor. Sharankumar Limbale, son of an Untouchable and a caste Hindu produced *Akkarmashi*, published as *The Outcaste* (Limbale 2003b). Mane, Gaikwad, Limbale, and Kale's works are available in English translation. Pawar's autobiography and other important autobiographies by Madhav Kondvikar (a Chambhar) Uttam Bandu Tupe (a Mang), and P. E. Sonkamble (a Buddhist), all of which deal with lives unknown to the middle class, have not been translated. The field of autobiography is ever expanding, and includes two works by minimally educated Marathi-speaking Buddhist women,[6] one by a tribal woman, and a number are planned, including that of the well-known short story writer, Urmilla Pawar. The anthology *Poisoned Bread* includes a selection from autobiographies by two Buddhist women, Shantabai Kamble and Kumud Pawade, one semi-literate and the other highly educated, as well as from the work of the late Shankarrao Kharat (see also Hardikar 1985, Shirwadkar 1981).

[6] Bebi or Baby Kamble is represented in the second volume of *Women Writing in India*, edited by S. T. and K. Lalita. New York: The Feminist Press, 1991; Shantabai Kamble appears in *Poisoned Bread*.

Bama's *Karukku*,[7] translated from the Tamil, was the first non-Marathi vernacular Dalit autobiography available in English, and the only one by a woman. The autobiography *Joothan: A Dalit's Life* by Omprakash Valmiki, translated from Hindi by Arun Prabha Mukherjee and published in 2003 by the Columbia University Press, was the first major translation of Dalit literature from Hindi (Valmiki 2003). The title refers to the leftover food that has been the lot of the Untouchable. The first translation from Gujarati is *The Stepchild* (Angaliyat) by Joseph Macwan, translated by Rita Kothari and published by Oxford University Press in New Delhi in 2004. *The Stepchild* makes vivid the complex community and village relationships of the Vankar (weaver) community. The initial translation in to English of a Kannada autobiography is, very fittingly, that of Siddalingaiah, a writer, poet, folklorist, founder of the Dalit Sangarsha Samhiti and a former member of the Karnataka Legislative Council. Translated by S. R. Ramakrishna, *Ooru-Keri: An Autobiography* was published by the Sahitya Akademi in 2003.

The first Dalit autobiography to be published in English in the West was Vasant Moon's (2001) *Vasti*, appearing as *Growing Up Untouchable in India*,[8] which evokes a colorful Mahar community in Nagpur and the changes brought by Ambedkar and the Buddhist conversion. Valmiki's story, titled *Joothan*, published by Columbia University Press, differs greatly from Moon's, since his north Indian village environment was much harsher than Moon's city life. When Valmiki does come to Maharashtra to work, he finds a much better life. Macwan's story, *The Stepchild*, published only in India, is also bleak but filled with the detail of the village life of the weaver Vankars. An autobiography which has been a bestseller in Marathi, Narendra Jadhav's *Amca Bap ani Amhi* (Our Father and Us), tells of the extraordinary success of a family influenced by Ambedkar and led by a challenging but illiterate father. It was published as *Outcaste: A Memoir* by Viking (Penguin) in 2003, and also recently by Scribners (New York) as *Untouchables*. It should be said that many of the autobiographies are brutally honest and the writers are criticized by their own communities for exposing faults to the outside world. When all four autobiographies become available in the United States in English, they will offer a vivid and varied study of Dalit life in India to outsiders.

Each autobiographical work introduces its readers to a new world, often with a new vocabulary. Punalekar (1997: 370) writes: "Dalit autobiography must be credited with the distinction of introducing us to a hitherto invisible and unknown social and cultural landscape, with their use of indigenous symbols and idioms." Since the castes of India are almost infinite, and those who succeed in

[7] Bama has won the prestigious Crossword Award for her work. *Karukku* is analyzed in Pandian (1998a).

[8] The late Vasant Moon was the editor of the *Dr. Babasaheb Ambedkar: Writings and Speeches* series published by the Government of Maharashtra (in seventeen volumes) that has led to much scholarly analysis of Ambedkar's thought.

raising themselves to be able to produce literature have a compelling story to tell, the autobiographical trend probably will continue (see, however, S. Anand 2003 for a discussion of why Dalit autobiographies are so readily published).

Is literature by Dalits written initially in English to be included within the Dalit Sahitya genre? This is not an issue yet discussed within the literary or Dalit communities. Two Uttar Pradesh writers have published their own English autobiographies: D. R. Jatava with *A Silent Soldier* (the Jatav or Chamar community) (2000) and Balwant Singh with *An Untouchable in the I. A. S.* (Indian Administrative Service) (1997). Additionally, I. D. Pawar's *My Struggle in Life* (1981, 1993) tells of the achievements of a Scheduled Caste Sikh, and Ashok Bhoyar's *Encounter with Dronacharya* (2001) reveals the problems of a Mahar surgeon. These four English autobiographies have not received the attention given to the Dalit autobiographies written in vernaculars, but reveal the almost desperate need of the highly educated and successful Dalit to express his struggles.

Dalit Rangabhumi (Dalit theater)

Theater and music have been part of Dalit life in the past in most areas of India. Modern Dalit theater may borrow from those forms, but is cast in the structure of modern Indian theater. The Marathi work of Datta Bhagat, now a retired Professor from Dr Babasaheb Ambedkar Marathwada University in Aurangabad, has not only appeared on TV but has been translated into English (see Bhagat 1994, 2000). His *Routes and Escape Routes* presents three ways in which Dalits dealt with the modern world, and his *Whirlwind* combines traditional *tamasha* and *jalsa* theater and presents life with memories of historic injustice. Premanand Gajvi's recent *Gandhi and Ambedkar* was performed on the Bombay stage and excerpts from his earlier *Ghotbhar Pani* (A Sip of Water) are included in a new anthology (Gajvi 2000). Early pioneers in Marathi Dalit Theater are B. C. Shinde, whose plays often dealt with Buddhist themes, and Ramnath Namdeo Chavan, whose controversial play *Sakshipuram*, on the conversion to Islam by Dalits in Tamil Nadu in 1984, has been translated from Marathi into Hindi but not English.

Dalit Rangabhumi (theater) conferences in Marathi are held regularly, and All India Dalit Theater conferences are convened from time to time. At the All India Dalit Drama Convention in 1992, Ramnath Chavan said, "More than a period of twelve to eighteen years has elapsed since the stream of Dalit theatre has started in our Maharashtra ... a small stream has now converted itself into a big one ... in ... Delhi, Karnataka, Tamil Nadu, Andhra Pradesh, Madhya Pradesh, Kerala and Goa, Dalit writers and artists who have been inspired by Dr Ambedkar's thoughts about social change have started the work of social awakening through the medium of drama and street theater." [9] Knowledge of

[9] "What is Dalit theatre?" http:\\ www.unet.univie.ac.at/-a8702482/cahvan.htm (2006).

Black theater in the United States resulted in presentations in Hindi translation of such plays as Langston Hughes' *Mulatto* by the Ahwan Theater in New Delhi and Amiri Baraka's *Slave* at an Asmitadarsh Conference in Chandrapur, Maharashtra.

The distinctive poetry and fiction of Dalit women

Marathi-speaking women are the most important group within women's Dalit literature, but Telugu women are gaining attention and have expressed some common concerns. Challapalli Swaroopa Rani claims that, in Telugu, "The poetry by dalit women . . . is far more powerful and has a far greater impact than the poetry of dalit male poets or upper caste women poets." (Challapalli Swaroopa Rani 1998: WS 21). Dalit women write about oppression from the caste system, but also from Dalit men as in this poem:

When has my life been truly mine?
In the home male arrogance
sets my cheek swinging
while in the street caste arrogance
splits the other cheek open. (p. WS 22)

Protest against patriarchy, however, is not the only mark of Dalit women writers. For many, there is a sense of common problems with all women. Hira Bansode, a well-known poet in Marathi, writes of this eloquently in *Gulam* (Slave). Even she mourns the continuing prejudice of a high caste friend in *Sakhi* (Bosom Friend) (see Zelliot 1996).

Dalit women poets, at least in Marathi, are more critical of the factionalism and hypocrisy within the group than are most men as can be seen in Mina Gajbhiye's *Shanti* (Peace) (in Deo and Zelliot 1994: 46–7). Women also seem to use subtle images more than men. See Surekha Bhagat's poem on Eklavya (below) and the poetry of Jyoti Lanjewar in Deo and Zelliot (1994: 47–9), as well as the work of these and other women in Zelliot (1996). Lanjewar is also distinguished by a very active commitment to social action. Her poem to *Ai* (Mother) is an eloquent tribute to all Dalit women, and includes a stanza on the campaign to change the name of Marathwada University to Ambedkar University, a campaign in which she took active part:

I have seen you
at the front of the Long March
the end of your sari tucked tightly at your waist
shouting "Change the Name,"
taking the blow of the police stick on your upraised hands
going to jail with head held high. (Zelliot 1996: 83)

The Marathi-speaking women had a journal edited by Meenakshi Moon, called *Maitrani* (village Marathi for woman friend), until her death in 2004. This journal produced a number of autobiographies and the well-known short story writer in

Urmila Pawar, whose stories may become better known through the current translation work of Veena Deo, a professor in the United States (see U. Pawar 1998, 2001).

Dalit women writers have the only example of a continuance of writing from one generation to the next: the late Daya Pawar's daughter, Padma Lokhande, has become a well-known poet (see also Thorat (2002) on Dalit women's poetry) and Satchidanandan (2001) on dissent in Indian poetry.

The spread of Dalit literature

Punjabi, Malayalam, Hindi, and Oriya

Dalit Literature remains most influential in the Marathi-speaking area, but has spread within ten years of its recognition as a movement to Maharashtra's neighbors, Gujarat and Karnataka, and then to Andhra and Tamil Nadu. Punjab and Kerala now have Dalit Sahitya organizations, but few translations into English or articles in English have come to light.[10] Translations from Hindi are still in their infancy, although the 16th Dalit Writers Conference was held in New Delhi in 2000. A very promising start has been made with the translation of Valmiki's autobiography, and with the work of Laura Brueck (University of Texas, Austin), whose article on a very important woman author and activist, "Dalit Writing: The Works of Kusum Meghval (2002)" is now available. The publication of a translation of Omprakash Valmiki's autobiography *Joothan* adds greatly to an understanding of Hindi Dalit literature. In Europe, Dr Heinz Werner Wessler (Bonn) reports a flowering of Hindi Dalit literature much like that of Marathi in the 1970s, and Sarah Beth (Cambridge) is working on Hindi Dalit women poets (see also Thorat 1996).

An article on Oriya literature by Raj Kumar suggests the ground is ready for Dalit literature, while one by Achintya Biswas on Bengali literature (1995: 199) indicates "The dawn is awaiting" (see also Anand and Zelliot 1992). There seems to be no end to the new literature coming up. For instance, recently found at a Dalit bookstore (Gautam Book Centre, Delhi), was a pamphlet *Selected Poems on Dalits* by Anil Sarkar, published by the Dalit Sahitya Kendra in Tripura, no date. It is clear that the geographic expansion of Dalit literature in the many tongues of India will continue, and that Punjabi and Malayalam speakers have entered the field although little is available in English.

Kannada

Kannada Dalit writing, which began in the mid-1970s, is best known for a poet, Siddalingaiah, and a fiction writer, Devanur Mahadeva. Dalit Literature seems

[10] A brief article on the "Dalit trend in Punjabi literature" by Chaman Lal (1998: 3) in Indian Literature 1 suggests literature by non-Dalits is more vivid than that by Dalits.

to have begun with Mahadeva's collection of short stories published in 1973, and he has continued to be productive. He is the only Dalit writer to be invited to the prestigious International Writing Program at the University of Iowa. One short story, "Tar arrives," has been included in English translation in *From Cauvery to Godavari* (Mahadeva 1992). His tale of motherhood, *Kusumabale*, published in 1988, received a national award with this citation: "For its powerful re-assertion of the dignity of man, this novel is considered an outstanding work in Indian literature written in Kannada."

Siddhalingaiah, the most popular Dalit poet–activist–orator of Karnataka, has written a well-known play, *Panchama* (The Fifth One, referring to those outside the *varna* system), as well as a play of the epic figure of Ekalavya. Siddhalingaiah was a Lok Shakti party Member of the Legislative Council in Karnataka. Both D. R. Nagaraj (1994) and A. M. Abraham Ayrookuzhiel (1990) discuss early radical poetry of Siddhalingaiah, as well as his more recent cultural affirmation. Nagaraj ends his 1994 article with the statement that the new definition of the Dalit movement, the "new birth," which Siddhalingaiah represents, will also "force the caste Hindu society to alter its definition of Dalits and their modes of creativity."[11] Nagaraj has also written on Mahadeva as one of the two most important writers (Nagaraj 1992). Shivapurkar writes of the conflicting poetic impulses of the caste-Hindu school Navya (Modern), and the Dalit-Bandaya (Protest) school led by Siddalingaiah in the 1970s and early 1980s, but calls the subsequent scene "dismal," although he notes the Kolar dialect work of Hosur Manishmappa and the song forms of K. Ramiah (Shivapurkar 1993a). In another study, however, Shivapurkar says that the Dalit-Bandaya movement, while not living up to its promise, has had significant indirect effects which the Navya poets do not admit (Shivapurkar 1993b).

Telugu

The Telugu movement is in its infancy, say some, while others point to thirty anthologies, and to lively discussions, such as "whether the poets with Marxist-Leninist persuasion are better than the Ambedkarites" (Murlidhar 1996: 213). Kalpana Rentalla goes so far as to say, "The Dalits, who have been in the lowest rung of the social hierarchy, have risen to the position of dictating terms to Telugu literary history," (*Indian Literature* 2000: 13). Most agree that there is a rich folk and epic Dalit heritage, including the rebel singer Gaddar and the early Christian poet Garram Joshua. The telling date for a mature Dalit School seems to be 1995 when the anthology *Chikkanavutunna Pata* (Thickening Song), brought

11 The late D. R. Nagaraj produced an excellent study of the whole Dalit movement in Karnataka in Nagaraj (1993). It is dedicated to Mahadeva and Siddalingaiah as the founders of the Dalit movement.

sixty poets to the fore. Interestingly enough, this initial effort indicated that "Dalit" meant Scheduled Castes, Scheduled Tribes, Backward Castes, and Minorities (i.e. Muslims), not just ex-Untouchables. This anthology was followed by a collection from students at Central University, Hyderabad, and the introduction of women poets in *Padunekkina Pata* (Sharpened Song). In contrast to earlier poetry by Jashua and others around the turn of the century, which was mostly Gandhian in outlook, a new school considers the teachings of Dr Ambedkar as its guideline. However, Jashua (born 1895), a Christian poet of mixed caste Yadava and Madiga (Untouchable) parentage, spoke to his daughter in terms that could easily be a credo for many of today's Dalit poets:

> I have learnt many lessons in life, under two gurus: poverty and caste-creed discrimination. The first taught me patience and the second taught me to protest against remaining a slave. I decided to tear myself free from the shackles of poverty and caste. I took up my sword to fight them. My sword was my poetry. I do not hate society, but only its life-patterns.[12]

Many critics and poets consider the Karamchedu massacre and the subsequent organization of the Dalitha Mahasabha in 1985 as Telugu Dalit literature's founding moment. Certainly Telugu literature has been full of protests against society's atrocities, but it also has engaged in sharp debate on Hindu religious traditions. Additionally, as in the Marathi tradition, Telugu Dalit literature has encouraged the poetry of women (see Challapalli Swaroopa Rani 1998, Satyanarayana 1994).

Tamil

Tamil literature has received a good deal of critical attention, but few translations into English. Bama's (2000) *Karukku*, an autobiography by a Christian Dalit, is an exception, as is Imayam's (2001) novel *Beasts of Burden* about a washerwoman, both translated by Lakshmi Holmstrom (see also Murugan 2004). V. Geetha has recently translated Murugan's *Seasons of the Palm* (2004) about Chakkili children. There are also two lengthy sections in *Indian Literature* 193 (1999) and 201 (2001). Swaminathan, in *Indian Literature* 193 (1999: 15–30), traces Dalit writing back to Nandan, the eighth-century Bhakti saint, and notes that Poomani built on the rich Dalit heritage to write in the 1970s. He suggests that some non-Dalits are accepted in the Dalit School, while some Dalits refuse to be called anything but contemporary Tamil writers. Swaminathan also reports that Cho. Dharman has received nationwide attention and the Katha award.

Included in *Indian Literature* 193 are five poets, seven short stories, and three essays by writers, two of which are very critical of Marxist domination of early

[12] Lavanam Hemalatha, *Ma Nanna* (My Father), 10, quoted in M. E. Prabhakar (1996: 7). Jangam Chinnaiah, Wagner College, Staten Island, NY, with a Ph.D. on Gurram Jashua, is one of the few Dalits in academics in the USA.

Dalit writing. The second Tamil issue of *Indian Literature* 201, contains four excerpts from Dalit novels, including ones by the pioneer Poomani and the well-known Cho. Dharman mentioned above.

An article by M. S. S. Pandian in *Wages of Freedom* (Pandian 1998b) brings to notice an unusual and interesting "Pondicherry Group" which challenges Tamil Dravidian nationalism, as well as Aryan domination, and even the mainstream Dalit discourse. For Raj Gowatham, who has analyzed the Sangam period and has reconstructed a social history of Tamil culture, only a few Siddhar poems echo the past voice of the Dalits. For him, the Dalit past is not one of glory but one of cultivators, hunters, and the like, without heroes but with total equality (Pandian 1998b: 304).

Gujarati

Critical work available in English about Dalit Gujarati literature is just beginning to be published, with an issue of *Indian Literature* appearing in 1994 and an *Economic and Political Weekly* article in 2001. The literature, however, became important much earlier with Joseph Macwan's novel, *Angaliyat* (The Stepchild), published in Gujarat in 1986, in Mumbai in 1988, and in English in 2004 by Oxford. The library of Congress listing contains the names of Macwan's many published works in Gujarati under the transliterated name of Yosepha Mekvan, but one of the few stories in English so far is in the *Indian Literature* 159 (1994). In the late 1980s, the poet Ramesh Chandra Parmar, Gujarat Dalit Panther chief, was asked to apologize for "obscene and inciting" poetry in his collection, "What did I do to be so black and blue?" (*Dalit Voice*, September 1–15, 1988: 14) a clear reference to American Black poetry and an indication of the growth of Gujarati Dalit poetry, but none of these poems are yet available in English.

An article by Rita Kothari on the short story in Gujarati Dalit Literature (2001: 4308–11) traces the beginnings of this field not to a larger political movement, as is the case in Maharashtra, but to the virulent attacks on the reservation policy in 1981. After the mid-1990s, a Dalit Sabha and Dalit Sahitya Akademi were established. She notes that although the Vankars have a considerable presence in the Christian community, only Joseph Macwan is considered a major writer. Her translation of his *Angaliyat* as "The Stepchild," to be published outside of India will bring his novel on the Vankars to a broader audience. Kothari also indicates that women are not served well in the literature. Several of the short story writers she mentions are represented by stories in *Indian Literature* 159 (1994): Joseph Macwan, Madhukant Kalpit, Mohan Parmar, and Harish Mangalam.

Indian Literature 159 (1994: 5) considered itself to be delivering a journal issue on "a rather nascent movement . . . comprehensively presented for the first time in English." The following essay by K. M. Sheriff, however, indicated that in the third decade of its existence, Gujarati Dalit writing had overcome the "teething troubles" caused by its being a poor cousin to Marathi literature, neglected by the Gujarati literary establishment. Sheriff notes that a remarkable achievement is the creation of a subaltern mythology with Ravana and Eklavya as epic heroes (9). Sheriff has assembled an impressive collection of ten poets (one of them Muslim), six short stories, and includes a conversation with Harish Mangalam, often translating from the Gujarati himself.

The Gujarat Dalit Sahitya Akademi has recently begun to publish a series of Dalit literary works. *Tongues of Fire* appeared in 2000. Edited by Darshana Trivedi and Ruplaee Burke, and published by the Akademi in Ahmedabad, it contains stories by thirteen writers (Trivedi and Burke 2000).

Identity

Dalit writers have a clear identity that crosses all language boundaries. They write of their own caste, and from their own experience, often using the language and vocabulary of the group they belong to, with honesty being of prime importance. Murlidhar has expressed the importance of this (1996: 213): "Telugu Dalit poetry has unfolded before the readers the hitherto unknown, unexpected, unimagined – the life in the raw. It has enlarged the scope of Telugu literature and redrawn its map by discerning and exploring a whole new continent of experience." It is this idea of a new continent of experience that creates the continuing explosion of autobiography, poems, and stories, which make real the enormous complexity of India.

Second in importance to Dalit identity is their sense of belonging to a group of Dalit writers. Many conferences are held every year, both of writers and dramatists, usually, but not always on a language basis. Recently publications in Marathi have included two collections of the Presidential speeches of these conferences. These conferences indicate a sort of brotherhood of Dalits, in spite of internal quarrels. There are yearly conferences begun by *Asmitadarsh*, the journal of Dalit writing which itself is an indication of a sense of identity; its name means "Mirror of Identity." Buddhist writers in Mumbai held early conferences, predating the eruption of Dalit literature in 1972. There are Dalit Theater conferences. An All India Phule-Ambedkar Literature Gathering was held in 2000. It is significant of literature's spread that the first All India Dalit Writers Conference was held in 1987 in Hyderabad, Andhra Pradesh, and the released commemorative volume is all in English. This *Who's Who of Dalit Writers, Poets, Journalists and Artists* (1885–1994) lists the names and accomplishments of several hundred men and women (Tharakam 1994). 528 delegates attended the conference, with the greatest numbers from Andhra (311), Karnataka (80), and Maharashtra (65), but even Assam, Himachal Pradesh and Rajasthan were represented by one delegate each. One

African-American attended, Runuko Rashidi from Los Angeles; caste Hindu writers on Dalit literature were also in attendance.

Dalit writers also hold that writing is, in itself, a form of social change. At least one critic agrees: J. H. Anand (1995) writes, "It is only in the writings of the Dalit writers that caste as an oppressive system is being attacked" (184). Poetry, in particular, often rises in response to atrocities, as if making the violence real through the written word might change the future. Waman Nimbalkar expressed this in an early poem entitled simply "Words":

Words it is that set aflame
house, homes, countries,
men as well.
Words extinguish even the fire
in men set aflame by words.
Were it not for words, the sparks of fire
would not have fallen from the eyes,
great floods of tears would not have flowed.
No one would have come near,
nor have gone far away –
were it not for Words. (Anand and Zelliot 1992: 124)

This sense of the importance of writing may be part of the Maharashtrian ethos, where the annual literary conference is one of the most important social (and, at times, political) events of the year. It also seems as if Gujarati, Kannada, Telugu, and Tamil writers have absorbed the same sense of urgency. On the other hand, this sense of a social impact may be related to the conflict that is portrayed – either with higher castes, or within the caste itself. One senses that depiction of the conflict may, it is hoped, lead to change.

Dalit writing is often linked to news of atrocities and violence against Dalits. Mina Gajbhiye, a young woman, wrote of her reaction to the extreme violence against Dalits in the area around Aurangabad when it was decided that Marathwada University would bear the name of Dr Babasaheb Ambedkar:[13]

I had sutured with difficulty
the weeping wound of centuries.
Those stitches are all ripped out,
ripped out by Marathwada.
Even our old bonds of give and take are snapped.
From now on I won't scream, "I want to live."
From now on I'll live to die.

[13] Mina Gajbhiye in *Asmitadarsh*, Diwali issue, 1980. Translated by Jayant Karve and Eleanor Zelliot. The university was eventually named Dr Babasaheb Ambedkar Marathwada University. The violence is still remembered, as is the "long march" to achieve the renaming. A book of poetry on *namanter* (name change) by many hands has been published in Marathi.

Let the village become a burning ground
along with me.
I will not live like a pariah dog, nowhere.

Another element in the identity of Dalit writers is belief in a culture counter to Indian Brahmanical culture by the use of the marginal figures of the great epics, the *Ramayana* and the *Mahabharata*, and religious mythology. Examples include Shambuk, the Shudra Rama killed for learning the Vedas, Karna, the rejected child of the mother of the three of the five Pandava brothers who are the heroes of the *Mahabharata*, Bali, whose kingdom was taken by trickery by Vaman, the dwarf incarnation of Vishnu and especially Eklavya, the low caste or tribal boy, whose archery rivaled that of Arjun and who cut off his thumb at the behest of Dronacharya, the Brahmin teacher (see Narayan and Misra 2004). Some women have evoked the image of Shurpanakha, mutilated by Rama as he spurned her advances. K. M. Sheriff writes: "A remarkable achievement of Gujarati Dalit literature is the creation of a subaltern mythology to counter classical Hindu mythology with its casteist, hegemonistic trappings. Ravana and Ekalavya are the epic heroes . . . " (*Indian Literature* 159, 1994: 10) and Svati Joshi quotes Yashwant Vaghela's Gujarati poem-Identity: "This head is Shambuk, this hand is Ekalavya, the heart is Kabir . . . and yet these feet still belong to a Shudra." (1990: 33)

Two poems on the story of Eklavya illustrate the way in which his act is interpreted by the Dalit poets. The first is by Trymbak Sapkale, a former ticket taker on the railway and a prize-winning poet in Marathi:

The round earth.
A steel lever
in my hand.
But no leverage?

O Eklavya,
you ideal disciple,
give me the finger you cut off.
That will be my fulcrum.[14]

A second version by Surekha Bhagat, a widow who works in a TB sanitarium in Buldhana, Maharashtra, indicates a sense of empowerment that needs no gurus:

He fondled the chisel.
Each chisel stroke
shapes a song into being.

[14] First published in the *Journal of South Asia Literature* XVII:1 (1982:100). Translated by Jayant Karve and Eleanor Zelliot with the assistance of A. K. Ramanujan.

He's found that out all right!
So that he could lay his hands on the chisel
he managed to learn everything.
No Dronacharya for Him!
Unlike Eklavya
this Eklavya was his own guru.
That was when they stopped
exacting the fee from the disciple
the way Dronacharya did. (Deo and Zelliot 1994: 29–30)

Punalekar (1988, 2001) has stressed the caste identity of each group of Dalit writers, along with the presence of a Bahujan (majority) identity, and also the total rejection of any upper caste pity. Another aspect of Dalit identity is identification with other oppressed groups, particularly Blacks in America- and Africans in South Africa (see Manavi 1990). Ralph Ellison's *Invisible Man* is widely known, as are some of Langston Hughes' poems and Amiri Baraka's plays. The relationship to earlier Dalit creativity in poem song, story, and theater is an unexplored field. The name of one Untouchable caste, "Pariah," however, revers to drum. Part of the identity of many, (but not all) Dalits is the creativity of Untouchables in the past (Gokhale-Turner 1980). There are clear suggestions that links modern Dalit identity with Dalits of even the very distant past. The pioneering writer Shankarrao Kharat, who died in April 2001, left a manuscript on the fourteenth-century saint–poet Cokhamela ready to be published by Sugawa Press in Pune. In Maharashtra, Cokhamela is no longer a symbol of Mahar pride, but rather an example of a wronged Dalit who nevertheless is honored as an example of early creativity. This may be the case in other language areas. Some critical writing also stresses earlier influences (Zelliot 2000). K. Satchitanadan, for example, notes the importance in Kannada literature of the oral epic of Manteswamy, an Untouchable saint, and the eleventh-century and twelfth-century Dalit saints Chenniah and Kalavve in *Indian Literature* 193 (1999: 5–8). See, however, Lele and Singh (1987).

The connections of writers outside Maharashtra to Buddhism remain unexplored, but there are many references to the Buddha along with Ambedkar and Phule, sometimes linking the three. For Marathi Dalit literature, Buddhism is all important. Baburao Bagul, Buddhist and Marxist, has said that Dalit literature could only emerge after the conversion of 1956 and that "love and compassion would have acquired significance in the Indian tradition if Buddhism had remained a shaping force influencing the psyche of the people." (Dangle 1992: 280). There has been much innovative poetry on the Buddha's wife Yashodhara (Hira Bansode), the figure of the robber Angulimala (Sapkale and Pawar), and other Buddhist images.

The importance of Ambedkar in this Dalit movement can hardly be exaggerated (Zelliot 1992). All Dalit writers, with no known exception, pay tribute to the memory of Dr B. R. Babasaheb Ambedkar. In all areas, but especially in Maharashtra, Ambedkar is the chief source of inspiration. "Ambedkarism is the philosophic soul of Dalit literature," claims G. Lakshmi Narasaiah (1999), writing about Telugu literature, and it seems very clear that all language schools of Dalit literature give credit to Ambedkar for inspiration and example. In the years since his death, Ambedkar has truly become an all-India figure. A Gujarati poet, Mangal Rathod has written a representative poem ending:

O, Babasaheb!
The first sip of water you drank
Quenched our thirst of ages.
We learned the taste of life!
We can never forget you
for your memory lingers
in each step we ascend. (*Indian Literature* 159, 1994: 24)

The poem refers to the 1927 satyagraha for water at the Chawdar tank in Mahad, just below Bombay, which was the first highly publicized effort of Untouchables to (unsuccessfully) test a law allowing them access to public water. Months later, Ambedkar returned to Mahad and portions of the classical Brahmanical law book, the *Manusmriti*, which indicated harsh punishment for overstepping caste lines, were burned.

Conclusion

The identity of the Dalit writer is one of many components. These include the need to write of his or her own experience, often in the idiom of the group or the place. Dalit identity also incorporates a sense of belonging to a great company of Dalit writers from all over India, and often other oppressed groups outside India, as well as a vision of their work as social activism (Bhoite and Bhoite 1977), with problems in society, especially atrocities and violence in the village, as both subject and stimulant. Dalit literature has been the creation of a counter culture to Brahmanical culture, especially evident in using marginal figures treated unjustly in the epics or in religious texts. Finally, the Dalit writer provides a link with past Untouchable creativity, often with Buddhism, and above all with Ambedkar and his life and thought.

24 Language and youth culture

Rukmini Bhaya Nair

Introduction

Two large and amorphous categories, namely "Indian youth" and "Indian English," intersect in this chapter to create a major analytic challenge. Youth, of course, has long been an intractable concept and no definition of the term has yet been found to hold across every culture. Hence, most researchers agree that only way out is to describe the group minimally as consisting of all those between 15 and 25 years of age.[1] I, therefore, use this measure as a starting point for discussion, although obvious problems exist with such a reductive strategy. The relevant bands in the demographic profile of India, present as well as projected, are the third and fourth in Table 24.1.

As the figures in Table 24.1 demonstrate, the "youth bulge", said to be the cause of much sociopolitical unrest in areas like Southwest Asia, for example, is also evident in India.[2] India's most recent census (2001) shows that

This chapter could not have been written without the generous and perceptive assistance of the author's students at the IIT. In particular, I think I have learnt more about language from the following students than I have ever managed to teach: Siddharth Mehla, Divyesh Mahajan, Ashoka, Ramnik Bajaj, Ankur Meattle, Shalabh Prasad, Gagan Kumar, and Saurabh Srivastava.

1 "Youth and children should be defined by their age – but in the absence of any accepted agreement on this issue, the size and identity of the group is likely to remain nebulous . . . the best definition is to allow the phrase 'young people' to refer to all people under 25. 'Youth' should be agreed to be all young people aged 15–25" (see David Woollcombe, *Peace Child International*).

"Today 1.05 billion is the biggest ever generation of young people between 15 to 24 years. This age group is rapidly expanding in many countries, especially in the third world, where children under the age of 15 constitute almost 40% of the population, as compared with the 21% of the developed world. In many developing countries the next 10 years will be the critical years . . . However, the operational definition and nuances of the term 'youth' often vary from country to country, depending on the specific socio-cultural, institutional, economic and political factors" (Source: *United Nations Division for Social Policy and Development*). It is the "factors" referred to in the last sentence of this UN document that are of special interest in the present chapter. Note 3, paragraph one, also relates to the issue of "age groups."

2 A typical instance of such an assessment appears in the following quotation: "Globalization has caught it [the Arab world] at a bad demographic moment. Arab societies are going through a massive youth bulge, with more than half of most countries' populations under the age of 25. Young men, often better educated than their parents . . . arrive in noisy, crowded cities like Cairo, Beirut and Damascus to work. In their new world, they see great disparities of wealth and the disorienting effects

Table 24.1. *Projected age distribution of population in India*

Age group (Years)	1996 (m)	2001 (m) (%)	2006 (m)	2010 (m)	2013 (m)	2016 (m)
0–4	119.5	108.5 (10.72)	113.5	119.7	120.8	122.8
5–14	233.2	239.1 (23.62)	221.2	215.5	220	227.6
15–19	90.7	109 (10.77)	122.4	117.4	110.1	104.9
20–24	82.1	90.2 (8.91)	108.5	120.8	120.9	114.6
25–34	141.9	156.6 (15.47)	170.6	190.8	210.7	228.6
35–44	104.8	121.6 (12.01)	139	151	158.6	167.6
45–54	73.3	85.7 (8.47)	100.2	113.1	123.3	133.7
55–59	26.4	31.1 (3.07)	36.9	41.5	45.8	50.8
60 and above	62.3	70.6 (6.97)	81.8	92.5	101.4	112.9
Total	**934.2**	**1,012.4**	**1,094.1**	**1,162.3**	**1,211.6**	**1,263.5**

Note: m = million.

approximately 60–70% of India's population is below the age of 30, making it not only one of the largest, but also one of the *youngest* countries in the world. The figures below are from the 2001 census:

> *Urban India*: **Age structure**:
> *1–14 years*: 30.8% (male 173,478,760/female 163,852,827)
> *15–64 years*: 64.3% (male 363,876,219/female 340,181,764)
> *65 years and over*: 4.9% (male 27,258,020/female 26,704,405) (2006 est.)

These figures reveal that the average age of Indians today stands at a little under 26 years. While the UN table cited as Figure 24.1 shows that the 15–25 segment comprises about 20% of the population in India in comparison with the percentage of youth in the world, which stands at a modest 17.5%., there thus seems to have been a radical upward revision of this trend in more recent estimates. In marked contrast to China, the other most populous nation with over a billion people where the 'one child' policy has impacted heavily on the demographic pattern of aging, 'the young-ing of India' appears to be an unstoppable process at the current time.

What is worthy of note is that this situation is likely to impact dramatically on the future of the region in the next fifteen years. At that time, the Indian youth, whose language and culture are recorded here, will be around 30–45 years and constitute a vocal majority, standing at over 30 percent of the total Indian population. The "battle of the youth bulge" will then have moved forward to the cultural frontlines. That is why it may be important to study the aspirations and

of modernity ... [heralding] a new politics of protest" (see Zakaria 2001). The current chapter seeks to describe exactly these "disorienting effects," mentioned by Zakaria, of the global processes of modernity, including the impact of educational and economic factors as they have conjoined to create a specific youth language "of protest" on the Indian subcontinent. See also note 3.

impulses concealed in the rapidly growing, as well as remarkably stable, argot used by the youth of South Asia over the last twenty years.

The cultural and psychological context of India

Their numerical strength may be one of the most apparent features characterizing South Asian youth, but it is suggested – a trifle controversially – that "youth" itself is perhaps less foregrounded as a conceptual category in the Indian subcontinent than in many other societies. Traditionally, the transitional years between childhood and full-fledged adulthood appear to be marked by a representational absence in literature and art. The ubiquitous Hindu God Krishna is a case in point. Krishna appears in many folk stories as a baby (*bal krishna*), playfully interacting with his mother. When we see him next, however, he is a grown male in full command, cavorting with Radha and her milkmaids in Vrindavan or advising Arjuna on the strategies of war in the *Mahabharata*. So where have the troubled teenage years disappeared? Those adolescent anxieties and the myriad psychological uncertainties that appear to beset contemporary youth never seem for a moment to disturb Krishna.

In a culture nurtured on the Krishna myth and similar legends, is "youth" then in some ways *as socially invisible as it is numerically significant*? Rather than search for counterexamples to the Krishna case, which no doubt can be easily located given our complex narrative past, the author is inclined to argue that "youth," as we understand it today, is in fact a category created by *the specific processes of modernity*. Increased lifespans and the institutions of the modern nation-state have combined to produce new social spaces within which the idea of youth, with a specialized culture of its own, has been psychologically extended and developed. University and college campuses, in particular, have provided ideal environments for introspection, for bonding, and for the contemplation of the rites of passage into adult life.

Today, the ideas of the psychologist Erik Erikson, whose profile of the young Gandhi is held to be a classic, and who first suggested that youth was a period dedicated, from the early modern period onward, to the resolution of "identity crises," are taken for granted (see Table 24.2 below).[3]

[3] See Erikson's (1958, 1968, 1969, 1974), which focuses on the "identity crisis" that youth in all cultures face. Not just his Pulitzer prize-winning *Gandhi's Truth: On the Origins of Militant Non-Violence* (1969), but many of his other books, including *Young Man Luther* (1958), *Identity, Youth and Crisis* (1968), and *Dimensions of a New Identity* (1974) dwell on this theme. Based on the plausible premise that human beings do not stop developing emotionally after the age of 12 or 13, Erikson added three other "epigenetic" stages of development to Freud's five, emphasizing adolescence and young adulthood in particular. Adolescence (stage V) typically begins at puberty and ends around 18–20, while young adulthood (stage VI) occupies the 20s. As it happens, these psychological stages, laid out in Table 24.2 (Source: *Internet site maintained by C. George Boeree*), appear to fit in quite well with the more pragmatic definitions of youth in note 1 as well

In this chapter, we are concerned with Erikson's stages V and VI in particular. Broadly following Erikson's approach, therefore, one of the main tasks that this author has set for herself is to ask: *exactly what sorts of crises of identity beset the youth of India at present and how are these reflected in the language that they use?* If Indian youth are indeed becoming increasingly "visible" nowadays, the first contention would be that it is not to the traditional sources of Indian wisdom that we should turn for an explanation of the phenomenon, since age rather than youth was typically valorized in that context. Rather, it is the ideology of post-Independence India – where "modernization" was a keyword from the 1950s to the late 1970s, augmented by the terminology of "globalization," "professionalism," and "liberalization" in the 1980s and 1990s – that has created the self-confident, pluralistic youth culture currently in evidence on the subcontinent.

Whereas the extent of the Indian contribution to the English tongue was once estimated in terms of the servility of "babu" and "butler" language, these familiar sites have been replaced by the subversive markers "bakra" and "bakwas" in the youth culture of the new millennium.[4]

as Table 24.1 pertaining to youth profiles in India, namely the stages of adolescence and young adulthood. "It was adolescence that interested Erikson first and most, and the patterns he saw here were the bases for his thinking about all the other stages" (C. George Boeree). Erikson contends that adolescence is the stage at which the young typically seek to formulate answers to the explicit query "Who am I?" However, in cases where a clearly defined adult culture that young people can unambiguously respect is absent, role confusion results, leading to a "crisis" of what he calls "ego identity." In this chapter, the author argues that, under conditions in which a traditionally complex society such as India's, where "youth" itself was possibly an "absent" category, is moving into modernity and seeking integration within a "global" context, ego identity becomes *communally unstable*. Hence, it is exactly at such points of cultural negotiation that the sort of bilingual "rites of passage," language, and subculture that the author has analyzed could significantly help youth "find themselves." The "disorienting effects" of ego crisis during adolescence and youth mentioned in Zakaria (2001) are also implicitly addressed by Erikson. When ego identity becomes overweening, Erikson points out that a maladaptive tendency toward "fanaticism" might manifest itself. "A fanatic believes that his way is the only way. Adolescents are, of course, known for their idealism, and for their tendency to see things in black-and-white. These people will gather others around them and promote their beliefs and life-styles without regard to others' rights to disagree. The lack of identity is perhaps more difficult still, and Erikson refers to the malignant tendency here as 'repudiation.' They repudiate their membership in the world of adults and, even more, they repudiate their need for an identity. Some adolescents allow themselves to 'fuse' with a group, especially the kind of group that is particularly eager to provide the details of your identity: religious cults, militaristic organizations, groups founded on hatred, groups that have divorced themselves from the painful demands of mainstream society. They may become involved in destructive activities, drugs, or alcohol, or may withdraw into their own psychotic fantasies. After all, being 'bad' or being 'nobody' is better than not knowing who you are!" (C. George Boeree)

My suggestion here has been that the youth of the Indian subcontinent have found a uniquely *linguistic* solution to these classic problems of identity crisis. They have thus managed to avoid, on the whole, the extremes of both fanaticism and repudiation that the move into "adulthood" and/or "modernity" can often entail.

4 A number of works have documented the rise, broadly speaking, of "Babu" and "Butler" Englishes, see Hobson-Jobson (1886), Nihalani *et al.* (1979), and B. Kachru (1983a,b).

Table 24.2. *Psychological stages*

Stage (age)	Psychosocial crisis	Significant relations	Psychosocial modalities	Psychosocial virtues	Maladaptations and malignancies
I (0–1) infant	Trust vs.mistrust	Mother	To get, to give in return	Hope, faith	Sensory distortion – withdrawal
II (2–3) toddler	Autonomy vs. shame and doubt	Parents	To hold on, to let go	Will, determination	Impulsivity – compulsion
III (3–6) preschooler	Initiative vs. guilt	Family	To go after, to play	Purpose, courage	Ruthlessness – inhibition
IV (7–12 or so) school-age child	Industry vs. inferiority	Neighborhood and school	To complete, to make things together	Competence	Narrow virtuosity – inertia
V (12–18 or so) adolescence	Ego identity vs. role confusion	Peer groups, role models	To be oneself, to share oneself	Fidelity, loyalty	Fanaticism – repudiation
VI (the 20s) young adult	Intimacy vs. isolation	Partners, friends	To lose and find oneself in another	Love	Promiscuity – exclusivity
VII (late 20s to 50s) middle adult	Generativity vs. self-absorption	Household, workmates	To make be, to take care of	Care	Overextension – rejectivity
VIII (50s and beyond) old adult	Integrity vs. despair	Mankind or "my kind"	To be, through having been, to face not being	Wisdom	Presumption – despair

Source: Internet site maintained by C. George Boeree. (http://webspace.ship.edu/cgboer/erikson.html, accessed 2001).

The former pair of concepts, as we know, had (1) little to do with youth and much to do with class hierarchy, and (2) usually denoted a certain bumbling linguistic incompetence. In contrast, the latter pair (1) arises directly of young people's usage and self-consciously derides establishment values, and (2) usually implies a cocky command over several languages, including English. The word "bakra," for example, literally means "a goat" but its metaphorical meaning is that everyone and everything can be the butt of ridicule. Nothing is sacred; similarly, "bakwas" means "nonsense" and illustrates a sophisticated use of metalanguage by the young to describe their own talk exchanges. Irreverence is thus, as shown later, built into the semantic structure of the current youth code.

Bilingualism and code switching naturally constitute the overarching features that link the "bakwas" variety of "Indian English" with its predecessor the "babu" variety. However, I aim to demonstrate, through as detailed a reading as space permits, that the functional significance of these varieties – related by history but separated across a generation divide – differs vastly. An attitudinal shift is revealed as, over the years, the stilted language contact between English and the other languages of the subcontinent has given way to a much freer and literally more "youthful" relationship. The eclectic data that are considered in pursuit of this goal comprise the following:

(1) an extract from a self-reflexive essay by the author's students on their own language;
(2) a lexicon of "youth" terms displaying productive morphological processes;
(3) an actual example from young subcontinentals "chatting" on the Internet;
(4) a series of advertisements in the "bakwaas" mode aimed at Indian youth.

Of the four samples above, the second and third serve as a basis for a discussion of observable semantic and pragmatic features of youth talk in India, while the fourth enables glimpses into the larger and more "artful" syntactic structures to which youth vocabulary can be adapted.

The self-reflexive mode

Since language is the main tool employed by the unabashedly elite, aggressive, urban and boundary-crossing architects of the "bakwaas" mode of communication, part of the author's investigative method consists in "allowing" the youth in question to speak in their own voices. The first item in the author's data set is justified on these grounds. At this point, it should be mentioned that this data was mainly collected in Delhi, with the invaluable help of the author's students at the IIT. The corpus is thus fairly homogenous and perhaps does not reflect the tremendous regional variation that attends almost all discourse genres in India. At the same time, it is suggested that the most potent aspects of youth culture in India, as elsewhere, are most readily to be discerned amongst the diverse student communities living in metropolitan centers. In this sense, the Delhi Indian Institute of Technology campus may not just be representative but *paradigmatic* of youth culture on the subcontinent. The essay below, written in 1999 by two of my students as part of a class-assignment, presents salient aspects of this paradigm as articulated by the youth themselves.

Enthu cutlets

It is not coincidental that the usage of slang gained popularity during the French revolution, as a mark of protest against state authoritarianism. The element of subversion has been defined everywhere as emblematic of youth culture. In our country, this element has gradually been taken over by the upwardly mobile "wannabes," referred to as "Puppys" in Delhi.

Delhi provides a vibrant culture of youth slang throughout its various campuses. A few years ago, it was mainly the English-speaking upper middle class which had a monopoly over words like K'Nags (Kamala Nagar, the main market behind Delhi University North Campus) and G'Jams and Hot Sams (Gulab Jamuns and Hot Samosas respectively). Then, even the predominantly Hindi-speaking crowd began using such words. For example, the phrase "pile on maarna" denotes "living at others expense."

The huge influx of people from different parts of the country in search of higher education is also beginning to be reflected in Dinglish or "Delhi English." Instead of the usual "cute," girls can use the Malayalam import "paavam," which denotes innocence and childlike qualities. "Machha" is an affectionate term hijacked from Mumbai. Another very popular word is "Fachha" which means a junior (also known as "junee"). And this flexibility is what is so significant about this culture. This reflects the "X, Y and Next" generation's constant striving to improvise and to create its own distinct identity. Thus, the various colleges come up with different vocabularies in tune with their different moorings. For example, the Lady Shri Ram College (LSR) girls are fed up of being "gated" continuously, that is complying with orders to remain inside the college gates. But these girls from high-class women's colleges also believe, like us, in cutting words short for colloquial use – as in "enthu" for enthusiasm, "obs" for obvious, "abso" for absolutely, and "ulti" for ultimate. Then, "John Peter" or "Peter" is used to refer to guys who talk only in English, while "Sean" for Sean Connery, the James Bond hero, denotes someone who's trying to look smart. The usage for Sean is always with "put": "he's putting a Sean, trying to put Sean."

A refreshing facet of youth slang is new coinages. Take "enthu cutlets": no, they have nothing to do with the menu or food. Instead, this adjectival form is used to refer to students who are, well, enthusiastic by nature! Some use "enthu pataani" which is a Tamil version of the term. Tamil slang used by some colleges run into pages. Thanks to the "Madras basai" influences, most of these are "swear" words.

The Tamil film industry is a major contributor to college slang. What started as mumbo jumbo introduced for the sake of "comedy" by film directors is today well in use. These are actually multidimensional words. "Jillako" and "Gilma" are exclamations that can be used to convey *anything* – the actual meaning being expressed by the way a word is spoken. For example, "That's jillako/gilma shirt you're wearing" could mean it's a nice shirt, it's a crazy shirt, it's a shirt in bad taste, or anything else. You can say this phrase is an Indian version of "yo."

As with any language, our slang reflects the experiences, beliefs, and values of the speakers. Yet, college slang is not a complete language. It is largely a descriptive and evaluative language, containing mainly synonyms for food or eating, money, effective or ineffective performance, relationships, intoxication, and local place names.

Why do we use slang? If you don't know, then obviously you lack the quality that makes slang popular: It's cool! When we speak, we are communicating not only the content of what we are saying but also a message about who we believe we are, our identity. Using slang artfully is a kind of performance and shows that the speaker is in tune with the times. Slanging is great fun and can be a form of play, arousing and entertaining both speaker and the listener

Youth slang draws upon common social experiences that go beyond a mere dictionary definition. It provides an efficient shorthand for communicating emotional experiences. Using slang sends the unstated message: "we are friends"; it indicates a kind of relational identity among the youth.

Despite its direct, perhaps "naïve" tone, attributable to the fact that it is written not by linguistics majors but by a couple of nineteen-year-old second-year students of engineering, this essay highlights several characteristics of youth language in India, namely:

(1) a medley of languages (Hindi, Malayalam, Marathi);
(2) the "marked" status of English ("John Peters" who "speak only in English" are singled out for special comment);
(3) economic and class rivalries (note the references to "pile on marna," and the "taking over" of upper-middle-class terminology by a "predominantly Hindi-speaking crowd" and the "high class" LSR girls);
(4) the ubiquitous influence of films including, interestingly, Tamil cinema (precisely because it is little understood in northern India, Tamil becomes a rich resource for supplying key nonsense or "bakwaas" terms like "jillako" which can be used for metarepresentational purposes);
(5) a self-conscious awareness of "college slang" as rooted in an international antiestablishmentarianism (indicated by allusions as distant as the French revolution and as local as the LSR girls' frustration at being "gated");
(6) an emphasis on interconnectedness of the everyday and the emotive (i.e. a practical vocabulary consisting of "food, money and local place-names" co-occurs with the terminology of "effective or ineffective performance, relationships, intoxication");

(7) an insistence that "slanging" is a form of performance "play" that marks a "cool" youth identity (the widely used slang word in Hindi for being cool is "bindaas," i.e. displaying a couldn't-care-less "attitude").

The lexicon of youth

As part of the author's work on the bilingual subcontinental youth patois described above, she has collected several hundred words.[5] Of these, only fifty representative terms are listed below. While the glosses for these terms comprise those of her students' as well as students from IIT, Bombay, she has sorted the selection into six standard morphological categories for ease of analysis:

(a) clippings;
(b) inflectional and derivational suffixes;
(c) abbreviations and acronyms;
(d) neologisms;
(e) nonce formations;
(f) relexicalized items that have undergone changes in meaning.

Clippings

(1) App (*Verb*) To app is to quit Desh (India) for greener pastures (!) to the west of the Atlantic. Every IITian worth his CGPA can app. Apping is a long-drawn process beginning in the summer of the penultimate year of one's stay on campus and culminating in a school maybe toward the end of one's final year.
(2) Arbit (*Adj.*) An abbreviation of "arbitrary," this word is used to describe something/someone weird, for example "That guy does arbit things" or "He's an arbit guy" implies that the person being referred to is a bit on the strange side.
(3) Disco (*Noun*). Double clipping from the conjunction of "disciplinary committee." Note the bitter irony of the pun.
(4) Funda/fundaes (*Adj.*) Abbreviations of "fundamental(s)". The "funda" of something means the basic principle behind it. "Fundaes" are a collection of several "fundas" and the person with the best fundaes is called a "funda man."

[5] Romaine (1989) identifies six types of bilingual speech of which the type noted in this author's mini-lexicon of youth language in India is Type 6, which Romaine terms "mixed languages." In this kind of bilingualism, children follow their parents in "code switching" between two or more languages, but the case that we record here has the interesting difference that it is the *parents* who are now adopting their children's usage throughout the metropolises of the subcontinent.

(5) Schol (*Noun.*) What almost every IITian lives for, a schol is a composite offer of admission and financial aid from a US University – for many, the finale of their stay in IIT.

Inflectional and derivational suffixes

(6) -aax (*Nominal derivation producing abstract nouns from nouns/verbs*) Used in many contexts, from "chillaax" to "scopeax" to "nabdaax." Has no independent existence and always attaches to another word.

(7) -giri (*Nominal derivation producing abstract nouns/ from verbs*) As in "dha" or "dhak" which is an abbreviated version of "dhakkan." (Hindi for "cap" or "lid" denotes a stupid person; so, to do "dhakkan-giri" is to do something stupid, also "dada-giri," to boss over someone.)

(8) -i (*Adjectival derivation from nouns, Hindi base*) For example, "canti," a generic term for the hostel canteen, "freshie" for "freshmen," and "futchi" for "fresh-woman." The word "futcha," with an "-a" ending is also a widely used form for referring to a "first year-ite." Similarly, "Insti" is short for the "Institute," meaning the IIT.

(9) -ite (*Derivational ending, noun to adj*) English suffix attached to words of Indian origin as in "Kailashite," a female from Kailash, the only girls' hostel in IIT Delhi.

(10) -ing, -s and -ed (*Inflectional calques*) English verb endings are regularly attached to words of Indian origin, as in "maro" (to filch), "maro-ed," "maro-ing," "maro-ed" or "kato-ed," "kato-ing," "kato-s" (to leave) and so on. An extremely productive process in youth slang. See also "kat le" (an expression of disbelief) and "kat gaya" (used when you feel let down). Likewise, the English plural morpheme "-s" is routinely affixed to Hindi nouns, e.g. "larka-larkis" (boys and girls), "buddhus" (idiots), and so on in youth language.

(11) -o (*Derivational calque, this very productive -o ending is peculiar to subcontinental English and does* **not** *derive from standard Hindi morphology*) For example, "despo" a clipping of "desperate" with an -o ending. "That guy is despo for a school." Or "Diro" for the Director of the Institute. The English suffix "-fy" can also be further attached to words with an "-o" or "-i" suffix as in "maro-fy" or "chutni-fy."

(12) -oo (*Derivational calque like* (8) *but restricted to adjectival forms*) For example, "to crib" is to raise objection(s) to something. In IIT cribbing is carried to great lengths by certain people, who are given the title of "cribboos" in recognition of their achievements.

Abbreviations and acronyms

(13) Dnot (*Noun*) Abbreviation of "dhandha not." A dnot is someone who has nothing to do in life or has absolutely no enthusiasm. Note the

phonological resemblance to the English word "dough-nut" – an object with a hole in the middle. To act like a dnot is to be a "dnotgir."

(14) DOSA (*Noun*) Dean of Student Affairs – the guy who's supposed to be on the side of the students – hmmm . . . (A "dosa" is also a very popular food item: a south Indian pancake).

(15) GKR (*Noun*) "Ganne ka ras" (sugarcane juice to pseuds).

(16) LT (*Noun*) Lecture Theatre, venue for a refreshing nap during the CS101 class.

Neologisms

(17) Bindaas (*Noun or Adjective*) Happy-go-lucky. A common attitudinal term signaling youthful insouciance.

(18) Bong (*Noun*) Someone from the state of West Bengal. See also "Maddu"/"Tam"/ "TamBram" to denote persons from the state of Tamil Nadu; "Mallu," indicating people from Kerala, speakers of Malayalam. "Ghat" or "ghati" describe persons from Maharashtra, the origins of these terms probably deriving from the nearby Western Ghats. "Punju" refers to someone belonging to Punjab, while "Surd" is a term for a Sikh (from "Sardarji"), with "Surdi" as an affectionate version. People from Andhra Pradesh are called "Gults." The etymology of this world is unclear, but it is thought to have originated from "Telugu," the language spoken by Gults. "Telugu" when spelt backwards sounds like "Gulutey," which possibly changed to "Gult" with the passage of time.

(19) Ghodagiri (*Verb*) Ironically, this word means "donkey work," whereas "ghoda" means "horse" in Hindi. "Ghodagiri" refers to any kind of work that's menial and/or involves little brainwork. Those engaging in this kind of thankless labor are referred to as "ghodas."

(20) Hadaaaaaaa . . . (*Speech act, exclamative*) An exclamation, its closest English equivalent is the phrase "No Way!" "Hadaa" is used when the person addressed is (1) farting away to glory or (2) generally wants putting down. Nothing beats the disbelief and contempt expressed by a loud "hadaaaaa," where the last "aaa . . . " can be as long as one wants.

(21) Hawa (*Noun*) Hindi for "air"; here stands for AIR, All India Rank in the Joint Entrance Examination or JEE.

(22) Hukkah (*Adj*) Applied to humanities courses at the IITs, implying that they consist of mostly smoke and very little substance – a cultural pun on the idea of the leisurely "hookah."

(23) Leching (*Verb*) An activity at which IITians excel, "leching" is the act of leering at any goodlooking female who passes by.

(24) Mug (*Verb*) To mug is to study/cram, an activity usually undertaken the night before the exam, but some people mug during other –

unseasonal – times too. Such characters are known as "muggoos"; "muggoos" who "hug" in exams are knows as "huggoo muggoos."

(25) P K Palta (*Verb phrase*) Fell over drunk (translation from Hindi *pī* ke *palṭā*).

(26) Poltu (*Noun*) Contraction of "politics," signifying campus politics and never ideological in nature; also refers to a person who indulges in the same.

(27) Talli (*Noun*) Drunkard.

(28) Rg/Rg-giri (*Noun and verb*) Derived from "Relative Grading" – supposedly – this term defines the act of doing something for one's own benefit at the expense of someone else. A good example is submitting an assignment/homework to a professor before everyone else.

Nonce formations

(29) Bhum-chaka (*Noun*) nonsense expression, term for making a nuisance.

(30) Sidey (*Adj*) Can mean "fart" or "shady" – another flexible, context-dependent word.

(31) Fundoo (*Adj*) Anything good is "fundoo." You can have a fundoo meal, watch a fundoo girl (not very likely inside the IIT campus, and equally improbable outside it, due to the "not hep" reputation of IITians). A multipurpose word which creeps into almost every sentence.

(32) Jing Bang (*Adj*) Context sensitive, whatever you take it to mean when you use it. Compare "jillako" from the Tamil.

(33) Types (*Noun*) A vestigial word added to sentences for no reason whatsoever. Lately "types" is being pronounced "taaps," a sign of the live and ever-changing nature of youth slang. "OK-types" is a further derivation that signifies anything that is good. This word can be used almost any place where a positive feeling/result is involved, as in "Okay alright!"

Relexicalized items that have undergone changes in meaning

(34) Boss (*Noun*) A word used while talking to someone whose name one (1) doesn't know, and (2) does know. In the second context, however, it is of no particular significance, a bit like the human appendix without its attendant problems.

(35) Chamkaa (*Verb*) The literal meaning of this word in Hindi is "lit up" or "glowed," but here it indicates an understanding of something that has been just explained/said/described to you. This use probably arose from the popular cartoon image of a bulb lighting up in a person's head when he gets an idea.

(36) Crack (*Verb*) This word, whatever its negative connotations in the real world, has a very positive meaning in IIT. Use of this term implies that

the person is referring to somebody's – perhaps his own – excellent performance/stroke of good fortune, e.g. "I cracked a school" or in true IIT style, "crack maar diyaa" or "crack scene hai boss."

(37) Fart (*Verb*) In IIT lingo, "to fart" means to say something patently untrue or wildly exaggerated. When someone "farts" he is essentially bullshitting big time. Such people are known as "fartoos." Another usage of this word indicates anything bad, that is a fart Prof., a fart movie/song, fart grub – anything which is not fundoo is fart.

(38) Fight (*Verb*) To "fight" over something means giving it your best shot. It's also used for encouraging people under stress who have to meet a challenge within a very short time.

(39) Gandh/gaandoo (*Adj*) These scatological terms derive from the Hindi ("dirt" and "from the butt" respectively) and have the same connotation as "fart."

(40) Give up (*Adj*) Also like "fart," in the sense of something bad, but milder, for example "That's a give up movie."

(41) Hug (*Verb*) Hugging is the act of performing badly at something, making a stupid mistake, or fouling up in general. The Hindi origin of this word lies in one of the necessary acts performed early in the morning, involving the expulsion of toxins from the body. Someone who hugs consistently is known as a "huggoo."

(42) Junta (*Noun, here a speech act, directive*) Meaning "the common people" in Hindi. In IIT, any notice or act directed at all and sundry begins with the word "junta" written on the notice board or shouted out to attract attention.

(43) Koi bhi (*Adj*) Used derogatively, and sometimes enviously, to indicate a person undeserving of a crack in academics or with some fundu chick, or a person of little importance who generates a lot of "awaaj" (Hindi for "noise").

(44) Kuchh bhi kyaa (*Speech act, exclamative*) This phrase, in typical Bombay Hindi, indicates disbelief and is also used to protest against an unreasonable request/demand.

(45) Night out (*Noun*) A "night out" is the act of staying awake all night, sometimes due to a crack session, or a combination of crack and intoxicants, or exam.

(46) Nachun (*Speech act, directive*) Interrogative, from the Hindi "should I dance?" Rumored to be a witty reply to boring information.

(47) Scene (*Noun*) Situation, as in "kya scene hai? (what's the situation?)," a popular greeting on campus.

(48) Scope/scope kyaa (*Speech act, exclamative*) Something impossible or beyond the capacities of the person talking about doing it – very commonly used.

(49) Stud (*Noun*) Someone extremely good at his/her field – even females can qualify as studs.
(50) Sutta (*Noun*) Cigarette; "sutta marna" means "to smoke."
(51) Tension (*Verb phrase*) In IIT, people are constantly "taking tensions" over several things and people (especially Profs.) and "giving tensions" too. Also used to refer to challenges, for example "A tense problem."

Prima facie, the mini-lexicon above appears to provide a rich observational base on which explanations of what the author's students at the IIT felicitously call "youth islands" could be founded. However, it should be noted that these very students whose evidence is so crucial inaugurate their efforts by advising caution:

> It's difficult to "explain" our grammar, since it was created in the first place to express things that English couldn't. New entrants to our hostels appear confused by our language. It's almost as if they're in a different country. The guideline seems to be to avoid using words of more than two syllables. The IITian, leading representative of the youth of India, does not, unfortunately, possess a long attention span – or vocabulary, for that matter. Although this sort of usage doesn't last very long and words keep getting replaced by newer ones, "slanguage" is real useful if you don't want outsiders to understand your idiom. It could also be useful if you're stranded on a youth-island and want to make peace with the leader. Hey, you never know.

With this warning in mind, we can now return to Erikson's fundamental query. What crises of emergent identity among subcontinental youth can we infer from a detailed study of their linguistic usage? Noam Chomsky has recently suggested that our representations of "child language" cannot but be implicitly teleological since they assume that such a language is one "caught in the act" of progressing toward its full-fledged adult form.[6] Similarly, my argument has been that the specific teleology of youth culture on the Indian subcontinent involves the struggle to transit from a tradition where "youth" was an obscure or nonexistent category to one where it attains an independent epistemological and "mature" status. It is this Eriksonian "crisis" that is evidenced by the febrile lexical processes outlined above.

[6] Noam Chomsky made these remarks at a lecture in St. Stephen's College, Delhi, in November, 2001.

In her own work on child language, I have tried to show how the "teleology" mentioned by Chomsky works in the case of bilingual language acquisition in India and in Singapore. See, in this connection, Bhaya Nair (1991a,b). A longer version of Bhaya Nair (1991b), where the author seeks to demonstrate that a richly bilingual environment seems to significantly enhance metacognitive abilities in children was presented at the Sixth Workshop of the European Science Foundation Network held in Paris in June 2001 on 'The Natural and Cultural Bases of Human Reasoning'. Erikson's epigentic stages I to III (toddler, infant, and preschool) would apply to the age groups in these particular studies.

Energetic lexical activity obviously indicates the burgeoning of a "semantic field," wherein a linguistic power base is "captured" as it is being established, but what is special about the Indian variety of youth language is its sophisticated ability to metarepresent its own quandaries. For example, the whole idea of "youth islands" headed by "leaders" with whom "outsiders" might be forced to parley reveals an underlying metaphor of a power struggle. The youth of India, in their own words, belong not just to a different generation but to a "different country" – a country whose boundaries are linguistically defined. As the commentators make clear, their youthful impatience with longwinded talk is revealed in their preference for words of two syllables or less. *Linguistically*, "clipping," represented in section 1, is the process whereby this desire is satisfied, but *metalinguistically* what is remarkable is the manner in which the authors of this language variety insist that the same preference pattern also *exposes their own inadequacy*. That is, they deliberately set themselves up as "bakras" or "goats" lacking both a vocabulary and an attention span.

In such a context, most interchanges lack a reliable Cartesian frame for assessing "true and certain knowledge" ("Hey you never know"). Indeed, it is within this "postmodern" perspective, where the ordinary logic of "one-word, one meaning" is itself rendered problematic that we should seek to analyze the reliance on the acronyms found in the section "Abbreviation and acronyms", the high proportion of nonce-words in the section "Nonce Formations", as well as the abundant bilingual codes used throughout. These choices are flatteringly described as "flexible" and "multipurpose" by the author's students. However, they may also be read as signs of an ironic rejection of complicated linguistic distinctions. By ridiculing their own fixation with evaluative indices (2, 7, 17, 22, 29, 30, 31) and obsession with competition (21, 36, 38, 48, 49, 51), these high-flying subcontinental youth insinuate that *everyone* is a "bakra" – including those judged brilliant academic performers like the IITians.

The Sections "Neologisms" and "Relexicalization or changes in meaning or usage", both of which produce "coinages," broadly speaking, betray a similar trend. *Grammatically* they are distinct as the neologisms seem to mainly produce nouns, while the relexicalization processes apply more to verbs, but *semantically* they cohere in their message: nothing and no one is to be taken too seriously. For example, the numerous slang terms for people from the different states and regions of India (18) display sensitivity to India's linguistic and ethnic pluralism. At the same time, the fact that these coinages are humorous rather than respectful shows how the "bakwaas attitude" permeates this idiom. Likewise, its quantum of scatological and abuse terms (37, 39, 41), as well as words relating to socially censured activities (23, 25, 50), may correspond to a general pattern in slang, but the linguistically salient factor here is the self-conscious mockery of their own achievements in *two languages at once* by Indian youth.

Even a rough inventory of the copious borrowings and adaptations in the mini-lexicon presented here shows that the boundaries between the grammars of Hindi and English are extremely fluid with the rich morphological processes outlined above cutting across these languages. Table 24.3 illustrates that words from both languages occur in almost equal proportions in this language variety.

Table 24.3. *Proportion of English and Hindi items*

	English[a]	Hindi[b]	Suffixes	Total
Nouns	9	10	—	19
Verbs	8	5	—	13
Adjectives	5	5	—	10
Speechacts, declarative	1	2	—	3
Speechacts, exclamative	0	1	—	1
Suffixes	—	—	6	6
Total	23	23	6	52[c]

Note: [a] One word functions as a noun as well as a verb.
[b] One word is a noun cum adjective.
[c] Hence the count is 52.

Given that this generation has been educated in accordance with the Three Language Formula, the balanced distribution of source languages found here is not surprising. This post-1947 policy adopted by most states in the country has meant that an Indian citizen is essentially defined as multilingual. He possesses a "core" self symbolized by his mother tongue, a "national" self represented by Hindi, and an "international" self epitomized by English. It is true that such a picture is ideal and that in reality the educational situation is both gravely unjust and terribly complicated. Yet it would be hard to deny the impact of these rich linguistic opportunities for "the presentation of self in every day life" on the current generation of urban Indian youth. The next section analyzes this interpersonal aspect of youth language, particularly in relation to issues of gender, as it affects the talk routines and self images not just of Indian, but of other subcontinental youth as well.

The private space of the chat room

Listing lexical items is insufficient. Showing how these are converted into robust conversational resources is logically the next sociolinguistic step. In this connection, the flourishing "chat culture" that has sprung up almost overnight across the world during the last decade is a rewarding observational site. The extracts below "capture" an IIT student in the act of chatting up a young

Bangladeshi girlfriend, illustrating the truly subcontinental, cross-cultural nature of the present "Indian chat room":

0:14:57 A: so . . . hoz life going . . . !!
0:16:01 B: i am bored these days
0:17:42 A: oh . . . kya baat hai
0:17:52 B: kuch nehi yaar

0:18:03 A: so . . . how is it that u re online this time
0:18:08 A: matlab . . .
0:18:08 B: i just come back from off and find the rest of the time very dull
0:20:49 A: soing nothing . . . is boring

0:20:53 B: but dhaka is so small
0:20:59 A: haha
0:21:10 B: and i have gone to every single place
0:21:16 B: theres nothing new to do
0:21:28 A: come to delhi then
0:21:32 A: hah
0:21:42 B: i have been to delhi dear

0:26:11 A: yaar . . . tumko lawyer hona chahiye
0:26:30 B: yeah rite
0:26:50 B: i thought about it
0:26:58 B: but the problem is . . .
0:27:18 A: kya problem hai
0:27:21 B: i would've been good in any field
0:27:29 B: he he
0:27:36 A: hehe . . . !!

0:30:51 A: aur sunao . . .
0:31:03 B: aur kya
0:31:10 B: tum sunao
0:31:16 B: say something interesting

0:31:44 A: kya boley yaar . . .
0:32:12 B: kuch bhi bolo janeman

0:32:19 A: haha
0:32:41 B: just few letters from ur side makes me delighted
0:32:50 B: he he
0:32:51 A: haha

0:33:09 B: achha sun
0:33:19 B: u better stop chatting and work
0:33:43 A: haan I also feel so . . .
0:34:38 B: bye
0:34:46 A: bye bye
0:35:26 B: ja bhag abhi

. . . .

22.41:04 A: so . . . how was ur flirting . . . that day . . . !!!!!
22:41:16 B: yaar off nehi hain, by off i meant to say office (off = office, i meant)
22:41:25 A: oh . . . k
22:41:44 A: so . . . kya irada hai. jan hai ki nahi
22:43:42 A: so . . . abhi tu busy hai kya . . . ?
22:47:46 A: A yaar. I was just kidding yaar
22:48:19 A: A to bhi serious ho gayii
22:48:29 B: B :-P
22:48:29 A: neways . . . I will have some more pics put on the net . . .
22:49:25 B: i honestly don't have any recent pic
22:49:35 B: now a days i have become too lazy to take photos
22:49:36 A: and I have scanned them
22:50:29 A: so haan . . . i still remember ur last pic a bit . . .
22:50:32 B: ji thanx
22:50:44 A: and u remem . . . that u told me abt ur vital stats
22:50:56 A: so . . . I can make out how u look like . . .
22:51:16 A: . . . MOTI
22:51:20 A: :-)
22:51:50 B: thanx
22:51:55 A: oyee . . .
22:52:01 A: thanx kisliye yaar
22:52:07 B: i am glad to picturised me perfectly
22:52:11 A: ahha haha

22:53:58 B: y don't u come to msn?
22:54:11 A: yaar. nahi aa sakta ...
22:54:14 A: nahi ...
22:54:19 A: A try sending me a msg ...
22:54:26 A: on msn
22:54:39 B: rehne do
22:54:45 A: hmmm ...
22:54:46 B: yahoo is ok
22:54:58 A: bhejiye to jara ... ma'am
22:55:08 B: u r not on msn
22:55:25 A: I am on "everybuddy" ...
22:55:32 B: how can i send u a msg from msn msg then
22:55:35 A: It is another messenger ... in LINUX
22:55:51 A: this is so because ... u are not allowed toi use msn here
22:56:04 B: rehne de yaar
22:56:04 A: chalo khair ...

22:56:39 A: How was the flirting bussiness ... !!
22:56:41 B: when r ya completing ur bachelors?
22:56:49 A: hmm ... next yr ...
22:56:59 B: oh aisi meri kismat kaha:P
22:57:07 A: then probably I will take a job or study some more

22:57:25 B: there were not a single interesting guy online
22:57:25 A: Kyon ... aapki kismat nahi to phir kiski hogi
22:58:03 A: vesey u must now be having enuf idea abt guys ... !!
22:58:20 A: aapne kya socha hai ..
22:58:31 A: u were planning to give GMAT I guess
22:59:00 B: hmm and i still plan to do that
22:59:07 A: haha
22:59:07 B: by the end of this yr
22:59:13 A: oh u serious ... !!
23:00:24 B: and where do u plan to go
23:00:33 B: i don't think i would try for USA
23:00:35 A: USA /or london
23:00:41 B: i don;t wanna go to US
23:00:45 B: i don't know y

23:00:47 A: oh y . . . ?
23:00:57 B: may be becos everyone is always crazy for US
23:01:05 A: yaar . . . I guess its the best place after . . . home . . .
23:01:11 B: and i don't like running after the same thing
23:01:16 A: ha ha
. . . .

23:34:24 A: hello dear.
23:34:46 A: tujjhe jana hai
23:34:46 B: i have to go to sleep now
23:35:02 A: have a sound sleep dear
23:35:08 B: hmm

23:35:15 B: kya haal hei?
23:35:39 A: doin gr8
23:35:42 A: tu suna
23:35:46 B: good

23:37:51 B: yaar i am hungry now
23:37:59 B: and asked ma to bring me something
23:38:13 B: when i am hungry i remain in a very short temper
23:38:34 A: hmm. kyon..?

23:37:26 A: par tu itna jaldi so kar kya karogi
23:37:36 A: abhi to time hi kuch nahin hua
23:38:01 B: its 12am

23:38:19 B: ok i better have a fag with ya b4 i leave
23:38:21 A: theek hai
23:38:25 B: if u don;t mind:P
23:38:31 A: oh . . . puhleex dear
23:38:36 B: thanx
23:38:45 A: I wud love to have one with u
23:38:54 A: u know . . . this is according to statistics
23:38:55 A: that
23:39:04 A: gurls look sexy taking a fag
23:39:04 B: ok then let me light it

23:39:14 A: do it hten
23:39:41 A: haan to ab bataiye
23:40:36 B: kya batau?

23:40:44 B: where r ya now?
23:40:50 B: in the lab?
23:41:22 A: haan
23:41:26 A: I m in the lab rt now

23:41:28 B: kaha hei aap?
23:41:32 A: lab mai
23:44:14 B: good night
23:44:35 A: lov ya
23:44:38 A: takle care

Tantalizingly poised between conversation and writing, "chat" offers a theoretically rich field for detailed conversational and speech act analyses of the pragmatics of discourse. Although the precise timing of turns, the management of openings and closings, topic shifts, and so on are independently interesting in this respect, this chapter concentrates on just the features of these transcripts that specifically relate to the formation of youth identities in India. If youth is a period of psychological preparation for adulthood, then it is possible that we may be witnessing here a striking twenty-first century, technologically supported, manifestation of a phenomenon that the anthropologist Brownislaw Malinowski (1920: 19) once called "phatic communion":

> a type of speech in which ties are created by a mere exchange of words ... by the special feelings which form convivial gregariousness, by the give and take of utterances which make up ordinary gossip ... Once more, language appears to us in this function not as an instrument of reflection but as a mode of action.

Like Malinowski's Trobriand islanders, the youth of the contemporary world seem to have revitalized "language ... as a mode of action." Typing away at their keyboards, usually late at night, these transcripts conjure up an atmosphere of latent sexuality and closet talk.[7] At the same time the tone is light and

[7] When we come to the discourse of the "Indian chat room," we reach Erikson's "stage VI." "If you have made it this far, you are in the stage of young adulthood. The task now is to achieve some degree of 'intimacy'. Intimacy is the ability to be close to others, as a lover, a friend, and as a participant in society. The young adult relationship should be a matter of two independent egos

bantering, consisting of "ordinary gossip" – far removed from "serious" courting. Romantic encounters literally lies at the heart of the psychology of youth, but these transcripts remind us yet again that the self-representation of Indian youth is in the "bakra" and "bakwaas" modes, where the main purpose of language is to question established societal norms and set up a *counteridiom*.

Evidence for this type of communication being essentially "phatic" – devoted, that is, to the construction of an antilanguage of youthful bonding – derives from the following features:

(1) Often the topic of discussion remains unspecified, and the conversation revolves in circles, since the primary intent is to bolster "convivial gregariousness" rather than exchange hard facts (0:30:51–0:32:12; 23:39:41–23:44:38). This "ordinary . . . give and take of utterances" is also mirrored in the references to everyday activities like sleeping (23:34:46–23:35:02), eating (23:37:51–23:38:34), and studying (22:58:31). At the level of discourse, these strategies effectively mirror the prolific use of lexical *nonce words* in this youth argot.
(2) Code switching and repetitions abound (0:14:57–0:18:08; 0:30:51–0:35:26; 23:34:24–23:38:01), with opening and closings as well as greetings and questions being duplicated in *both* Hindi and English (0:14:57–0:17:52; 23:40:44–23:41:32). Linguistically, such a plural attitude seems to imply mental "openness" as well, conforming once again to the "anything goes" formats of the "bakra" and "bakwaas" modes of youth talk. The processes of *suffixization* mentioned in connection with the subcontinental youth lexicon are especially noticeable here.
(3) Misspelling, colloquialisms both in Hindi and English, and wayward punctuation (0:14:57; 0:18:03; 0:20:49; 23:44:38) likewise create an informal atmosphere, where judgmental attitudes are eschewed and carefreeness is emphasized. Extended "joking" is typical (22:50:29–22:52:11) and "seriousness" is laughingly condemned (22:47:46–22:48:19; 22:59:13).
(4) Metarepresentation of different types of laughter – uproarious (0:27:36), measured (0:32:50), and skeptical (0:32:51) shows how adept these youth are at portraying the modalities of speech in the written mode. Other examples include pauses rendered with . . . (0:30:51; 22:41:04; 22:41:44; 22:43:42),

wanting to create something larger than themselves . . . If you successfully negotiate this stage, you will carry with you for the rest of your life the virtue or psychosocial strength Erikson calls 'love'. Love, in the context of his theory, means being able to put aside differences and antagonisms [and] includes not only the love we find in a good marriage, but the love between friends and the love of one's neighbor, co-worker, and compatriot as well" (George C. Boeree). In the chat-room transcripts analyzed here, we can clearly identify young adults exploring Erikson's stage VI region of love and friendship but with the added advantage of an "intimately" shared language.

expostulation with !! (22:41:04; 22:56:39) and "raised voice" with capitals (the most striking example of the latter is 22:51:16) when the Hindi word "MOTI" (fat) is immediately followed by a "smiling" emoticon.

(5) Emotional states are crucial in all phatic communion and the use of visual emoticons is frequent as well as innovative in this discourse (22:48:29; 22:51:20). Specifically, references to the typically "youthful" feeling of boredom occur throughout (0:14:57–0:20:49; 0:30:51–0:32:12). "Say something interesting" is a constant plea and "chat" is clearly perceived as a "talking cure" to the predicament of possible alienation, again underlining the fact that Eriksonian "identity crises" of emergence are a recurrent feature of this discourse.

(6) Thematically, the related discussion of "forbidden" activities such as flirting (22:41:04, 22:56:39), smoking, and sexuality (23:38:19–23:39:14) and the use of endearments such as "dear" and "janeman" from both English and Hindi are deployed to sustain the excitement of the chat. At one point, B even "fearlessly" indicates the presence of her mother nearby (23:37:59), while A explicitly indulges in an activity legally forbidden by the rules of IIT (22:55:51). Despite these instances of youthful bravado, however, it goes without saying that some of the conversation in this chat would be impossible for the interlocutors to manage in a face-to-face situation, as the IIT student in the present transcript confessed to me! It is this "hide-and-seek" feature that makes chat such an addictive medium for youth talk.

(7) Extended discussion of the actual medium of communication (22:53:58–22.55:51), showing awareness of different "codes" – msn, yahoo, LINUX – heightens the impression of metalinguistic savvy displayed in (4)–(6) above. The high tolerance of *neologisms* and *relexicalizations* shown in the youth lexicon are repeated here in the realm of discourse.

(8) Internationalization of a communication code that relies on a popular spelling system including "Americanisms" and innovative "short messaging" minus vowels (22:51:50; 22:55:08; 23:00:41–23:00:47; 23:35:08) mirrors the widespread recourse to *abbreviations, acronyms*, and *clippings* also noted in the youth lexicon we compiled.

(9) Acute consciousness of locative parameters and career options, so important in the psyche of an "internationalized" youth, is indicated by the way in which Dhaka, Delhi and, finally, the United States and the United Kingdom function as crucial coordinates of youth identity (0:20:49–0:21:42; 23:00:24–23:01:16). Other locations such as the "lab" (23:40:44–23:41:32) and "home" (23:01:05) form a "local" counterpoint to these "global" cities that define varying degrees of political power and metropolitan success. B endearingly confesses, for

> example, that her reason for not wanting to "go to US ... may be becos everyone is always crazy for US." This sort of reasoning may seem "perverse" at first sight, but read in light of the self-mocking "bakra" and "bakwas" idiom, it suddenly makes phatic sense.

The parameters above, taken as a cluster, duplicate significant lexical processes at the level of discourse, revealing the formal sophistication characteristic of this deceptively "casual" form. As is apparent, chat is a device adapted to both the creation and the concealment of crises of identity, where the breaking of linguistic norms psychologically reflects a challenge to other social barriers.

Gender, caste, and religious differences, sustained by a "babu" and "butler" linguistic syndrome, may have proved highly constraining within the family dominated scenarios of the Indian subcontinent, but they are now being bypassed or transcended in the virtual space of the chat room.[8] This is obviously so because the dangers associated with direct interaction are absent in a chat room, conferring on users a sense of freedom particularly important for the young subcontinentals engaged in constructing, as has been argued in this chapter, their own unobtrusively subversive "bakwaas" and "bakra" idiom. Age, sex, and other social parameters can easily be faked in this mode, which makes it a genre well suited to the open, critical, and adventurous exploration of identity typical of this age group. As a genre, "chat" thus demonstrates the originality and flexibility with which public space has been technologically redesigned – and redesignated – in the service of private intimacy by the youth of the Indian subcontinent. I shall now go on to show how the private enclosure of the chat room connects with an increasingly complex public arena.

The public space of performance

One measure of the vitality of "technological revolutions" consists in their capacity to foster new systems of communication.[9] Just as Gutenberg once "democratized" Europe and provided a key condition for the rise of the novel, a crucial question today is: will computer technologies similarly generate twenty-first century textual styles with radical epistemological consequences? In the last section, we examined subcontinental "chat" as a youth genre with well-defined stylistic features that managed to create a certain type of "bakwaas" psychology.

On the Indian subcontinent, the 15–25 year olds popularly known as "Generation Next" or "X" are – quite literally through their walkmans and music

[8] This chapter draws upon Bhaya Nair (1992, 1997a, 1999, 2000, 2001a,b).

[9] Some of these issues arising out of the interconnection of technology and cultural space in the sphere of education have been discussed in Bhaya Nair (1997a,b).

videos – "hooked into" an international culture dominated by television channels like MTV and Channel V. These channels encourage the fast and unselfconscious code switching between Hindi and English noted earlier by offering as role models youth who speak in this manner. In this connection, the case of the popular presenter Cyrus Brocha who actually runs a show called "MTV Bakra" is relevant. The aim of this program is to fool ordinary people into looking ridiculous (i.e. become "bakras" or goats) by giving them idiotic on-camera tasks (holding melting ice creams ad infinitum, jumping up every thirty seconds to speak into an allegedly faulty mike, etc.). While the idea behind this show is not unfamiliar, what is significant about it in the Indian context is (1) its name; (2) its predominant youthful orientation and (3) its instantly recognizable linguistic properties, which have combined to make it a pervasive ideological influence on metropolitan college and school goers. "Cyrus-talk" oneliners include:

(1)	*Hello ji.*	*Ek* favor *kar sakte ho*	[Can you do me a favor?]
	Hello (honorific)	one favor do can [you]	Expressive/Directive speech acts.

(2)	Sir *ji*	*aapko*	*yeh*	car award *mein*	*mili hai.*	[Sir, you have got this car as an award]
	sir (hon.)	you (hon.)	this	car award in	got is	Representative speech act.

(3)	*Baithiye,*	*hum*	long drive	*pe*	*chalte hain.*	[Please sit, let's go on a long drive]
	sit (hon.)	we	long drive	on	will go	Directive/Commissive speech acts.

(4) It is OK	*Bhaai Saab,*	*humko*	*gadi*	*chalaana*	*aataa hai.*	[It is okay. I know how to drive.]
it is okay	brother sahib	I (d ative case)	car	driving	know	Declarative speech acts.

Simple as these utterances are, they cover the entire range of basic speech acts, showing how serviceable this "new" bilingualism is, whether the matrix language is Hindi, as above, or English, as in the "chat" examples in the previous section. In this sort of idiom, the youth of India can both be seen publicly *performing* an innovative set of cross-cultural linguistic feats that will guarantee them an independent identity, as well as *forming* a linguistic vanguard in pursuit of "freedom of speech" across international boundaries.

The mind-set fostered by such a "liberated" verbal culture on television is simultaneously reinforced in the visual medium by a number of "hit" films, such as *Kaho Na Pyar Hai (KNPH), Dil Chahta Hai (DCH), Mujhe Kuch*

Kehana Hai (MKKH), and Kabhi Khushi Kabhi Gham (K3G). These films, aimed at a young bicultural, often nonresident Indian (NRI) audience, display a bilingual, "international" repertoire and exhibit all the processes of acronym formation, coinages, and code switching already noted. Small budget "campus films" that deal with the diasporic aspirations of young Indians are another recent addition to the youth repertoire: *Bombay Boys, Hyderabad Blues, B.A.L.S (or Bachelor of Arts Low Society)* and so on. Finally, Indian English fiction, placed on a "world-stage" by Rushdie and others who pepper English with subcontinental words without any apologetics, glossaries, or explanations, and foreground "the enigma of arrival" in connection with immigrant destinies, also contributes. In short, just as the "chat" analyzed above unabashedly mentions the United States as a desired destination, these genres too seem to have shaken off the "nationalist guilt" characteristic of an earlier generation schooled in "butler" or "babu" attitudes.

Overall, these developments attest the post-Independence rise of a nouveau "chattering class" of educated Indians, reared on television and well versed in the language of a technologically attuned, "multinational" world. Interestingly, serious world events and attitudes toward social issues are often conveyed to this youthful population via corporate advertising banners. I offer just one very striking example of this phenomenon below, consisting of a set of extracts from the aptly named "Bakwaas" advertisements of the Harvest Gold bread company. The first example, sent in by Nitin Sharma of New Delhi, lays out the "philosophy" of the idiom, and it is the only one quoted in full. The rest of the examples consist of extracts.

Bakwaas Advertising: First Class Bread

1. This is a marvellous contest, see it as a game
   Simple *tareeka* to get *paisa*, name and fame

   What's on your mind? Write all that *bakwaas*
   But style of writing should be *kuch khas*

   Main to ho gaya famous, you can be too
   Just write anything funny, *jhoota* or true

   Agar idea *nahi aata*, don't give up the fight
   Increase your IQ level with Harvest Gold *ki* bite.

On drug abuse among youth in the capital city:

2. So it has been proved. That be it uncle or *bhanja*
   Dilli sheher's bratpack is all on the *gaanja*

On cricket, India's beloved postcolonial sport:

3. Indian cricket's end is here. *Bauji*, what a drubbing
Ganguly on all our wounds is *ji* salt rubbing
Cricket was our only hope. That too we have got *dhakka*
By God *ji*, aside from Harvest Gold, life *mein aur kuch nahi rakha*

On Indo-Pakistan relations:

4. *Bauji, Agra mein*, I must say, *bahut bura hua*
General Musharraf scurried home like a *bheega chuha*

On recent political events:

5. The attack on America is barbaric. Innocent lives have been lost
The attackers should be punished. *Oh ji* at any cost

The images, they were horrible. *Nahi jaayegi yeh yaadein*
Sirji, we have to sort out this Osama Bin Laden

Why can't there be *aman* on earth. *Shanti kyon nahi hoti*
Why can't people have Harvest Gold *ki doubleroti* ?

On the post-September 11 trading downturns:

6. America *haadse ke baad*, stock market has crashed
Sensex is nonsensex. My *ji* hopes have dashed

Wife is asking *kya ho gaya?* She is wondering how
I said "*barbaad ho gaye*. Look at the bloody Dow!"

NSE, BSE, everywhere there is *kalesh*
Rupee has fallen down. Wipe out *ho gaya desh*

Apart from the exuberant and complex code switching which is by now only too familiar, we are able to identify the following broader semantic and pragmatic features of the language favored by the "bratpack" mentioned in (2) above:

(1) Clearly, no subject is too elevated to be excluded, or exempt, from a humorous treatment in this discourse, and socially significant topics, which can range from domestic discord to financial stress within a single ad (6), are commented upon with amazing swiftness and dexterity.
(2) Emotive opinions, however "politically incorrect" are expressed upfront. "Desh" or country occurs as a crucial signifier (6), contrasting with an international scenario. Feelings are continually foregrounded (3, 4, 5) as in any strongly phatic discourse.

(3) Recurrent honorifics (e.g. *ji, Sirji*, and *Oh ji* in 3, 5, and 6) and kinship terms (*Bauji* in 5) also indicate that this is primarily a language of bonding and phatic communion. Interestingly, regional (i.e. "north Indian") affiliation is concurrently marked as well.
(4) Crises of all kinds from dope addiction among youth (2) to a defeat in cricket (3) to a political fiasco (4) as the focus of affective attention reemphasizes the Eriksonian theme of youth as a period that marks an engagement with identity issues of all kinds.
(5) Self-reflexive, bilingual commentary on its own "style" is explicitly maintained at all times in this language variety (1).
(6) In terms of speech acts, this idiom is acutely performative, recognizing its own "playful" role, both marginal and central, in mediating and "advertising" attitudes toward critical social issues – national, international, *and* personal.

Conclusion

Many studies of bilingual competence have so far emanated from predominantly monolingual societies where borrowing, code switching, and language mixing are seen as indicative of a *lack* of command over the target language. In the Indian situation, however, these same features may offer evidence of *self-confidence* rather than inadequacy. This is an important interpretive insight that accrues from a study of the youth argot of the subcontinent, where huge interpersonal gains and an enhancement of visibility and power result from these very linguistic practices.

Among an earlier generation of users, the "babu" and "butler" modes marked a classical "subject positioning" vis-à-vis the "master language." Then, the model tongue was undeniably "British English"; today, the youth of the subcontinent seem much more strongly influenced by a relatively easy going brand of "American English" disseminated worldwide via a range of powerful public media. This postcolonial makeover highlights yet again the changing landscape of English as it is being rapidly and almost unrecognizably "internationalized" and "politicized."[10] Indeed, the world has recently witnessed several striking illustrations of the way in which the internet can serve the purposes of ideological transmission. In this chapter, I have considered the input of the youth of the Indian subcontinent to the formation of these new cross-cultural language "tribalisms", specifically arguing that linguistic transformations may in such a context be indicative of the *psychological struggle* for a less constrained group identity within a social structure where

[10] The growth of English as a global tongue and its varied consequences are examined in detail in Bhaya Nair (2002a,b).

"youth" was traditionally not an important category. It is for this reason that the author has analyzed this form of discourse as both intensely adapted to deal with a classical Eriksonian "crisis of youth" *and* as extensively "phatic" in the best Malinowskian sense.

Extremely local in its phonological, semantic, and syntactic choices but totally global in its reach, the youth idiom I have described is pervasive on the Indian subcontinent. Its most distinctive feature in my opinion is that, in it, *one language is used to comment on another language* with enormous, reflexive sophistication. The much-vaunted cultural pluralism and rooted democratic diversity of modern India are, it is argued, thus showcased in this language variety. As contended in this chapter, the present generation of middle-class, post-Independence Indians, schooled in at least two languages, are "natural born" translators.[11] Their skill at crossing linguistic boundaries aids their propensity to smoothly traverse other boundaries – such as those defined by nation and corporation. Nationalism and an allegiance to "desh" are still important motifs but the simplified diction of an earlier nationalism is being reinvented within a more skeptical, postnationalist frame by the technologically savvy Indian youth now represented by "outgoing" diasporic groups like the IIT undergraduates. When supported by "instant access" communication in the form of email and chat, these youth are thus particularly well poised to chart new "electronic" routes across the world.

In the process, subcontinental youth inevitably carry with them their "bakra" and "bakwaas" epistemic baggage, linguistic portmanteaus that help them identify and bond with their increasingly international and internationa*list* fraternity, whether in Delhi, Dhaka, or Dallas. The radical speech acts of affiliation promoted in this discourse thus derive paradoxically from the fact that the 15–25 year olds pioneering it have managed to create a stable argot that could ultimately serve the independent and "free" self-image of society as a *whole*. That is the signal contribution of this unique yet cosmopolitan form of "youth" language forged in contemporary India.

[11] India is a multilingual environment in which translation flourishes (See Bhaya Nair 2002b).

Part 10

Languages in diaspora

25 South Asian languages in the second diaspora

Rajend Mesthrie

Introduction

In a survey of South Asian diaspora, it is convenient to identify three focal periods and types of emigration, which I label the first, second, and third diasporas.[1]

The first diaspora, about which little is known, and even less of the languages involved saw Indians traveling to places in Asia, Africa, and Europe. These movements were voluntary and can be further divided into three very different types of movement. One movement was mercantilistic, resulting in settlements in places such as Sri Lanka, parts of South East Asia (Burma, Sumatra, Java, Malaysia, Cambodia), and on the coasts of Arabia, Persia, China, and Africa. Gregory (1971: 10) puts it thus: the fifth, sixth, and seventh centuries have been called the period of Hindu Imperialism, and the reign of Pulakeshi II of the Deccan in the early seventh century, when the imperial fleet consisted of "hundreds of ships," has been described as "the golden age of India's maritime activity."

Another movement involved more peaceful activities like the religious impulse which saw the spread of the teachings of the Buddha in Asia some five hundred years after his death (in *c*. 483 BCE). The languages of the first diaspora would have been south Indian languages and forms of Sanskrit and Prakrit. These languages did not survive long, though as expected many loanwords pertaining to culture and religion have spread in this way (e.g. forms like *dewa* "God" and *nirwana* "nirvana" in Malay).

Somewhat later between the ninth and twelfth centuries CE large-scale migrations of people who would be identified as gypsies took place out of north India to other parts of Asia and Europe, in a great wanderlust that was to eventually see some of them in the Americas. Romany is still classifiable as an Indo-Aryan language, despite centuries of acculturation to other "host" languages in different territories.

The second diaspora mainly involved the forced or semiforced migrations of Indian workers in the era of European imperialism. Within this period three

[1] For the 'second diaspora' section of this paper I would like to thank several scholars who took time to read and comment on an earlier version. These have been identified in Acknowledgments (see p. xviii of this volume).

groupings can be identified: (1) slavery; (2) indenture; and (3) movements of traders. Slaves were moved mainly by the French and the Dutch from parts of India to their territories such as Mauritius and the Cape. Slaves from south India were taken to Mauritius from 1729 to add to the numbers of African slaves there. Free laborers and artisans were also taken from various parts of India to develop Port Louis as a busy harbor. According to Domingue (1971: 10), at the beginning of the nineteenth century before the era of indentured immigration, there were about six thousand Indians on the island, speaking Tamil, Telugu, Marathi, Gujarati, and Bengali. Likewise in Cape Town the slave population from the late seventeenth century onwards included about 15–30 percent from India and environs (Armstrong and Worden 1989: 116). These were people from the coastal areas of India (Bengal, Coromandel coast, Malabar) who became part of the larger slave community from Indonesia, Madagascar, Mozambique, and Angola. Another strand of slavery saw Indians sold as slaves in the Central Asian markets like Kabul, which in the early seventeenth century was famous for its Indian slaves (Gautam 2000 personal communication).

The era of indenture remains the best researched part of the Indian diasporas, and much is known of its sociolinguistic consequences. This period saw the migration of over 1.2 million Indians from 1834 to 1920 to work the land in European colonies in which slaves had become free or in new colonies where slavery was not permitted. The term "indenture" refers to the contract between employer and employee in which the latter was tied or bonded to a particular employer for a fixed period (in this case five or ten years). Thereafter the employee was free to return to India, to sign up for a second term of indenture or to purchase a small plot of farming land. Historians have insisted that in practice indenture was not as benign as this: Tinker (1974: v) chose the title of his book on the subject from Lord John Russell who had characterized indenture as possibly leading to "a new system of slavery." The chief languages spoken by indentured workers were varieties closely associated with Hindi (especially Bhojpuri and Awadhi), Tamil, Telugu, Urdu, and Marathi. This part of the second diaspora is treated at length in the section on "The second diaspora – indenture and its aftermath." (A related movement of mainly south Indian workers to places within Asia, which also forms part of the second diaspora, is mentioned in this section)

Soon after the establishment of an Indian laboring populace in far-flung corners of the world, a voluntary movement of trading-class Indians into those territories followed. In this way Gujarati became established worldwide, and to a lesser extent Kacchi (also known as, Meman, a dialect of Sindhi, identified with Vohras (Muslims)), Konkani, and Panjabi.

The third diaspora involves the movement of Indians, Pakistanis, Bangladeshis and Sri Lankans essentially in the post-independence period in search of opportunities in the United Kingdom, the United States, Canada, Australia, the

Middle East, New Zealand, and so on. The third diaspora differs from the second in the following respects:

(1) It occurred more in the era of air travel, rather than of the sailing ship. This has consequences for communication and cultural links with the homeland.
(2) It included people from all walks of life (not just laborers and traders), filling professional as well as menial positions.
(3) It drew on migrants from mainly urban areas. This had consequences for the pace of assimilation within the host societies.
(4) It did not involve direct recruitment of people from specific areas.
(5) It involved people from post-Independence India and the rest of South Asia, having a different sense of "India" from their second diaspora predecessors.
(6) Proportions of third diaspora Indians to their host societies were minuscule in comparison to the ratio in second diaspora island and coastal societies.
(7) Panjabi was often the most spoken of the third diaspora languages.

The second diaspora – indenture and its aftermath

The second Indian diaspora is largely a consequence of the abolition of slavery in the European colonies in the early nineteenth century (1834 in the United Kingdom). Colonial planters in many parts of the world looked to migrant labor from Asian countries to fill the gap caused by the understandable reluctance of slaves to remain on the plantations once they were legally free. The British-administered Indian Government permitted the recruiting of laborers to a variety of colonial territories. This resulted in a great movement of hundreds of thousands of Indian laborers first to Mauritius (1834), then British Guyana (1838), Jamaica and Trinidad (1844), and subsequently to various other West Indian islands, Natal, Réunion, Suriname (Dutch Guiana), Fiji, East Africa, and the Seychelles (Table 25.1).The following discussion shows the great variety of languages spoken by the indentured workers:

(1) In Mauritius and British Guyana, the earliest indentured workers to be recruited were called Dhangars or hill coolies from the tribal areas of Bengal, Bihar, and the Chota Nagpur Plateau (Misra 1979: 17; Tinker 1974: 49). They would have been speakers of Austro-Asiatic languages such as Santali, Munda, and Ho. However, no trace of these languages or their speakers exist in the colonies, nor any appreciable influences seen on other Indian or creole languages of the territories, apart from surnames like Dhongoor and Dhingoor which attest to the former presence of Dhangars.

Table 25.1. *Major colonies importing Indian indentured labor*

Name of Colony	Years	Number of laborers imported
Mauritius	1834–1900	453,063
British Guyana	1838–1916	238,909
Trinidad	1845–1916	143,939
Jamaica	1845–1915	36,412
Grenada	1856–1885	3,200
St. Lucia	1858–1895	4,350
St. Kitts	1860–1861	337
St. Vincent	1860–1880	2,472
Natal	1860–1911	152,184
Réunion	1861–1883	26,507
Seychelles	1870–1916	6,315
Dutch Guyana	1873–1916	34,304
Fiji	1879–1916	60,965
East Africa	1895–1920	39,771

Source: Barz and Siegel 1988: 1.

(2) From the south of India, via the port of Madras (now Chennai), chiefly Tamil and Telugu, and in small numbers, Malayalam and Kannada were represented. The latter two languages did not have sufficiently large numbers of speakers to survive beyond a generation in most territories.
(3) From the north of India, via the port of Calcutta (now Kolkata), a variety of Indo-European languages including Bhojpuri, Awadhi, Magahi, Kanauji, Bengali, Rajasthani, Braj, and Oriya were represented. There was also what Tinker (1974: 52) called "the lingua franca of the emigration traffic, Hindustani".
(4) From the west central part of India, via the port of Mumbai (Bombay), Marathi-speakers from the state of Maharashtra (who went mainly to Mauritius) were represented.
(5) A small number of Muslims amongst the indentured laborers would have spoken the village language of their area as well as varieties of Urdu.[2]
(6) Similarly a small number of Christians would have spoken the language of their area of origin as well as English in many instances.

In Malaysia, Singapore, Burma, and Sri Lanka the system was slightly different. The *kangani* and the (closely related) *maistry* systems involved nonindentured laborers from south India. The kangani or maistry was a headman who was himself an Indian immigrant who supervised the work of a

[2] In addition, according to Grierson's maps, Awadhi seems to have been favored by Muslims in areas in (what are now) U.P. and Bihar, where another language might have predominated.

gang of 30 or so laborers from south India, which he usually recruited himself (see Kondapi 1951: 29).

Smaller numbers of Indians of trading background usually followed the laborers into the colonies, paying their own passage and having the status of free, rather than bonded, people. In this manner, languages such as Gujarati, Konkani (originally a variety of Marathi), Meman, Bengali, and Panjabi were established in the colonies.[3] In East Africa the presence of Indian traders and clerks preceded the period of British rule and of indentured immigrants. The majority of the latter returned to India after expiry of their contracts. Panjabi-speaking Indians went to Canada (*c.*1900–1914) as free immigrants in search of employment in an area where there had not been any prior indentured immigration (Basdeo 1999).

The sociolinguistic milieu in which Indians found themselves was a particularly complex one. Not only did they often lack a knowledge of the colonial languages (English, French, Dutch) and the local languages, but they would not always have been able to converse amongst themselves. In particular people from the north, speaking Indo-European languages, would not have been able to understand people from the south, who spoke Dravidian languages. Gujarati-speaking merchants and Marathi speakers would have been able to speak to indentured Indians from north India, often using a simplified variety of Hindi known as "Bombay Bazaar Hindustani," but they would not have been able to converse with speakers of Dravidian languages. The linguistic and social alienation among first generation migrants is well illustrated by Prabhakaran (1991: 74), who cites the case of a Telugu woman assigned to an estate in Natal where " the lady is continuously crying and speaks a language [Telugu] and neither she can understand the rest of the labourers in the mills nor they her. The other coolies won't have anything to do with her. She cannot or won't work and she does not earn her ration." (Letter to Protector of Indian Immigrants, November 9, 1903).

In such a situation we would expect a pidgin language (i.e. a rudimentary contact language) to thrive. In Fiji, for example, two pidgins arose for interethnic contact in the colonial period: one based on Fijian that arose prior to the introduction of Indians to the area and another based on Hindi (Moag 1979: 130–2). In Natal, the prior existing Fanakalo pidgin (originally arising out of contact between Europeans and Zulu and, to some extent Xhosa speakers) was taken up as a particularly useful language for communication not only with Europeans and Zulus, but between north and south Indians too (Mesthrie 1989). In the other territories Indians appear to have eventually learnt the preexisting creole language of the territory (Creole English in Jamaica, Guyana, Trinidad; Creole French in

[3] Panjabi speakers occasionally formed a small part of the indentured workforce. In East Africa they formed a main part of the workforce establishing the railways. In second diaspora communities it was only in Fiji that they went as a large group of free immigrants, in the main as agriculturists (Moag 1979: 125).

Mauritius, Seychelles, and Réunion; Sranan (an English-based creole in Suriname, which later came under the influence of Dutch). In East Africa the contact language learnt by Indians was Swahili; in Malaysia and Singapore, Malay.

In all of these territories English would have high status as language of learning amongst Indians, despite the dominance of French and Dutch in some colonies. Indians in Suriname, for example, are multilingual in Sarnami (the local variety that developed out of the north Indian experience of indenture, also known as Suriname Hindustani), Sranan, Dutch, and for the educated classes, English as well.[4] In Mauritius the repertoire of people of Indian ancestry often includes Bhojpuri, Creole, French, and English. Also introduced via schooling would be Hindi (as opposed to the usually low status vernaculars that evolved amongst north Indians). Hindi was often less successful in spreading as a language of learning than English; its value was more in the cultural and symbolic realm. In some territories, some north Indians learnt Tamil and some south Indians learnt a variety of Bhojpuri-Hindi (see Mesthrie 2000). In this chapter we use the term Bhojpuri-Hindi to denote a variety that has, or has been claimed to have, its roots in a variety of Bhojpuri of India, and in closely related varieties of (eastern) Hindi. We shall use the convenient abbreviation "OBH" for "overseas varieties of Bhojpuri-Hindi" in contrast to IB for "Indian Bhojpuri." Furthermore, we use abbreviations, such as MB for Mauritian Bhojpuri, TB (Trinidad Bhojpuri), GB (Guyanese Bhojpuri), SB (South African Bhojpuri), SH (Suriname Hindustani), and FH (Fiji Hindi). These are the labels used by linguists who have described the varieties and are not necessarily used by the communities. Nor do they suggest a single language antecedent in India.

Factors related to demographics and prestige sometimes prevented an Indian language from becoming a pan-Indian phenomenon in the colonies, with English or a form of creole often eventually supplying that function. A notable exception occurs in Fiji where it is the local Fiji Hindi, which is used by all people of Indian descent (Moag 1979). This was apparently the case in Burma where "until World War II, the lingua franca of Rangoon was not Burmese, but Hindustani. Even the South Indians and Chittagonians, whose mother tongue was other than Hindustani, conversed in that language" (Mahajani 1960: 26). Remarks in Gautam (1999) suggest that the Telugu community of Suriname also adopted Sarnami in time. This process of language shift also applies to the Tamil community of Suriname (Damsteegt 2000 personal communication), though many aspects of south Indian culture remain strong. Mohan (2000 personal communication) comments that although Tamil survives (tenuously) in Trinidad, at one stage Bhojpuri did become "an Indian" (rather than just

[4] Gautam (1999: 149) puts it thus: "[I]n order to keep relations with the neighbouring countries such as Guyana and Trinidad, Surinami Indians have to learn English as well as the standard Hindi/Urdu."

"North Indian") phenomenon. Descriptions of Tamil, Telugu, Gujarati, and Marathi in second diaspora communities are increasingly becoming available (e.g. Prabhakaran 1991, 1994; Mugler and Mohan Lal 1995; Mugler and Nair 1997; Mugler and Vijayasarathi 1997).[5] However, as such research does not yet permit detailed comparisons, I focus in the next section on research on the linguistic adaptations of indentured north Indians.

Linguistic adaptations

Koineisation

Indentured north Indian laborers came from a vast geographical territory, stretching from the Bengal coast on the east to well into north central and even northwestern India (mainly the present-day states of Bihar, Uttar Pradesh, and to a much lesser extent, West Bengal, Madhya Pradesh, Orissa, and Punjab). In this area a number of languages exist, the best known ones being Bengali, Bhojpuri, Awadhi, Braj, Hindi, Panjabi, and Rajasthani, though many other languages and dialects of these languages can be added to the list. British officials kept reasonably detailed records of all indentured workers, concerning their castes and places of origin, but not language. Fortunately, during the period of indentured immigration Sir George Grierson was undertaking his eleven-volumed (in nineteen parts) *Linguistic Survey of India* (published in 1903–1928, fieldwork began in 1894), with notes, skeleton grammars, and detailed speech samples of village speech throughout north India. Grierson's *Seven Grammars of the Dialects and Sub-dialects of the Bihari Languages* preceded the survey and was published in the period 1883–1887. These two sources serve as a baseline against which one can piece together a historical account of the linguistic adaptations that took place in the various territories. Table 25.2 gives a list of the ten most common districts of recruitment for Natal, Fiji, and Mauritius. In brackets are the (present-day) states to which these districts belong and the most common speech variety in these districts.

These districts mostly have Awadhi or Bhojpuri as their main vernacular languages, together with Hindi as supraregional language. Map 25.1 gives a display of the languages involved and the percentages of immigrants per district for Fiji.

Map 25.1 on p. 505 clearly indicates the diffuseness (heterogeneity) of the linguistic situation as people mingled together at the port depots, on board ship, and in the plantations of Fiji. It is not surprising that a "common denominator" speech form arose in each colony among north Indian immigrants. This process has been termed "koineization" (Mohan 1978; Pillai 1975; Siegel 1975) – the

[5] In Natal for example, South Indians speaking Telugu or Tamil made up 67.9% of the indentured population; in Mauritius the figure was 31.9%; in Fiji 23.8%.

Table 25.2. *Twelve most common districts of recruitment of laborers for three colonies and the language varieties of the districts*[6]

Natal	Fiji	Mauritius
Basti (UP; B)	Basti (UP; B)	Shahabad (Bihar; B)
Gonda (UP; A)	Gonda (UP; A)	Gaya (Bihar; M)
Azamgarh (UP; B)	Fyzabad (UP; A)	Ghazipur (UP; B)
Ghazipur (UP; B)	Sultanpur (UP; A)	Saran (Bihar; B)
Sultanpur (UP; A)	Azamgarh (UP; B)	Patna (Bihar; M)
Fyzabad (UP; A)	Gorakhpur (UP; B)	Varanasi (UP; B)
Patna (Bihar; M)	Allahabad (UP; A)	Ranchi (Bihar; B)
Gaya (Bihar; M)	Jaunpur (UP; A & B)	Lucknow (UP; A)
Allahabad (UP; A)	Shahabad (Bihar; B)	Puruliya (West Bengal; Be; M)
Rae Bareily (UP; A)	Ghazipur (UP; B)	Nagpur (Maharashtra; Ma)
Lucknow (UP; A)	Rae Bareily (UP; A)	Hazaribagh (Bihar; M)
Gorakhpur (UP; B)	Partabgarh (UP; A)	Azamgarh (UP; B)

Note: A = Awadhi, B = Bhojpuri, Be = Bengali, M = Magahi, Ma = Marathi, UP = Uttar Pradesh.

development of a new dialect from existing dialects of a language and/or other closely related languages. The first detailed discussion of the process of koineization was that of the Guyanese Bhojpuri koine (S. K. Gambhir 1981; repeated in 1984; see also Gambhir 1987). The process has also been considered in detail by Siegel (1987: 185–210). Gambhir provides an overview of Guyanese Bhojpuri koineization in tabular form, by grouping together features of GB shared by the source languages (see table 25.3, p. 506).

Although Table 25.3 gives a good overview of the koineization process, the number of features are not meant to be exactly comparable, since for classes like (a) rather broad grammatical subsystems are included (e.g. "tense and aspect"), while for others (e.g. (m)) very specific grammatical elements are referred to, like a particular noun or verb ending.

The only necessary process in koineization is that of the incorporation of features from several regional varieties of a language. In the early stages one can expect a certain amount of heterogeneity in the realization of individual phonemes, in morphology and, possibly, syntax. Trudgill (1986) has outlined how such dialect contact can be characterized in interactional and linguistic terms. He stresses the role of speech accommodation resulting from the unification of previously distinct groups (in terms of region and/or social status). The process of

[6] The table is based on Mesthrie (1991: 22), drawing on Swan (1985), Lal (1979: 21), and Carter (1995: 308–9). Details from the other colonies are not available, as analyses of the ships lists do not appear to have been undertaken. Shahabad and Saran are today known as Arrah and Chapra respectively. Bihar and UP have since been subdivided to include the new states of Jharkand and Uttarakhand. Spellings of place names have been modernized.

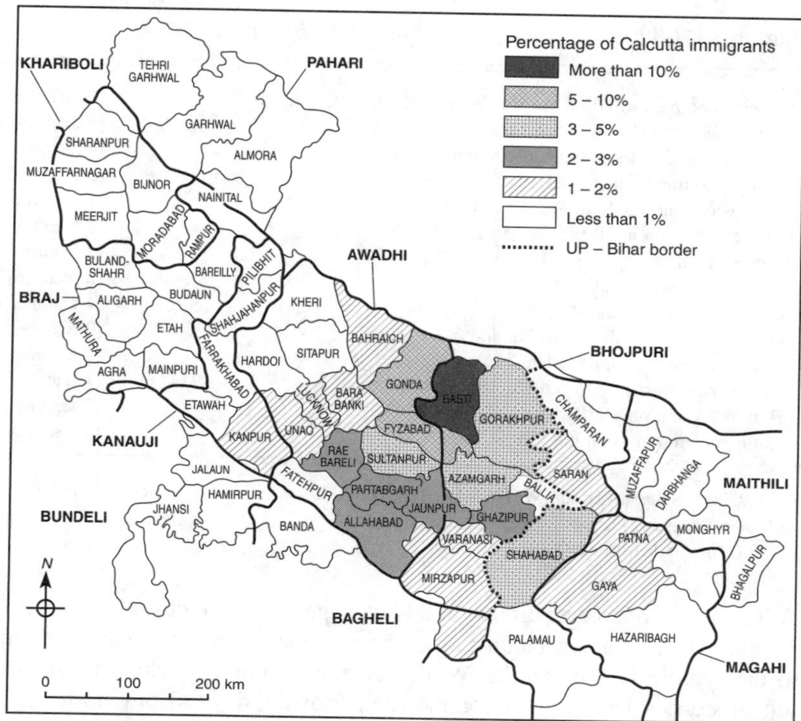

Map 25.1 *Places of recruitment for Fiji and the main languages spoken there Source:* Siegel 1987: 144.

accommodation between adult speakers will result in the neutralization of the social meaning attached to linguistic variants. That is, the variation in the early stages of koine formation will no longer correlate clearly with nonlinguistic factors such as region, function, and social status (Samarin 1971: 133). More salient variants will be retained, while minority and marked features will be "accommodated out" (Trudgill 1986). Forms which are more regular, and therefore more easily learnable (by adults), stand a better chance of being retained. Where several alternants occur, frequency of a particular form must assume some importance: the more dialects a form occurs in, the greater its chances of survival in the koine. In determining who accommodates to whom, and what forms win out, demographic factors involving proportions of different dialect speakers and relative prestige of groups will clearly play an important role.[7]

[7] Trudgill overstates the case for selection of features along purely linguistic grounds (e.g. the length of a morpheme where different choices are possible) – see Siegel (1993). The matter is, however, deserving of further research.

Table 25.3. *Multiple/koine origins of Guyanese Bhojpuri*

(a) Features common to all of Std Hn; W. Hn; E. Hn; IB; and GB	[18 features]
(b) Features common to all but Std Hn	[3 features]
(c) Features common to all but Std Hn and W. Hn	[6 features]
(d) Features common only to IB and GB	[6 features]
(e) Features common only to W. Hn and GB	[1 feature]
(f) Features common to all but Std Hn and IB	[2 features]
(g) Features common to all but IB	[2 features]
(h) Features common to all but E. Hn and IB	[2 features]
(i) Features found only in GB	[4 features]
(j) Features common only to Std Hn and GB	[0 features]
(k) Features found only in Std Hn	[1 feature]
(l) Features common only to Std Hn and W. Hn	[1 feature]
(m) Features found only in IB	[9 features]
(n) Features common to all but GB	[5 features]

Note: Std Hn = Standard Hindi; W. Hn = Western Hindi dialects; E. Hn = Eastern Hindi dialects; IB = Indian Bhojpuri; GB = Guyanese Bhojpuri.
Source: Gambhir 1981: 196–8.

With the rise of a generation of child language learners focusing takes place. Essentially this results in a reduction of the possible variants of linguistic forms and the stabilization of norms. While accommodation is a characteristically adult process, selection of accommodated forms and stabilization are more likely to be associated with child acquirers of the koine. Some of these postulated series of events are clear from an examination of present-day varieties of OBH. Our exemplification comes from SB, based on Mesthrie (1991: 55–76). The importance of demography in determining the blend of regionalisms has been the theme of this section, and needs no further discussion. The other processes are outlined below.

Variation in the early stages of koineization

In addition to the verb forms characteristic of SB there are some idiosyncratic forms used by a few older speakers. These forms are relics of the dialect input into SB, hinting at the great variety of forms prior to stabilization of the SB koine. Significantly, they occur in the speech of a few rural speakers who lead particularly isolated lives. In almost all instances these speakers had learnt the form from a parent born in India, prior to 1911, when immigration to Natal ceased. Among these idiolectal forms are present participles in *-it*, rather than the usual *-at*; second person future endings in *-ba*, rather than the usual *-be*; third person transitive past endings in *-le* or *-lis*, rather than the usual *-las* or *-lak*; and the use of the endings *-wa* for the third singular of past intransitive verbs. All of these forms show the marginalization of non-Bhojpurian features in the main coastal SB dialect. One pair of variants form a notable exception in that they occur equally frequently in coastal SB in apparent free variation. These are the 3rd person past transitive marker *-las* (from Bhojpuri) and *-lak* (its equivalent in Magahi and Maithili and some Bhojpuri dialects bordering upon them). Speakers are not sensitive to the difference in the phonological form of these items; that is, they are not indexical of social meanings.

Simplification

The term simplification is not an unproblematic one, as Mühlhäusler (1974: 67–75) shows. It is used here to indicate both reduction in the number of categories, as well as an increase in regularity in certain paradigms. Generally, all varieties of overseas Bhojpuri Hindi show drastic reduction in the expression of gender for verbs. Whereas grammars of all the input varieties specify separate verb paradigms according to gender, there is no trace of such gender variation in SB. For further details see Damsteegt (1988: 109); Gambhir (1981: 249–54); Mesthrie (1991: 94–5).

The same is true of the feature "respect," which is manifested systematically in Indic languages in verbal and pronominal paradigms. It seems this feature did not survive the koineization process in Natal, for there is no systematic morphological way of signaling respect in SB. Power relations between interlocutors once indexed by pronoun usage must have given way to the expression of solidarity on the plantations. When present-day SB speakers attempt to "soften" their speech in conversations with high-status addressees like priests, they do so in non-systematic ways (e.g. by leaving out the 2nd person pronoun; by use of the reflexive pronoun *āpan* "self," instead of *tū*; by borrowing the standard Hindi form *āp*, etc.) For an extended discussion of the feature "respect" the reader is again referred to Gambhir (1981: 260–9) and Mesthrie (1991: 100–2).

"*Accommodating out*" *of marked forms*

Although Bhojpuri features are well represented in SB and all other varieties of OBH, conspicuous by their absence are some irregular Bhojpuri verb forms, which would count as marked vis-à-vis equivalent structures in the other input varieties. For example, the special negative form of the copula *nahikhī̃*, *naikhī̃*, or *naikhe* does not survive in any OBH, being replaced by the analytic use of a negative particle *nahī̃*, plus the ordinary form of the copula, as in many of the (non-Bhojpuri) input varieties. The fate of IB's idiosyncratic features in the transplanted varieties is treated by Gambhir (1981: 271).

In each colony the new koine came to be considered a substandard version of Hindi and was strongly disparaged by those who had a knowledge of the latter. In official lists and censuses it is returned as *Hindi*, though it is often colloquially known by other names: *Kalkatiyā bāt* (Natal); *Puraniyā Hindi* (Guyana), or just *Hindustāni*, *Hindustaniyā* or *Hindi*. The name *Bhojpuri* is used in Mauritius, but rarely elsewhere, where more localized descriptors occur: *Sarnami*, *Naiṭali Hindi*, and *Fiji bāt*. Only in Suriname does an OBH seem to have gained a measure of recognition as a variety in its own right (M. K. Gautam 2003 personal communication). Although each colony developed its own koine, the strong parallels in terms of demographics, social change, and linguistic processes resulted in their being, on the whole, more similar to each other than to any of their parent Indic varieties. Linguists have tended to identify these koines as being closer structurally to Bhojpuri or to eastern varieties of Hindi like Awadhi. To the former group belong MB (Domingue 1971), TB (Mohan 1978), GB (Gambhir 1981), and SB (Mesthrie 1991). To the second group belong SH (Damsteegt 1988)) and FH (Moag 1977). Three examples will motivate this grouping:

(1) In Mauritius, Guyana, Trinidad, South Africa and Suriname the present habitual is formed by the verb stem + *-la* + auxiliary: *ham dekhilā* "I see." In Fiji the equivalent form is verb stem + *-tā* + auxiliary: *ham dekhtā hai* "I see."
(2) For the future tense first person Mauritius, Guyana, Trinidad, South Africa, and Suriname have *-b* (*ham dekhab* "I will see"), whilst Fiji has *-egā* (*ham dekhegā* "I will see").
(3) For the 3rd sg. past tense we have the following MB *ū dekhlak*; GB *ū dekhle*; TB *ū dekhal*; and SB *ū dekhlak* "I saw." On the other hand, SH *ū dekhis*; and FH *ū dekhā/dekhis* are used.[8]

A number of such features can be accounted for purely in terms of demographic factors: since recruiters started their operations in the more easterly parts of the north India and gradually moved inland, colonies that first imported Indian laborers have a more Bhojpuri character, whilst those settled last by Indians have a more interior "eastern Hindi/Awadhi flavour" (Gambhir 1981: 11; Mesthrie 1991: 76).[9] A second relevant principle would now be called the "founder principle" (after Mufwene's (2001) characterization for creole languages). Mufwene argues that in the prototypical Creole situation a variety that is socially

[8] For case of illustration we omit some variants in the different territories here (e.g. *dekhlas* is a viable free variant of *dekhlak* in SB).

[9] Natal was interesting in that two main dialects occur on the coast and uplands, with a third intermediate dialect in the Midlands. The coastal dialect is closer to the Bhojpuri based OBHs (Mauritius, Guyana, Trinidad), whilst the Uplands region variety, for which recruitment took place later than for the coast has a decidely Awadhi-based morphology for verbs, rather like Sarnami and Fiji Hindi. This was entirely in keeping with recruiting practice in India and Natal, (see Mesthrie 1991: 72–6).

prestigious and represented early in the input can have a lasting influence even if it is later outnumbered by other incoming varieties. For OBH it seems to be the case that more easterly varieties, especially Bhojpuri, show an influence that goes beyond their demographic proportion over the entire period of immigration, since they tended to provide more of the earlier shiploads of laborers. In Natal, for example, though Bhojpuri speaking districts made up approximately 36 percent of the immigrants in the full period of indenture, the basic structure of the koine tends to be Bhojpurian (with Awadhi verb morphology prominent in the interior dialect). This is probably a consequence of the greater importance of Bhojpuri speakers in the earlier period (43 percent in the first three years). Gambhir (1981: 60) suggests that Bhojpuri speakers in Guyana "later became the reference group for all immigrants in all cultural purposes, including linguistic." He cites Sankoff's (1980: 146) characterization of this as a "first past the post" principle. Of course, the founder principle is not infallible: there has to be some reinforcement from later immigrants for the founding variety to survive. Swamping of a variety that could have become a founding dialect can be seen from the early history of Indian settlement in Natal. Here the district which produced the most north Indian immigrants in the first year was Purulia, a predominantly Bengali-speaking district according to Grierson's maps, with some bilingualism in Bengali and Magahi. However, as further settlement from Bengali areas was minimal there is no trace of Bengali influence in Natal. Likewise, in Mauritius, as we have noted, the earliest indentured workers were "hill coolies" speaking an Austronesian language. Perhaps their languages did not have a founding effect for social reasons: as non-Hindus outside the structure of village society they would not have formed a reference point for the incoming indentured workers.

Language contact

Loanwords

Apart from the dialect convergence outlined above, the OBH show structural and lexical influences from the local languages they came into contact with. Indian languages also gave something in return to the local languages. Linguistic-cultural crossovers can be seen in the traditional African based sega songs in Mauritius and calypso in Trinidad sometimes including Bhojpuri words or lyrics. Food terms in Guyana and elsewhere draw heavily on Bhojpuri and the use of some choice Bhojpuri swear words is common across cultures in Trinidad.[10] In Mauritius, Bhojpuri was learnt as a lingua franca in the early period amongst various other communities like the Chinese and Creole

[10] I draw on information from Ramdat (1984) here and from comments and observations by delegates from the floor at conferences in University of the West Indies, Trinidad (1984) and Mahatma Gandhi Institute, Mauritius (2000).

Table 25.4. *Loanwords in OBH pertaining to the practice of indenture*

Term	Meaning	Source	Varieties
girmit	"indenture"	English *agreement*	all OBHs
girmityā	"indentured worker"	*girmit* + suffix *yā*	all OBHs
Kalkatiyā	"north Indian immigrant"	Calcutta (port)	all OBHs
Kalkatiyā bāt	"language of north Indians"	Hn *Kalkatiyā* + *bāt* "language"	all OBHs
arkatiyā	"recruiter"	Eng *recruiter*	MB,TB,SH
thagwā	"recruiter"	Hn *thag* "deceiver"	SB,SH
luterā	"recruiter"	Hn *luterā* "robber"	SB
damolā/mulẽ	"mill"	Mauritian Creole	MB, SB,[11] TB
kulambar	"European overseer"	Eng *call number*	FH, TB
ḍipū/ḍipuwā/ḍīpo	"emigration depot"	Eng *depot*	all OBHs[12]
jahājī-bhāī	"male ship mate"	Hn *jahāj* "ship", *bhāī* "brother"	all OBHs
jahājī-bahin	"female ship mate"	Hn *jahāj* + *bahin* "sister"	all OBHs
ḍipuā bhāī	"male depot mate"	Hn *dipū* + *bhāī*	SH
bārak	"long common housing structure"	Eng *barracks*	TB, GB, SB[13]
kantāp	"purple flower of sugar cane"	Eng *cane top*	FH, TB
sukhlāī	"replacing dead plants with new supply"	Eng *supply*	FH, TB[14]
kūlī	"Indian worker"	Eng *coolie*	SB, GB, SH, MB, TB[15]
sardār	"Indian supervisor of laborers"	Hn *sardar*	SB, MB, TB, GB,
rais	"ration"	Eng *rice*	GB, FH[16]
firīman(i)	"laborer freed from indenture"	Eng *free man*	FH, TB
latās	"task, ordinary task"	French *la tâche*	MB, SB, FH

Note: FH= Fiji Hindi, GB= Guyanese Bhojpuri, MB= Mauritian Bhojpuri, OBH= Overseas varieties of Bhojpuri Hindi, SB= South African Bhojpuri, SH= Suriname Hindustani, TB= Trinidad Bhojpuri.

populations. In this section some historical terms related to the experience of indenture are cited (see Table 25.4).

11 The form is *mulẽ/damolā* in Creole, which must have passed into MB and thence to SB. The example is one of a few that undoubtedly shows (minor) lexical influence of one OBH upon another, because of some managers and workers ending up in more than one colony. The form in FH is *mil* (from English) and in Trinidad *mule* (from French).

12 The exact forms are: FH: *dīpū*; TB *dīpū*; SB: *dippū*; SH *dīpū*.

13 The forms in other varieties are: FH *line* (from English), GB *lojī* (from Creole).

14 The TB form is *suplāī*.

15 The TB form is actually *bā̃kūlī* from English *bonded coolie*.

16 This etymology is from Siegel (1987: 279). In SB the word is *raicen* or *raisen*, based on English *ration*.

M. K. Gautam (2003 personal communication) notes additional terms from SH: *manjhā* "manager", *garmasrā* "plantation owner," *kantraki* "contract laborer," and *parnāsi* "plantation."

The influence of the different superstrates can be seen in terms for hospital: *aspatāl* (English) in SB; *lopital* (French) in MB; *ziekenhuis* (Dutch) in SH;[17] and in the word for "mill": MB, SB *damolā*; FH *mil*; and TB *mulẽ*.[18] The latter word illustrates another phenomenon, the influence of one OBH upon another by the movement of workers and plantation officials. It is clear that the SB form must have been adopted via the influence of Mauritian workers and planation managers whose presence in the nineteenth century on the plantations and railways of Natal was a significant one. The word for "task for the day" is *latās* in Mauritian Creole and Bhojpuri (ultimately from French *tâche*). In Fiji this turns up as *tās* apparently based on the English *task*. In Natal the word *latās* came to mean "task quickly and shoddily done" (Mauritian Creole *tap latas*). The similarities in the forms for *kantāp* and *sukhlāī* suggest a similar (minor) contact link between Fiji and Trinidad.

Parallel retentions and changes

An intriguing aspect of diasporic syntax is the parallel changes in certain areas of grammar. Certain modal auxiliaries seem to have been more susceptible than others to outside borrowing, rather than strict koineization. The modal *cuk-* "to complete" has been replaced by *khalās* in SB and FH (from Calcutta and/or Bombay Bazaar Hindustani), and to some extent by *don* in GB, TB, and SH (from Creole English *don*, ultimately English *done*).[19] There is variation in the use of *cah-* "to wish" in OBHs. Some of its space is taken over by *māng* (originally "to seek, ask for", extended in some OBHs to mean to "want, wish"). This influence probably occurs via Bombay Bazaar Hindustani and/or Calcutta Bazaar Hindustani (Siegel 1987: 195). Thus, in FH *māng-* may be used as an auxiliary as well as the main verb (see Siegel 1987: 195). In SB *cah-* is replaced by *honā*, a form from Bombay Bazaar Hindustani and/or Dakkhini Urdu (Mesthrie 1991: 91–3). Finally *mas* from English *must* has been incorporated into TB (e.g. *tū mas janā* "you must go") and SB (*ū mas kar ke jāī* "he must/is ever willing to go".[20] Some general principle involving the "renovation" of the

[17] The alternate form *(h) aspatal* also occurs in SH.

[18] In this case *damolā* is based on Mauritian Creole French (the SB form is a borrowing); the FH form is from English; the TB form is based on a French Creole form.

[19] In the case of SH the source word is Dutch *gedaan*. I have no information on MB here.

[20] Mohan (pc) suggests that *mas* in the TB sentence may well be a one-off occurrence for the benefit of the interviewer, showing a form from the prestige language, English. The SB form, however, is part of SB grammar, albeit a recent innovation.

meaning of salient/expressive grammatical items via borrowing seems to apply here.[21]

Language maintenance and shift

Given the original diversity of immigrants, the low status of the OBH koines, and the competition from local vernaculars and international superstrate languages, it is a noteworthy achievement that OBHs have survived for over a century.

However, it is likely that three of the OBHs – TB, GB, and SB – will not survive as colloquial languages, since fluent speakers are to be found only among more elderly groups. Although MB is receding in the cities and towns, the language can be heard in Mauritian villages, and has a degree of official recognition, even though it is conspicuously lacking in the educational system. The Mahatma Gandhi Institute in Moka was the host of the second World Bhojpuri Conference in 2000. Sarnami is alive and well, as is Fiji Hindi. However, Gambhir (2003 personal communication) warns that even for these varieties, there are unfavorable omens like "less use in the urban areas, less use in the younger generations, and less use amongst the more educated people." No clear explanation exists as to the differential success in language maintenance amongst OBHs. Time depth as an explanation is not enough since MB (the first colony for indentured Indian immigrants) survives far better than GB, TB, and SB. Philip Baker (1993 personal communication) once suggested to me that OBHs fare better in the non-English colonies compared to the English colonies. The "English as killer language" view is not, however, exceptionless, since FH is not just alive in a former English colony, but has spread to non-OBH communities of south Indians. Another explanation that comes to mind is that of urbanization and industrialization, processes which developed more rapidly in Trinidad and South Africa than elsewhere. But this will not explain why GB is obsolescent, since it exists in a largely rural environment. Perhaps the fact that at one time Indians were a slight but clear majority in Suriname, Mauritius, and Fiji is of significance. As in the broader field of language maintenance and shift, causes of shift are complex and multifaceted: in the case of South Africa, certainly, the fact that there were two major Indian languages SB and Tamil (and other prestigious languages such as Gujarati, Urdu, and Telugu) is also a contributory factor explaining why no Indian lingua franca emerged and consequently why SB is in decline. For a more detailed exploration of maintenance and shift in the OBHs see Siegel (1990) and Damsteegt (1993).

Space does not allow for more than a cursory mention of the role of standard Hindi in the various colonies (see further Barz 1980; Gambhir 1981; Moag 1979;

[21] This process seems to be the opposite of semantic bleaching.

Ramyead 1988). Though seldom the home language of indentured workers, it was (and remains) an important part of the cultural and educational life of Indians of the second diaspora. Its role was that of a diglossic complement to the OBH koines, commanding a great deal of overt prestige, making it the natural medium for formal speeches. It was often introduced via schooling, mostly outside the school curriculum (as in Natal) or as part of the mainstream curriculum (as in Fiji). Hindi films, religious discourses, and some popular Hindi books played a role too. However great the prestige of Hindi, it must be conceded that it was not mastered by the majority of the descendants of indentured immigrants. This is so partly because schooling in Hindi was not of sufficiently sustained duration and because of the need to master the dominant colonial codes like French, English, or Dutch (in addition to the local Creole vernaculars).

Issues for further research

There are many unresolved issues in the linguistic study of the OBH varieties. One issue concerns the role of lingua francas in the "immigration traffic" and their influence on the OBH koines. Tinker (1974: 52) cited "Hindustani" as fulfilling the role of lingua franca in the immigration traffic. Another issue concerns the possible role of Calcutta Bazaar Hindustani raised by Siegel (1975, 1987: 192–6) and disputed by Gambhir (1981) and others. Historians should look for more details of the places of origin of the communities in Trinidad, Guyana, Mauritius, and Suriname so as to allow systematic comparisons of demographics and koine formation in the various colonies which will match and extend work in Fiji and South Africa. The status and structure of OBH in some islands remains unchartered, for example in Réunion and Seychelles. Further information, however fragmentary, on the languages and dialects of the Bengal Presidency, Agra, and Oudh from sources other than Grierson would be welcome to aid our assessment of the koineization process – see for example Gautam's (1999) ongoing study of Munshi Rahman Khan's writing. Lexicographical work toward a Bhojpuri–Hindi–English dictionary has been recently completed in Mauritius, and a Fiji Hindi–English/English–Fiji Hindi dictionary (Hobbs 1985) exists. Such work would be welcome for all the OBH territories.

Conclusion

This chapter identified three broad groupings within the history of Indians abroad, with especial focus on the sociolinguistic history of the second and third diasporas. There are, of course, complications to the idea of discrete boundaries within the diaspora. These movements sometimes blend into one another. For example, as we mentioned in the section on the second diaspora, the arrival of

Indians in East Africa in the British period really continued a trend started in earlier times under Arab influence. The arrival of Panjabis in Canada at the turn of the nineteenth century (though classified as second diaspora here) was also intermediate, since it neither followed upon indentured immigration nor was part of a post-Independence third diaspora. Many second diaspora descendants have been forced by political and/or economic circumstances to move into "third diaspora territories." In this way a number of West Indian, East African, and Mauritian descendants of the second diaspora reside in the United Kingdom, Canada, or the United States. The descendants of the Panjabi settlers in Canada mentioned above later moved to take up agriculture in California. In almost all cases participants in this "double immigration" did not take an Indian language with them to their new ports of call: they had largely acculturated to the colonial and Creole languages of their countries of birth (see Sam Selvon's short story "When Greek meets Greek" about a Trinidadian in London, quoted in Ramchand 1973: 146–7).

It is appropriate to end this chapter with a reminder of the historic significance of the diaspora. It was one timid and shy Gujarati speaker, less than at ease in London, who was transformed by his experience with indentured Indians in South Africa. Whilst it is well known that Gandhi the politician was apprenticed in South Africa, it is perhaps less well known that Gandhi the language activist, was also apprenticed by his experience of the languages of indenture. It was in South Africa that he began to stress the value of the vernacular over English in certain contexts (Mesthrie 1992: 25–6). Years later in India in trying to inculcate Hindustani as a language of national unity, he cited his experiences in South Africa, where many south Indians had learnt Bhojpuri-Hindi (Mesthrie 1993). For all Indians in diaspora, the love of their home language and culture has been tempered by the need to survive and succeed in host societies that have sometimes been less than Gandhian in their ideas of tolerance.

26 South Asian diaspora in Europe and the United States

Kamal K. Sridhar

Introduction

The third diaspora of Asian Indians (see Chapter 25) involves migration to the United States, United Kingdom, Canada, and Australia, to mention just a few countries. This chapter concentrates on South Asian diaspora in the United Kingdom and United States. Detailed studies of South Asian languages in diaspora, as discussed in Chapter 25 are nonexistent for Asian Indian communities in these countries, except for some data on language use in select Asian Indian linguistic communities in the United States that this author has collected over the years. What we have is attitudinal surveys that discuss the users and uses of South Asian languages, primarily in the United States and United Kingdom. Two brief profiles of South Asian diasporic communities are presented here with special emphasis on the efforts being made to maintain the languages and cultures by the various ethnic groups.

The term "South Asian" needs some clarification, especially with reference to how these communities are identified in the censuses of these two countries:

(1) In the United Kingdom, most of the earlier immigrants (from British India) were identified as "Overseas Indians." Finer distinctions between South Asian communities did not start until 1947 when, after the formation of Pakistan, Pakistanis were identified as a distinct group. What was earlier East Pakistan became Bangladesh in 1971, and the Bangladeshis were listed in subsequent census reports (Mishra and Mohapatra 2001: i).

(2) In the United States, until recently, Asian Indians, Pakistanis, and Bangladeshis were lumped together under the broad category of "Other Asians," separating them from the East Asian (e.g. Chinese, Japanese, Korean) ethnic groups. Currently, only the Asian Indians are counted as

I am grateful to Tony Polson and Soma Phillipos for help in collecting the Malayali data and Hema Shah for the Gujarati data.

a separate ethnic group for census purposes. All others are listed under "Other Asians".

(3) The South Asian immigrants in the United States fall into three distinct groups. The first consists mostly of farmers from the British Indian province of Punjab who came to the United States in the late 1800s. Their descendants today are mostly in Yuba City and other places in California. The second is the post-1965 immigrants, who came subsequent to the liberalization of immigration laws in 1965. In a 1975 classification by the US Immigration Service, 93 percent of Indian immigrants were classified as "professional/technical workers" or as their spouses and children (Rangaswamy 2000: 47–8). They are referred to as the "New Ethnics." And, finally, the third group consists of relatives of the post-1965 arrivals, not as highly educated, nonprofessional, and employed in professions ranging from motel ownership to blue-collar jobs.

The profiling of South Asian immigrants is different in the two countries. In the context of the Untied States, Varma (1980) observes that:

> it is reasonable to assume that Indians are not considered "colored" in the United States today as they are in Britain. In England, Indians are a racial category; in the United States they are an ethnic group (30).

The South Asian immigrants in the United Kingdom and the United States may be living geographically apart, separated by the Atlantic Ocean; however, they share many experiences as immigrants, be it in establishing their own ethnic and cultural institutions, in creating their own ethnic media, or in their attempts to maintain their languages and cultures in their new surroundings. The circumstances may be different, but the experiences are similar.

The first section of this chapter is devoted to some general remarks about South Asian communities in the United Kingdom, followed by a section that provides a brief profile of South Asians (Asian Indians, Bangladeshis, and Pakistanis) in the United Kingdom based on recent census reports. A section on their socioeconomic profile comes next, as it is one of the major variables that determines how well the communities will be able to maintain their languages in the future. Subsequently, a discussion of language and cultural maintenance, and issues of identity and assimilation are discussed. South Asians in the United States are discussed following the same pattern.

South Asians in the United Kingdom

The South Asian presence in United Kingdom dates back to the eighteenth century, when they were simply identified as "Overseas Indians" (Vaughn 1996: 95), as mentioned earlier. The Census of Britain 1991 made the first

Table 26.1. *Estimated South Asian population in England and Wales, (1961–2001)*[a]

Country of birth/ethnic group	2001[e]	1961	1971	1981	1991[b]
India	10, 53, 411	81, 400	240, 730	673, 704	840, 255
Pakistan[c]	747, 285	24, 000	127, 000	295, 461	476, 555
Bangladeshi	283, 063	—	—	64, 562	162, 835
Other Asians[d]	—	—	45, 000	181, 000	211, 535

Notes:
[a] The numbers represent only people from South Asian region.
[b] Figures for 1991 come from Peach (1996).
[c] Figures for Pakistan 1951–1971 include Bangladeshis, as East Pakistan was part of Pakistan.
[d] Figures for East African Asians is from Vaughn (1996: 101).
[e] The 2001 figure are from the following source: http://www.statistics.gov.uk/cci/nugget.asp?id=273 (accessed March 10, 2007).
Source: Anwar (1998: 8).

attempt to identify the various South Asian groups residing in United Kingdom, and results revealed that the South Asian population (including people of South Asian origin from West Indies, etc.) was three million or roughly 5.5 percent of the total population. Table 26.1 presents the South Asian population in United Kingdom from various sources.

Indians were the largest individual ethnic category, numbering 1, 053, 411 (27.7 percent of the ethnic minority population and some 1.8 percent of the total population). Indians were followed by Pakistanis, those of Mixed ethnic backgrounds, Black Caribbeans, Black Africans and Bangladeshis. The remaining minority ethnic groups each accounted for less than 0.5 percent but together accounted for a further 1.4 percent of the UK population (Source: Census April 2001, Office for National Statistics).

The Pakistanis, except for the few Pathans and even fewer Muhajirs (those who first migrated from India to Pakistan, and eventually to the United Kingdom), are mostly of Punjabi descent. As Ballard (1996) points out, “While the census does not resolve ethnic differences to this level of fineness, my own estimate is that the great majority of British Pakistanis are from the Potohar region, and that the great majority of British Potohar’s have even more specific origins in the Mirpur district of Azad Kashmir” (122). The census also shows that exactly 50 percent of the Pakistani population was British born.

The Bangladeshis are the youngest and the fastest growing of all ethnic populations recorded in the 2001 Census of the United Kingdom. Although Bangladesh broke away from Pakistan in 1971, “The United Kingdom did not recognize the secession until 1972. Hence, Bangladeshis living in Britain up to and including the 1971 census were counted as Pakistanis” (Eade *et al.* 1996: 150).

While the census does not go into details of place of origin, most Bangladeshis are from the northeastern region of Sylhet, and more than 80 percent of the population is Muslim (Eade *et al.* 1996: 151). It is, on the whole, a highly male-dominated society, with an overall ratio of males to females of 100 : 64 (Eade *et al.* 1996: 152).

Profile of the South Asian community

Asian Indians in the United Kingdom have the highest qualifications compared to the other South Asian communities. The 1991 Census of the United Kingdom confirms that a higher percentage of Indians are qualified beyond the A-level – equivalent to a high school diploma. Comparable figures for the White, Pakistani, and Bangladeshi populations are given in Table 26.2 below.

Asian Indians in the United Kingdom tend to be self-employed in small businesses while Pakistanis are more likely to be in sales and driving (taxis) (Ballard 1996: 136).

Unemployment among the youth belonging to all South Asian communities is quite high considering their educational qualifications (Ballard 1994). 15.2% of Asian Indians have a high school diploma as compared to 12.5% of the whites. Yet, many Asian Indian youth are unemployed. Ballard (1996), however, points out,

> while rates of unemployment among Pakistanis in virtually all occupational sectors are substantially higher than among White workers, there is a good deal of variation among the South Asians. While Bangladeshis appear to be experiencing similar difficulties to the Pakistanis, the Indians' position is very much closer to that of the White majority (p. 137).

Anwar (1998) contends, "[r]esearch in this area has shown that racial discrimination is a contributory factor for such wide differences" (60).

The figures for unemployment are given in Table 26.3 below.

Sociocultural and economic profile

It is claimed that maintaining one's language is possible only when large support structures exist in the form of extended families and residence in ethnic neighborhoods. In an earlier work (K. K. Sridhar 1988), I have claimed that language maintenance is a luxury and can be accomplished only by those who need not struggle to put food on the table. If we examine the condition of South Asian communities in terms of support structure and economic status, we find that South Asians exhibit similar family and kinship patterns abroad as they do back home.

> The tendency among all three Asian groups remains towards living in a joint and extended family system as far as possible . . . Bangladeshi households were the largest,

Table 26.2. *Highest qualifications of Asian ethnic groups and Whites in Britain (in percent)*

Age group	White	Indian	Pakistani	Bangladeshi
18–29	12.5	15.2	7.2	3.4
30–34	19.7	17.0	7.6	6.0
45–pensionable age	14.0	14.7	6.4	6.5
Of pensionable age	6.6	3.8	1.8	1.6
All aged 18 and over	13.4	15.0	7.0	5.2

Source: 1991 Census, from Anwar (1998: 36).

Table 26.3. *Unemployment among Asian and White young people* (16–24), (in percent)

Indian		Pakistani		Bangladeshi		White	
Male	Female	Male	Female	Male	Female	Male	Female
25.3	21.0	40.8	35.2	25.1	36.7	18.0	12.3

Source: 1991 Census.

with a mean household size of (5.3) compared with Pakistani (4.8), Indian (3.8), and white (2.4) (Anwar 1998: 24–5).

Modood *et al.* (1997: 77–8) confirm this trend with the 1994 Survey, which shows that Asian households were larger than Whites: Indian, 3.9; Pakistani, 5.1; Bangladeshi, 5.7; and White, 2.4 dependent children per household. The 2001 census figures are: Indian, 3.3, Pakistani 4.2 and Bangladeshi, 4.7 (www.statistics.gov.uk/cci/nugget.asp?id=270). This would allow for use of the native language in the home environment, thereby ensuring its maintenance.

Many of the South Asians live in ethnic neighborhoods all over United Kingdom. Their experiences are similar to the early Chinese and Japanese immigrants to the United States, who formed Chinatowns and Little Japan to escape the wrath of the White Americans. In the long run, some ethnic minorities do move out of their initial places of residence to better residences, nevertheless, ethnic concentration often continues. Roughly, a quarter of the Bangladeshis are concentrated in Tower Hamlets. The Indians are concentrated in, for example Leicester, 22.3 percent; Brent, 17.2 percent; Harrow, 16.1 percent; Ealing, 16.1 percent; Hounslow, 14.3 percent; among others (Anwar 1998: 21). A little over 46 percent of the Pakistanis live in Greater Manchester, Birmingham, and West Yorkshire.

> By living with other members of their own ethnic group they find themselves in an environment where they can speak their own language and dialect and where they can protect themselves from the animosity of the native British. (Panayi 1999: 16).

All groups publish their own newspapers, in ethnic languages as well as in English, though newspapers such as *Eastern Eye* and *Voice* cater to more than one ethnic group, appealing to West Indians as well. All ethnic groups have their own radio stations, and several have their own television stations that show ethnic language movies, cultural programs, featured news from back home, as well as serials and soap operas from their respective home countries. All these are important for maintaining languages, and as in the United States, youngsters watch these shows with great interest and enthusiasm.

Religion, in addition to being the anchor for ethnic identity, helps the social networks and communicative patterns:

> Immigrants in post-war Britain have created an ethnicity revolving around religion, politics, and culture . . . Islam has taken off dramatically since 1945, leading to the construction of hundreds of mosques, together with schools and other institutions. Similarly Hindu temples and Sikh Gurudwaras have also taken off. (Panayi 1999: 20–1).

The SCRP/PSI Survey of 1994, reported in Modood *et al.* (1997), points out the importance of religion in the life of the South Asians in the United Kingdom. Muslims were more likely (74 percent) than Hindus (43 percent) and Sikhs (46 percent) to say that religion was very important in the way they lived their life (cf. Coward *et al.* 2000). Attending religious services at least once a week or more is a major priority for the Muslims (62 percent). The figure for Hindus is 27 percent.

Importance of religion, family life, and attitudes to schooling affect one's preference in choosing a partner for life. As is the custom in South Asia, parents and elders generally choose partners for the young men and women in the family in the United Kingdom, too, especially among the Muslims.

The Fourth National Survey of Ethnic Minorities (1997), quoted by Modood *et al.* (1997), shows that a majority of Indians, Pakistanis, and Bangladeshis of age 35 or over have their spouses chosen by their parents. It is clear that the pattern of parents choosing the partner was greatest among Pakistanis and Bangladeshis, and this extended to the 16–34 year olds as well. The Asian Indians in the United Kingdom, like their counterparts in the United States, seem to be either more liberal or are not given much role in the choice of life partners selected by their children. Parents, by choosing life partners belonging to the same linguistic community, ensure linguistic and cultural maintenance. Whether this will aid the survival of South Asian languages in the twenty-first century and beyond, time alone will tell.

Linguistic profile

While studies on specific language use, language maintenance, and language shift, or analysis of changes in the languages of South Asian immigrants are not available, indirect references to language use occurs in several of the works quoted above. The communities' educational achievements, employment patterns, residential practices, participation in social, cultural, ethnic, and religious practices can indirectly tell us something about language use and maintenance in these communities. There is a large number of South Asian languages spoken and used in the United Kingdom. The figures for the main languages spoken and their percentages are given in Table 26.4 below.

Indians were more likely to use English (32 percent) as their main medium of interaction compared with Pakistanis (22 percent) and Bangladeshis (10 percent). This is partly because Asian Indians are more educated and are more represented in professional and white-collar jobs.

The SCPR/PSI Survey of 1994 demonstrated that South Asians in the United Kingdom spoke a non-European language at home and a majority of them were also able to write it, indicating language maintenance. The results are given in Table 26.5 below.

The majority of Indians spoke Punjabi, as did Pakistanis; the majority of African Asians spoke Gujarati; and the majority of Bangladeshis spoke Bengali as well as Sylheti (Anwar 1998: 134).

The litmus test of maintenance is the use of the native language by the younger members of the community. In this respect, the same survey showed that while nearly all the younger generation (16–34 year olds) use the native languages to converse with elder members of the family, a significant percentage used them with their own age cohorts as well, indicating some degree of language maintenance. This was true of Bangladeshis as well as Punjabi and Gujarati speakers, but not so for speakers of Hindi. The details of language use by the younger members of the community are summarized in Table 26.6 below.

Rampton (1992) reports on the placement of all British-born South Asian students in ESL classes along with newly arrived immigrant students. These youngsters spoke fluent English, though they did have some problems with reading. He points out the prevalence of code mixing with Indian languages as well as with the indigenized variety of English (Indian English, Punjabi English, etc., but mostly "babu" English impersonation, to evoke laughter that youngsters use mostly in friendship groups (see B. Kachru 1990, 1992c, 1997b; B. Kachru and Nelson 1996; Y. Kachru 1997, 2001, among others, on varieties of South Asian English and their use). Rampton's study makes available concrete data on language use patterns of this community of young people.

Within the broad framework of linguistic profile, the next question relates to the commitment of the members of these ethnic communities to maintaining

Table 26.4. *Main languages spoken* (1992) (in percent)

Indian	%	Pakistani	%	Bangladeshi	%
Gujarati	36	Punjabi	48	Bengali	73
English	32	Urdu	24	Sylheti	17
Punjabi	24	English	22	English	10
Urdu	3	Other	6	All Languages	100
Hindi	3	All Languages	100		
Other	3				
All Languages	100				

Source: Anwar (1998: 133). Figures are from the 1991 Census.

Table 26.5. *Persons who speak and write a non-European language in Britain (in percent)*

	Indian	African Asian	Pakistani	Bangladeshi
Speak	88	92	92	97
Write	58	60	58	85

Source: SCPR/PSI Survey 1994 (from Anwar 1998: 134).

Table 26.6. *Use of Asian Languages (in percent)*

Language Use	Indian	African Asian	Pakistani	Bangladeshi
Hindi				
Speaks	33	44	5	22
With younger family	5	3	—	—
Gujarati				
Speaks	20	67	—	—
With younger family	17	44	—	—
Punjabi				
Speaks	62	30	74	4
With younger family	43	17	51	1
Urdu				
Speaks	13	18	73	21
With younger family	4	3	41	3
Bengali				
Speaks	2	1	—	56
With younger family	1	—	—	42
Sylheti				
Speaks	—	1	—	60
With younger family	—	—	—	55

Source: Adapted from SCPR/PSI Survey (Anwar 1998: 135)

their languages. In a 1975 survey, when asked whether they spoke their mother tongue at home, 91 percent of the parents and 85 percent of children claimed that they spoke the mother tongue instead of English. In Anwar's view (1998: 130):

> There was a relationship between the age of young people on arrival in Britain and the use of the mother tongue. Gujarati and Bengali speakers were marginally more likely to use their mother tongue than those whose main language was Punjabi, Hindi, or Urdu. In most cases, young people claimed that they spoke the mother tongue because there was someone in the household who did not understand English . . . in the 1983 survey, the pattern of the use of the mother tongue at home had not changed in any significant way compared to 1975.

This was also confirmed by a national survey of racial minorities in 1982. It showed that while 21 percent of Asian men spoke English "slightly" or "not at all," 47 percent of Asian women did not speak English. Two groups of women lacking in English skills were worth noting; "Bangladeshi women (76%) and Pakistani women (70%), who spoke either little English or none at all." (Anwar 1998: 132).

The figures for ethnic language use by younger generation in the United Kingdom is impressive, given that most of the younger people in the United States have just a smattering of their native language, and only a fraction can read and write them. The presence of the extended family seems to have played a role in the maintenance of ethnic languages, especially where the grandparents do not speak English it at all.

Issues of identity and assimilation

Majority of South Asians tend to live in ethnic neighborhoods because of their discomfort in speaking English, assurance of greater security, and protection from hostility of their White neighbors. As Anwar (1998: 139) shows, parents, particularly Asian mothers, and working class people of any age, want to spend their spare time with other Asians more than the middle class. Among religious groups, more Muslim young people prefer to spend their free time with other Asians than young people of other religions. As one young Asian interviewed in 1994 pointed out, "If you have a lot of Asian people living nearby then you can discuss problems because everybody has the same problems and you can visit them" (Anwar 1998: 140).

Young people, who have more opportunities to meet and interact with Whites, would prefer to stay away from ethnic neighborhoods. The difference in the percentages between the years 1975 (39 percent) and 1983 (25 percent) in preference for ethnic neighborhoods in Anwar's study (1998) is interesting.

There is less opposition to living in ethnic neighborhoods compared to 1975. There could be two explanations for this: one, Asian identities have become stronger after all the years of experience of racism and discrimination, and two, ethnic neighborhoods afford greater moral support. As one young Asian put it, "I do not feel foreigner living with people of my own background" (Anwar 1998: 140).

Preference for living in ethnic neighborhoods and wearing ethnic clothes are strong indicators of ethnic and cultural maintenance. According to the data presented in Anwar (1998), women tend to be more conservative, hence the figures are always higher for women in preference for Asian clothes. What is surprising, however, is the figures for Indian and African-Asian young women (16–34 year olds). The young are not very keen on wearing Asian clothes; they often do not speak their languages at home, nor do they prefer to live in ethnic neighborhoods. These are indicators of a second generation moving toward assimilation, rather than maintenance.

It is reasonable to conclude on the basis of the above description that the South Asians in the United Kingdom form distinct ethnic groups; the Indians, Pakistanis, and Bangladeshis have their own distinct identities. Evidence from educational achievements, living preferences, language use, preference for Western versus South Asian clothes among Asian parents as far as their daughters are concerned, marriage preferences, and religious practices, seem to demonstrate that Hindus and Sikhs are more assimilative than their Muslim counterparts from Pakistan and Bangladesh (for more on South Asians in Britain, see Bhatt 1999; Brah 1996; Burton 1998; and Candan 1986).

South Asians in the United States

Most Indians, Pakistanis, and Bangladeshis in the United States until recently were lumped together under the broad category "Asians" for Census counts. Since 1980, people of Indian origin are identified as Asian Indians, and are a separate category. Figures for this group are available, whereas only limited data is available about Pakistanis and even less about the Bangladeshis, for they were counted as Pakistanis until 1970's.

The history of South Asians in the United States is very similar to their brethren in Britain. They faced similar reception, harassment, and discrimination as their counterparts in Britain. Their numbers in the United States are significantly higher, and their community is economically bipolar. However, there are two major differences that emerge in the literature. First, the ethnic cultural organizations of the South Asians in the United States are mostly based along linguistic affiliations, for example Telugu, Tamil, Kannada, Hindi, Sindhi, Kashmiri, Rajasthani, and Bengali associations, to mention just a few. In addition, there are cultural associations based on particular interests, for example classical music group, and Indian film association. Second, compared to their counterparts in Britain, South Asian immigrants in the United States have a somewhat different history in terms of immigration. This is especially true of immigrants from the Punjab, who initially came to British Columbia (Canada) between 1904–1920 by Canadian steamships, to work for the Pacific Coast employers.

Those who came to Canada faced extreme discrimination and racism. They eventually made their way to Bellingham and Everett townships in Washington State in the United States where they found employment with Southern Pacific Railroad, the Northern Electric Company Railroad, and the Western Pacific Railroad. These 1,500 to 2,000 strong Indians were mostly Sikhs from farming communities of Punjab.

The records of the Immigration and Naturalization Service show a solitary Indian admitted to the United States in 1820 and a total of 716 arrivals from 1820 to 1900 (Rangaswamy 2000: 42). They formed the Asian Indian community in the United States; their descendants now live in Yuba City, California. Their farming background in Punjab made them well suited for agricultural work, and they found jobs as farmhands. Their increasing numbers created a clamor among the local residents in response to which the US. Supreme Court ruled in 1923 that East Asians were not eligible for citizenship because they were not White. (A 1790 naturalization law restricted citizenship only to "free White" people). This law, known as the *Indian Exclusion Act* was successfully challenged by an Asian Indian, Dr Sakaram Ganesh Pandit, a lawyer married to a White woman, who argued that East Asians are Aryans (hence White). Pandit won the case in 1927 and was allowed to retain his American citizenship. In 1946 the US Congress enacted laws allowing East Indians citizenship in the United States and allotted an annual immigration quota of 100 people.

In the post-Civil Rights movement era the immigration of Asian Indians crossed the marginal status. The 1965 *Immigration Reform Act* allowed every nationality equal immigration rights and gave preferential treatment to professionals. This led to an increase in immigration of Asian Indians to the United States. Almost the entire population of Asian Indians in the United States (except the Sikh communities in Yuba City) comprise of post-1960 arrivals. Detailed histories of the Asian Indians in the United States are available in Gibson 1988; Helweg and Helweg 1990; Leonard 1997; Minocha 1987; Petievich 1999; Rangaswamy 2000; Saran and Eames 1980; and K. K. Sridhar and S. N. Sridhar 2000, to mention just a few sources.

Profile of the community

According to Census 2000, the total population of Asians in the United States is 11, 898, 828 or 4 percent of the total. After the Chinese, Asian Indians have been the earliest immigrants to the United States; they are the largest group of South Asians, therefore more studies have been done and more data exist on this community. While some data is available on Pakistani immigrants, very little is available on the Bangladeshis in the United States. As Minocha points out (1987: 350):

> India sends the largest number of immigrants annually to the United States. After India come Pakistan, Afghanistan, Bangladesh, and Sri Lanka ... Indians and Pakistanis together account for about 90% of all South Asian immigrants, and India's share of South Asian immigrants is still by far the largest, although an increasingly higher percentage of Pakistan's population is emigrating.

The most recent Census (2000) shows that there are 1,678,765 Asian Indians in the United States. They are spread all over the country, with varying degrees of concentration. The largest numbers of Asian Indians are in California (314,819), followed by New York (251,724), New Jersey (169,180), Illinois (124,723), and Texas (129, 365), which may be termed High Density States. For lack of material on Pakistani and Bangladeshi communities, the major focus here is on Asian Indians in the United States, though wherever data is available, the other groups are also mentioned.

In terms of education, as of 1999, 20.4 percent of the South Asian immigrants have at least a college degree, compared to 15.7 percent of US-born population. In terms of specific immigrant groups, all South Asians' educational attainment rates are 25 percent above the US-born average; it is 64.9 percent for Indians, 53.7 percent for Pakistanis and 51.9 percent for Bangladeshis, according to US Census of 1990.

In terms of languages, according to the 1990 Census, Hindi/Urdu is ranked number 14 in terms of the size of speakers and Bengali is ranked number 44 out of the fifty most common languages spoken in the United States (the figure includes Indians from West Bengal and Bangladeshis). Over 91 percent of Hindi/Urdu speakers and over 92 percent of Bengali speakers are proficient in English.

Socioeconomic profile

The novelist Raja Rao has said, "What links the overseas Indians is the idea of India" suggesting that diasporic communities retain collective memories of the homeland, continue to relate to the homeland, and may even define themselves primarily with reference to it. But the new South Asian immigrants to the United States have more in common than ideas. They share socioeconomic characteristics, changing occupational and gender roles within the family, and organizational patterns (Leonard 1997: 76).

Compared to the earlier Asian Indian immigrants, the new generation of immigrants has encountered mostly opportunities rather than constraints. They are highly educated and mostly occupy professional jobs. Among the skilled South Asian professionals, many are physicians. One recent estimate puts Indians doctors at more than 20, 000 or nearly 4 percent of the nation's medical doctors (*India West*, February 26, 1993; *India Today*, August 1994: 481). Indian engineers are the second largest foreign-born group of engineers, just behind the Chinese (*India West*, December 1, 1995: A 29), and Indian business students outnumber any other international group (Leonard 1997: 78). Leonard continues (1997: 78):

> Occupational patterns for Asian Indian men and women in the United States suggest that, as in India, many Asian Indian women are working in professional positions. For example, in Bakersfield, California, forty of the ninety doctors from India are married to each other – that is ninety doctors include twenty couples.

This does not apply to the sponsored relatives of Indians in the United States, who arrived under the *Family Reunification Act*. It does not apply also to the illegal immigrants arriving into the United States via Mexico. While the initial post-1965 immigrants were mostly professionals, the arrivals since mid-1970s have been involved in small businesses (neighborhood stores such as 7-Eleven, Hallmark Cards, Subway (fast food chain), newspaper kiosks, etc.). Many South Asians are involved in ethnic businesses: jewelry stores, grocery stores, travel agencies, real estate agencies, restaurants, and so on, mainly catering to their ethnic communities, giving rise to Little India/Pakistan/Bangladesh in major metropolises with mostly South Asian clientele.

Language and cultural maintenance

Hossain (1982: 75) found that linguistic and religious affinities among immigrants were more important than the country of origin (quoted in Leonard 1997: 84–5). Since the US Census does not collect data on religion, it is difficult to estimate the religious affiliations of the communities from the South Asian subcontinent. Most estimates put the number of Hindus in the United States to be 1 million to 1.5 million (Gaustan and Barlow 2000; Leonard 1997). Regarding the Muslims, the American Muslim Council estimates that there are roughly 5 to 8 million Muslims in the United States, of which roughly 24 percent are from South Asia (Haddad 2000; Leonard 1997).

All languages of South Asia are probably represented in major metropolitan areas of the United States (see Leonard 1997: 20 for some figures). Given the diversity and the salience of regional languages and cultures as rallying points, it is advisable as an initial research strategy to study language maintenance and/or shift with reference to specific regional groups, and to arrive at generalizations inductively. Following this assessment, this author initiated studies of language maintenance among Asian Indian ethnic groups in the New York metropolitan area. Initial studies of language maintenance and/or language shift involved speakers of Kannada (referred to as Kannadigas), and expanded the scope of the study to include speakers of Gujarati (referred to as Gujaratis), and Malayalam (referred to as Malayalis). (K. K. Sridhar 1988, 1993, 1997; K. K. Sridhar and S. N. Sridhar 2000).

The primary data for the study came from a fifty-five-item questionnaire administered to a randomly selected set of tweny-one Kannadiga families, tweny-one Malayali families, and ninety-one Gujarati families, between 1985–1989, all in the New York City metropolitan area. The questionnaire elicited information pertaining to (1) demographic details; (2) opportunities for use of their respective native language(s); (3) indicators of rootedness in the ethnic tradition; (4) parents' use of languages in different domains; (5) children's proficiency in their respective ethnic tongue; (6) children's use of and attitude toward their ethnic language; (7) parents' efforts at language maintenance; and (8) parents' attitude toward the future of their ethnic tongue in the United States. Data from the questionnaire was supplemented by interviews and (participant) observation in the home setting, in the community setting (during picnics, concerts, meetings, and religious celebrations), and in the school/playground setting.

Since use and maintenance of native languages is under focus here, this chapter concentrates on statistics dealing with language. The data asking for opportunities for the use of the ethnic language in the New York/New Jersey area reveals that extensive "support networks" exist for the three communities. All three groups have several friends and relatives in the area, anywhere from twelve to thirty-four other families per respondent family. In addition, they attend social events organized by their respective cultural organizations, which are active. These data indicate a high degree of social interaction involving the use of the ethnic tongue. Most of the respondents entertain relatives and friends visiting from India on a regular basis. Given the extended family structure, hospitality is extended to even distant relatives and acquaintances; these visitors often stay as long as three to six months. It is also fairly common for the immigrants' parents to spend an extended period of time taking care of the grandchildren in the United States. The native language tends to be used more if the visiting relatives are of an older generation and do not speak English. Often, during holidays, children travel to India with their parents to visit the grandparents and other relatives, which exposes growing children to their parents' language and culture. Some pick up enough language during these visits to converse about daily life.

There are, however, discrepancies between what is claimed and what is the reality. While most parents were categorical in their support for maintaining their languages, the data in Table 26.7 present a different story.

Table 26.7. *Parents' use of ethnic language (in percent)*

	Kannada	Malayalam	Gujarati
Native language	19	14	56
Mostly in native language	24	57	16
Native language + English	57	48	33

The percentage that use native language exclusively is low for both Kannada and Malayalam speakers. Most parents agree that in conversing with their friends, they tend to use a variety somewhat code mixed with English. The Gujarati community is the only exception, but even here, about 33 percent of the parents report using a variety of language mixed with English. English is often used along with the native language in order to accommodate the younger generation who are sometimes not as fluent as their parents in the ethnic language. These findings are consistent with studies of Kannadigas in New Delhi (Satyanath 1982). This is pretty much the pattern in contemporary urban India as well, with most groups using a code-mixed variety, which is slowly moving into the home domain (Mukherjee 1980). As already noted, English is the most often used second language among the educated in India. These data are significant in that they indicate the use of English in the home domain for all the three groups. Considering the high level of education and the fact that they tend to use mostly English in their job-related conversations, this "intrusion" of English into the home domain is not surprising.

Code mixing/switching (S. N. Sridhar and K. K. Sridhar 1980) seems to be the norm in India also, as can be seen in Indian TV programs (serials, political discussion forums, movies, music shows, travel programs) that are intended for Indian audiences in India. These are also available on American TV (Subscription channels), such as Z TV, B4U (Bollywood for you), TVAsia, and SonyTV. Here are some examples from (1) travel programs and (2) popular film. Code-mixed elements in English are italicized; it is worth remembering that this is the model most children are exposed to.

(1) Travel

Gopalpur ek chota sa *fishing village* hai, *famous for its beaches*.
Gopalpur is a small fishing village, famous for its beaches

Yeh *lake* itna baDa hai ki *you can't tell* ki kahan *lake* khatam hota hai aur akash shuru.
This lake is so big that you can't tell where the lake finishes and the sky begins.

Orissa is an experience, I have given it full marks. Age aapki marzi (Later its your wish/decision).

(2) Popular film

Kabhi Khushi Kabhi Gham (Sometime happiness, sometimes sorrow) Rohan, the young hero of the movie, is victorious in the game of cricket and sends an e-mail to his dad:

"Hello dad, I won I won. I was the man of the match. They say I'm just the best.
Hey! *Aaj maine apko CNN per dekha.* (Today I saw you on CNN). *You look great!*
Now I know mere (my) *amazing good looks* mujhe kahan se mile (where I got them).
Anyway, mere (my) *final term* khatam ho chuka hai (is finished).
Aur mai dewali ke liye ghar vapas aa raha hu (And I am coming home for Diwali).
Can't wait to see you guys. Lots of love ... Rohan
PSPS: *ghar ane ke pahele mai Hardwar ja raha hu* (Before returning home, I am going to Hardwar) *to meet two of my favorite girl friends.*"

In another popular film *Monsoon Wedding*, set in middle-class India, the parents primarily speak English with a few words of Hindi mixed in:

Scene: Bride-to-be is sleeping. Parents come into the bedroom.
Father: "You know Pimmi, sometimes when I look at them I feel love which I almost cannot bear.
kaise itni jaldi badi ho gayi hai (How did she grow up so fast).
Han, And when did we grow old. If only their lives are happy, bas (that' all).
And for that I'm willing to take on every trouble, every sorrow in the world."

In the context of the United States, the true measure of maintenance is of course the use of the ethnic tongue by persons of the younger generation among themselves. There were a few questions that explored the children's attitude to the ethnic tongue. The children's pattern of socialization is much more assimilatory than that of their parents. They get together with children from different language and cultural backgrounds. When the native language background is shared, the Gujarati children tended to use more Gujarati, though the Malayali children did not use Malayalam much. Across the groups, however, English seems to be the preferred language among the second generation. The majority of the parents said, "they don't mind" (Kannadigas, 95 percent; Malayalis, 48 percent; Gujaratis, 66 percent). The often observed pattern of children asking their parents to speak to them in English was attested more often among the Malayalis (78 percent) as compared to the Kannadigas (5 percent) or the Gujaratis (11 percent).

As regards attitudes of the parents toward the future of their native language in their adopted land, while 86 percent of Gujarati parents and 100 percent of Kannada parents felt that "it will be maintained by a small number of people," the Malayali parents were more pessimistic: they felt that "it will disappear in the next generation." Parents were not comfortable with the possibility of their language not surviving them. While 80 percent of the Malayali parents felt "Children would be better off with English," 36 percent of the Kannadiga parents, and only 19 percent of the Gujarati parents felt this way. However, the parents are realistic. They realize that complete maintenance is not feasible. About 70 percent of the Gujarati parents and 64 percent of the Kannada parents pointed out that while they did not expect their children to be fluent in the native language, they hoped that the second generation would be aware of their roots, and make an effort to maintain the culture if not the language.

Issues of identity and assimilation

Regarding interaction and socialization patterns, the three groups indicated that they got together with friends and relatives at least once in two weeks, thus proving that they are very much rooted in their ethnic culture and traditions, with the Gujaratis and the Malayalis being more traditional. There seems to be relatively less interaction with Americans outside of the work domain, which indicates that the groups are self-contained to a certain extent.

There are several neighborhoods in the borough of Queens, New York, such as Jackson Heights and Flushing, where there are ethnic enclaves of Punjabis, Gujaratis, and other groups. People tend to interact socially on a regular basis primarily with members of their own language groups. During these get-togethers, the language of conversation is usually the ethnic tongue. Hegde's (1991) study confirms this. Her study explored the patterns of interactions of 133 Asian Indian immigrant families in the New York/New Jersey area. She observes that the immigrants maintained two distinct interpersonal networks: intraethnic (between members of the same language group) and interethnic (between speakers of different Asian Indian languages). Similar findings are reported in Alexander (1990) and Gibson (1988) about earlier settlements of Asian Indians in California.

The immigrants are still heavily rooted in their home culture, as is evidenced by their preference for Indian food, especially at dinner and on weekends. Members of the younger generation also eat Indian food, though they take interest in American fast food such as pizza, hot dogs, and hamburgers also. Most of the Gujaratis in the study indicated that they were vegetarians and their children ate mostly Indian vegetarian food.

Conclusion

This set of studies of patterns of language maintenance among the Asian Indians communities is an initial attempt to document and analyze the patterns of language use among Asian Indians in the United States. As we continue to observe the use of the language in the first generation, the interaction between the two generations, and between the second generation youth among themselves, we have to keep the following in mind. The pattern that emerges in the context of the United States is not very different from that we see in the South Asian communities in the United Kingdom. Unlike the older generation, the younger generation does not identify as much with their respective language groups. The children from all the three groups tended to identify themselves as Indian Americans and not so much as Gujaratis, Kannadigas, or Malayalis, unless pressed to do so. In fact, in the Malayali group, 40 percent of the children labeled themselves to be Asian Indians, 30 percent claimed themselves to be Americans, while only 10 percent identified themselves as Malayalis, and 20 percent did not respond to this question.

Informal observations indicate that the children are bicultural, aware of the cultural norms that have to be observed in the presence of other Asian Indians. Code mixing and code switching are a way of life in India, and abroad, too. In previous case studies, code mixing and switching have been used to support claims of language shift, and sometimes even attrition. But, in the Indian context, code mixing with English may account for the survival of not only minority languages but also majority languages. The mixing is so pervasive that one finds code-mixed languages in newspapers, popular magazines, books of fiction, poetry (Y. Kachru 1989), drama, media, including television news broadcasts, in advertising (T. Bhatia 2001b), and in published documents from state governments. Not only are words and phrases mixed and transferred freely between English and Indian languages but a free mixing of speech conventions from Indian languages into English and vice-versa is also rampant, for example, to express politeness, greetings, condolences, regret, etc. (Y. Kachru 1995b, and Chapter 17 in this volume). It is this sort of code-mixed language that is used by everyone, from politicians and film stars to the low-level shopkeepers and household servants (for a detailed discussion, see Dubey 1991; B. Kachru 1983b, 1990, 200X; S. N. Sridhar 1978; S. N. Sridhar and K. K. Sridhar 1980, among others).

Second, the children of Asian Indian immigrants may not be "bilingual" as the term is often used, that is, with full receptive and productive competence in all skills. Nevertheless, they are not completely monolingual either. Code-mixing is a prime example of a group or an individual's bicultural identity. The popularity of all genres of pop culture, that is music, TV serials, and films, which use code mixing freely, attest to a hybridization that is best described in terms of Gibson's (1988) characterization of the second and third generation Punjabi Americans in Valleyside, California. He suggests their identity involves "selective adaptation" or "accommodation without assimilation" rather than total assimilation.

The earlier stereotypes of bilingualism as the root cause of socioeconomic stagnation, poor educational performance, and low level of intelligence is, to say the least, groundless. None of these stereotypes fit the Asian Indian communities in the United Kingdom or the United States. On the positive side, compared to earlier immigrants to the United States (e.g. the Irish, the Italians, or the Germans), who were more or less forced to assimilate due to economic necessity, the South Asian linguistic groups have been able to achieve middle-class status without having to give up their native languages or cultures. This trend may continue with the future generations of South Asians in the United States as well as in the United Kingdom.

References

Abbi, Anvita. 1987. *Reduplicative Structures in South Asian Languages: A Phenomenon of Linguistic Area.* New Delhi: Jawahar Lal Nehru University, Centre of Linguistics and English.

Abbi, Anvita. 1992. *Reduplication in South Asian Languages: An Areal, Typological and Historical Study.* New Delhi: Allied Publishers Limited.

Abbi, Anvita. 1995a. "Language contact and language restructuring. A case study of tribal languages of Central India," *International Journal of the Sociology of Language*, 116, 175–85.

Abbi, Anvita. 1995b. "Small languages and small language communities," *International Journal of the Sociology of Language*, 116, 175–85.

Abbi, Anvita, R. S. Gupta, and Ravinder Gargesh. 2000. "Acceptance level of Hindi as a pan–Indian language, A pilot survey, ms. The ICSSR Project Report.

Abbott, Freeland. 1968. *Islam and Pakistan.* Ithaca, NY: Cornell University Press.

Abidi, S. A. H. 1960. "The influence of Hindi on Indo-Persian literature in the reign of Shah–Jahan (1628–1658)," *Indo-Iranica*, 13(2), 1–18.

Abidi, S. A. H. 1981. "A scientific study of Indo-Persian is necessary," *Indo-Iranica*, 34(1–4), 88–93.

Abidi S. A. H. 1998. "Contribution of the Chishti order to devotional music in India," in *Indo-Persian Cultural Perspectives*, edited by Mohammad A. Khan, Ravinder Gargesh, and Chander Shekhar. New Delhi: Saud Ahmad Dehlavi, pp. 33–53.

Abidi, S. A. H. 2000. "Ahade vusta meaccent Hindustani tamaddun ke irteqa meaccent faarsi adab ka hissaa" [Contribution of Persian Literature in the Evolution of Indian Culture in Medieval Period], *Islam aur Asr–e–Jadid Quarterly*, JMI 2000, 51–67.

Agesthialingom, S. and N. Kumaraswami Raja. 1975. *Studies in Early Dravidian Grammars: Proceedings of the Seminar on Early Dravidican Grammars.* Annamalainagar, India: Annamalai University, Department of Linguistics.

Agesthialingom, S. and S. Sakthivel. 1973. *A Bibliography of Dravidian Linguistics.* Annamalainagar, India: Annamalai University, Department of Linguistics.

Agnihotri, Rama Kant. 1992. "India: Multilingual perspectives," in *Democratically Speaking*, edited by N. D. Crawhill. Capetown: National Language Project, pp. 46–55.

Agnihotri, Rama Kant. 1994. "Campaign-based literacy programmes: The case of the Ambedkar Nagar experiment in Delhi," in *Sustaining Local Literacies*, edited by D. Barton. Special issue of *Language and Education*, 8, 47–56.

Agnihotri, Rama Kant. 1997. "Sustaining local literacies," in *Encyclopedia of Language and Education*, Vol. 2, edited by V. Edwards and D. Corson. Dordrecht: Kluwer, pp. 173–80.

Agnihotri, Rama Kant. 2001a. "English in Indian education," in *Language Education in Multilingual India*, edited by C. J. Daswani. New Delhi: United Nations Educational, Scientific and Cultural Organization, pp. 186–209.

Agnihotri, Rama Kant. 2001b. *Half the Battle and a Quarter*. CIIL Foundation Day Lectures. Mysore, India: Central Institute of Indian Languages.

Agnihotri, Rama Kant. 2002a. "A farce called literacy," in *Practice and Research in Literacy*, edited by A. Mukherjee and D. Vasantha. New Delhi: Sage, pp. 29–48.

Agnihotri, Rama Kant. 2002b. "On a pre-partition partition: The question of Hindi–Urdu," in *Pangs of Partition: The Human Dimension*, Vol. 2, edited by S. Settar and I. B. Gupta. New Delhi: Manohar, pp. 29–46.

Agnihotru, Rama Kant and A. L. Khanna. 1997. *Problematizing English in India*. Delhi: Sage India.

Agnihotri, Rama Kant and Anju Sahgal. 1986. "Is Indian English retroflexed and *r*-full?," *Indian Journal of Applied Linguistics*, 11, 97–108.

Ahmad, Imtiaz (ed.) 1978. *Caste and Social Stratification among Muslims in India*. New Delhi: Manohar.

Aiyar, L. V. Ramaswami. 1932. "Tulu prose texts in two dialects," *Bulletin of the School of Oriental Studies*, 6, 897–931.

Aiyar, L. V. Ramaswami. 1934–1935. "Semantic divergencies in Indo-Aryan loan-words in South Dravidian," *Journal of Oriental Research (Madras)*, 8–9.

Aiyar, L. V. Ramaswami. 1973. "A South Indian (Malayalam) evaluation of Sanskrit t (d) and ṭ(ḍ)," *International Journal of Dravidian Linguistics*, 2(1), 119–26.

Aklujkar, Ashok. 1972. "Stylistics in the Sanskrit tradition," in *Current Trends in Linguistics* (Papers in Linguistics, Monograph Series 2), edited by Braj B. Kachru and F. W. Herbert Stahlke. Edmonton, AB and Champaign, IL: Linguistic Research Inc., pp. 1–14.

Aklujkar, Ashok. 2001. "The word is the world: Nondualism in Indian philosophy of language," *Philosophy East & West*, 51(4), 452–73.

Alam, M. M. 1983. "Persian influence on Assamese language and literature," *Indo-Iranica*, 36(1–4), 160–73.

Alexander, G. P. 1990. "Asian Indians in the San Francisco valley," unpublished PhD dissertation, San Francisco, CA: Fuller Theological Seminary.

Ali, Ahmed. 1996. English in South Asia: A historical perspective," in *South Asian English: Structure, Use and Users*, edited by Robert J. Baumgardner. Urbana and Chicago, IL: University of Illinois Press, pp. 3–12.

Ali, H. M. T. 1985. "Persian studies in Bengal: Problems and prospects," *Indo-Iranica*, 38(1–2), 52–8.

Allardyce, Alexander. 1877. "The Anglo-Indian tongue," *Blackwood's Edinburgh Magazine*, 121, 541–51.

Allen, Charles (ed.) 1975. *Plain Tales from the Raj*. London: Andre Deutsch and the British Broadcasting Corporation.

Allen, David O. 1854. "The state and the prospects of the English language in India," *Journal of the American Orientel Society*, 4, 263–75. [Also in *Church of Scotland Magazine*, March–June 1836.]

Alleyne, Mervyn C. 1971. "Acculturation and the cultural matrix of creolization," in *Pidginization and Creolization of Languages*, edited by Dell Hymes. Cambridge: Cambridge University Press, pp. 169–86.

Alper, H. P. 1989. *Mantra*. Albany, NY: The State University of New York Press.

Amin, S. 1995. *Event, Metaphor, Memory: Chauri Chaura 1922–1992*. Berkeley, CA: University of California Press.

Anand, J. H. 1995. "Dalit literature is the literature of protest," in *Dalit Solidarity*, edited by Bhagwan Das and James Massey. New Delhi: Indian Society for Promotion of Christian Knowledge, pp. 177–84.

Anand, Mulk Raj. 1948. *The King Emperor's English; or, the Role of the English Language in Free India*. Bombay, India: Hind Kitabs.

Anand, Mulk Raj and Eleanor Zelliot (eds.) 1992. *An Anthology of Dalit Literature (Poems)*. New Delhi: Gyan Publishing House.

Ananthanarayana, H. S. 1975. "KannaDadalliruva samskruta pratyayagaLu" (Sanskrit affixes in Kannada), in *Sri: kanthatirtha*, edited by M. Chidanandamurti, T. S. Nagabhusana, and T. N. Shankaranarayana. Bangalore, India: Privately published.

Anderson, Benedict. 1983. *Imagined Communities: Reflections on the Origin and Spread of Nationalism*. London: Verso.

Andronov, M. 1964. "On the typological similarity of New Indo-Aryan and Dravidian," *Indian Linguistics*, 25, 119–26.

Andronov, M. 1966. *Materials for a Bibliography of Dravidian Linguistics*. Kuala Lumpur: University Malaya, Department of Indian Studies.

Annamalai, E. (ed.) 1979. *Language Movements in India*. Mysore, India: Central Institute of Indian Languages.

Annamalai, E. 1980. "The movement for linguistic purism: The case of Tamil," in *Language Movements of this Century in India*, edited by E. Annamalai. Mysore, India: Central Institute of Indian Languages, pp. 35–59.

Annamalai, E. 1997a. *Adjectival Clauses in Tamil*. Tokyo: Institute for the Study of Languages and Cultures of Asia and Africa, Tokyo University of Foreign Studies.

Annamalai, E. 1997b. "Questions on the linguistic characteristics of the tribal languages of India," in *Tribal and Indigenous Languages of India: The Ethnic Space*, edited by Abbi Anvita. New Delhi: Motilal Banarsidass, pp. 15–36.

Annamalai, E. 1998. "Language choice in education: Conflict resolution in Indian courts," *Language Sciences*, 20(1), 29–44.

Annamalai, E. 2001. *Managing Multilingualism in India: Political and Linguistic Manifestations*. New Delhi: Sage.

Ansal, Kusum. 1990. bas ek kraas. *India Today*. (Hindi edn.) Dec. 21, 1990, 96–99.

Anselmi, Dina L. and Anne L. Law (eds.) 1998. *Questions of Gender*. Boston, MA: McGraw-Hill.

Anwar, M. S. 1957. "Indo-Iranian philology," *Indo-Iranica*, 10(4), 23–32.

Anwar, M. S. 1958. "India's contribution to Persian lexicography," *Indo-Iranica*, 11(2), 1–8.

Anwar, Muhammad. 1998. *Between Cultures: Continuity and Change in the Lives of Young Asians*. London and New York: Routledge.

Appadurai, A. 1996. *Modernity at Large: Cultural Dimension of Globalization*. Minneapolis, MN: University of Minnesota Press.

Apte, Mahadev L. 1974a. "Pidginization of a lingua franca: A linguistic analysis of Hindi–Urdu spoken in Bombay," in *Contact and Convergence in South Asian*

Languages, edited by Franklin C. Southworth and Mahadev L. Apte. Special issue of *International Journal of Dravidian Linguistics*, 3, 21–41.

Apte, Mahadev L. 1974b. "'Thank you' and South Asian languages: A comparative sociolinguistic study," *International Journal of the Sociology of Language*, 3, 67–89.

Apte, Mahadev L. 1976. "Multilingualism in India and its sociopolitical implications: An overview," in *Language and Politics*, edited by William M. O'Barr and Jean F. O'Barr. The Hague: Mouton, pp. 141–64.

Arjunavādakara, Kṛṣṇa Srinivāsa [Arjunwadkar, Krishna Shriniwas]. 1992. *Marāthī Vyākaraṇācā Itihāsa* (History of Marathi grammar tradition). Mumbai, India: Mumbaī Viśvavidyālaya/Marāthī Vibhāga, Pune, India: Jñānamudrā

Armstrong, J. C. and N. A. Worden. 1989. "The slaves, 1652–1834," in *The Shaping of South African Society 1652–1840*, edited by R. Elphick and H. Giliomee. Cape Town: Maskew Miller Longman, pp. 109–83.

Aronoff, Mark and S. N. Sridhar. 1988. "Prefixation in Kannada," in *Theoretical Morphology*, edited by Michael Hammond and Michael Noonan. New York: Academic Press, pp. 179–91.

Arora, H. 2004. *Syntactic Convergence – The Case of Dakkhini Hindi-Urdu*. Delhi; Publication Division, University of Delhi.

Asher, R. E. 2007. "Southern Asia: From Iran to Bangladesh," in *Atlas of the World's Languages* (2nd edn), edited by R. E. Asher and Christopher Moseley. London and New York: Routledge, pp. 209–28.

Auroux, Sylvain, Konrad Koerner, Hans–Josef Niederehe, and Kees Versteegh (eds.) 2000. *History of the Language Sciences*. Berlin and New York: Walter de Gruyter.

Austin, Granville. 1999. *The Constitution of India: Cornerstone of a Nation*. Oxford, Oxford University Press.

Ayrookuzhiel, A. M. Abraham. 1990. "The ideological nature of the emerging Dalit consciousness," *Religion and Society*, XXXCII(3), 20–1.

Backstrom, Peter C. and Carla F. Radloff. 1992. *Languages of the Northern Areas*, Sociolinguistic Survey of Northern Pakistan, Vol 2. Islamabad: National Institute of Pakistan Studies; High Wycombe, Bucks: Summer Institute of Linguistics.

Bailey, Thomas Grahame. 1956. *Teach Yourself Urdu*. London: English Universities Press.

Bailey, Thomas Grahame. 1982. *Learn Urdu: For English Speakers*. Brooklyn, NY: Saphrograph Corp.

Bakhtin, Mikhail. 1981. *The Dialogic Imagination*. Austin, TX: University of Texas Press.

Baldauf, Richard B. Jr. and Robert B. Kaplan (eds.) 2000. *Language Planning in Nepal, Taiwan, and Sweden*. Clevedon, Avon: Multilingual Matters.

Ballard, Roger (ed.) 1994. *Desh Pardesh: The South Asian Presence in Britain*. Marcus Banks, London: Hurst.

Ballard, Roger. 1996. "The Pakistanis: Stability and introspection," in *Ethnicity in the 1991 Census*, edited by Ceri Peach. London: In the Service of Her Majesty: National Statistics.

Bama, 2000. *Karukku* (*Palmyra Leaves, Freshness*). Translated by Lakshmi Holmstrom. Chennai, India: Macmillan.

Banerji, Sures Chandra. 1996. *Historical Survey of Ancient Indian Grammars: Sanskrit, Pali, and Prakrit*. New Delhi: Sharada Publication House.

Bannerjee, Brajendra Nath. 1997. *Struggle for Justice to Dalit Christians*. New Delhi: New Age International.

Barnes, Sir Edward. 1932. *The History of Royal College* (Colombo). (It was earlier called Colombo academy.)

Barnet, Richard J. and John Cavanagh. 1994. *Global Dreams: Imperial Corporations and the New World Order*. New York: Simon & Schuster.

Barnouw, Eric and E. Krishnaswamy. 1963. *Indian Films*. New York: Columbia University Press.

Barton, D. (ed.) 1994. *Sustaining Local Literacies*, Special issue of *Language and Education*, 8.

Barz, R. K. 1980. "The cultural significance of Hindi in Mauritius," *Journal of South Asian Studies*, new series, 3, 1–14.

Barz, R. K. and J. Siegel (eds.) 1988. *Language Transplanted: The Development of Overseas Hindi*. Wiesbaden: Otto Harrassowitz.

Basdeo, S. 1999. "East Indians in Canada's Pacific coast 1900–1914: An encounter in race relations," in *Sojourners to Settlers: Indian Migrants in the Caribbean and the Americas*, edited by M. Gosine and D. Narine. New York: Windsor Press, pp. 236–52.

Bashir, Elena. 2006. "Pakistan: Research and developments in linguistics and language study," in *The Yearbook of South Asian Languages and Linguistics, 2006*, edited by Rajendra Singh. Berlin: Mouton de Gruyter, pp. 125–43.

Baumgardner, Robert J. 1992. "*To Shariat* or not *to Shariat*: Bilingual functional shifts in Pakistani England," in *The External Family: English in Global Bilingualism* (Studies *in Honor of Braj B. Kachru*), *World Englishes*, 11, 2/3, special issue, edited by Larry E. Smith and S. N. Sridhar. Oxford: Pergamon Press, pp. 129–40.

Baumgardner, Robert J. 1993. "The indigenisation of English in Pakistan," in *The English Language in Pakistan*, edited by Robert J. Baumgardner. Karachi, Pakistan: Oxford University Press, pp. 41–54.

Baumgardner, Robert J., Andrey A. H. Kennedy, and Fauzia Shamin. 1993. "The Urduization of English in Pakistan," in *The English Language in Pakistan*, edited by Robert J. Baumgardner. Karachi, Pakistan: Oxford University Press, pp. 83–203.

Bechert, H. (ed.) 1980. *The Language of the Earliest Buddhist Tradition*. Gottingen: Vandenhoeck and Ruprecht.

Benedict, Paul K. 1972. *Sino-Tibetan. A Conspectus*. Cambridge: Cambridge University Press.

Berger, Hermann. 1998. *Die Burushaski-Sprache von Hunza und Nager* (3 Vols., Neuindische Studien, Band 13). Wiesbaden: Otto Harrassowitz.

Bergsland, Knut and Hans Vogt. 1962. "On the validity of glottochronology," *Current Anthropology*, 3, 115–53.

Bergvall, Victoria L., Janet M. Bing, and Alice F. Freed. 1996. *Rethinking Language and Gender Research*. New York: Longman.

Bhagat, Datta. 1994. "Routes and escape-routes," Translated by Maya Pandit, in *Yatra: Writings from the Indian Subcontinent, III* edited by Satish Alekar. New Delhi: Indus.

Bhagat, Datta. 2000. "Whirlwind," in *Indian Drama since 1950*, translated by Georg Naggies, Vimal Thorat, and Eleanor Zelliot, edited by G. P. Deshpande. New Delhi: Sahitya Akademi.

Bhagwat, Vidyut. 1995. "Bombay in Dalit literature," in *Bombay: Mosaic of Modern Culture*, edited by Sujata Patel and Alice Thorner. Bombay, India: Oxford University Press, pp. 113–25.

Bhaskararao, Peri and Karumuri V. Subbarao (eds.) 2001. *The Yearbook of South Asian Languages 2001*. New Delhi: Thousand Oaks, London: Sage.

Bhaskararao, Peri and Karumuri V. Subbarao. 2004. *Non-nominative Subjects*, Vols. I and II. Amsterdam and Philadelphia, PA: John Benjamins.

Bhatia, Tej K. 1982. "English and the vernaculars of India: Contact and change," *Applied Linguistics*, 3(3), 235–45.

Bhatia, Tej K. 1987. *A History of Hindi (Hindustani) Grammatical Tradition*. Leiden: E. J. Brill.

Bhatia, Tej K. 1988. "English in advertising: Multiple mixing and media," *World Englishes*, 6, 33–48.

Bhatia, Tej K. 1992. "Discourse functions and pragmatics of mixing: Advertising across cultures," *World Englishes*, 11, 195–215.

Bhatia, Tej K. 1993. *Punjabi: A Cognitive-Descriptive Grammar*. London: Routledge.

Bhatia, Tej K. 1996. *Colloquial Hindi: The Complete Course for Beginners*. London: Routledge.

Bhatia, Tej K. 2000. *Advertising in India: Language, Marketing Communication, and Consumerism*. Tokyo: Institute for the Study of Languages and Cultures of Asia and Africa, Tokyo University of Foreign Studies.

Bhatia, Tej K. 2001a. "Grammatical traditions in contact: The case of India," *Ajia Afurika gengo bunka kenkyu (Journal of Asian and African Studies)*, 61, 303–31.

Bhatia, Tej K. 2001b. "Language mixing in global advertising," in *The Three Circles of English*, edited by Edwin Thumboo. Singapore: UniPress, pp. 195–215.

Bhatia, Tej K. 2003. "The Gurmukhi script and other writing systems of Punjab: History, structure and identity," in *International Symposium on Indic Scripts: Past and Present*, edited by Peri Bhaskararao. Tokyo: Research Institute for the Languages and Cultures of Asia and Africa, Tokyo University of Foreign Studies, pp. 181–213.

Bhatia, Tej K. and Shakuntala Chandana. 2002. *Colloquial Hindi*. Syracuse, NY: Taylor and Francis.

Bhatia, Vijay K. 1993. *Analyzing Genre: Language Use in Professional Settings*. London: Longman.

Bhatt, Rakesh. 1989. "Language planning and language conflict: The case of Kashmiri," *International Journal of the Sociology of Language*, 75, 73–86.

Bhatt, Rakesh. 1996. "On the grammar of code-switching," *World Englishes*, 15(3), 369–76.

Bhatt, Rakesh. 1999. *Verb Movement and the Syntax of Kashmiri*. Boston, MA: Kluwer Academic.

Bhattacharya, Sudhibhusan. 1957. *Ollari: A Dravidian Speech*. Calcutta, India: Anthropological Survey of India.

Bhatti, Ghazala. 1999. *Asian Children at Home and at School: An Ethnographic Study*. London and New York: Routledge.

Bhaya Nair, Rukmini. 1991a. "Monosyllabic English or disyllabic Hindi? Language acquisition in a bilingual child," *Indian Linguistics*, 52, 1–4.

Bhaya Nair, Rukmini. 1991b. "Pre-linguistic similarity and post-linguistic difference: Some observations on children's conceptualizations in a cross-cultural context," in *Child Language Development in Singapore and Malaysia*, edited by Anna Kwan-Terry. Singapore: Singapore University Press, pp. 35–76.

Bhaya Nair, Rukmini. 1992. "Gender, genre and generative grammar: Deconstructing the matrimonial column," in *Text and Context: Essays in Stylistics*, edited by M. Toolan. London: Routledge, pp. 227–54.

Bhaya Nair, Rukmini. 1997a. *Technobrat: Culture in a Cybernetic Classroom*. New Delhi: Harper Collins.

Bhaya Nair, Rukmini. 1997b. "Acts of agency and acts of God: The discourse of disaster," *Economic & Political Weekly*, March, pp. 535–42.

Bhaya Nair, Rukmini. 1999. "The mind has no sex," in *Stree*, special issue on *Indian Women*, pp. 6–10.

Bhaya Nair, Rukmini. 2000. "Stealing fire from the Greeks," in *Memories of the Second Sex: Gender and Sexuality in Women's Writing*, edited by Dominique S. Verma and T. V. Kunhi Krishnan. Delhi: Somaiya, pp. 33–66.

Bhaya Nair, Rukmini. 2001a. "The testament of the tenth muse: A perspective on feminine sexuality and sensibility among Indian women poets in English," in *Indian Poetry: Modernism and After*, edited by K. Satchidananadan. New Delhi: Sahitya Akademi, pp. 193–223.

Bhaya Nair, Rukmini. 2001b. "Is astrology different for feminists?" *Seminar*, 71–9.

Bhaya Nair, Rukmini. 2002a. *Lying on the Postcolonial Couch: The Idea of Indifference*. Minneapolis, MN: University of Minnesota Press.

Bhaya Nair, Rukmini (ed.) 2002b. *Translation, Text and Theory: The Paradigm of India*. New Delhi: Sage.

Bhoite, Uttam and Anuradha Bhoite. 1977. "The Dalit Sahitya Movement in Maharashtra: A sociological analysis," *Sociological Bulletin*, 26(1), 60–75.

Bickerton, Derek. 1977. "Pidginization and creolization: Language acquisition and language universals," in *Pidgin and Creole Linguistics*, edited by Albert Valdman. Bloomington, IN: Indiana University Press, pp. 49–69.

Birdwood, George. 1887. "Colonel Yule's Anglo-Indian glossary," *Quarterly Review*, 164, 144–66.

Biswas, Achintya. 1995. "Bengali Dalit poetry: Past and now," in *Dalit Solidarity*, edited by Bhagwan Das and James Massey. New Delhi: Indian Society for Promoting Christian Knowledge, pp. 190–200.

Bloch, Jules. 1934. *Indo-Aryan: From the Vedas to Modern Times*. Translated by Alfred Master. Paris: Librairie Adrien Maisonnneuve. (Original in French.)

Bloch, Jules. 1954. *The Grammatical Structure of Dravidian Languages*. Translated by R. G. Harshe. Poona, India: Deccan College, Post-graduate and Research Institute.

Bloomfield, Leonard. 1933. *Language*. New York: Holt.

Bly, R. (ed.) 1971. *The Kabir Book: Forty Four of the Ecstatic Poems of Kabir*. Toronto, ON: Fitzhenry and Whiteside.

Bolton, Kingsley and Braj B. Kachru (eds.) 2006a. *World Englishes: Critical Concepts in Linguistics*. 6 vols. London and New York: Routledge.

Bolton, Kingsley and Braj B. Kachru (eds.) 2006b. *Origin and Development of Asian Englishes*. 5 vols. London and New York: Routledge.

Borua, B. K. 1993. *Nagamese, the Language of Nagaland*. New Delhi: Mittal.

Bourdieu, P. 1991. *Language and Symbolic Power*. edited by J. B. Thompson. Cambridge: Polity Press.

Bradley, David. 1981. "Andaman and Nicobar Islands," in *Language Atlas of the Pacific Area*, edited by Stephen A. Wurm and Shirô Hattori. Canberra: Australian Academy of the Humanities.

Bradley, David. 1997. "Tibeto-Burman languages and classification," in *Tibeto-Burman Languages of the Himalayas* (Pacific Linguistics, Series A, 86; Papers in Southeast Asian Linguistics, no. 14), edited by David Bradley. Canberra: Department of Linguistics, Australian National University, pp. 1–71.

Brah, A. 1996. *Cartographies of Diaspora: Contesting Identities*. London and New York: Routledge.

Brass, Paul R. 1974. *Language, Religion, and Politics in North India*. Cambridge: Cambridge University Press.

Breton, Ronald J. -L. 1997. *Atlas of the Languages and Ethnic Communities of South Asia*. New Delhi: Sage; Walnut Creek, CA: AltaMira Press.

Brians, Paul, Mary Gallwey, Douglas Huges, et al. (eds.) 1999. *Reading About the World*, Vol. 1. Washington, DC: Harcourt Brace Custom Publishing.

Bright, William. 1960. "A study of caste and dialect in Mysore," *Indian Linguistics*, 21, 45–50.

Bright, William. 1990. *Language Variation in South Asia*. New York: Oxford University Press.

Bright, William. 1998. "The Dravidian scripts," in *The Dravidian Languages*, edited by Sanford Steever. London: Routledge, pp. 40–71.

Bright, William. 2000. "A matter of typology: Alphasyllabaries and Abugidas," *Studies in the Linguistic Sciences*, 30, 3–71.

Bright, William and A. K. Ramanujan. 1964. "Sociolinguistic variation and language change," in *Proceedings of the Ninth International Congress of Linguists*, edited by H. G. Hunt. Cambridge, MA: The Massachussetts Institute of Technology Press, pp. 1107–13.

Britto, Francis. 1986. *Diglossia: A Study of the Theory with Application to Tamil*. Washington, DC: Georgetown University Press.

Bronkhorst, Johannes. 2001. "Pāṇini and Euclid: Reflections on Indian geometry," *Journal of Indian Philosophy*, 29, 43–80.

Brown, L. 1980. *The Indian Christianity of St. Thomas*, 2nd edn. Cambridge: Cambridge University Press.

Brown, Penelope. 1980. "How and why are women more polite: Some evidence from a Mayan community," in *Women and Language in Literature and Society*, edited by Sally McConnell-Ginet, Ruth Borker, and Nelly Furman. New York: Praeger, pp. 111–36.

Brown, Penelope and Stephen C. Levinson. 1987. *Politeness: Some Universals in Language Usage*. Cambridge: Cambridge University Press.

Brueck, Laura. 2002. "Dalit writing: The works of Kusum Meghval," *Sagar: A South Asia Graduate Research Journal*, 8, 74–99.

Bryant, Arthur. 1932. *Macaulay*. Edinburgh: Edinburgh University Press.

Bühler, Georg. 1904. *Indian Paleography* [Reprinted in 1980, New Delhi: Oriental Books and Munshiram Manoharlal].

Bulletin of Concerned Asian Scholars, 1978, X(3), pp. 2–10.

Burke, A. K. 1982. "Persian literature in Kashmir in 18th C," *Indo-Iranica*, 35(1–2), 57–63.

Burrow, Thomas. 1965. *The Sanskrit Language*. London: Faber and Faber.

Burrow, Thomas and S. Bhattacharya. 1962–1963. "Gadaba supplement," *Indo-Iranian Journal*, 6, 45–51.

Burrow, Thomas and S. Bhattacharya. 1970. *The Pengo Language*. Oxford: Clarendon Press.

Burton, A. M. 1998. *At the Heart of the Empire: Indians and the Colonial Encounter in Late–Victorian Britain*. Berkeley, CA: University of California Press.

Butt, Miriam, Tracy Holloway King, and Gillian Ramchand. 1994. *Theoretical Perspectives on Word Order in South Asian Languages*. Stanford, CA: Center for the Study of Language and Information.

Caldwell, Robert. 1903. *A Comparative Grammar of the Dravidian or South Indian Family of Languages* (3rd edn). New Delhi: Orient Publications. [Reprinted in 1947.]

Cameron, Deborah. 1992. *Feminism and Linguistic Theory* (2nd edn). London: Macmillan.

Cameron, Deborah and Jennifer Coates (eds.) 1988. *Women in Their Speech Communities*. New York: Longman.

Canagarajah, Suresh. 1999. *Resisting Linguistic Imperialism in English Teaching*. Oxford: Oxford University Press.

Candan, A. 1986. *Indians in Britain*. New Delhi: Sterling.

Cardona, George. 1976. *Pāṇini: A Survey of Research*. The Hague and Paris: Mouton.

Cardona, George. 1983. *Linguistic Analysis and Some Indian Traditions*, Post-graduate and Research Department Series No. 20 (Pandit Shripad Shastri Deodhar Memorial Lectures). Poona, India: Bhandarkar Oriental Research Institute.

Cardona, George. 1987. "Sanskrit," in *The World's Major Languages*, edited by Bernard Comrie. New York: Oxford University Press, pp. 448–69.

Cardona, George. 1997. *Pāṇini: His Work and Its Traditions: Background and Introduction*. New Delhi: Motilal Banarsidass.

Cardona, George. 1999. *Recent Researches in Paninian Studies*. New Delhi: Motilal Banarsidass.

Cardona, George, and Dhanesh Jain (eds.) 2003. *The Indo-Aryan languages*. London and New York: Routledge.

Carter, M. 1995. *Servants, Sirdars and Settlers: Indians in Mauritius, 1834–1874*. New Delhi: Oxford University Press.

Census of India. 1961 *India, States and Union Territories*. Registrar General & Census Commissioner. New Delhi.

Census of India. 1991. *India, States and Union Territories*. Registrar General & Census Commissioner. New Delhi.

Census of India 2004. *Census of India: Language Atlas of India 1991*. Technical direction R. P. Singh, General direction Jayant Kumar Banthia. Delhi: Controller of Publications.

Chaitanya, Krishna. 1977. *A New History of Sanskrit Literature*. New Delhi: Manohar Book Service.

Chaklader, Snehamoy. 1987. *Minority Rights: A Sociolinguistic Analysis of Group Conflicts in Eastern Region of India*. Calcutta, India: K. P. Bagchi.

Chakrabarti, Sukla. 1996. *A Critical Linguistic Study of the Prātiśakhyas*. Calcutta, India: Punthi–Pustak.

Challapalli, Swaroopa Rani. 1998. "Dalit women's writing in Telugu," *The Economic and Political Weekly*, April 25, pp. 21–24.

Chandrasekhar, A. 1970. "Personal pronouns and pronominal forms in Malayalam," *Anthropological Linguistics*, 12(7), 246–55.

Chari, V. K. 1990. *Sanskrit Criticism*. Honolulu, HI: University of Hawaii Press.

Chatterjee, Kalyan K[umar]. 1976. *English Education in India. Issues and Opinions*. New Delhi: Macmillan.

Chatterji, Suniti Kumar. 1926. *The Origin and Development of the Bengali Language* (3 vols.). Calcutta, India: Calcutta University Press.

Chatterji, Suniti Kumar. 1931. *Calcutta Hindustani: A Study of a Jargon Dialect*. Lahore, Pakistan: G. D. Thukral [Reprinted in 1972, New Delhi: People's Publishing House, pp. 204–56].

Chatterji, Suniti Kumar. 1973. *India, a Polyglot Nation and its Linguistic Problems vis-à-vis National Integration*. Bombay, India: Mahatma Gandhi Memorial Research Centre.

Chatterji, Suniti Kumar. 1976. "The Persian language and Bengal," *Indo-Iranica*, 29 (1–4), 113–8.

Chatterji, Suniti Kumar. 1977. *Some Aspects of Indo-Iranian Literary and Cultural Traditions*. New Delhi: Ajanta.

Chatterji, Suniti Kumar. 1985. *The Origin and Development of the Bengali Language*. Calcutta, India: Rupa.

Chaturvedi, M. G. and B. V. Mohale. 1976. *The Position of Languages in School Curriculum in India*. New Delhi: National Council of Education Research and Training.

Chaturvedi, M. G. and S. Singh. 1981. *Language and Medium of Instruction in India Schools: Third All India Survey 1981*. New Delhi: National Council of Education Research and Training.

Chaudhry, Nazir Ahmad. 1977. *Development of Urdu as Official Language in the Punjab, 1849–1974*. Lahore, Pakistan: Punjab Government Record Office.

Chernyshev, V. A. 1971. "Nekotorye cherty Bombeiskogo govora khindustani" (na materiale sovremennoi prozy khindi), in *diiskaia i Iranskaia filologiia* (Voprosy Dialektologii), edited by N. A. Dvoriankov. Moscow: Izdatel'stvo "Nauka," pp. 121–41.

Chidananda Murthy, M. 1984. "Modernization of Kannada in the news media," in *Modernization of Indian Languages in the News Media*, edited by Bhadriraju Krishnamurti and Aditi Mukherji. Hyderabad, India: Department of Linguistics, Osmania University, pp. 54–63.

Chib, Som Nath. 1936. *Language, Universities and Nationalism in India*. London and Bombay, India: Milford and Oxford University Press.

Chion, Michel. 1999. *The Voice in Cinema*. New York: Columbia University Press.

Chitre, Dilip. 2001. *Namdeo Dhasal: Poet of the Underworld*. www.ambedkar.org/News/NamdeoDhasal.htm, accessed August 2005.

Chomsky, Noam. 1981. *Lectures on Government and Binding*. Dordrecht: Foris.

Cicourel, Aaron V. 1972. "Basic and normative rules in the negotiation of status and role," in *Studies in Social Interaction*, edited by David Sudnow. New York: Free Press, pp. 229–58.

Clarke, Hyde. 1890. "The English language in India and the East," *Asiatic Quarterly Review*, 10, 149–62.

Clements, J. Clancy. 1988. *The Genesis of a Language: The Formation and Development of Korlai Portuguese*. Amsterdam and Philadelphia, PA: John Benjamins.

Cohn, Bernard S. 1985. "The command of language and the language of command," in *Subattern Studies IV: Writings on South Asian History and Society*, edited by Ranjit Guha. New Delhi: Oxford University Press, pp. 276–329.

Collins, S. 2001. "Buddhism, Indian," in *Concise Encyclopedia of Language and Religion*, edited by J. F. A. Sawyer and J. M. Y. Simpson. Amsterdam: Elsevier, pp. 15–16.

Comrie, Bernard. 1978. "Ergativity," in *Syntactic Typology*, edited by W. P. Lehmann. Brighton, Sussex: The Harvester Press, pp. 329–94.

Comrie, Bernard. 1981. *Language Universals and Linguistic Typology*. Chicago, IL: University of Chicago Press.

Comrie, Bernard (ed.) 1987. *The World's Major Languages* London and Sydney: Croom Helm.

Cook, Nilla Cram. 1958. *The Way of the Swan*. Bombay, India: Asia Publishing House.

Coulmas, Florian. 1996. *The Blackwell Encyclopedia of Writing Systems*. Oxford: Blackwell.

Cowar, Nilmani. 1859. *Can English Be the Language of India?* An essay read at a bi-monthly meeting of students of the Presidency College in April 1859. Calcutta, India: Hurkabu Press, pp. 1–12.

Coward, Harold, John R. Hinnells, and Raymond B. Williams (eds.) 2000. *The South Asian Religious Diaspora in Britain, Canada, and the United States*. Albany, NY: State University of New York Press.

Crawford, Mary. 1995. *Talking Difference*. London: Sage.

Crosby, Faye and Linda Nyquist. 1977. "The female register: An empirical study of Lakoff's hypothesis," *Language in Society*, 6, 313–22.

Damsteegt, T. 1988. "Sarnami: A living language," in *Language Transplanted: The Development of Overseas Hindi*, edited by R. K. Barz and J. Siegel. Wiesbaden: Otto Harrassowitz, pp. 95–120.

Damsteegt, T. 1993. "Language maintenance among the East Indians in Suriname," in *Alternative Cultures in the Caribbean*, edited by T. Bremer and U. Fleischmann. Frankfurt am Main: Vervuert, pp. 95–120.

Dangle, Arjun (ed.) 1992. *Poisoned Bread: Translations from Modern Marathi Dalit Literature*. Hyderabad, India: Orient Longmans.

Dani, Ahmed Hasan. 1963. *Indian Paleography*. Oxford: Clarendon. [2nd edn, New Delhi: Munshiram Manoharlal, 1986.]

Daniels, Peter T. 2002. "The study of writing in the twentieth century: Semitic studies interacting with non-semitic," *Israel Oriental Studies*, 20, 85–118.

Daniels, Peter, T. and William Bright (eds.) 1996. *The World's Writing Systems*. New York: Oxford University Press.

Das Gupta, Bhidu Bhusan. 1966. *Assamese Self-taught*. Calcutta, India: DasGupta Prakashan.

Das Gupta, Jyotirindra. 1970. *Language Conflict and National Development*. Berkeley, CA: University of California Press.

Dasgupta, Probal. 1993. *The Otherness of English: India's Auntie Tongue Syndrome*. London and New Delhi: Sage.

Dasgupta, Probal. 2006. "Language policies and lesser-known language in India," in *The Yearbook of South Asian Languages and Linguistics, 2006*, edited by Rajendra Singh. Berlin: Mouton de Gruyter, pp. 193–205.

Das, Sisir Kumar. 1968. "Forms of address and terms of reference in Bengali," *Anthropological Linguistics*, 4(10), 19–31.

Das, Sisir Kumar. 1991. *A History of Indian Literature Volume VIII:1800–1910: Western Impact: Indian Response*. New Delhi: Sahitya Academi.

Davidar, David. 2002. *The House of Blue Mangoes*. New York: Harper Collins.

Davison, Alice. 1999b "Lexical anaphors in Hindi/Urdu," in Kashi Wali, K. V. Subbarao, B. Lust and J. Gair (eds.), *Lexical Anaphors and Pronouns in Some South Asian Languages: a Principled Typology*. Berlin: Mouton de Gruyter, 397–470.

de Silva, M. W. Sugathapala. 1972. *The Vedda Language of Ceylon, Texts and Lexicon*. Munich: R. Kitzinger.

Denny, J. Peter. 1991. "Rational thought in oral culture and literate decontextualization," in *Literacy and Orality*, edited by D. R. Olson and N. Torrance. Cambridge: Cambridge University Press, pp. 66–89.

Deo, Veena. 1996. "Dalit literature in Marathi," in *Handbook of Twentieth-Century Literature of India*, edited by Nalini Natarajan. Westport, CT: Greenwood Press, pp. 363–81.

Deo, Veena and Eleanor Zelliot. 1994. "Dalit literature – Twenty-five years of protest? Of progress?," *Journal of South Asian Literature*, XXIX(2), 41–67.

Deshpande, Madhav M. 1978. "Pāṇinian grammarians on dialectal variation in Sanskrit," *Brahmavidyā: Adyar Library Bulletin*, 61–114.

Deshpande, Madhav M. 1979a. "Genesis of Ṛgvedic retroflexion: A historical and socio-linguistic investigation," in *Aryan and Non-Aryan in India*, edited by Madhav Deshpande and Peter Edwin Hook. Ann Arbor, MI: Center for South and Southeast Asian Studies, The University of Michigan, pp. 235–315.

Deshpande, Madhav M. 1979b. *Sociolinguistic Attitudes in India: An Historical Reconstruction. Linguistica Extranea, Studia 5*. Ann Arbor, MI: Karoma Publishers.

Deshpande, Madhav M. 1985a. "Historical change and the theology of eternal Sanskrit," *Zeitschrift für vergleichende Sprachforschung*, 98, 122–49.

Deshpande, Madhav M. 1985b. "Sanskrit grammarians on diglossia," in *South Asian Languages: Structure, Convergence and Diglossia*, edited by Bh. Krishnamurti. New Delhi: Motilal Banarsidass, pp. 312–21.

Deshpande, Madhav M. 1991. "Diglossia in the writings of the Sanskrit grammarians," *Southwest Journal of Linguistics, Studies in Diglossia*, 10(1), 23–40.

Deshpande, Madhav M. 1992. "Sociolinguistic parameters of Pāṇini's Sanskrit," in *Vidyā-Vratin, Prof. A. M. Ghatage Felicitation Volume*, edited by V. N. Jha. New Delhi: Sri Satguru Publications, pp. 111–30.

Deshpande, Madhav M. 1993. *Sanskrit and Prakrit: Sociolinguistic Issues*. New Delhi: Motilal Banarsidass.

Deshpande, Madhav M. 1994. "Brahmanism versus Buddhism: A perspective on language attitudes," in *Jainism and Prakrit in Ancient and Medieval India, Professor J. C. Jain Felicitation Volume*, edited by N. N. Bhattacharya. New Delhi: Manohar Publishers, pp. 89–111.

Deshpande, Madhav M. 1996. "Contextualizing the eternal language: Features of priestly Sanskrit," in *Ideology & Status of Sanskrit, Contributions to the History of the Sanskrit Language*, edited by Jan Houben. Leiden: E. J. Brill, pp. 401–36.

Deshpande, Madhav M. 1999. "What to do with the Anāryas: Dharmic discourses of inclusion and exclusion," in *Aryan and Non–Aryan in South Asia (Harvard Oriental Series, Opera Minora, Vol. 3)*, edited by Madhav M. Deshpande and Jonannes Bronkhorst. Cambridge, MA: Department of Sanskrit and Indian Studies, Harvard University, pp. 107–27.

Deshpande, Madhav M. and Jonannes Bronkhorst (eds.) 1999. *Aryan and Non-Aryan in South Asia* (Harvard Oriental Series, Opera Minora, Vol. 3), Cambridge, MA: Department of Sanskrit and Indian Studies, Harvard University.

Deshpande, Madhav M. and Peter Edwin Hook (eds.) 1979. *Aryan and Non-Aryan in India*. Ann Arbor, MI: Center for South and Southeast Asian Studies, The University of Michigan.

Dhadphale, M. G. 1975. *Some Aspects of (Buddhist) Literary Criticism as Gleaned from Pāli Soures*. Bombay, India: Adreesh Prakashan.

Dhammika, Ven S. 1993. *The Edicts of King Ashoka*, Kandy, Sri Lanka: Buddhist Publication Society.

Dharmadasa, K. N. O. 1974. "The creolization of an aboriginal language: The case of Vedda in Sri Lanka (Ceylon)," *Anthropological Linguistics*, 16, 79–106.

Dharmadasa, K. N. O. 1977. "Nativism, diglossia and the Sinhalese identity in the language problem in Sri Lanka," *International Journal of the Sociology of Language*, 13, 21–31.

Dharmadasa, K. N. O. 1990. "The Vedda language," in *The Vanishing Aborigines: Sri Lanka's Veddas in Transition*, edited by K. N. O. Dharmadasa and S. W. R. de A. Samarasinghe. New Delhi: International Centre for Ethnic Studies, pp. 84–98.

Dharmadasa, K. N. O. 1992. *Language, Religion, and Ethnic Assertiveness: The Growth of Sinhalese Nationalism in Sri Lanka*. Ann Arbor, MI: University of Michigan Press.

Dharmadasa, K. N. O. (ed.) 1996. *National Language Policy in Sri Lanka, 1956 to 1996: Three Studies in Its Implementation*. Kandy, Sri Lanka: International Centre for Ethnic Studies.

Dharwadker, Vinay. 1994. "Dalit poetry in Marathi," *World Literature Today*, 68(2), 319–24.

Dharwadkar, Vinay. 2003. "The historical formation of Indian-English literature," in *Literary Cultures in History: Reconstructions from South Asia*, edited by Sheldon Pollock. Berkeley, CA: University of California Press, pp. 199–267.

Dhayagude, Suresh. 1981. *Western and Indian Poetics – A Comparative Study* (Bhandarkar Oriental Series no. 16). Pune, India: Bhandarkar Oriental Research Institute.

Dil, Anwar S. 1966. "The position of English in Pakistan," *Shahidullah Presentation Volume*, special issue of *Pakistani Linguistics*, 185–242.

Dil, Anwar S. 1969. "Linguistic studies in Pakistan," in *Current Trends in Linguistics. Vol. 5. Linguistics in South Asia*, edited by Thomas A. Sebeok. The Hague: Mouton, pp. 679–735.

Diringer, David. 1948. *The Alphabet: A Key to the History of Mankind*. New York: Philosophical Library.

Dissanayake, Wimal. 1985. "Towards a decolonised English: South Asian creativity in fiction," *World Englishes*, 4(2), 233–42.

Dissanayake, Wimal and Ashley Ratnavibhushana. 2000. *Profiling Sri Lankan Cinema*. Colombo: Asian Film Centre.

Dixon, David. 2006. *Characteristics of the Asian Born in the United States*. Washington, DC: Migration Policy Institute.

Dixon, Robert M. W. 1997. *The Rise and Fall of Languages*. Cambridge: Cambridge University Press.

Domingue, N. C. 1971. "Bhojpuri and Creole in Mauritius: A study of linguistic interference and its consequences in regard to synchronic variation and language change," unpublished PhD dissertation, University of Texas at Austin.

Doniger, Wendy. 1991. *The Laws of Manu*. Harmondsworth, Middlesex: Penguin Books.

Doniger, Wendy. 1999. *Splitting the Difference. Gender and Myth in Ancient Greece and India*. Oxford: Oxford University Press.

Dorian, Nancy. 1981. *Language Death: The Life Cycle of Scottish Gaelic Dialect*. Philadelphia, PA: University of Pennsylvania Press.

Dressler, Wolfgang U. 1991. "The sociolinguistic and patholoinguistic attrition of Breton phonology, morphology, and morphoponology," in *First Language Attrition*, edited by H. W. Seliger and R. W. Vago. Cambridge: Cambridge University Press, pp. 99–112.

Dryer, M. 1992. "The Greenbergian word order correlations," *Language*, 69, 81–138.

D'souza, Jean. 1986. "Toward a typology of modernization for India as a sociolinguistic area," paper presented at *The South Asian Languages Analysis Round Table*. Urbana, IL: University of Illinois.

D'souza, Jean. 1987. "South Asia as a sociolinguistic area," unpublished PhD dissertation, University of Illinois at Urbana-Champaign.

D'souza, Jean. 1988. "Interactional strategies in South Asian languages: Their implications for teaching English internationally," *World Englishes*, 7, 159–71.

D'souza, Jean. 2001. "Contextualizing range and depth in Indian English," *World Englishes*, 20(2), 145–60.

Dua, Hans R. 1985. *Language Planning in India*. New Delhi: Harnam Publications.

Dua, Hans R. 1986. *Language Use, Attitudes and Identity among Linguistic Minorities*. Mysore, India: Central Institute of Indian Languages.

Dua, Hans R. and Shakuntala Sharma. 1977. "Language diversity, bilingualism and communication in India," *Indian Linguistics*, 38(4), 210–20.

Dube, Leela. 1988. "On the construction of gender: Hindu girls in patrilinial India," *Economic and Political Weekly*, April 30, pp. 11–19.

Dubey, V. S. 1991. "The lexical style of Indian English newspapers," *World Englishes*, 10(1), 19–32.

Duff, Alexandra. 1837. *New Era of the English Language and Literature in India; or, An Exposition of the Late Governor-General of India's Last Act*. Edinburgh: Johastone.

Dulai, N. K. 1989. *A Pedagogical Grammar of Punjabi*. Patiala, India: Institute of Language Studies.

Dwivedi, Hazari Prasad. 1964. *Hindi Sahitya udbhav aur vikas*. New Delhi: Attarchand Kapoor and Sons.

Eade, John, Tim Vamplew, and Ceri Peach. 1996. "The Bangladeshis: The encapsulated community," in *Ethnicity in the 1991 Census*, edited by Ceri Peach. London: In Her Majesty's Service: National Statistics.

Eagle, S. 2000. "The language situation in Nepal," in *Language Planning in Nepal, Taiwan and Sweden*, edited by Richard Baldauf Jr. and Robert Kaplan. North York, ON: Multilingual Matters, pp. 272–327.

Eckert, Penelope and Sally McConnell-Ginet. 1992. "Communities of practice: Where language, gender and power all live," in *Locating Power: Proceedings of the Second Berkeley Woman and Language Conference*, edited by Kira Hall, Mary Bucholtz, and Birch Moonwomon. Berkeley, CA: Berkeley Women and Language Group, pp. 89–99.

Edwards, John. 1985. *Language, Society and Identity*. Oxford: Basil Blackwell.

Edwards, Viv and Savita Katbamna. 1988. "The wedding songs of British Gujarati women," in *Women in their Speech Communities*, edited by Deborah Cameron and Jennifer Coates. New York: Longman, pp. 158–74.

Ekka, Francis. 1979. "Language loyalty and maintenance among Kuruxs," in *Language Movements in India*, edited by E. Annamalai. Mysore, India: CIIL Publications, pp. 99–105.

Ekvall, R. B. 1964. *Religious Observances in Tibet*. Chicago, IL: University of Chicago Press.

Emeneau, Murray B. 1951. *Studies in Vietnamese (Annamese) Grammar* University of California Publications in Linguistics, Vol. 8. Berkeley, CA: University of California Press.

Emeneau, Murray B. 1955. "India and linguistics," *Journal of the American Oriental Society*, 75, 145–53.

Emeneau, Murray B. 1956. "India as a linguistic area," *Language*, 32, 3–16.

Emeneau, Murray B. 1962a. *Dravidian and Indian Linguistics*. Berkeley, CA: Center for South Asian Studies, University of California.

Emeneau, Murray B. 1962b. "Bilingualism and structural borrowing," *Proceedings of the American Philosophical Society*, 106(5), 430–42.

Emeneau, Murray B. 1971. *Toda Songs*. Oxford: Clarendon Press.

Emeneau, Murray B. 1980. "India and linguistic areas," in *Language and Linguistic Area: Essays by Murray B. Emeneau*, edited by A. N. Dil. Stanford, CA: Stanford University Press, pp. 126–66.

Emeneau, Murray B. and Thomas Burrow. 1962. *Dravidian Borrowings from Indo-Aryan*, University of California Publications in Linguistics 26. Berkeley, CA: University of California.

Erikson, Erik. 1958. *Young Man Luther. A Study Psychoanalysis and History*. New York: W. W. Norton.

Erikson, Erik. 1968. *Identity, Youth and Crisis*. London: Faber and Faber.

Erikson, Erik. 1969. *Gandhi's Truth: On the Origins of Militant Non-violence*. New York: W. W. Norton.

Erikson, Erik. 1974. *Dimensions of a New Identity*. New York: W. W. Norton

Europa World Year Book. 2000. London: Europa.

Excerpts from Khusrau's Persian Poetry. www.alif–india.com/love.html, accessed July 2005.

Fairclough, Norman. 1989. *Language and Power*. London: Longman.

Faruqi, Shamsur Rahman. 2001. *Early Urdu Literary Culture and History*. New Delhi: Oxford University Press.

Fatihi, A. R. 2003. *Language in India*, 3, 2–9, www.languageinindia.com, accessed August 25, 2005.

Ferdman, Bernardo M., Rose–Marie Weber, and Arnulfo G. Ramírez, (eds.) 1994. *Literacy across Languages and Cultures*. Albany, NY: State University of New York Press.

Ferguson, Charles A. 1945. "A chart of the Bengali Verb," *Journal of the American Oriental Society*, 65, 54–55.

Ferguson, Charles A. 1959. "Diglossia," *Word*, 15, 325–40.

Ferguson, Charles A. 1968. "Language development," in *Language Problems of Developing Nations*, edited by J. A. Fishman, Charles A. Ferguson, and J. Dasgupta. New York: John Wiley, pp. 27–35.

Ferguson, Charles A. 1976. "The structure and use of politeness formulas," *Language in Society*, 5, 137–51.

Ferguson, Charles A. 1992. "South Asia as a sociolinguistic area," in *Dimensions of Sociolinguistics in South Asia. Papers in Memory of Gerald Kelley*, edited by Edward C. Dimock, Jr., Braj B. Kachru, and Bh. Krishnamurti. New Delhi: Oxford University Press and India Book House, pp. 25–36.

Ferguson, Charles A. 1996. "English in South Asia: Imperialist legacy and regional asset," in *South Asian English: Structure, Use and Users*, edited by Robert J. Baumgardner Urban and Chicago, IL: University of Illinois Press, pp. 29–39.

Ferguson, Charles and John Gumperz (eds.) 1960. *Linguistic Diversity in South Asia: Studies in Regional, Social and Functional Variation*, special issue of *International Journal of American Linguistics*, 26(3), Part II.

Ferguson, Donald Williams. 1887a. "Anglo-Indianisms," *Ceylon Literary Register*, 1 (28), 231–32.

Ferguson, Donald Williams. 1887b. "Anglo-Indianisms," *Ceylon Literary Register*, (29), 238–40.

Fernando, Chitra. 1996. "The ideational function of English in Sri Lanka," in *South Asian English: Structure, Use and Users*, edited by Robert J. Baumgardner. Urbana and Chicago, IL: University of Illinois Press, pp. 206–17.

First Report of the Commissioner of Linguistic Minorities. 1957. New Delhi: Government of India.

Firth, John R. 1930. *Speech*. London: Benn's Sixpence Library, No. 121. [Reprinted edition, London: Oxford University Press, 1966.]

Fishman, Joshua Andrew. 1973. "Language modernization and planning in comparison with other types of national modernization and planning," *Language and Society*, 2(1), 23–43.

Fishman, P. M. 1983. "Interaction: The work women do," in *Language, Gender and Sex*, edited by Barrie Thorne, Cheris Kramarae, and Nancy Henley. Rowley, MA: Newbury House, pp. 89–101.

Fowler, Murray. 1954. "The segmental phonemes of Sanskritized Tamil," *Language*, 30, 360–7.

Fowler, R., B. Hodge, and T. Trew. 1997. *Language and Control*. London: Routledge.

Fox, J. A. 1973. "Russenorsk: A study in language adaptivity," unpublished manuscript, University of Chicago.

Frykenberg, Robert. 1988. "The myth of English as a 'colonialist' imposition upon India: A reappraisal with special reference to south India," *Journal of the Royal Asiatic Society*, 2, 305–15.

Gaeffke, Peter. 1978. *Hindi Literature in the Twentieth Century*, in the series *A History of Indian Literature*, edited by Jan Gonda, Vol. 8, fasc. 5. Wiesbaden: Otto Harrassowitz.

Ghaffar, Muzaffar A. 1990. "Which language do we speak: Engdu, Urdeng, or Urlish?," *Midasia*, Islamabad, April 12, 11.

Gaikwad, Laxman. 1998. *The Branded*, Translated by P. A. Koharkar. New Delhi: Sahitya Akademi.

Gair, J. W. 1998. *Studies in South Asian Linguistics: Sinhala and other South Asian languages*. New York, Oxford: Oxford University Press.

Gajvi, Premanand. 2000. "Ghotbhar pani" (A Sip of Water), in *Playwright at the Center: Marathi Drama from 1843 to the Present*, edited by Shanta Gokhale. Calcutta, India: Seagull, pp. 458–69.

Gambhir, S. K. 1981. "The East Indian speech community in Guyana: A sociolinguistic study with special reference to Koine-formation," unpublished PhD dissertation, University of Pennsylvania.

Gambhir, S. K. 1987. "Structural development of Guyanese Bhojpuri," in *Language Transplanted: The Development of Overseas Hindi*, edited by R. K. Barz and J. Siegel. Wiesbaden: Otto Harrassowitz, pp. 69–94.

Gambhir, V. 1981. "Syntactic restrictions and discourse functions of word order in standard Hindi," unpublished PhD. dissertation, University of Pennsylvania.

Gargesh, Ravinder. 1998. "Some reflections on the impact of Persian on word formation of Hindi–Urdu," in *Indo-Persian Cultural Perspectives*, edited by Mohammad A. Khan, Ravinder Gargesh, and Chander Shekhar. New Delhi: Saud Ahmad Dehlavi, pp. 79–90.

Gaustan, E. S. and P. L. Barlow. 2000. *New Historical Atlas of Religion in America*. New York: Oxford University Press.

Gautam, M. K. 1999. "The construction of the Indian image in Suriname: Deconstructing colonial derogatory notions and reconstructing Indian identity," in *Sojourners to Settlers: Indian Migrants in the Caribbean and the Americas*, edited by M. Gosine and D. Narine. New York: Windsor Press, pp. 125–79.

Gee, J. P. 1986. "Orality and literacy: From *The Savage Mind* to *Ways with Words*," *Teachers of English to Speakers of Other Languages, Quarterly*, 20, 719–46.

Geertz, C. 1995. *After the Fact: Two Countries. Four Decades. One Anthropologist*. Cambridge, MA: Harvard University Press.

Geocities. 2002. "Should Urdu continue as our national language?," www.geocities.com/paklanguage, Accessed July 2005.

Gerow, Edwin. 1971. *A Glossary of Indian Figures of Speech*. The Hague and Paris: Mouton.

Gerow, Edwin. 1977. *Indian Poetics*, A History of Indian Literature, Vol. V. Wiesbaden: Otto Harrassowitz.

Ghosh, Arunabha. 1998. *Jharkhand Movement: A Study in the Politics of Regionalism*. Calcutta, India: Minerva Associates.

Gibson, M. A. 1988. *Accomodation without Assimilation: Sikh Immigrants in an American High School*. Ithaca, NY: Cornell University Press.

Gluck, Sherna Berger and Daphne Patai. 1991. *Women's Words. The Feminist Practice of Oral History*. New York: Routledge.

Goffin, Raymond C. 1934. *Some Notes on Indian English*, S. P. E. Tract No. 41. Oxford: Clarendon Press, pp. 20–32.

Goffman, Erving. 1967. *Interaction Ritual: Essays on Face-to-Face Behavior*. Garden City, NY: Anchor Books, Doubleday.

Gokhale–Turner, Jayashree. 1980. "Bhakti or vidroha: Continuity and change in Dalit Literature," *Journal of Asian and African Studies*, 15(1–2), 29–40.

Goody, Esther N. (ed.) 1978. *Questions and Politeness*. Cambridge: Cambridge University Press.

Goody, Jack (ed.) 1968. *Literacy in Traditional Societies*. Cambridge: Cambridge University Press.

Goody, Jack. 1987. *The Interface between the Written and the Oral*. Cambridge: Cambridge University Press.

Gopal, Ram. 1966. *Linguistic Affairs of India*. London: Asia Publishing House.

Gopal, Sarvepalli (ed.) 1980. *Jawahar Lal Nehru: An Anthology*. New Delhi: Oxford University Press.

Gordon, Raymond G., Jr. (ed.) 2005. *Ethnologue: Languages of the World*. Fifteenth edition. Dallas, Tex.: SIL International. Online version: http://www.ethnologue.com/ (accessed 25/2/2007)

Goswami, Upendranath. 1978. *An Introduction to Assamese*. Guwahati, India: Mani-Manik Prakash.

Government of India. 1964. *Census of India*. New Delhi: Ministry of Home Affairs.

Government of India. 1978. *Background Papers on Tribal Development, Scheduled Tribes and Scheduled Areas in India*. New Delhi: Ministry of Home Affairs.

Government of India. 1991. *The Constitution of India* (3rd edn). New Delhi: Rajbhasha Khand.

Government of India. 1997. *Census of India*. New Delhi: Ministry of Home Affairs.

Grant, Charles. 1831–1832. "Observations on the state of society among the Asiatic subjects of Great Britain, particularly with respect to morals, and the means of improving it," in *General Appendix to Parliamentary Papers 1831–1832*, London.

Gray, John. 1992. *Men are from Mars, Women are from Venus*. New York: HarperCollins.

Greenberg, Joseph H. 1966. "Some universals of grammar with particular reference to the order of meaningful elements," in *Universals of Language* (2nd edn), edited by Joseph, H. Greenberg. Cambridge, MA: Massachussetts Institute of Technology Press, pp. 73–113.

Gregory, R. G. 1971. *India and East Africa – A History of Race Relations within the British Empire*. Oxford: Clarendon.

Grierson, George A. 1883–1887. *Seven Grammars of the Dialects and Sub-dialects of the Bihari Language*. Calcutta, India: Bengal Secretariat Press.

Grierson, George A. 1903–1928. *Linguistic Survey of India*. Calcutta, India: Government of India [Reprinted in 1967, New Delhi: Motilal Banarsidass (11 vols. 19 parts)].

Grierson, George A. 1967–1968. *Linguistic Survey of India* (11 vols). New Delhi: Motilal Banarsidass [Reprint of 1st edn, 1903–1928.]

Griffin, Michael K. Viswanath, and Dona Schwartz. 1994. "Gender advertising in the US and India: Exporting cultural stereotypes," *Media, Culture and Society*, 16, 487–507.

Grimes, Barbara F. (ed.) 1992. *Ethnologue: Languages of the World*. Dallas, TX: Summer Institute of Linguistics.

Gumperz, John J. 1961. "Speech variation and the study of Indian civilization," *American Anthropologist*, 63, 976–88.

Gumperz, John J. 1968. "The speech community," in *International Encyclopedia of the Social Sciences. Vol. 9*. London: Macmillan, pp. 381–86.

Gumperz, John J. and Robert Wilson. 1971. "Convergence and creolization: A case from the Indo-Aryan/Dravidian border in India," in *Pidginization and Creolization of Languages*, edited by Dell H. Hymes. London: Cambridge University Press, pp. 151–67.

Gupta, Dipankar (ed.) 1991. *Social Stratification*. New Delhi: Oxford University Press.

Guru, Kamata Prasad. 1920. *Hindi Vyakaran*. Banaras, India: Kashi Nagri Pracharini Sabha.

Gurung, Haraka. 1997. "Linguistic demography of Nepal," *Contributions to Nepalese Studies*, 24(2), 147–85.

Haas, Mary R. 1944. "Men's and women's speech in Koasati," *Language*, 20, 142–49. [Reprinted in 1964, in *Language in Culture and Society*, edited by Dell Hymes. New York: Harper and Row, pp. 228–33].

Haddad, Yvonne Yazebeck. 2000. "At home in the Hijra: South Asian Muslims in the United States," in *The South Asian Religious Diaspora in Britain, Canada, and the United States*, edited by H. Coward. Albany, NY: State University of New York Press, pp. 239–58.

Hale, Austin. 1982. *Research on Tibeto-Burman Languages*. Berlin: Mouton.

Hali, K. A. H. 1971. *Yadgaar-e-Ghalib* (Memoirs Pertaining to Ghalib). New Delhi: Maktabe Jamia and the Government of Jammu and Kashmir.

Hall, Kira and Veronica O'Donovan. 1996. "Shifting gender positions among Hindi speaking Hijras," in *Rethinking Language and Gender Research*, edited by Victoria L. Bergvall, M. Bing, and Alice F. Freed. New York: Longman, pp. 228–66.

Hall, Robert A. Jr. 1966. *Pidgin and Creole Languages*. Ithaca, NY: Cornell University Press.

Halliday, Michael A. K. 1970. "Language structure and language function," in *New Horizons in Linguistics*, edited by John Lyons. Harmondsworth, Middlesex: Penguin, pp. 140–65.

Halliday, Michael A. K. 1993. "The act of meaning," in *Language, Communication, and Social Meaning*, Georgetown University Roundtable on Languages and Linguistics 1992, edited by James E. Alatis. Washington, DC: Georgetown University Press, pp. 7–21.

Halliday, Michael A. K. and Ruqaiya Hasan. 1976. *Cohesion in English*. London: Longman.

Halverson, John. 1966. "Prolegomena to the study of Ceylon English," *University of Ceylon Review*, 24(1/2) 61–75.

Haque, Anjum Riyazul. 1993. "The position and status of English in Pakistan. The Urduization of English in Pakistan," in *The English Language in Pakistan*, edited by Robert J. Baumgardner Karachi, Pakistan: Oxford University Press, pp. 19–30.

Hardikar, Vinay. 1985. "Profiles in social transformation: Five Dalit autobiographies," *New Quest*, 49, 52–8.

Hardiman, D. 1987. *The Coming of the Devi: Adivasi Assertion in Western India*. New Delhi: Oxford University Press.

Hart, George L. 1976. *The Relation between Tamil and Classical Sanskrit Literature*, In the series *A History of Indian Literature*, edited by Jan Gonda, Vol. 10, fasc. 2. Wiesbaden: Otto Harrassowitz.

Harvey, David. 1990. *The Condition of Postmodernity*. Oxford: Blackwell.

Hasan, Ruqaiya. forthcoming. "Some clause types in Urdu: a tentative analysis," in *Describing Language: Form and Function: The Collected Works of Ruqaiya Hasan*, Vol. 5, edited by Jonathan Webster. London: Equinox Publishing.

Havanur, Srinivasa. 1989. *HosagannaDa AruNōdaya* (Dawn of Modern Kannada). Mysore, India: Institute for Kannada Studies.

Havelock, Eric Alfred. 1963. *Preface to Plato*. Cambridge, MA: Cambridge University Press.

Hawkins, R. E. 1976. "Supplement of words from India, Pakistan, Bangladesh and Sir Lanka," in *The Little Oxford Dictionary of Current English*, compiled by G. Ostler. New Delhi: Oxford University Press.

Hawkins, R. E. 1984. *Common Indian Words in English*. New Delhi: Oxford University Press.

Hazra, Kanai Lal. 1994. *Pāli Language and Literature: A Systematic Survey and Historical Study*, Emerging Perceptions in Buddhist Studies, Vols. 4–5. New Delhi: D. K. Printworld.

Hegde, R. S. 1991. "Adaptation and the interpersonal experience: A study of Asian Indians in the US," unpublished PhD dissertation, Columbus: Ohio State University.

Heimann, Betty. 1964. *Facets of Indian Thought*. London: George Allen and Unwin.

Helweg, Arthur W. and Helweg, Usha M. 1990. *An Immigrant Success Story*. Philadelphia, PA: University of Pennsylvania Press.

Hettiaratchi, D. F. 1969. "Linguistics in Ceylon, I," in *Current Trends in Linguistics. Vol. 5. Linguistics in South Asia*, edited by, Thomas A. Sebeok. The Hague: Mouton, pp. 736–51.

Hickey, Ramond. 2004. "South Asian Englishes," in *Legacies of Colonial English Studies in Transported Dialects*, edited by Ramond Hickey Cambridge: Cambridge University Press, pp. 536–58.

Hill, B., Sachiko Ide, S. Ikuta, A. Kawasaki, and T. Ogino. 1986. "Universals in linguistic politeness: Quantitative evidence from Japanese and American English," *Journal of Pragmatics*, 10, 347–71.

Hobbs, S. 1985. *Fiji Hindi – English, English – Fiji Hindi Dictionary*. Suva: Ministry of Education.

Hock, Hans Henrich. 1975. "Substratum influence on (Rig-Vedic) Sanskrit?," *Studies in the Linguistic Sciences*, 5(2), 76–125.

Hock, Hans Henrich. 1976. "Review article on R. Anttila: An introduction to historical comparative linguistics," *Language*, 52, 202–20.

Hock, Hans Henrich. 1991. *Principles of Historical Linguistics*. Berlin: Mouton de Gruyter.

Hock, Hans Henrich and Rajeshwari Pandharipande. 1976. "The sociolinguistic position of Sanskrit in pre-Muslim India," *Studies in Language Learning*, 11, 105–38.

Hock, Hans Henrich and Rajeshwari Pandharipande. 1978. "Sanskrit in pre-Islamic context of South Asia," Special issue of *International Journal of the Study of Language*, 16, 11–25.

Hodge, Robert and Gunther Kress. 1988. *Social Semiotic*. Cambridge: Polity Press.

Holle, K. F. 1877. *Tabel van oud- en nieuw-Indische Alphabetten*. Buttenzorg, Java, Dutch East Indies: C. Lang [Reprinted in 1999 as *Table of Old and New Indic Alphabets: Contribution to the Paleography of the Dutch Indies*. Translated by Carol Molony and Henk Pechler. *Written Lanuage and Literacy*, 2, 167–245].

Holm, John. 1989. *Pidgins and Creoles*, Vol. 2: *Reference Survey*. Cambridge: Cambridge University Press.

Hooper, John S. M. 1963. *Bible Translation in India, Pakistan, and Ceylon* (2nd edn). Bombay, India: Oxford University Press.

Hosali, Priya. 2000. *Butler English, Form and Function*. New Delhi: B. R Publishing.

Hosali, Priya and Jean Aitchison. 1986. "Butler English: A minimal pidgin?," *Journal of Pidgin and Creole Linguistics*, 1, 51–79.

Hossain, M. 1982. "South Asians in Southern California," *South Asia Bulletin*, 2(1), 74–82.

Hovell, Laurie. 1991. "Namdeo Dhasal: Poet panther," *Bulletin of Concerned Asian Scholars*, 23(2), 77–83.

Huebner, Thom (ed.) 1996. *Sociolinguistic Perspectives: Papers on Language in Society, 1959–1994*/Charles A. Ferguson. Oxford: Oxford University Press.

Hussainmiya, B. A. 1987. *Lost Cousins: The Malays of Sri Lanka*. Bangi, Malaysia: Institut Bahasa, Kesusasteraan dan Kebudayaan Melayu, Universiti Kebangsaan Malaysia.

Hunt, Cecil. 1931a. *Honoured Sir from Babujee*. London: P. Allen.

Hunt, Cecil. 1931b. *Babuji Writes Home: Being a New Edition of 'Honoured Sir' with Many Additional Letters*. London: P. Allen.

Hutton, J. H. 1921. *The Angami Nagas, with Some Notes on Neighbouring Tribes*. London: Macmillan.

Hwang, Juck–Ryoon. 1990. "'Deference' versus 'politeness' in Korean speech," *International Journal of the Sociology of Language*, 82, 41–55.

Ide, Sachiko. 1989. "Formal forms and discernment: Neglected aspects of linguistic politeness," *Multilingua*, 8(2), 223–48.

Imayam. 2001. *Beasts of Burden.* Translated by Lakshmi Holmstrom. Chennai, India: Manas (East West Books Madras).

Internet Indian History Sourcebook: The Laws of Manu, c. 1500 BCE. Translated by G. Buhler. www.fordham.edu/halsall/india/indiasbook.html, accessed August 2005.

Indian Literature 159. 1994. XXXVII(1).

Indian Literature 193. 1999. XLIII(5).

Indian Literature 200. 2000. XLIV(6).

Indian Literature 201. 2001. XLV(1).

Internet Public Library. www.ipl.org, accessed June 2001.

Ishtiaq, M. 1999. *Language Shifts among the Scheduled Tribes in India: A Geographic Study.* New Delhi: Motilal Banarsidass.

Itagi, N. H., B. D. Jayaram, and V. Vani. 1986. *Communication Potential in the Tribal Population of Assam and Madhya Pradesh.* Mysore, India: CIIL.

Itkonen, Esa. 1991. *Universal History of Linguistics: India, China, Arabia, Europe,* Amsterdam Studies in the Theory and History of Linguistic Science, Series 3, Vol. 65. Amsterdam and Philadelphia, PA: John Benjamins.

Iyengar, K. R. Srinivasa (ed.) 1983. *Asian Variations in Ramayana.* New Delhi: Sahitya Akademi.

Jadhav, Narendra. 2003. *Outcaste: A Memoir.* New Delhi: Viking Penguin.

Jaeggli, Osvaldo and Kenneth Safir. 1989. *The Null Subject Parameter.* Studies in Natural Language and Linguistic Theory. Dordrecht, Boston, MA, and London: Kluwer.

Jain, Dhanesh. 1973. "Pronominal usage in Hindi: A sociolinguistics study," unpublished PhD dissertation, University of Pennsylvania.

Jain, S. 1989. *Jaina Philosophy of Language.* New Delhi: Ahimsa International.

Jaina, Devendra Kumāra [Jain, Devendra Kumar]. 1965. Apabhraṁśa bhāṣā aura sāhitya *[Apabhramśa language and literature],* Jñāna-pīiḥa Lokodaya Grantha-mālā 152. Calcutta, Varanasi, and New Delhi: Bhāratīya Jñāna-pīṭha Hindi.

Jaina, Jagadīśa Candra [Jain, Jagdishchandra]. 1961. *Prākṛta sāhitya kā itihāsa* [History of Prakrit literature], Varanasi, India: Chowkhamba Vidya Bhawan.

Jaini, P. S. 1979. *The Jaina Path of Purification.* Berkeley, CA: University of California Press.

Jalibi, Jameel. 1984. *Tarikh-e-Adab-e-Urdu,* Vol. 1, History of Urdu literature. New Delhi: Educational Publishing Home.

James, Deborah and Sandra Clarke. 1993. "Women, men, and interruptions: A critical review," in *Gender and Conversational Interaction,* edited by Deborah Tannen. New York: Oxford University Press, pp. 231–80.

James, Deborah and Janice Drakich. 1993. "Understanding gender differences in amount of talk: A critical review of research," in *Gender and Conversational Interaction,* edited by Deborah Tannen. New York: Oxford University Press, pp. 281–312.

Jensen, Hans. 1969. *Sign, Symbol and Script: An Account of Man's Efforts to Write.* New York: Putnam's.

Jespersen, Otto. 1922. *Language. Its Nature, Development and Origin.* London: Allen and Unwin.

Jinnah, Mohammad A. 1948. Speech at a public meeting at Dacca, March 21, in *Quaid-I-Azam Mohammad Ali Jinnah: Speeches and Statements 1947–8.*

Islamabad: Government of Pakistan, Ministry of Information and Broadcasting.

Joshi, S. D. and S. D. Laddu. 1983. *Proceedings of the International Seminar on Studies in the Aṣṭādhyāyī of Pāṇini*. Pune, India: University of Poona.

Joshi, Svati. 1990. "Forging an epistemology of resistance: Dalit writing in Gujarati (A review of the anthology *Sarvanam* 1889)," *The Book Review*, 143, 32–3.

Kachru, Braj, B. 1965. "The 'Indianess' in Indian English," *Word*, 21, 391–410.

Kachru, Braj B. 1976. "The Englishization of Hindi: Linguistic rivalry and language change," in *Linguistic Method: Essays in Honor of Herbert Penzl*, edited by Irmengard Rauch and G. F. Carr. The Hague: Mouton, pp. 199–221.

Kachru, Braj B. 1977. "Linguistic schizophrenia and language census," *Linguistics*, 186, 17–32.

Kachru, Braj B. 1978a. "Code-mixing as a communicative strategy in India," in *International Dimensions of Bilingual Education*, edited by James E. Alatis. Washington, DC: Georgetown University Press, pp. 107–24.

Kachru, Braj B. 1978b. "English in South Asia," in Advances in *the Study of Societal Multilingualism*, edited by J. A. Fishman. The Hague: Mouton, pp. 477–551.

Kachru, Braj B. 1978c. "Toward structuring the form and function of code-mixing: An Indian perspective," *International Journal of the Sociology of Language*, 16, 21–40.

Kachru, Braj B. 1980. "The new Englishes and old dictionaries: Directions in lexicographical research on non-native varieties of English," in *Theory and Method in Lexicography: Western and Non-Western Perspectives*, edited by Ladislav Zgusta. Columbia, SC: Hornbeam Press, pp. 71–101.

Kachru, Braj B. 1981. *Kashmiri Literature*, In the series *History of Indian Literature*, edited by Jan Gonda, Vol. 8, fasc. 4. Wiesbaden: Otto Harrassowitz.

Kachru, Braj B. 1982a. "The bilingual's linguistic repertoire," in *Issues in International Bilingual Education: The Role of the Vernacular*, edited by Beverly S. Hartford, Albert Valdman, and Charles R. Foster. New York: Plenum, pp. 25–52.

Kachru, Braj B. 1982b. "Language policy in South Asia," *Annual Review of Applied Linguistics 1981*, 2, 60–58.

Kachru, Braj B. (ed.) 1982c. *The Other Tongue: English across Cultures*. New York: Pergamon Press.

Kachru, Braj B. 1983a. *The Alchemy of English: The Spread, Functions and Models of Non-native Englishes*. Oxford: Pergamon Press.

Kachru, Braj B. 1983b. "The bilingual's creativity: Discoursal and stylistic strategies in contact literatures in English," *Studies in the Linguistic Sciences*, 13 (2) 37–55. [Also in *The Alchemy of English: The Spread, Functions, and Models of Non-native Englishes, 1986*. Oxford: Pergamon Press, pp. 159–73]

Kachru, Braj B. 1983c. *The Indianization of English: The English Language in India*. New Delhi: Oxford University Press.

Kachru, Braj B. 1990. *The Alchemy of Engish: The Spread, Functions and Models of Non-native Englishes*. Urbana: University of Illinois Press.

Kachru, Braj B. 1992a. "Cultural contact and literary creativity in a multilingual setting," in *Dimensions of Sociolinguistics in South Asia*, edited by Edward C. Dimock, Braj B. Kachru, and Bhadriraju Krishnamurti. New Delhi: Oxford and India Book House, pp. 149–59.

Kachru, Braj B. 1992b. "South Asian broadcasting," in *The Oxford Companion to the English Language*, edited by Tom McArthur. Oxford: Oxford University Press, p. 958.

Kachru, Braj B. (ed.) 1992c. *The Other Tongue: English across Cultures* (2nd edn). Urbana, IL: University of Illinois Press.

Kachru, Braj B. 1994. "English in South Asia," in *The Cambridge History of the English Language, Vol. 5*, edited by Robert Burchfield. Cambridge: Cambridge University Press, pp. 497–553.

Kachru, Braj B. 1997a. "Language in Indian society," in *Ananya: A Portrait of India*, edited by S. N. Sridhar and N. K. Mattoo. New York: The Association of Indians in America, pp. 555–85.

Kachru, Braj B. 1997b. "World Englishes 2000: Resources for research and teaching," in *World Englishes 2000*, edited by M. Forman and Larry E. Smith. Honolulu, HI: University of Hawaii Press, pp. 48–67.

Kachru, Braj B. 2003. "On nativizing mantra: Identity construction in anglophone Englishes," in *Anglophone Cultures in Southeast Asia: Appropriations, Continuities, Contexts*, edited by Klaus Stierstorfer et al. Heidelberg, Germany: Heidelberg University Press, pp. 55–72.

Kachru, Braj B. 2005. *Asian Englishes: Beyond the Canon*. Hong Kong: Hong Kong University Press. [South Asian Edition: New Delhi: Oxford University Press, 2005.]

Kachru, Braj B., Yamuna Kachru, and Cecil L. Nelson (eds.) 2006. *The Handbook of World Englishes*. Oxford: Blackwell Publishing.

Kachru, Braj B. and Cecil L. Nelson. 1996. "World Englishes," in *Sociolinguistics and Language Teaching*, edited by S. L. Mckay and N. H. Hornberger. Cambridge: Cambridge University Press, pp. 71–102.

Kachru, Yamuna. 1966. *An Introduction to Hindi Syntax*. Urbana, IL: Department of Linguistics, University of Illinois.

Kachru, Yamuna. 1970. "The syntax of *ko*-sentences in Hindi–Urdu," *Papers in Linguistics*, 2(2), 299–316.

Kachru, Yamuna. 1979. "The quotative in South Asian languages," *South Asian Languages Analysis*, 63–77.

Kachru, Yamuna. 1980. *Aspects of Hindi Grammar*. New Delhi: Manohar Publications.

Kachru, Yamuna. 1981a. "On the syntax, semantics and pragmatics of the conjunctive participle in Hindi–Urdu," *Studies in the Linguistic Sciences*, 11(2), 35–50.

Kachru, Yamuna. (ed.) 1981b. *Dimensions of South Asian linguistics*, special issue of *Studies in the Linguistic Sciences*, 11(2).

Kachru, Yamuna. 1988. "Writers in Hindi and English," in *Writing across Languages and Cultures: Issues in Contrastive Rhetoric*, edited by Alan Purves. Newbury Park, CA: Sage, pp. 109–37.

Kachru, Yamuna. 1989. "Corpus planning for modernization: Sanskritization and Englishization of Hindi," *Studies in the Linguistic Sciences*, 19(1), 153–64.

Kachru, Yamuna. 1990. "Experiencer and other oblique subjects in Hindi," in *Experiencer Subjects in South Asian Languages*, edited by Manindra K. Verma and K. P. Mohanan. Stanford, CA: Stanford University, The Center for the Study of Language and Information, pp. 59–75.

Kachru, Yamuna. 1992. "Culture, style and discourse: Expanding poetics of English," in *The Other Tongue: English across Cultures* (2nd edn). edited by Braj B. Kachru. Urbana, IL: University of Illinois Press, pp. 340–52.

Kachru, Yamuna. 1993. "Social meaning and creativity in India English speech acts," in *Language, Communication and Social Meaning*, edited by James E. Alatis. Georgetown University Monograph Series on Languages and Linguistics 1992. Washington, DC: Georgetown University Press, pp. 378–87.

Kachru, Yamuna. 1994. "Self, identity, and creativity: Women writers in India," in *Self as Person in Asian Theory and Practice*, edited by Roger T. Ames, Wimal Dissanayake, and Thomas P. Kasulis. Albany, NY: State University of New York Press, pp. 335–56.

Kachru, Yamuna. 1995a. "Cultural meaning and rhetorical styles: Toward a framework for contrastive rhetoric," in *Principles and Practice in Applied Linguistics: Studies in Honor of Henry G. Widdowson*, edited by Barbara Seidlhofer and Guy Cook. London: Oxford University Press, pp. 171–84.

Kachru, Yamuna. 1995b. "Lexical exponents of cultural contact: Speech act verbs in Hindi–English dictionaries," in *Cultures, Ideologies, and the Dictionary: Studies in Honor of Ladislav Zgusta*, edited by Braj B. Kachru and Henry Kahane. Tübingen: Max Niemeyer Verlag, pp. 261–74.

Kachru, Yamuna. 1996. "Language and cultural meaning: Expository writing in South Asian English," in *South Asian English: Structure, Use and Users*, Edited by Robert J. Baumgardner. Urbana: University of Illinois Press, pp. 127–40.

Kachru, Yamuna. 1997. "Culture and argumentative writing in world Englishes," in *World Englishes 2000*, edited by Michael Forman and Larry E. Smith. Honolulu, HI: University of Hawaii Press, pp. 48–67.

Kachru, Yamuna. 1998. "Culture and speech acts: Evidence from Indian and Singaporean English," *Studies in the Linguistic Sciences*, 28, 79–98.

Kachru, Yamuna. 2001. "World Englishes and rhetoric across cultures," *Asian Englishes*, 4(2), 54–71.

Kachru, Yamuna. 2003. "Conventions of politeness in plural societies," in *Anglophone Cultures in South-East Asia: Appropriations, Continuities, Contexts*, edited by Rüdiger Ahrens, David Parker, Klaus Stierstorfer, and Kowk-Kan Tam. Heidelberg: Universitätsverlag Winter Heidelberg, pp. 39–53.

Kachru, Yamuna. 2006. *Hindi*. London Oriental and African Language Library. Amsterdam: John Benjamins.

Kachru, Yamuna and Tej K. Bhatia. 1977. "On reflexivization in Hindi–Urdu and its theoretical implications," *Indian Linguistics*, 38(1), 21–38.

Kachru, Yamuna and Tej K. Bhatia. 1978. "The emerging 'dialect' conflict in Hindi: A case of glottopolitics," *International Journal of the Sociology of Language*, 16, 47–56.

Kachru, Yamuna and Cecil L. Nelson. 2006. *World Englishes in Asian Contexts*. Hong Kong: Hong Kong University Press.

Kak, Aadil A. 2001. "Language maintenance and language shift in Srinagar," unpublished PhD dissertation, New Delhi: University of Delhi.

Kakar, Sudhir. 1979. *Indian Childhood: Cultural Ideals and Social Reality*. New Delhi: Oxford University Press.

Kakar, Sudhir. 1981. *The Inner World: A Psycho-analytic Study of Childhood and Society in India*. New Delhi and New York: Oxford University Press. [2nd revised and enlarged edition; 1st published in 1978.]

Kale, Kishore Shantabai. 2000. *Against All Odds* (*Kolhatyache por* "the child of a Kolhati"). Translated by Sandhya Pandey. New Delhi: Penguin.

Kandiah, Thiru. 1964. "The teaching of English as a second language in Ceylon," *Journal of the National Education Society of Ceylon*, 5(4) November, 8–12.

Kandiah, Thiru. 1984. "'Kaduva': Power and the English language weapon in Sri Lanka," in *Honouring E. F. C. Ludowyk: Felicitation Essays*, edited by Percy Colin-Thomé and Ashley Halpi. Dehiwala, Sri Lanka: Tisara Prakasakayo, pp. 117–54.

Kandiah, Thiru. 1991. "South Asia," in *English Around the World: Sociolinguistic Perspectives*, edited by Jenny Cheshire. Cambridge: Cambridge University Press, pp. 271–87.

Kandiah, Thiru. 1995. "Foreword: Centering the periphery of English: Towards participatory communities of discourse," in *De-hegemonizing Language Standards*, edited by Arjun Parakrama. London: Macmillan, pp. xv–xxxvii.

Kandiah, Thiru. 1996. "Syntactic 'deletion' in Lankan English: Learning from a new variety of English about – ," in *South Asian English: Structure, Use and Users*, edited by Robert J. Baumgardner. Urbana and Chicago, IL: University of Illinois Press, pp. 104–23.

Katre, Sumitra. Mangesh. 1957. "The language project at the Deccan College," *Indian Linguistics*, 18, 197–224.

Kedilaya, A. Shanker. 1970. *Foreign Loan Words in Kannada: Arabic and Persian*. University of Madras Kannada series, no. 17. Madras: University of Madras.

Keenan, Elinor. 1974. "Norm-makers, norm-breakers: Uses of speech by men and women in a Malagasy community," in *Explorations in the Ethnography of Speaking*, edited by J. F. Sherzer and R. Baumann. New York: Cambridge University Press, pp. 125–43.

Kejariwal, O. P. 2002. *Ghalib in Translation*. New Delhi: UBSPD.

Kelkar, Ashok R. 1969. "General linguistics in South Asia," in *Current Trends in Linguistics. Vol. 5 Linguistics in South Asia*, edited by Thomas A. Sebeok. The Hague: Mouton, pp. 532–42.

Kellogg, Samuel Henry. 1875. *A Grammar of the Hindi Language*. London: Routledge and Kegan Paul.

Kemper, Steven. 2001. *Buying and Believing: Sri Lankan Advertising and Consumers in a Transnational World*. Chicago, IL: University of Chicago.

Kerswill, Paul. 2004. "Coineization and accommodation," in *The Handbook of Language Variation and Change*, edited by Jack Chambers, Peter Trudgill, and Natalie Schilling-Estes. Oxford: Blackwell, p. 12.

Keshari, Biseshwar P. 1982. "Problems and prospects of Jharkhandi languages," in *Fourth World Dynamics: Jharkhand*, edited by Nirmal Sengupta. New Delhi: Authors Guild, pp. 137–64.

Kevichusa, M. 1996. "Relative clause formation in Tenyidie (Angami)," unpublished MPhil dissertation, New Delhi: University of Delhi.

Khan, Farhat. 1991. "Final consonant cluster simplification in a variety of Indian English," in *English Around the World: Sociolinguistic Perspectives*, edited by Jenny Cheshire. New York: Cambridge University Press, pp. 288–307.

Khubchandani, Lachman M. 1978. "Distribution of contact language in India. A study of the 1961 bilingual returns," in *Advances in the Study of Societal Multilingualism*, edited by Joshua Fishman. The Hague: Mouton, pp. 553–85.

Khubchandani, Lachman M. 1983. *Plural Languages, Plural Cultures*. Honolulu, HI: East West Center, University of Hawaii Press.

Khubchandani, Lachman M. 1992. *Tribal Identity. A Language and Communication Perspective*. Simla, India: Indian Institute of Advanced Study.

Khubchandani, Lachman M. 1997a. "Demographic indicators of language persistence and shift among tribals: A sociolinguistic perspective," in *Tribal and Indigenous Languages of India: The Ethnic Space*, edited by Anvita Abbi. New Delhi: Motilal Banarsidass,.

Khubchandani, Lachman M. 1997b. *Revisualizing Boundaries: A Plurilingual Ethos*. New Delhi: Sage.

Kindersley, A. F. 1938. "Notes on the Indian idiom of English: Style, syntax, and vocabulary," *Transactions of the Philosophical Society*, 25–34.

King, Christopher R. 1994. *One Language, Two Scripts: The Hindi Movement in Nineteenth Century North India*. Bombay, India: Oxford University Press.

King, Robert D. 1986. "The language issue revisited," in *India 2000: The Next Fifteen Years*, edited by James R. Roach. Riverdale, MD: The Riverdale Company, pp. 135–43.

King, Robert D. 1997. *Nehru and the Language Politics of India*. New Delhi: Oxford University Press.

King, Robert D. 2001. "The poisonous potency of script: Hindi and Urdu," *International Journal of the Sociology of Language*, 40, 43–60.

Kiparsky, Paul. 1979. *Pāṇini as a Variationist*. Cambridge, MA: The Massachussetts Institute of Technology Press; Pune, India: University of Poona.

Kishore, Satyendra. 1987. *National Integration in India*. New Delhi: Sterling.

Kishwar, Madhu. 2000. Personal Interview. *Manushi*, October 30. New Delhi.

Klaiman, M. H. 1987. "Bengali," in *The World's Major Languages*, edited by Bernard Comrie. London: Croom Helm, pp. 490–513.

Kluyev, Boris I. 1981. *India: National and Language Problem*. New Delhi: Sterling.

Koerner, E. F. K. and R. E. Asher. 1995. *Concise History of the Language Sciences from the Sumerians to the Cognitivists*. New York, Oxford: Pergamon.

Koh, T. J. 2003. "Agreement in Ho," unpublished MA dissertation, New Delhi: University of Delhi.

Kondapi, C. 1951. *Indians Overseas, 1838–1949*. New Delhi: Indian Council of World Affairs.

Kothari, Rita. 2001. "Short story in Gujarati Dalit literature," *Economic and Political Weekly*, XXXVI(45), 4308–11.

Koul, Omkar N. 1984. "Modes of address in Kashmiri," in *Aspects of Kashmiri Linguistics*, edited by Peter Hook. New Delhi: Bahri.

Koul, Omkar N. and Madhu Bala. 1989. *Modes of Address and Pronominal Usage in Punjabi. A Sociolinguistic Study*. Mysore, India: Central Institute of Indian Languages.

Kramarae, Cheris. 1981. *Women and Men Speaking*. Rowley, MA: Newbury House.

Krishan, Shree (ed.) 1990. *Linguistic Traits across Language Boundaries*, A Report of All India Linguistic Traits Survey. Calcutta, India: Anthropological Survey of India.

Krishna, Sumi. 1991. *India's Living Languages: The Critical Issues*. New Delhi: Allied Publishers.

Krishnamurthy, K. 1997. "Sanskrit literature," in *Ananya: A Portrait of India*, edited by S. N. Sridhar and Nirmal K. Mattoo. New York: Association of Indians in America,.

Krishnamurti, Bh. 1978. "Language planning and development: The case of Telegu," *Contributions to Asian Studies*, 2, 37–56.

Krishnamurti, Bh. (ed.) 1986. *South Asian Language: Structural Convergence and Dialogue*. New Delhi: Motilal Banarasidas.

Krishnamurti, Bh. 1992. "On verbalizing politeness in Telugu," in *Dimensions of Sociolinguistics in South Asia: Papers in Memory of Gerald B. Kelley*, edited by Edward C. Dimock, Jr. Braj B. Kachru and Bh. Krishnamurti. New Delhi: Oxford & IBH; 1992, pp. 87–99.

Krishnamurti, Bh. 1993. "Dravidian languages," in *The International Encyclopaedia of Linguistics*, edited by William Bright. Oxford: Oxford University Press, pp. 373–76.

Krishnamurti, Bh. 1995. "Official language policies with special reference to the Eighth Schedule of the Constitution of India," in *Language and the State*, edited by Gupta, R. S., Anvita Abbi, and Kailash N. Aggarwal. New Delhi: Creative Books, pp. 8–23.

Krishnamurti, Bh. 2003. *The Dravidian Languages*. Cambridge: Cambridge University Press.

Krishnaswamy, N. and Archana S. Brude. 1998. *The Politics of Indians' English: Linguistic Colonialism and the Expanding English Empire*. New Delhi: Oxford University Press.

Krishnamurti, Bh. and J. P L. Gwynn. 1985. *A Grammar of Modern Telugu*. New Delhi: Oxford University Press.

Krishnamurti, Bh. and Aditi Mukherji (eds.) 1984. *Modernization of Indian Languages in the News Media*. Hyderabad, India: Department of Linguistics, Osmania University.

Kuiper, F. B. J. 1967. "The genesis of a linguistic area," *Indo-Iranian Journal*, 10, 81–102.

Kulke, Hermann and Dietmar Rothermund. 1991. *A History of India*. Calcutta, India: Rupa.

Kulli, Jayavant S. 1991. *History of Grammatical Theories in Kannada*. Trivandrum, India: International School of Dravidian Linguistics.

Kumar, Braj Bihari. 1978. *Nagami vyakaran ki ruparekha*. Kohima, India: Nagaland Bhasha Parishad.

Kumar, N. (ed.) 1994. *Women as Subjects: South Asian Histories*. New Delhi: Stree.

Kumar, Raj. 1995. "Oriya Dalit literature: A historical perspective," *The Fourth World*, 2, 91–111.

Kunjunni Raja K. 1972. "The influence of Sanskrit on the Dravidian literatures with special reference to Malayalam," in *Indian Literature*, edited by Arabinda Poddar. Simla, India: Indian Institute of Advanced Study.

Labov, William. 1972. *Sociolinguistic Patterns*. Philadelphia, PA: Pennsylvania University Press.

Labov, William. 1982. "Objectivity and commitment in linguistic science: The case of Black English trial in Ann Arbor," *Language in Society*, 11, 165–201.

Labru, G. L. 1984. *Indian Newspaper English*. New Delhi: B. R Publishing.

Lakoff, Robin. 1975. *Language and Woman's Place*. New York: Harper and Row.

Lakshmi Narasaiah, G. 1999. *The Essence of Dalit Poetry: A Socio-Philosophic Study of Telugu Dalit Poetry*. Hyderabad, India: Dalit Sana Publications.

Lal, B. 1979. "Girmityas: The background to banishment," in *Rama's Banishment: A Centenary Tribute to the Fiji Indians, 1879–1979*, edited by V. Misra. London: Heineman Educational, pp. 12–39.

Lal, Chaman. 1998. "Dalit trend in Punjabi literature," *Indian Literature* 185, XLII(3), 13–7.

Lalitha Murthy, B. 1994. "Participial constructions: A cross-linguistic study," unpublished PhD dissertation, New Delhi: University of Delhi.

Lalitha Murthy, B. and Karumuri V. Subbarao. 2000. "Lexical anaphors and pronouns in Mizo," in *Lexical Anaphors and Pronouns in Selected South Asian Languages*, edited by Barbara Lust, James Gair, Kashi Wali, and Karumuri V. Subbarao. Berlin: Mouton de Gruyter, pp. 777–840.

Lankshear, Colin. 1987. *Literacy, Schooling and Revolution*. London: Falmer Press.

Law, Bimala Churn. 1933. *History of Pāli Literature*. London: K. Paul, Trench, Trubner & Co. [Reprinted in 1983: New Delhi: Indological Book House].

Law, Narendra Nath. 1915. *Promotion of Learning in India by Early European Settlers*. London: Longman.

Lee, Motoko. 1976. "The married women's status and role as reflected in Japanese," *Signs*, 1, 991–9.

Lele, Jayant and Rajendra Singh. 1987. "Language and literature of Dalits and Sants: Some missed opportunities," in *Literature, Social Consciousness and Polity*, edited by Iqbal Narain and Lothar Lutze. New Delhi: Manohar, pp. 28–60.

Leonard, Karen I. 1997. *The South Asian Americans*. Westport, CT: Greenwood Press.

Lewis, Ivor. 1991. *Sahibs, Nawabs and Boxwallahs: A Dictionary of the Words of Anglo-India*. Bombay, India: Oxford University Press.

Lingat, Robert. 1998. *The Classical Law of India*. New Delhi: Oxford University Press.

Limbale, Sharankumar. 2003a. *Towards an Aesthetic of Dalit Literature: History, Controversies and Considerations*. Translated by Alok Mukherjee. Hyderabad, India: Orient Longman.

Limbale, Sharankumar. 2003b. *The Outcaste: Akkarmashi*. Translated from Marathi by Santosh Bhoomkar. New Delhi: Oxford University Press.

Lokpriy. 2005. Demographic Profile Scheduled Tribes in India, 1981–2001. Seminar Paper submitted for Diploma in Population Studies, International Institute for Population Sciences, Deonar, Mumbai.://www.iipsindia.org/sp05%5Clokpriy.pdf (Accessed August 21, 2005)

Luke, A. 1998. "Ideology," in *Concise Encyclopedia of Pragmatics*, edited by J. L May. Pergamon, pp. 366–68.

Lust, Barbara, James Gair, Kashi Wali, and Karumuri V. Subbarao (eds.) 2000. *Lexical Anaphors and Pronouns in Selected South Asian Languages*. Berlin: Mouton de Gruyter.

Macmillan, Michael. 1895. "Anglo-Indian words and phrases." *The Globe Trotter in India Two Hundred Years Ago and Other Indian Studies*. London: Sonnenschein, pp. 77–114.

Macwan, Joseph. 2004. *The Stepchild: Angaliyat*. Translated by Rita Kothari. New Delhi: Oxford.

Madan, T. N. 1986. *Foreword to Vaudeville's Barahmasa in Indian Literature*. New Delhi: Motilal Banarsidass, v–vii.

Mahadeva, Devanur. 1992. "Tar arrives," Translated by Manu Shetty and A. K. Ramanujan. In *From Cavery to Godavari: Modern Kannada Short Stories*. Edited by Ramachandra Sharma. New Delhi: Penguin.

Mahadevan, Iravatham. 2003. *Early Tamil Epigraphy. From the Earliest Times to the Sixth Century A.D.* (Harvard Oriental Series, v. 62). Chennai: Cre-A / Harvard: The Department of Sanskrit and Indian Studies, Harvard University.

Mahajani, Usha. 1960. *The Role of Indian Minorities in Burma and Malaya*. Bombay, India: Vora and Co.

Mahapatra, Bijoy P. 1979. "Santali language movement in the context of many dominant languages," in *Language Movements in India*, Edited by E. Annamalai. Mysore, India: Central Institute of India Languages, pp. 107–17.

Mahapatra, Bijoy P. 1989. "The problems in learning minority languages with special reference to tribal languages," *International Journal of the Sociology of Language*, 75, 61–72.

Mahboob, A. and Ahmar, N. 2004. Pakistani English: A historical and phonological overview. In B. Kortmann & E. Traugott (eds.), *A Handbook of Varieties of English*, Vol. 1, Berlin: Mouton de Gruyter, pp. 1003–16.

Majumdar, Ramesh C., H. D. Raychaudhuri, and Kalikindar Datta. 1961. *An Advanced History of India*. Bombay, India: Bharatiya Vidya Bhavan.

Malinowski, Bronislaw. 1920. "War and weapons among the natives of the Trobriand Islands," *Man*, 20, 10–12.

Malla, Kamal Prakash. 1977. *English in Nepalese Education*. Kathmandu: Ratna Pustak Bhandar.

Mallikarjun, B. 2001. "Languages of India according to the 1991 census," *Language in India*, 1, November 7, www.languageinindia.com, accessed June 2002.

Mallikarjun, B. 2004. "Indian multilingualism, language policy and the digital divide," *Language in India*, 4(4), www.languageinindia.com/april2004/ kathmandupaper1.html, accessed September 2004.

Maltz, Daniel and Ruth Borker. 1982. "A cultural approach to male–female miscommunication," in *Language and Social Identity*, edited by John J. Gumperz. Cambridge: Cambridge University Press, pp. 196–214.

Mane, Laxman. 1997. *Upara: An Outsider*. Translated by A. K Kamat. New Delhi: Sahitya Akademi.

Manoharan, S. 1989. *A Descriptive and Comparative Study of the Andamanese Language*. Calcutta, India: Anthropological Survey of India, Government of India.

Mansoor, Sabiha. 1993. *Punjabi, Urdu, English in Pakistan: A Sociolinguistic Study*. Lahore, Pakistan: Vanguard.

Marek, Jan. 1968. "Persian literature in India," in *History of Iranian Literature*, edited by Jan Rypka. Dordrecht-Holland: D. Reidel, pp. 711–34.

Mascarenhas–Keyes, Stella. 1994. "Language as diaspora: The use of Portuguese, English and Konkani by Catholic Goan women," in *Bilingual Women*, edited by

Pauline Burton, Ketaki Kushari Dyson, and Shirley Ardener. Oxford: Berg, pp. 149–66.

Masica, Colin P. 1976. *Defining a Linguistic Area: South Asia*. Chicago, IL: University of Chicago Press.

Masica, Colin P. 1991. *The Indo-Aryan Languages*, Cambridge Language Surveys. Cambridge: Cambridge University Press.

Mathai, Samuel. [1979]2004. "Preface," in *Indian and British English: A Handbook of Usage and Pronunciation*, 2nd edn, edited by Paroo Nihalani, R. K Tongue, Priya Hosali, and Jonathan Crowther India: Oxford University Press, pp. v–viii.

Matilal, Bimal Krishna. 1991. *The Word and the World: India's Contribution to the Study of Language*. Oxford: Oxford University Press.

Maurer, Walter H. 1981. "The origin of grammatical speculation and its development in India," *Indo-Pacifica, Occasional Papers*, 1, 1–27.

Maurer, Walter H. 1981. "The origin of grammatical speculation and its development in India," *Indo-Pacifica, Occasional Papers*, 1, 1–27.

McAlpin, David W. 1981. *Proto-Elamo-Dravidian: The Evidence and Its Implications (Transactions of the American Philosophical Society, 71, 3)*. Philadelphia, PA: The American Philosophical Society.

McConnell–Ginet, Sally. 1988. "Language and gender," in *Linguistics: The Cambridge Survey*, Vol. IV, edited by Frederick J. Newmyer. Cambridge: Cambridge University Press, pp. 75–99.

McCormack, William. 1960. "Social dialects in Dharwar Kannada," in *Linguistic Diversity in South Asia: Studies in Regional, Social and Functional Variation*, edited by Charles Ferguson and John Gumperz. Special issue of *International Journal of American Linguistics*, 26(3), 79–91.

McDonald, Hamish (1993/1994). Review 200-India. *Far Eastern Economic Review* (Dec. 30/Jan. 6), 46–47.

McGregor, Ronald Stuart. 1972. *Outline of Hindi Grammar*. London: Oxford University Press.

McGregor, Ronald Stuart. 1974. *Hindi Literature of the Nineteenth and Early Twentieth Centuries*, in the series A History of Indian Literature, edited by Jan Gonda, Vol. 8, fasc. 2. Wiesbaden: Otto Harrassowitz.

Mead, Margaret. 1949. *Male and Female*. New York: William Morrow.

Mehrotra, Arvind Krishna (ed.) 2003. *An Illustrated History of Indian Literature in English*. New Delhi: Permanent Black.

Mehrotra, Raja Ram. 1981. "Non-kin forms of address in Hindi," *International Journal of the Sociology of Language*, 32, 121–37.

Mehrotra, Raja Ram. 1985. *Sociolinguistics in Hindi Contexts*. New Delhi: Oxford University Press and India Book House.

Mehrotra, Raja Ram. 1998. *Indian English: Text and Interpretation*. Amsterdam: John Benjamins.

Meraj, Shaheen. 1993. "The use of English in Urdu advertising in Pakistan," in *The English Language in Pakistan*, edited by Robert J. Baumgardener. Karachi, Pakistan: Oxford University Press, pp. 221–52.

Mesthrie, Rajend. 1989. "The origins of Fanagalo," *Journal of Pidgin and Creole Languages*, 4(2), 211–40.

Mesthrie, Rajend. 1991. *Language in Indenture: A Sociolinguistic History of Bhojpuri-Hindi in South Africa*. Johannesburg: Witwatersrand University Press. [International edition, 1992, London: Routledge.]

Mesthrie, Rajend. 1992. *English in Language Shift: The History, Structure and Sociolinguistics of South African Indian English*. Cambridge: Cambridge University Press.

Mesthrie, Rajend. 1993. "Gandhi and language politics," *Bua*, 8(4), 4–7.

Mesthrie, Rajend. 2000. "Dravidian Hindi in South Africa: An historical variety," in *Yearbook of South Asian Languages*, edited by Rajendra Singh. London: Sage, pp. 49–59.

Metz, Christian. 1982. *Imaginary Signifier*. Bloomington, IN: Indiana University Press.

Minocha, Urmilla. 1987. "South Asian immigrants: Trends and impact on the sending and receiving societies," in *Pacific Bridges: The New Immigrants from Asia and the Pacific Islands*, edited by James T. Fawcett and Benjamin Carino. New York: Center for Migration Studies, pp. 347–74.

Miranda, Rocky V. 1978. "Caste, religion, and dialect differentiation in the Konkani area," *International Journal of the Sociology of Language*, 16, 77–91.

Mirza, Mohammad Wahid. 1974. *The Life and Works of Amir Khusrau*. New Delhi: Idareh-e-adabiyaat-e-Delhi.

Mishra, Pramod and Urmila Mohapatra. 2001. *South Asian Diaspora: A Bibliographical Study*. New Delhi: Kalinga.

Misra, Vijay (ed.) 1979. *Rama's Banishment: A Centenary Tribute to the Fiji Indians, 1879–1979*. London: Heineman Educational.

Mitry, Jean. 2000. *Semiotics and the Analysis of Films*. Bloomington, IN: Indiana University Press.

Moag R. F. 1977. *Fiji Hindi*. Canberra: Australian National University Press.

Moag R. 1979. "The linguistic adaptations of the Fiji Indians," in *Rama's Banishment: A Centenary Tribute to the Fiji Indians, 1879–1979*, edited by Vijay Misra. London: Heineman Educational, pp. 112–38.

Modood, Tariq, Richard Berthoud, Jane Lakey, James Nazroo, Patten Smith, Satnam Virdee, and Sharon Beishon (eds.) 1997. *Ethnic Minorities in Britain: Diversity and Disadvantage*. London: Policy Studies Institute.

Mohan, Peggy Ramesar. 1978. "Trinidad Bhojpuri: A morphological study," unpublished PhD dissertation, University of Michigan.

Mohanty, Chandra Talpade. 1984. "Under Western eyes: Feminist scholarship and colonial discourses," *Boundary*, 2(12), 333–58.

Monier-Williams, Monier. 1899. *A Sanskrit–English Dictionary*. London: Oxford University Press. [Reprinted in 1990, New Delhi: Motilal Banarsidass.]

Montaut, Annie. 2004. *A Grammar of Hindi*. LINCOM Studies in Indo-European Linguistics 02. Munich: Lincom.

Moon, Vasant. 2001. *Growing up Untouchable in India*. Translated by Gail Omvedt. Blue Ridge Summit, PA: Rowman and Littlefield.

Morey, Stephen. 2005. *The Tai Languages of Assam: a Grammar and Texts* (Pacific Linguistics 565). Canberra: Research School of Pacific and Asian Linguistics, Australian National University.

Mufwene, S. 2001. *The Ecology of Language Evolution*. New York: Cambridge University Press.

Mugler, F. and S. Mohan Lal. 1995. "Fiji Tamil: The structure of a language under threat," *International Journal of Dravidian Linguistics*, 24(2), 118–133.

Mugler, F. and V. Saratchandaran Nair. 1997. "Fiji Malayalam," *PILC Journal of Dravidic Studies*, 7(1), 1–14.

Mugler, F. and G. Vijayasarathi. 1997. "Telugu in Fiji," *PILC Journal of Dravidic Studies*, 7(1), 129–43.

Mühlhüusler, Peter. 1974. *Pacific Linguistics, B-26. Pidginization and Simplification of Language*. Canberra: Australian National University Press.

Mühlhäusler, Peter. 1986. *Pidgin and Creole Linguistics*. Oxford: Basil Blackwell.

Mukherjee, Aditi. 1980. "Language maintenance and language shift among Panjabis and Bengalis in Delhi: A sociolinguistic perspective," unpublished PhD dissertation, New Delhi: Delhi University.

Mukherjee, Sujit (ed.) 1981. *The Idea of an Indian Literature*. Mysore, India: Central Insitute of Indian Languages.

Mukherji, Amulyadhan. 1976. *Sanskrit Prosody: Its Evolution*. Calcutta, India: Saraswat Library.

Mukta, Parita. 1994. *Upholding the Common Life: The Community of Mirabai*. New Delhi: Oxford University Press.

Munda, Ram D. 1989. "In search of a tribal homeland," *The Saturday Statesman*, February 4.

Munshi, Kanhaiyalal M. 1971. *Pilgrimage to Freedom*, Vol. 1. Bombay, India: Bhartiya Vidhya Bhavan.

Murlidhar, T. 1996. "Exhibiting wounds: Dalit self-consciousness in Telugu poetry," *New Quest*, 118, 213–16.

Muthiah, S. 1991. *Words in Indian English: A Reader's Guide*, New Delhi: Harper Collins.

Nadkarni, M. V. 1970. "NP-embedded structures in Kannada and Konkani," unpublished PhD dissertation, University of California at Los Angeles.

Nadkarni, M. V. 1975. "Bilingualism and syntactic change in Konkani," *Language*, 51 (3), 672–83.

Nadkarni, Mangesh V. 1983. "Cultural pluralism as a national resource: Strategies for language education," in *Language Planning and Language Education*, edited by Chris Kennedy. London: George Allen and Unwin, pp. 151–59.

Nagamma Reddy, K. 1991. "Woman, gender and language structure," *International Journal of Dravidian Linguistics*, 20(2), 83–90.

Nagaraj, D. R. 1992. "Grasshopper versus a horse for the sun – A critical narrative on social change in Kannada fiction," *Indian International Centre Quarterly*, Monsoon, 127–36.

Nagaraj, D. R. 1993. *The Flaming Feet*. Bangalore, India: South Forum Press.

Nagaraj, D. R. 1994. "From political rage to cultural affirmation: Notes on the Kannada Dalit poet-activist Siddalingaiah," *India International Centre Quarterly*, 21(4), 15–26.

Nagaraj, S. 1995. "Gauri Vishwanathan's Masks of Conquest," *Jodhpur Studies in English*, 6.

Nagendra. 1973. *Hindi Sahitya ka Itihas*. New Delhi: National.

Nair, B. G. 1971. "Caste dialects of Malayalam," in *Proceedings of the First All India Conference of Dravidian Linguistics*, pp. 409–14.

Naipaul, V. S. 1990. *India: A Million Mutinies Now*. New York: Viking.

Nakebandi. 1999. Translations by V. D Chandanshive. Mumbai, India: Sanjana Publication.

Nanda, Serena. 1990. *Neither Man Nor Woman. The Hijras of India*. Belmont, CA: Wadsworth.

Nandy, Ashis. 1983. *The Intimate Enemy. Loss and Recovery of Self under Colonialism*. New Delhi: Oxford University Press.

Nandy, Ashis. 1988. "Woman vs. womanliness in India: An essay in social and political psychology," in *Women in Indian Society. A Reader*, edited by Rehana Ghadially. New Delhi: Sage, pp. 69–80.

Naqvi, Dr S. 1962 *Farhang Navisi Faarsi dar Hindo-Pakistan*. Tehran: Inteshrat Idara'E' Kul Nigarish Vizarate Farhang.

Narasaiah, G. Lakshmi. 1999. *The Essence of Dalit Poetry: A Socio–Philosophic Study of Telugu Dalit Poetry*. Hyderabad, India: Dalit Sana.

Narasimhaiah C. D. (ed.) 1969. *Gandhi and the West*. Mysore, India: University of Mysore.

Narawane, Vishwanath Dinkar. 1978. *Bharatiya Kahavat Sangrah* (Proverbs of India). Pune, India: Triveni Sangam.

Narayan, K. 1997. "Towards an integrated theory of developing writing system for oral language," in *On Writing*, Edited by K. P Acharya. Mysore, India: Central Institute of Indian Languages, pp. 15–20.

Narayanan, Vasudha. 1994. *The Vernacular Veda*. Columbia, SC: The University of South Carolina Press.

National Institute of Adult Education. 1993. *Statistical Database for Literacy*. New Delhi: National Institute of Adult Education.

Nayak, H. M. 1967. *Kannada: Literary and Colloquial – A Study in Two Styles*. Mysore, India: Rao and Raghavan.

Nayar, Baldev Raj. 1969. *National Communication and Language Policy in India*. New York: Praeger.

NCERT (National Council of Education Research and Training). 1992. *Fifth All India Educational Survey*. New Delhi: National Council of Education Research and Training and New Delhi: Sage.

Nichols, Patricia. 1980. "Women in their speech communities," in *Women and Language in Literature and Society*, edited by Sally McConnell-Ginet, Ruth Borker, and Nelly Furman. New York: Praeger, pp. 140–49.

Nida, Eugene and Harold W. Fehderau. 1970. "Indigenous pidgins and koinés," *International Journal of American Linguistics*, 36, 146–55.

Nigam, R. C. 1972. *India: Language Handbook on Mother Tongues in Census*. New Delhi: Ministry of Home Affairs.

Nihalani, Paroo., R. K. Tongue, and Priya Hosali. 1979. *Indian and British English: A Handbook of Usage and Pronunciation*. New Delhi: Oxford University Press.

Nimbalkar, Waman. 1973. *Gaokushabaheril Kavita* (Poems from beyond the village boundary). Translated by Graham Smith. Aurangabad, India: Asmitadarsh Prakashan.

Nitti–Dolci, Luigia. 1938. *Les Grammairiens Prakrits*. Paris: Adrien Maisonneuve. [The Prākṛta Grammarians by Late Luigia Nitti-Dolci. Translated by Prabhākara Jha. New Delhi: Motilal Banarsidass, 1972]

Noonan, Michael. 1996. "The fall and rise of the Chantyal language," *Southwest Journal of Linguistics*, 15, 121–35.

Norman, K. R. 1983. *Pāli Literature: Including the Canonical Literature in Prakrit and Sanskrit of all the Hī nayāna Schools of Buddhism*, A History of Indian Literature, Vol. VII. Wiesbaden: Otto Harrassowitz.

Oakley, Ann. 1981. *Subject Women*. New York: Pantheon.

Ohala, Manjari. 1983. *Aspects of Hindi Phonology*. New Delhi: Motilal Banarsidass.

Olson, David R. 1985. "Introduction," in *Literacy, Language, and Learning: The Nature and Consequences of Reading and Writing*, edited by David R. Olson, Nancy Torrance, and Aangela Hildyard. Cambridge: Cambridge University Press, pp. 1–18.

Olson, David R. 1991. "Literacy as metalinguistic activity," in *Literacy and Orality*, edited by David R. Olson and Nancy Torrance. Cambridge: Cambridge University Press, pp. 251–70.

Olson, David R., Nancy Torrance, and Aangela Hildyard (ed.) 1985. *Literacy, Language, and Learning: The Nature and Consequences of Reading and Writing*. Cambridge: Cambridge University Press.

Omar, Kaleẹm. 1986. "The Pakistanisation of English," *The Star*, Ḳarachi, February 27, 11.

Ong, Walter J. 1982. *Orality and Literacy: The Technologizing of the World*. London: Methuen

Oxenham, John. 1980. *Literacy: Writing, Reading and Social Organization*. London: Routledge and Kegan Paul.

Padgaonkar, Dilip (ed.) 1973. *Times of India* Weekly supplement, Vol. 4(7), special issue on Dalit Literature. November 25.

Pakistan Broadcasting Corporation. (PBC) n.d. *Basic Facts*. Islamabad.

Pakistan Languages. 2002. "The Excellence Network," www.excellence.com.pk/explorepakistan/pakistan%20languages.htm, accessed June 2002.

Panayi, Panikos. 1999. *The Impact of Immigration: A Documentary History of the Effects and Experiences of Immigrants in Britain since 1945*. Manchester and New York: Manchester University Press.

Pandharipande, Rajeshwari. 1979. "Passive as an optional rule in Hindi, Marathi, and Nepali," *South Asian Languages Analysis*, 1, 89–106.

Pandharipande, Rajeshwari. 1983. "Linguistics and written discourse in particular language: contrastive studies: English and Marathi," *Annual Review of Applied Linguistics*, 3, 118–36.

Pandharipande, Rajeshwari. 1992a. "Language of religion in Soth Asia: The case of Hindi," in *Dimensions of Sociolinguistics in South Asia. Papers in Memory of Gerard Kelly*, edited by E. Dimmock, Braj B. Kachru, and Bhadriraju Krishnamurti. New Delhi: Oxford University Press and India Book House, pp. 271–84.

Pandharipande, Rajeshwari. 1992b. "Defining politeness in Indian English," *World Englishes*, 11. 2/3: 241–50.

Pandharipande, Rajeshwari. 1997. *Marathi*. London and New York: Routledge.

Pandharipande, Rajeshwari. 1999. "Metaphors as a mechanism of language change," paper presented at *South Asian Languages and Linguistics Roundtable*. Urbana and Champaign, IL: University of Illinois at Urbana-Champaign.

Pandharipande, Rajeshwari. 2001. "The role of language of religion in the convergence of South Asian languages," in *The Yearbook of South Asian Languages and Linguistics*, edited by Rajendra Singh. New Delhi: Sage, pp. 289–310.

Pandian, M. S. S. 1992. *The Image Trap*. Delhi: Sage.

Pandian, M. S. S. 1998a. "On a Dalit woman's testimonio," *Seminar*, 471, 53–6.

Pandian, M. S. S. 1998b. "Stepping outside history? New Dalit writings from Tamil Nadu," in *Wages of Freedom: Fifty Years of the Indian Nation-State*, edited by Partha Chaterjee. New Delhi: Oxford University Press, pp. 293–309.

Pandit, Prabodh B. 1963. "Sanskritic clusters and caste dialects," *Indian Linguistics*, 24, 70–80.

Pandit, Prabodh B. 1969. "Parameters of speech variation in an Indian community," in *Language and Society in India*, edited by A. Poddar. Simla: Indian Institute of Advanced Studies, pp. 207–28.

Pandit, Prabodh B. 1972. *India as a Sociolinguistic Area*. Poona, India: University of Poona.

Pandit, Prabodh B. 1977. *Language in a Plural Society*. New Delhi: Dev Raj Chanana Memorial Publication; Pune, India: Ganeshkhind.

Pandit, Prabodh B. 1979. "Perspectives on sociolinguistics in India," in *Language and Society: Anthropological Issues*, edited by W. C McCormick and S. A Wurm. The Hague: Mouton.

Pantawane, Gangadhar. 1986. "Evolving a new Identity: The Development of a Dalit Culture," in *Untouchable! Voices from the Dalit Liberation Movement*, edited by Barbara Joshi. London: Zed Books, pp. 79–87.

Parakrama, Arjuna. 1995. *De-hegemonizing Language Standards: Learning from (Post)colonial Englishes about "English."* Basingstoke, Hampshire: Macmillan.

Parpola, Asko. 1994. *Deciphering the Indus Script*. Cambridge: Cambridge University Press.

Pasoloni, Pier Paolo. 1978. *Heretical Empiricism*. Bloomington, IN: Indiana University Press.

Pathak, R. S. 1985. "Language variation in a bilingual setting: A North Indian case study," *Indian Linguistics*, 46(1–2), 9–24.

Pattanayak, Debi Prasanna. 1973. *Indian Languages: Bibliography of Grammars, Dictionaries, and Teaching Materials* (2nd revised edn). New Delhi: Educational Resourses Center.

Pattanayak, Debi Prasanna. 1981. *Multilingualism and Mother-Tongue Education*. New Delhi: Oxford University Press.

Pattanayak, Devi P. (ed.) 1990. *Multilingualism in India*. Philadelphia, PA: Multilingual Matters.

Paulston, Christina Bratt. 1994. *Linguistic Minorities in Multilingual Settings*. Amsterdam: John Benjamins.

Paulston, Christina Bratt. 2000. "Ethnicity, ethnic movements, and language maintenance," in *Assessing Ethnolinguistic Vitality: Theory and Practice. Selected Papers from The Third International Language Assessment Conference*,

SIL International Publication in Sociolinguistics No. 3, edited by Gloria Kindell and M. Paul Lewis. Dallas, TX: Summer Institute of Linguistics, pp. 27–38.

Pawar, Urmila. 1998. *Amhihi Itihas Ghadawala* (We made history too). Mumbai, India: Sparrow.

Pawar, Urmila. 2001. *Chauthi Bhint* (The Fourth Wall). Translated by Gail Omvedt. *Manushi*, 122, 23–31.

Peach, Ceri (ed.) 1996. *Ethnicity in the 1991 Census*. London: In the Service of Her Majesty: National Statistics.

Peng, Fred C. C. *et. al.* 1981. *Male/Female Differences in Japanese*. Special issue of *Language Sciences*, 3(1).

Peterson, Indira Viswanathan. 1989. *Poems to Shiva*. Princeton, NJ: Princeton University Press.

Petievich, Carla (ed.) 1999. *The Expanding Landscape: South Asians and the Diaspora*. New Delhi: Manohar.

Pillai, Anavartavinayakam S. 1924. "The Sanskritic element in the vocabularies of the Dravidian languages," in *Dravidic Studies*, III, edited by Mark Collins. Madras, India: University of Madras, pp. 27–48.

Pillai, R. C. 1975. "Fiji Hindi as a Creole language," unpublished MA thesis, Southern Illinois University.

Pind, Ole Holten. 1989. "Studies in the Pāli grammarians I: Buddha-ghosa's references to grammar and grammarians," *Journal of the Pāli Text Society*, 1, 33–82.

Pind, Ole Holten. 1990. "Studies in the Pāli grammarians II," *Journal of the Pāli Text Society*, 14, 175–218.

Pind, Ole Holten. 1995. "Pāli and the Pāli grammarians: The methodology of the Pāli grammarians," in *Studies in Honour of Siegfried Lienhard on his 70th Birthday*, edited by Sauhṛdya-maṅgalam. Stockholm: The Association of Oriental Studies, pp. 281–97.

Pind, Ole Holten. 1997. "Pāli grammar and grammarians from Buddha-ghosa to Vajira-buddhi: A survey," *Buddhist Studies (Bukkyo Kenkyu)*, 26, 23–88.

Pollock, Sheldon. 1998. "India in the vernacular millennium: Literary culture and polity 1000–1500" in *Collective Identities and Political Order*, edited by Shmuel Eisenstadt and W. Schlichter, special Issue of *Daedalus*, 127(3), pp. 41–74.

Polomé, Edgar C. 1982. "Language, paleoculture, and religion," in *Language, Society, and Paleoculture*, edited by Anwar S. Dil. Stanford, CA: Stanford University Press, pp. 285–368.

Possehl, Gregory L. 1996. *The Indus Age: Writing System*. Philadelphia, PA: University of Pennsylvania Press.

Prabhakar, M. E. 1996. "Doing theology with poetic traditions of India with special reference to the Dalit poetry of poet-laureate, Joshua," in *Doing Theology with the Poetic Traditions of India: Focus on Dalit and Tribal Poems*, edited by Joseph Patmury. Bangalore, India: Program for Theologies and Cultures / South Asia Thealogical Research Institute, pp. 3–20.

Prabhakaran, Varijakshi. 1991. "The Telugu language and its influence on the cultural lives of the Hindu 'Pravasandhras' in South Africa," unpublished PhD dissertation, University of Durban-Westville.

Prabhakaran, Varijakshi. 1994. "Tamil lexical borrowings in South African Telugu," *South African Journal of Linguistics*, 12(1), 26–31.

Prasad, M. Madhava. 1998. *Ideology of the Hindi Film*. New Delhi: Oxford University Press.

Punalekar, S. P. 1988. "Identities and consciousness: An overview of Dalit literature in Maharashtra," *Man and Development*, X(4), 111–40.

Punalekar, S. P. 1997. "Sociology of Dalit autobiography," in *Social Transformation in India: Essays in Honour of Professor I. P Desai* (2 vols.), edited by Ghanshyam Shah. Jaipur, India: Rawat, pp. 370–96.

Punalekar, S. P. 2001. "Dalit literature and Dalit identity," in *Dalit Identity and Politics*, edited by Ghanshyam Shah. New Delhi: Sage, pp. 216–41.

Pushp, P. N. 1996. "Kashmiri and the linguistic predicament of the state," in *Jammu, Kashmir and Ladakh: Linguisitic Predicament*, edited by P. N. Pushp and K. Warikoo New Delhi: Har-Anand, pp. 13–29.

Pushp, P. N. and K. Warikoo. 1996. *Jammu, Kashmir, and Ladakh: Linguisitic Predicament*. New Delhi: Har Anand.

Radhakrishna, B. 1971. "Diglossia in Telugu," *Proceedings of the First All India Conference of Linguists*, pp. 218–26.

Raghavan, Venkatarama (ed.) 1980. *The Ramayana Tradition in Asia*. New Delhi: Sahitya Akademi.

Raghavan, Venkatarama and Nagendra. 1970. *An Introduction to Indian Poetics*. Bombay, India: Macmillan.

Raheja, Gloria Goodwin. 1994. "Women's speech genres, kinship and contradiction," in *Women as Subjects: South Asian Histories*, edited by Nita Kumar. Charlottesville, VI: University Press of Virginia, pp. 49–80.

Rahman, M. L. 1978. "Guru Govind Singh and his contribution to Persian literature," *Indo-Iranica*, 31(3–4), 37–62.

Rahman, S. S. A. 1957. "Glimpses of Indo-Persian literature," *Indo-Iranica*, 10(2), 1–25.

Rahman, Tariq. 1991a. *Pakistan Engilsh*. Islamabad: National Institute of Pakistan Studies, Qaid-i-Azam University.

Rahman, Tariq. 1991b. *A History of Pakistani Literature in English*. Lahore, Pakistan: Vanguard.

Rahman, Tariq. 1996a. *Language and Politics in Pakistan*. Karachi, Pakistan: Oxford University Press.

Rahman, Tariq. 1996b. *The History of the Urdu–English Controversy in Pakistan*. Islamabad: National Language Authority.

Rahman, Tariq. 2004. Language policy and localization in Pakistan: Proposal for a paradigm shift. Paper presented at SCALLA 2004, Kathmandu, www.elda.org/en/proj/scalla/SCALLA2004/rahman.pdf, accessed August 19, 2005.

Rai, Amrit. 1984. *A House Divided: The Origin and Development of Hindi/Hindavi*. New Delhi: Oxford Univsersity Press.

Raina, A. M. 2002. "The verb second phenomenon in Kashmiri," in *Topics in Kashmiri Linguistics*, edited by O. N. Koul and K. Wali. New Delhi: Creative Books, 113–29.

Raj, Sebasti L. and G. F. Xavier Raj (eds.) 1993. *Caste Culture in Indian Church: The Response of Church to the Problem of Caste within the Christian Community*. New Delhi: Indian Social Institute.

Ram, Tulsi. 1983. *Trading in Language: The Story of English in India*. New Delhi: GDK.

Ramanujan, A. K. 1968. "The structure of variation: A study in caste dialects," in *Structure and Change in Indian Society*, edited by Milton Singer and Bernard S. Cohn. Chicago, IL: Aldine, pp. 461–74.

Ramanujan, A. K. 1973. *Speaking of Shiva*. Harmondsworth, Middlesex: Penguin.

Ramanujan, A. K. 1989. "Is there an Indian way of thinking?," *Contributions to Indian Sociology*, 23(1), 41–58.

Ramanujan, A. K. (ed.) 1993. *Folktales from India*. New Delhi: Viking.

Ramanujan A. K. 1999. "Who needs folklore? The relevance of oral traditions to South Asian studies," in *The Collected Essays of A. K. Ramanujan*, edited by Vinay Dharwarkar. Delhi: Oxford University Press, pp. 532–52.

Ramanujan, A. K. and Colin P. Masica. 1969. "Toward a phonological typology of the Indian linguistic area," in *Current Trends in Linguistics: Linguistics in South Asia*, edited by Thomas A. Sebeok. The Hague: Mouton, pp. 543–77.

Ramarao, C. and B. Ramakrishna Reddy. 1984. "Some influences and non-influences of English on the syntax of Telugu newspapers," in *Modernization of Indian Languages in the News Media*, edited by Bhadriraju Krishnamurti and Aditi Mukherji. Hyderabad, India: Department of Linguistics, Osmania University.

Ramchand, K. 1973. "The language of the master," in *Varieties of Present-Day English*, edited by R. W. Bailey and J. Robinson. New York: Macmillan, pp. 115–46.

Ramdat, K. 1984. "Some aspects of Indic pejorative usage among Hindus in Guyana," paper presented at *The Third Conference on East Indians in the Caribbean*. Trinidad: University of the West Indies, August 28–September 5.

Rampton, M. B. H. 1992. "Scope for empowerment in sociolinguistics," in *Researching Language: Issues of Power and Method*, edited by D. Cameron, E. Frazer, P. Harvey, M. B. H. Rampton, and K. Richardson. London: Routledge, pp. 29–64.

Ramyead, Lutchmee Parsad. 1988. "Hindi in Mauritius: A perspective," in *Language Transplanted: The Development of Overseas Hindi*, edited by R K. Barz and J. Siegel. Wiesbaden: Otto Harrassowitz, pp. 23–40.

Ranade, R. D. 1933. *Mysticism in Maharashtra*. New Delhi: Motilal Banarsidass.

Rangaswamy, Padma. 2000. *Namaste America: Indian Americans in an American Metropolis*. University Park, PA: Pennsylvania University Press.

Rao, B. Raamchandra. 1984. "Modernization of Kannada in news media," in *Modernization of Indian Languages in the News Media*, edited by Bhadriraju Krishnamurti and Aditi Mukherji. Hyderabad, India: Department of Linguistics, Osmania University, pp. 64–72.

Rao, Subba G. 1954. *Indian Words in English: A Study in Indo-British Cultural and Linguistic Relations*. Oxford: Clarendon Press.

Rasheed, Abdur. 1996. *Farsi mẽ Hindi alfaaz* (Hindi Words in Persian). New Delhi: Rabita Publications.

Raza, Moonis and Aijazuddin Ahmed. 1990. *An Atlas of Tribal India*. New Delhi: Concept Publications.

Remlinger, Kathryn A. 1994. "Language choice and use: Influences of setting and gender," in *Differences that Make a Difference*, edited by Lynn H. Turner and Helen M. Slerk. Westport, CT: Bergin and Garvey, pp 163–73.

Renou, Louis and Jean Filliozat. 1947. *L'Inde Classique*. Paris: Payot.

Report of the States Reorganization Commission. 1955. New Delhi: Government of India.

Report of the States Reorganization Commission. 1956. New Delhi: Government of India.

Richter, Julius. 1908. *A History of Missions in India*. Translated by Sydney H. Moore. New York: F. H. Revell.

Roberts, T. T. 1800. *An Indian Glossary Consisting of Some Thousand Words and Forms Commonly Used in East Indies ... Extremely Serviceable in Assisting Strangers to Acquire with Ease and Quickness the Language of That Country*. London: Murray and Highley.

Robertson, Roland. 1992. *Globalization: Social Theory and Global Culture*. Newberry Park, CA: Sage.

Robinson, Francis (ed.) 1989. *The Cambridge Encyclopedia of India, Pakistan, Bangladesh, Sri Lanka, Nepal, Bhutan and the Maldives*. Cambridge: Cambridge University Press.

Robinson, Vaughan. 1996. "The Indians: Onward and upward," in *The Ethnic Minority Populations*, edited by Ceri Peach. London: In the Service of Her Majesty: National Statistics, pp. 95–121.

Roland, Alan. 1988. *In Search of Self in India and Japan: Toward a Cross-Cultural Psychology*. Princeton, NJ: Princeton University Press.

Romaine, Suzanne. 1988. *Pidgins and Creoles*. London: Longman.

Romaine, Suzanne. 1989. *Bilingualism*. Oxford: Basil Blackwell.

Romaine, Suzanne. 1999. *Communicating Gender*. Mahwah, NJ: Lawrence Erlbaum.

Roy, Ramashray. 1985. "Region and nation: A heretical view," in *Region and Nation in India*, edited by Paul Wallace. New Delhi: American Institute of Indian Studies.

Roy, Rammohan. 1823. "Letter to Lord Amherst, December 11," in *Selection from Educational Records, Part 1 (1781–1838)*. Calcutta, India: Bureau of Education, Government of India, pp. 99–101.

Ruberu, Ranjit. 1962. *Education in Colonial Ceylon*. Kandy, Sri Lanka: Kandy printers.

Ruegg, David Seyfort. 1978. "Mathematical and linguistic models in Indian thought: The case of zero and śūnyatā," *Weiner Zeitschrift für die Kunde Südasiens and Archiv fur indische Philosophie*, 22, 171–81.

Rushdie, Salman. 1991. "Hobson-Jobson," in *Imaginary Homelands: Essays and Criticism 1981–1991*. London: Viking, pp. 81–83.

Russell, Ralph. 1980. *A New Course in Hindustani for Learners in Britain*. London: School of Oriental and African Studies.

Rypka, Jan. 1968. "History of Persian literature up to the beginning of the 20th century," in *History of Iranian Literature*, edited by Jan Rypka. Dordrecht-Holland: D. Reidel, pp. 69–351.

Safavi, K. 2002. "Re-evaluating the emergence of Hindi style in Persian poetry," paper presented at *The Seminar on Dialogue between Civilizations: India and Iran*. Bareilly, India, December 15–18.

Saghal, Anju. 1991. "Patterns of language use in a bilingual setting in India," in *English Around the World: Sociolinguistic Perspectives*, edited by Jenny Cheshire. Cambridge: Cambridge University Press, pp. 299–307.

Salomon, Richard. 1989. "Linguistic variability in post-Vedic Sanskrit," in *Dialectes dans les Littératures Indo-Aryennes. Publications de l'*Institut de Civilisation

Indienne (Fascicule 55), edited by Colette Caillat. Paris: Institut de Civilisation Indienne, pp. 275–94.

Salomon, Richard. 1998. *Indian Epigraphy: A Guide to the Study of Inscriptions in Sanskrit, Prakrit, and the Other Indo-Aryan Languages*. New York: Oxford University Press.

Samarin, W. J. 1971. "Salient and substantive pidginization," in *Pidginization and Creolization of Languages*, edited by Dell Hymes. Cambridge: Cambridge University Press, pp. 117–40.

Sankoff, Gillian. 1980. *The Social Life of Language*. Philadelphia, PA: University of Pennsylvania Press.

Sapir, Edward. 1949. "Male and female forms of speech in Yana," in *Selected Writings of Edward Sapir on Language, Culture and Personality*, edited by David Mandelbaum. Berkeley, CA: University of California Press, pp. 206–12.

Saran, Parmatma and Edwin Eames. 1980. *The New Ethnics: The Asian Indians in the U.S.* New York: Praeger.

Sarju Devi, T. and Karumuri V. Subbarao. 2003. "Reduplication and case copying: The case of lexical anaphors in Manipuri and Telugu," in *Perspectives in Honor of P. J. Mistry*, edited by Ritva Laury, Gerald McMenamin, Shigeko Okamoto, Vida Samiian, and Karumuri V. Subbarao. New Delhi: Indian Institute of Language Studies, pp. 55–81.

Sarkar, J. N. 1985a. "The age of Akbar," *Indo-Iranica*, 38(3–4), 16–25.

Sarkar, J. N. 1985b. "A study of Sufism – Its background and its syncretic significance in Medieval India," *Indo-Iranica*, 38(1–2), 1–24.

Saroop B. 1998. *'Taj-ul-Maathir' of Hasan Nizami*. (Translated from Persian to English). Delhi: Saud Ahmed & Co.

Sastri, Korada Mahadeva. 1969. *Historical Grammar of Telugu – With Special Reference to Old Telugu, c. 200 BC – 1000 AD*. Anantapur, India: Sri Venkateswara University, Post-graduate Centre.

Satchidanandan, K. 2001. "The tradition of dissent in Indian poetry," in *Culturation: Essays in Honour of Jawaharlal Handoo*, edited by Udaya Narayana Singh. Mysore, India: Central Institute of Indian Languages, pp. 35–78.

Sathasivam, A. 1969."Linguistics in Ceylon, II," in *Current Trends in Linguistcs. Vol. 5. Linguistics in South Asia*," edited by Thomas A. Sebeok. The Hague: Mouton, pp. 752–59.

Satyanarayana, A. 1994. "Dalit protest literature in Telugu: A historical perspective," *Economic and Political Weekly*, XXX(3), 171–5.

Satyanath, T. S. 1982. "Kannadigas in Delhi: A sociolinguistic study," unpublished PhD dissertation, Delhi: Delhi University.

Sawhney, Sabina. 1997. "Feminism and hybridity," *Surfaces*, VII(113), 1–12.

Scharfe, Hartmut. 1971. *Pāṇini's Metalanguage*. Philadephia, PA: American Philosophical Society.

Scharfe, Hartmut. 1977. *Grammatical Literature*, A History of Indian Literature, Vol. V. Wiesbaden: Otto Harrassowitz.

Schimmel, Annemarie. 1973. *Islamic Literatures of India*. Wiesbaden: Harrassowitz.

Schirmer, Jennifer G. 1989. "'Those who die for life cannot be called dead:' Women in human rights protest in Latin America," *Feminist Review*, 32, 3–29.

Schuchardt, H. [1891] 1980. "Indo-English," in *Pidgins and Creole Languages: Selected Essays*, edited and translated by G. G. Gilbert. London: Cambridge University Press, pp. 38–64.

Schulz, Muriel R. 1975. "The semantic derogation of woman," in *Language and Sex: Difference and Dominance*, edited by Barrie Thorne and Nancy Henley. Rowley, MA: Newbury House, pp. 64–73.

Schwartzberg, Joseph E. 1985. "Factors in the linguistic reorganization of Indian states," in *Region and Nation in India*, edited by Paul Wallace. New Delhi: American Institute of Indian Studies.

Scmidt, Ruth Laila. 1999. *Urdu, an Essential Grammar*. London: Routledge.

Sebba, Mark. 1997. *Contact Languages: Pidgins and Creoles*. New York: St. Martin's Press.

Sekhar, Anantaramayyar Chandra. 1969. *Evolution of Malayalam*. Poona, India: Deccan College Post-graduate and Research Institute.

Sen, A. P. 1902. "Does education breed sedition in India?," *Westminster Review*, 158, 168–78.

Sen, Sukumar. 1979. *Women's Dialect in Bengali*. Calcutta, India: Jijnasa.

Shackle, Christopher. 1970. "Punjabi in Lahore," *Modern Asian Studies*, 4(3), 239–67.

Shackle, Christopher. 1977. "Siraiki: A language movement in Pakistan," *Modern Asian Studies*, 11(3), 239–67.

Shackle, Christopher. 1983. *An Introduction to the Sacred Language of the Sikhs*. London: The School of Oriental and African Studies.

Shackle, Christopher. 2001. "Christianity in South Asia," in *Concise Encyclopedia of Language and Religion*, edited by John F. A. Sawyer. Amsterdam: Elsevier, pp. 39–41.

Shah, A[mritlal] B. (ed.) 1968. *The Great Debate: Language Controversy and University Education*. Bombay, India: Lalvani.

Shah, Ijlal Hussain. 1994. *The Pragmatics of Formality and Politeness in Burushaski and Shina*. Islamabad: Quaid-i-Azam University (Unpublished M.Phil. Thesis).

Shanmugam Pillai, M. 1960. "Tamil: Literary and colloquial," in *Linguistic Diversity in South Asia: Studies in Regional, Social, and Functional Variation*, edited by Charles A. Ferguson and John Gumperz. Bloomington, IN: Indiana University Press, pp. 27–42.

Shanmugham Pillai, M. 1965. "Caste isoglosses in kinship terms," *Anthropological Linguistics*, 7(3), 59–66.

Shanmugan, S. V. 1975. "Modernization in Tamil," *Anthropological Linguistics*, 17 (3), 53–67.

Shapiro, Michael. 2003. *A Primer of Modern Standard Hindu*. Seatlle, WA: University of Washington Press.

Shapiro, Michael C. and Harold F. Schiffman. 1981. *Language and Society in South Asia*. New Delhi: Motilal Banarsidass.

Sharma, Aryendra. 1958. *A Basic Grammar of Modern Hindi*. New Delhi: Government of India, Ministry of Education and Scientific Research.

Sharma, Rama Nath. 1981. "On the notion of grammar in Pāṇini," *Indo-Pacifica Occasional Papers*, 1, 29–58.

Sharma, Rama Nath. 1987. *The Aṣṭādhyāyī of Pāṇini: Introduction to the Aṣṭādhyāyī as a Grammatical Device*. New Delhi: Munshiram Manoharlal.

Sharma, Shri Ram. 1964. *Dakkhinī Hindī kā Udbhav aur Vikās* (The Origin and Development of Dakkhini Hindi). Prayag (Allahabad), India: Hindi Sahitya Sammelan.

Shastri, K. G. 1986. "Modernization of Kannada," paper presented at *The Eighth South Asian Languages Analysis Roundtable*. Urbana, IL: University of Illinois.

Shekhar, Chander. 1998. "Some peculiarities of Persian poetry at the court of Shahjahan," in *Indo-Persian Cultural Perspectives*, edited by Mohammad A. Khan, Ravinder Gargesh and Chander Shekhar. New Delhi: Saud Ahmad Dehlavi, pp. 91–106.

Sherring, Matthew A. 1884. *The History of Protestant Missions in India from Their Commencement in 1706 to 1871*. London and Edinburgh: Religious Tracy Society.

Shirwadkar, K. R. 1881. "Stranger than fiction: Dalit memoirs in Marathi," *New Quest*, 27, 173–7.

Shivapurkar, H. S. 1993a. "One earth – many words: The new generation," *Book Review*, 17(12), 10–11.

Shivapurkar, H. S. 1993b. "Modernism and after: Some reflections on contemporary Kannada poetry," *Indian Literature*, 36(6), 151–56.

Shrestha, Balgopal and Bert van den Hoek. 1994. "Education in the mother tongue: The case of Newari," *Nepalese Linguistics*, 11, 46–47.

Shukla, Ramchandra. 1929. *Hindi Sahitya Ka Itihas* (History of Hindi Literature). Benaras, India: Nagri Pracharini Sabha.

Siddalingaiah. 2003. *Ooru-Keri: An Autobiography*. Translated by S. R. Ramakrishna. New Delhi: Sahitya Akademi.

Siegel, Jeff. 1975. "Fiji Hindustani," *University of Hawaii Working Papers in Linguistics*, 7(3), 127–44.

Siegel, Jeff. 1987. *Language Contact in a Plantation Environment: A Sociolinguistic History of Fiji*. Cambridge: Cambridge University Press.

Siegel, Jeff. 1990. "Language maintenance of overseas Hindi," in *Learning, Keeping and Using Language* (Selected papers from *The Eighth World Congress of Applied Linguistics*, Sydney, 16–21 August 1987), edited by M. A. K. Halliday, J. Gibbons, and H. Nicholas. Amsterdam: John Benjamins, pp. 91–113.

Siegel, Jeff. 1993. "Dialect contact and koineization: A review of dialects in contact by Peter Trudgill," *International Journal of the Sociology of Language*, 99, 105–21.

Siegel, Jeff. 2001. "Koine formation and creole genesis," in *Creolization and Contact*, edited by Norval Smith and Tonjes Veenstra. Amsterdam and Philadelphia, PA: John Benjamins, pp. 175–98.

SIL (Summer Institute of Linguistics) International. 2002. *Ethnologue: Languages of the World* (14th edn). www.ethnologue.com, accessed August 2005.

Silverstein, Michael. 1979. "Language structure and linguistic ideology," in *The Elements: A Parasession on Linguistic Units and Levels*, edited by Paul R. Clyne, William F. Hanks, and Carol L. Hofbauer. Chicago, IL: Chicago Linguisitc Society, pp. 193–247.

Simelane, Sandie E. 2002. "The population of South Africa: An overall and demographic description of the South African population based on Census '96," Occassional paper 2002/01.

Singer, Milton. 1972. *When a Great Tradition Modernizes: An Anthropological Approach to Indian Civilization*. New York: Praeger.

Singh, Harjinder (ed.) 1977. *Caste among Non-Hindus in India*. New Delhi: National Publishing House.

Singh, Harjinder (ed.) 1995–1998. *The Encyclopedia of Sikhism*. Patiala, India: Punjabi University.

Singh, K. S. and S. Manoharan. 1993. *Languages and Scripts*. New Delhi: Oxford University Press.

Singh, M. P. 1994. *V. N. Shukla's 'Constitution of India.'* Lucknow, India: Eastern Book Company.

Singh, M. P. 1997. *Outline of Indian Legal and Constitutional History*. New Delhi: Universal Law Publishing Co.

Singh, Rajendra. 1985. "Grammatical constraints on code-switching: Evidence from Hindi–English," *Canadian Journal of Linguistics*, 30, 33–45.

Singh, Rajendra (ed.) 1998. *The Native Speaker: Multilingual Perspectives*. New Delhi: Sage.

Singh, R. and R. K. Agnihotri. 1997. *Hindi Morphology: A Word-based Description*. New Delhi: Motilal Banarsidass.

Singh, Udaya Narayana. 1989. "How to honor someone in Maithili," *International Journal of the Sociology of Language*, 75, 87–107.

Singh, Udaya Narayana. 1992. *On Language Development and Planning*. Simla, India: Indian Institute of Advanced Study.

Singh, Udaya Narayana. 2001a. "Multiscriptality in South Asia and language development," *International Journal of the Sociology of Language*, 150, 61–74.

Singh, Udaya Narayana (ed.) 2001b. *Culturation: Essays in Honour of Jawaharlal Handoo*. Mysore, India: Central Institute of Indian Languages.

Sinha, A. K. 1998. "Influence of Indian languages on Persian," in *Indo-Persian Cultural Perspectives*, edited by Mohammad A. Khan, Ravinder Gargesh and Chander Shekhar. New Delhi: Saud Ahmad Dehlavi, pp. 53–64.

Sjoberg, Andrée F. 1962. "Co-existant phonemic systems in Telugu," *Word*, 18, 269–79.

Sjoberg, Andrée F. and Gideon Sjoberg. 1956. "Problems in glottochronology: Culture as a significant variable in lexical change," *American Anthropologist*, 58(2), 296–300.

Smith, Ian R. 1979. "Substrata vs. universals in the formation of Sri Lanka Portuguese," *Papers in Pidgin and Creole Linguistics*, No. 2. Canberra: Pacific Linguistics, pp. 183–200.

Smith, Ian R. 1998. "Introdução," in *Dialecto Indo-Português de Ceylão* [Re-issue of a description of Sri Lanka Portuguese by Sabastião Rodolpho Dalgado, 1900]. Lisbon: Comissão Nacional para as Comemorações dos Descobrimentos Portuguêses, pp. 13–36.

Smith, Ian R. forthcoming. "Sri Lanka Portuguese," in *Encyclopaedia of Linguistics*, edited by Christy Prahl and Philipp Strazny. Chicago, IL: Fitzroy Dearborn.

Smith-Pearse, T. L. N. 1934. *English Errors in Indian Schools*. Bombay, India: Oxford University Press.

Sommer, Anton F. W. 1991. *Kurzgefasste Grammatik des Assamesischen mit ausgewähltem Wörterverzeichnis und einigen Textproben*. Wien: Anton F. W. Sommer.

Sontaag, Salma. 1995. "Ethnolinguistic identity and language policy in Nepal," *Nationalism and Ethnic Politics*, 1(4), 108–20.

Sopher, David E. (ed.) 1980. *An Exploration of India*. Ithaca, NY: Cornell University Press.

Southworth, Franklin C. 1971. "Detecting prior creolization: An analysis of the historical origins of Marathi," in *Pidginization and Creolization of Languages*, edited by Dell Hymes. Cambridge: Cambridge University Press, pp. 255–76.

Southworth, Franklin C. 1979. "Lexical evidence for early contact between Indo-Aryan and Dravidian," in *Aryan and Non–Aryan in India*, edited by Madhav Deshpande and Peter Edwin Hook. Ann Arbor, MI: Center for South and Southeast Asian Studies, The University of Michigan, pp. 191–233.

Spender, Dale. 1980. *Man-Made Language*. Boston, MA: Routledge and Kegan Paul.

Sreedevi, B. 1991. "Language of women," *International Journal of Dravidian Linguistics*, 20, 261–82.

Sreedhar, M. V. 1974. *Naga Pidgin: A Sociolinguistic Study of Inter-lingual Communication Pattern in Nagaland*. Mysore, India: Central Institute of Indian Languages.

Sreedhar, M. V. 1976a. "Standardization of Naga pidgin," *Anthropological Linguistics*, 18, 371–9.

Sreedhar, M. V. 1976b. *Sema Phonetic Reader*. Mysore, India: Central Institute of Indian Languages.

Sreedhar, M. V. 1985. *Standardized Grammar of Naga Pidgin*. Mysore, India: Central Institute of Indian Languages.

Sreedhar, M. V. (ed.) 1988. *Pidgins and Creoles: Languages of Wider Communication*. Mysore: Central Institute of Indian Languages.

Sreekantaiya, T. N. 1956. "Notes on loans and native replacements in Kannada," *American Anthropologist*, 58, 306–8.

Sridhar, Kamal K. 1988. "Language maintenance by Asian Indians in the U.S.: Kannada speakers in the New York area," *International Journal of the Sociology of Language*, 69, 73–87.

Sridhar, Kamal K. 1989. *English in Indian Bilingualism*. New Delhi: Manohar.

Sridhar, Kamal K. 1991. "Speech acts in an Indigenized variety: Sociocultural values and language variation," in *English around the World: Sociolinguistic Perspectives*, edited by Jenny Cheshire. Cambridge: Cambridge University Press, pp. 308–18.

Sridhar, Kamal K. 1993. "Meaning, means, maintenance," in *Language, Communication, and Social Meaning* (Georgetown University Roundtable on Languages and Linguistics), edited by James. E. Alatis. Washington, DC: Georgetown University Press, pp. 56–65.

Sridhar, Kamal K. 1997. "Languages of India in New York," in *The Multilingual Apple: Languages in New York City*, edited by Ofelia Garcia and Joshua A. Fishman. Berlin: Mouton de Gruyer, pp. 257–80.

Sridhar, Kamal K. and S. N. Sridhar. 2000. "At home with English: Assimilation and adaptation of Asian Indians in the US," in *Language Diversity: Problem or Resource*, edited by Sandra Mckay and Sau–ling C. Wong. Cambridge: Cambridge University Press, pp. 369–92.

Sridhar, S. N. 1975. "On the Indo-Aryanization of the Kannada lexicon: A study of the Hindi–Urdu loanwords in Kannada," in *Language Borrowing*, edited by Herman van Olphen. Austin, TX: University of Texas at Austin, pp. 99–108.

Sridhar, S. N. 1978. "On the functions of code–mixing in Kannada," in *Aspects of Sociolinguistics in South Asia*, edited by Braj B. Kachru and S. N. Sridhar. Special issue of *International Journal of the Sociology of Language*, 16, 109–17.

Sridhar, S. N. 1979a. "Dative subjects and the notion of subject," *Lingua*, 49, 99–125.

Sridhar, S. N. 1979b. "In defense of spontaneous demotion," *South Asian Languages Analysis*, 1, 115–24.

Sridhar, S. N. 1980. "Diglossia in Kannada," paper presented at *The Second International Conference on South Asian Languages and Linguistics*, Hyderabad, India.

Sridhar, S. N. 1981. "Linguistic convergence: Indo-Aryanization of Dravidian languages," *Lingua*, 53, 199–220.

Sridhar, S. N. 1984. "The role of English in expanding the stylistic repertoire of Indian languages," in *Perspectives on English Language Teaching*, edited by J. M. Ure and S. Velayudhan. Bangalore, India: Macmillan.

Sridhar, S. N. 1987. "Language variation, attitudes, and rivalry: The spread of Hindi in India," in *Language Spread and Language Policy: Issues, Implications and Case Studies*, Georgetown University Roundtable on Languages and Linguistics, edited by Peter Lowenberg. Washington, DC: Georgetown University Press, pp. 300–19.

Sridhar, S. N. 1988. "Language modernization: Structural and sociolinguistic aspects," in *Euskara Biltzarra*, Conference on the Basque Language, Vol. 1: *Description of the Language*. Victoria-Gasteiz: Eusko Jauriaritzaren Argitalpen–Zerbitzu Naguisa, pp. 351–62.

Sridhar, S. N. 1990. *Descriptive Grammar: Kannada*. London: Routledge.

Sridhar, S. N. 1992. "Language modernization in Kannada," in *Dimensions of South Asia as a Sociolinguistic Area: Papers in Honor of Gerald B. Kelly*, edited by Edward Dimmock, Jr., Braj B. Kachru, and Bh. Krishnamurti. New Delhi: Oxford and India Book House, pp. 223–36.

Sridhar, S. N. 1995. *Indina Kannada: Racane Mattu Balake* (Contemporary Kannada: Structure and Function). Hampi, India: Kannada University.

Sridhar, S. N and Kamal K. Sridhar. 1980. "The syntax and psycholinguistics of bilingual code–mixing," *Canadian Journal of Psychology*, 34(4), 409–18.

Srinivas, M. N. 1966. *Social Change in Modern India*. Berkeley and Los Angeles, CA: University of California Press.

Srinivas, M. N. 1976. *The Remembered Village*. New Delhi: Oxford University Press.

Srinivas, M. N. 1989. *The Cohesive Role of Sanskritization and Other Essays*. New Delhi: Oxford University Press.

Srinivas, M. N. 1997. "Caste: A systemic change," in *Ananya: A Portrait of India*, edited by S. N. Sridhar and Nirmal K. Mattoo. New York: Association of Indians in America, pp. 297–312.

Srivastava, Gopi Nath. 1970. *The Language Controversy and The Minorities*. New Delhi: Atma Ram and Sons.

Srivastava, Ravindra Nath. 1980. *Language Teaching in Bi- or Pluralingual and Multilingual Environment*. [Academic Report]. Paris: United Nations Educational, Scientific and Cultural Organization.

Srivastava, Ravindra Nath. 1984a. "Linguistic minorities and national language," in *Linguistic Minorities and Literacy: Language Policy Issues in Developing Countries*, edited by Florian Coulmas. Berlin: Mouton, pp. 99–114.

Srivastava, Ravindra Nath. 1984b. "Consequences of initiating literacy in a second language," in *Linguistic Minorities and Literacy: Language Policy Issues in Developing Countries*, edited by Florian Coulmas. Berlin: Mouton, pp. 39–46.

Srivastava, Ravindra Nath. 1987. "Theory of planning and language planning," in *Perspectives in Language Planning*, edited by Uday N. Singh and Ravindra Nath Srivastava. Calcutta, India: Mithila Darshan, pp. 137–52.

Srivastava, Ravindra Nath. 1988. "Address to the Indian linguists," *International Journal of Dravidian Linguistics*, 17, 1–13.

Srivastava, Ravindra Nath. 1992. "Theory and reality in Indian linguistics," in *Dimensions of Sociolinguistics in South Asia*, edited by Edward C. Dimock, Braj B. Kachru, and Bh. Krishnamurti. New Delhi: Oxford and India Book House, pp. 329–38.

Srivastava, Ravindra Nath. 1994. *Hindi bhasha ka samaj shastr*. Compiled and edited by Mahendra Beena Srivastava and Dilip Singh. New Delhi: Radhakrishna Parkashan.

Srivastava, Ravindra Nath and R. S. Gupta. 1983. "A linguistic view of literacy," *Journal of Pragmatics*, 7, 533–49.

Srivastava, Ravindra Nath and R. S. Gupta. 1990. "Literacy in a multilingual context," in *Multilingualism in India*, edited by Debi P. Pattanayak. Clevedon, Avon: Multilingual Matters, pp. 67–78.

Srivastava, Ravindra Nath and Ashok Kalra. 1984. "Modernization of Hindi in news media," in *Modernization of Indian Languages in the News Media*, edited by Bhadriraju Krishnamurti and Aditi Mukherji. Hyderabad, India: Osmania University.

Srivastava, Ravindra Nath and Ira Pandit. 1988. "The pragmatic basis of syntactic structures and the politeness hierarchy in Hindi," *Journal of Pragmatics*, 12, 185–205.

Staal, J. Frits (ed.) 1972. *A Reader on the Sanskrit Grammarians*. Cambridge, MA: The Massachussetts Institute of Technology Press.

Staal, J. Frits. 1989. "The mantra in Vedic and Tantric ritual," in *Mantra*, edited by H. P. Alper. Albany, NY: The State University of NewYork Press, pp. 48–95.

Stearns, Peter (ed.) 2001. *The Encyclopedia of World History*. Boston, MA: Houghton Mifflin Company.

Steever, Sanford B. (ed.) 1998. *The Dravidian Languages*. London and New York: Routledge.

Stegmuller, Henning, Dilip Chitre, Namdeo Dhasal. 1996. *Bombay Mumbai: Bilder einere Mega Stadt*. Translated by Lothar Lutze. Munich: A–1 Verlag.

Street, Brian V. 1994. "What is meant by local literacies?," in *Sustaining Local Literacies*, edited by D. Barton. Special issue of *Language and Education*, 8, 19–30.

Street, Brian V. 1997. "Social literacies," in *Encyclopedia of Language and Education*, Vol. 2, edited by V. Edwards and D. Corson. Dordrecht: Kluwer, pp. 133–42.

Subbarao, Karumuri V. 1984. *Complementation in Hindi Syntax*. New Delhi: Academic Publications.

Subbarao, Karumuri V. 1998a. "Linguistic theory and syntactic typology: A proposal for a symbiotic relationship," in *Vaagbhaarati: Proceedings of the International*

Conference on South Asian Languages, edited by L. V. Khokhlova and Atul Sawani. Moscow: Institute of Asian & African Studies, Moscow State University, pp. 5–23. [Reprinted in 1999, *Indian Linguistics*, 60, 95–110.]

Subbarao, Karumuri V. 1998b. Fieldnotes.

Subbarao, Karumuri V. 2000. "Syntactic typology and South Asian languages," in *The Yearbook of South Asian Languages and Linguistics 2000*, edited by Rajendra Singh. New Delhi, Thousand Oaks; London: Sage, pp. 93–103.

Subbarao, Karumuri V. 2001. "Agreement in South Asian languages and minimalist inquiries: The framework," in *The Yearbook of South Asian Languages 2001*, edited by Peri Bhaskararao and Karumuri V. Subbarao. New Delhi: Thousand Oaks, London: Sage, pp. 457–492.

Subbarao, Karumuri V. and B. Lalitha Murthy. 2000. "Lexical anaphors and pronouns in Telugu," in *Lexical Anaphors and Pronouns in Selected South Asian Languages*, edited by Barbara Lust, James Gair, Kashi Wali, and Karumuri V. Subbarao. Berlin: Mouton de Gruyter, pp. 217–273.

Subbarao, Karumuri V. and A. Saxena. 1987. "Language universals: Inductive or deductive?," in *Select Papers from SALA-7*, edited by Elena Bashir, Madhav Deshpande, and Peter E. Hook. Bloomigton, IN: Indiana University Linguistic Club, pp. 337–342.

Subbarao, Karumuri V., C. Viswanath Rao, A. Saxena, and N. Rau. 1989. "The verb 'say' in South Asian languages: A study in linguistic convergence," in *Language Variation and Change*, edited by Aditi Mukherjee. Hyderabad, India: Centre for Advanced Study in Linguistics, Osmania University, pp. 89–103.

Subramoniam, V. I. and P. C. Ganeshsundaram. 1954. "Marathi loans in Tamil," *Indian Linguistics*, 14, 104–23.

Sukthankar, V. S. 1941. "The position of linguistics studies in India," *Proceedings of the 10th All India Oriental Conference*, 593–609. [Reproduced in *Bharatiya Vidya* 2: 23–35; *Sukthankar Memorial Edition 2*, 1945, Bombay, India: Karnatak, pp. 386–99.]

Swan, Maureen. 1985. *Gandhi: The South African Experience*. Johannesburg: Ravan.

T. W. J. 1890. *'Baboo English' ; or, Our Mother-Tongue as Our Aryan Brethren Understand It. Amusing Specimens of Composition and Style, or, English as Written by Some of Her Majesty's Indian Subjects*. Calcutta, India: Kent.

Tagare, Ganesh Vasudev. 1948. *Historical Grammar of Apabhraṃśa*, Deccan College Dissertation Series 5. Poona, India: Deccan College.

Tannen, Deborah. 1990. *You Just Don't Understand*. New York: Ballantine.

Tannen, Deborah (ed.) 1993. *Gender and Conversational Interaction*. New York: Oxford University Press.

Tannen, Deborah. 1994. *Gender and Discourse*. New York: Oxford University Press.

Tannen, Deborah. 1998. *Argument Culture*. New York: Random House.

Taylor, Douglas. 1971. "Grammatical and lexical affinities of creoles," in *Pidginization and Creolization of Languages*, edited by Dell Hymes. Cambridge: Cambridge University Press, pp. 293–96.

Taylor, Gordon and Tingguang Chen. 1991. "Linguistic, cultural and subcultural issues in contrastive discourse analysis: Anglo-American and Chinese scientific texts," *Applied Linguistics*, 12, 319–36.

Taylor, Issac. 1833. *The Alphabet*, 2 Vols. (2nd edn, 1899). London: Edward Arnold.

Thapar, Romila. 1966. *A History of India*, Vol. I. Harmondsworth, Middlesex: Penguin.

Thapar, Romila. 1973. *The Past and Prejudice*. New Delhi: Publications Division, Government of India.

Tharu, Susie and K. Lalita (ed.) 1991. *Women Writing in India*. New York: The Feminist Press.

The World Almanac and Book of Facts 2002. New York: World Almanac Books.

Theva Rajan, A. 1995. *Tamil as Official Language: Retrospect and Prospect*. Colombo: International Centre for Ethnic Studies.

Thirumalai, M. S. 2005. "The roots of linguistics reorganization of Indian provinces: Dr. Annie Besant and her Home Rule Movement," *Language in India*, 5(5), May 2005. www.languageinindia.com/may2005/motilalnehrureport1.html, accessed august 21, 2005.

Thirugnanasambandhan, P. 1992. *Sanskrit–Tamil Contact*. Thiruvananthapuram, India: International School of Dravidian Linguisitcs.

Thomason, Sarah G. and Terrence Kaufman. 1988. *Language Contact, Creolization and Genetic Linguistics*. Berkeley: University of California Press.

Thompson, John B. 1990. *Ideology and Modern Culture*. Stanford, CA: Stanford University Press.

Thorat, Vimal. 1996. "Social movement and literary consciousness: A comparative study of Hindi and Dalit poetry in the sixties," translated by Raj Kumar and Eleanor Zelliot, *The Fourth World*, 3, 58–64.

Thorat, Vimal. 2002. *The Silent Volcano: English Translation of Dalit Women's Poetry*. Bangalore: National Federation of Dalit Women.

Thumboo, Edwin (ed.) 2001. *The Three Circles of English*. Singapore: Unipress, The Center for the Arts, National University of Singapore.

Tikku, Girdhari Lal. 1961. *Shu'ara-I-Kashmir* (The Poets of Kashmir). Tehran: Hind-I-Nau.

Tinker, Hugh. 1974. *A New System of Slavery: The Export of Indian Labour Overseas 1830–1920*. Oxford: Oxford University Press.

Tirumalesh, K. V. 1979. "Movement rules in Kannada," unpublished PhD dissertation, Hyderabad, India: Central Institute of English and Foreign Languages.

Tiwary, Kapil Muni. 1978. "Tuneful weeping: A mode of communication," *Frontiers*, 3(3), 24–7.

Toynbee, Arnold J. 1927. *Survey of International Affairs*, Vol. I. London: Oxford University Press.

Treichler, Paula, Richard Frankel, Cheris Kramarae, Kathleen Zoppi, and Howard Beckman. 1984. "Problems and problems: Power relationships in a medical encounter," in *Language and Power*, edited by Cheris Kramarae. Beverly Hills, CA: Sage, pp. 62–88.

Trivedi, Darshana and Rupalee Burke (ed./trans.) 2000. *Tongues of Fire*. Ahmedabad, India: Gujarat Dalit Sahitya Akademi.

Tröemel-Plöetz, Senta. 1991. "Selling the apolitical," *Discourse and Society*, 2(4), 489–502.

Trudgill, Peter. 1972. "Sex, covert prestige and linguistic change in the urban British English of Norwich," *Language in Society*, 1, 179–95.

Trudgill, Peter. 1986. *Dialects in Contact*. Oxford: Basil Blackwell.

Trubetzkoy N. S. 1928. Proposition 16. In *Actes du 1er Congrès international de linguistes*. Leiden: A. W. Sijthoff's Uitgeversmaatschappij, pp. 17–18.

Tulpule, Shankar Gopal. 1979. *Classical Marathi Literature*, in the series *A History of Indian Literature*, edited by Jan Gonda, Vol. 9, fasc. 4. Wiesbaden: Otto Harrassowitz.

Turner, Barry (ed.) 2001. *The Statesman's Yearbook: The Politics, Cultures, and Economies of the World 2001*. New York: St. Martin's Press.

T. W. J. 1890. *Baboo English or Our Mother Tongue as Our Aryan Brethren Understand It. Amusing Specimens of Composition and Style. Or English as Written by Her Majesty's Indian Subjects*. Calcutta: Kent.

Ukyab, Tamla and Shyam Adhikari. 2000. *The Nationalities of Nepal*. Kathmandu, Nepal: Government of Nepal, Ministry of Local Development, National Committee for Development of Nationalities.

Ullrich, Helen E. 1992. "Sociolinguistic change in language attitudes: A Karnataka village study," in *Dimensions of Sociolinguistics in South Asia*, edited by Edward C. Dimock, Braj B. Kachru, and Bhadriraju Krishnamurti. New Delhi: Oxford and India Book House, pp. 113–27.

Umar, M. 1979. "Indigenous elements in Persian literature and language produced during the 18th century in India," *Indo-Iranica* 32(1–2), 3–8.

UNESCO. (United Nations Educational, Scientific and Cultural Organization) 1984a. *Literacy Situation in Asia and the Pacific: Bangladesh*. Bangkok: Regional Office for Education in Asia and the Pacific.

UNESCO. (United Nations Educational, Scientific and Cultural Organization) 1984b. *Literacy Situation in Asia and the Pacific: India*. Bangkok: Regional Office for Education in Asia and the Pacific.

UNESCO. (United Nations Educational, Scientific and Cultural Organization) 1984c. *Literacy Situation in Asia and the Pacific: Nepal*. Bangkok: Regional Office for Education in Asia and the Pacific.

Underwood, Ellis. 1885. *Indian English and Indian Character. Calcutta, India*: Thacker, Spink.

Unger, Rhoda and Mary Crawford. 1996. "Sex and gender – The troubled relationship between terms and concepts," in *Questions of Gender*, edited by Dina L. Anselmi and Ann L. Law. Boston, MA: McGraw–Hill, pp. 18–21.

Upadhyaya, U. P. 1971. "Effects of bilingualism on Bidar Kannada," *Indian Linguistics*, 32(2), 132–8.

Upadhye, A. N. 1975. *Prakrit Languages and Literature* Dr. P. D. Gune Memorial Lectures. Poona, India: University of Poona.

Vagartha. Serial Publication. New Delhi: Joshi Foundation.

Vaidyanathan, S. 1971. *Indo-Aryan Loanwords in Old Tamil*. Madras, India: Rajan Publishers.

Valentine, Tamara. 1983. "Sexism in Hindi: Form, function and variation," *Studies in the Linguistic Sciences*, 13(2), 143–58.

Valentine, Tamara. 1985a. "Cross–sex conversation in Indian English fiction," *World Englishes*, 4(3), 319–32.

Valentine, Tamara. 1985b. "Sex, power and linguistic strategies in the Hindi language," *Studies in the Linguistic Sciences*, 15(1), 195–211.

Valentine, Tamara. 1986. "Language and power. Cross-sex communicative strategies in Hindi and Indian English," *Economic and Political Weekly*, 21(43), WS75–WS87.

Valentine, Tamara. 1987. "Sexist practices in the Hindi Language," *Indian Journal of Linguistics*, 14, 25–55.

Valentine, Tamara. 1988. "Developing discourse types in non-native English: Strategies of gender in Hindi and Indian English," *World Englishes*, 7(2), 143–58.

Valentine, Tamara. 1993. "What's the point? Storytelling by women of India," *Studies in the Linguistic Sciences*, 25(2), 77–102.

Valmiki, Omprakash. 2003. *Joothan: An Untouchable's Life*. Translated from Hindi by Arun Prabha Mukherjee. New York: Columbia University Press.

van Bekkum, Wout, Jan Houben, Kneke Sluiter, and Kees Versteegh (eds.) 1997. *The Emergence of Semantics in Four Linguistic Traditions: Hebrew, Sanskrit, Greek, Arabic*. Amsterdam Studies in *The Theory and History of Linguistics Science*, Series 3, Vol. 82. Amsterdam and Philadelphia, PA: John Benjamins.

Van de Walle, Lieve. 1993. *Pragmatics and Classical Sanskrit: A Pilot Study in Linguistic Politeness*. Pragmatics and Beyond New Series 28, Amsterdam, John Benjamins.

van Driem, George. 2001. *Languages of the Himalayas: an ethnolinguistic handbook of the Greater Himalayan region*. 2 vols. (*Handbuch der Orientalistik* 10/1, 2). Leiden/Boston/Köln: Brill.

van Driem, George. 2007. 'South Asia and the Middle East'. In *Encyclopedia of the World's Endangered Languages*, Christopher Moseley ed. London & New York: Routledge. 282–347.

van Elteren, Mel. 1996. "Conceptualizing the impact of US popular culture globally," *Journal of Popular Culture*, 30, 47–81.

Varma, Baidya Nath. 1980. "Indians as new ethnics: A theoretical note," in *The New Ethnics: The Asian Indians in the United States*, edited by Parmatma Saran and Edwin Eames. New York: Praeger, pp. 29–41.

Varma, Ram Kumar. 1947. *Hindi Sahitya ka Alocńaatmak Itihas*. Allahabad, India: Nav Sahitya Press.

Varma, Siddheshwar. 1972–1976. *G.A. Grierson's Linguistic Survey of India: A Summary*, 3 vols. Hoshiarpur, India: Vishveshvaranand Institute, Punjab University.

Varma, Udayanarayana. 1983. *Diglossia in Bangladesh and Language Planning*. Calcutta, India: Gyan Bharati.

Vasanthakumari, T. 1991. "Language of women: A focus on the impact of stratification and socialization," *International Journal of Dravidian Linguistics*, 20(2), 49–60.

Vatuk, Sylvia. 1969. "Reference, address, and fictive kinship in urban north India," *Ethnology*, 8, 255–72.

Vaudeville, C. 1986. *Barahmasa in Indian Literature*. New Delhi: Motilal Banarsidass.

Vaughn, Robinson. 1996. The Indians: onward and upward. In Ceri Peach ed. *The Ethnic Minority Populations*. London: In the Service of Her Majesty: National Statistics.

Velten H. V. 1943. "The Nez Perce verb", *Pacific Northwest Quarterly*, 34, 271–92.

Verghese, Anila. 2002. *Hampi*. New Delhi: Oxford University Press.

Verhagen, Pieter C. 1994. *A Sanskrit of Grammatical Literature in Tibet. Vol 1: Transmission of the Canonical Literature*. Leiden: E. J. Brill.

Verma, Dhirendra. 1933. *Hindi bhasa ka itihas*. Allahabad, India: Hindustani Academy.
Verma, Manindra K. and K. P. Mohanan. 1990. *Experiencer Subjects in South Asian Languages*. Stanford, CA: Center for the Study of Language and Information.
Verma, Tugeshwar P. 1996. "Some features of Nepali newspaper English," in *South Asian English: Structure, Use and Users*, edited by Robert J. Baumgardner. Urbana and Chicago: University of Illinois Press, pp. 82–87.
Vetterling-Braggin, M. (ed.) 1981. *Sexist Language*. Lehigh U: Littlefield, Adams.
Vinaypatrika: Tulsidas Letter to Sri Ram, compiled by Camille Bulcke (presented by "Khristnath") Patna: Navajyoti Niketan, 1988.
Vogel, Claus. 1979. *Indian Lexicography* (A History of Indian Literature, Vol. V). Wiesbaden: Otto Harrassowitz.
von Hinüber, Oskar. 1994. *Selected Papers on Pali Studies*. Oxford: Pali Text Society.
Viswanathan, Gauri. 1987. "The beginings of English literary study in British India," *Oxford Literary Review*, 9, 2–26.
Viswanathan, Gauri. 1989. *Masks of Conquest: Literary Study and British Rule in India*, New York: Columbia University Press.
von Hinüber, Oskar. 1994. *Selected Papers on Pali Studies*. Oxford: Pali Text Society.
Vyas, B. S., Bhola Nath Tiwari, and Ravindra Nath Srivastava. 1972. *Hindī vyakaran aur rachna*. New Delhi: National Council of Educational Research and Training.
Vygotsky, L. S. 1978. *Mind in Society: The Development of Higher Psychological Processes*, edited by M. Cole, V. John-Steiner, S. Scribner, and E. Souberman. Cambridge, MA: Harvard University Press.
Wadhwa, Kamlesh K. 1975. *Minority Safeguards in India*. New Delhi: Thomson Press.
Wadia, Ardeshir R. 1954. *The Future of English in India*. Bombay, India: Asia Publishing House.
Wadley, Susan. 1986. "Women and the Hindu tradition," in *Women in India: Two Perspectives*, edited by Doranne Jacobson and Susan S. Wadley. New Delhi: Manohar, pp. 113–39.
Wali, Kashi and Omkar N. Koul. 1997. *Kashmiri: A Cognitive Descriptive Grammar*. London and New York: Routledge.
Wali, Kashi, Omkar N. Koul, Peter E. Hook, and Ashok K. Koul. 2000. "Lexical anaphors and pronouns in Kashmiri," in *Lexical Anaphors and Pronouns in Selected South Asian Languages*, edited by Barbara Lust, James Gair, Kashi Wali, and Karumuri V. Subbarao. Berlin: Mouton de Gruyter, pp. 471–512.
Warder, A. K. 1972. *Indian Kavya Literature*, Vol. 1. New Delhi: Motilal Banarsidass.
Watters, Steve. 2001. "Language death: A review and examination of the global issue in the Nepalese context," a working paper presented at *The National Symposium on Language Death or Suicide: An Examination of the Issues in the Nepalese Context*. Kathmandu, Nepal.
Weil, Shalva. 1983. "Women and language in Israel," *International Journal of the Sociology of Language*, 41, 77–91.
Weinreich, Uriel. 1958. "On the compatibility of genetic relationship and convergent development," *Word*, 14, 374–79.
Whinnom, Keith. 1971. "Linguistic hybridization and the 'special case' of pidgins and creoles," in *Pidginization and Creolization of Languages*, edited by Dell Hymes. Cambridge: Cambridge University Press, pp. 91–115.

Whitworth, George C. 1885. *An Anglo-Indian Dictionary: A Glossary of Indian Terms Used in English, and of Such English or Other Non-English Terms as Have Attained Special Meanings in India*. London: Kegan Paul.

Whitworth, George C. 1907. *Indian English: An Examination Made by Indians in Writing English*. Letchworth: Garden City Press.

Whorf, Benjamin Lee. 1940. "Linguistics as an exact science," *Technology Review*, 43, 61–3, 80–3. [Reprinted in 1996 in the collection of Whorf's selected writings, *Language, Thought, and Reality*, Cambridge, MA: The Massachussetts Institute of Technology Press, pp. 220–32.]

Williams, Colin (ed.) 1991. *Linguistic Minorities, Society, and Territory*. Clevedon, Avon: Multilingual Matters.

Williams P. M. 2001. "Buddhism, Tibetan," in *Concise Encyclopedia of Language and Religion*, edited by J. A. Sawyer. Amsterdam: Elsevier, pp. 39–41.

Williams, Walter L. 1986. *The Spirit and the Flesh: Sexual Diversity in American Indian Culture*. Boston, MA: Beacon Press.

Wolpert, Stanley. 1991. *India*. Berkeley, CA: University of California Press.

Wolpert, Stanley. 1993. *A New History of India* (4th edn). New York: Oxford University Press.

Woollcombe, David. *Peace Child International*, www.global–vision.org/sustainability/rescuemission.html, accessed August 2005.

Wright, Arnold. 1891. *Baboo English as 'Tis Writ: Being Curiosities of Indian Journalism*. London: Fisher Unwin.

Yadava, Yogendra P. 2006. "Linguistic activities in Nepal (1999–2004)," in *The Yearbook of South Asian Languages and Linguistics, 2006*, edited by Rajendra Singh. Berlin: Mouton de Gruyter, pp. 153–64.

Yule, Henry. 1886. "Hobson-Jobsoniana," *Asiatic Quarterly Review*, 1, 119–40.

Yule, Henry and A. C. Burnell. 1886. *Hobson-Jobson: A Glossary of Colloquial Anglo-Indian Words and Phrases and of Kindred Terms, Etymological, Historical, Geographical, and Discursive*. [New edition. by W. Crooke (1903). London: J. Murry.]

Zakaria, Fareed. 2001. "The roots of rage," Special report of *Newsweek*, October 15, p. 20.

Zelliot, Eleanor. 1992. *From Untouchable to Dalit: Essays on the Ambedkar movement*. New Delhi: Manohar. [3rd end. 2001].

Zelliot, Eleanor. 1996. "Stri Dalit Sahitya: The new voice of women poets," in *Images of Women in Maharashtrian Literature and Religion*, edited by Anne Feldhaus. Albany, NY: State University of New York Press, pp. 65–93.

Zelliot, Eleanor. 2000. "Sant Sahitya and Dalit movements," in *Intersections: Socio-cultural Trends in Maharashtra*, edited by Meera Kosambi. Hyderabad, India: Orient Longman, pp. 187–93.

Zelliot, Eleanor and Philip Engblom (eds.) 1982. "A Marathi sampler," *Journal of South Asia Literature*, 17(1), 1–169.

Zimmerman, D. H. and C. West. 1975. "Sex roles, interruptions, and silences in conversation," in *Language and Sex: Difference and Dominance*, edited by B. Thorne and N. Henley. Rowley, MA: Newbury House, pp. 105–29.

Zvelebil, Kamil Veith. 1973. *The Smile of Murugan. On Tamil Lieterature of South India*. Leiden: E. J. Brill.

Zvelebil, Kamil Veith. 1974. *Tamil Literature*, in the series *A History of Indian Literature*, edited by Jan Gonda, Vol. 10, fasc. 1. Wiesbaden: Otto Harrassowitz.

Zvelebil, Kamil Veith. 1995. *Lexicon of Tamil Literature* (Handbuch der Orientalistik 2). Leiden and New York: E. J. Brill.

Zwilling, Leonard and Michael J. Sweet. 2000. "The evolution of third-sex constructs in ancient India: A study in ambiguity," in *Invented Identities: The Interplay of Gender, Religion and Politics in India*, edited by Julia Leslie and Mary McGee. New Delhi: Oxford University Press, pp. 99–132.

Subject Index

Language Index

Author Index